THE PAPERS OF

Andrew Jackson

•

HAROLD D. MOSER,
EDITOR-IN-CHIEF

THE PAPERS OF

Andrew Jackson

VOLUME IV, 1816–1820

HAROLD D. MOSER
DAVID R. HOTH
GEORGE H. HOEMANN
EDITORS

•

THE UNIVERSITY OF TENNESSEE PRESS
KNOXVILLE

•

*The paper in this book meets the minimum
requirements of the American National Standard
for Permanence of Paper for Printed Library Materials.*

∞

*Binding materials have been chosen
for strength and durability.*

•

Library of Congress Cataloging in Publication Data
(Revised for vol. 4)

Jackson, Andrew, 1767–1845.
The papers of Andrew Jackson.
Vol. 2 edited by Harold D. Moser and Sharon Macpherson.
Vol. 4 edited by Harold D. Moser, David R. Hoth,
George H. Hoemann.
Includes bibliographical references and indexes.
Contents: v. 1. 1770–1803.—vol. 2. 1804–1813—[etc.]—v. 4. 1816–1820.
1. Jackson, Andrew, 1767–1845. 2. United States—
Politics and government—1829–1837—Sources. 3. Presidents—
United States—Correspondence. I. Smith, Sam B., 1929– .
II. Owsley, Harriet Fason Chappell. III. Moser, Harold D. IV. Title.
E302.J35 1980 1980 973.5′6′092 79-15078
ISBN 0-87049-219-5
ISBN 0-87049-441-4 (v. 2 : alk. paper)
ISBN 0-87049-650-6 (v. 3 : cloth : alk. paper)
ISBN 0-87049-778-2 (v. 4 : cloth : alk. paper)

Advisory Board

Publication of
The Papers of Andrew Jackson
was assisted by grants from
THE LADIES' HERMITAGE ASSOCIATION
THE UNIVERSITY OF TENNESSEE
THE NATIONAL HISTORICAL PUBLICATIONS
AND RECORDS COMMISSION
THE TENNESSEE HISTORICAL COMMISSION
THE PROGRAM FOR EDITIONS OF THE
NATIONAL ENDOWMENT FOR THE HUMANITIES,
AN INDEPENDENT FEDERAL AGENCY,
and from
THE BELZ FOUNDATION
THE GEORGE NEWTON BULLARD FOUNDATION
FIDELITY FEDERAL SAVINGS & LOAN ASSOCIATION
WILLIAM G. AND FLETCH COKE
WILLIAM C. AND JEAN E. COOK
ROBERT S. DOOCHIN
SAM S. HAYS, JR.
THE SOCIETY OF THE LEES OF VIRGINIA
(in memory of Julia Page McCall Robbins)
M & W WALLER TRUST
CHARLES E. AND ANN H. WELLS
WILLIAM RIDLEY WILLS, II
WERTHAN FOUNDATION

In memory of
Charles M. Wiltse

Contents

For the page number on which each document of The Papers begins, see the Calendar.

Illustrations

Survey of Creek Treaty, with Chickasaw and Cherokee Boundaries, [1817], adapted from map drawn by Hunter Peel and approved by William Barnett and John Coffee, Records of the Bureau of Land Management, Record Group 49, National Archives. Adaptation prepared by William Fontanez, University of Tennessee Cartographic Services Laboratory.

John Adair, oil on canvas by Nicola Marschall. Courtesy of the Kentucky Historical Society, Frankfort.

Isaac Shelby, oil on canvas by Matthew H. Jouett. Courtesy of the Kentucky Historical Society, Frankfort.

Winfield Scott, Plaster bust by William Rush. Courtesy of The National Portrait Gallery, Smithsonian Institution, Washington, D.C.

Stephen Harriman Long, oil on canvas by Charles Willson Peale. Courtesy of Independence National Historical Park, Philadelphia, Pennsylvania.

Andrew Jackson, Terra-cotta bust by William Rush. Courtesy of The Art Institute of Chicago, Restricted gift of Jamee J. and Marshall Field, and the Brooks and Hope B. McCormick Foundation; Bessie Bennett, W. G. Field, Ada Turnbull Hertle, Laura T. Magnusson, and Major Acquisition funds, 1985.251.

The Seminole Campaign in East Florida, 1818, adapted from Hugh Young's "Map of the Seat of War in East Florida during the Seminole Campaign," Records of the Office of the Chief of Engineers, Record Group 77, National Archives. Adaptation prepared by Brian Williams, University of Tennessee Cartographic Services Laboratory.

"*American Justice!! or The Ferocious Yankee Genl. Jack's Reward for Butchering Two British Subjects!!!,*" cartoon by George Cruikshank. Courtesy of The Tennessee State Museum, Nashville.

Pushmataha, oil on canvas by Charles Bird King. Courtesy of The Warner Collection of Gulf States Paper Corporation, Tuscaloosa, Alabama.

Colonel William McIntosh, oil on canvas by Nathan Negus. Courtesy of Alabama Department of Archives and History, Montgomery.

Abner Lacock, engraving by Stephen James Ferris after a portrait by unknown artist. From *The Pennsylvania Magazine of History and Biography,* 4(1880):facing p. 133.

Rufus King, engraving by T. Kelly after a portrait by Gilbert Stuart. From James B. Longacre and James Herring, *The National Portrait Gallery of Distinguished Americans* (4 vols.; Philadelphia: H. Perkins, 1834–39), Volume 3.

David Brydie Mitchell, oil on canvas by Richard West Habersham. Courtesy of Georgia Historical Society, Savannah.

John Clark, oil on canvas by W. R. Freeman. Courtesy of Georgia Department of Archives and History, Atlanta.

Rachel Jackson, watercolor on ivory attributed to Mary Catherine Strobel. Courtesy of James F. Ruddy.

Andrew Jackson, watercolor on ivory by Ralph E. W. Earl. Courtesy of Dr. Benjamin H. Caldwell, Jr.

Introduction

ANDREW JACKSON, 1816–1820

Between 1816 and 1820, the new American nation experienced political adjustment and economic turmoil unparalleled in its twenty-seven-year history. The Treaty of Ghent brought peace and abated the rankling and sectional squabbling that had marred the war effort. In 1816, the Federalist party was near death, and Federalists and Republicans united behind the president-elect, James Monroe, to pay off the war debt and to return the country to a peacetime economy.

Economic recovery was slow in coming. The nation did not experience prosperity until mid-1817, when money became plentiful, credit flowed, and trade flourished. Land sales boomed as settlers flocked west and south to newly opened lands. Prosperity, however, was short-lived, and by mid-1819 financial collapse had displaced the flush times. Trade and commerce languished. Prices fell precipitously; money was in short supply. The Panic of 1819 brought failure to many and left others scrambling to salvage their investments.

Political harmony proved even more fragile than prosperity. At the time of Monroe's inauguration in early 1817, ambitious politicians in the cabinet and in Congress were already organizing for succession to the presidential office. Monroe managed to survive and to run again unopposed in 1820, but the rivalries had resulted in many an acrimonious fight. Moreover, as Congress debated statehood for Missouri and Maine and the balance of power between slave and free states, the years 1819 and 1820 marked the introduction of a new form of sectionalism, one that was to influence the organization of the second party system and dominate the political arena for the next forty years. All in all, the years were ones of extreme contradictions—boom and bust, harmony and discord. Whatever "good feelings" there were derived mainly from General Andrew Jackson's decisive victory at New Orleans in January 1815.

In the five years from 1816 through 1820, the Hero of New Orleans was not at the center of politics, but he was often the center of political debate. Following the Gulf campaign, Jackson remained in the army, one of two major generals in the peacetime reorganization. As commander of the Southern Division, he was charged with maintaining the security of an area that extended from Norfolk, Virginia, on the eastern seaboard, south to Amelia Island, west beyond the Mississippi River, and north to the Dakotas. His chief duties, chronicled in this fourth volume of *The Papers,* involved maintaining peace between whites and Indians and establishing an adequate line of fortifications along the Gulf Coast and frontier settlements to secure the areas against foreign influence and incursion.

In keeping the peace between whites and Indians, Jackson's role was to safeguard the interests of both, and those demands often placed him in the contradictory positions of removing white intruders from Indian lands and of negotiating with Indians for relinquishment of titles to those lands. Jackson's view was that harmony between the two could exist only when the Indians were assimilated, whereupon they would lose their national identity, or removed, the only realistic way to preserve that identity. As treaty commissioner, Jackson favored removal, and over the course of these five years, he pursued that policy, concluding a total of five treaties with the Cherokees, Chickasaws, and Choctaws, all extinguishing titles. His success with the southern Indians freed millions of acres of land for white settlement and speculation, but his policy brought him into open conflict with William Harris Crawford, secretary of war in 1816, for, according to Jackson's notion, the administration policy of negotiating and recognizing Indian claims instead of dictating removal often promoted hostility rather than peace and harmony.

Protecting the peace won at New Orleans proved to be Jackson's chief concern during these years, and the security of the Gulf Coast against foreign intervention remained foremost in his mind. To accomplish this objective, Jackson proposed to Washington the erection of an armory in the southwest to ensure the availability of munitions in the event of war. He oversaw the construction of a military road from Nashville to New Orleans to allow rapid movement of troops should attack come. He monitored topographical surveys of western lands and of the Gulf and Atlantic coasts, and he directed the construction of fortifications in Louisiana, Alabama, and along the Georgia-Florida border. In the course of improving defense posts, forces under his command destroyed Negro Fort, regarded by Jackson and some others to be still a bastion of British influence.

Jackson's preoccupation with Gulf Coast security led to one of the most important, and one of the most controversial, decisions of his long career: the invasion of Florida in early 1818. The Treaty of Ghent had established peace between the United States and Great Britain, but it had not ended rumors of British intrigue with the Seminole Indians in Spanish Florida or even of British buildup in the area. Spain was also at peace with the United States, but it lacked the strength to curtail Seminole depredations. As they increased, President Monroe directed Jackson to take personal command in the area, whereupon Jackson crossed the border, attacked Indian towns, and captured Spanish forts at St. Marks and Pensacola. At St. Marks, Jackson found what he considered conclusive evidence of continuing British intrigue in the persons of Alexander Arbuthnot and Robert Christie Ambrister, and he ordered their execution. For a brief period, Washington politicians feared retaliation from both Great Britain and Spain. In large measure, the documents of the last three years of this volume concern the debate over this First Seminole War.

Jackson's seizure of Pensacola, the capital of Spanish West Florida, ignited a political explosion. The event and its repercussions helped shape the politics of Tennessee and the nation for more than a decade. The act saddled Jackson with baggage that he never lost: for one faction, it offered irrefutable proof that he was the "savior" of his country; for another, it was merely additional evidence that Jackson was a "military chieftain." In response to the events, Congress, through Abner Lacock of Pennsylvania, Henry Randolph Storrs of New York, and Henry Clay of Kentucky, demanded to know from President Monroe whether Jackson had violated international law and presidential orders. Neither Monroe's responses to the Senate and House investigations nor Jackson's memorial to the Senate settled the issue. The matter quickly became a political weapon, as William H. Crawford and other aspirants for office not only assailed Jackson but used him as a foil to destroy Monroe. In Tennessee, the invasion and resulting investigations gave cohesion to Jackson's opponents, and in the ensuing decade the leaders of that opposition—John Williams, John Cocke, Newton Cannon, and Andrew Erwin, all Crawfordites during these years—would increase their efforts to deprive Jackson of the presidency.

Jackson's responses to the Seminole investigations, his lengthy exchanges with Monroe over the war power, and his recommendations to Monroe in 1816 on the role of the president disclosed a man who had already given considerable thought to the constitution, the presidency, and the separation of powers. The Jackson revealed in these documents is one dedicated to Union, honor, and integrity in government, a man who had already concluded that the president was the direct representative of all the people, not of special or local interests.

The Jackson of these years also remained highly sensitive to—even intolerant of—criticism. He continued to debate with John Adair the performance of the Kentucky troops at the Battle of New Orleans. He scolded the Tennessee delegation and Congress for the vote on Cherokee reparations, which he regarded as an affront to his and his troops' honor, integrity, and discipline. He quarreled furiously with the war department over chain of command and came close to challenging General Winfield Scott for questioning his order to the Southern Division on that issue. During the Seminole invasion, he denounced Governor William Rabun for issuing orders to the Georgia militia, announcing that during a state of emergency final authority, even over state militia, must rest with the field commander. To Jackson, on this occasion as at New Orleans, the ultimate goal was to preserve the "substance," not just the "shadow," of the constitution.

Jackson's nearly endless series of quarrels invoked simultaneously within him both a longing for retirement and a dogged determination to remain at his post so long as there was any hint of tarnish to his name and reputation. The Jacksons, Andrew and Rachel, were both in their early fifties and they experienced frequent bouts with poor health. Their adopted son, Andrew, Jr., had not yet reached his teens. Family and friends made increasing demands on the general's time and finances, but Jackson seemed to relish the opportunity to offer assistance when needed or requested. For many of his subordinate officers, he became something of a father figure, offering career advice, marital counseling, and sometimes financial help. For many of the orphans of friends and family, he became surrogate father, directing not only their informal but also their formal education, often even providing the funds. Consequently, the demands of family and duties as major general precluded close attention to the construction of a new residence at the Hermitage and the farming operations there and on plantations in Alabama. For Jackson, health, family, and friends proved strong lures to retirement between 1816 and 1820, but the need to vindicate his name and acts proved the greater, and despite the longing for repose, he remained at his post, ever ready, as he assured President Monroe in 1818, to serve his country so long as he was needed.

ACKNOWLEDGMENTS

This volume of *The Papers of Andrew Jackson,* like the third, is the product of a major collaborative effort involving thousands of institutions and individuals. The list is too long to mention each separately, but to all of those who responded to our requests for documents, we are grateful, and especially to those furnishing manuscripts for this volume.

Several institutions deserve special mention, mainly for the magnitude of their contributions. Chief among these are the Library of Congress, the National Archives, the Tennessee State Library and Archives, the John C. Hodges Library, University of Tennessee, and the Alabama Department of Archives and History. At the Library of Congress, John McDonough, Manuscript Historian, has assisted the project at every turn: he has made the Library's Jackson collection readily available, he has answered innumerable research questions, and he continues to share with us his extensive knowledge. At the National Archives, the research staff of the National Historical Publications and Records Commission, and particularly Timothy Connelly, have been indefatigable in unearthing documents and answering difficult questions. Our demands at Hodges Library, University of Tennessee, have been incessant, but Nancy Laemlein in Interlibrary Loans and James B. Lloyd, Bill Eigelsbach, Curtis Lyons, and Nick Wyman in Special Collections have always gone out of their way to service our requests and to make their collections available. The staff of the Tennessee State Library and Archives—and especially Marylin Bell-Hughes, Fran

Schell, and John Thweatt—has been equally cooperative and helpful. At the Alabama Department of Archives and History, Rickie Louise Brunner, Public Services Division, has helped us above and beyond the call of duty, saving us endless hours and considerable cost in locating materials.

We are also deeply obligated to several individuals who have assisted us far beyond any normal expectations: to Bill Cook in Lebanon, to Colonel James S. Corbitt in Jackson, to Fletch Coke and Ann Harwell Wells in Nashville, past regents and chairwomen of the Jackson Papers Committee, Ladies' Hermitage Association, to Jerry W. Cook in Wartrace, and to Milly Wright in Florence, Alabama. As always, Mary-Jo Kline and Joseph Rubinfine have shared their expertise on and knowledge of manuscripts. To each of them we offer our sincere thanks.

Our sponsors have seen to it that the work continued, and our indebtedness to them is great and our appreciation sincere: to George Anderjack, Director, and Sharon Macpherson, Deputy Director of Programs, at The Hermitage, to Anna Wadlington, Regent, and to the other regents, past and present, the Board, and the membership of the Ladies' Hermitage Association; to the National Historical Publications and Records Commission and its staff, Gerald George, Executive Director, Nancy Sahli, Program Director, and Richard N. Sheldon, Assistant Director for Publications; to the National Endowment for the Humanities, Research Programs Division, and especially Margot Backas, David Nichols, Gordon McKinney, and Douglas M. Arnold; to the Tennessee Historical Commission, Herbert L. Harper, Executive Director, Robert E. Corlew, Chairman, and Linda T. Wynn, Administrative Assistant; and finally, to our fiscal agent, the University of Tennessee-Knoxville. At the University, we are fortunate to receive the encouragement and support of Joseph E. Johnson, President, and John J. Quinn, Chancellor; but we are particularly appreciative of the Office of the Dean, College of Liberal Arts—Deans Lorman A. Ratner and Charles O. Jackson, Administrative Assistant Phyllis Cole and Executive Assistant Ann Robinson-Craig—for their patience, understanding, and guidance in the day-to-day administration of the project.

The supporting staff of the Jackson papers has made our work easier and, indeed, more pleasant. We have been fortunate to have as NHPRC Fellow for 1991–92 Mark A. Mastromarino, who has saved us from many errors in his critical reading of this volume, and we indeed appreciate his input and advice. We have continued to rely upon student assistant Robert Haas to relieve us of eyestrain by reading hundreds of reels of microfilm and to save us countless steps by hauling books to and from the library; his graduation will prove a great loss to the project. In addition, Jesús F. de la Teja has continued to provide invaluable assistance with Spanish documents; and, above all, Dorothy Brooks has generously kept the office running while the editors were too engrossed in Jackson to notice anything else.

And finally, in recognition of our deep indebtedness to Charles M. Wiltse for his contributions to Jacksonian scholarship and his influence on the policies and procedures of The Papers of Andrew Jackson, we issue this volume in his memory.

Editorial Policies

PLAN OF WORK

The goal of the Papers of Andrew Jackson is to bring together the literary remains of Andrew Jackson and make them accessible to both the general reader and the serious scholar. An international search of almost 6,000 repositories, contacts with hundreds of private collectors, and an examination of newspapers, magazines, journals, and monographs has yielded a collection of some 100,000 documents. To make this material available, complementary letterpress and microfilm series will be published.

The microfilm publication, thirty-nine reels issued in 1987, is a supplement to the Library of Congress Andrew Jackson Papers and the National Archives microfilm series. It includes *all* Jackson documents found in the project's search to that date and *not* included on those two publications. The entire body of Jackson papers in the three publications—the Supplement, the Library of Congress Presidents' Papers Series, and the National Archives records—can be accessed through *The Papers of Andrew Jackson: A Guide and Index to the Microfilm Editions* (Scholarly Resources, Inc., 1987). Microfilm supplements will make available newly located documents when sufficient numbers accumulate.

The letterpress series will be a selective edition of sixteen volumes, accompanied by a cumulative index. With its annotations, it will stand alone as a unit, but it will also facilitate access to the much larger body of material available on the microfilms. Each volume will include a calendar in which all unselected documents, except the most routine, will be described by their writer or recipient, subject matter, provenance, and location on the film collections. The letterpress series will thus serve as an indispensable guide to the entire body of papers.

EDITORIAL METHOD

In the interest of stylistic continuity in the letterpress series, the present editors have adopted generally the editorial practices established in the previous three volumes.

The editors have broadly defined "papers" as outgoing and incoming correspondence, financial records, deeds, records of litigation, speeches and essays, memoranda, and military orders. In addition the editors have included in the Calendar all of Rachel Jackson's correspondence, whether or not with Jackson, and a small number of particularly significant third-party items essential to the understanding of an otherwise obscure event in Jackson's life. All documents are listed in the Calendar following The Papers, with page numbers indicated for those selected, and writer or recipient, provenance, and subject matter described for the others. Certain routine documents have been omitted from the calendar, notably ration returns, orders for payment of military accounts, passes, military furloughs, and muster rolls. With few exceptions, the routine military correspondence, signed by aides-de-camp on Jackson's orders, has also been omitted unless the letter was part of a chain including letters directly to or from Jackson.

Documents in this volume are arranged in chronological sequence. The only exception is with enclosures, which generally appear immediately following the document they accompanied. All letters are reproduced in full, except when the only surviving text is incomplete. If several copies of a document are available, the editors have relied upon the recipient's copy (whether AL, ALS, or LS) for the text. Where that is missing, they have selected the most authoritative manuscript available. Generally, printed copies have been used only in the absence of manuscript versions, or when the manuscript has been mutilated or is a badly garbled copy. In several instances, variant manuscript copies of documents have been found containing additional text. If short, it has been incorporated into the document, with attention called to the source of that portion in footnotes. When lengthy or when some portion of the document may still be missing, the text source has been identified in an unnumbered provenance note immediately following that portion. Texts are taken from the first cited source.

The prime consideration in preparing the documents for publication has been fidelity to the original text. With the few exceptions noted below, the editors have made an effort to reproduce the papers exactly as written with all their peculiarities of spelling, capitalization, and punctuation. To aid readability dashes after commas, semicolons, colons, or periods have been omitted. Abbreviations, including the commonly used ampersand and contractions, have been allowed to stand as written, with expansion in square brackets only when necessary for the understanding of the contemporary reader. Apostrophes below the line have been raised to their modern position above the line, and superscripts have been dropped to the line, retaining punctuation as in the original. Addressees' names, often written at the end of a document, have been omitted, as have words inadvertently repeated in the text. Dates written at the end of a document have been transferred to the beginning; interlineations and marginalia have been incorporated into the text as indicated by the writer.

Occasionally bracketed matter has been introduced into the text to clarify otherwise questionable or unrecognizable words, to supply characters in mutilated documents, to indicate with ellipses a missing portion of a document (italicized in these last two instances), and to insert the full name(s) of persons. Dates and names furnished by the editors for undated, misdated, unsigned, and unaddressed documents are also enclosed in brackets, with a question mark if conjectural. Significant cancellations have been incorporated in angle brackets.

Immediately following each document is an unnumbered note giving the provenance of that item and, if appropriate, identifying the writer or recipient. Significant postmarks, address instructions, endorsements, and dockets have also been included here. The symbols used in this note appear in the List of Abbreviations. The document's location on microfilms is also noted in parentheses, with reel number alone referring to the Jackson Papers on the Library of Congress Presidents' Papers Series; with reel and frame number separated by a hyphen, to the Jackson Papers Series (Scholarly Resources, Inc., 1987); and M or T followed by a hyphen and reel number, to the National Archives publications, which are conveniently listed in the Repository Symbols of this volume.

Introductory notes and footnotes are used to supply context and continuity and to identify persons, places, and events, usually at their first appearance in the text. Persons in the *Dictionary of American Biography* and the *Biographical Directory of the United States Congress, 1774–1989,* have been identified only briefly, and symbols at their names in the index have been used to direct the reader to additional biographical information in those publications.

DOCUMENT SYMBOLS

AD	Autograph Document
ADS	Autograph Document Signed
AL	Autograph Letter
ALS	Autograph Letter Signed
AN	Autograph Note
ANS	Autograph Note Signed
DS	Document Signed
LC	Letterbook copy
LS	Letter Signed

REPOSITORY SYMBOLS

A-Ar	Alabama Department of Archives and History, Montgomery

ABAU	University of Alabama in Birmingham
AMobM	City of Mobile Museum, Mobile, Ala.
CLU-C	University of California, Los Angeles, William Andrews Clark Memorial Library
CSmH	Henry E. Huntington Library, San Marino, Calif.
CoHi	Colorado State Historical Society, Denver
CtY	Yale University, New Haven, Conn.
DLC	Library of Congress, Washington, D.C.
DNA	National Archives, Washington, D.C.
	RG 11, General Records of the United States Government
	RG 11, M668, Ratified Indian Treaties, 1722–1869
	RG 15, Records of the Veterans Administration
	RG 21, Records of the District Courts of the United States
	RG 21, M1213, Minute Books of the U.S. District Court for West Tennessee, 1797–1839, and of the U.S. District Court for the Middle District of Tennessee, 1839–65
	RG 45, Naval Records Collection of the Office of Naval Records and Library
	RG 45, M124, Letters Received by the Secretary of the Navy: Miscellaneous Letters, 1801–84
	RG 45, M125, Letters Received by the Secretary of the Navy: Captains' Letters, 1805–61, 1866–85
	RG 45, M147, Letters Received by the Secretary of the Navy from Commanders, 1804–86
	RG 46, Records of the United States Senate
	RG 49, Records of the Bureau of Land Management
	RG 59, General Records of the Department of State
	RG 59, M40, Domestic Letters of the Department of State, 1784–1906
	RG 59, M116, State Department Territorial Papers, Florida, 1777–1824
	RG 59, M179, Miscellaneous Letters of the Department of State, 1789–1906
	RG 59, M439, Letters of Application and Recommendation during the Administration of James Monroe, 1817–25
	RG 75, Records of the Bureau of Indian Affairs
	RG 75, M15, Letters Sent by the Secretary of War Relating to Indian Affairs, 1800–24
	RG 75, M208, Records of the Cherokee Indian Agency in Tennessee, 1801–35

RG 75, M271, Letters Received by the Office of the Secretary of War Relating to Indian Affairs, 1800–23
RG 75, T494, Documents Relating to the Negotiation of Ratified and Unratified Treaties with Various Indian Tribes, 1801–69
RG 77, Records of the Office of the Chief of Engineers
RG 84, Records of the Foreign Service Posts of the Department of State
RG 92, Records of the Office of the Quartermaster General
RG 94, Records of the Adjutant General's Office
RG 94, M565, Letters Sent by the Office of the Adjutant General (Main Series), 1800–90
RG 94, M566, Letters Received by the Office of the Adjutant General, 1805–21
RG 98, Records of United States Army Commands, 1784–1821
RG 99, Records of the Office of the Paymaster General
RG 107, Records of the Office of the Secretary of War
RG 107, M6, Letters Sent by the Secretary of War Relating to Military Affairs, 1800–89
RG 107, M7, Confidential and Unofficial Letters Sent by the Secretary of War, 1814–47
RG 107, M22, Register of Letters Received by the Office of the Secretary of War, Main Series, 1800–70
RG 107, M221, Letters Received by the Secretary of War, Registered Series, 1801–70
RG 107, M222, Letters Received by the Secretary of War, Unregistered Series, 1789–1861
RG 153, Records of the Office of the Judge Advocate General (Army)
RG 156, Records of the Office of the Chief of Ordnance
RG 159, Records of the Office of the Inspector General
RG 192, Records of the Office of the Commissary General of Subsistence
RG 217, Records of the United States General Accounting Office
RG 233, Records of the United States House of Representatives
RG 279, Records of the Indian Claims Commission
RG 391, Records of the United States Regular Army Mobile Units, 1821–1942

DSC — Scottish Rite of Freemasonry, Southern Jurisdiction U.S.A., Supreme Council Library, Washington, D.C.

FHi	Florida Historical Society, Tampa
G-Ar	Georgia State Department of Archives and History, Atlanta
GU	University of Georgia, Athens
ICHi	Chicago Historical Society, Chicago, Ill.
ICU	University of Chicago, Chicago, Ill.
ICarbS	Southern Illinois University, Carbondale
InHi	Indiana Historical Society, Indianapolis
InU-Li	Indiana University, Lilly Library, Bloomington
KyClHi	Hickman County Archives, Clinton, Ky.
KyLoF	Filson Club, Louisville, Ky.
LN	New Orleans Public Library, New Orleans, La.
LNHiC	The Historic New Orleans Collection, New Orleans, La.
LU	Louisiana State University, Baton Rouge
MB	Boston Public Library, Boston, Mass.
MH-H	Harvard University, Houghton Library, Cambridge, Mass.
MHi	Massachusetts Historical Society, Boston
MNS	Smith College, Northampton, Mass.
MiDbEI	Edison Institute, Henry Ford Museum, and Greenfield Village Library, Dearborn, Mich.
MiU-C	University of Michigan, William L. Clements Library, Ann Arbor
MoHi	Missouri State Historical Society, Columbia
MoSM	St. Louis Mercantile Library Association, St. Louis, Mo.
Ms-Ar	Mississippi Department of Archives and History, Jackson
MsSM	Mississippi State University, State College
NHi	New-York Historical Society, New York City
NHpR	Franklin D. Roosevelt Library, Hyde Park, N.Y.
NIC	Cornell University, Ithaca, N.Y.
NN	New York Public Library, New York City
NNC	Columbia University, New York, N.Y.
NNMAI	Museum of the American Indian, New York, N.Y.
NNPM	Pierpont Morgan Library, New York, N.Y.
NWM	United States Military Academy, West Point, N.Y.
NcD	Duke University, Durham, N.C.
NcU	University of North Carolina, Chapel Hill
NhD	Dartmouth College, Hanover, N.H.
NjMoHP	Morristown National Historical Park, Morristown, N.J.
NjP	Princeton University, Princeton, N.J.
OClWHi	Western Reserve Historical Society, Cleveland, Ohio

OHi	Ohio Historical Society, Columbus
OkTG	Thomas Gilcrease Institute of American History and Art, Tulsa, Okla.
PCarlMH	United States Army, Military History Research Collection, Carlisle Barracks, Pa.
PHC	Haverford College, Haverford, Pa.
PHi	Historical Society of Pennsylvania, Philadelphia
PPRF	Rosenbach Foundation, Philadelphia, Pa.
Sc	South Carolina State Library, Columbia
ScU	University of South Carolina, Columbia
SpSAG	Archivo General de Indias, Seville, Spain
Sw	Kungliga Biblioteket, Stockholm, Sweden
T	Tennessee State Library and Archives, Nashville
TBHay	Haywood County Archives, Haywood County Court, Brownsville, Tenn.
TDRh	Rhea County Archives, Rhea County Court, Dayton, Tenn.
TGSum	Sumner County Archives, Sumner County Court, Gallatin, Tenn.
THer	Ladies' Hermitage Association, Hermitage, Tenn.
THi	Tennessee Historical Society, Nashville
TKKn	Knox County Archives, Knox County Court, Knoxville, Tenn.
TKL	Public Library of Knoxville and Knox County, Knoxville, Tenn.
TLWil	Wilson County Archives, Wilson County Court, Lebanon, Tenn.
TM	Memphis Public Library, Memphis, Tenn.
TMM	Memphis State University, Memphis, Tenn.
TMSh	Shelby County Archives, Shelby County Court, Memphis, Tenn.
TNDa	Davidson County Archives, Davidson County Court, Nashville, Tenn.
TNJ	Joint University Libraries, Vanderbilt University, Nashville, Tenn.
TPGil	Giles County Archives, Giles County Court, Pulaski, Tenn.
TSBe	Bedford County Archives, Bedford County Court, Shelbyville, Tenn.
TU	University of Tennessee, Knoxville
Tx	Texas State Library and Historical Commission, Austin
TxU	University of Texas, Austin
UkENL	National Library of Scotland, Edinburgh, United Kingdom
ViHi	Virginia Historical Society, Richmond

ViU	University of Virginia, Charlottesville
WHi	State Historical Society of Wisconsin, Madison

SHORT TITLES

ABPC	*American Book Prices Current.*
Annals of Congress	*The Debates and Proceedings in the Congress of the United States . . . .* 42 vols. Washington, D.C., 1834–1856.
ASP	*American State Papers: Documents Legislative and Executive, of the Congress of the United States . . . .* 38 vols. Washington, D.C., 1832–1861.
Bassett	John Spencer Bassett, ed., *Correspondence of Andrew Jackson.* 7 vols. Washington, D.C., 1926–1935.
Calhoun Papers	Clyde N. Wilson et al., eds., *The Papers of John C. Calhoun.* 20 vols. to date. Columbia, S.C., 1959–.
Heiskell	S. G. Heiskell, *Andrew Jackson and Early Tennessee History.* 3 vols. Nashville, Tenn., 1921.
HRDoc	U.S. Congress, House of Representatives, *House Documents.*
HRRep	U.S. Congress, House of Representatives, *House Reports.*
Jackson	Harold D. Moser et al., eds., *The Papers of Andrew Jackson.* 4 vols. to date. Knoxville, Tenn., 1980–.
mAJs	Microfilm of *The Papers of Andrew Jackson,* Supplement (forthcoming).
Memoirs of John Quincy Adams	Charles Francis Adams, ed., *Memoirs of John Quincy Adams, Comprising Portions of His Diary from 1795 to 1848.* 12 vols. Philadelphia, Pa., 1874–77.
Nichols, *Missouri Expedition*	Roger L. Nichols, ed., *The Missouri Expedition, 1818–1820: The Journal of Surgeon John Gale with Related Documents.* Norman, Okla., 1969.
Parton	James Parton, *Life of Andrew Jackson.* 3 vols. New York, 1860.
RegKyHi	*Register of the Kentucky Historical Society.*
SDoc	U.S. Congress, Senate, *Senate Documents.*
TPUS	Clarence E. Carter and John Porter Bloom, eds., *The Territorial Papers of the United States.* 28 vols. Washington, D.C., 1934–1975.

Williams, *Beginnings of West Tennessee*	Samuel Cole Williams, *Beginnings of West Tennessee in the Land of the Chickasaws, 1541–1841*. Johnson City, Tenn., 1930.

Chronology

1816

Jan 2	Left New London, Virginia, with family en route to the Hermitage from Washington
Jan 18	John Reid, Jackson's aide-de-camp, died in Virginia; President James Madison recommended congressional approval of Cherokee land grants to Jackson, Benjamin Hawkins, and Alexander Cornells
Feb 1	Arrived at Hermitage on return from Washington
Feb 8	White settlers Daniel Johnston and McGaskey killed near Fort Claiborne by Indians
Feb 22	Appointed James Gadsden and Isaac Lewis Baker as aides-de-camp
Feb 26	Departed Nashville to tour Gulf Coast defenses
March 11	Feted at St. Stephens, Mississippi Territory
March 16	Congressional caucus nominated James Monroe for president
March 22	Arrived at New Orleans on tour of defenses; Cherokee treaty signed at Washington
March 27	House of Representatives Committee on Public Lands recommended against confirmation of Cherokee land grants to Jackson, Hawkins, and Cornells
April 10	President Madison signed bill chartering Second Bank of the United States
April 23	Arrived at Natchez en route home from tour of southern defenses
April 24	Wrote William Harris Crawford expressing reservations about transfer of Eleazar Wheelock Ripley to the Southern Division
April 27	Tariff act approved, imposing a 25% duty on many woolen, cotton, and iron manufactures
April 29	Senate approved appointments of Robert Butler as adjutant general, Arthur Peronneau Hayne as inspector general, and George Gibson as quartermaster general for Southern Division
May 7	*Nashville Whig* denounced March 22 Cherokee treaty

May 8	Reached Hermitage after tour of southern defenses
May 12	Wrote James Monroe denouncing March 22 Cherokee treaty
June 4	Appointed with David Meriwether and Jesse Franklin to negotiate for cessions of Chickasaw and Cherokee lands; Abram Maury announced that John Henry Eaton would complete John Reid's biography of Jackson
June 17	Appointed William Orlando Butler as aide-de-camp vice Isaac L. Baker
June 21	Public meeting in Nashville condemned the March 22 Cherokee treaty
July 6	Nashville citizens in public meeting adopted memorial protesting March 22 Cherokee treaty
July 24	Commenced enquiry of Tennessee's congressional delegation on their votes for Cherokee spoliations
July 27	United States naval vessels in support of troops from Jackson's division destroyed Negro Fort in Spanish Florida
Aug 14	Ordered William O. Butler to survey a route for a military road from Nashville to New Orleans
Aug 20	Left Nashville en route to Chickasaw and Cherokee treaty negotiations
Aug 27	Three Spanish ships fired on U.S.S. *Firebrand* in the Gulf of Mexico and captured it
Aug 29	Arrived at Chickasaw Council House
Sept 8	Formally opened treaty negotiations with Chickasaws and Cherokees
Sept 14	Concluded treaty with Cherokees for relinquishment of lands south of the Tennessee River
Sept 20	Concluded Chickasaw treaty
Oct 4	Obtained ratification by Cherokee council of treaty agreed to September 14
Oct 11	Returned to Nashville from treaty negotiations
Oct 22	William H. Crawford transferred from the war to the treasury department
Oct 23	Wrote to advise James Monroe regarding appointment of secretary of war
Oct 26	Appointed James McMillan Glassell as aide-de-camp vice William O. Butler
Nov 1	Edmund Pendleton Gaines found not guilty at court-martial in New York
Nov 12	Attended public dinner in Nashville honoring Eleazar W. Ripley; wrote advising Monroe to announce sale of lands recently ceded by Indians and to make cabinet appointments "without any regard to party"

Nov 22	Purchased with John Hutchings the Melton's Bluff plantation on the Tennessee River in northern Mississippi Territory
Dec 4	James Monroe elected president; Daniel D. Tompkins vice-president
Dec 9	Wrote proposing terms for purchasing lands in Mississippi Territory for Daniel Parker and friends in Washington
Dec 11	Indiana admitted as nineteenth state
Dec 27	Empowered George Washington Martin to contract for the purchase of Mississippi Territory lands
Dec 28	American Colonization Society founded in Washington

1817

Jan 1	Named a vice-president of American Colonization Society
cJan 12	Andrew Jackson Donelson left Tennessee for Military Academy
Jan 14	Denounced war department for orders to Stephen Harriman Long
Jan 16	Alexander James Dallas, Madison's secretary of the treasury and ad interim secretary of war, died
Feb 20	Banks of Philadelphia, New York, Baltimore, and Richmond resumed specie payments
cFeb 22	Ralph Eleazar Whitesides Earl painted his first portrait of Jackson
March 3	Act creating Alabama Territory passed
March 4	James Monroe inaugurated as president
March 7	Andrew Erwin submitted answer in lawsuit, *Jackson* v. *Erwin,* involving Duck River lands
March 11	Wrote editors of Lexington *Kentucky Reporter* disputing their discussion of conduct of Kentucky troops at New Orleans
April 11	Suspended removal of intruders from Cherokee lands
April 21	Received from Edmund P. Gaines a report of Alexander Arbuthnot's activities with the Seminoles in Florida
April 22	Issued division order forbidding officers to obey war department orders unless routed through division headquarters
April 28–29	Rush-Bagot agreement concluded, providing for mutual disarmament of United States and British forces on the Great Lakes

May 24	President Monroe issued proclamation for sale of portion of Creek lands to commence in August at Milledgeville
May 29	Left Nashville to commence negotiations with Cherokees at Hiwassee Garrison
June 11	Arrived at Huntsville
June 18	Arrived at Cherokee Agency
June 20	Commenced Cherokee negotiations
June 29	Gregor MacGregor seized Amelia Island
July 4	Ground broken to begin construction of the Erie Canal
July 8	Signed Cherokee treaty
July 13	Reached John Coffee's residence in Rutherford County, Tennessee, en route from the Cherokee negotiations
Aug 2	*New-York Columbian* criticized Jackson's April 22 order
Aug 4	Arthur P. Hayne began purchasing land for himself and friends at the Milledgeville sale
Aug 19	*Nashville Clarion* published Jackson's letter of July 23 to John Adair re the performance of Kentucky troops at the Battle of New Orleans
Sept 2	Offered to resign if his disagreement with the administration over the April 22 Division Order could not be adjusted
Sept 3	Received anonymous letter from New York asserting that Winfield Scott had denounced Jackson's April 22 Division Order as mutiny
Sept 8	Queried Scott about his criticism of the April 22 Division Order
Oct 5	Monroe requested that Jackson remain in the army
Oct 27	Left Nashville for Melton's Bluff
Oct 30	War department ordered Edmund P. Gaines not to attack Indians in Florida without authorization
Nov 12	Edmund P. Gaines ordered to Amelia Island
Nov 20	John Hutchings died; Jackson named guardian of his son Andrew Jackson Hutchings
Nov 21	U.S. troops battled Indians at Fowltown
Nov 30	Returned to Nashville from John Hutchings's funeral; supply boat ascending Apalachicola River attacked by Indians, and Lt. Richard W. Scott and most of his party killed
[Nov-Dec]	John Jackson, John McCrea, James Jackson, Sr. and Jr., John Donelson, Jr., John Christmas McLemore, Thomas Childress, and John Henry Eaton formed Pensacola land speculation company; rumor circulated that John Adair had killed Jackson in duel

Dec 1	Received Winfield Scott's reply of October 4, denying authorship of the *New-York Columbian* charges but stating that he regarded the order as a "reprimand" to the president
Dec 2	President Monroe proposed arrangement for settlement of Jackson's concerns about war department orders
Dec 3	Wrote to Winfield Scott denouncing him as "contemptible"
Dec 10	Mississippi admitted as twentieth state
Dec 16	Secretary of War John Caldwell Calhoun authorized Edmund P. Gaines to attack Indian towns in Florida
Dec 23	United States forces seized Amelia Island, driving off filibusters
Dec 26	Ordered to take command in Georgia and suppress Seminole hostilities

1818

Jan 1	Copyright notice for Reid and Eaton, *Life of Andrew Jackson,* registered in Philadelphia
Jan 11	Requested selected officers to recruit Tennessee volunteers for Seminole campaign
Jan 22	Left Nashville to commence Seminole campaign
Jan 26	Arrived at Huntsville en route to Georgia
Jan 30	James Monroe directed Secretary of War Calhoun to instruct Jackson not to attack any post occupied by Spanish troops
Jan 31	Tennessee volunteers rendezvoused in Fayetteville
Feb 9	Arrived at Fort Hawkins, Georgia
Feb 12	Arrived at Hartford, Georgia
cFeb 12	Allegedly received a letter from John Rhea conveying Monroe's approval for invasion of Florida
Feb 14	Reported to John C. Calhoun allegations of David Brydie Mitchell's involvement in slave smuggling from Amelia Island
March 2	John Coffee on behalf of self and Jackson signed agreement to associate with John Childress, James Jackson, and John Donelson, Jr., to purchase land in Alabama for Philadelphia investors
March 10	Assumed command of troops at Fort Scott; commenced march to former site of Negro Fort

March 12	Cypress Land Company formed, with Jackson as a stockholder
March	Andrew Erwin's mercantile business in Georgia collapsed, prompting his settlement in Tennessee
March–April	Acquired land at Evans Spring, Lauderdale County, Alabama
April 1	Destroyed Seminole town of Mikasuki
April 3	Isaac McKeever captured Josiah Francis and Homathlemico, Red Stick leaders
April 7	Seized Fort St. Marks in Florida; arrested Alexander Arbuthnot
April 8	Ordered Josiah Francis and Homathlemico hanged
April 9	Left Fort St. Marks for Suwannee towns
April 12	Tennessee volunteers and Indian auxiliaries skirmished with Seminoles near Econofina River
April 15	Elected to membership in the American Antiquarian Society
April 16	Destroyed Bowleg's Town on Suwannee River
April 17	Commissioned, with Isaac Shelby, to negotiate Chickasaw treaty
April 18	Captured Robert Christie Ambrister; George Gibson appointed commissary general of subsistence
April 22	Georgia militia attacked Chehaw, a friendly Creek town
April 25	Returned to Fort St. Marks
April 29	Ordered execution of Alexander Arbuthnot and Robert C. Ambrister
May 2	Returned to Fort Gadsden
May 7	Appointed Richard Keith Call aide-de-camp vice James M. Glassell; ordered arrest of Obed Wright of the Georgia militia for attack on Chehaw town
May 7–8	Left Fort Gadsden for Pensacola
May 24	Occupied Pensacola
May 28	Received surrender of Fort San Carlos de Barrancas
June 1	Reached Fort Montgomery on return from Florida; *Savannah Republican* reported that Jackson planned to challenge Winfield Scott
June 16	Daniel Smith, grandfather of Andrew J. Donelson, died
June 18	Isaac McKeever captured the slavetrading vessels *Louisa* and *Merino* near Mobile
June 26	Reached Columbia, Tennessee, and discharged Tennessee volunteers
June 28	Arrived, to celebrations, at Nashville
July 8	Spanish minister Luis de Onís demanded that the United States return captured forts in Florida to Spain

July 15–21	President Monroe's cabinet met to discuss Jackson's actions in Florida and to draft response to Luis de Onís
July 19	President Monroe wrote Jackson about transcending orders and provoking a state of war, which only Congress, not the executive, could declare
July 22	Cypress Land Company opened sales of lots in Florence, Alabama; Jackson, James Gadsden, and James Craine Bronaugh jointly acquired nine lots
July 27	Washington *National Intelligencer* reported President Monroe's decision to surrender forts in Florida taken by Jackson and stated that Jackson had attacked forts on his own responsibility
Aug 5	Requested Richard K. Call to collect evidence justifying incursion into Florida
Aug 10	Winfield Scott published article in the *New-York Evening Post* criticizing the execution of Robert C. Ambrister
Aug 28	James Gadsden arrived in Washington with communications from Jackson
Sept 5	John H. Eaton appointed to Senate seat vacated by George Washington Campbell
Sept 9	President Monroe suggested to John C. Calhoun that he note for the record that Jackson had exceeded his orders during the Seminole campaign
Sept 18	Attended dinner at Nashville Inn in honor of Isaac Shelby, who was visiting the Hermitage en route to Chickasaw negotiations
Sept 20	Appointed Richard Ivy Easter as aide-de-camp vice James Gadsden
[Sept]	Hired William White Crawford as overseer on the Alabama plantations
Oct 10	Hugh Young and Richard K. Call arrived in Nashville with depositions about the situation in Pensacola prompting the previous spring's invasion
Oct 12	Purchased town lots at Marathon, Alabama
Oct 17	Severn Donelson, Jackson's brother-in-law, died
Oct 19	Concluded Chickasaw treaty
Oct 20	Convention signed at London setting boundary between British North America and the United States at the 49th parallel from the Lake of the Woods to the crest of the Rocky Mountains
Nov 5	Attended land sales at Huntsville and purchased section in Franklin County, Alabama, at minimum price when none bid against him

Nov 12	Arrived at the Hermitage from the Chickasaw negotiations
Nov 20	Attended Nashville ball in honor of Chickasaw treaty
Dec 3	Illinois admitted as twenty-first state
Dec 12	Conveyed half of his quarter interest in the Chickasaw Bluff lands (Memphis) to James Winchester
Dec 22	"Algernon Sidney" began publishing anti-Jackson letters in the *Richmond Enquirer*

1819

Jan 3	Mary Donelson Hamblen, Jackson's niece, died
Jan 6	Chickasaw treaty ratified by the Senate
cJan 7	Left for Washington
Jan 12	Reached Knoxville en route to Washington; House Committee on Military Affairs condemned executions of Alexander Arbuthnot and Robert C. Ambrister
Jan 20	Henry Clay attacked invasion of Florida in House of Representatives
Jan 23	Arrived in Washington
Jan	Purchased in Washington slave girl Sally for Rachel Jackson
Feb 2	Supreme Court rendered verdict in *Trustees of Dartmouth College* v. *Woodward*
Feb 3	Denied to John Quincy Adams that he had invaded Pensacola to protect his and his friends' land speculation
Feb 8	House debate on Seminole campaign ended, exonerating Jackson
Feb 11	Left Washington for tour of East and arrived in Baltimore; Jane Caffery Earl, Jackson's niece, and infant died during childbirth
Feb 17	Sat for portrait by Thomas Sully in Philadelphia
Feb 20	Arrived in New York
Feb 22	Adams-Onís Treaty signed in Washington
Feb 24	Lacock committee report condemned Florida invasion
Feb 28–March 1	Returned to Baltimore and sat for portrait by Rembrandt Peale
March 2	Returned to Washington; Arkansas Territory created
March 6	Supreme Court handed down decision in *M'Culloch* v. *Maryland*

March 9	Left for Tennessee; "Strictures" against the Lacock report published in the Washington *National Intelligencer*
March 25	Reached Knoxville en route from Washington
March 29	Commissioned as Choctaw treaty negotiator
March 30	James Monroe embarked on southern and western tour
March	John Cocke published *Letter to the Hon. John H. Eaton, December 16, 1818*, questioning the reliability of Eaton's biography of Jackson
April 2	Arrived at the Hermitage
April 6	Feted in Nashville; DeWitt Clinton denounced Winfield Scott and denied authorship of the anonymous letter to Jackson of August 14, 1817
April 9	*Correspondence between Major General Jackson and Brevet Major General Scott* published in the *Richmond Enquirer*
April 12	John Rhea letter detailing President Monroe's approval for invasion of Florida reportedly burned
April 18	Willie Blount characterized Jackson's detractors as "poor minded bitches"
April 20	Began to solicit from John Clark of Georgia information on William H. Crawford's activities
April	John H. Eaton responded to John Cocke's publication with *To the Public*
May 2–12	Suffered severe health problems
May 3	James Gadsden informed Jackson, confirming Jackson's suspicion, that William H. Crawford was the rumored author of the Lacock committee report on the Florida invasion
May 24	John Clark disclosed to Jackson that William H. Crawford had revealed the division in President Monroe's cabinet over Jackson's invasion of Florida
June 5	President Monroe arrived at the Hermitage
June 9	Nashville citizens officially welcomed the president
June 11	President Monroe returned to the Hermitage
June 12	Jenkin Whiteside filed amended bill of complaint in *Jackson* v. *Erwin*
June 14	Left with President Monroe for tour of Kentucky
June 17	Criticized by "C" for failure to complete military road
July 2	Arrived with President Monroe in Lexington, Kentucky
July 11	Returned to the Hermitage from tour of Kentucky
July 31	Chastised Eleazar W. Ripley for failure to complete the military road

July	John Cocke responded to John H. Eaton's pamphlet with a second publication
cAug 7	Left for Florence, Alabama
Aug 12	Hired Malachi Nicholson as overseer of Andrew J. Hutchings's Alabama plantation; Choctaw council refused to meet with Jackson and other commissioners, aborting treaty negotiation
Aug 14	Andrew Erwin published anti-Eaton piece in the Shelbyville *Tennessee Herald,* which also accused Jackson of complicity in the 1818 Chickasaw salt lick reserve for William Berkeley Lewis
Aug 16	Returned to Nashville
Aug 21	Contracted with Benjamin Decker for carpentry and construction of the new Hermitage
Aug 25	Prompted James Jackson and Jenkin Whiteside on their public response to Andrew Erwin and the Duck River land controversy
Aug 20–25	Prepared report to Tennessee legislature re salt lick reserve
Aug 26–Sept 6	Remained bedridden at Hermitage because of illness
Sept 4	*Nashville Whig* carried article discussing the Duck River lands
Sept 9	Advised Richard K. Call, John H. Eaton's second in expected duel with Andrew Erwin, on code duello
Sept 14	Robert Hays, Jackson's longtime friend, died
Sept 15	John Overton published *Vindication of the Measures of the President and His Commanding Generals*
Sept 21	Attended meeting of Tennessee legislature
Sept 23	Report on salt lick reserve submitted to legislature
Sept 24	Eaton-Erwin duel cancelled
Sept 29	Advised President Monroe that Andrew Erwin, candidate for federal marshal in West Tennessee, was involved in the David B. Mitchell slave-smuggling affair
Oct 8	Denied that he wished a reconciliation with Senator John Williams
Oct 9	John H. Eaton elected to the U.S. Senate for remaining two years of George W. Campbell's term
Oct 22	Left for northern Alabama and inspection of military road
Nov 9	Alabama legislature commended Jackson's career
Nov 14	Returned to Nashville
Nov 22	Tennessee legislature commended Jackson's career
Nov 29	Forwarded to Washington his memorial to the Senate on the Seminole War; informed President Monroe of his intention to resign

Dec 11	Contracted with Nelson P. Jones to superintend Evans Spring farm
cDec 12	Left for Florence, Alabama
Dec 14	Alabama admitted as twenty-second state
Dec 26	Returned to the Hermitage

1820

Jan 7	Attended Nashville ball honoring Battle of New Orleans
Jan 12	Thomas Childress deposed that Jackson was neither directly nor indirectly interested in the Pensacola land speculation
Feb 2	Tennessee and Kentucky negotiators agreed to settlement of disputed boundary between the states
Feb 23	Rufus King of New York submitted to the U.S. Senate Jackson's revised memorial answering Lacock committee
Feb 26	Ordered removal of intruders from Cherokee lands
Feb 28	Storrs committee criticized Florida invasion
March 3	First Missouri compromise completed
April 13	William Donelson, Jackson's brother-in-law, died
May 11	House of Representatives called for reduction of the U.S. Army
cMay 17	Left for tour of military road and Creek and Cherokee nations, and to obtain duplicate deed of release from David Allison's heirs
[May]	Military road completed
June 3	Received duplicate deed of release from Allison heirs
July 1	Andrew J. Donelson and Edward George Washington Butler commissioned officers in U.S. Army
July 12	Travelled to Murfreesboro to protest proposed state loan office
July 13	Commissioned as Choctaw treaty negotiator
July 15	Davidson County citizens adopted memorial denouncing the state loan office bill
July 17	Memorial of Davidson County citizens presented to legislature
Aug 6	Arthur P. Hayne resigned from U.S. Army
Sept 14	Left for Choctaw negotiations
Sept 20	Andrew J. Donelson appointed aide-de-camp vice Richard I. Easter
Sept 28	Arrived at Choctaw treaty ground

Oct 1	James Gadsden appointed inspector general, Southern Division, vice Arthur P. Hayne
Oct 3	Pushmataha and Apuckshunnubbe, principal chiefs of the Choctaw Nation, arrived for treaty negotiations at Doak's Stand
Oct 18	Signed Treaty of Doak's Stand
Nov 4	Terminated contract with Nelson P. Jones at Evans Spring farm
Nov 10	Returned to Nashville; ill until November 13
Dec 6	James Monroe reelected president of the United States

The Papers, 1816–1820

1816

On December 24, 1815, General Andrew Jackson set out from Washington on his return to Tennessee, retracing the route he had taken in October and November, when he journeyed to the capital to discuss the peacetime reorganization of the army and to obtain vindication of his conduct at New Orleans. The Jackson party arrived at Lynchburg, Virginia, on December 31 and spent the following day visiting the family of his aide-de-camp, John Reid (1784–1816), at Poplar Grove near New London in Campbell County. When Jackson left on January 2, Reid, his pregnant wife Elizabeth, and two children remained, intending to return to Tennessee in a few months.

Jackson had expected to reach the Hermitage on January 28, but because of the severe weather he did not arrive until late on February 1. It was at that time that he learned of Reid's death on January 18 from influenza.

Intending to leave immediately on a tour of southern defenses, Jackson postponed his departure until February 26 because of a bad cold and the "Kentucky plague," as the influenza epidemic was called in Nashville. In the interim, he sought to secure his papers at Poplar Grove in Virginia and to identify a writer to complete the biography of the Hero of New Orleans that Reid had begun in 1815. It was not until May, after consideration of several candidates, that Jackson and his advisers settled upon John Henry Eaton (1790–1856) for the task.

To John Reid

Major Goodsons January 15th. 1816

Dr. Sir

after a detention of four days by breaking of my Carriage, & bad weather I reached here this evening all well, and hope in two days more to reach Rogersville—

The weather has been extremely cold, the ground hard frozen, which added to the quantity of rock in the road, has made it rough travelling.

you will please recollect, that I left Fanny for your use and as your property—If you can exchange for a good horse that will draw your carriage, it might save the expence of sending horses to you—but I beg you to advise me on this head immediately, as I intend if an opportunity offers to send on to you two draft horses as soon as I reach home—

I need not say to you my anxiety for your success in your book—there are many weighty reasons, that create this anxiety—you like myself have your enemies, and I have no doubt some there are, who would rejoice at its failure to be published—you will I know in this disappoint them, if once published success must & will attend you—On reflecting on the official report of the Battle of Emuckfa—I am apprehensive, that the death of Genl [John] Coffees' aid de camp and the wound recd by the Genl has been omitted to be noted—I beg you to look over the official report, and if I am correct in my apprehension be pleased to correct it in your history—[1]

Please write me, to reach Nashville by the 28th. instant, I hope to be there on that day—endeavour to be out before the sale of the lands and prevail upon your father to sell & remove to the west—did I not clearly see his benefit & that of his rising family in this, I assure you I would not recommend it—[2]

I have not heard from the city since I left you—Capt [Joseph H.] Coleman has not overtaken me—[3]

Be pleased to present Mrs. [Rachel] Jackson & myself afectionately to your lady & children your father & the whole of the family, and believe me to be sincerely your friend

Andrew Jackson

Andrew [Jackson, Jr.] often speaks of you & William & enquires when you will overtake us[4] The citizens as I pass make particular enquiry about your welfare, and appear anxious for the appearance of your book—should there be any dificulty in getting it printed—write me & I will procure the means—& the sale of the Book will fully indemnify.

ALS, NjP (4-1360). Published in *Cincinnati Commercial Gazette,* January 13, 1883 (extract). Postmarked Abingdon, Virginia, January 18, where Jackson had probably taken lodging with John Goodson, sometime justice of the peace in Washington County.

1. Coffee (1772–1833), friend and comrade in arms during the Creek War and the Battle of New Orleans, had married Jackson's niece Mary Donelson (1792–1871), daughter of John (1755–1830), in 1809. In his report to Thomas Pinckney, January 29, 1814, Jackson had mentioned both Coffee's wound and the death of Alexander Donelson (1784–1814), Coffee's aide-de-camp, at the Battle of Emuckfau on January 28, 1814. See John Reid and John Henry Eaton, *The Life of Andrew Jackson* . . . (Philadelphia, 1817), pp. 128–29, for the incorporation of Jackson's suggestion.

2. General sales of land in the Creek cession did not begin until mid-1817, two years after legislation authorizing the boundary survey. John Reid's father, Nathan (1753–1830), veteran of the revolution, did not move west.

3. Coleman (d. 1819), a Nashville merchant and paymaster for the Tennessee troops in the Gulf campaign, had gone to Washington to settle his accounts.

4. Rachel Donelson (c1767–1828). Their adopted child, Andrew Jackson Donelson (1808–65), called Andrew Jackson, Jr., was the son of Severn (1773–1818) and Elizabeth Rucker Donelson (1782–1828). In 1809 John Reid had married Elizabeth Branch Maury (c1793–1852), the eldest child of Abram Maury (1766–1825), a Williamson County planter

and sometime state legislator. Their children were William Steptoe (1813–99), Sophia (1811–87), and John, Jr. (1816–85).

From Arthur Peronneau Hayne

Philadelphia 24th. January 1815 [1816]

Dear General,

I have had the pleasure to hear of tho' not from you. Major Read says you suffered much from the Cold. My business is completed so far as relates to myself. I have not yet heard from Genl. [Jacob Jennings] Brown.[1] Nothing else now keeps me. Doctor [Philip Syng] Physick says if yr breast should be affected you must take Bark, & regrets as well as the whole City, that Mrs. Jackson and yourself did not visit Philadelphia. From my description of yr Arm, he says the *upper* part must be laid open, the *lower* part on no consideration whatsoever. There are pieces of bone resting on the Artery which *must* be removed.[2] I find Congress have not yet acted in yr case. I expect to hear from Mr. [John] Gaillard in the course of the ensuing week, & should I believe my persona would be of advantage to you, shall then take Washington in my route to Nashville.[3] As relating to our mutual friend Major Read & his Book, Judge [Thomas] Cooper and myself are now busily engaged on that subject[4]—We shall sift the matter. I shall call at his Father's on my way out, & then give him the result of our joint exertions. If he has Ten Thousand subscribers he must do well. I shall fix myself and family on the Alabama. My mind is made up on this Point. I hope to be with you on the lst. March—shall [write] you before I start.

God bless and preserve you is the prayer of your sincere obliged and affectionate friend—

A.P. Hayne

P.S. I beg to be remembered to Mrs. Jackson and your son, also Col. [Robert] Butler & his family[5] & all enquiring friends A.P.H

ALS, DLC (15). Published in Bassett, 2:226–27 (extract). Hayne (1790–1867), a South Carolinian, served as inspector general of the Southern Division, 1816–20.

1. Hayne had requested a transfer to Jackson's command and was awaiting approval from Brown (1775–1828), commander of the Northern Division.

2. Physick (1768–1837), surgeon and leading medical authority in Philadelphia, was recommending the use of quinine (Peruvian or red "bark"). The bullet and bone splinters in Jackson's left arm, resulting from his brawl with Jesse and Thomas Hart Benton in September 1813, were not removed until 1832 in Washington.

3. Gaillard (1765–1826) was U.S. senator from South Carolina. Two matters involving Jackson—the land claims of the heirs of John Donelson (c1718–86), Jackson's father-in-law, and the Creek donation to Jackson—were pending before Congress. Hayne was here clearly referring to the Creek donation. For discussion of both issues, see Hayne to AJ, March 27, below, and George W. Campbell to AJ, February 18.

4. Cooper (1759–1839), professor of chemistry at the University of Pennsylvania and for-

mer state judge, and Hayne were negotiating for the publication of Reid's biography of Jackson. On January 25, Cooper sent Hayne a publication offer from John Conrad (DLC-20), but the contract went to Mathew Carey (1760–1839) of Philadelphia.

5. Butler (1786–1860), son of Thomas Butler (1754–1805) and Adjutant General of the Southern Division, had married Jackson's niece Rachel Hays (b. 1786) in 1808; by this time they had at least three children.

By an act of March 3, 1815 (3 U.S. Statutes at Large *228–29), Congress had created a three-man commission to survey the boundaries of the lands ceded by the Creeks at the Treaty of Fort Jackson, but the commission's work was already much delayed when John Sevier died in September. To prevent further delay, when the war department notified Edmund Pendleton Gaines (1777–1849), commander of the eastern section of Jackson's Southern Division, of his appointment to replace Sevier, it also enclosed a commission for John Coffee, who had been recommended by Jackson. Coffee's commission was to be used only if Creek agent Benjamin Hawkins (1754–1816) could not serve. Gaines, however, sent the commission on to Coffee, and Coffee accepted in December.*

Encouraged by Jackson, Coffee soon embarked on a survey of the northern boundary of the Creek cession, but since only three commissioners were authorized by law and Gaines, Hawkins, and original commissioner William Barnett (1761–1832), a former congressman from Georgia, were also acting as commissioners, the legality of Coffee's actions was questionable. The resolution of this embarrassing situation would contribute to strained relations between Jackson, who supported Coffee's actions, and Secretary of War William Harris Crawford (1772–1834), who did not (see AJ to Coffee, February 2, 13, to James Monroe, May 12, and Crawford to AJ, May 20, all below).

To John Coffee

Hermitage February 2nd. 1816

Dr. Genl

Late last night we reached home, after a tedious Journey occasioned by bad roads & inclement weather, all in good health, bad colds excepted— On this morning I had the pleasure of receiving yours of the 27th of Decbr., it passed me twice upon the road—

At the city I was informed of your appointment, rejoiced at it, and gave assurances that the line would now be run without delay—

I am happy to see from your letter that you are determined to act promptly and run the line agreable to the best information you Possess, the commissioners are the proper Judges, & must act from the best information they can obtain, I have but little doubt, that Justice will be done by persuing the information you possess as it respects the cherokees, and the choctaws have no claim that is well founded East of the Tombigby—[1]

I believe no dificulty will be experienced by you in the settlement of your accounts at the war office your receipts were deposited with the accountant, and as soon as the press of business will permit, a statement will be made & Inclosed to you—Q.M. [Robert] Andrews due bills to your regt. will not be paid, I deposited them with the accountant, Took his recpt, & statement in writing, why payment was refused[2]—Our mutual friend Major Reid *is no more,* I have this moment recd a letter from the Postmaster New London stating that on the 20th ult. he was *buried*[3]—he was taken on the 18th. & lived but 18 hours—Thus has one of the bravest & best of men Escaped ten thousand dangers in the field of Battle to fall a Victim to a burning fever—the Town of Nashville is visited with a pestilence that (report says) carries off three & four of a night—I shall if health permits set out in a few days to Ft Bowyer[4] & the southern boundary of the cession from the Creeks, to Establish some garrisons, & cause to be commenced, some auxiliary fortifications for the better protection of that frontier & Neworleans, I wish to fall in with you & Genl Gains, & will thank you to write me at what point you will be at a given date—

I have read with no less astonishment & surprise than yourself, the information relative to the secrete attempt of Doctor [John Robertson] Bedford & Genl [William] Carroll to injure you & myself—such base ingratitude will meet its reward—It is evidence of such wanton wickedness & depravity of heart that I can scarcely believe it myself, that I have huged such monsters to my boosom, called them friend, and risqued my life for the preservation of the charector & feelings of such a man as it appears Genl Carroll is[5]—I shall see Mr James Jackson, hear with patience, & determine with firmness, I cannot disguise to either when I meet them my feelings & contempt for such base conduct—under the auspices of undisguised friendship.[6]

your friends are all in good health Betsy Maclemore excepted, who (as the old scotch Irish says) is *Grunting*—I hope in a few days she will present Mr M. with a fine son—[7]

Mrs. J. Joins me in best wishes for your health & happiness & believe me to be, respectfully yr mo. ob. serv.

Andrew Jackson

P.S. I have the express promise that you will be appointed receiver of Publick money—[8] A.J.

ALS, THi (4-1372).

1. The Choctaws ceded their claims to land east of the Tombigbee River in the treaty of October 24, 1816.

2. Andrews was an assistant deputy quartermaster general; his receipt and statement have not been found. It has not been determined whether Coffee's disputed accounts grew out of the Natchez expedition in 1813 or the New Orleans campaign in 1814.

3. Letter not found.

4. Fort Bowyer was located at Mobile Point.

5. The Bedford-Carroll matter involved, as Coffee reported on December 27, 1815, rumors of fraudulent land purchases by AJ, Coffee, and others. Bedford (1782–1827), a native of Mecklenburg County, Virginia, was a physician in Rutherford County. Later, he abandoned medicine for a mercantile business in Alabama and Louisiana. Carroll (1788–1844), elected major general of the Tennessee militia after Jackson's appointment to the U.S. army in 1814, later served as governor of the state. On the issue, see also AJ to Coffee, February 13, below. Other rumors of the abuse of public trust for private gain against Jackson, family, and friends grew out of the 1818 Chickasaw treaty and the invasion of Pensacola (all discussed below), and emerged during the Seminole investigation and the presidential campaigns of 1824 and 1828.

6. James Jackson (1782–1840), at this time a Nashville merchant, was Jackson's partner and agent in a number of land speculations in Tennessee and Alabama. About 1818 he relocated to Florence, Alabama.

7. Elizabeth Donelson (1796–1836), sister to Mary Coffee, had married John Christmas McLemore (1790–1864) in 1815. Their daughter Mary was born on February 16.

8. In 1817 Coffee was appointed surveyor, instead of receiver, for the northern section of Mississippi Territory (later Alabama), and he held the post until his death.

To Nathan Reid, Jr.

Hermitage near Nashville
February 8th 1816

Dr Sir

Your letter of the 24th ult. containing the unpleasant information of the sudden & unexpected death of my dear, & much Esteemed friend Major John Reid reached me yesterday.

I came home on the first day of this month, on the second received a number of letters that had reached Nashville. The first I opened was from Major Reid, of date the 10th. of January amonghst other things advising me of his & his families good health—the next I opened was one from the postmaster New London of date 21st. January stating that on the day preceding he had accompanyed the remains of my friend to his grave. The shock that this produced is more easily Judged of than explained, having Just before finished the reading of his letter of the 10th. stating that he enjoyed good health. It is wrong to murmur at the decrees of heaven, *the lords will be done,* but such is the frailty of human nature that it will repine at the untimely loss of dear & valuable friends, and often exclaim why were they not spared a little longer. I can well figure to myself the distress of his parents wife, & brethern, he was there darling, they like myself knew his vallue as a man and as a child & brother and like myself appreciated his merit. We must cease to mourn for the dead and endeavour to cheer, aid, and comfort the living. On the receipt of the letter from the postmaster

New London, I lost not a moment, to write Major A. Murry giving him the melancholly intelligence[1] I have not yet heard from him, but have no doubt if his health will permit will immediately go to his daughter The interest of his Dear little family must be attended to, and the Book must be finished for there benefit—if none of his friends or acquaintances in Virginia will undertake to finish the work, I will endeavour to get some person, whose talents and integrity can be relied on to do Justice to the work to compleat it for the benefit of his little family.

It is all important to me that all the papers of a Publick nature, and all others appertaining to my office be carefully preserved—Those who finishes the work must have free access to the originals or copies must be made out & furnished them—The original papers must be carefully preserved & sent on to me by a safe hand, well bound up, the expence of which I will pay. On the event of none of his friends or acquaintances in Virginia will undertake to compleat the work, please to send on the whole papers, books & manuscript, contained in the Trunk and Major A. Murry & myself will endeavour to have the work compleated, and the neat proceeds applied to the benefit of his family—

I will depend upon your care of the papers untill a safe opportunity offers for their convayence to me. If Mrs. Reid returns to this country let the Trunk & papers be sent on with her, The Filley I left, was a present from me to Major Reid, as a small Token of my Esteem—If Major Murry goes on horses &c &c will be forwarded, on the receipt of this please write me & give me information whether any of Major Reids friends will undertake finishing his Book, young Mr [William] Steptoe I am Told, is a young man of good education & competent to the Task[2]—give me a statement of the progress of the work, any labour or information in my power shall be freely bestowed, to have the work compleated.

Make a tender of Mrs. Jackson & my best wishes to your father mother & family, and to Mrs. J. Reid and the dear little children, say to them we sincerely regret & feel the loss they have sustained in Major Reid our exertions will not be wanting to render his little family any services in our power, & accept assurances of our friendship & Esteem

Andrew Jackson

ALS, T (4-1386). Published in *Cincinnati Commercial Gazette,* January 13, 1883 (extract). Nathan Reid, Jr., was a younger brother of John.

1. None of the the letters mentioned have been found.

2. Steptoe, a Bedford, Virginia, physician, for whom John Reid's oldest son was named, did not undertake the completion of Reid's biography of Jackson, but he did publish "A Sketch of the Life of Maj. John Reid" in the *Lynchburg Press,* May 23.

In late May 1814, Secretary of War John Armstrong (1758–1843) issued a general order calling for dismissal from service of any commissioned of-

ficer who engaged in a duel. Two months later, on August 1, the order was enforced in the case of Charles Henry Roberts and John B. Rose, both second lieutenants with the 15th Infantry, for a duel on July 11 in which Roberts suffered a broken thigh bone.

The case became something of a cause célèbre, in part because it was the first instance of enforcement of the order and in part because of the efforts of the prominent Morris family of New York to gain Roberts's reinstatement. Jackson's letter, below, to William Harris Crawford, then James Madison's secretary of war, responded to a request from William W. Morris (letter not found) for an appeal. Roberts, Staats Morris's stepson, descended from a distinguished South Carolina family: his grandfather, Owen, a member of the South Carolina provincial assembly, died at the Battle of Stono, at which Jackson also served and lost a brother; his father, Richard Brooke, also lost his life in service. Jackson's intervention perhaps stemmed more from his sense of honor than from any personal involvement.

Roberts was not reinstated, but the evidence suggests that in other instances the war department did not vigorously enforce the anti-dueling order (see AJ to Edmund P. Gaines, November 22, 1815, in Jackson, *3:394).*

To William Harris Crawford

Headquarters D. of the South.
Nashville, February 11. 1816.

Sir,

The Enclosed letter reached me since my return to this place, & I think it proper that it should be laid before you. Subordination & strict obedience of orders, in all cases, ought to be required of officers in the Service of the U. States—But in the ⟨present⟩ case before us, as long as officers of the Army possess those exalted, honorable feelings that lead them on to heroic achievments, cases will arise, when honor & every noble sentiment as officers will compel them to appeal to this mode for redress: if they do not, in many cases they will be branded with the Epithet *coward*. Every officer possessing proper Military pride, recollects that noble motto, which is & ought always to be before the eyes of the honorable & brave, "Death before Dishonor." It does therefore appear to me that the conduct towards Lt. Roberts, in striking him from the Rolls, was severe; that if he had been brought before a Court Martial, circumstances might have been shewn, that notwithstanding the act was a disobedience of orders, that would have mitigated the sentence from the *highest* penalty of the law, that, he was still a brave, honorable & useful officer, & his services retained for the benefit of his country. I *cannot dissemble,* this is the kind of officers, when my country is in danger I like to command. They will always bravely support the Eagles of their Country, & never disgrace themselves by cowardice.[1] The *brave* are always virtuous. I am &c.

A. Jackson

LC, DLC (62).

1. The national colors carried by U.S. Army regiments featured an eagle as the central motif.

To John Coffee

February 13th 1816

Dr. Genl.

By the express you will receive several official communications[1]—This is private—I was scarcely in Town untill the Genl waited upon me, I was surrounded with company—his looks denoted the sensations of his mind, he knew I was advised, of his conduct, and I thought I saw that a guilty conscience *needs* no accuser—[2]

write me where you will be in ten, fifteen & twenty days, I will see you on my rout and I am compelled to wait untill the next Tuesdays Mail, for dispatches I expect to receive, and for some information of the Engineer—[3]

I have said, write to the other commissioners, inform them of the information, and your intended rout, have either there unqualified approbation or disapprobation—But do you progress with the line—I have enclosed you an order to have raised 25 mounted gunmen as a guard & I have also enclosed you a letter to Mr. J[ohn] M Armstrong[4]—If you have confidence in him (for I have none) send it to him—If not you can raise the men in one day, and any person who is able will furnish the supplies—& notwithstanding I am not Legally authorised, to call for such a force they will be as punctually paid as any others—go on my Dear Genl & compleat the line & show them that you are as prompt in the cabinet as in the field—But mark one thing we have found that all Generals are not confidential men possessing gratitude, & let me repeat have the approbation or disapprobation of the other commissioners, the promptitud with which you have commenced the delay of others, will create a Jealousy in there minds excuse must be sought for, & censure if possible will be endeavoured to be thrown on the active agent to *Screen* the *drone* from blame & punishment—Therefore as you have taken upon yourself the responsibility of acting alone,[5] have the whole honor, or the whole blame, or the unamous approbation of the commissioners. There is but little doubt if promptly applied to they will approve the whole, to participate in the approbation that must accompany your industry—Have either there full approbation or there dissent—you can fully Justify your conduct & proceed promptly, finish the line with as little delay as possible The object of the Govt. is to bring into markett this land & have it populated—& I expect your report of the compleating the line will reach the war department as soon as that of the commissioners who ran the line to Georgia.[6] This will be as it ought to be, and as I have assured the Goverment—then finish it without delay—and realise the opinion I have assured the goverment ought always to be entertained of you—I will be with you—shortly—& run the line agreable to the best information you have & can obtain—your own Judgt is your guide, and proceed thereon and you a*[re]* right, *Cold water* is in the Creek Country,[7] *[the]* Choctaws has no claim well found East of Tombigby—By running the line to Tombigby, will leave it open to the Choctaws to shew there claim, and combat the proofs of the Creeks. This will open the field to Justice you are right to persue your line of conduct adopted—I am yours affectionately

Andrew Jackson

P.S. I write in haste—I neither have time to read it over, correct or keep a copy—I wrote you your accounts would easily be settled—[8]

Andrew Jackson

I have no money I can appropriate to the quartermaster department or commissioners. I have assumed the amount of the expense of your express one dollar 75/100. charge it in your account I shall charge it to yours

ALS, THi (4-1398). Published in Bassett, 2:230–31.

1. See AJ to Coffee and to John M. Armstrong, February 13.

2. Jackson was alluding to General William Carroll and the Bedford-Carroll rumors (see above, AJ to Coffee, February 2).

3. Jackson was awaiting the arrival of James Gadsden (1788–1858; Yale 1806) of the Corps of Engineers, whom the war department had sent to tour the southwestern district and to select sites for the defense of New Orleans and Mobile. Gadsden joined Jackson by February 21, was appointed aide-de-camp on February 22, and remained a member of Jackson's "military family" until 1821.

4. Armstrong, a resident of Williamson County and lieutenant in the 21st Regiment, Tennessee Militia, had served with Jackson on the Natchez expedition. In June 1813 Armstrong and Jackson had been seconds for Jesse Benton's and William Carroll's duel.

5. See Coffee to AJ, January 21 and February 8.

6. On December 12, 1815, Edmund P. Gaines had announced the completion of the survey to the Georgia line.

7. Coldwater or Spring Creek flows through Colbert County, Alabama, and empties into the Tennessee River below Tuscumbia.

8. See above, AJ to Coffee, February 2.

To George Colbert

Nashville 13th. Feby 1816

Friend & Brother

I have recvd. a letter from Genl. Jno Coffee who is now running the line agreeably to the treaty with the Creek Indians. he has extended it to the Tennessee between the US. & the Cherokees & is about to proceed with it to the Chickasaw and Choctaw lines: He informs me that your people has threatened to stop him from running the line:[1] He is ordered to proceed & you will notify your people that the line will be run, & if they attempt to oppose it or insult Genl. Coffee or his guard, your people will bring down immediate punishment upon them: Your father the President of the U States wants no land but what belonged to the Creek nation; Genl. Coffee is running the line agreeably to what they claim, & the Cherokee chiefs tell him the Creeks were entitled to, and if he runs upon ground the Chickasaws are entitled to upon producing good evidence of their claim, it will be given up to this nation. But you will remember the Cold water was occupied by the Creeks; from that point the Creek Warriors committed every kind of rapine & murder on our women & children, untill we destroyed & drove them from there. Those that escaped collected on the Black Warrior & there continued to murder our Citizens & steal our property untill Genl. Coffee drove them from there & burnt there houses:[2] The Chickasaws therefore cannot claim Cold water that was so long possessed by our enemies the Creeks & to which they never put up claim untill long after the Creeks were driven from there; I do not know that they now claim it but if they do they must be prepared to shew their right & to account why they suffered our enemies to occupy their ground whilst they were killing our Citizens & stealing our property:[3] I have to repeat, the line will be run by Genl. Coffee & if yr. people attempt to interrupt him you will bring destruction on yourselves: The President I repeat wants not any land that you have a good claim for, & if the line includes any of it he will restore it on your shewing that you are entitled to it—But either insult or opposition to Genl Coffee will meet with prompt & immediate punishment. The President of the U States loves his red children, & will do justice to them; but he will punish his red children when they attempt by force to do wrong

I write you this as your friend & brother & as a frind of your nation to save you from involving yourselves in trouble—Some bad men has been lately on the road stealing horses, this you must prevent—our Citizens on that road must pass in safety & undisturbed in their property, this will ensure you our friendship; If our property is stolen you must deliver up the bad men that they may be punished; this will keep us frinds I am yr friend & Brother

Andrew Jackson

Copy in John H. Eaton's hand, DLC (20). Published in Bassett, 2:233–34. Colbert (c1764–1839), the son of a Scottish trader and a Chickasaw woman, operated a store and ferry on the Tennessee River about fifteen miles west of the site of Florence, Alabama.

1. See Coffee to AJ, February 8. On March 1, Colbert responded that the Chickasaws had heard nothing of the survey until Coffee arrived.

2. See Coffee to AJ, October 22, 1813, *Jackson,* 2:438–39.

3. Chickasaw claims to lands in the area of Coldwater Creek were extinguished by the treaty of September 20.

To Rachel Jackson

Judge [Harry] Toulmans
March 13th. 1816

My Love—

I reached this place this morning in good health, will set out for Mobile in a few minutes, by water having sent my horses across by land to the Mississippi. I shall make but little stay at Mobile, will I hope reach New-orleans in ten days where I shall expect to hear from you.

If you see Genl Coffee say to him I was within a few hours of meeting him at the Cotton gin Port.[1] I will write him at the first stage I stop for a day—in the mean time you may say to him, that from all the information I can collect I am still more inclined to believe that the Choctaws have no real claim to any lands East of the Tombigby—

Say to my son if he will learn his Book well his sweet papa, will bring him a *pretty* from Neworleans,[2] kiss him for me, & say to him I send him my blessing, say to my young friend Lemuel (who I hope has recovered) that I miss him much, and I have regretted that I left him in franklin indisposed without biding him farewell,[3] accept of my prayers for your health untill I return, & believe me to be afectionately yours

Andrew Jackson

ALS, DLC (20). Published in Bassett, 2:236. Toulmin (1766–1823) was a superior court judge for Mississippi, later Alabama, Territory. He lived near Fort Stoddert, at the junction of the Tombigbee and Alabama rivers.

1. A town located at the point where the Tombigbee tributaries meet to form the main channel in Monroe County, Mississippi.

2. It has not been established who was teaching Andrew Jackson, Jr., or what school he might have been attending at this time. Later in the year, however, he enrolled in the grammar school at Cumberland College.

3. Lemuel Donelson (1789–1832), Jackson's nephew, had been invited to join Jackson on the tour of the southern defenses.

Following the Treaty of Ghent, Seminoles and recalcitrant Creeks still marauded white settlements along the Spanish Florida border, and more than three hundred blacks and Indians including runaway slaves also harassed American and Spanish outposts from Negro Fort, built by the British in 1814 at Prospect Bluff about sixteen miles upriver from the mouth of the Apalachicola.

In response to continuing raids and murders, Jackson ordered the construction of fortifications just above the Georgia border on the Escambia and Apalachicola rivers. Simultaneously he sought authority to attack Negro Fort, but Washington, as shown in Secretary of War Crawford's letter below, recommended diplomacy before invasion.

With diplomacy failing, Jackson continued to solicit orders to destroy the fort, but before he received anything more than discretionary authority, American forces in the region attacked the site. In late June, a detachment of the 4th Infantry under Lieutenant Colonel Duncan Lamont Clinch (1787–1849) and auxiliary Creek forces under William McIntosh (c1775–1825) moved to erect what later became Fort Scott, on the west bank of the Flint River just above its junction with the Chattahoochie to form the Apalachicola. To supply the troops, Edmund P. Gaines, in immediate command of the threatened district, and Clinch called for naval support from New Orleans. By July 10 a naval contingent under the command of Jarius Loomis had reached the mouth of the Apalachicola, where they awaited Clinch, who was marching downriver to meet the supply ships. Fire from the fort, however, impeded Clinch's march, and three American sailors were killed while searching for water near the fort.

Clinch prepared to respond, based on the discretionary authority to attack that Jackson had granted Gaines on April 8 and on Gaines's subsequent order that Clinch reduce the fort if attacked. Clinch requested gunboat support; and as the gunboats approached on July 27, they exchanged fire with the fort and then resorted to hot shot. The first volley hit the fort's magazine, setting off a massive explosion that killed 270 and wounded 61 of the 334 occupants.

The destruction of Negro Fort, though later investigated in connection with the 1819 congressional inquiry into Jackson's 1818 invasion of Florida, immediately removed one of the main problems facing Jackson's forces on the southern border, leaving them, however, with the continuing problem of Indian depredations from the haven of Spanish Florida.

From William Harris Crawford

Department of War, 15th. March, 1816.

Sir,

It appears from the representations of Colonel Hawkins, that the negroe fort, erected during the war, at the junction of the Chatahouchie and Flint rivers, has been strengthened since that period, and is now occupied by between two hundred and fifty and three hundred blacks, who are well armed, clothed and disciplined. Secret practices to inveigle negroes from the frontiers of Georgia, as well as from the Cherokee and Creek nations, are still continued by the negroes, and hostile Creeks. This is a state of things which cannot fail to produce much injury to the neighbouring settlements, and excite irritations which may ultimately endanger the peace of the nation. The President has therefore directed me to instruct you to call the attention of the governor or military commander of Pensacola to this subject. The principles of good neighbourhood require the interference of the Spanish authority, to put an end to an evil of so serious a nature.[1] Should he decline this interference, it will be incumbent on the Executive to determine what course shall be adopted in relation to this banditti. Should it be determined that the destruction of this fort does not require the sanction of the legislature, measures will be promptly taken for its reduction. From the representations of its strength, heavy cannon will be necessary to batter it. It is presumed, that a cooperation of the naval force may be useful, at least, in transporting the battering train. I have the honor to be, Your most obedt. & very humble servant,

Wm H Crawford

LS, DLC (20); LC, DNA-RG 107 (M6-8); Copy, DNA-RG 233 (4-1413). Published in Bassett, 2:236–37.

1. See AJ to Mauricio de Zuñiga, April 23, below, for Jackson's compliance with Crawford's orders. Zuñiga became governor of West Florida, December 1815, and died nine months later.

At the conclusion of the negotiations of the Treaty of Fort Jackson on August 9, 1814, the friendly Creek chiefs offered three square miles of land each to Jackson and Benjamin Hawkins and one square mile each to interpreters George Mayfield (c1778–1848) and Alexander Cornells (d. 1815) as tokens of their appreciation for assistance against the warring faction. All accepted the donations, pending approval in Washington, but Jackson expressed a wish that the value of his portion of the land be appropriated to charity—clothing destitute Creek women and children. The donors protested, stating that the land on which they hoped Jackson would reside was for the benefit of Jackson and his heirs.

Officials in Washington took no formal action on the donation until early 1816, some three weeks after Jackson departed. On January 18, President James Madison (1751–1836; Princeton 1771) recommended that Congress approve the gift. It was, he advised, "an inviting opportunity for bestowing on an officer, who has rendered such illustrious services to his country, a token of its sensibility to them—the inducement to which cannot be diminished by the delicacy and disinterestedness of his proposal to transfer the benefit from himself" (Annals of Congress, *14th Cong., 1st sess., p. 90).*

Congress gave the matter only casual consideration. On March 27, the Committee on Public Lands of the House of Representatives reported approval as "inexpedient" and a month later the full House indefinitely postponed further consideration. On April 13, a special committee of the Senate reported a bill to confirm the grant, but on April 24, one week before Congress recessed, Abner Lacock (1770–1837) of Pennsylvania blocked further consideration with a motion to postpone the discussion until July. In January 1817 and again in November 1818, congressmen James B. Reynolds (1779–1851) and John Rhea (1753–1832) of Tennessee gained referral of the donation to the Committee on Private Land Claims, but on both occasions the committee failed to report.

In the absence of any written comment from Jackson, it has been impossible to determine his attitude toward Madison's recommendation or the congressional proceedings, but several of his close associates, as with Hayne below, zealously worked for the confirmation of the grant.

From Arthur Peronneau Hayne

Baltimore 27th. March 1816.

Dear General.

I have this moment stepped out of the Stage from Washington. I would have written you while there, but I was so much indisposed, that I was induced to postpone it, till my arrival at this place. Since the President of the U.S. has communicated a special message to both Houses of Congress, on the subject of the Donation from the Creek Nation, to yourself & others, it has progressed no further, & being myself at leisure, and also being persuaded that I could promote your Interest in this business by being on the Spot, I repaired to Washington. I had an interview with Mr. Madison. (Mr. [James] Monroe was present) I also saw our Secy Mr. Crawford, Governor [David] Holmes & my Carolina friends generally &c. These gentlemen seem well disposed towards you—Mr. [James] Brown is the Chairman of the Committee appointed by the Senate, Mr. [Thomas Bolling] Robertson, that appointed by the House.[1] These gentlemen both assure me that they are friendly disposed towards the Bill, & that the reason why they have not yet made their Report, is that they fear that a Majority of the Committee are opposed to the Bill. But they have promised me to act promptly & suffer no longer delay to take place. Col. Hawkins & the Interpreters seem to be the great cause of difficulty—Your friends think & with great justice in my mind, that a separation ought to be made between your *Case* & *theirs*. As it respects them it might open a Door for the Commission of Frauc., as to yourself the reverse is the fact. And *should* the *Committee* Report *against* the *Bill, yet* by *bringging* it before both *Houses* of *Congress,* they may *decide otherwise*. I know yr high mind &

delicate feelings, and in my conduct I have never for a moment lost sight of them. Mr. [William] Lowndes still thinks the business will have a favorable issue; and will not fail to give it his support—so will Mr. Gaillard.[2] But these gentlemen could do nothing before the Committee had made their Report. Time must soon determine the matter, & I cannot but believe that the Decision of Congress will be such, as not to cause us to Blush for them. But this much I am certain of, if you do not succeed this session, you never will succeed at any future period. Services Genl. are soon forgotten. But yrs never can, for you must ever be looked upon as only next to Washington.

While in Washington I had the pleasure to meet with my friend Judge [William] Johnson, of the Supreme U.S. Court & of So. Ca.[3] The Judge made the following Proposition to me & which I promised him to communicate to you & to the Major's Father. He says if the materials which have collected are placed in his hands, *He Will write The Book, and Present it to Mrs. Reid.* That he will devote the whole of the ensuing summer, to that employment, & will leave nothing undone on his part, to make it worthy of the occasion & the nation. The Copy Right would sell for at least $3,000. in Philadelphia. And this arrangement you will at once perceive will not cost Mrs Reid a single cent. The Judge wishes it expressly understood that he does not wish to obtrude his services. I know it would be unpleasant for your private papers to be perused by any one but a friend. I think in the hands of Judge Johnson, they would be safe. Pray let me hear from you on this subject as I wish to write the Judge, as he tells me if he does not engage in this work he wishes to travel the ensuing Summer.[4]

The Bank Bill has passed the Lower House & I am of opinion that it will pass the Senate.[5] The most perfect harmony prevails in Congress—I think Congress will continue the session about 6 weeks longer.

I understood you that our friend Genl. Coffee was to receive the Appointment of Receiver of Public Monies, in the section of Country on the Alabama. Let me advise you to keep a good look out, as I understand it may be given to another.

The Staff Bill has passed the Lower House, & will pass the Senate. I will shortly be yr Inspr. Genl.[6] You know not how happy this will make me. I shall then be content.

I was honored a few days previous to my leaving Carlisle with a letter from his *Excellency Major General Jacob Brown,* who says "I presumed I should have had the pleasure to see you at Washington" &c. He has granted me a Furlough for six months.

We have set our hearts on yr passing the summer at the North. Will you not come to Carlisle & we pledge ourselves to give you as good a Constitution as you had before the Creek War.

So soon as I am Transferred, I will Report myself to you & join you at any moment you please. My dear Frances is to be confined in May.[7] I wish to take her to Charleston in October next. She will remain there during the

Winter & Spring. I was to visit the Alabama in Novr. or Decr. next. A part of the Lands on the Alabama will be sold in Jany. 1817. But that part of the Country which extends from a little above Fort Claiborne to Fort Jackson, which according to my view embraces all the Good Land, will be sold at a future period but when I know not.[8] Remember me affectionately to Col Butler & Lt. Gadsden. God bless and preserve you is the prayer of your affectionate friend.

A.P. Hayne

P.S. At one time I fondly flattered myself I should have planted a crop on the Alabama in 1817; but now I know not when.[9]

P.S. This is the fourth letter, I have written you since we parted at Washington.[10]

ALS, DLC (20). Published in Bassett, 2:237–38 (extract). Endorsed by AJ: "*Private*—answered & forwarded 11th of May 1816—& all points noted in the answer—*Private.*" Jackson's reply has not been found.

1. Monroe (1758–1831) was secretary of state. Holmes (1770–1832) was governor of Mississippi Territory. Both Brown (1766–1835) and Robertson (1779–1828) were from Louisiana.
2. Lowndes (1782–1822), congressman, and Gaillard, senator, were from South Carolina.
3. Thomas Jefferson had appointed Johnson (1771–1834) a justice of the court.
4. After learning that Eaton would finish the biography, Hayne wrote, "Judge Johnson's proposition was predicated on the supposition that *he* was to be the *Author,* and altho' I have a high opinion of Judge Johnson, yet nevertheless I am well convinced that the *Love* of *Literary Fame,* induced him to make the offer" (see Hayne to AJ, May 31).
5. The act to incorporate the Bank of the United States passed the House on March 14. Amended, it passed the Senate April 3, the House April 5, and was approved April 10.
6. An act for organizing the general staff passed the House March 23. Amended in the Senate, it was finally approved April 24. The Senate approved Hayne's appointment as inspector general for the Southern Division on April 29.
7. Frances Duncan (c1797–1820), the daughter of Judge Thomas Duncan of Pennsylvania and Hayne's wife, was expecting a child, Martha Ann (1816–20).
8. Fort Claiborne was at the site of present-day Claiborne, Alabama; Fort Jackson was located in present-day Elmore County, Alabama, about three miles south of Wetumpka and twelve miles northeast of Montgomery.
9. Upon his resignation from the army in 1820, Hayne settled in Autauga County, Alabama.
10. Only the letter above, Hayne to AJ, January 24, has been found.

From Big Warrior

Camp on Ofuckshee
April 16th. 1816

General Jackson my friend

I am going now to answer your letter. I wish to know whether you want me to search out for those murderers. I thought I had put all that power in General Gaines so far as I was able to do it.[1]

I recollect the treaty at Fort Jackson; I told you your enemy was just over the river, that they were not Completely cowed & that they would be yet killing of us & said let us follow them & kill them. You replied, if you kill them I will kill you, let them alone the war is ended with the Indians.

I told you of this that whenever they quit their towns, & lost their lands, they were like a parcel of wolves, had no home to go to & would be doing mischief; that they would never return to the friendly party & were like wild people in the woods.

You Cannot expect such fellows as these will return to their native Country, nor expect from me to make a search for them.

It appears that I am suspicioned by these murderers coming into their former towns. If it was found out that they Came over the line on our side,[2] our warriors are ready, I would turn them out & put the law in force & see they were punished; But as the murder has been done below the line on your side it is out of my power to do any thing in it. They have never returned to the settlements of the friendly Indians Since they were driven off by General Jackson.

My friend Jackson, I remember the speech you made at Fort Jackson, that you were going to have a line directly.[3] You told me all the damage done above the line I should be answerable for. That line was to cut me off from all those below the line & from having any Connection with foreign powers or others; you were the only commander below the line. I recollect what I have stated & for that reason cannot have any agency below the line.

This is all I have to say to my friend & brother General Jackson in answer to his letter.

I have now to speak to him on a subject that Concerns us. Since the treaty at Fort Jackson there has been several murders Committed above the line by Soldiers & by Citizens. One in particular at the Council house (Tookabatchee) I did not think the murderer would be carried out of the country, but would be executed; but instead of that he was taken over the line. One was killed at Ocmulgee ferry & buried on the hill when the regular troops were there One at the big spring on the west side of Fort Mitchell by the militia & one by a Captain of the Army at Fort Jackson.[4] I think hard about the female killed at Tookabatchee, she was a beloved woman. The officer Commanding the Regiment there, told me the murderer should be confined in irons. In place of that he was seen the other day travelling along the road with his wife. If the Indian murderers were as Completely in my power as this murderer was in yours, you should see what I would have done with them, but as the Case now stands I am sorry for it.[5]

This is what I wished you to know had been done above the line, which I send to my friend General Jackson. your friend & brother

James Cornells — Big BW Warrior
Interpreter — Speaker for Upper Creeks

Written as interpreted by J[eoffrey] Robinson
Capt 7th Inf Actg Brgd. major[6]

LS by proxy, DLC (20); Copy, DNA-RG 107 (M221-69). Published in Bassett, 2:239–40. Big Warrior (Tustunnuggee Thlocco; d. 1825) was Creek war chief at Tuckabatchee, on the west bank of the Tallapoosa River just below Tallassee in Elmore County, Alabama. Oakfuskee Creek follows the Macon-Montgomery County line, emptying into the Tallapoosa River.

1. Jackson's letter has not been found, but Big Warrior was referring to Jackson's demand that the Creeks assist Edmund P. Gaines in apprehending Indians who, in late February, had killed two men, Daniel Johnston and [?] McGaskey, above Fort Claiborne near the Alabama River.

2. Big Warrior was referring to the southern boundary of Creek lands as set by the Treaty of Fort Jackson.

3. See AJ to Big Warrior, August 7, 1814, *Jackson,* 3:109–111.

4. Either Fort Mitchell near the western border of Pulaski County, Georgia, or Fort Mitchell, Alabama, a half mile from the Chattahoochee in Russell County.

5. Sergeant William Cherry of the 7th Regiment had been arrested for killing the Creek woman and taken to Huntsville for trial, but a civil judge released him on a writ of habeas corpus. Gaines ordered him rearrested and confined at Fort Montgomery, where he remained from April 25 to mid-August (see Gaines to AJ, June 3). Although reduced to private, he remained in the army until his term of duty expired in 1819.

6. Cornells, part Creek, was Alexander's brother; Robinson, a Tennessean, died in August 1816.

From Benjamin Hawkins

Fort Jackson 21 April 1816

General Gaines who is with me, will give you details in his department. The Commissioners will in a few days complete the line designated in the last Treaty with the Creeks. The friendly Indians do not oppose and will not aid us.[1]

The Chiefs are making an effort of themselves, to aid the Seminolie Chiefs in destroying the negro establishment in that country, capturing and delivering up Negro's belonging to Citizens of the United States, to me, or some of our military establishment. The Little Prince and some warriors are by the last report on the march for effecting this object[2] They have applied for some aid in corn which after conferring with the General is sent them 300 bushels.

On the 16th. having an occasion to write the Secretary of War I stated to him, "I am just informed by Mr. Barnett 'it is currently reported General Jackson thro' me negotiated the donation of the Indians to him.' I declare upon honor, and am willing to add to it the solemnity of an oath, that he never directly or indirectly thro' me or any person within my knowledge, attempted any such thing; and I have reason to believe, and do believe, the first intimation he ever had of their intention on this subject, was from me, in the way reported. He rejected the idea as soon as presented, and I heard no more until the morning that the gift was mentioned, and made to him as stated in my report."

"The foregoing I owe to the General, and if it was true, that I had an agency from myself in producing it I should not disown it. as from my particular situation I know how much he merited from the friendly Indians, as well as from his Country for services all things considered which have [never] been excelled."[3]

We continue in the dark as to the further operations of the Commissioners. The last mail from the North failed, That, and the one due this night may bring us something important. Colo Samuel Daile of Monroe County, is laying off the County in Militia districts, advertising for the election of officers, assessing the Inhabitants, collecting their taxes and taking the Census of the Inhabitants. I have stated these facts to the government.[4] I write you in pain having a gouty hand, and am your friend

Benjamin Hawkins

ALS, DLC (20). Published in Clement L. Grant, ed., *Letters, Journals, and Writings of Benjamin Hawkins* (2 vols.; Savannah, Ga., 1980), 2:781–82. Endorsed by AJ: "answered 15th of May 1816." Jackson's reply has not been found.

1. See Edmund P. Gaines to AJ, April 21. Hawkins was referring to the survey of the southern part of the treaty line. For the survey report, see "Field notes of a survey of the boundary line designated in the Treaty made at Fort Jackson," in the Creek Boundary File, DNA-RG 94 (M566-68).

2. Hawkins was referring to Negro Fort. Little Prince (Tustunnuggee Hopoie; d. 1828) was a chief of the Broken Arrow towns of the Coweta tribe and speaker for the lower Creek towns (see Little Prince to AJ, April 26).

3. See Hawkins to William H. Crawford, April 16 (DLC-20).

4. In his letter to Crawford, Hawkins cited the actions by Dale (1772–1841) as proof "that the officers of the Mississippi Territory are by all means in their power counteracting the proclamation of the President" closing the ceded lands to white settlers.

To [Mauricio de Zuñiga]

Head Quarters Divison of the South
Washington Mississippi Territory.
23. April—1816

Sir,

I am charged by my government to make known to you that a Negroe Fort, erected during our late war with Britain at or near the Junction of the Chatahouche and Flint Rivers, has been strengthened since that period, and is now occupied by upwards of two hundred & fifty negroes, many of whom have been enticed away from the service of their Masters, Citizens of the United States, all of whom are well armed clothed and disciplined[1]

Secret practises to inveigle Negroes from the frontier citizens of Georgia as well as from the Cherokee and Creek nations of Indians are still continued by this Banditti and the Hostile Creeks. This is a state of things which cannot fail to produce much injury to the neighboring settlements and excite Irritations which may ultimately endanger the peace of the nation and interrupt that good understanding that so happily exists between our governments.

The principles of good faith which always insure good neighborhood between Nations require the immediate and prompt interference of the Spanish Authority; to destroy or remove from our frontier this Banditti, put an end to an evil of so serious a nature, and return to our citizens and the friendly Indians inhabiting our Territory those Negroes now in the said fort and which have been stolen and enticed from them.

I cannot permit myself to indulge a thought that the governor of Pensacola or the military commander of that place will hesitate a moment in giving immediate orders for this Banditti to be dispersed and the property of the citizens of the United States forthwith restored to them and our friendly Indians—particularly when ⟨you⟩ I reflect that this Banditti's conduct will not be tolerated by our government and if not put down by the Spanish Authority will compel us in self Defence to destroy them.

This communication is entrusted to Captain [Ferdinand Louis] Amelung of the 1st. Regt. U.S. Iy. who is charged to bring back such answer as you may be pleased to make to this letter. In your answer you will be pleased to state whether that fort has been built by the government of Spain—and whether the negroes, who garison it, are considered the subjects of his Catholic Majesty; and if not, by the Authority of Spain—by whom, and under whose orders, it has been established[2]—I have the honor to be Sir—Very Respectfully your. Mo: Obt. Servt.

Andrew Jackson
Major Genl comdg
D of the South

LS and Translation, SpSAG (5-0045); Copies, DNA-RG 107 (M221-70), DNA-RG 46 (5-0050), DNA-RG 233 (5-0054). Published in *ASP, Foreign Relations,* 4:499, 555–56; and in Bassett, 2:241–42 (from Copy, DNA-RG 107).

1. See above, William H. Crawford to AJ, March 15.

2. See Isaac L. Baker to Ferdinand L. Amelung, April 23. Amelung (d. 1821) was a captain in the 1st Infantry from 1815–19, when he resigned, serving thereafter as sheriff in Baton Rouge, Louisiana, until his death. Amelung's command of languages was a major consideration in his appointment to the mission. For Zuñiga's reply of May 26, see pp.41–43, below.

From Abner Lawson Duncan

(Duplicate) New-Orleans April 23d. 1816

Dear Sir

By our mutual friend Capt. [Robert] Sprig, I am afforded an opportunity of answering yours, of the 19th. Inst., so as to reach you before your arrival at Nashville.[1] The Tract of Land (now mine and lately Donaldson's) contains fifteen Acres or Arpans in front, or fronting the River; with eighty in

Depth; the lines so diverging, as to embrace two thousand five hundred Arpans; the adjoining Tract, (now the property of Scott's heirs, but offered to me on very good Terms, for ten thousand dollars, that is two thousand in Cash, and the remaining Eight thousand, in one, two, three, and four Years,) contains fourteen Acres in front, with the same depth of mine; and the lines diverging in the same manner; so that the two tracts would give nearly five thousand acres, or arpans of Land, all susceptible of cultivation.[2] I fear we have not understood each other well on the subject of the sale; I proposed to give you my Tract at Cost, that is Ten thousand, three hundred dollars; to purchase the adjoining one, and to hold jointly the whole; what with your Negroes, those of your Nephew,[3] and an equal proportion of mine, we might fairly calculate upon being able, to establish an elegant, and not less profitable Plantation: the management, to be under the entire and sole direction of your Nephew: If however, you should be disappointed in uniting with your Nephew; indeed in any event, if you wish to purchase on your own account; I will most cheerfully convey my Tract, upon the Terms mentioned; and relinquish all pretensions to the purchase of the adjoining one: In a word, make precisely such arrangements, as will suit your Convenience; take the whole, or part; If the whole, advise me in Season; so as to secure for you the purchase of Scott's, on the Terms offered to me.[4] The purchase money of my Tract, will be due on the 15th. day of Decr. next; but if it should not be perfectly convenient for you to meet the payment, I will do it for you; and give you any further time you may require. Yrs. Very truly

A L. Duncan

LS duplicate, DLC (20). Duncan (d. 1823) was a volunteer aide at the Battle of New Orleans and had defended Jackson during his trial before Judge Dominick A. Hall in 1815.

1. Sprigg (d. 1827), a resident of Natchez whom Jackson had known at least since 1812, was a trader and boat owner. He commanded a company of volunteer boatmen during the Battle of New Orleans and later represented East Baton Rouge in the Louisiana House, 1823–24. Jackson's letter of April 19 has not been found.

2. The land in question was the William Donaldson-John Scott portion of the Houmas grant in Ascension Parish, about twenty-two leagues above New Orleans and across the Mississippi River from Donaldsonville. The depth of the property remained a matter of dispute until 1884, when the Supreme Court, in *Slidell* v. *Grandjean,* 111 *U.S. Reports* 412 (1884), set it at eighty arpents.

3. John Hutchings (c1776–1817), the son of Thomas (1750–1804) and Catherine Donelson Hutchings (c1752–1834).

4. On continuing efforts to forge this deal, as well as AJ's attempt to purchase a sugar plantation on the Gulf coast, both of which came to naught, see Duncan to AJ, June 9, AJ to Duncan, July 9, and AJ to John Hutchings, April 22.

William H. Crawford's decision to transfer Eleazar Wheelock Ripley (1782–1839; Dartmouth 1800) from the Northern to the Southern Division of the army, the major topic in Jackson's letter below, was only one in a long series of events that contributed to a deteriorating relationship between Jackson and the secretary of war.

Jackson's objections to the transfer grew out of his concern over the impact that Ripley's presence might have on the morale and discipline of Southern Division officers. The uneasiness grew out of a dispute between Ripley and Charles Kitchel Gardner (1787–1869), Jacob J. Brown's adjutant general.

In September 1815, Gardner had demanded of Ripley satisfaction for rumors Ripley had spread about Gardner's cowardice at the battles of Chippewa, Lundy's Lane, and Fort Erie. Ripley responded by ordering Gardner's arrest and court-martial on charges of cowardice and dereliction of duty, conduct unbecoming an officer, and disrespectful conduct and language. The court, convening on October 4, 1815, rendered its verdict on January 22, 1816: it found Gardner not guilty of the first three charges, guilty of some of the specifications of the fourth and guilty of the fifth, and sentenced him to be reprimanded. When General Brown reviewed the decision, he used the opportunity more to criticize Ripley than to reprimand Gardner. He ordered Gardner to resume his sword and duties as adjutant general. He expressed, however, strong disapproval of Ripley's method of originating the arrest and court-martial, saying that the important charges involved events long past and that the arrest grew out of a personal quarrel. He concluded that "the discipline of the Army would not have suffered" if Ripley had applied to his superior, and he demanded Ripley's transfer. On May 21, Crawford wrote that, despite Jackson's objections, Ripley would be transferred to the Southern Division.

To William Harris Crawford

Head Quarters Div. of the South
Greenville M.T. april 24th. 1816

Sir,

Your two letters of the 15th. ultimo I had the honor to receive last evening at Natchez.[1] I immediately addressed a note to the governor of Pensacola on the subject of the negroe fort which I placed in the hands of Colonel [Thomas Sidney] Jessup to be handed to Captain Amelung of the 1st. Regt. Iy: whom I have instructed to be the bearer of it.[2] It is accompanied with the necessary Instructions to Capt Amelung for his government copies of which with an extract of a letter of mine to Genl. Gaines on this subject of the 8th. Inst shall be forwarded you as soon as I reach Nashville[3]—at which point I have advised Genls. Gaines & [Thomas Adams] Smith I should be on the 8th. proximo; at which time and place I expect to receive communications from each of those gentlemen.[4] I have a hope that General Gaines has attended to the subject of this negroe fort and put an end to the lawless Depradations of this Banditti of *Land Pirates*. He has been left to his Discretion to act on this subject with my opinion, if certain facts can be proven against them that their fort must be destroyed. I trust he has taken the Hint. So soon as I receive the governor or commanding officer's answer I shall forward you copies of the corospondence[5]

On the subject of General Ripley I can only say that the officers live in the most perfect Harmony with each other in my Division and I should be sorry that a transfer should be made that would interrupt this good understanding. The conduct of General Ripley as regards the arrest of Majr Gardner of the 3d. Iy. has produced sensations respecting him in the minds of the officers of the Division that I have heard converse on the subject highly unfavourable to Genl. Ripley from which feelings I must acknowlege I am not free: but not having seen the charges against Majr Gardner or his acquittal I do on this as on all other occasions where the feelings of honorable men are concerned suspend my opinion untill I am better advised; but if it is true that Genl Ripley arrested Majr Gardner on the disgraceful charge of cowardice, (and made this charge of himself) and if a court martial has honorably acquitted the Majr of this charge I hesitate not in declaring that General Ripley or any other officer of the army who makes such a charge against his brother officer and fails in the proof ought to be dismissed for lying. You may Judge then of my feelings of Genl Ripley if this should be the fact: otherwise I am free to declare that I have been impressed favourably towards the General before this transaction and would have felt happy to have had him with me in the day of danger: I should have thought him a safe and valuable companion on all occasions

After this candid declaration on my part you will from the facts attending the arrest of Majr Gardner judge of the propriety of transfering General Ripley, with this assurance, that I shall acquiesce in any transfer you may think proper to make: but I cannot pretend to hazard an opinion as it regards the general feeling of the officers composing my division[6] I have the honor to be sir with high consideration your Obt. Servant—

Andrew Jackson
Major Genl comdg
D. of the South.

LS, DNA-RG 107 (M221-70); Extract, DNA-RG 233 (5-0065). Published in *HRDoc* 122, 15th Cong., 2nd sess. (Serial 22), p. 6 (extract).

1. See above and Calendar.

2. See above, AJ to Mauricio de Zuñiga, April 23. Jesup (1788–1860), appointed quartermaster general of the army in 1818, had served with distinction on the staff of General William Hull in the War of 1812 and was at this time in temporary command at New Orleans.

3. Jackson forwarded copies of Isaac L. Baker to Ferdinand L. Amelung, April 23, and AJ to Edmund P. Gaines, April 8, on May 12.

4. For Gaines's report, see Gaines to AJ, May 14, below. Smith (1781–1844), brevet brigadier general, was a colonel of the rifle regiment; his report has not been found.

5. Jackson forwarded Zuñiga's reply of May 26 on June 15.

6. Jackson requested a copy of the Gardner court-martial proceedings in June, and Gardner transmitted a copy in August (see Report of the charges and verdict re Gardner, February 5, DLC-20; Robert Butler to Gardner, June 26, 4-0131; and Gardner to Butler, August 5, DLC-21). By November 12, when he attended a public dinner in Nashville honoring Ripley, Jackson had apparently cast off his apprehensions regarding the transfer.

Rachel Jackson to Sophia Thorpe Reid

Tennessee State Aprill 27th 1816

My Dear

Maddam I received your Frendly and affectionate Letter of March 26th[1] I never wisched more sincerely for aney thing than to heare from you at the time your Letter came to hand you perhaps will Screcly believe me when I Declare to you that I was as much Distressed the Day I Left youre house as if you had all been my nearest relations oh my will you pardon me for not writeing to you I fully Itended it the next Day & nothing prevented it But my writeing so bad a hand Mrs. E Reade did not call on me She passed above some Distance say 20 miles[2]—how sincerely I have sympathised in your sorrows, it has not ben in the power of an absent Friend To suth or Eleviat one sorrowfull hour or rest asured it would have been done—ther is none Exempt from trouble And the great Disposur of all who holds the Disteny of nations in his hands sees and knows what is best for us Let us my Friend resine to His will—your son was an honour to his Friends and Country a bright gem pluct from among Them but alas he has gon the ways of all Erth I Cannot Disscribe my feelings on the The Day I Left your house Dear Maria often did I see her in my imigination so strongly it was Impresst on my mind to say something to her in that most sollam hour but she was in the hands of her god he altogeather murcy and goodness[3]—I hav writen to Mrs Read at her fathers but hav received no Answer as yet[4] Genneral Jackson has been from Home since some time Fby through the Mobile and all that Section of the 7th Destrict he was three weeks in New orleans I frequently have Letters he will return Tennessee in May he says to me his health is something Better then usual what my dear Madam have you herd of this Dreadfull Epedemic that has swept nearely one third of our Cittizens so maney instances of men and ther wives going togeather six and seven oute of some famalys—

nothing would give me more pleasure on Erth then to see you all once more Except see Mr Jackson Remember me to Mrs Harris[5] & all her famaly Capt Reade and youre famaly and except for yourself my prayers that happyness may visit your aboad once more a gleame of joy set on your Evening hours is my wish

Rachel Jackson

ALS, DLC (71). Published in *Cincinnati Commercial Gazette,* January 13, 1883. Sophia Thorpe Reid of Bedford County, Virginia, John Reid's mother, had married Nathan in 1784.

1. Not found.
2. John Reid's widow, Elizabeth, had returned to the home of her father, Abram Maury, in Williamson County.
3. John Reid's sister Maria Cabell (c1797–1816) died of pneumonia in early January.
4. Letters not found.
5. Not identified.

With the Creek capitulation at Fort Jackson in August 1814, southwesterners anticipated that Indian claims to western Georgia, northern Mississippi Territory, and southern Tennessee would be quickly extinguished and the land opened for settlement. For most, however, the course of events leading to the survey and sale of the land proved disappointing.

Although the Creeks had ceded all their lands west of the Coosa River, the exact extent of the lands obtained by the United States remained unclear because Chickasaw and Cherokee claims directly south of the Tennessee River and Choctaw claims east of the Tombigbee River overlapped with the northern and western portions of the territory ceded by the Creeks. More than a year elapsed before John Coffee, acting without the cooperation of other commissioners, finally completed a survey of the western and northern boundaries of the cession in March 1816. In the same month, a treaty negotiated in Washington with Cherokees recognized their claims to lands in the northwestern part of the cession and authorized compensation for depredations on Cherokee property committed by Tennessee troops during the Creek War.

The treaty evoked strong protests in the Southwest. On May 7, the Nashville Whig *condemned the treaty, and, over the next few months, citizens in Davidson County and elsewhere adopted resolutions opposing it. But the federal government refused to yield to the protestors. Jackson himself repeatedly denounced the recognition of Cherokee claims until mid-1816 when, in instructions to negotiate a treaty with the Chickasaws, he was given the opportunity to bargain for Cherokee claims as well; his complaints about the spoliation provisions continued even longer.*

To James Monroe

Hermitage near Nashville May 12th 1816

Dr Sir

Since I wrote you on the 8th. instant, I have had the pleasure of seeing Genl Coffee.[1] The Genl has shewn me the whole correspondance between him & the other commissioners. The whole evidence of the right of Territory ceded by the creeks, which he included in the lines ran by him, The evidence of right in the creeks to the Territory Thus included in the lines ran by Genl Coffee appear clear & conclusive.[2]

From a view of the whole correspondance, I am amazed at the conduct of the other commissioners, and particularly at that of Genl Gains, in forming a board after the commission filled up for Genl Coffee by the President, had been forwarded by him to Genl Coffee, with a request that he should immediately as commissioner enter on the duties as such, and proceed, to run the line between the cherokees & Creeks &c &c.

Genl Coffee's feelings under these circumstances are not alltogether at ease—and it would afford him some satisfaction to be informed whether the survayor chain carriers &c, have or will be ordered to be paid by the Goverment will you sir have the goodness to give this information.[3]

The late hasty convention with the Cherokees, is much regretted & deprecated in this quarter. It is believed that the President has been badly advised on this subject; and the Instrument obtained by the cherokees, from Major McIntosh after the creeks had concluded, signed & fully executed with me the treaty, has been held forth to him as an instrument executed in full council of the creeks.[4] I hope this has not been the fact. Colo [Return Jonathan] Meiggs,[5] knew this instrument was of no avail, that the creeks had positively refused to do any thing on the subject of boundary with the cherokees and this paper was merely given by McIntosh who had married a cherokee woman, to please the cherokees for the moment, and not as a national act of the creeks, and being subsequent to the execution of the treaty with the U.S. could have no binding effect upon the U. States—The Territory ceded contains between four and five millions of acres, to which it is believed the cherokees never had the least semblance of claim. This Territory ceded was of incalculable Vallue to the U States, as it opened a free communication to the lower country through our own soil, strengthened that frontier, cut off all communication & intercourse between the southern & northwestern Indians, gave us roads unshakelled by Indian claims, & supplies for our army on these roads from the certain industry of our own citizens, and hardy soldiers to meet an invading enemy at the threshold. By this convention all these benefits are lost and as is believed wantonly surrendered—a free communication is restored between the northern & southern tribes of Indians, which again exposes our frontier to savage murders & depredation—the intercourse with the lower country closed except through an Indian country, our citizens as at present & heretofore, subjected to every contribution that Indian avarice can suggest, supplies of the worst kind and at all times scarce & precarious, and never can be calculated on for the supply of an army—when you open roads, as at present, they will be stopped and turned at the pleasure of the Indians, your bridges destroyed, others marked & opened to lead to there turnpikes, to which you cannot pass without endangering the legs or neck of the horse and rider—and what is still worse, the minds of your citizens irritated & disgusted, that so much blood has flown, & privations sufferred, to give security to our country, which is wantonly surrendered to an Indian tribe, that never had a claim to it, and which the creeks inhabited untill they were drove from it & destroyed by the exertions of those verry citizens who now complain—and if there services are again wanted will have a banefull effect upon their former spirit of patriotism—and I am fearfull that this thing in the end will involve our Goverment in much trouble & perplexity.

It affords your friends here much pleasure that you are not involved in the general deprecation that this act has brought upon the Goverment. I sincerely regret that the administration of the best of men should be deprecated by the citizens for this act—but neither upon the grounds of right Justice or national policy can his best friends step forward to Justify—as to right the cherokees never had any to the soil, and national policy forbade the surrender to them—be it right or wrong, the whole is ascribed to the Secratary of war, and he has forever forfeighted in this act the confidence of the people of this section of the country—

Present Mrs. J. & my respects to your lady[6] & family, and accept assurances of my respect & Esteem

Andrew Jackson

ALS, DLC (5-0079). Endorsed on page three in Monroe's hand: "will the surveyor & chain carriers be orderd to be paid by the govt. They will be paid. Genl Coffee is acting as Comr." Endorsed on cover, by James Madison: "The boundaries between the Indian tribes are very uncertain in themselves, and difficult to be understood. As the expense of extinguishing their claims is inconsiderable, humanity and policy also may prescribe to the U.S. a double purchase as preferable to the risks of doing injustice or creating hostile dispositions. On this principle the Govt. is proceeding, and will, as fast as circumstances admit or the public interest requires endeavor to accomodate the reasonable wishes of our Citizens. In this proceeding it is not meant nor has it tried to diminish the merit of Genl J's conquests or the value or validity of the cessions of lands by the Creeks."

1. See AJ to Monroe, May 8.

2. See DNA-RG 75 (M271-1) for the evidence and correspondence that Coffee submitted to the war department.

3. In his letter of June 18, Monroe reported, in accordance with his endorsement on this letter, that the survey crew would be paid.

4. For discussions of the McIntosh document, see John Donelson to AJ, July 23, 1815 (*Jackson*, 3:373–75), and AJ to William H. Crawford, June 4, below.

5. Meigs (1740–1823) was U.S. Cherokee agent.

6. Elizabeth Kortright Monroe (c1763–1830), the daughter of a New York merchant, married Monroe in 1786.

From Edmund Pendleton Gaines

Fort Stoddert M.T. 14th May 1816

General

I had the honor to receive on the eve of my departure from Fort Jackson the 30th. your letters of the 8th and 12th of last month.[1]

The officers Commanding posts within the ceded Territory have been instructed to carry into effect your orders, and for this purpose to keep out reconnoitreing parties accompanied by friendly half breeds and Interpretors, until the Murderers of [Daniel] Johnson and McGaskey are detected.[2]

The little Prince with other chiefs and Warriors have engaged to take the Negro Fort on the Apa'la'cha'co'la, and deliver the negroes at 50$ each. Col Hawkins is of opinion they will succeed, and, although I have little faith in Indian promises, it seems to me proper to encourge the undertaking and wait a reasonable time for the result. I have sanctioned Col Hawkins requisition for 300 bushels corn for the subsistence of the Indians. They are not however to be considered as in our service or entitled to Pay. Should they fail, I shall then avail myself of the discretionary power which you have been pleased to confide to me and shall adopt such measures as may appear best Calculated to Counteract Indian hostility and at the same time to break up the Negro establishment, which I have reason to believe is acquiring strength and additional numbers.[3] The Fort (as described by a Nephew of Durant,[4] and some other persons) stands upon the left Bank of the Apalachacola, about 50 miles below the mouth of Flint river. The ramparts and parapets built of hewn timber filled in with earth, mounting 9 to 12 pieces of Cannon, several of which very large, with some Mortars and Howitzers. It has a deep ditch intended to be filled with water, but was dry when last seen by my informants, two or three months ago. The work is nearly square and extends over near two acres of ground, has Comfortable barracks and large stone houses inside. It is rendered inaccessible by land, excepting a narrow pass up near the margin of the river, by reason of an impenetrable swamp in the rear and extending to the river above. The Negroes are attempting to raise Corn, and some of them are reported to have gone to St Marks.[5] The number at and near the Fort is stated to be upwards of three hundred men. They have red Coats and are supplied with a large quantity of British muskets, Powder and other supplies.

Major [David Emanuel] Twiggs arrived at Fort Montgomery on the 8th instant with the advance detachment of the 7th Infantry in march for Escambia. This detachment of four Companies will be followed by the remaining four Companies from Fort Hawkins, in a few days.[6]

I shall make an attempt to supply the posts on the Escambia and Apalachicola with provisions by water, in the manner which you have suggested. I have the honor to be Most Respectfully Your Obt. Sert.

Edmund P. Gaines

LS, DLC (20). Fort Stoddert was on the west bank of the Mobile River, about four miles south of the confluence of the Alabama and Tombigbee.

1. Only AJ to Gaines, April 8, has been found.

2. In his letter of March 12 to Gaines, Jackson had ordered that "until the perpetrators of the late murders on the ceeded territory are delivered up, and the property which they have stolen is restored, you will suffer no Creek Indian to remain within the ceeded limits," except those friendly chiefs granted exemptions in the treaty. On June 3, Gaines informed Jackson that friendly Indians had delivered to Fort Jackson two of the murderers, who had been sent to Fort Montgomery to await trial by civil authorities. A longtime resident of the territory, Johnston had a plantation on the Alabama River about thirty-five miles above Fort Claiborne. McGaskey has not been identified.

3. For Gaines's discretionary authority regarding Negro Fort, see AJ to Gaines, April 8.

4. The Durants were a part-Creek family related by marriage to Alexander McGillivray. The individual to whom Gaines was referring has not been identified.

5. A Spanish post, Fort St. Marks was located at the junction of the St. Marks and Wakulla rivers, six miles above the entrance to Appalachicola Bay.

6. Twiggs (1790–1862), from Georgia, later served in the Mexican and Civil wars. Fort Montgomery was located opposite the cutoff of the Alabama River, about twelve miles above its confluence with the Tombigbee. Fort Hawkins, located on the east side of the Ocmulgee River, is now within Macon, Georgia.

In March Secretary of War Crawford announced plans to negotiate with the Cherokees, Chickasaws, and Choctaws before the final survey of the Creek cession, and he accordingly suspended Coffee's operations. Crawford's hope was that after the government had fairly recognized all tribal claims, the Indians could be induced to cede their rights to the disputed lands. In the letter below, he informed Jackson of the progress of his plans for dealing with the Choctaws and Chickasaws. Because the March 22 treaty recognized the Cherokee right to lands also claimed by the Chickasaws, the Cherokees were eventually included at the Chickasaw negotiations in September.

From William Harris Crawford

Department of War, 20th. May 1816

Sir,

Your communication of the 11th. ulto. has been received.[1] The view which you have taken of the treaty with the Cherokees, and the boundaries which you have assigned to the Creek cession, have not in any degree changed the opinion of the President upon that subject. The commissioners certainly had power to run the lines of that cession, which were defined in the treaty, but they manifestly had no power to run lines not defined. The Northern and Western boundaries of the cession were not defined, and as they necessarily affected the rights of others, it is difficult to conceive how the commissioners who had no power to make conventions with the tribes whose interests might be affected, could undertake to define and run them. But giving to the commissioners all the power contended for, it is still more difficult to conceive how their power could be exclusive of the executive and legislative authority. This authority has defined the Northern limits of the cession, in conjunction with the cherokee deputation, conformably to existing treaties to which the United States were parties.[2]

The people of Tennessee have deserved well of their fellow citizens during the late war, and it is confidently believed that they will not forfeit their claim to the respect of the government by a different course of conduct in time of peace.

Considering the short distance that the road from the Tennessee river to Mobile and Orleans, will run thro' the Indian country, and the extent of the settlements below, no great inconvenience in peace or war can be apprehended from this circumstance. The Southern settlements will be able to supply any number of troops, which the defence of the coast from the Perdido to Pearl river shall require, and two or three days march, will pass from Tennessee river to those settlements. The President is as sensible as any other person of the advantages which the extension of the settlements to the Tennessee would have secured, and every exertion was made to procure the relinquishment of the Cherokee title to the lands in question, which were unavailing. He knew that the Chickasaws claim most of those lands, yet he offered them an annuity of six thousand dollars for their relinquishment.[3] The advantages however important, would have been too dearly bought by an act of injustice, which might have changed a friendly tribe into inveterate foes.

The importance of the navigation of the Tombigby river, renders it highly important to obtain the lands up to its Eastern margin. For this purpose Genl. John Coffee, John Rhea esqr. and Colo. [John] McKee have been appointed commissioners to treat with the Choctaw nation.[4] No exertion will be spared to obtain their consent to this boundary, either by an acknowledgement that the Creek cession extends that far to the West, or by the relinquishment of their title for a valuable consideration.

It is understood that a deputation of the Chickasaws are on their way to this city, for the purpose of adjusting their Eastern boundary with the United States. The geographical situation of the Flat Rock is not exactly known; nor is the direction of the Chickasaw line from thence to the Northern line of the Choctaws distinctly understood. It is, however, believed that the convention with the cherokees must have removed much of their cause of complaint. Should it be found impracticable to adjust this question, either from the defect of power in the deputation, or from the defect of evidence, it will become necessary to hold a treaty with that nation. In this event, the President will avail himself of your services.[5] They would have been required in the Choctaw treaty, but the situation in which Genl. Coffee had been placed by the mistake of Genl. Gaines, rendered his employment indispensable. The President's desire to give Mr. Rhea a mark of respect for his long and faithful services in Congress, could not be foregone on the present occasion.[6] I have the honor to be &c

Wm. H. Crawford.

LC, DNA-RG 75 (M15-3).

1. Only the abstract of Jackson's letter of April 11 has been found.

2. Crawford was referring to the treaties of 1802 and 1806.

3. There was no provision for an annuity in the March 22 treaty, only $25,500 spoliations. In the treaty negotiated at the Chickasaw Council House on September 14 and approved on October 4, the Cherokees accepted a $6,000 annuity for ten years.

4. The treaty with the Choctaws was concluded on October 24 and included an annuity of $6,000 for twenty years in exchange for relinquishment of claims to lands east of the Tombigbee. McKee (1771–1832) was Choctaw agent.

5. On April 17 Chickasaw agent William Cocke had written the war department enclosing a talk by Tishomingo criticizing Coffee's survey and AJ's attitude toward Indian claims and announcing the departure for Washington of a delegation (DNA-RG 107, M221-68). When the delegation—Chiefs William Colbert, Tishomingo, and Arpasarshtubby; interpreter James Colbert; and two warriors—arrived in early June, Crawford decided that the points at issue precluded immediate settlement, and he appointed AJ, David Meriwether, and Jesse Franklin as Chickasaw commissioners (see Crawford to AJ, June 4, July 5).

6. Rhea had been unsuccessful in his bid for reelection to the Fourteenth Congress.

To James Gadsden

May 30th. 1816

Dr Sir

your letter of the 10th Instant with its accompanying copy of your report is duly to hand[1]—and fully meets my approbation except in this, you appear to think that the fortification proposed for Mobile point will not be effectual to prevent the entrance of an invading fleet—I am of the opinion that the works proposed will prevent the entrance of all ships of war & large transports—others will not if they could pass up unprotected by large vessels, when there retreat might be cut off by a Battery at the point of Pass Heron, and a Temporary Battery on The Dauphin, hence I conclude that the work proposed will be effectual—[2]

a few days ago I wrote you addressed to New york, Major [Isaac Lewis] Baker being absent, I have not the copy, and cannot give you the date to which I refer you[3]—and here will only add that the discontent of the citizens at the surrender of the Territory to the Cherokees in the late convention rather increase than abate—the more there pretensions of cherokee right is investigated, the more unfounded it appears—and the attempt to give them possession, I fear will lead to consequences more disagreable than any that has occured since the commencement of our happy Goverment—this is a Territory so important to the defence of the lower country and the frontier of this and so long the Den of the marauding & murdering Creek that one foot ought not to have been given up, unless on the proof of right in the Cherokees, every principle of sound national policy forbade it, as well as national Justice—it would have united the upper with the lower country, by a strong & thick population afforded abundant supplies for a road & advancing army, and cut off all communication between the northwestern Indians with the creeks & Seminoles—the late convention has destroyed all these national benefits, and we have with our blood & Treasure drove the lion from his Den, & placed the wolf in it to devour our innocent lambs—already have the Indians become insolent, they have lately flogged two Whitemen, who were settled on the creek lands ceded—a party of whites raised & followed, and gave this party a dreadfull beating the seeds of hostility is sown, and I expect to hear of murders next—If that should be the case the arm of Goverment is not strong anough to prevent the anihilation of that part of the cherokee tribe living East of the Mississippi for the arm of the west will be raised in support of the citizen instead of the support of the govt.

I do believe that the President & secratary of war has both been imposed on by the information of the agent[4]—if he has represented any right to this land in the cherokees, or any acknowledgement of there right by the creeks south of wills creek the waters of the coose and the mouth of Thompsons creek[5] waters of Tennessee he has openly & wilfully sinned, by stating that which he must have knew was untrue—Frankness is due to our goverment by all its officers—This induced me when at the city[6] to tell the Honble. sec of war that the cherokees would set up claim to Territory they had no right to, and that they had no right to the land ceded & explained to him the importants of this Territory to the defence of the lower country & security of this, and I now beg you to tell him, that it will cost the Govt more blood of our citizens to give the cherokees possession of this Territory than all the battles of the south in the late war. on the recpt of this write me, when I will instruct you at what point I wish you to Join me—&c &c &c

AL draft, DLC (20).

1. See Gadsden to AJ, May 10. For the surviving portion of Gadsden's report, see Document 72, Reports on Fortifications and Topographical Surveys, DNA-RG 77 (mAJs).

2. Pass Heron, now Grants Pass, connects Mobile Bay with the Mississippi Sound between the coast and Dauphin Island.

3. Letter not found. Baker (1792–1830), brevetted major for gallantry at the Battle of New Orleans, served as Jackson's aide, February 22–June 15, 1816. He returned to Louisiana, where he was a planter, lawyer, and sometime member of the state legislature.

4. Return J. Meigs (1740–1823). Jackson continued to attack Meigs's statements, calling them blatant misrepresentations. See, for example, AJ to William H. Crawford, June 4, and AJ to James Monroe, July 9, both below.

5. Fort Deposit was located at the mouth of Honey or Thompson's Creek in present-day Marshall County, Alabama.

6. Jackson was referring to his stay at Washington in November and December 1815.

Confident of the superiority of Creek claims to the disputed region in northern Mississippi Territory, Jackson had given little thought to Cherokee boasts to have an "instrument of writing" supporting their claim to the land. But from the moment he first saw the provisions of the March 22 treaty and the printed instrument the Cherokee delegation had taken to Washington (DNA-RG 75, M208-6), he suspected that the Cherokees had gulled Washington officials with inaccurate accounts of the meetings at Fort Jackson.

The Cherokee document printed the boundary proposals the Cherokees had submitted for Creek acceptance and the agreement signed by the two tribes and linked them by a short narrative suggesting that when the Creeks agreed to allow Cherokee settlement pending resolution of the boundary they, in effect, acquiesced to the Cherokee proposals. That suggestion was not according to Jackson's understanding of the August 1814 negotiations, and in the letter below he so informed Crawford.

On June 19, Crawford responded to Jackson's denunciation of the treaty. "I am very far from believing," he wrote, "that we have yielded any thing to the Cherokees, which they had not a right to demand. . . . The lands south of the Cherokee line, when settled, will furnish a population equal to the repulsion of any enemy which may be brought to act against it. There is, therefore, no inducement to reexamine this subject, or to question its validity. In an enlightened nation, submission to the laws is the fundamental principle upon which the social compact must rest. No apprehension is entertained of the consequences which you appear to forebode. The treaty with the Cherokees, has been approved by the Senate and House of Representatives, and is the supreme law of the land. Submission to it is a duty which will not be neglected."

To William Harris Crawford

Nashville June 4th. 1816—

Sir

The inclosed paper was a few days ago sent me with this remark; that it was believed a copy of it had been laid before the President as an evidence of the Consent of the Creeks to the Cherokee claim to the Territory lately ceeded to them by convention at Washington & that Col Meigs had urged it to the President as affording an evidence of that claim.[1] I can scarcely believe the statement and until it is in my power to hear from you, will not forego the good opinion entertained of the Col. by believing that he could so far sin against light & knowlege as to act in direct opposition to the information he possessed

This paper was drafted by Col Meigs and presented to the Creek Indians and 'tho as I understood from him an assurance was had that they would sign it, yet when presented they possitively refused to do it.

At an early period after reaching what is now called Fort strother information was given me by the Creek chiefs that the Lands of their Nation extended much higher up than Wills creek the boundary shewn by the Cherokees, that they extended as high as the mouth of Hightower & along the Creek path to the Tennessee where it crossed that River.[2] They stated that the Cherokees were settled on lands belonging to them as low down the Coosa as the mouth of Wills Creek which had been loaned them by their Nation.

When ordered to receive the capitulation of the Creeks and a surrender of as much land as would indemnify the United States for the expences of the war I wrote to Col. Meigs and requested that the Cherokee Chiefs should attend the Council at Fort Jackson to settle their boundary before the Treaty should be finally concluded.[3] This was important as well to ascertain what bounds should be secured to the Creeks as to know certainly how far the residue would offer to the U. States complete indemnity for the expences of the war. Himself and some of the Cherokee Chiefs attended & many conferences were held; not being invited I was present at none of them, and only learned what was passing, by information derived from the Creeks. They stated that it was insisted by the Cherokees that now as they were about to cede a portion of their Country to the U. States they should previously to concluding the Treaty recognise their boundary to include lands to which as they alledged the Cherokees had not nor ever had a tytle; this they possitively refused. Learning from Col. Meigs and the Creek Chiefs that nothing could be concluded on in relation to boundary, I proceeded to a confirmation of the Treaty without calling therein for any points that might prejudice the claims of either party, leaving what might not be sufficiently certain to be ascertained by the commissioners whom the President might appoint

On the 9th. of August after much warmth had as I understood been manifested both by the Creeks and Cherokees, this paper was bro't by Col. Meigs to my tent and requested to be attested by Col. Hawkins and myself as the only thing that could then be done and for the purpose as was expressly declared to secure the Cherokees who might be settled on the Creek Lands in quiet and undisturbed possession until the question of boundary could be settled between them; and to prevent them in the interim from being in any manner subject to the Creek laws.[4]

These are the facts & if representations different from them have been made, or if it has been suggested that the Creek Chiefs in Council ever made any acknowlegement of boundary which was attested by me; or having agreed to a boundary were prevented by me from signing it; there will be no hesitation on my part in declaring it absolutely false. Be the representation what it may I request of you if knowing to it, to detail it to me as it is & by whom made: Can so uncandid and illiberal statements have been made by Col Meigs or countenanced by him Let it tho have been made by whom it may it is unfounded; altho well calculated to have induced the President to enter into this hasty convention, a convention by which the best portion of Country ceeded by the Creeks amounting to 5,000000 of acres has been surrendered & with it the security of the lower Country & our own frontier. Below the mouth of Wills Creek on the Coosa & Thompsons on the Tennessee the Cherokees never had a claim a fact I am persuaded well known both to the Indians & their agents. Understanding when at the City that Col Meigs was coming on with the Cherokee Chiefs I declared my belief that they would assert claims to Lands to which they never had a right, & urged the propriety of leaving with the commissioners appointed by the Government to designate the points of the Treaty, not doubting but that full & complete justice would be done & that all parties would at once acquiese in the boundary they might establish I must tho here be permitted to remark that the idea never was indulged that the inclosed paper would be attempted to be palmed on the Government as an evidence of right in the Cherokees or consent to that right by the Creeks The paper speaks for itself & conveys no such idea; if it has been used differently from what it purports, it deserves to be investigated, that the odium may be thrown at the proper door; & the contract set aside because clearly founded in fraud The evidence of Col. Butler adjt. Genl., Col Hawkins, Capt. Thomas [Langford] Butler then my aid, Major [Howell] Tatum & Mr. [Charles] Cassedy can fully explain this whole transaction[5]

I regret exceedingly that this Convention has been thus hastily entered into without that clear & satisfactory information which might have been had & which would have clearly negatived all idea of right on the part of the Cherokees. The western people are loud in their complaints against it. They consider that, that security for which they fought & bled is taken from them, & the Country gained at the expence of some of the best blood of their Land, taken as they believe without evidence of right & bestowed on a nation of Indians whose hatchet and scalping knife has left many an orphan & many a parent without a child.

Many of these people are settled down on the Villiages from whence they by their valor drove the hostile Creeks, & many of the Volunteers who against the orders of their goverment marched against the Cherokees at Nicajack, destroyed it & gave security to their frontier are also there.[6] When they shall see themselves removed from these Villiages which were the dens of the murderers of their wives & children, not to answer any general policy of the Government, but to benefit the prowling Lyon of the forest who has already done them so much injury; your forebodings will be something like mine that evil may result. I hope it will be believed that I am not often alarmed at trifles, but that in all my acts, in all my expressions and information to the Government I am swayed alone by disinterested motives—publick good[7]—I am Respectfully Yo Mo. Obt Svt

Andrew Jackson

LS in John H. Eaton's hand, NcD (5-0140); ALS draft, DLC (58); Copy, DNA-RG 233 (5-0133). Published in *HRDoc* 108, 20th Cong., 2nd sess. (Serial 186), pp. 6–8; and in Bassett, 2:246–49 (from ALS draft with ascribed date of June 13).

1. Jackson's copy of the Cherokee document may have been forwarded by Joseph McMinn, who had recently discussed the Cherokee claims with Meigs.

2. Fort Strother, Jackson's headquarters during the Creek War, was on the Coosa River in northern Mississippi Territory, in what is now St. Clair County, Alabama. The Hightower, now the Etowah, joins with the Oostanaula, to form the Coosa River in Floyd County, Georgia. The Creek Path ran north from Wills Creek near Attalla in present Etowah County to the Tennessee River east of Fort Deposit, near its southernmost point in present Marshall County, Alabama.

3. See Robert Butler to Return J. Meigs (1740–1823), June 14; Meigs to AJ, July 6; and Meigs et al. to AJ, August 4, 1814.

4. See Agreement between Creeks and Cherokees, August 9, 1814.

5. Butler (1789–1881), cousin of Robert, served as Jackson's aide during the Pensacola and New Orleans campaigns in 1814–15. Tatum (1753–1822), a revolutionary veteran, lawyer, surveyor, and officeholder in the Mero District, had served as a topographical engineer, 1814–15. Cassedy (c1782–1858), a native New Yorker, had moved to Tennessee about 1810 and served as Jackson's secretary in the Creek negotiations.

6. Tennessee volunteers destroyed Nickajack in September 1794.

7. In the draft after this point, AJ indicated that he was enclosing a copy of a letter to Meigs (not found) on the subject of the Cherokee publication.

From Ferdinand Louis Amelung

New Orleans June 4. 1816

Sir

In obedience to your order received on the 6th. May last, I proceeded the next day for Panzacola but owing to adverse winds (having to wait 12 days at the Bay St. Louis) I only arrived at that place on the 24th. May I was received and treated with great attention by the governor and his officers, and after receiving his answer to your Letter I left there on the 27th. and arrived here on the 2nd. Inst.[1]

I have the honor to transmit herewith the answer of the Governor (which I think embraces all the points touched upon in yr. letter) and also take the liberty to subjoin a translation thereof, as it might happen that no person is near you understanding the spanish Language[2] I am firmly of opinion that the Governor asserts the truth in his communication, and am convinced that the Inhabitants of Panzacola have suffered and do now suffer more than our Citizens from the existence of the Fort and its Garrison. I also take the Liberty of communicating such intelligence as I have been able to collect from good authority and which might perhaps be of some use.

The Fort in question is situated at Bonavista on the Eastern Bank of the Apalachicola River 15 miles above its mouth and 120 miles East of Panza. The River discharges itself into St. George's Sound and vessels drawing not more than 10 feet water may come in between St. George's and St. Vincent's Islands; the Bar however is dangerous and requires a skillful pilot.

The fort was constructed by [Edward] Nichols & [George] Woodbine[3] and the British occasionally resorted thither but on their final evacuation of this country, left it in possession of a Garrison composed of Negroes and Indians with 4 heavy pieces of ordnance and 10,000 lb. of Powder &c.

About 20 Choctaws, a number of Seminoles and a great number of runaway negroes are supposed to have been there some time ago but a great part of these Brigands have abandoned the Fort on account of scarcity of provisions and have gone to Savannah (alias St. Josephs) River in East Florida, whither they will no doubt all retire in case of an attack by land, as they have a Schooner and several large Boats to make good their retreat, if not intercepted by Sea.

From this spot they can easily annoy our Settlements on Flint River and the whole Georgia Frontier, and are in a country, where they can procure subsistence with facility

Panzacola itself is, I can assure you, entirely defenceless; the Garrison consists of from 80 to 100 effective men exclusive of a Batallion of color'd troops say abt 150 men, of whom the Inhabitants themselves stand in constant dread They have about 150 serviceable muskets about 500 musket cartridges and not enough Gunpowder to fire a salute; one gun was mounting at Barancas on the day I left there[4] To this is to be added the dissatisfaction of the Inhabitants and even of a number of the officers of Government and the desire of the majority to see a change effected. I must not forget to present to you on the part of the Governor the thanks of the Inhabitants of Panzacola for the examplary and humane conduct of the Army under your command while at Panzacola, and I verily believe their professions to be sincere[5]

The Governor also, on my mentioning in conversation that I was persuaded you would willingly assist in destroying the Fort, said that if the object was sufficiently important to require the presence of General Jackson he would be proud to be commanded by you, and that if the Captain General of Cuba[6] could not furnish him with the necessary means, he might perhaps apply to you for assistance.

Having nothing further to add I remain Very Respectfully General Your most obdt. Servt.

Ferd. L Amelung
Capt 1st. Inf

ALS, DLC (20); Copies, DNA-RG 107 (M221-70), DNA-RG 46, DNA-RG 233 (5-0124). Published in *ASP, Foreign Relations,* 4:557, and in Bassett, 2:242–43.

1. See Isaac L. Baker to Amelung, and (above) AJ to Mauricio de Zuñiga, April 23; Zuñiga to AJ, May 26, below.

2. See below for Amelung's translation of Zuñiga's reply and the Appendix for the original.

3. Nicolls (1770–1865) and Woodbine (d. 1837), British marines, had led Indian troops during the attack on Mobile Point in September 1814. After the war, they continued to urge the Creeks in Florida to resist the terms of the Treaty of Fort Jackson.

4. Fort San Carlos de Barrancas, which guarded the entrance to Pensacola bay about nine miles south-southwest of Pensacola, had been destroyed by the British during Jackson's 1814 invasion of Florida, but fortifications remained at the site.

5. Amelung was referring to the brief occupation of Pensacola by Jackson's troops in November 1814.

6. Juan Ruíz de Apodaca (1754–1835).

ENCLOSURE: FROM MAURICIO DE ZUÑIGA

(*Translation*) Panzacola May 26th. 1816

Excellent Sir,

On the 24th. Inst. Capt Amelung of the 1st. U:S: Infry put into my hands Your Excellency's letter dated Washington M.T. 23rd. April 1816 in which (after informing me that you are charged by yr. Government to acquaint me, that the negro Fort erected during the late war with Great Brittain near the Junction of the Rivers Chatahouche & Flint has been reinforced and is now actually occupied by more than 250 Negroes, of which many have been seduced from the service of their masters, citizens of the U:S:, and that all are well armed, provision'd and disciplined) you make several pertinent remarks about the serious inconveniencies that may result from the toleration of a similar Establishment, not only as it regards the interruption of the tranquillity of the neighbouring people, but also the harmony which happily reigns between our respective Governments; You give your opinion on what the Spanish authorities ought to do, in order to put a stop to an evil of such a serious nature, in the manner conformable to those principles of good faith which form the basis of the friendly intercourse between the two nations.

You declare that this Government will have to take the necessary steps immediately otherwise that you will be compelled to provide yourself for the safety of the Inhabitants of the U.S., and you conclude by demanding that in my answer to your Letter, I may inform you, whether the said Fort has been constructed by the spanish Government, and if the negroes, who garrison it at present are considered as vassals of H. C: M:, and if not by whose authority and order it has been established[1] In reply I assure Yr. Excy with that truth inherent to an officer of honor, in which class I consider myself, that I arrived at this place about the End of March last, and having been informed of that which forms the subject of yr. Eys' Letter (with this only difference that the Fort instead of being situated in the place you mention, stands on the Eastern Bank of the Apalachicola River at the distance of about 15 miles of its mouth) I lost no time in proposing to my Captain General the measures which appeared to me the most proper, as well to shelter the Inhabitants of the District under my command against the Losses and damages which had resulted and might yet result from a similar Establishment, as also to prevent the citizens of the U.S: and the neighbouring friendly Indians to continue experiencing them. I have as yet received no answer and consequently Your Excy (who knows the limits of the powers of a subor[d]inate officer) will not blame me if I say, that (although my sentiments coincide entirely with yours on the particular point & the necessity of dislodging the Negroes from said fort, occupying it by spanish troops or Destroying it, and returning to their Lawful owners all negroes that may be retaken) I cannot act unless I receive the orders of my Captain General and the necessary Supplies, in order to undertake the Expedition with the probable prospect of ending it successfully

I am convinced that the determination of said chief will be made known to me ere long and should he authorize me to act your Excy may be assured that I shall not lose an instant to take the most efficacious measures on my part in order to cut at the root of an Evil which, besides what is mentioned in Yr. Excys Letter, has afflicted and occasioned great Losses to the Inhabitants of this district, subjects of my sovereign, whose wellfare and tranquillity I am bound to watch over and preserve

After this exposition, and informing you that the Fort of Apalachicola, occupied by the negroes, (whose destruction I think as necessary) was not constructed by the Spanish Government, and that the Negroes (altho' those belonging to the Inhabitants of this district and as natives of this place are vassals of the King my master) are by me considered in the light of Insurgents or Rebels against the authority not only of that of H.C.M. but also of that of the proprietors from whose Service they have withdrawn, some by the seductions of the British Colonel Edward Nichols and Major Woodbine and his agents, and others thro' their natural propensity to desert, after this exposition I say I might consider your letter entirely answered, but as Yr. Ey has manifested a particular desire, that in case the Fort had not been constructed by spanish authority, I might inform you under whose authority and by whose order it had been done, I feel no reluctance to satisfy yr. curiosity

I have learnt since my arrival at this place that said Fort and an other near the Junction of the Chatahouche and Flint River (which does not appear to exist now) were constructed by order of the above mentioned Colo. Nichols, whether authorized therein by his government I will not pretend to say, but he proceeded to provide it with artillery ammunition and provisions by order of Rear Admiral [Pulteney] Malcolm,[2] and when Col: Nichols and his troops, after the final conclusion of the Expedition against Louisa., retired from this point, he left with the Negroes orders totally contrary to the incontestable rights of sovereignty, which the King my master excercises from the 31st. Degree of N: Latitude towards the South

Of all these transactions my predecessors in this Government have given notice to the authority, from which Panza. depends, that satisfaction may be claimed correspondent to the violations.

I think I have satisfied Yr E. on all points mentioned in your Letter in such terms, as will leave no doubt on your mind about the sincerity of my Intentions in favor of the cause which is common to the Inhabitants both American and Spaniards, and that my present inaction does not proceed from backwardness. I therefore flatter myself that until my Captain General makes known to me his decision, neither the Government of the U.S: nor Yr. Exy. will take any step to the prejudice of the sovereignty of the King, my master, over the district of Apalachicola dependent on this Government, and in conclusion beg leave to assure Yr. Ey that it will give me always the most particular Satisfaction to meet with opportunities, where I can prove that my wishes are not only to contribute as much as lies in my power towards cementing the harmony which exists between our Respective countries but also to convince your Excy that I have formed the most exalted opinion of your virtues and military talents God keep your Excy many years

(signed) Mauricio de Zuñiga

Translation by Amelung, DLC (20); LS and Translations, DNA-RG 94 (mAJs); Translations, DNA-RG 46 (5-0091), DNA-RG 233 (5-0102); Copy, SpSAG (mAJs). Published in *ASP, Military Affairs,* 1:714–15 (dated May 26, 1818); *ASP, Foreign Relations,* 4:499–500 (dated March 26, 1816) and 4:556–57 (dated May 26, 1818).

1. See above.

2. Malcolm (1768–1838), third ranking officer of the British forces in the Gulf during the War of 1812, commanded the Gulf fleet after February 1815.

To William Harris Crawford

Nashville 9th. June 1816

Sir,

I have the honour to acknowlege the receipt of your letters of the 20th. & 21st. ultimo:

The orders contained afford much gratification. I have directed my adjutant General, to make the necessary detail of officers, and issue orders for the recruiting service; which will be made known to you, thro the Adjutant & Inspector General's Office. I have no doubt, but our ranks will be speedily filled, and that no necessity will exist, for a transfer from the Infantry to the Artillery.[1]

It affords me equal pleasure to be informed, that the Appropriations, for fortifications, are ample, and that our frontier will be placed in a state of safety, from a sudden attack of an Enemy, by their speedy completion. The exposed situation of the lower Mississippi requires this.

I hope the government and country may profit much by the Skill and talents of General [Simon] Bernard.[2] He stands high as a military character, and I doubt not deservedly so; but I have been so much deceived in the ostensible talents of French Engineers, warmly recommended and found to be grossly ignorant of their profession, I must confess I am not sanguine, that in this instance, the expectations of the government will be realized.

Foreign Engineers, having been so accustomed to large armies, and fortifications to be defended by a large force, and funds at will—that they may look at the works without calculating the means we have of defending them. I have never yet seen a work, planned and executed by a French

Engineer, that was not too large for the force we had to defend it. However if general Bernard can reduce, his Ideas, and plans to our means, his genius and skill may be of great utility.

It affords me satisfaction, that the measures, adopted for the pursuit of the Indians, who murdered Johnson & Mcgaskey, are approved of by the president; and I flatter myself, if the president of the United States, were as well acquainted with the Depravity, intrigue, cunning, and native cruelty of the Indians as I am, from his known humane dispositions, and desire to spare the effusion of Blood, he would also approbate the order I gave, for all Indians to depart from the ceded Territory, unless those secured under the treaty, and those for whose good conduct they would vouch.[3] An unprovoked murder of the most aggravated kind, about that time, had been committed; by whom it was not then, nor is it yet known. The only fact, established was that it was done by Indians: pursuit was necessary: and the innocent Indian could not be told from the Guilty. Steps were necessary to prevent other murders from being committed, or if perpetrated to secure to the actor immediate punishment. At that time the friendly party expressed objections to the extension of the Lines, and there were strong grounds for believing, that this murder was planned, if not executed, by the friendly party, to deter people from setling down in that country, or the commissioners from running the Lines. No other efficient course presented itself, but the one adopted, to keep the innocent from suffering, and our citizens from being slaughtered. There is but little game on this land; the Indians cannot support themselves by hunting: they must labour or live by robbing their Neighbours. The latter I have told them will not do—punishment awaits it—If they are permitted to range over this country, how easy it will be for them to murder our surveyors, be fed and secreted by the connivance of the friendly Indians, & through their means escape punishment. I have but little doubt, these murders were committed by the excitement, of what is termed, the friendly party, the property sent to the Seminoles, to prevent detection, by which it was thought the threat of Nichols, would be understood, by us as about to be executed, and the land resurrendered to them, under a dread of War.[4] I should suspect the Big Warrior for devising this plan. You may recollect when I was at the City I told you he was an Artful, cunning, double faced man, and a great coward; and capable of plotting, but not of executing mischief. If the hunting is essential to them, they can controll the hostile, and bad men of their Nation, & surrender the murderers, with a pledge that a repetition of such scenes shall not take place. If they will not, security, to our citizens and the innocent Indian, requires the order to be enforced untill the surveying ordered is completed. But if the President of the United States will devise any other plan, and direct it, I will cause it to be forthwith executed.

If on the one hand I have been solicitous for the safety of the citizens, on the other, I have been careful, that punishment should await them, for every act of injustice or hostility, towards the Indian, as you will perceive, by the enclosed extract of my letter to General Gaines on this subject, under date of the 15 ultimo.[5] I have the honour to be, Sir, Your obedient humble Servant

Andrew Jackson
Major Genl comdg.
D. of the South—

LS, DNA-RG 107 (M221-70).

1. See Crawford to AJ, May 20 and 21. For the recruiting orders, see Robert Butler to Daniel Parker, June 10, DNA-RG 94 (M566-87).

2. Bernard (1779–1839; École Polytechnique) had served in Napoleon's armies before he came to the United States in 1815. During the fifteen years he served as a U.S. Army engineer, he planned and directed the building of the coastal defense system.

3. See AJ to Crawford, March 15, for his report of measures to apprehend the murderers of Johnston and McGaskey. Crawford's May 21 letter relayed the president's approval of plans for their pursuit and conveyed Madison's reservations about barring friendly Creeks from the ceded land.

4. For Edward Nicolls's warning regarding the line survey, see Nicolls to Benjamin Hawkins, June 12, 1815 (DLC-8).

5. Not found.

To William Harris Crawford

June 16th. 1816—

I have the honor to acknowledge the receipt of your letter of the 24th. ult. have duly noted that part that relates to the settlers south of the Tennessee river which will be duly attended to.[1]

The ballance of your letter contains a system of Ethics at open war with those practised by Mr. Madison president of the u states, through a long & well spent life, therefore I cannot believe the doctrine advanced by you have been sanctioned by him, but is the offspring of your own mind, and shall thus view them so far as I conceive it necessary to reply—

I must in the first place premise; that I never did expect to hear it announced through the organ of our Goverment whose main pillers are virtue, that to be charged with Robery was no disgrace to an officer & soldiers and that it was inconsistant with the dignity of our Goverment to investigate fraud, when it had been practised against the U.S

I made the request in my letter of the 8th of april that Justice might be done the W Tennesseans,[2] and a discrimination might be made between the guilty & innocent—& if charges had been made against their actions they were unjust that the might be investigated This Justice being witheld, and a determination displayed to mingle us with the guilty measures will be taken at a proper time to procure that Justice to them that I know there good conduct entitle them—

your observation "that it is well known that the march of the best diciplined troops, thro there own country is always attended with loss," must have proceeded from inexperience, for when it ever happens the officer ought to be cashierd. for neglect of duty—and it is the well known fact, that the west T. troops marched in the year 1812–13 & 1815 to the lower country & back through the cherokee & creek country and entered Pensacola under circumstances that might have induced disorder from thence to new orleans & back and the Tongue of truth cannot point to a single act of private property being infringed without Just compensation—The concurrent Testimony referred to, to produce a conviction of my mistake, in asserting that no losses were sustained by depredation committed by the west Tennesseans, are too absurd to obtain credit by a reflecting mind, unless indeed those Gentlemen by some kind of instinct or intuitive knowledge after a lapse of two years could tell, by the track—how many cattle, hogs & horses, the cherokees two years before possessed, that they had been stolen, not made use of or sold by themselves—and if stolen, that they were carried away by the west Tennesseans, I am sorry the names of those inspired gentlemen were not given, that the publick might admire them for there wisdom & divinity—however I shall inclose an extract from Colo. [Leroy] Popes letter, who was some times present, which I hope will obtain as much credit as those Gentlemen who passed through the nation two years after the depredations are alledged to be committed, and will refer you to the accounts on file in the quartermasters department—filed by Colo. S[tockley] D[onelson] Hays & Major Wm B[erkeley] Lewis.[3]

I enclose for your information a copy of a letter from Colo Barnett to Genl Coffee from which you will discover more particularly how the cherokees has been tampering with the creeks to filch the U States out of the land which they well knew had been ceded by the creek treaty[4]—I should have noticed your concluding sentence, but I cannot believe you to be serious, no man who possesses honourable feelings and brought up in a country, where the laws punish vice, & applaud virtue, can believe that the charectors of the west Tennesseans are not implicated, when they are recorded as the worst kind of robers, Taking from the poor Indian. I shall here close the subject, making an appeal for Justice, to a source, who may appreciate, virtuous conduct of the american officers and soldiers, more than you appear to do and who I hope will think it Justice, that the innocent should not suffer for the crimes of the guilty—

AL draft, DLC (21). Published in Bassett, 2:249–50.

1. On May 24, Crawford had agreed to suspend the removal of settlers south of the Tennessee River pending settlement of the Chickasaw boundary.

2. Jackson meant his letter of May 8, which requested a statement of the Cherokee claims.

3. See Leroy Pope to AJ, May 29. Pope (1765–1844), a founder of Huntsville, Alabama, was a merchant and banker. In the course of a general protest against the March 22 treaty, Pope wrote, "I am fully persuaded that I have paid myself the full amount of all there property made use of by the Army. . . ." Hays (1788–1831), Jackson's nephew and judge advocate

general of the Southern Division, had been quartermaster for the Tennessee militia, 1812–14; Lewis (1784–1866), Jackson's long-time friend and confidant, had been U.S. assistant deputy quartermaster general.

4. Not found.

To Nathan Reid

Nashville June 23rd. 1816

Dr Sir

I have no doubt but you have been surprised at my long Silence. I should have written you immediately on my return from Neworleans, but publick business that had accumulated by my absence took up my whole attention, except the hours that was necessary to promote the work began by our deceased friend. This has engrossed much of my time & thoughts, and I flatter myself by the pen of Major Eaton it will be compleated in a manner to meet the expectations of the publick, to the interest of his dear little family, and in a style worthy the original author. Major Eaton will exert his best talents, his industry & research will give to the publick a Just narative of facts.

I hope the work will be ready for the press in less than three months. I have wrote Colo. A. P. Hayne to make an engagement with some artist to engrave the plates promised in the prospectus of the work.[1]

Mrs. Jackson has shewn to me a letter from Miss Martha to her, in which she requests that I would give you my opinion on the subject of your removal to this country[2]—when at your house I gave you fully my opinion, it corisponded, with the opinion of our friend since deceased—notwithstanding a principle inducement has ceased to exist by his death, still the interest of your family, could not fail to be promoted by a sale of your real property there and an investment of half the amount of sales in land in the newly acquired country. It is true that the late hasty convention with the cherokees has greatly curtailed the benefits that was expected to result to the u states from the creek cession, and has rendered that section of country less valuable for the present, by leaving it less secure, but in time those encumbrances, will be removed when land in that country will be more Valuable than in any other, except in the climate adapted to the growth of the sugar cain, in which much health cannot be expected.[3] This country being so well calculated for the culture of cotton—which is & must continue to be a staple—I therefore would recommend you to come out, explore this country and be prepared to purchase at the public sales of this land which is now preparing ⟨for sale⟩ by the orders of the Goverment. by adopting this plan, from a view of the country you can better Judge for yourself, and have also the pleasure of seeing your daughter & her three sweet little children—Mrs. Reid has been very unwell, but has recovered, the children enjoy good health. I called to see them on my return. I never saw a finer child than the youngest—If you come & explore the country I am sure you will like it, and it will aford me much pleasure, that you should purchase in the neighbourhood that I do, it will give Mrs. J & myself great pleasure to have you & your family near us. Have the goodness to present us affectionately to them, and say to Miss Martha that Mrs. Jackson will give her letter a full answer shortly, she has hitherto been prevented by a crowd of company, & busied in preparing to move to Nashville, where I find it necessary to be for a few months, to wind up my publick business, where, should you visit this country, I shall expect to see you. I shall be happy to hear from you often, and will always reply when I have leisure, accept of our good wishes for your welfare & happiness and that of your amiable family and believe me to be, respectfully yr mo. ob. serv.

Andrew Jackson

ALS, DLC (71).

1. Letter not found. The prospectus of the biography promised "accurate drawings of the positions of the armies in the several engagements, and a current engraving of the General" (*Nashville Whig,* September 5, 1815).

2. The letter from Nathan's daughter, Martha Reid (1791–1859), has not been found.

3. Jackson was referring to the March 22 Cherokee treaty.

From William Harris Crawford

War Department, July 1. 1816.

Sir,

Your letter of the 13th. ultimo has been received. The omission on the part of the Adjutant & Inspector General to send you a copy of the order to General Gaines, has produced the remarks which it contains. From the perusal of that order, which the Adjutant and Inspector General has been directed to forward, you will discover that no absolute arrest has been directed.[1] The Executive has been induced to take this course, as well from the nature of the case, as from the situation of affairs in the Department more immediately under his command. It was believed, that his services might be necessary in the Department, as long as it was practicable for him to remain there consistently with his punctual attendance at the Court instituted for his trial. The distant period assigned for the Convention of the Court, was intended, among other things to give you an opportunity of assigning the Command of the Department to any other officer in your division, should the aspect of affairs render the selection an object of importance.

The ferment produced in the public mind in the State of Tennessee, by misrepresentations in relation to the Cherokee convention, is the more regretted, as it can only tend to the injury of those who are led astray.[2] That Convention, as well as every other which has been, or shall be ratified by the President, with the advice of the Senate, will be strictly executed, unless the Cherokee & Chickesaw title to the lands, in question, shall be extinguished by the Commissioners appointed to treat with the latter tribe.[3]

The idea attempted to be imposed upon the public, by the intruders, that they are ready to remove from their settlements, as public property, but not as Indian lands, is too shallow a device to deceive the most inconsiderate. The most of these intruders have entered upon the land in question, since the running of Genl. Coffee's line, and are as liable to be removed, as tho' the act of Congress had never passed. That act provides only for those who had intruded before the first day of February last, on the ground that the proclamation was not known before they had entered upon the public land.[4]

The intruders upon the land in question, acted with full knowledge upon the subject; or, at least, they had the means of knowing that their intrusion was in violation both of the law,[5] and the proclamation, and yet they have the effrontery to talk of submission to the laws. It is easy to make professions, and nearly as easy to devise pretexts for an unlawful act, especially if it is not thought necessary that they should even be plausible. This appears to be the case in the present instance. This delusion must be terminated. The idea of resisting the authority of the government, must not be admitted for a moment. As the execution of the law should it be resisted, will immediately devolve upon you, as the Commanding General of the Southern division, it is expected, that you will use your influence to arrest this momentary delusion, which otherwise, may possibly be carried so far as to make the interference of the military indispensable. This unpleasant alternative is by no means apprehended; but the very idea of it ought not to be permitted to exist. I have the honor to be, With great respect, Yr. Obt. Servant,

(signed) Wm. H. Crawford.

I Certify the foregoing to be a true copy of a letter on record in this Department. Dept. of War, August 3. 1816. Geo: Graham[6]

Certified copy and Copy, DLC (21); LC, DNA-RG 75 (M15-3); Extracts, DNA-RG 46 (5-0249), DNA-RG 107 (5-0246). Published in Bassett, 2:250–51.

1. In his letter of June 13, Jackson had protested the war department's failure to route through Southern Division headquarters its order for Edmund P. Gaines to attend a court of inquiry into his conduct at Fort Erie in 1814. For Daniel Parker's order to Gaines, May 22, see DNA-RG 94 (M565-5).

2. See above, for example, AJ to James Monroe, May 12.

3. On June 4, Jackson, David Meriwether, and Jesse Franklin had been appointed commissioners to negotiate the Chickasaw boundary.

4. Crawford was referring to the act of March 25, 1816, which provided that those who had settled on public lands prior to February 1 could register to remain as tenants until the land was sold (3 *U.S. Statutes at Large* 260). The presidential proclamation of December 12, 1815, directed public land intruders to leave and authorized the military to enforce removal.

5. Of March 3, 1807 (2 *U.S. Statutes at Large* 445–46).

6. The original (not found) of this letter was apparently sent to Jackson without signature, who returned it to the adjutant and inspector general for clarification. On August 3, George Graham (1772–1830; Columbia 1790), the war department's chief clerk, in the absence of Crawford, made a copy from the war department letterbooks, certified it, and returned it to Jackson with the observation that although the secretary had failed to sign the letter, Crawford had franked it.

To James Monroe

(Private) Nashville 9th July 1816

Dear Sir

I have just received your letter of the 18th. of June last. The justice done General Coffee, is truly Grattifying to me, and will be duly appreciated.[1]

The feelings you express toward the Citizen and the Soldier who have fought the battle of their Country will endear you to them much, and in case of emergency ensure their services to the government.

I feel it a duty I owe to my Country, to undertake any service wherein it may be thought I can be usefull. This consideration *alone,* induces me to enter on the duties assigned me as Commissioner.[2] But unless my instructions will authorize a full investigation and adjustment, of the Territory ceded by the Creeks, with the Cherokees, as well as the Chickesaws; no benefit can result to the United States; for in this Convention, all the difficuty, ⟨and⟩ evil exists. If a delegation, should be authorized from the Cheokees, with full power to investigate theirs, and the Creek boundary; I have no doubt but that all things could be adjusted to the satisfaction of all, upon the broad principles of Justice; and that security restored to our frontier and to the lower country which has been so unfortunately surrendered. But untill the convention can be got rid of, every foot of land obtained from the Chickesaws in that quarter, will tend to the agraizement of the Cherokees only. By that Convention all that portion of Country belonging to the Chickesaws, which would be usefull to the United States is given to the Cherokees It follows of course that [the] moment the United States are vested with a right to it, it vests in the Cherokees. Hence the necessity of geting clear of this convention, which I think could be done by proper management if another convention with that Tribe was ordered. The Cherokees Know they never had a right to that land; they see the irritation of the whites on this subject, and they begin to dread (what is really to be feared) their own destruction, by an irritated people.

Colnl Meigs ought to exert himself on this occasion. I fear he has not acted with his usual candour with the goverment, or this hasty convention with the Cherokees would not have been entered into. He, as Agent can still cause Justice to be done, by a surrender of this Territory, for a small annuity. And candour compells me to say to you, that from the present feeling of the people they will never permit the Cherokees to inhabit the country from which the Creeks have been expelled What follows? Treaties are the supreme law of the land; they must be executed. the consequence may be that the Cherokees will be annihilated; which will compell the arm of Government to be raised against her own Citizens for the violent infraction of the Treaty. This subject has caused me much reflection, and filled me with sincere regreat. I hope a remedy may, and will be found in another Convention with this Nation, and that shortly.

A Whiteman has lately been Killed on the Georgia Road; as soon as it was known, Majr Russell raised four hundred men to penetrate their Nation, but was prevented from doing so, by a speedy surrender of the Cherokees, who commited the murder.[3] From this you may see what may result to that nation. From the contents of a letter from Colonel Lowery to Major Russell, (as I am informed) there is but little doubt but if proper application was made to the Cherokees, they would yeild up all pretensions to this Teritory for a very small consideration.[4] In fact they had agreed on a boundary with gen Coffee in case nothing had been done at the city.[5]

You will see from the newspapers what are the feelings of the People on this subject, and more particularly from the Remonstrance sent the President this feeling is unanimous[6]

We learn with much regreat the indisposition of Mrs [George] Hay and tender our best wishes for her speedy recovery. Mrs Jackson and myself desire our best respects to your lady, Mr and Mrs Hay,[7] and accept for your self our best wishes for your individual health and happiness. Believe me respectfully your sincere friend and humble servant

Andrew Jackson

LS in William O. Butler's hand, DLC (5-0296); ALS draft, dated July 8, DLC (21). Published in Bassett 2:252–53 (extract of ALS draft). "(Private)" in AJ's hand.

1. In that letter Monroe promised pay for Coffee's supernumerary officers for their war service and for Coffee's Creek cession survey crews.

2. Jackson was referring to his appointment as Chickasaw negotiator.

3. On June 29 Governor Joseph McMinn wrote Jackson that Major John Walker, a half-Cherokee chief who fought in the Creek War, had escorted into Knoxville two of the three accused of the murder. The trial before the U.S. District Court for East Tennessee was dismissed for lack of jurisdiction. Jackson was probably referring to William Russell (c1760–1825) of Franklin County, who had commanded a contingent of spies in 1814.

4. Letter not found. John Lowry (1768?–1820?), a half-Cherokee, had served as lieutenant colonel of Indian troops at Horseshoe Bend and at other Creek War battles.

5. Jackson was referring to an agreement reached on February 8 (DNA-RG 75, M271-1), which provided for a boundary "beginning on the Coosa river at the mouth of Will's creek—running from thence up the eastern bank of said Wills creek, with its meanders, to a point oposite to Camp Wills. . . ." Coffee stated that the agreement was offered to the Cherokees but they "declined accepting untill they recd. information from the deputation the nation had sent to see the President."

6. On June 21 a public forum in Nashville denounced the Cherokee treaty and the failure of the federal government to complete payment of the troops. Several speakers blamed Crawford for both problems. Reconvening on July 6, the citizens of Nashville and adjacent counties adopted a memorial to the president, again protesting the Cherokee treaty, and requesting extinguishment of Chickasaw claims in Tennessee.

7. Eliza Monroe Hay (1786–1835), Monroe's daughter, had married George Hay (1765–1830) in September 1808.

To John Coffee

(Private) Nashville July 21rst. 1816

Dr. Genl

I have this moment recd. by mail the letter to your adress here enclosed, having opened it and finding it from Colo McKee and being on the subject of the choctaw treaty, I enclose it—[1]

From the late date of the meeting of the chiefs it will afford sufficient time for you to attend to the duties on the line. It is really strange that you & Colo. Barnett has not recd instructions to desist from running the line for the present untill, the event is known, of the treaty ordered with the cherokees, for a recession of those lands lately ceded south of the Tennessee, was it not for so many plunders being lately committed, I would conclude, that there was no reallity in this show of a treaty with the cherokees, or there would have been some others aded to the commission[2]—it proves one thing at least, that they have not attached so much ⟨confidence⟩ importance to this thing, as to the other treaties to be holden, when I view it as the key to all things that can benefit the U.S. and can be obtained by treaty—I really am not sorry that you are without advice, your orders will compell you to go on & will authorise you to call for the chiefs to attend you—and you can do more with the chiefs, by advice, than will be done by Colo. Meigs—I wish you & Colo. Barnett could see Colo. [Richard] Brown Lowry the Pathkiller & the ridge—should you, you can sound them to the Bottom & obtain from them a declaration that they will resign all claim for a very small sum, they know they never had any right & they will be glad as I believe to swindle the u states out of a few thousand dollars, and bury there claim, which they know if persisted in, might bury them & there nation. By obtaining a declaration from the chiefs that the will sell, you can tell them I am authorised to buy from them, & expect a full delegation from there nation at the chikesaw treaty to be held on the first of Sept. next at the old council house[3]—Colo Meiggs is instructed to have a full delegation there, But as all this may be for the Public eye—when really under the Rose advice may be given contrary we ought to be on our guard, to detect duplicity (if it exists) and expose it, and do all we can Justly, to do away that *cursed convention* that may deludge our country in blood—They Cherokees are alarmed and Justly, and with a little Vigilence & good policy, all the evils can be averted only the sum that will have to be paid for the recession—The hight of my diplomattic ambition is that we may restore to the u states the territory fairly & Justly ceded by the creeks, if the convention with the cherokees can be set aside the ballance will follow, as a thing of course, if that cannot be done all that can be obtained from the chikesaws will agrandize the cherokees, whom it delighteth the sec to honour—when I take a View of this whole thing with all its ramifications I cannot determine whether it proceeded from shear ⟨ignorance⟩ weakness or corruption—or from what else it could have proceded, to say the least, it was a wanton, hasty, useless thing calculated to injure the best interests of the u states, without affording the least hope of benefit to her—we must exert ourselves to get the goverment honourably clear of this convention that they may by more Vigilence & care regain the good opinion of the good citizens of the west, with my best wishes to you & respects to Colo. Barnett—adieu—

Andrew Jackson

ALS, THi (5-0321). Published in Bassett, 2:254–55.

1. Enclosure not found. Coffee, McKee, and John Rhea had been appointed Choctaw treaty commissioners.

2. Article 3 of the March 22 Cherokee treaty required the Cherokees to appoint two representatives to advise the commissioners surveying the Creek boundary line.

3. In his instructions to the Chickasaw treaty commissioners, Crawford empowered them to negotiate a purchase of the Cherokee claims if a sale had not been negotiated earlier. Ridge (Major Ridge; Kah-nung-da-cla-geh; c1771–1839) commanded Cherokee auxiliaries to Jackson's troops in the Creek War and Seminole campaigns. Brown (d. 1819), a Cherokee chief, had organized and led Cherokee warriors in the Creek War. Pathkiller (d. 1827) served as principal chief of the Cherokees from 1811 until his death.

Throughout the summer of 1816, Jackson was relentless in his efforts to stop depredations payments to the Cherokees, for which an appropriation bill of $28,600 had passed Congress on April 29 (3 U.S. Statutes at Large *326). When Jackson learned of the act, he lambasted Tennessee congressmen and demanded that they reexamine the accounts and defend their votes. As Jackson warned in the letter below, the March 22 treaty and the April appropriations bill were significant issues in the fall congressional campaigns and sparked a confrontation at Nashville between Jackson and the incumbent congressman, Newton Cannon (1781–1841). When one of Cannon's campaign speeches touched upon the March treaty, Jackson interrupted to criticize the congressman for his vote for the bill. In the colloquy that followed, Jackson, by one report, accused Cannon of telling "five damned infernal lies." (See Jesse Benton,* An Address to the People of the United States, on the Presidential Election, *Nashville, 1824, p. 31; and William B. Lewis to [Stephen Simpson], September 20, 1824, NN.) Only one of the six Tennessee congressmen—William Grainger Blount (1784–1827), son of William—was reelected to the Fifteenth Congress.*

To Isaac Thomas

Head quarters D. of the South
July 24th. 1816

Sir

By yesterdays mail I was furnished (in part) with a roster of the accounts exhibitted by the cherokees for depredations committed by the Troops & stipulated to be paid for by the 5th article of the late convention with the cherokees.[1]

I would forward you a copy but the sec. of war observes to me under date of the 24th of May last, that these accounts were certified by Colo. Meiggs, in due form of his agency, laid before the senate & house of representatives, and approved of by them, you then being a member, (if his statement is correct) you must have seen, examined, and approved them—[2]

It is equally astonishing that these accounts met with the approbation of you & others as it is that Colo Meiggs should have certified them—

My army is charged with taking six hundred & seven head of cattle & seven hundred & seventy one head of Hoggs & sundry horses. you were present with that army, and know its wants & privations, was well acquainted with the police established & fully executed, & did know that not a cent was permitted to be taken from the Indians that was not fully paid for, that you should have sanctioned by your vote, such a wicked & unjust slander against yourself and the whole army, is as unacountable as the accounts are unjust & untrue, one item in the account is for three hundred head of Cattle from [William] Ratcliff, you were present when we entered the nation and did know that we recd not half that amount, from every source & that Ratcliff was paid as well for his own cattle as for many he claimed from the drove brought from Littefutche belonging to Bob Catauley of these things you must have some recollection and under such circumstances, that you would by your Vote sanction his charge for $2700— and hand down to posterity, yourself & those brave honest citizens as robers in the solem form of a treaty requires some explanation[3]—To afford this is the object of my letter—I do not profess to be the guardian of the national purse, this is the province of you & others, representatives of the ⟨nation⟩ people but it is my duty to protect the well earned ⟨reputation of my self &⟩ fame of those honest & brave men I had the honor to command, & to prevent them on such, false groundless & corrupt exhibits, to be handed down to posterity as Vile delapidators and that too in the solem form of a treaty sanctioned by the Vote of the national Legislature. I must have your affidavit or certificate on this subject, to lay a ground, for rescinding the vote of censure contained in the Ratification of the 5th art and the act for carrying it into execution—of the late cherokee convention with the corruption that has swindled the goverment out of $25,000 cash, & ten millions worth of land that we fought & bled for I have nothing to do, this belongs to the representatives of the people, & in which I am not more concerned than any other citizen who has to participate in the burthens of the goverment. But our Reputation is dear to us, it must not, nor shall not be taken unjustly from us—I wish you to come in, ⟨see the⟩ reexamine these accounts, and if you can, exonerate yourself, from the blame that is attached to you for your Vote on this occasion.

This is a subject that will give rise to considerable animadversion at the next election—added to this, there is a Justice due to your reputation, and those brave men who fought with you. ⟨If you have not seen them⟩ I wish you therefore to reexamine them, and give such an explanation as Justice & truth requires.[4] ⟨It is due to yourself, it is due to the fair fame of those honest citizens—who fought & bled for there countrys rights, that Justice should be done them &⟩ for this purpose I adress you, I am respectfully yr mo. ob. serv.

Andrew Jackson

ALS draft, DLC (21). A Creek War veteran of John H. Anderson's 2nd Regiment of Volunteer Infantry, Thomas (1784–1859) served only one term in Congress.

1. See William H. Crawford to AJ, July 5.
2. See Crawford to AJ, May 24.
3. Some of the property of Ratcliff, a wealthy half-Cherokee, had been confiscated and Ratcliff himself arrested in December 1813 on suspicion of collaborating with hostile Creeks. Bob Cotalla (Catawla), a hostile Creek chief, lived near Littafuchee (Litafatchi), on Big Canoe Creek south of Fort Deposit. Jackson's troops had destroyed his village and captured him in October 1813 (*Jackson*, 2:443, 445).
4. Thomas replied on August 12, claiming that he had not seen the accounts nor did he recall voting on them. Newton Cannon, whom Jackson also queried on the matter, had a similar lapse of memory (see Cannon to AJ, November 3, and AJ to Cannon, November 6).

From Return Jonathan Meigs (1740–1823)

Cherokee Agency
7th. August 1816.

Sir

I have now before me your letter of the 23rd. ult., the subject of which is principally relating to depredations on the property of the Cherokees committed by the troops, (either taken or destroyed) in the expeditions against the hostile Creeks.[1] For your satisfaction I transmit to you true copies of the accounts exhibitted to the War Department of the spoliations therein said to have been committed by the troops.[2] The remarks made & attached to these accounts were made at the time. they the accounts were brought to me in the shape you now see them. It was my indispensable duty to present them to the war department and it has been done without partiality or the least possible private interest. some of the people who complain were rich; but the greater number were poor & helpless people who had a right decently to ask for redress from the Government, no inconsiderable part of these depredations were probably made by Deserters flying from their duty; some it is said were done for mere sport, or to try their Rifles, & some from ancient prejudices; this will appear from the statements that much of the meat was suffered to rot in the woods. some carcasses mutilated, & some untouched after being shot down, some wounded & left to perish by the wounds received; this proves that these disorders were not induced by necessity. The heads of some of the suffering families were at the same time fighting in the common cause of our Country. It appears that in one instance when an officer interfered his life was threatend, this will be found stated in the notes of explanation No. 15.[3]

It will be found by examination of these cases of complaint that a great part of the depredations are laid to waggoners by the complainants.

If Sir you will read over the tedious detail of these claims it may surprize you as it did me. I always knew that it was impossible for you to know the extent of these depredations. It cannot be understood that I certified these accounts from my personal knowledge. I never undertook to do anything that would require superhuman agency. I only certified these claims as being exhibitted to me in such a shape of credibility as induced my belief that they were true; and in that state they were submitted to the proper Department. there may have been instances of fraud—I know of no such instance. Ratcliffs claim being very great I had some doubts about it, and enquired of many about it. they generally only reply'd to me that Ratcliffs stocks were very large: one person only expressed any doubt about it. when he came for his money I questioned him about the greatness of his claim. he averred it to be right. I then explained to him the nature of an Oath, & required of him to make affirmation in the presence of the Great Spirit, which he did, before I paid him.

In all our transactions amongst men both in public & private transactions, we are sometimes compelled to put our confidence in men: there is necessity for it in some cases, and humanity & justice imperiously demand it other cases.

I will mention some of the claimants. Some of which I presume have your esteem, & in whom on trying occasions you have placed your confidence, & have not been deceived by them—Among the claimants we find the Path Killer, Major John Walker, Captain [John] Mclemore, Mr. D[aniel] Ross, Mr. Joseph Coody, Mr. Eliphalet [M.] Holt, Major Ridge, Major James Brown, Colonel Richard Brown, Mr. John Gunter & Captain John Thompson[4]—from such men I could not with propriety withhold my confidence and the simplicity of the statements made by other individuals are such as I was bound to notice—I presented the whole to the proper Department accompanied by Certificates of officers of high rank at that time in the Army, *copies of* which I now transmit. You will find sir by reading the notes annexed to the proper number that Colonel [William] Lillard was applyd to for redress. he replied "that he had already paid a great deal of money to save the credit of his regiment." this was his answer. Another claimant says that he applied to General [John] Cocke. & that the General observed that, "the soldiers had got clear of the fetters of the law & could not be restrained.["][5]

These circumstances were intirely unknown to you—and do not reflect on the Discipline or Morality of the Army under your immediate command—

That great disorder was apparent in that part of the Army on the eastern section of the Cherokee Country was true or I have been egregiously misinformed. disorders of a mutinous, disorganizing character large squads of Deserters went through the Country, and some of the depredations complained of were laid to those deserters. Some horses were probably taken by them. With respect to the duty and the interest of the Cherokees to make the Cession or cessions in question, I expressed my sentiments in my letter of yesterday,[6] and I am confident it will be readily done by them. In the existing state of the public mind, it is perhaps absolutely necessary to their security—besides being their duty. it is right in itself, & they owe it to the Government—perhaps their national existence requires it to be done. With respect to the fair fame of the Army under your command, I never in a single instance heard it impeached; but on the contrary always eulogized. You despise adulation and I need say no more on that subject.

You will permit me sir [to] differ in opinion with you that by the 5th. article of the convention an attempt was made to deprive your Army of their good character, & to brand them with the character of plunderers. I declare upon my honor I never discovered anything having that tendency; but directly the contrary in the administration every member of the Executive department—and as to my own nonimportance I will only say that when I do it the magnetic needle will change its direction at right angles.

with respect to the treaty making power I do not believe there is more wisdom or more integrity in any administration under heaven than in ours. I have the Honor of being with the greatest respect Your Obt. Servant

Return J Meigs.

ALS, DLC (21); Copy, DNA-RG 75 (M208-7). About 1816 Meigs moved the Cherokee Agency from the Hiwassee Garrison, at the junction of the Hiwassee and Tennessee rivers near Dayton in Rhea County, to a site about ten miles east on the north bank of the Hiwassee at Agency Creek in what is now Meigs County.

1. Letter not found.

2. The Cherokee accounts can be found on DLC (66, 69, 70).

3. Meigs was referring to the claim of Amoy'atau'whee (DLC-66).

4. All were prominent Cherokees. Their claims ranged from $12.00 for Major Ridge to $1,784.00 for James Brown.

5. Meigs was referring to the claims of Joseph Coody and James Lesley (DLC-66). Lillard (1744–1832), a former state legislator from Cocke County, had commanded the 2nd Regi-

ment of East Tennessee Volunteers during the Creek War. Cocke (1772–1854) had been major general of the East Tennessee militia.

6. See Meigs to AJ, August 6.

From Return Jonathan Meigs (1740–1823)

Cherokee Agency 19th. August 1816.

Sir

I have the honor to acknowledge the receipt of your letter of the 17th. Ult: I only received it three days ago, it was 30 days on its passage to me; probably by having been mislaid in some post office.[1]

I thank you sir for your writing to Colonel R. Brown & Colonel Jno. Lowrey.[2]

I take this opportunity to mention that in our Negotiations with the Cherokees—they made no kind of objection to the consideration offered by government for the land South & West of the eastern boundary of Madison County $6000 pr. annum and they need not; for it is abundantly sufficient—they objected to the price offered for the land on the North side of Tennessee 20,000: but it will be observed that by my instructions there was besides 5000$ to be disposed of at *discretion.* add to this I was authorised to pay Colonel Lowrey the value of his possessions: for this object the sum remained uncertain: but in my estimation this may be considered as 5,000 dollars more, making the agregate disposable at *Discretion 10,000 dollars.*[3] now Sir I will state my view of the prospect of obtaining the lands on the north side of Tennessee. For although they objected to the principal sum for that land, to wit, 20,000 dollars, this was not in my opinion the principal difficulty to be got over—the principal difficulty appeared to me to be to satisfy or remunerate Colo. [John] Lowrey & others for the loss of their possessions—Geo: Lowry, Major James Brown, & Lieut. John Brown have nearly equal claim for remuneration on account of their places[4]—there may be others; but no other appeared—If these men can be satisfied I think the principal sum 20,000 dollars will not be urged as an inadequate sum for the lands—

Success therefore may perhaps depend on the disposal of the discretionary funds, to wit, 10,000 dollars according to my estimation—& to effect the object I woud draw in favor of those who are to receive it, on the War Department, say at thirty days sight—this may be considered as prompt payment—for the Bills if not too large could be sold for cash in Nashville or Knoxville, to the merchants—or to the Banks—

I mention this because I have always found that prompt payment in such cases has a greater effect than the *sum itself.* it is sensibly felt, it acts on the senses physically & morally; it is tangible, it reaches from the fingers ends to the brain, it directly becomes enjoyment. I am very anxious to have you succeed in both cases: but think the attainment of the lands on the north side of Tennessee the most difficult. but to quiet the minds of the Citizens both cessions are necessary—and the Cherokees ought to do it. they owe it to the government & they owe it to their own tranquility & Safety.

They have no proper conceptions of their own true standing—their ideas of their own absolute independence are erroneous—they are voluntarily in the hands of a just government; a government that will never injure them: & in which they ought entirely to confide.

The government seem determined to raise them up. A Gentleman has arrived from Massachusetts to open a Lancasterian school on an extensive scale—at the expense of the Missionary Societies of Massachusetts & Connecticut & under the patronage of the government. these schools are worth more to them than half their lands.[5]

I have received orders to build houses for the teachers & for the Schools. I have the honor to be respectfully yr. Obt. Servant.

Return J Meigs.

P.S. I hope sir you will not consider me as officiously touching the subject of the pending treaty. I have very recently acted as Commissioner in this business, & I thought it my duty to State to you as you have to me—my view of the subject—& I have done it as it appears to me now—things may have changed the aspect—As a Citizen of the United States, and as Agent for the U. States in this nation, I am extremely anxious to have such arrangements now made, as will have the effect of removing the irritation of the people & the securing the enjoyment of tranquility. I transmit a Copy of a letter from Colonel Richard Brown giving an account of the Killing of two Cherokees by Whitemen at or near the Muscle Shoals.[6] this unhappy circumstance ought not to affect the negotiations—the misconduct of a few individuals is not chargeable on the whole community: but the men who have committed the outrage ought to be punished. and I hope the Executive authority will be exerted to have the perpetrators apprehended. R.J.M.

ALS, DLC (21).

1. Letter not found.

2. Only the letter to Richard Brown, [July 19], has been found.

3. Meigs had been authorized to negotiate for Cherokee lands north and south of the Tennessee River (see above, AJ to John Coffee, July 21). At meetings from July 20 to August 3, he was joined by Governor Joseph McMinn and John Williams of Tennessee, but the negotiations failed. For Meigs's instructions, see William H. Crawford to Meigs, May 27, DNA-RG 75 (M208-7).

4. Lowry (1770–1852), John's brother, was a member of the Cherokee council and later assistant principal chief. James Brown (1779?–1863) commanded Cherokee troops in the Creek War and later served on the Cherokee supreme court. Lieutenant John Brown later became a leader of the "old settler" faction of Cherokees.

5. In 1817 the Reverend Cyrus Kingsbury established the Brainerd school and mission under the auspices of the American Board of Commissioners for Foreign Missions, east of Ross's Landing.

6. See Brown to Meigs, August 14, DLC (21).

To Thomas Sidney Jesup

Head Quarters Chickasaw Council House—
Sept. 6. 1816

Sir

I have to acknowledge the receipt of your several letters of the 12, 18, & 21 August—

Your sentiments, as expressed in your correspondence with the Governor of Louisiana, accord with my own—[1]

Any act of aggression committed by Spain on our Territory, must be met by correspondent hostilities on our part, and from that moment she can be viewed in no other light than as an open Enemy—You will be cautious however & by no means provoke offensive movements. Spain must be the assailant—Your project against Cuba, is a good one provided the means in our power are such as to ensure success.[2] In the event of its execution being deemed advisable be assured your military Talents & enterprise will not be overlooked. with respect your most ob Serv

Andrew Jackson
Major Genl comdg
D. of the South

LS in James Gadsden's hand, NcD (5-0455). The home of George Colbert, near Tupelo, was designated as the Chickasaw Council House for the treaty meetings. Jackson and David Meriwether arrived there together on the evening of August 29.

1. See Jesup to AJ, August 12, 18, and 21. Jesup had sent Jackson his correspondence of August 4 and 10 with William C. C. Claiborne.

2. Jesup's August 18 letter announced his intention to "take immediate possession of Cuba" in the event of any Spanish assault on American posts.

To William Harris Crawford

Chickasaw Nation Old Council House
7th. Septr. 1816

Sir,

I have the honor to enclose you the Copy of a dispatch received this day from Lt. Col. Clinch, giving an account of the Capture & destruction of the negro Fort on the Appalachicola.[1]

I have this morning received two communications of a late date from the Commandant of the 8th. Military Department, Col. Jesup, extracts from these letters are herewith inclosed, for your consideration.[2] From the tenor of these communications, it would appear, that a War with Spain may take place. If we take into consideration the actual condition of Spain there would seem to be but little ground, for such a belief, but the present Ruler of that Nation approaches so near the character of a madman, that we may be deceived in our calculations.[3] I have thought it prudent to be prepared to meet events, as they may occur. From such a course of conduct is often to be realized the most important results. It would be superfluous for me to dwell on the importance of the *Lower Country,* including Orleans and Mobile and the Command of the Rivers Mississippi & Mobile. Nothing that could have the tendency to give security to the Western World should be left to chance. Under these circumstances, I beg leave to submit for your consideration the propriety of making such arrangements as will enable me to bring to the support of the *Lower Country,* at the shortest possible notice, the 8th. Regiment & the Rifle Corps. My object is to make surety doubly sure—to be ready, promptly to meet every Contingency & thus be able to act Offensively or Defensively, as circumstances may authorize. The only mode which I can devise, that will enable us to realize this object, and to apply it practically if necessary, will be to direct the Commandant at Detroit, to make arrangements to relieve the Posts & Cantonments under the Command of Brevet Brigr. Smith. At all events immediate arrangements to relieve & place the 8th. Regt. Infy. at my disposal, I look upon as highly important. I should not make this proposition to you, for I am aware of its delicacy, if I did not suppose in the course of events it may prove highly advantageous to the security of this most important section of our Country.

The enclosed communication from Brevet Brigr. Smith, with the accompanying papers, will convince you of the impossibility of having my Division in that efficient state, which I could wish & which the public good requires. I trust a re-transfer of the Detachment in question will take place. Brevet Majr. Genl. [Alexander] Macomb's conduct & the sanction given it by Majr. Genl. Brown is unauthorized & cannot be supported upon Military principles. The Rifle Regt. has been arranged on the peace establishment to my Division.[4] I have the honor to be Sir with greatest respect yr mot. obt. Sert.

Andrew Jackson
Major Genl comdg
D. of the South

LS, DLC (5-0460).

1. See Duncan L. Clinch to Robert Butler, July 28 and August 2.

2. Probably Thomas S. Jesup to AJ, August 18 and 21.

3. Jackson was referring to Ferdinand VII (1784–1833) of Spain.

4. See Thomas A. Smith to Butler, July 22. In the peacetime army, the rifle regiment had been assigned to the Southern Division but had been allowed to remain on a temporary basis (with Jackson's approval) within the Northern Division. In April 1816, Jackson had ordered the regiment to St. Louis. Willoughby Morgan, captain and brevet major of the regiment, reported the order to Macomb (1782–1841), commander of the 5th Department, whereupon Macomb and subsequently Brown protested against Jackson's interference in Northern Di-

vision affairs; and the war department warned Jackson against such interference. Within weeks, however, the regiment was transferred to Jackson's Southern Division.

To Rachel Jackson

Chikesaw council house Sept. 18th. 1816

My Love

I have this moment recd. your affectionate letter of the 8th. Instant, I rejoice that you are well & our little son.[1] Tell him his sweept papa hears with pleasure that he has been a good boy & learns his Book, Tell him his sweet papa labours hard to get money to educate him, but when he learns & becomes a great man, his sweet papa will be amply rewarded for all his care, expence, & pains—how thankfull I am to you for taking poor little Lyncoya home & cloathing him—I have been much hurt to see him there with the negroes, like a lost sheep without a sheperd.[2]

we have had a long and disagreable time of it here, our servants have been all sick, Doctor [James Craine] Bronaugh very low, Jame had like to have went, but is on the mend[3]—I hope we will get through our business tomorrow & leave here day after for Turkey town in the cherokee nation, I hope to reach home about the 5th. or 6th. of october we have made a conditional Treaty with the cherokee delegation and are to meet a full council at Turkey Town on the 28th. Instant to have it fully ratified[4]—I have a sanguine hope we will be fully successfull with the chikesaw and once more, regain by tribute, what I fairly, & hardly purchased with the sword, so much trouble & cost has been occassioned by the rashness, folly, & Ignorance of a great little man.[5] But as successfull as I have reason to believe we will be at present, I shall be contented—I have truly noted the conduct of the overseer, & negroes, as soon as I return will take a satisfactory order on all—and you will charge him to sell nothing without your express orders—or I will make him more than answerable for the Vallue[6]—with my sincere prayers for your health & happiness, and my little son & all the family believe me to be affectionately yours.

Andrew Jackson

P.S. I thank you for your admonition I hope in all my acts & conduct through life they will measure with propriety and dignity, or at least with what I believe true dignity consists, that is to say honesty, propriety of conduct, & honest independance—A.J.

Mr James Jackson on your application will take order on Sampson if necessary, that family will sell any where, better below than in Nashville, but I suppose in Nashville for $14. or 1500—[7]

ALS, OkTG (5-0485).

1. Not found.

2. Lyncoya (c1812–28), a Creek orphan found on the site of the Battle of Tallushatchee, grew up at the Hermitage.

3. Bronaugh (1788–1822), an army surgeon and later surgeon general of the Division of the South, served as aide to Jackson in Florida in 1821. He was president of the first territorial legislative council and was campaigning for election as delegate to Congress when he died of yellow fever during an epidemic in Pensacola. The slave Jame (c1794–1829) served as one of Jackson's allotted military servants both during and after the War of 1812.

4. The Cherokees ratified the treaty at Turkey Town, a Cherokee village situated in a bend of the Coosa River about one mile south of present-day Centre, in Cherokee County, Alabama, on October 4.

5. Jackson's reference to a "great little man" is unclear. He may have been referring to either James Madison or William H. Crawford.

6. Harrison Saunders, hired in April, was overseer at the Hermitage at this time.

7. No evidence has been found that a sale was concluded. There were two Sampsons with families on the 1825 and 1829 slave inventories of the Hermitage: Old Sampson with wife Priss and seven children; and Big Sampson with wife Pleasant and son George. It seems likely that the Big Sampson family was meant here.

To John Coffee

Chikesaw council house Sept. 19th. 1816.

Dr Genl

On the 14th. Instant we concluded a treaty with the Cherokee delegation, for all the lands south of the Tennessee subject to the ratification of a full council of the nation at Turkey Town on the 28th instant, for the sum of six thousand dollars pr annum, five thousand dollars for Meltons & other improvements & some small presents to the fifteen chiefs that attended here[1]—with this variation from your line, Beg. at camp coffee, south to the ridge, then Eastwardly, along the ridge leaving all the waters of the Blackwarior on the right to where the ridge is oposed by the west fork of wills creek, thence down the east side of said fork & wills creek to the coosee then down the coosee—all south of the Tennessee & west of that line is ceded to the U.S.[2] on tomorrow we are to have an answer from the chikesaws & we are told by their chief, that a cession will be made of all lands north of the Tennessee, and all South East of your line—

we have had much to encounter, we were obliged to take a firm & decided stands—we took the evidence of the chikesaws, then produced the creek claim, with all evidence in its support, then made them the proposition as a peace offerring telling them the creek claim was the best—but their father the President of the u states—hearing they had a claim offerred the compensation as a peace offerring—that from the evidence he had a right to hold it as a conquored country—& sell it to pay to there nations & the choctaws the expence of the war, that it was demanded for this purpose from the creeks, ceded for this purpose & our citizens being in possession could not be removed, nor would they be taxed to pay the expence of the war untill this land was sold for that purpose—That they must clearly see not only the Justice but the generosity of their father the President in the offer—he first proposed to pay each nation a fair price for their claim, that the land might be sold for the benefit of all, to pay the debt due to the cherokees, the chikesaws & the choctaws and the ballance to pay their white brothers[3]—In this stand I was well supported by Genl [David] Meryweather who is a fine old fellow, and this stand was what has & will procure us success, & the choctaws are prepared to receive the offer of the Goverment—But an Indian is fickle, & you will have to take the same firm stand, & support it & you are sure of success—[Jesse] Franklin was detained by the sickness of his son, and fortunately did not get up untill the Indians had received our proposals & were deliberating upon them—he is Butting at every thing—his horns are getting sore & I believe he will be docile & Butt no more[4] I should have posponed writing you untill we had finally closed, but our time is so short & after we hear there answer if favourable as I now expect, will be so much hurried that I am fearfull I would not have time I therefore give you the outlines of the course we have steered—a firm stand & you will be successfull—all the chiefs said they had listened & the talk of there father the President was a good talk—you must tell them to lay aside all ideas of hunting become farmers like us—& that for this purpose the anuity is offered—& that this land being disputed no reservation to the nation can be granted—[5]

May the gods bless & protect you, & grant you success is the fervent wish of your unalterable friend

Andrew Jackson

ALS, THi (5-0489). Published in Bassett, 2:260–61.

1. Jackson was referring to the Melton property at Melton's Bluff, which he purchased in November. Tochelar, Oohulookee, Wososey, and the two interpreters (Thomas Wilson and Alexander McCoy) each received $100; the other Cherokee delegates, $50 each. The annuity was for ten years only.

2. The new boundary left to the Cherokees most of present-day DeKalb, Marshall, and Jackson counties in Alabama. The Cherokees also retained their claims to lands north of the Tennessee River.

3. See the September 11 entry from the Journal of Chickasaw and Cherokee treaty proceedings, August 19–October 4, for testimony offered at the meetings in support of Creek claims.

4. Meriwether (1755–1822), a revolutionary veteran, was a former Georgia congressman. Franklin (1760–1823), former North Carolina state legislator and United States senator and representative, did not arrive at the treaty ground until September 13. He returned to attend his son James rather than accompanying Jackson and Meriwether to the Cherokee ratification meeting, but on October 11 he expressed satisfaction with the result.

5. Jackson's advice was for the commissioners' guidance at the Choctaw negotiations, which convened at the Choctaw trading house at St. Stephens in mid-October.

To William Harris Crawford

Chickasaw Council House
September 20. 1816—

Sir.

In a communication to you of the 4th. Inst from Generals Jackson & Meriwether, you was advised of the Big Warriors having sent a runner to this nation, excusing himself & chiefs of the Creek Nation from attending at this convention, but inviting the Four Southern Tribes to assemble at Turkey Town on the 1st. of October next.

It was stated that this was believed to be in combination with the Cherokees to defeat the objects of this conference & that to counteract it; George Mayfie[l]d, accompanied by a Creek chief, had been sent on a second mission to the Creek Nation, to invite their attendance & bring on if possible the Upper chiefs of said nation.[1]

The Cherokee Delegates arrived here on the 6th. Inst. and on the 8th Generals Jackson & Meriwether held a conference with the Chiefs of the Chickasaws, Cherokees & Choctaws, for the substance of which as well as the proceedings of the subsequent meetings, you are respectfully referred to the Journal that will be forwarded you.[2] As was anticipated much difficulty was encountered in negotiating with the Chickasaws; The conference being held with the whole nation, every individual had to be consulted, and the Chiefs, together with the Agent, seemed more anxious to maintain their popularity, than to promote the views of Government, or the best interests of the Nation they ruled. Much embarrasment was occasioned by your letter of the 16th of April to the agent having been read to the Chickasaws previous to the arrival of the Commissioners & the interpretation given it; The Charter from General Washington was supposed unobjectionable & an idea prevailed that it would be supported in preference to any other title.[3] Generals Jackson & Meriwether, The Two Commissioners present (Jesse Franklin Esqr not having arrived) believing that no Creek Title to territory actually occupied and settled could be impaired by any charter to which the Creeks did not give their assent, deemed it an act of justice & sound policy & absolutely necessary to the correct discharge of the duties assigned them, to examine the Testimony on which the conflicting claims of the Three parties were founded. They accordingly proceeded to take all the evidence offered which has been recorded in the Journal for your information From that Testimony it appears that the Creeks were the earliest settlers of this section of country, that they were found here by the other nations on their first arrival, That they continued in possession untill 1813 when they were driven away by the American Troops. It also appears from the declaration of the whole Chickasaw Nation, that the Cherokees never had any land adjoining them on the South side of the Tennessee River & that the Creeks were always their neighbours; That the Chickasaws never complained of Creek encroachments while settled at Cold Water, but permitted the Creeks to remain in peaceable possession untill destroyed by General Robinson in 1786, but that the moment a settlement was attempted on Bear Creek, Piomingo notifies the Intruders to remove, or he will destroy them & takes part of their goods for rent (see [John] Gordons Testimony).[4] It further appears, That the Creeks were in possession not only of Cold Water, but had settlements on the Tennessee a little below Flint or Tanchecunda Creek & at Thompsons Creek; At Black Warrior a very old Town, & at Littefutche on Canoe Creek, near Wills Creek, the lower boundary of lands stated to have been loaned by the Creeks to the Cherokees.[5] From this collective testimony & a belief that possession is the best, if not the only substantial Evidence of Indian title; The Commissioners then present (Generals Jackson & Meriwether) expressed their conviction of the Creek claim being the strongest, in an address to the Council on the 12 Inst. & then made proposals to the Chickasaws & Cherokees as will be found recorded in the journal.[6] The Cherokees on the 14th. made a communication in writing, refusing to yield any lands on the North side of the Tennessee, but proposing to cede their claim to the disputed Territory on the south for certain considerations, which were acceded to, embodied in the form of a Treaty & duly executed & signed by all the Commissioners (the Honbl Jessee Franklin having previously arrived).[7] As the Cherokee Delegates seemed doubtful as to the extent of their powers, This Treaty has been concluded subject to the ratification of the Cherokee Nation & it is provided that the said nation shall meet the Commissioners on the 28 Inst. at Turkey Town to express their approbation or not. In concluding this Treaty with the Cherokees, it was found both wise & politic to make a few presents to the Chiefs & Interpreters—

The execution of the Treaty with the Cherokees, alarmed and seemed to iritate the Chickasaws, and the death of a principal chief (The Factor) appeared to distract their counsels; Confusion amongst them was visible.[8] When solicited for an answer to the propositions made them on the 12 Inst. They invariably beged time to deliberate. It was soon found that a favourable result to the negotiation was not to be anticipated unless we addressed ourselves feelingly to the predominant & governing passions of all Indian Tribes, ie. Their avarice or Fear; our instructions pointed to the former & forbid the latter; We therefore were compelled not from choice, but from instructions to apply the sole remedy in our power. It was applied & presents offered to the Influential Chiefs amounting to Four Thousand five hundred Dollars to be paid on the success of the negotiation. This measure seemed to produce some sensible effect. Time was asked for reflection, The Chiefs that had left the ground were sent for & we have this day concluded a Treaty, That secures to the West a free & uninterrupted intercourse with the low country. Independent of the accession of a rich &

large body of lands to the U States, the objects otherwise obtained by this Treaty are of incalculable political advantage, to our country. We have obtained a connection of Tennessee with the Low Country, The free use & navigation of the Coosa, Black Warrior & Tombigby rivers & what is truly grateful to the human mind prevented the destruction of many of our Red Brethren & possibly a civil war, secured the affections of the Population of the south & west to the present administration & restored that confidence that formerly existed between the Rulers & the People—If the annuity given has been larger than usual, it is not more than proportionate to the benefits obtained.

We have drawn upon the Department of War for the amount of those presents distributed to the Principal Chiefs & which could not appear on the Treaty: Secrecy was enjoined as to the names; Secrecy is necessary, or the influence of the Chiefs would be destroyed, which has been & may be useful on a future occasion. The Chiefs will accompany the Drafts, which we have no doubt will be duly honored & paid—[9]

The Land within the state of Tennessee & ceded by this Treaty, being within the Congressional District & all the vacant lands being the property of the United States, we did not conceive it necessary to make any discrimination. We did not consider it of any importance when compared with the value of the cession in a political point of view & we were more particularly urged to the measure from a belief that an adjustment between the U States & State was practicable & the ratification of the Treaty thereby not hazarded by a reference to a State Legislature—[10]

Finding the Jealousy of the Chickasaw Indians aroused, when we obtained the cessions embraced in the Treaty we did not think it prudent to urge them on the other points of our Instructions, we conceived it not prudent & of course did not name it to them—[11]

Agreeably to our Instructions we put to the Council the question whether their agent had the confidence of the nation, on this day the question was answered by Tishomingo, That they did not want their Present Agent and gave this as the full sence of the whole nation—The Chiefs have spoken to us this evening to say to you that They want an agent sent them from the east, capable of doing justice to their red & white Brethren—[12]

The Enclosed Petition of James Colbert & Turner Brashears Indian Interpreters is referred for your consideration.[13] We remain respectfully your mo ob hu Servants

Andrew Jackson
D. Meriwether
J Franklin
Commissioners

LS, InU-Li (5-0494); Copies, DLC (62), NcU (5-0501), DNA-RG 11 (M668-4), DNA-RG 46 (5-0511). Published in *ASP, Indian Affairs,* 2:104–105.

1. See AJ and David Meriwether to Crawford, September 4; and AJ to Big Warrior, August 30.

2. See the Journal of Chickasaw and Cherokee treaty proceedings, August 19–October 4.

3. In his letter of April 16 to William Cocke (DNA-RG 75, M15-3), Crawford (1) explained that the March 22 Cherokee treaty did not interfere with Chickasaw claims to lands south of a line from the Tennessee River to Flat Rock and east of Coffee's survey line; (2) directed him to forward evidence supporting Chickasaw claims in that area; and (3) urged him to canvass the Chickasaws regarding the cession of their claim in exchange for indemnity. Washington's guarantee of Chickasaw territory, July 21, 1794 (Copy, DLC-1), included a large portion of western Kentucky and the Southwest Territory.

4. In 1787 (not 1786) James Robertson (1742–1814) led about 120 Tennesseans in the destruction of a Creek-French trading town at Coldwater (Tuscumbia) below Muscle Shoals. Piomingo, the major chief of the Chickasaws and Robertson's friend, was murdered by Creeks and Cherokees in 1799. The testimony of Gordon (1763–1819), ferry and innkeeper on the Natchez Trace and spy commander in the Creek War, concerned the dispersal of a settlement of French traders on Bear Creek in 1791 (see Journal of the treaty proceedings, September 1).

5. Flint Creek enters the Tennessee River at the eastern edge of present-day Decatur, Alabama. Black Warrior's Town, on the Black Warrior River possibly at present-day Tuscaloosa, was destroyed by Jackson's troops in October 1813.

6. The commissioners' speech urged the Chickasaws and Cherokees to cede their claims to all lands north of the Tennessee and lands within Coffee's survey of the Creek cession south of the river for annuities of $10,000 per year for ten years to the Chickasaws and $8,000 per year for ten years to the Cherokees.

7. The Cherokee communication has not been found. See above, AJ to John Coffee, September 19, for the substance of the draft treaty.

8. The Old Factor was listed among the Chickasaw chiefs present at the opening session, September 8. His death was not noted in the journal.

9. The abstract of the commissioners' letter, September 20, advising Crawford of drafts in favor of Chickasaw chiefs, indicated that William, George, Levi, and James Colbert and Tishomingo received $1,000 each.

10. The Congressional District, established in 1806 by act of Congress, was the area of unappropriated lands in Tennessee west of a line where the Elk River crossed the Tennessee-Mississippi Territory border, due north to the Duck River, and westward along the Duck River to the "Military Line" and on along the Duck to the Tennessee River, thence north to the Kentucky border. A small portion of the lands ceded by the Chickasaw treaty were within this area; and the commissioners' reference to an adjustment of differences between the United States and Tennessee stemmed from Tennessee's pledge to pay part of the annuities for a cession of these lands (see 2 *U.S. Statutes at Large* 381–83).

11. Jackson was referring to the instructions to attempt to secure cession of the Chickasaw hunting grounds in western Kentucky (see Crawford to the Commissioners, July 5).

12. The war department had heard frequent complaints from the Chickasaws about their agent, William Cocke (1748–1828), mainly about incompetence and nepotism. Tishomingo (d. 1841) was Speaker of the Chickasaw Nation.

13. Colbert (c1768–1842), a half-brother of George and Levi Colbert, and Brashears, [cSeptember 20], had asked the commissioners to cover the costs of the unusual amount of entertaining required at the treaty meetings.

Once the probable outcome of the presidential election of 1816 became clear, Jackson began to offer advice to James Monroe in hopes of healing the wounds and ending the bitterness left by the War of 1812. The letter below is the first in a series of six they exchanged in late 1816 and early

1817 concerning the course of the new administration. Although important in their own context, they enjoyed great notoriety in 1824 when Crawfordites referred to the letters to demonstrate that Jackson was a closet Federalist. Forced to clarify the recommendations to Monroe, Jacksonians published the letters in 1824 to prove that Jackson held national above partisan interests.

To James Monroe

Head Quarters, Division of the South,
Nashville, 23d of October, 1816.

Dear Sir:

I returned from the nation on the 12th inst. and seize the first moment from duty to write you.

I have the pleasure to inform you that we have obtained by cession from the Cherokees and Chickasaws all their claim south of the Tennessee, that interfered with the Creek cession.

We experienced much difficulty with the Chickasaws, from what they call their guarantee, or charter given by President Washington, in the year 1794, and recognized by the treaty with that nation in 1801; which not only guarantied the territory, but bound the United States to prevent intrusions, within the limits defined, of every kind whatever.[1] In the treaty with the Cherokees lately entered into at the City of Washington, the greater part of the land guarantied by the treaty of 1801 to the Chikasaws was included.[2] The fact is, that both President Washington, and the present Secretary of War, must have been imposed on by false representations, as neither the Cherokees or Chickasaws had any right to the territory south of the Tennessee, and included within the Creek cession, as the testimony recorded on our journal, and forwarded with the treaty, will shew; it being in the possession of the Creeks until conquered by us in the fall of 1813. I feel happy that all these conflicting claims are accommodated by the late treaties,[3] and at a moderate premium, payable in ten years; and that extensive fertile country west of the county of Madison, and north of the Tennessee, which at once opens a free intercourse to, and defence for, the lower country, is acquired: In a political point of view, its benefits are incalculable. We will now have good roads, kept up and supplied by the industry of our own citizens, and our frontier defended by a strong population. The sooner, therefore, that this country can be brought into market the better. By dividing this country into two districts, by a line drawn due East from the mouth of the Black-warrior to the Coosa river; and appointing an enterprising individual to superintend the Northern District as surveyor, he can have all the lands North of the line ready for sale by the first of June next. The vast capital now held up for the purchase of this land, if offered for sale before the holders turn it to other objects, will ensure the Treasury an immense sum of money, and give to the government a permanent population, capable of defending that frontier, which ought to induce the government to prepare it for market as early as possible.

Having learnt from General David Merriwether, that Mr. Crawford is about to retire from the Department of War, I am induced, as a friend to you and the government, to bring to your notice, as a fit character to fill that office, Col. William H. Drayton, late of the army of the United States.[4]

I am not personally acquainted with Col. D. but believing it of the utmost importance that the office of Secretary of War should be well filled, I have, for some time, through every source that has presented, been making inquiry on the subject. From information that I can rely on, the result is, that he is a man of nice[5] principles of honor and honesty, of military experience and pride—possessing handsome talents as a lawyer and statesman.

I am told, before the war he was ranked with the Federalists, but the moment his country was threatened, he abandoned private ease and a lucrative practice, for the tented fields. Such acts as these speak louder than words—"the tree is best known by its fruit," and such a man as this, it matters not what he is called, will always act like a true American. Whether he would accept the appointment I cannot say, but if he would, his talents, experience, and energy, would prove highly useful to his country. It is all important in peace and in war, as you well know, to have this office well filled; at present, when there exists such strife in the army as appears in the North, it is important to select a character of such firmness and energy as cannot be swayed from strict rule and justice.[6] From every information I have received, Col. Drayton fills this character; and is better qualified to execute the duties of the Department of War than any other character I have any knowledge of, either personally or from information. I write you confidentially. It is said here . . .[7] is spoken of to succeed Mr. Crawford. Rest assured this will not do—when I say this I wish you to understand me, that he does not possess sufficient capacity, stability, or energy—the three necessary qualifications for a war officer. These hints proceed from the purest motives, that you may be supported in your administration by the best talents and virtue of our country, that you may be hailed in your retirement from the executive chair, with that unanimous approbation that has brought you to it.

Present Mrs. J. and myself respectfully to your lady and family, in which is included Mrs. Hay, and accept for yourself my warmest wishes for your happiness.

Andrew Jackson.

Printed, Washington *National Intelligencer,* May 12, 1824 (mAJs); ALS draft, DLC (21); Typed copy of ALS, T (5-0545). Published in other contemporary newspapers and in Bassett, 2:261–62 (from ALS draft).

1. The treaty with the Chickasaws, October 24, 1801, chiefly secured a right-of-way through the nation for a road connecting Nashville and Natchez, but in response to the anxieties of the Chickasaws over maintaining their landholdings, an article was added acknowledging Washington's certificate of 1794 and providing that the president "shall take such measures, from time to time, as he may deem proper, to assist the Chickasaws to preserve, entire, all their rights against the encroachments of unjust neighbors, of which he shall be the judge . . ." (*ASP, Indian Affairs,* 1:648–49).

2. Jackson was referring to the March 22 treaty.

3. For "treaties," the typed copy reads "treaty."

4. William H. Crawford transferred to the treasury department on October 22, leaving the war department under the guidance of chief clerk George Graham, whom John C. Calhoun superseded in December 1817. Jackson meant not William H. but William Drayton (1776–1846) of South Carolina, a cousin by marriage to James Gadsden. Although Drayton had accepted a commission in the army as early as March 1812 and had been made colonel commandant of the new 18th Infantry, his unit saw no action, and he finished the war as inspector general. In 1831, Jackson as president considered him for successor to John H. Eaton in the war department.

5. For "nice," the typed copy reads "true."

6. For "justice," the typed copy reads "virtue."

7. Richard Mentor Johnson's name was deleted from the 1824 publications, but his identity is revealed in the ALS draft. It has not been determined why Jackson at this time had such a low opinion of Johnson (1780–1850), later vice-president under Martin Van Buren.

To Edward Livingston

Nashville Octbr. 24th 1816

Dr. Sir

I have Just returned from the nation, and have the pleasure to say to you, that a free communication is opened from the upper to the lower country, and a fertile country well calculated to afford a strong population fully adequate to the defence of the lower country—we will soon have good roads kept in repair & supplied by the certain industry of our own citizens.

Since my return to this place I have heard much of Spanish insolence and the attack upon the fire brand, I was sorry to hear that any communication had been made on this subject to Govert. untill Comodore [Daniel Todd] Patterson had sunk those three Spanish vessels—for if it was an unauthorised attack by Spain, it ought to have been repelled by another unauthorised act by us—If authorised by the goverment of Spain, it was an act of war, and ought to be met as such—I hope in this, my friend the commodore will take every responsibility necessary to wipe from our flag the stain it has recd. there is but one way & that is by sinking one or all of those vessels and then reporting the circumstance to our Goverment—Be good anough to give me the earliest inteligence of all these matters & things & your opinion as it respects a Spanish war. My eyes are open, my horses in keeping, the 8th. & 4th Regts in motion, & you have nothing to fear as I hope & trust from the result of war with Spain—But as a Just nation, no act of ours ought to provoke a war with Spain or any other nation—But our national rights ought not to be trampled on with impunity[1]

I have Just heard of the result of your elections, the parties ran high, and I hear that Major [Auguste G. V.] Davasac had an afair of honor, in which Major Butler informs me he acquitted himself with honor, this is gratifying to me, as he was once a member of my family present him my respects[2]—& say to my Neworleans friends, that I am wide awake to their security & defence—and only await the sound of war to be with them.

Present me affectionately to your lady[3] & family & believe me to be very respectfully yr mo ob Serv

Andrew Jackson

P.S write me on the receipt of this[4]

ALS, NjP (mAJs). Published in Bassett, 6:459–60. Livingston (1764–1836) had served as a volunteer aide to Jackson during the Battle of New Orleans; in 1831 Jackson appointed him secretary of state.

1. Jackson was referring to the Spanish capture of the American schooner *USS Firebrand* in the Gulf of Mexico on August 27 (see Thomas S. Jesup to AJ, September 11). Anticipating a Spanish attack on the Gulf coast, Jackson informed Crawford on October 18 that he had ordered the 8th Regiment down the Mississippi River from St. Louis and the 4th Regiment to Fort Montgomery. Patterson (1786–1839), a career naval officer, had commanded the American naval forces at the Battle of New Orleans.

2. Jackson was probably alluding to the Louisiana gubernatorial election in which Jacques P. Villeré had been elected the state's first Creole governor. Davezac (1780–1851), a New Orleans lawyer and brother-in-law of Livingston, had served as Jackson's judge advocate during the New Orleans campaign and was later appointed by Jackson to various diplomatic posts. The details of his "afair of honor" have not been established, nor has Thomas L. Butler's letter been found.

3. In 1805, Livingston had married Louise Moreau de Lassy (1786–1860), the sister of Davezac and the widow of a French officer.

4. For reply, see Livingston to AJ, November 7.

From George Graham

(Confidential) Department of War, 5th. Novemr. 1816.

Sir,

I have the honor to acknowledge the receipt of your letter of the 18th. inst., advising this department of the disposition which you were about to make of the troops within your division of the Army.[1] The proposed arrangements are entirely approved, tho' at present the government is in possession of no information, that would justify a belief, that there is any imminent danger of an immediate collision with Spain. The facts on which Colonel Jesup has founded his apprehensions, have not as yet been communicated to this department.[2] Govr. Holmes has forwarded his general orders of the 3d of Oct. together with a copy of a letter to him from Colo.

Jesup; in which he observes that "I shall demand the citizens (seized at Pensacola) and if they are not surrendered, I shall release them by force, unless otherwise instructed by the General."[3] It is a matter of much surprise that, that officer should, for a moment, contemplate the commission of such an act of retaliatory warfare, as would place the country in a state of actual hostility with a foreign nation, to which the power of Congress *only* is competent. I therefore trust that you have given to Colonel Jesup such instructions as will confine him within the limits of his legitimate authority, as commanding officer of a department.[4] I have the honor to be, with great respect, Your Obt. Servant.

Geo: Graham

P.S. The last information from the Governor of Georgia, stated that a party of negroes and Indians were embodied on the Chatahouchee below fort Crawford: Should that information be correct, it would perhaps be advisable not to remove all the troops from that post—[5]

Ten thousand dollars have been remitted to Major [Christopher] Van de Venter at Augusta, on account of the Quarter master's department.[6]

LS, DLC (21); AL draft, DNA-RG 107 (5-0564); LC, DNA-RG 107 (M7-1).

1. Graham meant "ultimo." See AJ to William H. Crawford, October 18.

2. Graham was referring to Thomas S. Jesup's failure to confirm the rumors Jesup had communicated to James Monroe on August 21.

3. Jesup wrote Jackson on September 23, "I have just received information that the Spanish Commandant at Pensacola has seized three American citizens, whom he has employed as slaves upon the fortifications which he is erecting at that post," but he did not reveal plans for liberating the captives in this or subsequent communications.

4. On December 11 Jackson wrote to Graham that he had dispatched an order to Jesup and Eleazar W. Ripley "*to permit no act to be done to provoke war with Spain.*"

5. Graham was referring to Jackson's order for the 4th Regiment to move from Fort Crawford (later Fort Scott) to Fort Montgomery.

6. Vandeventer (1789–1838; Military Academy 1809) had received an interim appointment as deputy quartermaster general after the recess of Congress in April. He served as chief clerk of the war department, 1817–27.

To James Monroe

(*Private*) Nashville Novr. 12th. 1816

Sir,

Permit me to introduce to your notice Liut. Gadsdone, who will hand you this letter; and, who is also, the bearer of the Treaties lately concluded with the Creeks, Chickasaws and Cherokees.

In my last to you, I took the liberty of drawing your attention to the benefits that would result both, to the Treasury of the United States and the defence of the lower Mississippi and its dependencies, by bringing into market those tracts of country lately acquired by the Treaties above named.[1]

I am so deeply impressed with the importance of this subject that I cannot forego the present opportunity of again bringing it to your view. I have this moment wrote the comptroller on this highly interesting and important business.[2] If the plan proposed is adopted; the land can be brought into market, within a very short time, which will immediately give to that section of country a strong and permanent settlement of American citizens, competent to its defense. Should the Goverment divide the surveyors district, as proposed, and appoint Genl. Coffee surveyor of the Northern ⟨District⟩ his energy and industry will bring it into market in all June next. Should the District be divided, as contemplated, and Genl. Coffee appointed surveyor ⟨of the Northern⟩ it will leave open the appointment of Reciver of public monies, heretofore, promised to the Genl.—which vacancy I warmly recommend to be filled by Liut. Gadsdone, who, owing to the late, indeed I might say present, delicate state of his health, is desireous of resigning his appointment in the army.[3] In this as in all my recommendations I have the public good in view.

From the acquirements of Liut. Gadsdone the army will sustain a great loss by the withdrawal of his services from it; but, by retiring at present and avoiding the insalubrious climates where his duty as an officer, calls him, his health may be restored and his life preserved for the benefit of his country at some future period. There are few young men in the army, or else where, possessing his merit—his education is of the best kind, and his mind is richly stored with the most useful sort of knowledge; he should, therefore, be fostered as capable, at some future day, of becoming one of his country's most useful and valuable citizens. Liut. Gadsdone's situation requires some office the profits of which will yield him a competency while preparing himself for some professional persuit—this office will afford it.

These are the reasons that induce me so warmly to recommend him; I hope, should the events, alluded to occur, he will receve the appoint.

Being deeply impressed with the importance of an other subject which relates to yourself, as well as the Government, I hope I may be permitted, once more, to obtrude my opinions. In filling the vacancy occasioned by the transfer of Mr. Crawford from the War Office to the Treasury, it is of the *highest moment* that some *proper* and *fit* person should be selected.

Your hapiness and the Nation's welfare materially depend upon the selections which are to be made to fill the heads of Departments. I need not tell you that feuds exist, and have existed, to an injurious degree in the Northern Army. To fill the Dept. of War with a character who has taken a part in those feuds, or whose feelings have been enlisted on the side of party, will be adding fuel to a flame which, for the good of the service, already burns too fiercely. This and other considerations induced me to enter on the enquiry for a character best calculated to fill that Dept.—it has resulted in the selection of Col. William Drayton. Since my last to you, in which this subject was then named, Genl. Ripley has arrived here, who heartily concurs with me in the opinion, that Col. Drayton is the best selection that can be made.[4]

Pardon me, my dear Sir, for the following remarks concerning the next presidential term—they are made with the sincerity and freedom of a friend. I cannot doubt they *will* be recd. with feelings similar to those which have impelled me to make them. Every thing depends on the selection of your ministry. In every selection, party, and party feelings should be avoided. Now is the time to exterminate that *Monster* called Party spirit. By selecting characters most conspicuous for their probity, Virtue, capacity and firmness, without any regard to party, you will go far to, ⟨if not entirely,⟩ eradicate those feelings which on former occasions threw so many obsticles in the way of government; and, perhaps, have the *pleasure,* and *honor,* of uniting a people heretofore ⟨now⟩ politically divided. The Chief Magistrate of a great and powerful nation should never indulge in party feelings. His conduct should be liberal and disinterested, *always* bearing in mind that he acts for the *whole* and not a *part* of the community. By this course you will *exalt the national character* and acquire for *yourself* a name as imperishable as monumental marble. Consult *no party* in your choice—persue the dictates of that unerring judgment which has so long, and so often benefitted our country, and rendered conspicuous its Rulers ⟨Possessor⟩. These are the sentiments of a friend—they are the feelings, if I know my own heart, of an undissembled patriot. Accept assurances of my sincere friendship, and believe me to be respectfully your obt. Sert.

Andrew Jackson

LS in William B. Lewis's hand and ALS draft, DLC (21); Copy in Lewis's hand, DLC (71). Published in the Washington *National Intelligencer,* May 12, 1824, and other contemporary newspapers; republished again in 1832, 1834, 1835, 1836; and in Bassett, 2:263–65 (from ALS draft). For Jackson's discussion of Lewis's copying of the letter, see AJ to Lewis, February 22, 1824.

1. See above, AJ to Monroe, October 23.

2. Letter not found. Joseph Inslee Anderson (1757–1837), former Tennessee senator, served as comptroller of the treasury from 1815 to 1836.

3. John Coffee was offered the surveyor's position in northern Mississippi Territory created by the act of March 3, 1817, but the act did not provide for appointment of additional registers and receivers. Instead, it attached the new district to Madison County, with headquarters in Huntsville where John Brahan had been receiver since 1809. Gadsden remained in the army until 1822.

4. See above, AJ to Monroe, October 23. Ripley arrived in Nashville on October 31 en route to his New Orleans assignment.

To George Washington Campbell

Nashville Decr. 22d. 1816.

Sir,

Since my last, the order for the removal of all intruders from the land ceded by the Chickasaws lying north of the T. has reached me.[1] It is my duty to carry into effect promptly all orders from the P. of the U. States, this will of course be executed, with as little delay as the troops that I have within striking distance will permit. The execution of it, will produce great distress, and destruction to all the stock owned and drove on the land by the intruders, and many of the people must suffer if not die with hunger. The stock drove back within our former limits must die for want of food, there not being a supply for their existence—If the government does intend to bring this land into market shortly, it is a pity that the order could not be suspended until that period, those people have moved on it, not expecting any benefit from their improvements, unless they bid more for it than any other—and every improvement however small will increase the value and sale of those lands—These things your own judgt. & knowledge of the country without argument will suggest. I am anxious before I enter upon the execution of the order to be advised, whether the tenants of [Charles] Hicks & [David and Betsy] Melton are to be removed from that reservation, and I hope you have ere this recd. my letter on that subject and has obtained the Presidents instruction for me thereon.[2] I have suggested to the secy. of war that a number of citizens holding patent grants from the State of North Carolina, and which lie within the Congressional reservation, are within the bounds of the Chickasaw cession, quere—as soon as the treaty is ratified, can those individuals holding under grants be removed by military force, (constitutionally) without first making just compensation—and will not the officer executing this order, be liable to be harrassed with suits for a trespass. I want on this subject precise instructions, as the order expresses "all intruders, and particularly those on the reservations" which I construe to include the Congressional reservation, as well as all others.[3]

Extract (enclosed in Campbell to George Graham, January 11, 1817), DNA-RG 107 (M221-73). Campbell (1769–1848; Princeton 1794) was U.S. senator from Tennessee; from 1818–21 he served as minister to Russia.

1. For the order, see Graham to AJ, November 7. Jackson's previous letter to Campbell has not been found.

2. Jackson had forwarded to Washington the October 10 petition of Charles Hicks (d. 1827), David Melton, and Betsy Melton requesting confirmation of their sale to Louis Winston of the land reserved to Hicks and Moses Melton by the Cherokee Treaty of January 7, 1806 (DNA-RG 107, M221-68). Jackson evidently asked if Winston and his tenants should be expelled as intruders. On December 28, Graham directed that the Melton-Hicks reservees retained only an "Indian title" and ordered removal of "all persons found upon those reservations in contravention of the right of the United States, whether with or without the consent of the reservees." In petitioning for a ruling on the Winston claims, Jackson may also have been concerned about settlers on the land he had bought from David Melton on November 22. When Graham received this letter from Campbell, he replied on January 13 by authorizing Jackson to purchase the reservations for the United States.

3. See AJ to Graham, December 11. In his letter of January 13, 1817, Graham did not reply specifically to Jackson's query regarding North Carolina land patents to veterans in the

Congressional District, which had been confirmed by Tennessee, perhaps concluding that his instructions of the same date regarding intruder removal sufficiently answered the inquiry.

To John Coffee

Nashville Decbr. 26th. 1816

Dr. Genl

your letter on the eve of your departure enclosing Major Bakers, & Genl [Daniel] Parkers was duly recd.[1]

I wrote to Genl Parker as directed, and farther added, that I was determined, to engage in purchasing or entering lands for any Individual or company, on the following terms—1rst. any Individual or company furnishing ten thousand dollars & upwards Scrip that I would furnish the amount in cash directed by law, purchase & enter to the amount, at my own expence, having one third of the land so purchased or entered. 2nd. on any Individual or company furnishing as above Scrip within three years from the ending of the sales of the public lands, for which the same is receivable, I would pay in lands at Valluation the nominal amount of said scrip. 3rd & lastly, that any Individual furnishing scrip or M. Stock as above, that I would within five years from the termination of the sales of the lands for which the stock is receivable, pay to the Individual &c &c in cash the nominal amount of said stock or scrip so furnished—whether any of those terms will suit the Genl and his friends I expect to learn shortly[2]—I have heard nothing from congress yet, The Sec of war writes me of date 4th. Instant that the land ceded will be brought into markett with as little delay as possible, and the treaties has met with the entire approbation of the President[3]—Lt. Gadsden writes me of the 3d. instant that Mr Crawford is oposed to bringing this land into markett spedily[4]—he says it would glutt the markett, & the u states would loose by it—Mr C. has a better reason than this, he does not like us, wishes at the hazard of the safety of the union to cramp our growing greatness, & wishes to prevent the population of Georgia to be drained by the emigration to this new country—and he oposes it because I have recommended it. But the tenor of the sec of wars letter of the 4th. breaths a differrent sentiment than Mr C. I therefore conclude he has but little influence in the cabinett.

I am directed to remove all intruders north of the Tennessee—to lay off a site for an armory & foundery near the Shoals, with a reservation of thirty thousand acres of land[5]—below the Shoals will, (you see) become a great & important place—I shall set out shortly to explore that country

I heard the other day from your family, they were all well.

I have removed to the Hermitage, I landed last monday—I wanted to lay myself up in dry Dock for repairs, but the Goverment will not let me—

I cannot bear whilst eating the public bread, to report unfit for duty—accept of my best wishes. adieu.

Andrew Jackson

ALS, THi (5-0636). Published in Bassett, 2:270–71. Addressed to Huntsville, where Coffee had gone to run the Chickasaw-Cherokee boundary.

1. Coffee's letter has not been found, but for the enclosures, see Isaac L. Baker to Coffee, November 7, and Daniel Parker to Baker, August 29 (DLC-21). Parker (1782–1846; Dartmouth 1801), adjutant general of the army, requested someone to enter lands on the Alabama River for him, redeeming the Mississippi stock he had inherited from a Yazoo claimant.

2. See AJ to Parker, December 9. For response to the proposals, see Parker to AJ, February 10, 1817, below.

3. See George Graham to AJ, December 4.

4. Letter not found.

5. See Graham to AJ, November 7 and December 4.

1817

To George Graham

Head Quarters D. S. Nashville
6th. Jan. 1817

Sir

In mine of the 18th. Oct. last, in answer to yours of the 10th & 12th Sepr., I advised you that the definition of the lines established by the late treaties, would be furnished the Commissioners, with instructions to commence running them as early as possible.[1]

On the 20th. Oct. I wrote Colo. Barnett enclosing him a definition of the treaties, & requesting him to repair to this place, immediately, for the purpose of joining Genl. Coffie so soon as he returned from the Choctaw treaty, that no delay might be experienced in the commencement of their duties.[2] I have had no answer from Colo. Barnett to the above communication.

As soon as Genl. Coffie returned, he was furnished with a deffinition of the treaties, & ordered to proceed to run the lines, under the expectation that Colo. Barnett would certainly meet him in due time. I also wrote to Colo. Cocke (agent for the Chickesaws) to notify the Chiefs, to have their commissioners in readiness to unite with ours; and afterwards notified him of the time Genl. Coffie would be on the line:[3] It appears from Colo. Cocke's letter (herewith enclosed) that some delay in the receipt was occasioned by the conduct of the Post Master. It is just such conduct as I should expect from such a man as Wigdon King: and how such a character has obtruded himself upon the Post Master General I am unable to divine. Wigdon King is unworthy of any confidence whatever.[4]

By a letter recd from Genl. Coffie, dated Huntsville, 29th Ult. I am advised that he has accomplished the line between the United States & Chickesaws; that their commissioners having failed to meet him as directed, & not hearing from them, he, after some delay, proceeded on his duties, & when he had reached the Cotton Gin Port was met by Levi Colbert and Wm. McGilvary (Chickesaw Commrs.) who, on the part of the Nation gave their consent to the line as run & marked. He has been advised by Col. Brown, of the Cherokee Nation, that their Commissioners would meet him on the 1st. Jan. when that line would be commenced, which he expected to compleat by the 10th. & has requested me to name to the Dept. his expectation of being ready by the 15th. Inst to make his report.[5]

The General has again been compell'd to act alone,[6] but I trust that the duty will be performed to the satisfaction of all concerned, & that his report will reach the Department in due time for the Govt. to make any order on the lands ceded, that it may judge most expedient for the general good I am, very Respy Yo. Mo. Obt. Sevt—

Andrew Jackson
Major Genl Comdg

LS in James M. Glassell's hand, DNA-RG 107 (M221-74). Published in *TPUS,* 18:10–11.

1. Jackson was referring to the treaties signed on September 20 and October 4, 1816, with the Chickasaws and Cherokees settling their overlapping claims to lands ceded by the Creeks at the Treaty of Fort Jackson in August 1814. See William H. Crawford to AJ, David Meriwether, and Jesse Franklin, September 10, 12, 1816; AJ to Crawford, October 18, 1816.
2. Letter not found. John Coffee returned to Nashville in early November after negotiating a treaty with the Choctaws on October 24, 1816.
3. Letters not found.
4. See William Cocke to AJ, December 19, 1816. King (d. 1833), the Chickasaw postmaster, had intrigued to replace Cocke as Chickasaw agent.
5. See Coffee to AJ, December 29, 1816. Colbert (c1759–1834), a member of a prominent mixed-blood family, became principal chief of the Chickasaws in 1825. McGillivray (c1754–1844), a Chickasaw chief, had served as a lieutenant of a Chickasaw detachment in the Creek War.
6. Jackson was referring to Coffee's previous survey of the northern boundary of the Creek cession.

To James Monroe

Nashville January 6th 1817

Dear Sir

I have the pleasure to acknowledge the receipt of your letter of the 14th Decbr last, which I have read with great interest and much satisfaction.[1]

your Ideas of the importance of the late acquired territory from the Indians is certainly correct, and all the importance you attach to it will be reallized. The sooner these lands are brought into markett, a permanent security will be given to what I deem the most important, as well as the most vulnerable part of the union. This country once settled, our fortifications of defence in the lower country compleated, all urope will cease to look at it with an eye to conquest. There is no other point america united, that combined urope can expect to invade with success.

On the other subjects embraced in my letter as well as this, I gave you my crude Ideas with the candour of a friend, under a recollection of the old adage, that the bee may suck honey from the mire[2]—I am much gratified that you received them as I intented; It was the purest friendship for you, individually, combined with the good of our country, that dictated the liberty I took in writing you. The importance of the station you were about to fill to our country & yourself—The injury in reputation that the chief magistrate may sustain from the acts of a weak minister—The various interests that will arise to recommend for office their favorite candidate—& from experience in the late war, the mischief that did arise to our nation & national charector, by the wickedness or weakness of our war minister,[3] induced me to give you my candid opinion on the importance of the charector that should fill this office. I had made for this purpose, the most extensive enquiry in my power, from the most impartial sources, for the most fit charector, combining—*virtue, honor,* & *energy,* with *talents,* and all united in the individual named.

I am fully impressed with the propriety as well as the policy you have pointed out, of taking the head of departments from the four grand sections of the U. States where each section can afford a charector of equal fitness—where that cannot be done—fitness and not locality ought to govern—the executive being entitled to the best talents when combined with other necessary qualifications, that the union can afford.

I have read with much satisfaction that part of your letter on the rise, progress & policy of the Federalists—It is in my opinion a Just exposition—I am free to declare, had I commanded the Military Department where the Hartford convention met—if it had been the last act of my life I should have punished three principle leaders of the party—I am certain an independant courtmartial would have condemned them under the 2nd. section of the act establishing rules & regulations for the goverment of the army of the U States[4]—These kind of men altho called Federalists, are really monarchrists, & traitors to the constituted Goverment. But, I am of opinion that there are men called Federalists that are honest, virtuous, and really attached to our goverment, and altho they differ in many respects and opinions with the republicans, still they will risque every thing in its defence—It is therefore a favourite adage with me that the "tree is known by its fruit."[5] Experience in the late war taught me to know, that it is not those who cry patriotism loudest who are the greatest friends to their country or will risque most in its defence—The Senate of Rome had a Sempronious—america has hers;[6] when, therefore I see a charector with manly firmness give his opinion, but when overruled by a majority fly to support that majority—protecting the Eagles of his country, meeting every privation & danger; for a love of country & the security of its independant rights—I care not by what name he is called—I believe him to be a true american, worthy the confidence of his country, & every good man—such a charector will never do an act injurious to his country—Such is the charector given to me of Colo. D, & believing in the recommendation I was & still am confident he is well qualified to fill the office with credit to himself and benefit to his country, and aid you in the arduous station a gratefull country has called you to fill—Permit me to add, that names are but Bubbles and sometimes used for the most wicked purposes—I will name one instance I have been once upon a time been denounced ⟨as⟩ a federalist—you will smile when I name the cause—when your country put up your name in opposition to Mr M. I was one of those who gave you the preferrence[7]—and for reason, that in the event of war (which was then probable) you would steer the vessel of state with more energy &c &c—That Mr M. was one of the best of men and a great civilian but I always believed that the mind of a philosopher could not dwell on blood & carnage with any composure, of course, not well fitted for a stormy sea—I was immediately branded with the epithet Federalist, & you also—But I trust when compared with the good old adage, of the tree being known by its fruit, it was unjustly applied to either—To conclude My Dear Sir My whole letter was predicated, to put you on your guard against the american Sempronius—that you might exercise your own Judgt. in the choice of your own ministry—by which you would glide smoothly through your administration with honor to yourself & benefit to your country. This was my motive—this, the first wish of my heart, to see you, when I am in retirement, endeavouring to nurse a broken & debilitated constitution, administering the goverment with the full approbation of all goodmen—persuing an undeviating course—alone dictated by your own independant, matured Judgt.

Present Mrs. J & myself respectfully to your lady and accept for yourself our best wishes & believe me to be yr mo. ob. serv.

Andrew Jackson

ALS, DLC (71); ALS draft, DLC (22). Published in Bassett, 2:272–73 (from ALS draft). In the campaign of 1824 John H. Eaton released two official versions of the letter: the ALS, with revisions on the original, went to the Washington *National Intelligencer* for publication; a slightly different copy (not found) went to Stephen Simpson for publication in the Philadelphia *Columbian Observer.* The transcription above omits revisions made for publication in 1824.

1. See Monroe to AJ, December 14, 1816.

2. See above, AJ to Monroe, November 12, 1816.

3. Jackson was probably referring to John Armstrong. In the 1824 publications, the *Columbian Observer* version included the phrase "by the wickedness or weakness of our war minister;" the Washington *National Intelligencer* version omitted it. When Armstrong questioned Jackson about the reference on June 6, 1824, Jackson denied that he meant Armstrong (see AJ to Armstrong, June 29, 1824).

4. Section 2 of the act, April 10, 1806 (2 *U.S. Statutes at Large* 371) provided "that in time of war, all persons not citizens of, or owing allegiance to the United States . . . , who shall be found lurking as spies, in or about the fortifications or encampments of the armies of the United States . . . shall suffer death . . . by sentence of a general court martial." Jackson was probably referring to George Cabot (1752–1823), Harrison Gray Otis (1765–1848; Harvard 1783), and Daniel Lyman (1756–1830; Yale 1776).

5. Jackson was probably quoting from Matthew 12:33.

6. Jackson was probably referring to Tiberius Sempronius, tribune in 133 B.C., to Gaius Sempronius, tribune in 123 B.C., both of whom championed a popular party in opposition to the authority of the Roman Senate, or to Joseph Addison's Sempronius in *Cato.* It has not been established whom Jackson regarded as the American Sempronius.

7. In 1808 Jackson had supported Monroe for president in preference to James Madison (see *Jackson,* 2:194–95).

From Joseph McMinn

Knoxville 10 January 1817

Sir

The Subject of the cherokees exchanging their lands for others on the west the Miss. has been laid before the head, of Departments, and as I am advised little doubt exists of their friendly disposition, Provided the cherokees wish to go into the measure, To ascertain which fact I have Sent Colo [John] Lowry of Maryville (who possess's great influence) with dispatches to the agent and Several of the chiefs with whom I had frequent opertunities of Conversing on that subject last fall at this place.[1]

He has not returned nor am I able to venture an opinion. Tho From the result of diliberations here I was very much flattered yet their then friendly impressions might soon be efface'd after their return home. I will advise you on the return of Colo Lowry

On the 8th Inst we had some firing of Cannon, an elegant Ball &c in Commemoration of the Distinguished victory near New Orleans. We have a very fine Season, and the citizens in excellent health

Crops have proved in housing much more abundant than the Farmer had anticipated

please Tender the friendly Salutations of Mrs Mc.Minn[2] & my Self to Mrs Jackson and accept the same for your Self from Sir your Friend

Jos. Mc.Minn

(please write)

ALS, DLC (22). McMinn (1758–1824) was governor of Tennessee.

1. Following his meeting with Cherokee chiefs in Knoxville on October 21, 1816, to explore the land exchange, McMinn had recommended to William H. Crawford and the Madison administration the formal adoption of the policy. Lowry, a lawyer, represented Blount County in the Tennessee House, 1809–11, and the Tennessee Senate, 1817–21, 1827–29.

2. McMinn had recently married his third wife, Nancy Glasgow Williams (c1770–1857) of Nashville.

To Joseph Gardner Swift

Nashville Janry 12th 1817.

Sir

Without preface or apology for the want of a personal acquaintance with you, with the frankness of a soldier, I present to your acquaintance and friendly attention, my Nephew Andrew J[ackson] Donelson who will hand you this.[1]

He has obtained a warrant to enter the military academy at west point. I have furnished him with funds for necessary expence, which when exausted I have authorised him to draw on me for such sums, as may be necessary to meet his wants.[2] I have recommended him to practice oeconomy—but to draw a proper distinction, between that and parsimony.

This youth is young & inexperiencd, but possessing an amiable disposition—from which I trust & hope he will conduct himself with such propriety as will not only merit your Esteem & friendship, but that of his professors & fellow students—he was fortunate at the college here at which he graduated, to obtain the good will & friendship of all, I hope he may be equally fortunate with you—and I ask for him your friendly care and attention so far as he merits it—I much wish that he may deserve it.

I cannot forego, this opportunity by my nephew of making you a tender of my gratefull thanks for your friendly attention to my ward Edward [George Washington] Butler who has lately entered the military academy and request your farther attention to him—he is the son of a meritorious officer & good man[3]—The virtues of the father creates in me, a great solicitude for the respectability of his son—he has also authority to draw on me for necessary funds—I want Edward & Andre[w] both, if in need, supplied, But it is necessary that there wants should be confined within proper bounds, & to your care I ask permission to recommend them I am with due reguard & Esteem yr mo. ob. serv.

Andrew Jackson

P.S. I take the liberty to ask a line from you when leisure will permit it, informing me with the frankness of a soldier, how these youths conduct themselves.

ALS, NWM (5-0692). Swift (1783–1865; Military Academy 1802), chief engineer of the army, was charged with supervision of the United States Military Academy.

1. Donelson (1799–1871; Military Academy 1820), son of Samuel (c1770–1804) and Jackson's ward, graduated from Cumberland College, Nashville, in 1816.

2. See AJ to Donelson, January 12.

3. Butler (1800–1888; Military Academy 1820) was the son of Edward Butler (1762–1803).

To George Graham

Head Quarters
Division of the South
Nashville 14th. Jan. 1817

Sir

A report from Major [Stephen Harriman] Long, Topographical Engineer, has just reached me through the medium of the Adjutant General's

Office, and I enclose a copy, by which you will perceive, he has, by orders from the Dept. of War, left the duties assigned him, & is now on duty in the Nothern Division.[1]

If this report be correct it at once shews the impropriety of ordering & transfering an officer from one Division to another, except through the medium of the commg General thereof: it is inconsistent with all military rule, and subversive of the first principles of that subordination which ought, & must be maintained, either to make an Army usefull or efficient.

This officer had been ordered on a special duty by the Commandant of the 9th. Dept. and that at a time when his prompt execution of the order, & report thereon, was deem'd all important, and would so have been, provided a war with the Indians, which was highly probable at that time, had to have ensued.[2] Instead of completing the duty assigned him, by furnishing a perfect sketch of the topography of the Country, he is, without any notice thereof to the officer commanding the Department "ordered to Washington by the Secy of War" & thence to N. York; and that too, without any notice to the Officer commanding the Division, who is held responsible for its safety & Defence.

Without Topographical Engineers are kept at duty within their Divisions in time of peace we can expect but little benefit from them in time of War, and they might as well be stricken from the rolls of the Staff; for as yet, as far as my information extends they have rendered no beneficial service in my Division, and Major Long is the only one who has made the least effort under orders from the Divn. of the South.

I have to request an explanation how it has happened that Major Long has been ordered from duty in my division to the Nothern, without due notice, thereof, to me; and, if any, what T. Engineer has been transferred to the Southern Division in his stead. And I have further to request, that, if Major Long has not been transferred to the North, he be ordered to report himself, without delay, at the Head Quarters of the Southern Division.[3] I am Sir, very Respy. Yr. Mo. Obt. St.

Andrew Jackson
Major Genl Comdg.

LS in James M. Glassell's hand and Copy, NN (5-0697, -0700). Published in Bassett, 2:273–74.

1. Long (1784–1864; Dartmouth 1809) had been promoted to major and topographical engineer in April 1816. The "report" Jackson enclosed was probably a newspaper clipping, since, according to his endorsement on William H. Crawford to Long, July 2, 1816 (DLC-21), he learned of Long's presence in New York from a newspaper. See Memorandum re assignment of Stephen H. Long, [cApril].

2. On October 4, 1816, William Lawrence (d. 1841), acting commander of the 9th Department in the absence of General Thomas A. Smith, had ordered Long to reconnoiter the area between Fort Bellefontaine, just north of St. Louis, and Fort Wayne, in northeast Indiana, and to return in the spring of 1817 via Prairie du Chien (DLC-21).

3. For the war department response, see Graham to AJ, February 1, below.

Robert Butler to William King

Head Quarters Division of the South
Adjutant Genls. Office.
Nashville, Jany 21st. 1817:

Sir,

In answer to your letter of 23d. November last, (which did not reach in due time) I am instructed by the Commanding General, to order, that you attempt the supply of Provisions for the Troops at Coneka from New Orleans, by Pensacola and Escambie and persist in the right to navigate these waters with provisions for our Troops until opposed by force, but you are *to distinctly understand,* that no force must be used to compel a passage through the way of Escambie[1]—Shou'd the Spanish authority not interfere, provisions will be supplied in this way, but care must be taken not to hazard too much by a discontinuance of the land supply—On the contrary should they oppose by force your attempt to throw in Provisions, to Coneka, you will report the same forthwith.[2] I have the honor to be very respectfully

(signed) Robert Butler
Adjutant General

LC, DNA-RG 98 (mAJs). King (d. 1826), a colonel of the 4th Infantry, commanded the troops at Fort Montgomery in Edmund P. Gaines's absence.

1. Letter not found.

2. For further discussion of the continuing efforts to supply Fort Crawford on the Conecuh River near Brewton, Alabama, see Gaines to AJ, April 2, below.

From George Graham

Department of War,
1st. February, 1817.

Sir,

I have the honor to acknowledge the receipt of your letter of the 14th. ultimo, which seems to have been founded on an erroneous impression of the instructions which had been given to Major Long; extracts from which are enclosed.[1] When Major Long reported himself to this department in pursuance of those instructions, he applied for leave to go to New York for the purpose of arranging some private business: this permission was granted on his representation, that his report and topographical plans could be executed by him with greater facility, in consequence of the instruments which he had there, and which he could not readily procure at this place. He was, also, verbally instructed to act temporarily, if necessary, as topographical Engineer to the Board of Fortifications; provided, Major

[Isaac] Roberdeau, who had been assigned to that duty, should be prevented from joining the board.[2] It is not understood, however, that he has been called on to perform any duties of that kind.

So soon as Major Long has made his report to this department, he will in pursuance of the original intention of the department, be ordered to report himself to you at Nashville. It is distinctly to be understood, that this department at all times exercises the right of assigning officers to the performance of Special duties, at its discretion.[3] I have the honor to be, With great respect, your obt. Servant.

Geo: Graham
Acting Secty. of War

LS, DLC (22); LC, DNA-RG 107 (M6-9); Copies, NN (5-0715, -0718). Published in Bassett, 2:274–75.

1. See above. For enclosures, see William H. Crawford to Stephen H. Long, June 18, July 2, 1816, DLC (21).

2. Roberdeau (1763–1829) was appointed chief of the army topographical division in 1818.

3. For AJ's response to the Long affair, see Division Order, April 22, below.

From John Henry Eaton

Washington City Feby 4 1817—

Dr Sir

To day is Tuesday; Saturday morning we reached the city and certainly few travellers to this place ever had a more disagreeable jaunt; the Country is every where covered with snow six or 8 inches deep & has been so for ten days the Potomack is entirely frozen over and at this time the weather continues extremely cold—we wait only for the opportunity & honor of attending her majesties levee on Wednesday and shall the next day set out for Philadea and Baltimore

I have visited for two days the Congress of the U States and have seen nothing either of men or measures calculated to excite astonishment or interest. I have heard in debate Lownds [Daniel] Sheffy [John] Forsyth & [John] Randolph,[1] the latter is & must be no doubt partially deranged; on the subject of chartering the district banks to day, he assumed a lattitude of remark that evinced a mind evidently disordered;[2] you saw no connection of idea—no system—no fancy, nor in fact any thing else but an asperity & ill natured mode of expression that delighted in torturing the feelings of others rather than attempting to produce conviction. At the moment you are rather pleased at the manner of the man, but so soon as reflection is restored & what he has said is rightly considered, that feeling which at first is excited dwindles away & sinks to contempt If that mans mind, talents & consequence has not been greatly overated I am indeed under a serious mistake. His ideas are grovelling & his expressions striped of every thing like manliness and dignity: He was very severe to day on all within his reach—of Mr. Campbell he said that his appointment to the Treasury Dep was as ill timed & unfortunate as the appointment of a certain man in the British cabinet of whom it was said he could not count 20£ if put in three parcels[3]—The President—Mr [Albert] Gallatin & the speaker all drank of his gall[4]—[John] Henrys conspiracy was also detailed;[5] & yet they were as remote from his subject as is the Potomack from the Cumberland—I have heard no body yet that at all meets the idea I had formed of the eloquence to be heard in Congress—Our great men here are like the will O wisps of the night, that always loom largest at a distance

I have been to see Mr. Madison & Monroe; with *[the]* appearance of the latter I am much the most pleased independent of a mind highly cultivated, a stranger is won to him from the conviction his looks inspire that he is a good man

Mr. Campbell went with Andrew [Jackson Donelson] to day to see about his warrant[6]—Mr. Monroe or Madison have not yet been seen Mr. C. informs me that the acting secty of war Graham states that a warrant can be procured & will be granted him; but by a regulation extending to that seminary the only periods of admission are in September that untill then Andrew will be unable to make his entrance. Tomorrow or next day complete information will be had on this subject, but I apprehend it will certainly not be in his power to get in previously to that time: what shall be done in the interim? If it shall be impracticable for him to gain admittance would his friends prefer his proceeding to some good school until that time or would it be better for him to return? I apprise you thus early of the situation of things that a timely decision may be made

We sold our horses at Beans station and took the stage[7]—once turning over was all the accident met with, no injury was sustained except having to ride 7 or 8 miles bare back—

Andrew and myself are quite well My best respects to Mrs. Jackson Yours very respectfully

Jno H. Eaton

It is stated to day in the city that the banks of Phila New york & Baltimore have agreed to pay specie on the 20 Inst.[8] Mr. [Alexander James] Dallas is dead—[9]

ALS, DLC (71).

1. Sheffey (1770–1830) and Randolph (1733–1833) represented Virginia, and Forsyth (1780–1841; Princeton 1799), Georgia in the House of Representatives.

2. For a summary report of Randolph's speech on February 3 (his remarks of February 4 were not reported), see *Annals of Congress,* 14th Cong., 2nd sess., pp. 846–47.

3. George W. Campbell had served as secretary of the treasury from February 9 to October 6, 1814.

4. Gallatin (1761–1849; Geneva 1779) was at this time minister to France; Henry Clay (1777–1852) was speaker of the House.
5. Henry (b. c1776) was an Irish adventurer whose 1808–09 reports to the governor-general of Canada had been published in March 1812 as evidence that Great Britain had intrigued with Federalist leaders to dismember the Union.
6. For admission to West Point.
7. A village in Grainger County, Tennessee, thirty miles northeast of Knoxville.
8. On February 1, the chartered banks of Philadelphia, New York, Baltimore, and Richmond announced resumption of specie payments on February 20 in compliance with a congressional resolution of April 30, 1816.
9. Dallas (1759–1817), secretary of the treasury and ad interim secretary of war under Madison, died January 16.

On March 31, 1814, as part of the settlement of the Yazoo land claims in the aftermath of Fletcher *v.* Peck *(6 Cranch 87), Congress had passed a law that provided for issuance of non-interest-bearing stock, payable out of the proceeds of land sales in Mississippi and Alabama territories, to the Yazoo claimants (3* U.S. Statutes at Large *116–20). In the summer of 1816 the army's adjutant and inspector general Daniel Parker decided that the Mississippi stock he had inherited had so depreciated that he could obtain reasonable value only by investing in land, since by law the stock was redeemable for 95 percent of the purchase price of territorial land. Through Jackson's former aide, Isaac L. Baker, he requested advice from Jackson and John Coffee regarding the purchase of Alabama lands about to be placed on the market.*

On December 9, 1816, upon learning of Parker's interest, Jackson wrote, proposing terms. For the use of any stock valued at $10,000 or more, he offered to furnish the five percent cash required and enter the lands at his own expense in return for one-third of the lands so purchased; to pay the owner the stock's nominal value in Alabama lands purchased, figured at their cash value three years hence; or to give security and pay within five years the nominal value in cash. Having asked Parker to publicize his proposals among friends, Jackson dispatched George Washington Martin (1792–1854), stepson of Stockley Donelson (c1759–1805) and a major in John Coffee's cavalry during the Creek War, to Washington with a power of attorney to obtain Mississippi stock (see AJ to Martin, December 27, 1816).

From Daniel Parker

Washington Feby 10th 1817

Dear Sir,

We have with us your young friend Major Martin Business & curiosity have divided his time for a few days past—he visits Congress & some our great men—I understand he proposes to go to Maryland very soon—From the best information I can obtain he will not find Mississippi stock so low as to answer his views—The holders of it would generally prefer to *cash it* & vest the proceeds in bank stock rather than have its nominal value five years hence—The meeting of the money changers at Phila. to organize the *great* bank last fall increased the price of all kinds of stock, or as some financiers have it, reduced the price of specie[1]—The Treasury report of this session of Congress states that the Missi. stock will be cancelled in three years[2]—Congress as you perceive by the papers do little more than scold—They threaten the army, but will do nothing unless it be to deprive *brevet* of pay &c. that is they say to make it the *legion of honor* in our service—[3]

When I introduced Major Martin to Mr. Monroe I took occasion in the conversation to bring his attention to the expediency of having the lands on the Tennessee early surveyed & sold—Several things were mentioned by the Major & myself which seemed to strike him with some force in favor of such arrangement—Several of the members of Congress in both houses are urging the importance of having a new surveying district to promote the important object of bringing the lands of the northern part of the Missi. into the markett as early as possible[4]—I understand the agents for the French imigrants wish to get a location on the south side of the high lands which divide the waters of the Tennessee & Mobile[5]

We cannot *guess* who will be Secretary of War—The knowing ones say Mr. [John Quincy] Adams is to be Secy. of State, Mr. Crawford remains in the Treasury & Mr. [Benjamin Williams] Crowningshied in the Navy—A few days will now determine the new organization—Report says Mr. Clay & Mr. Lowndes have both been offered the War Dept.[6] With great respect & regard I have the honor to be Dr Sir Your Ob Sevt

D. Parker

ALS, DLC (22).

1. Following a meeting of public stockholders of the newly chartered second Bank of the United States on October 28 and 29, 1816, expectations rose that specie payments would be resumed shortly.

2. For a discussion of Mississippi stock in the treasury report, December 20, 1816, see *ASP, Finance,* 3:142.

3. A bill to strip the added pay and emoluments from brevet ranks passed the House on February 22, but was indefinitely postponed by the Senate.

4. The act authorizing the appointment of a surveyor for the northern part of the Mississippi Territory was approved March 3 (3 *U.S. Statutes at Large* 375–76).

5. In response to a petition from the French Agricultural and Manufacturing Society, a Philadelphia group of Napoleonic exiles, for a grant of land within the Creek cession, Congress had under consideration a bill to sell the society four townships at $2 per acre. In 1818, a year after the enactment of the bill, a number of the exiles founded the town of Demopolis on the Tombigbee River in Alabama (3 *U.S. Statutes at Large* 374).

6. Adams (1767–1848; Harvard 1787), Crawford, and Crowninshield (1772–1851) accepted the indicated appointments. Clay and Lowndes declined their offers.

To Andrew Jackson Donelson

Nashville Febry 24th. 1817

Dear Andrew

Since writing you yesterday, on reflection I have concluded, that your best plan will be to proceed on to West Point, taking Newyork in your rout, where you will find Genl Swift, to whom I have written by yesterdays mail and receive his instructions, as to the best plan for your goverment & employment during the time that is to elapse before you can enter the M. academy.[1] I have a great wish that you should be near West Point, where you can become acquainted with the rules & regulations of the academy, prepare yourself for your examination, & make such progress in the academical studies that will enable you to overtake, if not at once Join the senior class who has Joined since last Septbr. I enclose you a letter to my friend Mr Saml Carswell,[2] which I request you to deliver yourself—it is open for your inspection—put a wafer in it before you deliver it. This will procure you the means of spending the summer, in the most beneficial mode for your future wellfare & greatness.

My Dear Andrew, you are now entered on the theatre of the world amonghst stranger, where it behoves you to be guarded at all points. in your intercourse with the world you ought to be courteous to all, but make confidents of few, a young mind is too apt, to form opinions on spacious shows, & polite attention by others and to bestow confidence, before it has had proofs of it being well founded, when often, very often, they will be deceived, & when too late find to their sorrow & regret that those specious shows of proferred friendship, are merely to obtain confidence the better to deceive, you therefore must be carefull on forming new acquaintances, how & where you repose confidence. I have full confidence in your Judgment, when ripened with experience I have full confidence in your morality & virtue, I well know, you will part with existance, before you will tarnish your honor, or depart from the paths of virtue & honesty—But you must recollect, how many snares will be laid for the inexperienced youth to draw him into disapation, vice & folly, against these snares I wish to guard you. This will be attempted first by obtaining your confidence, by specious display of sacred reguard to virtue, honor & honesty, and deriding morality & religion as empty hypocritical shows, endeavouring to draw you into little vices & dissapation, & then step by step into those of a more destructive kind, from all which I wish you to be guarded—I do not mean by these observations, that you should, shut yourself up from the world, or deprive yourself from proper relaxation, or innocent amusement but only, that you should alone intermix, with the better class of society, whose charectors are well established for their virtue, & upright conduct, amonghst, the virtuous females, you ought to cultivate an acquaintance, & shun the intercourse of the others as you would the society of the viper or base charector—it is an intercourse with the latter description, that engenders corruption, & contaminates the morals, and fits the young mind for any act of unguarded baseness, when on the other hand, the society of the virtuous female, enobles the mind, cultivates your manners, & prepares the mind for the achievement of every thing great, virtuous, & honourable, & shrinks from every thing base or ignoble. you will find Genl Swift in New york, when you reach there wait upon him & deliver the letter I gave you for him,[3] take his instructions for your guide, I have requested his patronage for you under his admonitions, you are safe, from them I hope you will not depart.

I have barely to add, whilst I recommend oeconomy to you as a virtue, on the other hand shun parsomony never spend money uselessly, nor never withold it when necessary to spend it. I have notified Genl Swift that you are authorised to draw on me for what sum of money may be necessary for your education & support.

all friends are well, & your aunt Joins me in prayers for your health happiness & prosperity, & requests that you should write often—let me hear from you from Philadelphia before you leave that, from New york, & then from West Point as soon as you reach that place—& believe me to be affectionately your friend,

Andrew Jackson

P S Since writing the above I have mad arangements with Mr. James Jackson for any funds you may want & enclose you his note to Mr [Thomas] Kirkman, which you will present—I have therefore not written to my friend Saml Carswell as noted in this letter—but ⟨wish for your Esteem to introduce you to him⟩ barely a letter of introduction to him—A.J.[4]

ALS, DLC (mAJs; 5-0739). Published in Bassett, 2:275–76 (extract).

1. See AJ to Donelson, February 23. Jackson's letter to Swift has not been found.

2. Carswell (c1765–1822) was a Philadelphia merchant and sometime alderman.

3. See above, AJ to Joseph G. Swift, January 12.

4. See AJ to Carswell, February 23; the enclosed note from James Jackson to Kirkman has not been found. Kirkman (1779–1826) was James Jackson's brother-in-law and partner with Washington Jackson (1784–1865) in the mercantile firm of Kirkman & Jackson of Philadelphia. Kirkman's daughter, Mary, later married Jackson's protegé, Richard Keith Call.

To James Monroe

Head Qrs. D. of the South
Nashville 4th. March 1817

Sir

I have waited with anxious solicitude for the period to arrive, when I could congratulate my Country and myself on your being placed into the Presidential chair of this rising Republic.

Your Predecessor accomplished much for his Country. None could have served with more virtuous zeal—yet there still remains undone, much for you to perform—The safety of the Country has its first claim upon your attention; next its general welfare, and I am convinced that you will pardon me, and ascribe to its proper motives, my having, at so early a period, after your instalment to the Executive chair, brought to your notice the defenceless situation of New Orleans Mobile and their dependencies, in consequence of the want of repairs to the old Fortifications and the erection of others which are absolutely necessary for their safety and defence—On file in the War Department you will find the result of the examination of that Country, which was made by Lieut. Gadsden and myself, contained in his report; which met the approbation of the then Secretary of War; yet so far as I am informed nothing has been either done, to the old Fortifications, nor preparations made towards the erection of new ones—[1]

Next to the completion of the Fortifications of defence, I would beg leave to call your attention to strengthing that Frontier by a permanent settlement of all the Lands acquired from the Creek Indians[2]—Short sighted politicians may urge that by bringing too much land into market at once, it will reduce the price, and thereby injure the finances of the Country—others, still more blind, may contend that it will drain the old States of their population, to prevent which, that the land ought not to be brought into market for twenty years—suc*[h]* are the reasons which have been used, but they are too weak to have any influence upon strong and experienced minds; The lower country is of too great importance to the Union for its safety to be jeopardized, by such short sighted policy—all the Lands to be sold, are, in a national point of view, but as a drop in the bucket when brought in competition with the value of that Country to the Union, or when compared with the amount which it would cost the United States to retake it, should it once fall into the hands of an Enemy possessing a superiority on the Ocean—every moment then should be employed, and all the means in the power of the Nation used, to add to its strength, & insure its defence, with the least expense—In what manner then can this be accomplished with so much certainty as by giving it a permanent population, able to defend it, who will by their industry afford ample supplies for an Army, good roads, & improve the navigation, so as to render the transportation of every thing necessary for an Army, easy and cheap—Permit me here to repeat, that, the fortifications compleated, and a permanent settlement on those Lands made, Louisiana may be considered safe, and the lower Country impregnable to an enemy. Closely connected with this subject is the Foundry and Armory contemplated on the waters of Tennessee, on the site lately selected by me under the order of the President[3]—this can be erected in six months, and will produce a sufficient supply of metal for all purposes of defence; the Tennessee River below the Shoals, and within eighteen Miles of the site, affords at all seasons of the year a free communication to all points on the Mississippi. From this situation on the Tennessee, where a general depot ought to be established, to the Cotton Gin Port, will not exceed fifty Miles, and may not be more than Forty five; here, on the event of War and an invasion of Mobile (should the water communication between Orleans and Mobile be cut off) might be a Depot of Arms and supplies, which could with ease be transported to the operating Army. This situation on the Tennessee is highly advantageous, it being perfectly secure from the approach of an enemy, & on the contingency mentioned could supp[l]y, at very little expense, the temporary Depot at the Cotton Gin Port. The Site chosen for a Foundry and Armory in point of ore, water, Timber, and appearance of Stone coal, cannot be surpassed. The ore is of the richest quality, and from every appearance inexhaustible—taking into consideration all these advantages, I do not hesitate to recommend it as the most advantageous site in America. I may add that the military road ordered to be laid out and opened will pass directly through the reserve, and by the Foundry; this road I hope to be able to commence opening in a few weeks; I expect Capt. [Hugh] Young Asst. Topographical Engineer, who is now engaged in running an experimental line, to return to the Tennessee during this month—so soon as he reports, the work will be commenced.[4]

Connected with the safety and defence of the Southwestern section of the union is another subject, (which altho more intimately united with the defence and safety of the North West) I beg leave to present to your view. It is that the Lands on the Ohio, within the State of Kentucky and on the East bank of the Mississippi be obtained from the Chickasaws and immediately settled.[5] Although it may be said that we have sufficient Territory already, and that our settlements ought not to be extended too far—yet every thing should be done to lessen our frontier and *consolidate* our settlements; this would at once have that effect, it would not only cut off all intercourse between the Northern Indians, & the Chickasaws and Choctaws but insure safety to our commerce on the Ohio and Mississippi, and afford a strong defence within striking distance of the settlements on the Mississippi and Missouri Rivers. I would also add another important reason why just policy should dictate the acquirement of this Territory—Within that part which lies within the chartered limits of the State of Tennessee a great portion was sold as early as 1783 to redeem the public debt of the revolution and Patents have been issued for the same—The individuals purchasing expected immediate possession—They believed that the State of North Carolina possessed a good title as no other was set up or acknowledged; and by the treaty of Peace Great Britain acknowledged it conquered, and ceded it without any kind of reservation whatever—The policy of the Government in open violation of the constitution which secures property from being taken for public use without just compensation being made, has by law, prevented the individuals from taking possession of their Lands, & reserved them for hunting grounds for the Indians—The game being destroyed as acknowledgd by all, the right of possession, granted to the Indians for the purpose of hunting ceases, and justice, sound policy & the constitutional rights of the Citizen, would require its being resigned to him[6]—It may be asked how this land is to be obtained from the Indians, they having refused to relinquish their claim to the commissioners lately appointed instructed and authorised to make this purchase from them one of whom, I was—I will answer, and I beg you will not be astonished at the ground I assume until you examine it well—I have long viewed treaties with the Indians an absurdity not to be reconciled to the principles of our Government. The Indians are the subjects of the United States, inhabiting its territory and acknowledging its sovereignty, then is it not absurd for the sovereign to negotiate by treaty with the subject—I have always thought, that Congress had as much right to regulate by acts of Legislation all Indian concerns as they had of Territories; there is only this difference, that the inhabitants of Territories, are Citizens of the United States and entitled to all the rights thereof, the Indians are Subjects and entitled to their protection and fostering care; the proper guardian of this protection and fostering care is the Legislature of the Union—I would therefore contend that the Legislature of the Union have the right to prescribe their bounds at pleasure, and provide for their wants and whenever the safety, interest, or defence of the country should render it necessary for the Government of the United States to occupy and possess any part of the Territory, used by them for hunting, that they have the right to take it and dispose of it. In the mean time justice would require, that their wants, in return, should be provided for, and that protection should be granted them, and certainly Congress is as competent to do them justice, as a commissioner appointed for that purpose—The wisdom of the Government has wisely provided, that the property of a Citizen can be taken for public use, on just compensation being made—and can it be argued that an Indian, thrown on the bounty of the Government, subject to its sovereignty, not possessing the right of soil or domain merely having the possessory right, yielded by the liberality of the United States through humanity, when they were ceded by a treaty with a conquered Country, without a reservation of any kind in their favor, I ask can it be contended with any propriety that their rights are better secured than our Citizens, and that Congress cannot pass laws for their regulation, when it is acknowledged, that they live within the Territory of the United States and are subject to its sovereignty, and would it not be absurd to say that they were not subject to its laws—If they are viewed as an independent Nation, possessing the right of sovereignity and domain, then negotiating with them and concluding treaties, would be right and proper. But this is not the fact—all Indians within the Territorial limits of the United States, are considered subject to its sovereignty, and have only a possessory right to the soil, for the purpose of hunting and not the right of domain—hence I conclude that Congress has full power, by law, to regulate all the concerns of the Indians—To this might be opposed the policy and practice of the Government so long pursued towards them; to which I would answer, that this policy grew out of the weakness of the arm of Government, and the circumstances under which the nations were placed, and not from rights acknowledged to be possessed by them, by the confederated Government—The Arm of Government was not sufficiently strong to enforce its regulations amongst them, it was difficult to keep them at peace, and the policy of treating with them was adopted from necessity—circumstances have entirely changed, and the time has arrived when a just course of policy can be exercised towards them—their existance and happiness now depend upon a change in their habits and customs which can only be effected by a change of policy in the Government. The game being destroyed, they can no longer exist by their bows & arrows & Gun—They must lay them aside and produce by labour, from the earth a subsistance; in short they must be civilized; to effect which their territorial boundary must be curtailed; as long as they are permitted to roam over vast limits in pursuit of game, so long will they retain their savage manners, and customs: good policy would therefore point to just and necessary regulation, by law, to produce this grand object—circumscribe their bounds—put into their hands, the utensils of husbandry—yield them protection, and enforce obedience to those just laws provided for their benefit, and in a short time they will be civilized—and by placing near them an industrious and virtuous population you set them good examples, their manners habits, and customs will be imbibed and adopted—and by circumscribing the Chickasaws to the limits mentioned, you leave them sufficient extent of Territory, you do justice to those Citizens who have been so long and so unjustly deprived of the possession of their property, & you place your landmarks at a permanent point, from which neither justice or sound policy will require a removal—you give content at home, and peace on your frontier by the consolidation of your settlements. Justice to the Citizen, the interest and security of the United States, and the peace and happiness of the Indians require that this should be done, and it can only be effected, by the Legislature of the Union whose powers are coextensive with the object, and, under the change of circumstances, the arm of Government sufficiently strong to carry them into execution. There can be no doubt, but that, in this way more justice will be extended to the Nation, than by the farce which has been introduced of holding treaties with them, for it is too true that avarice and fear are the predominant passions that govern an Indian—and money, is the weapon, in the hand of the commissioner, wielded to corrupt a few of their leaders, and induce them to adopt the plans embraced by the views of the Government, when the poor of the Nation receive but little, and are, by the influence of their Chiefs, (thus managed by corruption) induced to assent to their wills. Honor justice and humanity certainly require that a change of Policy should take place.

Not knowing who may fill the Office of Secretary of War, and from powers assumed by the late incumbent, which strike at the very root of all subordination, that ought and must exist in an Army, I cannot forbear bringing it thus early to your notice, that it may find a correction before its disorganizing features, take root, and be hereafter quoted as precedents. It is the right, assumed by the Secretary of War to direct the Topographical Engineers to perform special duties, the manner in which they shall report, and even directing them to report to an independent department, and all this without the knowledge of the Commanding Genl.

The case alluded to, is, instructions given to Major Long Topo: Engineer, who had reported to this Division, and been ordered on duty; after which, the first that is known of him, is, his report from New York, stating that he is there by an order from the Secretary of War. A letter is written and a request made of that department, to be informed, whether any orders have been given that officer—and in answer the Letter and Extracts enclosed, marked No. 1. 2. & 3. was received[7]—It is expressly declared that, that department reserves the right to order subordinate Officers to perform special duties when it may think proper, without that order even going through, or being made know to the commanding General—such a doctrine, is a violation of all military etiquette, and subversive of every principle of subordination, and could only originate in an inexperienced head, perfectly unskilled in military matters, & really unacquainted even with the duties prescribed by the rules and regulations for the government of the Army, or the act organizing the General Staff.[8] Admit for a moment this modern doctrine, and you destroy all subordination, deprive, at the pleasure of the Secretary the Commanding Genl. (who is responsible for the safety & defence of his Division) of the services of his best Officers—to whom he has assigned the execution of duties, for the most important purposes—and that too without his knowledge, with out their report, and kept for a considerable time ignorant of their situation, when he is in daily expectation of receiving their report upon which depends an important movement of the Army—a sudden attack of the enemy. It will be at once acknowledged by all military men that the duties and labour of a Topo: Engineer are alone important to the Officer directing the operations of an Army; it can be of no benefit to him that the Topography of a Country has been obtained & locked up in the War Department, or even, which is more ludicrous, instead of being reported to him, reported to the chief of Engineers. It is the correct knowledge of the Topography of a country that enables the commander of an Army to strike the enemy with certainty and effect, and act with promptness and success; for this purpose that part of the General Staff was created by law and attached to the Divisions, and made subordinate to the orders of their Commanders, and cannot be removed without their knowledge and consent—unless it is by establishing in the person of the Secretary of War a Tyrant superior to the law, whose will is the constitution, his caprice the law.

Ours is a Government of laws and this wise principle pervades the whole from the President down both in the civil and military departments, with that regular subordination and responsibility, which at once not only beautifies, but gives regularity and system to the whole machinery; destroy one link, and you disorganize this well regulated system, & every thing becomes insubordination and chaos. Every Military order must pass through the regular channel; the responsible Officer is then enabled to calculate his strength, and means, make all the necessary regulations for the safety and security of his command & be prepared at all points—If he fails in duty or preparation for defence and a failure ensues, his head ought to pay the forfeit. Justice cries aloud against making him responsible, when another department assumes the right, at pleasure, and his own caprice, to deprive him of the means without his knowledge or consent and this too when the duties assigned to the Officer taken, is all important to the security and defence of his Division. I will barely add, what your great experience teaches, that a time of peace, is the proper time to obtain the true Topography of the Country, and make the necessary preparations for a state of War. I have the honor to be Sir With great Respect Your Obt. St.

Andrew Jackson
Major Genl Comdg.

LS in James C. Bronaugh's hand, NN (5-0749). Published in Bassett, 2:277–82.

1. See James Gadsden to AJ, May 10, 1816. Only a portion of Gadsden's fortification report has been found. Gadsden informed Jackson, July 2, 1816, that he had obtained Secretary of War William H. Crawford's approval of the report. At this time, Gadsden was en route to New Orleans to reexamine Gulf Coast defenses.

2. Jackson was referring to the lands ceded by the Creeks at the Treaty of Fort Jackson.

3. At the request of the war department, Jackson had selected a site on Shoal Creek, in what is now Lawrence County, Tennessee (see George Bomford to AJ, October 15, 1816; AJ to George Graham, November 12, 1816, January 19 and February 12, 1817; and Graham to AJ, December 4, 1816).

4. See Hugh Young to AJ, March 14. In November 1816, Jackson had named Young (d. 1822) from Baltimore to replace William O. Butler as surveyor for the new military road from Nashville to New Orleans.

5. In 1816, Jackson, David Meriwether, and Jesse Franklin had been instructed to try to obtain title to Chickasaw land in western Kentucky, but having with difficulty overcome Chickasaw resistance to other cessions, the commissioners elected not to raise the issue (see above, AJ, Meriwether, and Franklin to Crawford, September 20, 1816). Jackson later negotiated cession of the Chickasaw land west of the Tennessee River in Kentucky and Tennessee by the treaty of October 19, 1818.

6. Jackson was referring to the Fifth Amendment to the Constitution and to the act of April 18, 1806, which allowed Tennessee to perfect titles on lands in East and Middle Tennessee but reserved the Congressional District lands in West Tennessee to the United States (2 *U.S. Statutes at Large* 381–83).

7. See above, AJ to Graham, January 14, and Graham to AJ, February 1.

8. See *Military Laws, and Rules and Regulations for the Army of the United States,* issued by the Adjutant and Inspector General's Office, September 1816, p. 97, and "An Act for organizing the general staff, and making further provisions for the army of the United States," April 24, 1816 (3 *U.S. Statutes at Large* 297–99).

The controversy aroused by Jackson's criticism of the conduct of the Kentucky troops at the Battle of New Orleans subsided briefly after his exchange of letters with John Adair (1757–1840), adjutant general of the Kentucky troops, in March and April 1815. Two years later, however, the issue resurfaced, as some Kentuckians still smarted from Jackson's allegations and Jackson refused to brook any questions of his veracity.

Despite Jackson's suspicions that the renewed debate was a partisan scheme concocted by Adair and the editors of the Lexington Kentucky Reporter, *William W. Worsley (d. 1852) and his brother-in-law Thomas Smith (d. 1866), to promote Adair's political career, the resumption of the debate on the valor of the Kentucky troops seems more to have been part of a lingering need to assess successes and failures of various officers and troops in the War of 1812 nationally. The Kentucky reexamination began when the editors of the* Reporter, *in response to a critical comment regarding the Kentuckians' courage in the Boston* Columbian Centinel, *countered with an editorial defending the troops. In large measure the defense was drawn from* History of the Late War in the Western Country, *by Robert Breckenridge McAfee (1784–1842), which the* Reporter *editors had published in late 1816. In his study, McAfee claimed that David Bannister Morgan (1773–1848), a brigadier general of the Louisiana drafted militia who commanded the west bank troops on January 8, and U.S. naval commander Daniel Todd Patterson (1786–1839), who manned the west bank artillery, had "induced" Jackson to criticize the Kentucky troops in order to hide their own failures (see Lexington* Kentucky Reporter, *February 26).*

Jackson found Worsley and Smith's editorial (and also McAfee's allegations) filled with inaccuracies, and he lost little time in taking up his pen to assail them in the letter below, insisting on its publication. To avoid a public argument with Jackson, Worsley and Smith pleaded mea culpa, acknowledged misattribution of a quotation from General John Thomas to Jackson, and urged Jackson to retract his demand, but Jackson flatly refused (see Worsley and Smith to AJ, March 22, and AJ to Worsley and Smith, April 11). The editors then printed Jackson's correspondence on April 23, accompanied by a critical editorial. After another editorial on April 30, Jackson bombarded the editors with additional documents (see AJ to Robert Butler, May 7, and Kentucky Reporter, *May 27). Adair also entered the* *controversy with a May 6 letter to the editors (*Kentucky Reporter, *June 4). The subsequent argument, widely published in newspapers and reprinted in a pamphlet,* Letters of Gen. Adair and Gen. Jackson Relative to the Charge of Cowardice, Made by the Latter against the Kentucky Troops at New Orleans, *[Lexington, Ky., 1817], was so bitter as to engender a rumor that Adair, second for Jackson in his fight with Waightstill Avery in 1788, had now killed Jackson in a duel. Although the controversy again died when Jackson apparently took the advice of friends and lapsed into an uncharacteristic silence on the issue (see William Carroll to AJ, September 11, below), and Isaac Shelby was reported to have "honorably adjusted" Jackson's dispute with Adair by 1819, the issue resurfaced in Kentucky during the 1828 campaign (*Knoxville Register, *January 26, 1819).*

To William W. Worsley and Thomas Smith

Nashville, March 11, 1817.

Gentlemen,

In your paper of the 28th of Feb., I perceive that the Kentucky detachment under the command of Col. [John] Davis, on the right bank of the Mississippi, on the 8th of January, 1815, is again brought before the public; and I have seen in that publication, with extreme regret, a forgery of the blackest kind, under the declaration of my name, for the express purpose of making it appear to the world, that I had joined in the censure of Com. Patterson and Gen. Morgan, for having done injustice to those troops, in their official report of that affair.[1] Had nothing but genuine extracts, from official documents, been attempted to be given to the world, you might have mutilated them at pleasure, and commented upon them at will, and I should have remained silent; but to permit a forgery of that kind to pass uncontradicted, to posterity for a truth, and for such base and infamous purposes, would be, in me, highly criminal. I allude to the following, which is inserted immediately before the extract of my answer to Gen. Aadair's letter.[2] "A few days after the above was written, the general subjoined the following remarks to the opinion of the court of inquiry. [']The general is impressed with a belief that the conduct of the detachment of Kentucky militia, composing Col. Davis's command, on the 8th of January, has been misrepresented, and that their retreat was not only excusable, but absolutely justifiable, owing to the unfortunate position in which they were placed. New Orleans, April 4th, 1815.[']" The foregoing I pronounce a wicked, wilful, and corrupt forgery; and state positively that no additional remarks were ever made by me, to those which appear in the general order, promulgating the proceedings of the court of inquiry, and signed by H[enry] Chotard, assistant adj. gen.[3] I have therefore to request, that you will furnish me a copy of the paper, bearing my signature, and the name of the individual from whom you received it—that the author of this forgery may be made known, and receive merited punishment. I have further to request, that you will give publicity to this in your paper, and as you have published Gen. Adair's letter to me, entire, that you again publish it, with my answer in full; "*these papers speak for themselves,*" a copy of my letter is here enclosed; although when written I did not expect it to be published; but as it contains the facts which existed, and my feelings on that occasion, I now wish it given to the world, not in mutilated scraps, ushered forth to suit party purposes, but in full that the public may judge of it.[4] But I must here remark, that it is most strange and unaccountable, that the 400 Kentuckians which were detached from Gen. [John] Thomas's Division, and ordered to cross the river, should not have been armed, when it is acknowledged by Gen. Adair, that he received on that day, from a corps of exempts in the city, between 4 and 500 muskets and bayonets on a loan for three days.[5] Why these arms were not placed in the hands of Col. Davis's detachment, and how it happened that as but 200 of them were furnished with arms, and those indifferent, the fact was not immediately reported through the adjutant general's office to the commander in chief, remains for general Adair, who is well acquainted with military etiquette, to explain. Should the real facts relative to this affair, and all others, in which those troops acted, be wanted for publication, all the reports and official documents which are in my office, or in that of the adjutant general's of division, will be furnished upon proper application being made. These fully before the public, the merits and demerits of all the troops acting on that station, from the commencement of the siege of New Orleans, until the declaration of peace, can be fairly judged of by an impartial public. My only wish on the subject is, that the truth may appear, and that the villain who would basely, either forge or fabricate a falsehood, may be dragged before the public and receive his just punishment. I am yours, &c.

ANDREW JACKSON

Printed, Lexington *Kentucky Reporter,* April 23 (5-0774).

1. Davis (d. 1816) commanded the detachment of Kentucky militia sent to reinforce the west bank troops just prior to the January 8, 1815, battle. For Morgan's report, see Morgan to AJ, January 8, 1815. No report from Patterson to Jackson has been found. Worsley and Smith may have intended reference to his report to the secretary of the navy (see Patterson to Benjamin W. Crowninshield, January 13, 1815, DNA-RG 45, M147-6).

2. See Adair to AJ, March 20, 1815 (*Jackson,* 3:318–21), and AJ to Adair, April 2, 1815.

3. See the general order reporting verdict of the court of inquiry, February 19, 1815. On March 22, Worsley and Smith informed Jackson that the quotation to which he objected was not forged, but misattributed, being actually taken from General John Thomas's order written by his aide-de-camp Henry P. Helm. Chotard (1787–1870) served with the 3rd Infantry before becoming assistant adjutant general under Jackson during the Gulf Campaign.

4. Worsley and Smith printed Jackson's letter on April 30.

5. Thomas (1765–1838) was major general in command of the Kentucky militia at New Orleans. When the Kentucky troops arrived at New Orleans on January 4, 1815, they were

mostly unarmed, much to the disgust of Jackson, who was already concerned about a shortage of arms for the Louisiana militia. For Adair's account of the muskets obtained from the corps of exempts, see Adair to AJ, March 20, 1815.

To James Monroe

(Private) Nashville March 18th. 1817
Dear Sir

I had the pleasure this day of receiving your letter of the 1rst. Instant, That by Genl [Simon] Barnard I have not received,[1] I learn by this days mail that he has reached Knoxville & will be on in a few days.

My friend Judge Campbell was instructed, & fully authorised to make the communication to you that he did, & I hope gave you fully, my reasons for my determination, & wishes on that subject.[2]

I have no hesitation in saying, you have made the best selection, to fill the Department of State that could be made—Mr Adams in the hour of dificulty will be an able helpmate, and I am convinced his appointment will afford general satisfaction.

No person stands higher in my estimation than Governor [Isaac] Shelby—he is a well tried patriot, and if he accepts, will with a virtuous zeal, discharge the duties of the office, as far as his abilities will ⟨admit⟩ enable him.[3] I cannot disguise to you my opinion on this occasion, my anxious solicitude, for your public & private wellfare, requires of me canduer on all occasions—and I am compelled to say to you, that the acquirements of this worthy man, is not competant to the discharge of the multiplied duties of this Department; I therefore hope he may not accept the appointment, I am fearfull if he does, he will not add much splendor to his present well earned standing as a public Charactor—Should he accept rest assured that as long as I remain in the army it will afford me great pleasure in obaying your orders through him, & rendering his situation & duty easy & pleasant as far as circumstances will place it in my power.

I am aware of the dificulties that surround you in the selection of your Cabinet. But the plan you have adopted of making all considerations, yield to the general weal, will bring you to retirement, with the salutations & applause of all the virtuous, wise & good—& should you be properly seconded by the congress of the u states, ⟨(of which I have much fear)⟩ you will be enabled to place the union in a state of security, & prosperity that cannot be shaken by the convulsions of urope—To this end you can calculate with confidence on my feeble exertions, so long as my constitution may permit me to be usefull—I have looked forward to that happy period, when under your guidance our goverment would be in the "full tide of successfull experiment,"[4] when I would retire from public life, & endeavour to regain a much enfeeble constitution—Should you be properly seconded in your views, this period will arive, as soon as the measures you adopt for the defence of the frontier is caried into effect, by completing those fortifications, that have & may be selected for its defence, by erecting foundries & armories—organizing & classing the militia ⟨agreably to the plan you recommended to Congress in the spring 1815⟩[5]—Then *we will have peace,* for then we will be prepared for war—every man having a gun in his hand, all urope combined cannot hurt us—Then all the world will be anxious to be at peace with us—because all will see we wish peace with all—but are prepared for defence against those ⟨all⟩ who may attempt, to infringe our national rights. Accept assurances of my best wishes & believe me to be respectfully yr mo. ob. serv.

Andrew Jackson

ALS, MNS (5-0781); ALS draft, DLC (22); Typed copy, DLC (71). Published in Washington *National Intelligencer,* May 12, 1824, other 1824 newspapers, and Bassett, 2:282–83 (from ALS draft).

1. See Monroe to AJ, March 1. The letter Bernard carried en route to New Orleans to inspect coastal defenses has not been found.

2. At this point an asterisk appears referring to a phrase inserted in a different hand at the bottom of the page: "for declining the appointment of Secty of War." The change was probably made during editing for publication in 1824, as the printed versions show the phrase as a footnote. Jackson had apparently authorized George W. Campbell to inform Monroe that he did not wish the war department post.

3. Shelby (1750–1826), a Revolutionary War veteran and former governor of Kentucky, was also under consideration for secretary of war.

4. The source of Jackson's quotation has not been identified.

5. Jackson's meaning here is unclear. He may have been referring to the reorganization and reassignment of the peacetime army.

From John Henry Eaton

Philadelphia March 20. 1817—

Dr Sir

Your two letters have been receved: Andrew has already as he informs me given you a detail of his situation and prospects, & the unexpected difficulties he has encountered in seeking admission at West Point. The acting Secty at War was positive that he would not be able to obtain an entrance untill the recommencemt of the Session in Sept; information tho obtained at this place shews that such things have been done, & unless the regulation referred to by the Secty be of modern enaction Andrew may be able to effect the same thing. He sets out at one to day in the mail stage for New York where he will wait upon genl. Swift & proceed then to West point to execute what can best be effected.[1]

A day or two ago he reced a Letter from young Mr Butler who stated to him that he would be able to procure private boarding & to pursue privately the studies of the accademy if he can do this & also be admitted to the right of instruction it will have the effect with proper industry on his part to enable him to join in Sept an advanced class; this he has promised he will endeavour to effect.[2] On reaching the place of his destination he will apprise you of the result. Gel. Swift is said to be at this time at Washington, if so he will have to proceed without seeing him & seek to effect his purpose through the Superintendant at the point.[3]

I think you may rest satisfied, that the prudence and correct conduct of your nephew will shield him against the allurements of vice; it is very true he is now at an age tender and dangerous, when the mind is most open to seduction, and easily to be led away; but I have seen few young men in my life whose reflections conduct & deportment were as correct: if he persevers in his present course of steadiness, he will never want a welcome passport to the confidence and friendship of the good and deserving

I am moving on in my business, not as speedily as I could wish—fast tho as I can. I have but 140 pages yet completed It is neatly executed on good paper & looks remarkably well: the type is wholly new.[4] I regret not being able to get off home sooner, but I much expect not to leave this untill perhaps the last of May; fifty pages a week is all that can be done, and the work can not be divided out to different printers, because not knowing how many pages the manuscript will make, the pages could not be arranged in a manner to meet. There is no doing any thing here through agents, & if I had not come on, this book would have just gone on at the leasure & convenience of the parties engaged in it: I must stay then untill all is completed; how long this may be I dont know, for no application is yet made to a book binder or any thing known of the time it may take to have them bound—M. Carey is my publisher. He insisted on having it, not, as he said and I believe with a view to benefit himself, but that you might come forth to the world in as unacceptionable an attire as possible: between us I hope it will be done; a proof sheet comes to each of us, he suggests any alteration or improvemt he pleases & sends it to me to be judged of—he has been highly servicable & I feel myself under obligations to him for it

Major Gadsden has executed & forwarded all the plats, & Mr Tanner has finished their engraving neatly & handsomly[5]—I have not been able to procure a likeness. Mr West who had a minature painting is at new orleans. The one sent Mr. Munroe is in the hands of the Society of fine arts at this place, I have applied to Mr [Joseph] Hopinkson for it, but cant procure it.[6] I have written to Mr. Munroe on the subject & expect an answer in a day or two. I have an engraved likeness executed by [David] Edwin which all who know you say is an excellent one, I think so too: it was done for a gentleman in N. York, to whom thro' some gentlemen here I have applied to get the plate & am in hopes of succeeding. Should this & the application to Mr. Munroe fail I know not what will be done—I must then prevail on you to send me one from Nashville; in the event of failure you will hear from me in *[thr]*ee or four days after this.[7] My respects to Mrs. Jackson very respectfully

Jno. H Eaton

ALS, DLC (22). Published in Bassett, 2:283–84 (extract). Endorsed as received April 8.

1. Neither Jackson's letters to Eaton nor Donelson's letter to Jackson has been found. Donelson obtained admission to West Point, June 20.

2. Edward G. W. Butler's letter to Donelson has not been found.

3. Alden Partridge (1785–1854; Military Academy 1806) was acting superintendent at West Point.

4. Eaton was overseeing publication of *The Life of Andrew Jackson*.

5. Either Henry Schenk Tanner (1786–1858) or Benjamin Tanner (1775–1848), Philadelphia engravers noted especially for their work on maps.

6. Eaton may have been referring to either John B. West or William Edward West (1788–1857), a student under Thomas Sully, who had recently moved to New Orleans. The war department had sent the John B. West miniature (now lost) to Hopkinson (1770–1842), president of the Philadelphia Society of Fine Arts, for the engraving of Jackson's congressional medal.

7. Although Jackson forwarded Eaton a portrait by Ralph Eleazar Whitesides Earl (1788–1838), as he informed Abram Maury on April 22, Eaton used as the frontispiece a stipple engraving made in 1815 by Edwin (1776–1841) of Philadelphia from a painting by Nathan W. Wheeler (c1794–1849) of New Orleans.

To Francis Smith

Nashville March 29th 1817

Dr Sir

Having this moment recd information that the lands ceded by the Creeks have been divided into two survayors Districts, & that Genl Coffee has been appointed survayor of the nothern District.[1]

Looking in my memorandom Book, I find in the hand writing of my young friend Mr. L Donelson who accompanyed me to the city of Washington, that you have a wish to procure some land in this Territory ceded from the Creeks—knowing the enterprise & industry of Genl Coffee, I have little doubt, but he will Bring in to markett, the land in his District next fall, should you be inclined to invest funds in those lands, it will afford me pleasure to give you any aid in my power, and I trust my general knowledge of that country is equal to any other individuals—I have no hesitation in saying that this section of country present to the capitalist greater prospects of advantage—than any other what little I can command will be invested in land in that quarter.[2]

Should you still be inclined to become an adventurer in those lands, please to advise me, & I will with pleasure, keep you advised, of the progress made by the survayors, & the time of sale—& if I can be servicable, it will afford me great pleasure—Mrs. J. Joins me in good wishes to you & your amiable lady, & we beg you to present us affectionately to Genl F[rancis] Preston & his amiable family[3]—Should he wish to invest any capital in those lands—say to the Genl it will afford me equal pleasure to be usefull to him—accept assurances of my Esteem & believe me to be respectfully. yr. mo. ob. Serv.

Andrew Jackson

ALS, ICU (5-0799). Smith (c1772–1841) of Abingdon, Virginia, managed the King Salt Works.

1. The surveyor's districts in Mississippi Territory were divided by the act of March 3, 1817 (3 *U.S. Statutes at Large* 375–76). Coffee's appointment was approved March 6.

2. Memorandum book not found.

3. Mary Trigg King (d. 1839) married Smith in 1811. Preston (1765–1835; William and Mary 1787) of Abingdon, Virginia, who had served with Jackson in the Fourth Congress, leased the Preston Salt Works to Smith.

From Edmund Pendleton Gaines

Hd. qrs. Camp Montgomery M. T.
April 2. 1817

General

The prospect of Pensacola being shortly assailed by the spanish revolutionists seems to have vanished; and, to the credit of our white and red *people of the woods,* be it spoken, though disposed to see Pensacola change masters, they had felt too sensibly the pressure of the late war, (which possessed the advantage of being sanctioned by their country) to volunteer in one which might prove to be even more disasterous to them, and in which their government and country had not seen fit to authorise their participation.[1]

I have ordered the supplies for Fort Crawford to be sent in future, agreeable to your instruction, by water. With the first cargo, I have sent Lieut [French Strother] Gray, to superintend the transportation, and to make a temporary arrangement for a place of deposite; where the supplies may be discharged from coasting vessels and put on board Barges or Batteaux adapted to the navigation of the Escambia and Conaka rivers. And I deemed it proper to put into the hands of Lieut. Gray a letter to the Spanish Governor, of which and of my Instructions to the Lieut I enclose copies Nos. 1 & 2.[2] The Governor is at this time I understand, disposed to be unusually civil towards us, and I think it not likely that he will so far lose sight of his true policy as to attempt to prohibit the passage of our supplies.

I received, not until the 24th. ultimo, your order through the Adjutant Generals Office, of the 15th. february, to station a company of artillery at Fort Scott. The enclosures No. 3 and 4 will inform you of the measures I have taken pursuant to that order.[3]

The rumours mentioned to you some time past that the Indians had burnt the Barracks at Fort Scott, has been corroborated by subsequent reports from the vicinity of that place;[4] and, although the reports of Indian countrymen should mostly be taken at a considerable discount; yet I have no reason to doubt, & much reason to rely on the truth of those just mentioned.

I received by the last weeks mail a letter from the Honble. Archd. Clark, Intendant of the town of St. Mary's, by which it appears that another outrage of uncommon cruelty and barbarism has recently been perpetrated on the southern frontier of Georgia. a party of Indians attacked a defenceless family and massaccred a woman (Mrs. Garrot) and her two children—the woman and eldest child were scalped, the house robbed and set on fire. The high respectability of the gentleman who communicated these facts, leaves no doubt of their truth. I enclose his letter No. 5.[5]

The failures of the mail prevented my receiving this, as well as several other accounts, corroborative of the settled hostility of the Seminolas until a delay of many days had intervened. Two of those communications I send you herewith, No. 6 and 7. I enclose also, (No. 8) a letter signed "A[lexander] Arbuthnott."[6] This letter appears to have been written by one of those *self-styled Philanthropists* who have long infested our neighboring Indian villages, in the character of British Agents—fomenting a spirit of discord, ⟨calculated to work the destruction of the deluded savages⟩ and endeavoring by pretended care and kindness, to effect the destruction of these wretched savages. I have the honor to be, most respectfully Your obdt Servt.

Edmund P. Gaines

ALS, DLC (22). Endorsed as received April 21 and answered April 22.

1. For Gaines's earlier report regarding a rumored expedition against Pensacola, see Gaines to AJ, February 14.

2. For Jackson's instructions regarding the supply of Fort Crawford, see above, Robert Butler to William King, January 21. Gray (d. 1819) enlisted as an ensign in 1813 and rose to captain in the 7th Infantry before his death. José Masot (1756–1820), a career officer in the Spanish army, served as interim governor of Spanish West Florida from November 1816 to May 1818. For enclosures, see Gaines to Gray and to Masot, March 18, both DLC (22).

3. For Jackson's order, see Robert Butler to Gaines, February 15. For enclosures, see Gaines to James Bankhead and to Georgia contractor, March 24, both DLC (22).

4. See Richard M. Sands to [Gaines], February 2, which Gaines enclosed to AJ on February 14.

5. See Archibald Clark to Gaines, February 26, DLC (22). Clark (1783–1848) was collector of customs as well as mayor at St. Mary's. Mrs. Garrett was the wife of Obediah, an overseer on Israel Barber's farm, about 3 miles above Clark's mill at Spanish Creek in Camden (now Charlton) County, Georgia.

6. See George Periman to Richard M. Sands, February 24; Sands to William King, March 15; and Alexander Arbuthnot to Sands, March 3, all DLC (22). Arbuthnot (c1748–1818), a trader from the West Indies, was later court-martialed and executed by Jackson for his alleged support of the hostile Indians.

To George Graham

Head Quarters
Division of the South
Nashville 11th. April 1817

Sir

From many respectable, & disinterested reports, and from my own knowledge, I ⟨have Learned⟩ find that the unfortunate situation of the intruders on the two reservations, embraced in the Cherokee treaty of 1806, is such, as even to preclude the possibility of ⟨a⟩ their removal, without the means are furnished by government. They are actually in a starving condition. Under these feelings, together with the knowledge that there is not an individual on those reservations who have settled there in *contravention* to the right of the United States; I have taken upon myself to suspend the order for their removal, untill, after, making a statement of those facts, I could learn the farther decision of the War Dept.[1]

Yours of the 22d Ult. is just received, and I have this moment, notified the Cherokee Agent that the meeting of the Chiefs, contemplated to take place on the 1st. May, is postponed to the 20th. June next, & requested him to make the necessary arrangements to that effect.[2] I have the honor to be, Very Respy Yo. Mo. Obt St.

Andrew Jackson
Major Genl Comdg

LS in James M. Glassell's hand, OkTG (5-0806).

1. On May 20 Graham reported President Monroe's approval of Jackson's order suspending removal. See Graham to AJ, November 7, 1816, ordering removal; and Samuel Houston to Robert Houston, April 15, suspending action.

2. See Graham to AJ, March 22. Jackson's letter to Return J. Meigs has not been found.

To avoid white settlers a small group of Cherokees had settled in what is now Arkansas in the 1790s. Continuing white intrusions onto Cherokee lands in Tennessee and Georgia led agent Return J. Meigs to suggest in 1808 that a solution might be found by encouraging the nation to exchange their lands east of the Mississippi for lands in the west. The proposal exacerbated the already present divisions over cessions made in their January 7, 1806, treaty with the United States. Many Lower Town chiefs favored removal, while the Upper Towns opposed. A mixed delegation sent to Washington reached no agreement either with the government or among themselves, but in his January 9, 1809, farewells to the Upper and Lower Town delegates (DNA-RG 75, M15-2), President Jefferson authorized the Lower Towns to locate a suitable western tract "not claimed by other Indians" and promised that the government would arrange "the exchange of that for a just portion of the country they leave and to a part of which, proportioned to their numbers, they have a right." Accordingly, about 1,000 Cherokees emigrated to Arkansas in January and February of 1810.

Exchange of eastern for western lands, however, continued to divide the Cherokees; and when Jackson called for a meeting with them in 1817 to negotiate a cession of the 1806 treaty reserves, Cherokee removal reemerged as a major issue, especially as the Arkansas Cherokees found their land claimed by the Osage and Quapaw Indians.

From Arkansas Cherokees

[April 18, 1817]

To the Honourable Major Generall Andrew Jackson
Sir

We the Cherokees that live on the Arkansas River beg leave to present to you our best wishes for a long life and prosperity

Father and friend we live a long way from you and cannot all be present to see you. we have therefore in full Councill appointed two of our party agents vested with full power to transact our business with our Father the President and the Chiefs of the old Nation—we hope Sir you will Receive them and consider them as if we were here present ourselves we have directed them to speak with you ask your advice for our good.[1]

For Colonel Megs

3700 is our Standing Number. Since last fall that we talked with Govenor [William] Clark, we have not aded the Numbers that have come since and is on the River coming[2]—My Fathers and friends G Jackson & Colonel Meggs we understand are about holding a treaty with the Chiefs of the Cherokees about Land. Colonell Meggs you Remember very well & know that the Cherokees sent a deputation to federall City in the year 1807 how they were divided concerning coming to this Country and that the President agreed with both parties and I was advised to come to this Country and I have the papers to shew. you have the papers also.[3] My friends & Brothers your Chiefs of the Cherokees you remember the Councill at Broom Town. when my coming to this Country was fully digestd and talked off and you all agreed.[4] I did not steal it from you. Now I understand some of you since that you turned your talks another way What I am talking about is a long time back I am not bred of you—My friends you are still in your houses. I still think of you I keep hearing crooked talks about me from you Now the time is I will speak about Land this day I think myself very strong and my people is coming to me every day ⟨I Expect⟩ we do not think of looking back nor going back—we love our Country here. My friends your Chiefs our fathers General Jackson and Col. Meggs: I Expect you understand what I say we send our talk by John D Chisholm and James Rogers[5] I Expect when I hear from my father the President I shall hear that all is done to satisfaction I hold his arm fast. My father General Jackson & Col Meggs there are two roads leading to [6] help my people keep the Roads open and ⟨help my people⟩ clear for them I never loose sight of the Presidents talks to hold all peoples by the hands I have done so.

I am now compelled to let go the hands of the Osages because they let mine go & the Presidents also. they are daily stealing my property & killing my people & white people also—you ask to know the size of the Osage purchas we do not wish the Goverment to Run it, it will be a bad President if you agree to pay their damages—their will be and end to their stealing—My young men have now took their guns in their hands we mean to make our Crops before we begin.[7] I expect a great many of my friends from the old Nation. I mean to have provision for them I mean to wait three months to work the Corn I also expect my friends from the old nation in that time to assist me. General Jackson & Col Meggs I ask your advise should I conquer the Osages and drive them off will not the Land be mine the depredations committed on us and on the whites & French are not Resented by them I now *resent it I cannot take it any longer.* My friends and Brothers your Chiefs of the Old Nation I am informed by Govenor Clark—that you was to see the President last you denied us and said that none of the anuity or Land belonged to us.[8] Why say you so if we Cherokees in the Old Nation we are Cherokees here also and we have not changed our notion nor rights. Colonell Meggs and, General Jackson we ask you to let our deputies to have their expences paid to them: as we have no agent we look to our fathers. We conclude by saying we are your Children and friends.

Done in full Councill this 18th day of Aprill 1817 Signed by the Chiefs in behalf of the whole In the presence of Joseph Severe & William Ware[9]

Kacuttokah
Tallan Tuskey
Black Fox
Sanawney
Waterminer
Kiami
Thomas Graves

LS by proxy, DLC (22). Published in Bassett, 2:289–91. The letter is addressed to Jackson and Return Jonathan Meigs (1740–1823). Kacuttokah is probably Takatoka (c1755–c1825), a principal chief in Arkansas. Tahlonteskee (d. c1819), a kinsman of Doublehead and a principal chief, led a migration of Lower Town Cherokees to Arkansas in 1810. Black Fox (d. c1834) was also a chief of the Arkansas Cherokees. Waterminer remained a powerful leader at least until 1824. Sawnawney (Senaneh), emigrating to Arkansas by 1811, was a former chief of the Creek Path towns. Graves remained a chief of the Arkansas Cherokees at least until 1828, when he served on their delegation to Washington. Kiami has not been further identified.

1. The power of attorney, April 17 (DLC-22), authorized John D. Chisholm, who carried the letter to the treaty ground, and James Rogers to negotiate on their behalf.

2. Clark's report on the tribes in Missouri Territory, November 4, 1816 (DNA-RG 75, M271-1), showed 3,600 Cherokees. Clark (1770–1838), governor of Missouri Territory, had been appointed in March 1815 a commissioner to negotiate with Indian tribes on the waters of the Mississippi River. In November 1816 a Cherokee delegation met with him and other commissioners to discuss an Osage boundary line.

3. Almost certainly a reference to the delegation that attended Washington, December 1808–January 1809, and Jefferson's addresses of January 9, 1809.

4. The Cherokee national council had met at Broomstown in September 1808, but it did not resolve the removal question. Shortly after that meeting, a hastily called council at Hi-

wassee, dominated by Upper Town chiefs opposed to removal, voted to depose the Lower Town chiefs, Black Fox (d. 1811), Tahlonteskee, Chisholm, and The Glass.

5. Chisholm (d. 1818), a white trader who married into the tribe, was the grandfather of Jesse Chisholm of Texas fame. Rogers, who was probably the son of John Rodgers (b. c1749), was an interpreter for Arkansas Cherokees as late as 1831; employed by the war department in 1828 to encourage emigration, he became a pariah to Eastern leaders.

6. Left blank in manuscript.

7. In May 1816 Secretary of War William H. Crawford had directed the treaty commissioners to have the boundary set by the Osage treaty of November 10, 1808, surveyed.

8. In his September 17, 1816, letter to Clark, Crawford informed the governor that during the negotiations at Washington in February and March 1816 the Eastern Cherokees had refused to consider any aid to the Arkansas branch of the tribe (DNA-RG 75, M15-3).

9. Sevier (1763–c1825), a son of former Tennessee governor and congressman John Sevier, was an Indian trader in Arkansas. Ware has not been identified.

To George Graham

Head Quarters
Division of the South
Nashville 22d Apl. 1817

Sir

I have to acknowledge the receipt of your letter of the 5th. Inst with its enclosure.[1]

Measures have been adopted, as far as the physical force in the upper Mississippi will authorize, to protect that section of country, and promptly chastise the Indians for any acts of murder or treachery, that they may attempt.

I trust the Government have taken prompt measures to send out of that country any British traders, who have by imposition, or otherwise, obtained a licence from her Agents: I have directed that all such characters, in the event of War, be immediately apprehended; and those found with the enemy, treated with the greatest rigor known to civilized Warfare.[2] By these fiends the savages are led to acts of hostility that will involve them in general destruction, and they ought to feel the keeness of the scalping knife which they excite.

My Aid, Lieut [James McMillan] Glassell, acknowledged the receipt of yours of the 25th and advised, you of the instructions, consequent on the receipt of yours of the 22d. March, that had been given to Colo. Meigs, to adopt such measures as he might deem most proper to obtain a full meeting of the chiefs on the 20th. June, the day to which it was postponed.[3]

In yours of the 25th. Ult. you say "As circumstances may probably make it inexpedient to enter into a negotiation with the Cherokees, for an exchange of Territory, at so early a period as that mentioned in my letter of the 22d Inst it will be unnecessary to take any measures" &c, &c —If the President finds the grounds for protracting the time of the exchange, in the belief that the minds of the nation is not sufficiently made up to meet that question; I will barely remark my belief that it might be brought before them without any prejudice at the ensuing meeting, stating to them the necessity of an immediate understanding on that subject, that a section of country might be appropriated at once, & the whites prevented from settling on it: and also stating to them the necessity, to prevent a division of the nation, the President would be under, if a change was not effected, to remove those back who had already settled on the Arkansas river: and it might be further urged that altho' the President felt the necessity, for the reasons above stated, to come to an immediate understanding, yet their immediate removal would not be insisted on.

Should the President conclude to bring this subject before them at the next meeting, it would be pleasing to have Genl. Meriwether associated with me in that duty. If this cannot be done I could wish that the Adjutant Genl. Col. Butler, might be his substitute, as I conceive a necessity for some assisstance, in my infirm health, as, then, in the event of my sickness the business might nevertheless progress.

The Cherokee Agent is now here, & says he has, and will impress the policy of an exchange on the minds of the chiefs. It is certainly their true policy, and, in my opinion, will be adopted by the mass of the nation; a few half breeds may oppose it; these might be provided for by the reservation of a section, so long as they chose to occupy it, but when abandoned, for it to accrue to the United States: and whilst they remained, for them to be subject to the laws of the United States.

Pursuant to the sugge[s]tion contained in yours of the 22d Ult. endeavors will be made to ascertain whether any locations have been made on the late survey for a foundery, under warrants issued by the state of North Carolina, that may be considered valid, and the result reported to the Dept. of War.[4] I have the honor to be Very Respy Yo. Mo. Obt. St.

Andrew Jackson
Major Genl Comdg.

LS in James M. Glassell's hand, DNA-RG 107 (M221-74). Published in Bassett, 2:292–93 (extract).

1. See Graham to AJ, April 5. Graham enclosed a letter from Ninian Edwards, February 21, warning of "a hostile disposition" of the Indians in Missouri and Illinois territories.

2. Order not found.

3. See Graham to AJ, March 22 and 25; Glassell to Graham, April 18. Glassell (1790–1838), of Virginia, had accepted appointment as Jackson's aide in October 1816.

4. On December 30, 1817, Jackson reported to John C. Calhoun that no "patented land" lay within the foundry survey.

Dissatisfied with acting Secretary of War George Graham's response to his protest of the reassignment of topographical engineer Stephen H. Long, Jackson acted unilaterally to enforce his view of the proper chain of command by issuing the division order, below. The April 22 order became one of the most controversial acts of Jackson's military career, since his critics found it insubordinate. As newspaper editors debated the order, the controversy was further inflamed by a rancorous and ultimately public exchange of letters between Jackson and Winfield Scott, who had criticized it (see below). Meanwhile the Monroe administration sought to mollify Jackson while maintaining the principle of presidential control over the military, but not until December was a formula found to extinguish the disagreement (see James Monroe to AJ, December 2, below, and December 28).

Division Order

Adjutant-General's Office,
Head-Quarters,
Division of the South.
Nashville, April 22, 1817.

The commanding General considers it due to the principles of subordination, which ought and must exist in an army, to prohibit the obedience of any order emanating from the Department of War, to officers of this Division, who have reported and been assigned to duty, unless coming through him as the proper organ of communication. The object of this order is to prevent the recurrence of a circumstance which removed an important officer from the division, without the knowledge of the commanding General, and indeed when he supposed that officer engaged in his official duties, and anticipated hourly the receipt of his official reports, on a subject of great importance to his command; also to prevent the Topographical reports from being made public through the medium of newspapers, as was done in the case alluded to,[1] thereby enabling the enemy to obtain the benefit of all our Topographical researches as soon as the general commanding, who is responsible for the defence of his division. Superior officers having commands assigned them, are held responsible to their government for the character and conduct of that command; and it might as well be justified in an officer senior in command to give orders to a *guard* on duty, without passing that order through the officer of that guard, as that the Department of War should countermand the arrangements of commanding generals, without giving their order through the proper channel. To acquiesce in such a course, would be a tame surrender of military rights and etiquette, and at once subvert the established principle of subordination and good order. Obedience to the lawful commands of superior officers, is constitutionally and morally required; but there is a chain of communication that binds the military compact, which, if broken, opens the door to disobedience and disrespect, and gives loose to the turbulent spirits, who are ever ready to excite mutiny. All Physicians able to perform duty, who are absent on furlough, will forthwith repair to their respective posts. Commanding officers of regiments and corps, are required to report, *specially,* all officers absent from duty after the 30th of June next, and their cause of absence. "The army is too small to tolerate idlers, and they will be dismissed the service." By order of Major-General JACKSON,

Robert Butler
Adjutant-General.

DS (printed forms signed), DLC (69), NN (5-0836); LC, DNA-RG 98 (5-0838); Copies, DNA-RG 94 (5-0840), DNA-RG 107 (M222-19). Published in contemporary newspapers and in Bassett, 2:291–92.

1. Stephen H. Long's March 4 report to George Graham regarding the topography of the Old Northwest was published in the Washington *National Register,* March 29.

To Isabella Butler Vinson

Hermitage near Nashville
May 9th. 1817.

My Dear Madam

I had the pleasure to receive your letter of the 1rst ult. by due course of mail. It should have had an Earlier answer, but my indisposition has prevented me untill now, added to a wish I had to converse, & make some erangements with Mr Robert Bell, to emeliorate if possible your present situation, and to have the lands mentioned by you, to have been sold for the Taxes redeemed—[1]

I regret My Dear Madam, yea, I much regret your present, unpleasant, & unfortunate situation, & will with pleasure, yield every aid in my power to relieve you, but when you reflect the situation of some of my near connections & how much they want, pecuniary aid, added to the sums necessary for the support of those, of an advanced age, now finishing their education, you will readily conceive, my streitened circumstances with regard to funds, when I add, that my farm for years has been unproductive—& my expence double to my pay, untill the last four or five months—added to the serious encumbrances, of securityship that forced me to pay large sums—

It was well understood, when I was appointed guardian of your children that I could not undertake the superintendance of their property, beyond the limits of this state[2]—I have said to Mr Bell, If he will have, the situation of the land in that country enquired into—The sum necessary for its redemption—assertained, I will advance the sum to redeem it so that the rents & profits, of your right of dower, or of the whole, (with the consent of the children of age) may result to your support—

I have discovered amonghst my papers a patent, granted to Nathaniel

Smith 3d by the state of Pensylvania, Westmoreland County for 200 acres of land, Transferred on the back of the patent to Edward Butler the 30th. of Decbr 1786—This I will place in the hands of Mr Bell that enquiry may be mad into its situation with the other lands, from which I hope relief may be afforded you—[3]

I have Just had letters from Edward & Anthony they are both well, & doing well, Edwards' Teacher, gives me a very flattering account of Edwards' application & propriety of conduct—[4]

I can now scarcely write with a pain in my left side, that has confined me for some days, but with copious repletion I am getting better, as soon as my health permits, I will have another interview with Mr Bell, & will again write you—accept my Dear Madam, my sincere prayers for your health & happiness—& p*[lea]*s to excuse this hasty scrall written with much pain—I am respectfully yours &c &c

Andrew Jackson

ALS, LNHiC (5-0847). The widow of Edward Butler, Isabella (d. 1821) had married William B. Vinson by 1810.

1. Vinson's letter has not been found, and the lands in question, near the Pennsylvania-Ohio border, have not been specifically identified. Bell (d. 1842) was Isabella B. Vinson's son-in-law, having married her daughter Caroline Butler (d. 1864). They settled in Louisiana. For Jackson's efforts in the redemption of lands belonging to the Butler estate, see Robert Bell to AJ, October 21, and Memorandum of Accounts between Edward G. W. Butler and AJ, [August 7, 1820].

2. Jackson was appointed guardian for Caroline, Eliza Eleanor (1791–1850), Edward George Washington, and Anthony Wayne Butler (1803–1824) on October 20, 1803. No written agreement regarding the conditions of guardianship has been found.

3. The patent has not been found, nor has Smith been identified.

4. Not found.

To George Graham

Head Quarters
Division of the South
Nashville 13th. May 1817

Sir

Major [Paul Hyacinte] Perrault of the Topographical Department having a few days since reported himself at this place[1] I have determined not to await the return of Capt. Young but immediately to commence opening the contemplated military road from the nothern boundery of the Mississippi Territory to the lake Ponchertrain, commencing at the first named point with the troops (one company) ⟨now⟩ at Fort Hampton, untill the affairs of the upper Mississippi will justify the removal of the two companies of the 8th. Infantry now there[2]—Orders have been given to General Ripley to furnish two companies, to commence cutting at the southern extremity of the road under the directions of Capt. Young, Topo. Engineer, who has been instructed to open it thirty feet wide, causway all marshes & swamps 20 feet wide, raising them above high water mark, and to make bridges of durable materials over all streams that their means will permit.[3]

It is much to be regretted that the Topo. Engineers have not been furnished with the necessary mathematical instruments, as none can be procured here, and Major Perrault's total want thereof, will, I am apprehensive, cause delay untill they can be obtained from Philidelphia, as it is improbable that he can procure either a quadrant or Sextant to take the latitude, necessary on commencing the road at the north point of beginning. But as it appears to be important to connect the different sections of land cut by this road, and Genl. Coffee having commenced the duty enjoined upon him; I shall loose no time in compleating it as far south as the hundred Townships, which he is directed to lay out, extends; and shall leave this, for the Tennessee river for that purpose, between the 15th and 20th. Inst. or as soon as my health is sufficiently re-established to encounter the fatigue of travelling.[4]

Before I proceed to meet the Cherokee Chiefs at Hiwassee on the 20th June next, I shall expect your instructions to what specific in subjects, I shall be confined in that conferrence; not having, as yet, received an answer to my letter to you of the 22d April last.[5] I am Sir Very Respy. Yo. Mo. Obt. St.

Andrew Jackson
Major Genl Comdg

LS in James M. Glassell's hand, TU (5-0852).

1. Perrault (d. 1834), a veteran of the War of 1812, accepted reappointment as major of the topographical engineers on February 24.

2. Fort Hampton was built in 1809 on the Elk River in what is now Limestone County, Alabama, seventeen miles west of Athens. See Robert Butler to Eleazar W. Ripley and to Thomas A. Smith, April 22, for Jackson's arrangements regarding the transfer of the 8th Infantry companies from the upper Mississippi to road-building near Muscle Shoals.

3. See Robert Butler to Ripley, May 9; the order to Hugh Young has not been found.

4. On March 18, the commissioner of the general land office, Josiah Meigs, had directed John Coffee to survey fifty townships on the north side of the Tennessee River immediately contiguous to the western boundary of Madison County, Mississippi Territory, and fifty townships south of the river, extending from the eastern limits of the Cherokee cession of 1816 to a point no farther west than the western boundary of the survey north of the river. Jackson left Nashville May 29.

5. See above, AJ to Graham, April 22. Jackson received Graham's response of May 14 at Huntsville on June 11. Graham authorized Jackson to negotiate an exchange of eastern Cherokee lands for lands on the Arkansas River adjoining the Osage boundary line and to obtain a cession of the reserves granted in the treaty of 1806. On the negotiations, see also Graham to AJ, May 16.

To Rachel Jackson

Nashville May 29th. 17

My love

I leave this immediately after closing this, & have to beg of you to reconcile my absence always recollecting, that, that, all seeing being who has so often shielded me from the shafts of death can preserve me from a sick bed, and when he commands, to yield up our existance, the summons must be obayed—I have therefore thought it wrong to repine at the acts of the duty on any occasion—I have long, very long, looked forward to that moment, when I could retire from the bustle, of Public life to private ease, & domestic happiness—Thus far I have been disappointed—but I hope a few months (if I live) will bring about this long wished for period. I therefore beg of you on the present absence, exercise your philosophy. I enclose you a note to Mr Sanders *[o]*n the subject of Tobacco plants, read & deliver *[i]*t to him[1]—accept of my prayers for your *[hea]*lth & happiness & that of our Dear Andrew—*[du]*ring my absence—adieu—

Andrew Jackson

ALS, MH-H (5-0883).

1. The note, which has not been found, was probably addressed to Hermitage overseer Harrison Saunders.

To Rachel Jackson

Huntsville May [June] 11th. 1817.

My Love

I reached here to day, on yesterday dined with your sister Hutchings, found her & family well, she has lost a great deal of her flesh, I am fearfull she is not contented—Kitt. lives on the poorest place I ever saw, but is healthy & fine water I hope this fall at the sales of the lands, it will be in our friend Jack's power to purchase a good tract, & settle her comfortably for life.[1]

I was at the Bluff Two days & nights, Major Hutchings deserves a Meddle—he has the finest Prospect of a good crop I ever saw, his cotton far excells any crop I have seen, & I think we may calculate, on, from Eighty, to Ninety Bales[2]—he will be in, perhaps before I return he has a bad cough, I have urged him to come in & apply proper remedies for it—

I have enjoyed only tolerable health, since I left you, troubled with my bowells, which perhaps has kept me free of the pain in my side & breast—I have been truly fortunate in not getting wet—on tomorrow I shall proceed to Highwassee, from whence I shall write you—I expect to reach there on the 18th. Instant, and hope not to be detained there longer than ten days, however I have to await the slow movements of the Indian chiefs, & cannot calculate with any certainty how long I may be detained, but as soon as the conferrence can be closed, I shall set out for home—[3]

I enclose a letter to Jackey Cafferey, which you will please send him—I hope our Andrew is well, & learning his Book well, kiss him for me & say to him I shall expect him at the head of his class when I come home—Tell him that Jack & George sends howde, to Master Andrew—Present me to Mrs. [Mary Donelson] Caffery & Jane.[4]

If Colo. Hayne & Lady is with you please present me to them.

Say to Colo. [Robert] Hays I have seen a fine country present me to him & the family[5] & believe me to be affectionately yrs

Andrew Jackson

P S. have a wife Chosen for Major H—he is determined to marry—his life is too loansome—[6]

ALS, MH-H (5-0892). The reference to Jackson's arrival at Huntsville indicates a June date.

1. Catherine Donelson Hutchings, John Hutchings's mother.

2. Hutchings was operating the Melton's Bluff plantation that he had purchased with Jackson in November 1816.

3. Jackson was travelling to the Cherokee treaty negotiation at Hiwassee Garrison, scheduled for June 20. On that date, the commissioners met at the Cherokee Agency, where the negotiations were moved, but they waited until June 28 for the Cherokee delegation to assemble. The treaty was signed on July 8.

4. Letter not found. John (Jackey) Caffery, Jr. (b. c1795), and Jane Caffery (c1801–19), who married Ralph E. W. Earl in 1818, were children of Mary Donelson Caffery (c1756–1823). Andrew Jackson, Jr., who had attended classes in Nashville at the grammar school of Cumberland College in 1816, began taking instruction at William McKnight's school near the Hermitage in June or July. Jack and George were most likely Hermitage slaves temporarily employed on Jackson and Hutchings's plantation at Melton's Bluff.

5. Hays (1758–1819), married to Jane Donelson Hays (1766–1834), resided in Rutherford County.

6. Mary Smith Hutchings, John's wife, had died in 1813.

To Robert Butler

Cherokee agency June 21rst. 1817.

Dr Colo.

I reached this place on the 18th. having got to Highwassee Garrison on the 17th. where I learned that Colo. Meiggs had notified the chiefs to meet here believing public good would result from the change.

yesterday being the day appointed, none but the chiefs & delegation from the arkansaw attended. These appear verry solicitous for an exchange, in fact I believe every native of the nation left to themselves, would freely make this election—But they appear to be overawed by the council of some whitemen and half breeds, who have been and are fattening upon the annuities, the labours, and folly of the native Indian, & who believe, that their income would be destroyed by the removal of the Indians—[1]

These that I have named are like some of our bawling politicians, who loudly exclaim we are the friends of the people, but who, when the obtain their views care no more for the happiness or wellfare of the people than the Devil does—but each procure influence through the same channels & for the same base purpose, *self agrandisement.*

Genl Meryweather is with me, & it becomes our duty to endeavour to counteract this policy & clearly explain, the true interests of the natives & I am of the opinion, that at least one half of the nation will relinquish their right here and go to the Arkansaw, perhaps the whole with very few exceptions, for as soon as the native says he will go, few of the whitemen or half breeds can live under civilized laws, & will follow—

I see from the National Intelligencer that the lands on the Allabama are proclamated for sale in the month of august next[2]—Colo. Hayne I know, must be there—If he wishes to set out before I return, give such written Permission to him as may be necessary for the occasion—

I enclose a letter for Mrs J. which I hope you will please forward to her.[3]

Present me affectionately to your lady & family & kiss Jackson for me[4]—& accept for yourself my best wishes.

Andrew Jackson

ALS, DLC (23). Published in Bassett, 2:299 (extract).

1. Although this could be taken as a general complaint, Jackson may have intended a specific reference to the Cherokee reform council at Amohee, which had adopted a new constitution requiring unanimous consent for any disposal of land and explicitly disinheriting Cherokees who emigrated from the nation (see Charles Hicks to Return J. Meigs, May 11; Cherokee constitution, May 6; Protest of Nancy Ward et al. against emigration, May 2; and Petition of Georgia Cherokees against intruders, n.d., all DLC-22).

2. Monroe's proclamation of May 24, calling for sales of a portion of the Creek cession lands at Milledgeville in August, was published in the Washington *National Intelligencer* on May 28 and in subsequent issues.

3. Letter not found.

4. Jackson Orleans Butler (1816–26), son of Robert and Rachel Hays Butler.

Having waited eight days for the Cherokee chiefs to assemble and organize, the treaty commissioners were finally able to open the meetings with an address on July 28. Jackson, speaking for the commissioners, asserted that the "first Object" of the treaty was to arrange an exchange of eastern lands for lands allotted to Cherokees now in Arkansas or soon to move there. He promised assistance to those who removed and fee simple reservations to those who wished to remain and become citizens. Annui-

ties, he suggested, should be divided between the Arkansas and Eastern Cherokees.

The commissioners' proposals were supported by the Arkansas delegates and a few eastern chiefs openly committed to removal, but most Eastern Cherokee leaders resisted. When the commissioners badgered them to include the Arkansas delegates in their council (AJ, Joseph McMinn, and David Meriwether to Charles Hicks, July 2), the national committee replied (Richard Brown and Thomas Wilson to AJ, McMinn, and Meriwether, July 3) in words judged too "insolent" for inclusion in the official minutes of the negotiation. Hoping to push the negotiations forward, the commissioners again assembled the chiefs and warriors on July 4, at which time the Eastern Cherokees responded with the address below that they had prepared on July 2.

From Eastern Cherokees

Cherokee Agency July 2nd 1817

Friends & Brothers We have now convened in a general Council of all the principal chiefs and head men of this nation to deliberate on your talk to us.[1] you give us to understand that you are appointed by the President of the United States to meet the Chiefs of this nation and the chiefs and head men of the Cherokees now residing on the Arkansas. We hear with Sincere Gratitude and pleasure with respect to the frienship of our Father the President of the United States which he has expressed towards us through his commissioners. It is well known to our Father the President of the United States, that it always have been our universal desire to meet and promote the views of the General Government so far as is consistent with Justice and good reason.

Friends & Brothers You say about nine years ago a Deputation from our nation duly authorised were sent on to see our Father Mr. Jefferson to transact the important concerns of our nation. We acknowledge they were sent, But we can assure the Honorable Commissioners that they were not authorised to transact any business as respects the division of the nation. It was merely to take leave of our Father the President Mr. Jefferson who was about to retire to a private life which being communicated through Col. Meigs our Agent to the Chiefs that our Father the President of the U. S. had invited his red children the Cherokees to visit him previous to his retiring from a publick life that of a division was proposed by a few chiefs of the lower part of the nation, Nor was it Known to the nation untill a few days before the delegation started to the city of washington that such were the intentions of the lower Delegates, who were sent from the River or lower Towns. The delegates from the upper Towns knew nothing of the designs of the Delegates from the lower Towns untill they arrived at the City of Washington.

Friends & Brothers. As soon as the idea became doubtful to the Chiefs and head men of our nation who were friendly disposed towards their country. We then appointed two other delegates in addition to those who were first chosen in order to frustrate the designs of that part of the delegation who would attempt to do any thing that would be in any wise injurious to the nation in general. But unfortunately when the delegation arrived at the City of Washington City the two delegates in whom the faith and confidence of the nation were placed were rejected and were not admitted to a hearing & in consequence of their not being allowed their voice, the first chosen delegates were divided when the subject of Division took place.[2]

Friends & Brothers We feel assured that our father the president will not compell us into measures so diametrically against the Will and Interest of a large majority of our nation. A part of those very men who were on at the City of Washington, who made the proposals for an Exchange of lands, have in a general Council held at Oostenally in april 1810 signed a talk that was sent to our agent with instructions to communicate it to the Secretary of War insomuch that the Secretary of War might know the resolutions we had made with a determination not to dispose of any part of our country. As it will more fully appear from the tenure of the letter[3]

Brothers We Wish to remain on our lands & hold it fast. we appeal to our Father the President of the United States to do us Justic[e] We look to him for protection in the hour of distress, we are now distressed with the alternative proposal, to remove from this Country to the Arkansas or stay and becom[e] Citizens of the United States. We are not yet civilized enough to become citizens of the united States nor do we wish to be compelled to move to a country so much against our inclinations and Will. Where we would in the course of a few years return into the same Savage State of life that we were in before the U. S. Our white brothers extended their fostering hand towards us and brought us out of a savage state into a state Similar to theirs

Brothers you tell us to speak freely and make our choice. Our choice is to remain on our lands and follow the pursuits of agriculture & Civilization as all the Presidents our Fathers have recommended & advised us to do. and we hope by the benevolent societies of our white brothers to the north that in the course of time, if we should be allowed to keep our country that our White Brothers will not blush to own us as Brothers.

Brothers. The Cherokees are near as free as the breeze which fans the Shade. We are not yet prepared to adapt ourselves to the laws of the united States, We as yet have but few laws and agreeable to the advice of our former father Mr. Jefferson. we ought not to have many only those which will be Suitable to our Situation. if we accede to your propositions loaded with a burthen of laws which we do not understand we would have eventually to surrender the little, which your proposals offer us. we therefore request that you will press this subject no further at present. but Suffer us to remain in peaceable possession of this our country presented to us by our Great father the Good Spirit from the Creation for our inheritance and Suffer us to keep it for the Sake of the doner.

Brothers. The emigration of a small part of our people to the Arkansas were unauthorized by the chiefs and head men of this nation We have always wished them to remain in their native country.

This we acknowledge to be the week and feeble defense, for our beloved country.

his
Richd. X Brown Prest.
mark
Cabbin Smith X
Kelachuly X
Roman Nose X
X Sleeping X Rabbit
Geo. Saunders X
Currohe Dick X
Jno. X Walker
James Brown
George Lowry
Walter Adair
Richd Taylor
Richd. Riley
By Order of the National Committee
Thos. Wilson Clk

---

their
Toochalar X
marks
Glass X
Chickasawtihee X
Duck X
the big halfbreed X
Sour mush X
the Boot X
the Bark X
the Rabbit X
Tee ahstiskee X
Beaver carrier X

---

by the Principle Chiefs
Ch. Hicks
Whiteman Killer X
John X Watts
John X McIntosh

Oowatachuyota X
Yeooyokee X
Bone Cracker X
Jno. Butler X
Chilioa Mn. town X
Oo-ne-yohetta X
Tesquei X
Chillaugatehee X
Dreadfull Water X
Esaya X
Jno. Ratliff X
Kahchetowy X
John Mn. town X
Pheasant X
Chenowee X
Kunsceilooya X

Tunnatahee X
Echyula X
Katehee X
Bridgemaker X
Doct. Kilakee X
Little Nettle Carrier X
Kulsuttehee X
Two Killer X
John X
Te Kunequatosky X
Five Killer X
Bushy head X
Oowawasety X
Tekenwahyeecaty X
Eight Killer X

Geo Harlin
Thomas X Foreman
Going X Snake
Davis X son
Thos. X Saunders
Oonola X
Kee Kea X
Big rattling X Gourd
Woman X Killer
Jno. Doherty X
Jas. Downing X
Oo le nowae X

LS and Copy, DLC (23); Copy, DNA-RG 46 (5-0905). Published in *ASP, Indian Affairs*, 2:142–43. Addressed to Cherokee commissioners, Jackson, Joseph McMinn, and David Meriwether. All seventy-two signers were Cherokee chiefs and warriors; the first twelve constituted the Cherokee national committee. The national committee and about one-third of the other chiefs ultimately signed the treaty on July 8.

1. See AJ, McMinn, and Meriwether to Cherokees, June 28.

2. The Cherokees were referring to the delegates appointed by councils at Broomstown in September and Hiwassee in November 1808. The original delegation consisted of Major Ridge, John Walker, John McIntosh (Quotaquskee), Tochelar, Skiuka, and The Seed, to which were added John Rodgers and Thomas Wilson.

3. See Charles Hicks et al. to Return J. Meigs, April 11, 1810 (DLC-4).

The commissioners, "deeming that their address had been either misunderstood, or a misunderstanding imposed upon the Chiefs by a few designing men," responded to the Eastern Cherokees' appeal above by interrogating the chiefs on its meaning. Although the commissioners cannily began by questioning two chiefs committed to emigration, who asserted that they had signed the document without understanding it, other chiefs respectfully denied that their answer contradicted President Jefferson and insisted that the tribe had never agreed to a division of their nation. The commissioners then offered a talk, summarizing the terms of their opening address, stating that "the promise of the President to the arkansaw, must be full filled," and recommending "a friendly intercourse" with the Arkansas Cherokees regarding the division of land (AJ, McMinn, and Meriwether to Cherokees, July 4). Afterwards some of the Cherokees indicated a willingness to reconsider, and the meeting adjourned, pending their reply. Still the chiefs delayed, remaining in council on July 5. On July 6, the commissioners tried to speed the process by sending them "a rough draft of their final terms" and summoning them to meet the next morning. At that time the Cherokees again reported themselves in council, but on the evening of July 7 they capitulated and on July 8 signed a treaty that embodied the commissioners' proposals (see Minutes of Cherokee negotiations, June 20–July 8).

The document below was apparently prepared in response to the Eastern Cherokees' reply (above), perhaps to accompany the rough draft of treaty terms sent on July 6. Although no reference to the address appears in the minutes of negotiations, the ideas, whether formally delivered as a speech or expressed in informal conversations with the attending chiefs, surely influenced the Cherokees' decision to sign a treaty.

To Eastern Cherokees

[cJuly 6, 1817]

Friends & Brothers We met you the other day in full council: Before we broke up, you told us you were desirous to do justice to your brothers on the Arkansas: We adjourned to let the chiefs of this nation, and the delegation from the Arkansas, whom you had promised to invite to your councils, arrange the business in a just & friendly manner. We told you then, that that was the way you ought to do: that was the road to friendship; but if you could not do it, your father the President, as the friend of both parties, must arrange it, & we were bound, and would carry his promise into compleat effect.

F. & B. We have been told that threats have been made, and even the deputy from the Arkansas (Capt. Rodgers) when in council with you had been threatened & insulted; that other insults have been offered; and even (as we are told) Capt. Chisholm was threatned while sitting with the U.S. Commissioners. Let such conduct cease; for woe be to that man, that again attempts such conduct, and wo to this nation if they permit blood to flow on this occasion when every man is asked to speak freely & do as he chooses. Let it be remembered, that your father, the President, who never lies, has said to you, the fool has his choice as well as the wise; the poor is as free as the rich.

F. & B. When we talk with you & your chiefs in council & out of council, they say your brothers on the Arkansas shall have justice, that they are your friends, your people & your brothers; but we find that when they make the most just propositions, it is not agreed to by your council. We know they are generous; we have seen them converse with, & explain to Major Hicks & Mr. [Walter] Adair,[1] two members of your committee, chosen, as we understand, by your nation to meet & confer with the Arkansas delegation; when we told them we would, and did send to your council the following propositions, which we know are fair to both parties, & liberal from the United States. They are these.

(See the propositions, herewith, marked)[2]

F. & B. Can any person of this nation say that these terms do not hold out justice, peace & good will to all; who can object to it; who does object to it! none except those who have become wealthy; who have seated themselves on public roads & at ferries. Do those ferries benefit the nation at large, or only individuals? The answer is individuals only. Is then the interest of all your poor, your national existence, and the name of the Cherokees to be drowned in the interest of those few individuals, who are offered the choice to remain where they now are, or if they do not choose to do that, to pay them a fair price for their improvements, or give them other improvements of equal value, in bounds left for this part of the nation, and for which your father the P. has agreed to pay. Here is justice offered to those few who are interested—We ask then, is the justice due to your brothers on the Arkansas, which you have acknowledged & promised, and the best interests of the whole nation to be sacraficed to the interests of a few, who, we are told, will neither take reservations where they live, nor exchange their lands for others. They say they cannot leave their homes, nor will they come under the laws of the United States. Is this such a talk you ought to give to your father the President of the United States; who, for twenty four years, has been using his best endeavors to promote your interests, and to bring you into a state of civilization, and full membership with his own great family. We hope you will give to every part of the President's talk, full consideration,[3] and we wish you to agree with your brothers on the Arkansas, what part of the lands you will surrender to them. If you cannot agree, we will on tomorrow, in full council, commence the negotiation with the Arkansas Chiefs & deputies, to which you are all invited: nothing has been done in secret; nothing will be done in secret; all things will be done in open council.

Copy in James M. Glassell's hand, DLC (59, 5-0901).

1. Adair (1783–1835) was the half-Cherokee son of the Scots trader John Adair.

2. Not found.

3. See AJ, Joseph McMinn, and David Meriwether to Cherokees, June 28. In the twenty-four year reference, Jackson and the other commissioners were probably alluding to the establishment of the Cherokee agency in 1792.

To George Graham

Cherokee agency July 9th. 1817

Sir

Since my arival at this place sundry application have been made to me by the wives of those indians who fell in the Battle of the horse shoe in the creek war. I had instructions from the goverment, to call, all Indians within the then 7th. Military District, into the service of the u states, and when so called they should be entitled to the same pay and emoluments as any other troops ordered into the service of the u states.[1]

I did believe they were to be considered in every respect on the same footing with the militia and entitled to every benefit that ⟨would⟩ might be secured to them by law. I made this promise believing it was Just. I hope it will be complied with and directions given to Colo. Meiggs to procure the proper evidence of the number killed in Battle or who have died with wounds, that they may be placed in the same situation of the wives & children of our soldiers who have fell in Battle,[2] they warriors are going to arkansaw, it will attach them to us, it will continue their friendship—I am respectfully yr mo. ob. serv.

Andrew Jackson

ALS, DNA-RG 107 (M221-74); Copies, DNA-RG 99 (5-0914), DNA-RG 217 (mAJs).

1. On March 27, 1814, Jackson broke the power of the hostile Creek Indians by destroying their stronghold at the Horseshoe Bend of the Tallapoosa River in what is now Tallapoosa County, Alabama. Jackson reported eighteen killed and thirty-six wounded among his Cherokee allies at that battle.

2. On August 12, Graham directed Return J. Meigs to certify the names of Cherokee widows eligible for pensions (DNA-RG 75, M15-4).

To John Coffee

July 13th. 1817

Dr. Sir

I reached here this morning to breakfast with a hope to find you at home, in this I was disappointed, but hearing from Mrs. Coffee, that you intend visitting Nashville before you return to your Survaying District, I flatter myself with the pleasure of seeing you shortly.[1]

We were detained in council with the cherokees 17 days, before we concluded a treaty, which was signed on the 8th. instant, we obtained a cession of the lands adjoining Georgia, and west to the chatehouchie river &c &c, and a small part north of the Tennessee, a little more in all, than two millions—This of itself would be unimportant, was it not for the principle Established by the treaty, which will gives us the whole country in less than two years—a few of its provisions, are first that the census is to be taken next June by commissioners appointed by the u states accompanied by a commission, from the cherokees East of the M. and one from those settled on the arkansaw, Those on the arkansaw, those who are going there, and those who when the enumeration is taken, declare their intention of removing there, are to be considered as the numbers on the arkansaw, and the cherokee nation has agreed to cede to the u. states, the proportion of land agreable to their numbers, compared with the whole number of the nation, and the whole quantity of land owned by the cherokees East of the M. and the u states bind themselves to convay to the cherokees on the arkansaw acre for acre so to be ceded, including the quantity ceded by the nation by the late treaty—This at once secures half the whole country, as at least half is there & enrolled to go there—in short Sir my opinion is that but few will remain, none except those prepared for agricultural persuits, civil life, & a goverment of laws, There are but few in comparrison prepared for this, or at least will make a choice of a goverment of laws

We have stipulated, to furnish all with transportation & provisions who choose to go, we have further stipulated to give every poor man in the nation who chooses to go, a rifle gun, amunition a blanket, and a brass Kettle or in lieu of the latter a Beaver trap—This is to be in full of their improvements, and will induce hundreds to go—Those who stay & choose to become under the laws of the u states, will be laid off for Each head of family 640 acres to include his improvement in the center—To those who remove & have improvements that add real Vallue to the land, the Possessor is to receve the Vallue of his improvement to be assessed by a commissioner of the u states—from the features here stated you will Easily discover, the permanant happiness of the cherokee nation, and those who wish to become citizens of the u states laid and also, the Extinguishment of the name of the cherokee nation East of the M. and its perpetuation on the arkansaw, in short the happiness of the cherokees, and the connection of the state of Georgia & the state of Tennessee, at a short day, and the country that has long been, & now is a harbour of theeifs, who has long prayed upon the honest industry of all, become a peacefull abode for the honest citizen protected by our laws—This is the outlines of what we have done, & rest assured it was not done without considerable labour and adress—We had to counteract the machinations of a corrupt & designing few, wielded by the councils of Colo. Gideon Morgan [Jr.], under the rose, who at one time produced an answer to us signed by seventy two of their principl chiefs, with the intention of giving us that answer as the answer of the whole nation, and breaking up as they had done the year before without doing any thing[2]—we believing that this was not the Sentiments of the nation but a trick under the management of Morgan & others—Took it up in full council had it read & explained, to them, when we called on each chief one by one unroobed, the rascally imposition, and before we rose they asked permission to reconsider their answer[3]—This lead to the treaty which is signed by all in open council we had to take stronger ground than was taken by the commissioners last year, and convince them we intended to keep it—or we would have effected nothing—a farther explanation when we meet—expecting to see you shortly & before you go out, I shall not touch any other subject—It is raining, I do not expect you to day, I am anxious to be at home for sundry reasons, therefore encounter the inclement day—with my best wishes adieu—

Andrew Jackson

ALS, THi (5-0928). Published in Bassett, 2:307–308.

1. Coffee's Sugar Tree plantation lay on the east fork of Stones River about two miles above Jefferson in Rutherford County.

2. See above, Eastern Cherokees to AJ, Joseph McMinn, and David Meriwether, July 2. Morgan (1788–1851), a white married to a part-Cherokee granddaughter of John Sevier, had organized and commanded the regiment of Cherokee warriors at Horseshoe Bend.

3. See the Record of the chiefs' responses to individual interrogations, [July 4], DLC (4); see also Minutes of Cherokee negotiations, June 20–July 8. For the commissioners' further explanation, see AJ, McMinn, and Meriwether to Cherokees, July 4.

To George Graham

Head Quarters
Division of the South
Nashville 22d July 1817

Sir

on my return from Hiwassee to this place, I had the honor to receive your note of the 6th. of June enclosing a copy of a letter of the same date, to the Marshal, for the District of West Tennessee.[1]

From the various treaties, and Acts of Congress regulating intercourse with the Indians, I clearly understand that the United States have stipulated to prevent intrusions, by its Citizens ⟨on⟩ or trespasses by driving their stock on their lands.[2] Experience has proven that it is useless to remove themselves or stock therefrom, without prosecution for the infraction of the law: The experiment made last fall shewed the inutility of the bare⟨ly⟩ destruction of improvements, & removal of stock: The Intruders returned within a few days after the soldiers had retired, drove back their stock & recommenced their plan of robbery. From the tenor of the treaties & acts of Congress, I have always believed that, where cattle were found Trespassing on the Indian lands, and this trespass by the owner driving his stock thereon, the cattle were liable, & ought to be seized, (damage feasant)[3] delivered over to the civil authority, and made answerable for the damage: It is the only way to put an end to the villianies practised within the Indian bounderies. Under these impressions I ordered Capt. [Robert] Houston to seize & deliver all intruders ⟨into the hands of⟩ over to the Civil Authority, & their stock into the hands of the Marshal, and if he refused to receive them to note it before evidence and let them go:[4] The Marshal in one instance received, and being perishable property, sold them at public sale; this, on legal principles, I have no doubt can be justified, but with his duty I have nothing to do: my orders still are, to take all persons and stock, found trespassing on the Indian Territory, and deliver them over to the civil authority for prosecution. If the military is not aided by the civil authority, in executing the laws and treaties, it will be useless to harrass the former in pursuit of trespassers & their stock; all of the troops on the Military peace establishment (without horsemen) could not carry into effect the treaties with the Cherokees & prevent intrusions; the late procedure has had more beneficial effects than all other measures that had been previously adopted: and I am convinced that none else will have the desired effect.

On this subject I shall expect your full instructions, and until I receive them shall continue to pursue the mode previously adopted.[5] I am Sir Very Respy. Yo. Mo. Obt. St.

Andrew Jackson
Major Genl Comdg
D. of the South

LS in James M. Glassell's hand, DNA-RG 107 (M221-74); Copy, DNA-RG 46 (5-0935). Published in Bassett, 2:308–309.

1. See Graham to AJ, enclosing Graham to John Childress, both June 6. Childress (d. 1819) reported to Graham, May 6, that on April 10 he had sold some seized stock delivered to him under Jackson's orders, but that he had determined not to receive such property in the future (DNA-RG 107, M221-73). Graham's reply supported Childress's position. Subsequently, when one of the intruders petitioned Congress in 1820 asking compensation for the cattle seized, the House Committee of Claims concluded that Jackson had exceeded his orders and should be "personally and individually responsible for any invasion of private rights, committed without authority." Thus, the committee ruled, the government had no responsibility to compensate (see *HRRep* 14, 16th Cong., 2nd sess., Serial 57).

2. For the applicable laws, see 2 *U.S. Statutes at Large* 139–46, 445–46. The July 8 Cherokee treaty bound the United States to prevent intrusion on the ceded Cherokee lands, pending ratification.

3. Doing damage or injury, spoken of cattle straying upon another's land.

4. See Robert Butler to Robert Houston, October 22, 1816. Houston (d. 1818), an older brother of Samuel Houston, was in the 8th Infantry.

5. On August 14 Graham replied that the federal courts lacked jurisdiction to seize stock, but he authorized Jackson to take such action if it were "sanctioned" by the Tennessee courts.

To James McMillan Glassell

Hermitage July 24th. 1817

Dr. Glassell

On yesterday, Mr J. Jackson obtained a promise from me, to detain the publication of my letter untill he could, write Genl Adair and Enclose him a copy—as we rode up, and on reflection, that there would be a great impropriety, in Mr Jackson doing this, as base minds are always apt to put the worts construction on the most magnanimous act; and Adair might construe it, as begging an apology through our friend, I have his writen absolvement—and enclosed it to Doctor Bronaugh[1]—I thought it my duty as soon as I heard Genl Adair was in town to notify him, that I was preparing a letter for him, and request that he would not leave Town untill he recd. it, he precipitated himself off—after receiving this information, of course, I am entitled, when I think proper to publish the letter, and will give this fact to the world with it the ⟨*letter*⟩—I have to request that you will ⟨it⟩ copy & correct the letter,[2] transposing any of the sentences, that may be necessary, giving the facts clear & distinct—and on that point, which again asks him the question why! if he had the 400 or 500 arms borrowed as he has alledged from a corps of exempts,[3] he did not place them in the hands of Davises Detachment ⟨retained⟩, or report⟨ed⟩, them to me ⟨retained⟩, and point out his unmilitary conduct in this particularly clearly & have it stronly commented on—I have stated, that by this unmilitary act, which he cannot Justify the country might have been lost &c, I wish you to place this when you copy it in the strongest point of view, & the strongest language—I wish you with the Doctor to give it your best consideration, & cloath it with your best genius, stating the facts, clearly, so that they will be clearly understood—and placing the referrences, & spreading them, where they most, properly apply—I shall expect you up with the Doctor on tomorrow, with the letter. If you cannot finish it before you come up, it can be done here—

Please send me some wafers by Dunwoody who will hand you this[4] accept assurances of my respect

Andrew Jackson

ALS, NjMoHP (5-0942). Published in *Magazine of American History,* 16(1886):399.

1. Jackson was referring to the publication of his letter of July 23 to John Adair. Neither Jackson's letter to James C. Bronaugh nor James Jackson's statement has been found.

2. The surviving copy of AJ to Adair, July 23, is in the hand of Anthony Palmer, a clerk in the office of the Southern Division adjutant general, not Glassell's.

3. See Adair to AJ, March 20, 1815.

4. Dinwiddie (c1774–c1844–46), a slave purchased by Jackson in 1806, served primarily as his horse trainer.

From Arthur Peronneau Hayne

Private Milledgeville 5th. August 1817

My Dear General,

I reached this place on the morning of the 4th. instt. about three hours before the commencement of the Sails, when I had the pleasure to receive from Mr. Js. Jackson yr kind & affectionate letter of the 24th. ultimo.[1] How can I sufficiently thank you for yr kind & affectionate conduct towards me, but how utterly incapable am I to thank Mrs. Jackson & yourself for yr parental conduct towards my beloved Wife & child. Such conduct is deeply engraven on my mind & neither time or distance or change of circumstances can make any impression on it. It affords me great pleasure to hear that yr health is better & that you have some thoughts of taking a trip to the Harodsburgh Springs.[2]

The successful termination of yr Cherokee mission, has given universal satisfaction & you will have the pleasure of daily seeing that your exertions in behalf of the South Western Country, will make it a great & growing Quarter of the American Community.

I am happy to tell you that we have succeeded in acquiring an accurate Knowledge of all the sections of good Lands to be sold at the present sales. Two Townships will I think cover all the good Lands. Six Townships have already been exposed for sale, & not more than three or four of the Qr. sections disposed of. Mr. Leake is with us, but can be of no service to us, as our information is much more correct than his & my wish to have his notes, was thro' a belief that they would cost but a trifle & might be the means of making surely doubly sure.[3]

To tell you with any degree of certainty, what our prospects are, is at present impossible, but I am sanguine that it will terminate in a handsome little speculation. The Bibbites I hear talk very largely, even go so far as to say that they will go as high as $100 for the Lands in the Big Bend & in the opposite Bluff where they contemplate to have their Town.[4] If they are to get these Lands they shall pay for them. My determination is to get Lands of the first quality—regarding the quality rather than the price, yet I do not feel disposed to give more for Lands than what they are actually worth. A set of men from Georgia who have explored the Lands in question, have alarmed the original settlers by thus talking largely, & but few of the men at present settled in that Country are or will be present at the sales & many others who are not so easily alarmed & who would have been present have not horses capable of bringg. them so far, such has been the starved condition of the Country. On a view of the whole subject I am disposed to believe that the Lands of the first quality will sell for their value. I wish you could be possessed of the Four sections mentioned in my letter by Mr. Owens, it would form a most desirable establishment for yr old age.[5] I should greatly prefer them to any other four sections to be sold. I shall hope to be with you early in Septr. Pray remember me most affectionately to Mrs. J. & Andrew. and believe me to be, in great haste, yr most affectionate & obliged friend & humble servant.

A. P. Hayne

ALS, DLC (23).

1. Not found.

2. The Harrodsburg Springs are near the source of the Salt River in Kentucky.

3. Probably John M. Leake (c1771–1830), a Madison County, Mississippi Territory, surveyor in 1816 and Alabama state representative, 1820–23. On July 19 Hayne had written Jackson of his arrangements to purchase from Leake, then in Nashville, notes regarding land available at the Milledgeville sale.

4. Dr. William Wyatt Bibb (1781–1820), appointed provisionally as first territorial governor of Alabama, and his brother Thomas (1784–1839), were investors at the Milledgeville and later Huntsville land sales. Newspapers reported that a 170 acre fraction on the Big Bend of the Alabama sold for $70 per acre while a projected townsite on Ten Mile Bluff opposite went for $50 per acre. The average price of all sold was $5.35 per acre. Thomas Bibb and his associates joined with Nashville investors, including Hayne and James Jackson, to found the town of Alabama at the Ten Mile Bluff in Montgomery County, near what is now Montgomery.

5. See Hayne to AJ, July 19. The letter carrier was probably William Purnell Owen

(c1792–1822), who served as a Tennessee ranger under Jackson during the Creek and Gulf campaigns and as a Creek cession surveyor.

To John Coffee

Nashville August 12th. 1817.

Dr. Sir

On the 10th. instant yours of the 5th was handed me by Mr [Lemuel] Donelson, who is to call on me to day and receive my answer.[1]

On the subject of information of proper *sites* for Towns on the T. river, for the information of the President of the u states, you can recommend the points on the north & south side of the T. river, where the military road X the same, this is the point at which, I have recommended a military Depo. to be Established—and on both sides are good sites for a Town—on the north, the site is about half a mile from the river, at the head of navigation up cypress creek. I can say nothing on the subject of the site at the cotton ginn port—never having explored it, with an eye to that object, but your own knowledge will be competant to afford the President information of this point—Double heads place on the north side, the head of the shoals, or Meltons Bluff on the south, with the site below the mouth of Flint on the south side are the only places, that I could suppose would be proper sites for Towns, and some of those only, that ever can be expected to grow into any beneficial size[2]—so soon as the lands are sold, the Legislative authority will have the right to lay off counties, Establish Towns, &c &c—no place therefore either on, or, above the shoals, ever can become of any great importance, unless fixed upon as the seat for county Towns—below the shoals it will be differrent—at the crossing of the military road where I have recommended the Establishment of a military Deposit—I have but little doubt, will become one of the largest towns in the western country—here will capital concentrate itself—and it will become the *Nashville* of the Tennessee The others will be the *Cairo*.

you will please to observe that the above remarks are made, that, you, if you please may make an extract of them, and forward it to the president—What I have stated is my candid opinion but few will invest money in Town lotts, untill the site is recognised by a legislative act—witness *Cairo* on cumberland, & *Clarksville*—[3]

The contents of your letter, will be, as you have requested.

I have waited for two weeks to hear from Genl Adair in answer to my letter—as yet I have heard nothing—he passed through Nashville, he arived late in the Evening, in the morning, hearing he had arived, I requested Doctor Brunaugh, to wait upon & inform him I was preparing an answer to him, to his letter to the Editors of the Reporters, with a request that he would wait a few hours for it to be copied, he replied his business was so pressing he could not stay—he immediately left Town, I sent the letter by mail, as yet I have heard nothing from him, and unless I do to day, I shall give it to the publick, in the next Clarion, you will find it pretty tough—[4]

In my letter to him, I have stated Major Butlers statement to me, that no arms were obtained from the exempt corps, to his knowledg untill after the Battle of the 8th. of January & that this corps reported to him daily. I have expected the Major here for some days, hearing by Mr Donelson that he has embarked again in survaying, I have wrote him by Mr Donelson, requesting him to send me his statement in writing, least it may be wanted—If Major Butler is not coming in shortly will you obtain it for me & send it by a safe hand, or bring it when you come in—[5]

all friends are well, [Thomas] Claibourne elected by a majority of nearly 1700 votes with my best wishes adieu—[6]

Andrew Jackson

ALS, THi (5-0964). Published in Bassett, 2:321–22 (extract).

1. Letter not found.

2. In June Coffee had been directed to propose town sites for the area he was surveying (see *TPUS,* 6:794–95). Jackson recommended what are now the approximate locations of Tuscumbia and Florence, Alabama, near which he later purchased land. Doubleheads town lay west of Bluewater Creek on the north Bank of the Tennessee River.

3. Cairo in Sumner County was the site of a land speculation by James Winchester and William Cage in 1799 with the first lots sold in 1800. The town was incorporated by the Tennessee legislature in 1815. The site of Clarksville was obtained in a 1784 land grant, and the town was officially established by the General Assembly of North Carolina in late 1785.

4. Jackson's letter to John Adair, July 23, in answer to Adair's May 6 letter to the editors of the Lexington *Kentucky Reporter,* appeared in the *Nashville Clarion,* August 19.

5. See AJ to Thomas L. Butler, August 12; and Butler to AJ, [August]. Butler was one of Coffee's deputy surveyors.

6. In balloting held August 7 and 8, Claiborne (1780–1856) defeated Newton Cannon and Robert Weakley in the contest for representative of Tennessee's Fifth Congressional District.

The author of the letter below has not been identified with certainty. The endorsement of Jackson's aide, James M. Glassell, "Annonymous," indicates that Jackson himself may not have known his correspondent. William G. Terrell (1829–1900), who had access to the Jackson papers in the late nineteenth century, asserted in "Quarrel with General Scott," Cincinnati Commercial, *January 8, 1880, that the letter was "believed to have been written by Samuel Swartwout" (1783–1856), whom Jackson knew from the Burr trial and later appointed as collector of the port of New York. The handwriting of the letter, however, offers no conclusive evidence, and the basis for Terrell's assertion is unknown.*

The anonymous letter instigated a dispute between Jackson and Winfield Scott (1786–1866), the New-York-based commander of the 1st and 3rd Military Departments. On receipt of the letter, Jackson wrote Scott on September 8, asking him as "a man of honor" about his criticism of the April

22 Division Order. Scott's reply of October 4 (below) did not satisfy Jackson, setting off an additional exchange between them on December 3 (also below) and on January 2, 1818.

Evading the war department regulation of February 21, 1818, forbidding "publications relative to transactions between officers of a private and personal nature," both Jackson and Scott subsequently circulated manuscript copies of their correspondence to those they hoped would support their positions. Ultimately Scott's version was published as a pamphlet, Correspondence between Major General Jackson, and Brevet Major General Scott, on the Subject of an Order, Bearing Date the 22d April, 1817; Published by the former, to the Troops of His Division, and Printed about the Same Time, in Most of the Public Papers *([Richmond], 1819). For further discussion of the dispute, see AJ to William B. Lewis, January 30, 1819, below.*

From Unknown

[August 14, 1817]

Your late order has been the subject of much private and some public remark. The War office gentry and their adherents, pensioners, and expectants have all been busy: but no one (of sufficient mark for your notice) more than Major Gen. Scott who I am credibly informed goes so far as to call the order in question an act of mutiny. In this district he is the organ of Government insinuations and the supposed author of the paper enclosed—which however (the better to cover him) was not published untill after he had left this city for the lakes.[1] Be on your guard—as they have placed spies upon Brown here; so it is probable you are not without them. The Eastern Federalists having now all become Good republicans & pledged to the support of the president, as he to them, Government can now do well without the aid of Tennessee &c. &c. a word to the wise is enough. The enclosed is taken from the Columbian a paper of much Circulation in this state. New York.

AL, T (5-0982); Copies, THi (5-0983), NWM (mAJs). Published in *Correspondence between Major General Jackson, and Brevet Major General Scott,* p. 6. Postmarked, New York, August 14, and endorsed as received September 3.

1. The enclosed article was A Querist, "General Jackson's Doctrines of Obedience," *New-York Columbian,* August 2, which suggested that Jackson's position regarding the chain of command could be used to save the military position of a favored subordinate "in defiance of Government itself."

To James Monroe

Nashville 2d. Sept. 1817

Dr. Sir

Yours of the 4th. Ult was received on yesterday, and I shall await the further communication, referred to, with patience.[1]

Permit me to assure you that I will continue to support the Government in all respects where the orders of the War Dept. do not, in my opinion, go to infringe all law and strike at the very root of subordination & the discipline of the Army. Should it, ultimately, be found that my opinion of subordination & legal authority, as excercised by the Dept. of War, does not coincide with yours, be assured that on my part it will be viewed as an honest differrence of opinion, and in my retirement, will, with that zeal for your welfare and the public good, as heretofore, continue to lend my feeble aid to the administration of the Government under your Presidency.

When your promised communication reaches me I will give it my best attention; in the mean time this subject shall remain, as you have desired, until I have the pleasure, either of seeing or hearing from you. Accept of my best wishes for your health and happiness, and believe me to be with great Respect Yo. Mo. Obt. St.

Andrew Jackson

LS in James M. Glassell's hand, NN (5-1004). Published in Bassett, 2:324–25. Endorsed by Monroe: "Sepr 2 1817 gen Jackson—reply to mine of augt 4—in which he perceives, that I disagreed with him, as to the right of the dept to issue orders, to officers under him, directly."

1. See Monroe to AJ, August 4. For Monroe's detailed response to the April 22 Division Order, see Monroe to AJ, October 5, below.

To James Monroe

Head quarters D. of the South
Nashville Sept 9th 1817

Sir

This moment has been Shewn to me an order from the adjt & Inspector Genl to Major [Charles] Wolstoncraft, a copy of which I enclose you.[1]

I cannot bring myself to believe that such wanton and unmilitary interference with the police of my Divisions is directed by you particularly when I view your request, to let things rest untill I hear from, or have an interview with you,[2] and this too, when persuing the proper rotine of military rule would be more certain and expeditious—and when no necessity exists for departing from it.

On the 21rst. ult. Genl Ripley was directed to order Major Wolstoncraft to the city to settle his accounts, he having requested it, the order has been this day reiterated, and the unmilitary order of the adjt. & Inspector Genl, as being useless returned to him.[3] It is high time for me to be informed whether these subordinate officers of the executive staff will be permitted, Thus to insult my feelings, by attempting to disorganise the whole military system of subordination & which is calculated to bring subordinate officers in to dificulty, for disobedience of orders, for it is certain that Major Wolstoncraft, could not, nay dare not, leave his post, or duty assigned him without the permission of his immediate commanding officer. There never has been an order directed to me that I have not promptly obayed, there never has been an interference with the police of my command similar to the present, that I have n*[ot]* resisted. This I conceived to be a sacred duty I owed to myself, to the service, and safety of my country which has given me room to think all things considered, that this was a wanton attack upon me on the eve of my quitting service, to irritate my feelings, and induce a belief of want of confidence in me. I cannot believe that it has originated from your instructions, but it must be thus presumed by the world, untill you disavow it, because by positive law, the sec of war has no right to Issue an order without your express instructions.[4] Therefore, you can easily conceive, that I must have some anxiety to receive your promised communication. I am Sir with great respect your mo. ob. serv.

Andrew Jackson
Major Genl Comdg
D. of the South—

ALS, DNA-RG 107 (M222-19).

1. See Daniel Parker to Charles Wollstonecraft, August 22, DNA-RG 107 (M222-19). On June 11 Parker had requested that General Eleazar W. Ripley order Wollstonecraft to Washington to settle his accounts. When Ripley sent a copy of Jackson's April 22 order in response, Parker himself ordered Wollstonecraft to Washington, directing the order through Southern Division Adjutant General Robert Butler (see Parker to Secretary of War, October 7, DNA-RG 107, M222-19). Wollstonecraft (1770–1817), a brother of the British writer Mary Wollstonecraft, had come to the United States in 1792. At this time he was an artillery major serving as a quartermaster at New Orleans.

2. See Monroe to AJ, August 4.

3. See Robert Butler to Ripley, August 21; James M. Glassell to Parker, September 9.

4. Jackson was referring to the act establishing the department of war, August 7, 1789 (1 *U.S. Statutes at Large* 49–50). On October 5 Monroe sent Jackson's letter to the war department and requested an explanation. George Graham's response, October 8 (DNA-RG 107, M222-19), denied any disrespect for Jackson. He stated that upon receiving notice of the April 22 order, he had determined that orders would be issued as usual but with particular attention to informing the commanding generals.

From William Carroll

Nashville Sept 11th. 1817

Dr. Sir,

I have this moment received your letter of yesterday: and as Mr. Butler sets out immediately I cannot give so satisfactory an answer as I could wish[1]—Will you permit me to say that I think the contemplated publication ought not to be made by you—You stand on too high an eminence to gratify the Editors of the Kentucky news papers with any thing more on the subject—

If you will furnish the documents you have, and may be able to procure, Majr. [William] White and my self, under your direction, will make such an exposition of the conduct of the officers, throughout the whole campaign, as will silence them and make even their villianous [sublity?] blush—[2]

Yesterday I had an opportunity of seeing the capt of [Thomas] Maples's boat, and procured his certificate, which you will find inclosed[3]—Majr. White has promised to throw all the documents together on the subject of the Kentuckians, with such reflections as they deserve. Should you approve the plan, he will see you and consult on the best ⟨plan⟩ method of making the publication—Should you however, still believe that the publication had best be made by yourself I will be ready at any time, to comply with your request, and make any statement of facts, coming within my own knowledge that may have a bearing on the subject—I have always said that the evidence before the court of Enquiry was of so contradictory a nature, that it was dificult to believe a word of it; and had it not been for the peculiar circumstances of the times, the court would have found much to sencure in the conduct of all the officers concerned on the right bank of the Mississippia—But the war was over, and little could be gained by punishment, and it was extreamely desireable on our part, to enable every individual to return home to his family and friends, without a stain on his character and reputation—hence I say that much was looked over in the investigation by the courts of enquiry—[4]

I conclude with remarking that if you leave the publication to Majr. White and my self it will be done without delay: if on the contrary, you do it yourself, I shall always be ready to serve you—I am respectfully Yr. friend

Wm. Carroll

ALS, DLC (23).

1. Letter not found. The reference is probably to Thomas L. Butler.

2. White (1781–1833), a Gallatin attorney, had served as judge advocate of West Tennessee militia under Jackson in 1813–14. Jackson issued no further publication on the Ken-

tucky militia controversy. A detailed response to John Adair's last letter did, however, appear as an editorial series in the *Nashville Clarion,* December 2, 9, 30.

3. See certificate of Thompson Moss, September 10, DLC (23). Maples had contracted to ship arms from Pittsburgh to New Orleans in late 1814. When the arms did not arrive until after the battle, Jackson had Maples arrested, but he was acquitted by a court-martial. Moss testified that his boat had met the Kentucky troops en route to New Orleans, but they had failed to order him to join them.

4. Carroll had presided over the February 1815 court of enquiry into the causes for the defeat of American forces on the west bank on January 8.

To John Coffee

Meltons Bluff Sept. 28th. 1817.

Dr. Genl

I left this for the military encampment on the 23d. reached there on the 24th. where I met Capt. Young who gives me a favourable report of the whole rout to the lake, and states that an excellant road can be made to Russells settlement[1]—he returned with me to this place—which we reached on the evening of the 26th. when I found three more of my hands taken down in my absence—George, Aron, and Squire I have them up again & all appear on the recovery—Capt Scott, out of danger—Mrs. Wilson Dead, but the family on the mend—Mr & Mrs. Mitchell very ill, and Mrs. Shannon, this morning again taken down—what the Doctor here may do with her the lord only knows—If he & her husband, had taken other advice she would have been well[2]—I hope to leave here on tomorrow (29th) and will be happy to see you on Tuesday or Wednesday next at Mrs. [Catherine Donelson] Hutchings—I am very uneasy about Major [John] Hutchings & will see him as soon as I can—I wish you to speak to Stockley [Donelson] Hutchings and get him to engage the overseer spoken of, and send him to Mrs. Hutchings on Wednesday next Mr [James] Cummins, wishes to go on to Virginia as soon as he can[3]—and he is too low, to Superintend the farm—an active man must be had or our crop cannot be got in, or the hands restored to health, which with attention could be done in a few days—let me see you as I pass and I would be glad you could bring with you the survey of the 3rd. Township & 8th. range—and that including cold water or spring creak[4]—I have but little doubt, but something can be done at the sales—on which subject I wish to see you least I may be compelled to the Eastward, before I have the opportunity of again seeing you. Present me to [Leroy] Pope [John] Brahan & Stockley Hutchings, their ladies & families, I have a wish to see Major [John Williams] Walker on my return If I can[5]—yours respectfully

Andrew Jackson

ALS, THi (5-1023).

1. A settlement of Tennesseeans near the present site of Greensboro, Alabama.

2. Probably Hermitage slaves sent temporarily to Melton's Bluff: George was possibly the slave that Rachel inherited from John Donelson in 1791; Aaron (c1785–1878) was purchased in 1791 and worked as the Hermitage blacksmith; Squire (b. c1799) was born at the Hermitage and served as a slave foreman in the 1840s. The local residents, other than the Mitchells, former residents of Nashville, have not been further identified.

3. Stockley D. Hutchings (d. 1821) was John Hutchings's brother. Cummins, the overseer at Melton's Bluff, was replaced by Richard Massey.

4. Coldwater or Spring Creek, near where Jackson purchased in November 1818 and June 1820, was in Colbert County, Alabama.

5. Brahan (1774–1834) and Pope of Huntsville had served as principal contractors for Jackson's army during the Creek War. Mary Weakley Brahan (1792–1837), a daughter of Robert Weakley, married John Brahan in 1810. Judith Sale Pope (1770–1827) married Leroy in Virginia before their removal to the Mississippi Territory. Elizabeth Atwood Hutchings (c1794–1854) married Stockley in 1816. In June Jackson had recommended Pope's son-in-law Walker (1783–1823; Princeton 1806), who lived near Huntsville, for governor of the Alabama territory in the event of its separation from Mississippi. The governor's post, however, went to William W. Bibb.

From Tochelar and The Glass

Lookout mountain Cherokee Nation
Sept 30th. 1817—

Dear friend and brother I have taken this opportunity to inform you of the intenson of our people respecting our late treaty for an Exchange of Countries—the people who are in opposition to this Exchange have been exerting Ever Since the treaty to prevent our treaty from being ratifide—they have Chosen Seven Deligates to Send on to head quarters to Stop the ratification of our treaty—and the Deligation is now Call'd together to Receive their instructions and it is Said they will Setout in a few Days[1]—they have appointed Charles hicks king of the Nation which he Shall only Command one half after this year[2]—and we the arkinsaw people will Command the other half in the new Country—we are at a great loss as our agent Colo meigs is Set out fifteen Days and we arkinsaw people Did not know that he was going until we heard he was gone[3] we Do not know who is to forward us to Setout as the time is now at hand that we Should be Seting out we are looking for the arkinsaw Delegates Every Day and as the other party has Seven Delegates we Shall take the Same number of Delegates as we Shall Exchange Every foot of land that will Come to our Shair ther is a number of people that will go to the arkinsaw that have Declare'd there minds Since the treaty—there is a number of our people now wanting to move this fall if they ware furnished with Cotes and other thing that you promisd them to move with—

we think it is nessasary for you to rite on for our reception Seven in number—the opposet holds them-Selves a majority and would prevent us if they Can from making use of any of our public funs to acquip our Selfs for our Journy we hope that General Jacson will not let us be Neglected and left two far behind—we have Chosen a young glass and Eli[phalet] M Holt a white man Suitable for our use and to Conduct us on the rods—the sd holt is Exesary to our Exchange being a member of our Country we hope we Shall be Receiv'd as Seven Deligates in number[4]—the opposet party is threatning our lives Daily we live in greate pain

The glass and Tochaler

LS by proxy, DNA-RG 107 (M222-19). Endorsed, "forwarded, to be laid before the President of the u states—A.J," and sent to George Graham, October 17. Tochelar (Toochelar, Toochalah), a Lower Town Cherokee chief, had served as speaker of the nation in 1809 and later as second principal chief, but he was deposed in 1817 for his support of removal. The Glass (Tauquitee, b. c1744), a Lower Town Cherokee chief since the 1770s, had been deposed as a principal chief of the nation in 1808 for favoring removal, but he was restored to his position in 1809. Both chiefs signed the 1816 and 1817 Cherokee treaties.

1. The delegates—Going Snake (1758?–1839), George Harlin, James Brown (1779?–1863), Roman Nose, Richard Taylor (1788–1853), and Richard Riley (c1790–1828)—visited Washington in November and December, meeting with the secretary of war and Congress but failing to block ratification. For their instructions, adopted on September 19, see DNA-RG 75 (M208-7).

2. Hicks replaced Tochelar as second principal chief when the latter was deposed.

3. Return J. Meigs arrived in Washington, October 4, to settle his accounts for payment of the Cherokee spoliation claims.

4. Although Eastern Cherokees protested (see Pathkiller to Meigs, August 6, DNA-RG 75, M208-7) and sent their own delegation partly in response, the July treaty had authorized the visit of a delegation of Arkansas Cherokees to Washington. The Arkansas contigent, increased to seven by the inclusion of eastern chiefs who had stated an intent to relocate, consisted of Tahlonteskee, Tochelar, The Glass, John McLemore, John Speer (1780?–1828), Richard Brown, and John Thompson, accompanied by James Rogers as interpreter and Samuel Houston as guide. They arrived in Washington, February 5, 1818. Neither Young Glass, of either Hiwassee or Running Town and later an Arkansas chief, nor Holt, who had married a Cherokee woman and resided in Running Town, were delegates.

From Edmund Pendleton Gaines

(Duplicate) Head Qrs. Camp Montgomery A. T.
October 1st 1817.

General,

I have the honor to lay before you a letter which I have received from the Chiefs of ten of the Seminnola towns, in reply to my demand for the delivery of the murderers of our Citizens.[1]

By this communication it appears that instead of a compliance, the Chiefs have set up a claim against us for the lives of three Indians, for whom they allege they have not yet taken satisfaction. They charge us with having killed ten of their warriors—and allowing a balance of three to be due them, they consequently admit, that they have killed seven of our Citizens. They acknowledge the murder of a woman (Mrs. Garret) and her two children—but justify the act upon the ground that the Warriors who committed this outrage had lost friends, had entered our Settlements to take satisfaction, found at the house of Garret a kettle belonging to the Indians that had been killed, and therefore "Supposing the murder had been committed by the husband of the woman," killed her and her children.

I am convinced that nothing but the application of force, will be sufficient to ensure a permanent adjustment of this affair. I shall therefore put the First Brigade in motion for Fort Scott as soon as I can possibly obtain transportation, and I trust that I shall at least by the 20th or 25th reach that place.

As soon as I can obtain transport I shall report to you by Express. My heavy supplies will go by water with suitable guards; the principal part of the force however will go by Land; and in any event we shall finish the new road, near one third of which is already completed.[2]

By a letter from Major Twiggs the Commandant of Fort Scott, I learn that he had been warned, some weeks past, by the principal Chief of the Fowl Town (fifteen miles above the Fort, and nearly twenty above the national Boundary), "not to cut another Stick on the East of Flint River," adding that "the land was his, and he was directed by the powers above to protect and defend it, and should do so; and it would be seen that talking could not frighten him." Major Twiggs adds that he had not seen the Chief nor any of his people since he made the above threat, and that the Indians of this town alone had recently stolen and killed an hundred head of cattle in one drove.[3]

I shall confer with the agent upon the subject of punishing and removing out of our limits these disorderly Indians

To put at rest any doubt upon the subject of limits, and to enable us to confine the Indians to their own territory, it is very desirable that the national Boundary should be surveyed and marked from the East bank of the appalachicola river to the Okafonoka Swamp. Should the President be pleased to authorise the work there can be no period more suitable for its execution than the next two months whilst the troops are in that quarter. This part of the line it will be recollected has never been run. Whether it can or cannot be completed without an agent or Commissioner on the part of Spain, is a question about which I know nothing, but which I presume the President could at once determine.

I have understood, I think from Colonel Hawkins, that the Commissioners after completing their observations upon the line at the junction of Flint and Chattahouchie, and at or near the head of the St. Mary's in the Okafonoka Swamp; and ascertaining the Latitude and Longitude of those places, agreed that the intermediate part of the line should be run by one of our Surveyors—and I have recently learned from Major [Thomas] Freeman the Surveyor General, that he was once authorised or requested to complete that part of the line.[4] He is now at or near St. Stephens in this Territory. I have the honor to be very Respectfully yr obt Servant.

Edmund P. Gaines,
Major General by Brevet.
Comm

LS duplicate, DLC (23). Published in Bassett, 2:326 (extract). Endorsed as received at Nashville November 7 and answered November 24. Robert Butler held the letter until November 19, expecting Jackson's immediate return from Huntsville, which was delayed by John Hutchings's illness.

1. See Seminole chiefs to commanding officer at Fort Scott [David E. Twiggs], September 11, and Gaines to Seminoles, May 10, both DLC-23. Regarding the murders, see above, Gaines to AJ, April 2.

2. Gaines's subsequent report of his troops' movements, October 23, was received by Jackson at the same time as this letter. For the proposed new road, see Gaines to AJ, July 10.

3. See Twiggs to Gaines, August 11, DLC (23). Neamathla (E'ne'he'e'math'la) was the Fowltown chief.

4. Gaines was referring to the survey of the United States southern boundary, 1798–1800, by United States commissioner Andrew Ellicott and Spanish commissioners Stephen Minor and William Dunbar. Freeman (d. 1821), United States surveyor of public lands south of Tennessee, had been surveyor for the commission.

From Winfield Scott

Head Qrs, 1st & 3rd Mil. Depts.
New York, Octr. 4th, 1817.

Sir,

I have the honour to acknowledge the receipt of your letter of the 8th ultimo, together with the two papers therein enclosed.[1]

I am not the author of the miserable and unmeaning article copied from "The Columbian," and (not being a reader of that Gazette) should probably never have heard of it, but for the copy you have sent me. And whilst on the subject of *writing* and *publishing*, it may save time, to say, at once, that, with the exception of *the substance* of two articles which appeared in "The Enquirer," last fall, and a journal kept whilst a prisoner in the hands of the enemy, I have not written, nor caused any other to write a single line for any Gazette whatever, since the commencement of the late war.

Conversing with some two or three private gentlemen, about as many times, on the subject of the Division Order, dated at Nashville, April the 22nd, 1817, it is true, that I gave it as my opinion, that that paper was, as it respected the future, mutinous in its character and tendency; and, as it respected the past, a reprimand of the Commander-in-Chief, the President of the U. States; for altho' the latter be not expressly named, it is a principle well understood, that the War Department, without, at least, his *supposed* sanction, cannot give a valid command to an ensign.

I have thus, sir, frankly answered the queries addressed to me, and which were suggested to you by the letter of your anonymous correspondent; but on a question so important as that which you have raised with the War Department, or in other words with the President of the U. States; and in which I find myself incidentally involved, I must take leave to illustrate my meaning a little; in doing which I shall employ almost the precise language which was used on the occasions above alluded to.

Take any three officers. Let A be the common superior, B the intermediate commander & C the common junior. A wishes to make an order which shall affect C. The good of the service, etiquette and courtesy, require, no doubt, that the order should pass thro' B; or, if expedition and the dispersed situation of the parties make it necessary to send the order direct to C (of which necessity A is the judge)—the good of the service, etiquette & courtesy require, with as little doubt, that A notify B thereof, as soon as practicable. Such notice, of itself, has always been held, as sufficient, under the circumstances last stated. But we will suppose that A sends the order direct to C, and neglects to notify B thereof; and such appears to be the precise case alluded to in the order before cited. Has B no redress against this irregularity? He may, unquestionably remonstrate with A, in a respectful manner, and if remonstrance fail, and there be a higher military authority than A, B may appeal to it for redress. Now, in the case under consideration, there existed no such higher authority; the War Department, or in other words, *the President*; being the common superior (A), & the general of division the intermediate commander (B). A private & respectful remonstrance, therefore, appears to have been the only mode of redress which circumstances admitted of. An appeal to the army or the public, before or after such remonstrance, seems to have been a greater irregularity than the measure complained of; to reprobate that measure, publicly, as the Division Order does, was to mount still higher in the scale of indecorum; but when the order goes so far as to prohibit to all officers in the division an obedience to the commands of the President of the U. States, unless received thro' division Head Quarters, it appears to me, that nothing but mutiny & defiance can be understood or intended.

There is another view of this subject which must have escaped you, as I am persuaded there is not a man in America less disposed to shift responsibility from himself, to a weaker party, than yourself. Suppose the War Department, by order of the President, sends instructions direct to the commanding officer, perhaps, a captain, at Natchitoches (a post within your division) to attack the body of Spanish royalists nearest to that frontier. If the Captain obeys, you arrest him; but if in compliance with your prohibition he sets the commands of the President at naught, he would find himself in direct conflict with the highest military authority under the Constitution, and thus would have to maintain against that "fearful odds" the dangerous position laid down in your order. Surely this consequence could not have been foreseen by you when you penned that order.

I must pray you to beleive, sir, that I have expressed my opinions on this great question, without the least hostility to yourself, personally, and without any view of making my court in another quarter, as is insinuated by your anonymous correspondent. I have nothing to fear or hope, from either party. It is not likely that the Executive will be offended at the opinion, that *it* has committed an irregularity in the transmission of one of its orders; and, as to yourself, altho' I cheerfully admit that you are my *superior,*

I deny that you are my *commanding* officer, within the meaning of the 6th. article of the rules & articles of war.[2] Even if I belonged to your division, I should not hesitate to repeat to you all that I have said, at any time, ⟨whenever⟩ on your subject, if a proper occasion offered; and, what is more, I should expect your approbation; as, in my humble judgment, re⟨futation is out of the question⟩futation is impossible.

As you do not adopt the imputations contained in the anonymous letter, a copy of which you enclosed me, I shall not degrade myself by any further notice of it.

I have just shown the article from "The Columbian" to some military gentlemen of this place, from whom I learn, that it was probably intended to be applied to a case which has recently occurred at West Point. The writer is supposed to proceed upon a report (which is nevertheless believed to be erroneous) that Brig. General Swift had orders from the War Department, more than a twelve month since, to remove Captain Patridge from the Military Academy, & that he suppressed those orders, &c. The author is believed to be a young man of the army, & was at the time of publication in this city, but not under my command, & with whom I have never had the smallest intimacy. I forbear to mention his name, because it is only known by conjecture.[3] I have the honour to remain, Sir, With much respect Y most Ob. Servt.

W. Scott.

ALS, DLC (23); Copies, THi (5-1075), NWM (mAJs). Published in 1819 and 1828 newspapers and in Bassett, 2:326–29. Endorsed by James M. Glassell: "Recd. by J.M.G. on the 22d Oct 1817 & delivered by him to Major Genl. Jackson 1st. Decr. 1817 he having been absent until that time, the answer enclosed by J.M.G. to Mr. Thos. R. Mercein (of N. York) on the 5th Decr."

1. See AJ to Scott, September 8, enclosing Unknown to AJ, [August 14], above.

2. Article 6 of the rules and articles for the government of the army (2 *U.S. Statutes at Large* 359–72 at 360) provided that any soldier who behaved "with contempt or disrespect towards his commanding officer" should be punished. Jackson outranked Scott, but Scott was assigned to the Northern Division and thus not under his command.

3. Complaints regarding Alden Partridge's supervision at West Point had led to a court of inquiry, March 15–April 12, 1816. Although the court generally exonerated Partridge, Secretary of War William H. Crawford wrote Joseph G. Swift, September 9, 1816, that the academy superintendent must be either Swift or his second in command William McRee. Neither Scott's informants nor the conjectured author has been established.

From James Monroe

Albemarle near Milton Virga.
Octr 5. 1817.

Dear Sir

I will now communicate to you, without reserve, my sentiments, on a subject of great national importance, in which you are particularly interested. I need not mention that this is a painful office for me to enter on; among the most painful that could have occurrd; for united as we have been on principle, and connected in operations, in which you renderd the most important services to your country, and acquird for yourself an imperishable fame, nothing could be more distressing to me, than that a difference of opinion should have arisen between us, on a point, involving such serious consequences and on which it is my indispensible duty to decide. In performing this duty, my own feelings, will be a sufficient guard, against my saying any thing, to wound yours, intentionally. An honest difference of opinion daily takes place between the best friends, and that, that, which you entertain in this instance, is founded in the most upright motives, I sincerely believe.

In expressing my sentiments on this subject, it is necessary to advert only, to the real point in issue. The causes leading to it are known to us both and need not be here recited. Your order of the 22d. of april makes the issue, by prohibiting obedience to any order from the dept. of war, by the officers of your division, or by any officer who had reported & been assignd to duty in it, which did not pass thro' you its commander.[1] This order involves the naked principle, of the power of the Executive, over the officers of the army, in such cases, for the department of war cannot be separated from the President. It is instituted to convey his orders to the army, & to perform other services under him. The orders of the dept are therefore the orders of the President. To this point therefore, I shall confine my remarks in the first instance. Whether it is expedient to give orders, to an officer, performing service, in a division directly, and not through its commander, in any case, and if in any, under what circumstances, is a different question to which I will next attend.

According to my view of the subject, no officer of the army, can rightfully disobey, an order from the President. By the constitution of the UStates the Executive is a Coordinate branch of the government, and vested with all the Executive power, delegated by the people, to the government. He is also made Commander in chief of the army & navy & of the militia when called into the service of the UStates. By virtue of these powers the President nominates, and, by and with the advice & consent of the Senate, appoints, all the officers of the army & navy, and has power to remove them, when in his judgment, there shall be good cause for it. He has the control of the public force; directs its operations in war & positions in peace; assigns commanders to the divisions, prescribes the extent of their respective commands, & designates the troops they are to command. In short, he is vested with the power, and made responsible, according to the constitution & laws of the UStates, for the wise direction and government of the military & naval force of the nation both in war & peace. Under these circumstances I cannot perceive on what ground an order from the ch. Magistrate, within the limitation stated, can be disobeyd.

If the question is examind on military principles, it appears to me, that all those principles require a short and prompt obedience to the orders of the chief Magistrate. I do not think that any officer of either of our divisions, would disobey an order from its commander, given, directly, in person, or thro' an aid, or in writing, for the reason that it did not pass thro' the immediate commander of the post. I am satisfied that he ought not to disobey it, because on sound military principles, every thing appertaining to the government of the division, under the control of the Executive, emanates from the commander of the district. By the arrangment of the Executive, the commander of a district & division, is commander in chief thereof, and knows no superior within that limit, except the President. The commander of another district & division, tho' of superior rank has nothing to do with him, nor ought his orders to be obeyd. In peace when the force is dispersed, and the corps are cantoned at a distance from each other, as is now the case, greater authority necessarily devolves on the commander of each post, than he would have, if the whole division were assembled together, under the immediate command, of the commander of the division; nevertheless, he is, for all military purposes, supposd to be always present, every where, and his orders, even in the most minute detail, should he think proper to give them, must be obeyd.

Whatever may be said of the right of a commander of a district and division, to command within his district & division, applies with full force to the President as commander in chief of the army. In that character, he is present every where, and no officer, can, in my judgment, rightfully disobey his order, provided it be conveyd to him, thro the dept of war, or other proper channel. In another view, the argument, is still more conclusive. The Executive power of the nation is vested in the President. If any officer of the army, can disobey his order, for the reason assignd, or for any such reason, the government is suspended, and put aside, than which I confidently believe nothing is more remote from your views.

The commander of a district, is, it is true, charged with its defense, & has duties to perform connected with it, which it is highly important that he should execute, in due time; but still he is no further responsible, than for the faithful application of the means committed to him for the purpose, by the Executive. The whole means provided by law, for the defense of the union, are committed to the Executive, who is held responsible, for a proper application and direction thereof, on that great scale. He must therefore be the judge how those means are to be applied, and have full power to apply them, to such objects, and in such quarters, as he may find expedient. He must also be the judge, of the expediency, of augmenting the force in one quarter, and diminishing it, in another, and of transferring officers, from one to another station. Emergencies may occur, requiring prompt agency, for which, in the vast extent of our country, the opportunity might be lost, and the calamity inevitable, if the Executive could not apply the force nearest at hand, but must send the order, circuitously, through the commander of the district.

As to the policy of exercising the power to the full extent of the right, of giving orders, invariably, to officers in any division, without passing them thro' the commander of the division, I am far from advocating it. In general, I think that the practice, should be otherwise, & be deviated from, in cases, of urgency ⟨of⟩ only, of which, the dept. should be the judge. The reasons which you urge, have in this view, great weight,[2] but yet I cannot think, considering the nature & extent of our districts, the whole union being divided into two only, & the remotest parts of each five, or 6,00. miles from the center, the Head Quarters of its commander, the maritime frontier liable to attack by a naval force from the ocean, and the Inland frontier, by savages, combined with foreign powers, with other possible causes of occasional disturbance, at each extreme, & in the intermediate spaces, that it would be safe to adopt it, as an invariable rule. As a general rule, I think that it would be proper, and that in all cases, when departed from, the commander of the district should be promptly advisd of it, and a copy of the order sent to him.

These being my opinions, formed on great consideration, and in conformity to which I must act, I hope to hear from you soon on the subject, and shall be much gratified should you concur with me in them.

I have read with great interest the observations containd in your letters, & particularly in that of the 4th of March last, on several very important subjects. Your report with that of Lt Gadsden respecting the fortifications necessary for the defense of Louisiana, will be duly considerd. Your reasons for promoting the rapid settlement of the alabama country, the establishment of a foundry on the Tennessee river, near the muscle shoals, and for the extinguishment of the title of the chickasaws, on the Eastern bank of the Mississippi, have great weight. The view which you have taken of the Indian title to lands is new but very deserving of attention. The hunter or savage state, requires, a greater extent of territory to sustain it, than is compatible with the progress and just claims of civilized life, and must yield to it. Nothing is more certain, than, if the Indian tribes do not abandon that state, and become civilized, that they will decline, & become extinct. The hunter state, tho maintain'd by warlike spirits, presents but a feeble resistance to the more dense, compact, and powerful population of civilized man. Within our limits, where the Indian title is not extinguished, our title is good, against European powers only, and it is by treaties with the latter, that our limits are formed. It has been customary to purchase the title of the Indian tribes, for a valuable consideration, tho' in general that of each tribe, has been vague & undefined. A compulsory process seems to be necessary, to break their habits, & to civilize them, & there is much cause to believe, that it must be resorted to, ⟨civilize &⟩ to preserve them. On these, and every other subject, mentiond, in your letters, I shall avail myself of the light shed on them by your experience and judgment, on every proper occasion, and I shall always be happy to promote your wishes respecting individuals when circumstances will permit it.

I need not state that it is my earnest desire that you remain in the service of your country. Our affairs are not settled, and nothing is more uncertain than the time, we shall be permitted to enjoy our present tranquility & peace. The Spanish government has injur'd us, & shews no disposition to repair the injury; while, the revolutionary struggle, in the colonies, continues, to which, from a variety of important considerations, we cannot be indifferent. Should we be involved in another war, I have no doubt, that it will decide the fate of our free government, and of the independance of Spanish America. I should therefore much lament your retir'ment. with great respect and esteem I am dear Sir yr very obt servant

James Monroe

ALS, DLC (23); Copies, NN (5-1079, -1087). Published in Bassett, 2:329–32.

1. See above.

2. See above, AJ to Monroe, March 4.

To James Monroe

(Private) Nashville 22nd. of Octbr 1817—

Dear Sir

I have recd your friendly letter of the 27th ult. *and* your letter of the 5th. Instant.[1] They both reached me by this days mail. I have given them as attentive a perusal as my situation would permit, being on the eve of my departure to see my friend and Nephew Major Hutchings, who lies very ill and dispaired of near Huntsville, and has requested me to take to him his little and only son about six years old[2]—under these circumstances I have to request the indulgence of a few days untill my return to answer your letter of the 5th inst. However I must remark, that I can never abandon principle, be the personal consequences what they may—The causes which gave rise to my order of the 22nd. april, being the improper interferrence of the Department of War, with a Topographical Engineer of my Division, after he had reported and was ordered on duty by me, in open violation of the regulations of the army of the u states page 91 which defines his duty and makes him subordinate to the directions of the comdg. General—and also the act of the 24th of April 1816 organizing the Genl Staff—which I trust viewing your constitutional duty, "to see the laws faithfully executed" in connection with your duty as ["]commander in chief of the army & navy" you cannot Justify.[3] These being remonstrated against by me to the Sec of War, and fifty four days having elapsed without receiving an answer[4]—and being an interference, that my duty as a commander of a Division compeled me to resist. These I say being withdrawn, as they were the basis of my order, I shall have no hesitation in withdrawing my General order—& that rules and regulations may hereafter be adopted, which may tend to harmonize the army and keep up subordination. I am induced from the conciliatory features of your letter to make these remarks—and that you may have the causes which gave rise to my order again before you, I inclose you a copy of my letter to the sec of war of the 14th. of Janury, with the extracts of the orders and instructions given by the sec of war to Major Long.[5]

I would barely remark that cases of necessity, creates their own rule, and when really they exist—forms an exception from the general rule—altho not expressed allways implied—hence I have never complained of any order being Issued in cases of necessity—where I was immediately advised thereof—nor is it a real ground of complaint.

I shall await your answer to this letter before I forward my answer to yours of the 5th Instant.[6] I am Sir with Sincere respect yr mo. ob. Serv.

Andrew Jackson

P S Should the accomodation proposed, not meet your wishes, you will please return this enclosed to me. A. J.

ALS, NN (5-1118); Copy, DLC (23). Published in Bassett, 2:332–33 (from copy).

1. See Monroe to AJ, September 27, and above, October 5.

2. Jackson was referring to John Hutchings and his son, Andrew Jackson Hutchings (1811–41), who on November 20 became Jackson's ward upon the death of his father.

3. See above, Division Order, April 22. Jackson meant to refer to page 97, not 91, of *Military Laws, and Rules and Regulations for the Army of the United States* and to section 1 of the act for organizing the general staff (3 *U.S. Statutes at Large* 297), which assigned three topographical engineers to each division.

4. For the remonstrance, see AJ to George Graham, February 26.

5. See above, AJ to Graham, January 14; and William H. Crawford to Stephen H. Long, June 18, July 2, 1816, DLC (21).

6. See Monroe to AJ, December 2, and AJ to Monroe, December 20, both below.

With the Seminoles unresponsive to demands for the apprehension of marauders along the Georgia-Florida border, General Gaines ordered a detachment of troops to arrest Neamathla, the Fowltown chief (see Edmund P. Gaines to AJ, August 21 and, above, October 1). The resulting skirmish, reported below, can be considered the first offensive action of the army in the Seminole campaign.

*During the 1819 congressional debate over Jackson's Florida invasion, Charles Fenton Mercer of Virginia and Timothy Fuller of Massachusetts countered the argument that his actions were justified on principles of national self-defense by asserting that the United States and not the Indians were aggressors (*Annals of Congress*, 15th Cong., 2nd sess., pp. 804, 989–90). Both cited the Fowltown incident, Fuller going so far as to argue that the November 30 attack on Richard W. Scott's party ascending the Apalachicola River was "the inevitable consequence of the recent massacre and pillage of Fowltown" (see Gaines to AJ, December 2, below). Moreover,*

Creek agent David B. Mitchell declared that the destruction of Fowltown was "the immediate cause of the Seminole war" (ASP, Military Affairs, *1:749). The report inspired Gaines to defend his conduct, a defense which Jackson fully supported (see Gaines to John C. Calhoun, October 17, 1819; and AJ to Gaines, April 24, 1819, below).*

From Edmund Pendleton Gaines

Head Quarters, E. S. D. of the South
Fort Scott Georgia
21st November 1817

General,

The first Brigade arrived at this place on the 19th instant. I had previously sent an Indian runner to notify the foul-town Chief E'ne'he'maut'ly of my arrival, and, with a view to ascertain whether his hostile temper had abated, requested him to visit me—he replied that he had already said to the Commanding officer here, all he had to say, and that he would not come.

He had warned Major Twiggs not to cross, or cut a stick of wood on the East side of Flint river, alleging *[that the land]* was his, that he was directed by the powers *[above and below]* to protect and defend it and should do so.[1] This *[being the talk ref]*ered to, and his town having continued to *[be hostile ever since]* the last war—having participated as the *[friendly Indians]* assert in the predatory war carried on for *[some time past]* against the Georgia frontier, I yesterday detached *[2]*50 men (supposed to be about the strength of the town) under the Command of Major Twiggs, with orders to bring to me the Chief and warriors and in the event of resistance to treat them as Enemies.

The detachment arrived at the town early this morning and were instantly fired upon, but without effect. The fir*[e was]* briskly returned by the detachment, and the Indians put to f*[light,]* with the loss of four warriors slain—and as there is reason to believe many more wounded.[2]

It is with deep regret I have to add that a woman was accidentally shot with some warriors in the act of forcing their way through our line formed for the purpose of arresting their flight. The unfortunate woman had a blanket fastened round her (as many of the warriors had[)] which amidst the smoke in which they were enveloped, rendered it impossible as I am assured by the officers present, to distinguish her from the warriors.

Among the articles found in the house *[of the Chief,]* was a British uniform coat (Scarlet) *[with a pair of]* gold Epaulettes, and a certificate si*[gned by a british]* Captain of Marines, "Robert White, in *[the absence of Colonel]* Nichols," Stating that the Chief "had al*[ways been a true]* and faithfull friend to the British*[."]*[3]

Major Twiggs reports that the officers and *[men of]* the detachment generally performed their duty with zeal and propriety.

The reports of friendly Indians concur in Estimating the number of hostile warriors including the red sticks & seminolas at more than two *[th]*ousand, besides the blacks amounting to near four *[hu]*ndred men & increasing by runaways from Georgia. They have been promised, as several Indians inform me, assistance from the British at new Providence—this promise though made by Woodbine, is relied on by most of the seminola Indians. I have not a doubt but they will sue for peace as soon as they find their hopes of british aid to be without foundation.

I regret to be under the necessity of saying to you that Major [Peter] Muhlenburg [Jr.] with the detachment and supplies sent around by water, has not yet arrived—nor have I heard of his having entered the river.[4] *[Yet he may]* have been in the river for several *[days, with]*out my being able to hear of it. I have the honor to be most *[respectfully]* Your obdt. Servt.

Edmund P. Gaines

ALS, DLC (23); Copy, DNA-RG 107 (M222-19); Extracts, DNA-RG 46 (5-1136, -1137), DNA-RG 233 (5-1140, -1143). Published in Bassett, 2:333–34 (extract). Where the ALS is torn, the missing material has been supplied from the copy. James M. Glassell's endorsement on the ALS indicates that the copy was forwarded to the secretary of war on December 16 (see below) and that Gaines's letter was answered on the same day (not found).

1. See above, Gaines to AJ, October 1.

2. For the orders, see Gaines to David E. Twiggs, November 20; for a report of the action, see Twiggs to Gaines, November 21, both DLC (27). Both items were forwarded to Jackson in 1819.

3. During the British Gulf campaign of 1814–15, Edward Nicolls had responsibility for organizing and training Indian allies. White has not been identified further.

4. Muhlenberg (d. 1844), a captain (brevet major) of the 4th Infantry and the son of John Peter Gabriel Muhlenberg (1746–1807), revolutionary general and Pennsylvania congressman and senator, had been assigned to bring supplies from Mobile to Fort Scott and was at this time in Apalachicola Bay with five vessels ready to ascend the river.

To George Graham

Head Quarters, Divn of the South
Nashville 1st Decbr 1817.

Sir,

On the 27th of Oct last, I left this to visit a friend and nephew of mine who was lying dangerously ill,[1] of which you have been advised by the Adjt General already, and having performed the last duty to him who expired on the 20th ulto. I reached this on the 30th.

On my return journey I received your letter of the 25th Octr marked private, also a copy of the Adjutant General's to you of the 19th ult.[2]

I perfectly coincide with Colo Butler, and for the reasons he has assigned, that nothing can be done with the Chickasaws on the subject named until the arrearages due them are paid as it would, in my opinion completely jeopardise the objects in view which, I fully agree with you, are of the greatest importance. Indeed it is my opinion that, until their arrearages are paid, even to name the subject, would tend to frustrate the object of the Government.

So soon as the money arrives I will proceed to the Chickasaw Nation, and use my best exertions to obtain a relinquishment to their title to the lands proposed, of which, altho' not sanguine, I do not despair of effecting, so soon as they are made friendly disposed by the change of their Agent and the receipt of their Annuities.[3]

I sincerely hope that Genl [Jonas] Platt will accept of the Agency as the chiefs of that nation have expressed their wish to Genl Meriwether and myself that their Agent should be taken from the Eastward; should Genl P not accept and you will forward the amount due the Chickasaw nation to Col Robt Butler, who has been for a long time doing the extra duty of Qr Mr. General, from real necessity, and furnish him with particular instructions for its appropriation, I will undertake to see the faithful distribution thereof, and take that moment to obtain their relinquishment to the lands proposed.[4]

Your several communications of the 11th and 30th Oct, and the 6th & 13th of Novbr with their respective enclosures have been received, and attended to.[5] Notification has been made and proposals will be received for the repair of the old Natchez road, from where the Reynoldsburg road intersects to the Mississippi ⟨River⟩ line.

The Adjt. General has been directed to order Lt Col [William] Lindsay to form the recruits of the 4th Battalion into two companies and have them marched to Mobile without delay[6] I am Sir &c

Andrew Jackson
Maj Genl Comdg.

Copy, DNA-RG 46 (5-1149). Published in *ASP, Indian Affairs,* 2:172–73.

1. John Hutchings.

2. See Graham to AJ, October 25, and Robert Butler to Graham, November 19.

3. The appointment of Chickasaw agent William Cocke in 1814 had disappointed some Chickasaws, who had requested an agent from the northern states. The 1816 Chickasaw treaty commissioners, requested to investigate complaints of Cocke's nepotism and incompetence, reported that the tribe wished him removed (see above, AJ, David Meriwether, and Jesse Franklin to William H. Crawford, September 20, 1816). The war department had consequently not sent Cocke the $12,000 annuity promised the Chickasaws by the treaty, and Jackson did not wish to press the cession of Chickasaw claims to lands west of the Tennessee River in Kentucky and Tennessee until the annuities were paid.

4. Platt (1769–1834), a former congressman from New York, declined the appointment, and Henry Sherburne (1747–1824), a revolutionary war officer and former treasurer of Rhode Island, was appointed in December. In the meantime, the annuities were sent to Butler.

5. See Graham to AJ, October 11, 30, November 6, 13.

6. See Butler to Lindsay, December 1. Lindsay (d. 1838; William and Mary), from Virginia, was a lieutenant colonel of artillery.

From Edmund Pendleton Gaines

Hd. Qrs. Fort Scott Ga
December 2. 1817

General

It is my painful duty to report to you an affair of a more serious and disastrous character than has heretofore occurred upon this frontier; and which leaves no doubt of the deep hostility of the Indians, or the necessity of prompt and efficient measures on our part.

A large party of Seminola Indians on the 30th. Ultimo formed an ambuscade on the Appalachicola river a mile below the junction of the Flint and Chattahoochie, attacked one of our boats ascending near the shore, and killed, wounded and took the greater part of the detachment consisting of forty men commanded by Lieut. R[ichard] W. Scott of the 7th. Infantry; there were also on board killed or taken Seven women the wives of Soldiers.[1] Six men of the detachment only escaped, four of whom were wounded. They report that the strength of the current at the point of attack had oblidged the Lieutenant to keep his boat near the shore; that the Indians had formed along the Bank of the River and were not discovered until their fire commenced, in the first volley of which Lieut. Scott and his most valuable men fell.

The Lieutenant and his party had been sent from this place some days before to assist Major Muhlenberg in ascending the River with three Vessels laden with military stores brought from Montgomery and Mobile. The Major instead of retaining the party to assist him as I had advised (see the inclosure No 1.)[2] retained only about Twenty men and in their place put a like number of sick, with the women and some Regimental clothing. The Boat thus laden was detached alone for this place. It is due to Major Muhlenberg to observe that at the time he detached the Boat I have reason to believe he was not apprised of any recent hostilities having taken place in this quarter. It appears however from Lieut. Scott's letter received about the hour in which he was attacked (Enclosure No 2.)[3] that he had been warned of the danger. Upon the receipt of this letter I had two Boats fitted up with covers and port holes for defence, and detached Captain [Joseph John] Clinch with an officer and forty men; with an order to secure the movement of Lieut. Scott and then to assist Major Muhlenberg (see enclosure No. 3).[4] This detachment embarked late in the evening of the 30th. and must have passed the scene of action below, at night, and some hours after the affair terminated. I have not yet heard from Captain Clinch. I shall immediately strengthen the detachment under Major Muhlenberg with another Boat secured against the Enemy's fire. He will therefore move up with safety by keeping near the middle of the river. I shall moreover take a position with my principal force at the junction of the Rivers, near the line,[5] and shall attack any force that may attempt to intercept our vessels and supplies below, as I feel persuaded the order of the President prohibiting an attack upon the Indians below the line, has reference only to the past, and not to the present or future outrages, such as the one just now perpetrated, and such as shall place our troops strictly within the pale of natural law where self defence is sanctioned by the principal of self preservation.[6]

The wounded men who made their escape concur in the opinion that they had seen upwards of five hundred hostile warriors at different places on the river below the point of attack. Of the force engaged they differ in opinion; but all agree the number was very considerable—extending about one hundred and fifty yards along the shore, at the edge of a swamp, or thick woods.

I am assured by the friendly chiefs that the hostile warriors of every town upon the Chattahoochie set about preparing canoes and moving off down the river to join the Seminolas as soon as the account of my movement from Montgomery reached them.

The Indians now remaining upon the Chattahoochie, I have reason to believe are well disposed. One of the new settlers, however, has recently been killed; but it has been clearly proven that the perpetrator of this act together with most of the young warriors of his town (High Town) belonged to and have joined the hostile party. The friendly chiefs in the neighborhood, when apprised of the murder assembled a party and sent in pursuit of the offender, followed him to this river on the route to Mickasukee, whither he escaped.[7] Onishajo and several other friendly chiefs have tendered me their services, with their warriors, to go against the Seminolas.[8] I have promised to give them notice of the time that may be fixed for my departure, and then to accept their services.

The inclosure No 4. contains the substance of what I have said to the chiefs who have visited me; several of whom reside south of the Spanish line and west of the Appalachicola river. The chiefs were desirous I should communicate to them my views and wishes—I felt authorised to say but little, and deemed it necessary in what I should say, to endeavor to counteract the erroneous impressions by which they have been misled by pretended british agents.[9] I have the honor to be most respectfully your obdt. servant

Edmund P. Gaines
Major General by Brevet Commg

LS, DLC (23). Endorsed as received and answered, December 31. Published in Bassett, 2:337 (extract); a longer extract appeared in the *Nashville Clarion,* January 6, 1818, and other newspapers.

1. Scott, of Virginia, had served as an army officer since 1813.

2. See Gaines to Peter Muhlenberg, Jr., November [18], DLC (23).
3. See Scott to Gaines, November 28, DLC (23).
4. See Gaines to Clinch, November 30, DLC (23). Clinch (1789–1827), a brother of Duncan L., was in the 7th Infantry.
5. The junction of the Flint and Chattahoochee rivers, forming the Apalachicola.
6. On October 30, George Graham ordered Gaines not to attack the Indians in Florida without war department authorization (*ASP, Indian Affairs,* 2:159).
7. Mikasuki, a principal Seminole town destroyed by Jackson's troops in April 1818, lay west of Lake Miccosukee in northern Florida.
8. Onishajo, a chief of the friendly village of Oak'le'o'kene, captained a company of seventy-five Creek warriors in the Seminole campaign.
9. See Gaines to Chiefs and Warriors, [December 2], DLC (23).

From James Monroe

private — Washington Decr 2. 1817

Dear Sir

I have the pleasure to enclose you a copy of my message to Congress, which was communicated to day.[1]

I expected to have receiv'd a letter from you before this, or at least I inferr'd it, from your last of the 22d. of Octr. I suspect from what Mr Rhea states, that you never saw, the order of the dept. of war, under which Major Long went to St. Louis, & acted on the Mississippi. It was under that order, that he return'd. None other, was, as I am assurd, ever given him untill after his return. I merely suggest this for your information, not meaning to enter further ⟨at⟩ into the subject.[2]

My earnest desire is, to terminate this unpleasant affair, in the most honorable manner for you, that it may be possible, consistent, with principles, which it is my duty to maintain, & are explaind in my last, to you.[3] The mode, which, suggests itself, is, for the Secretary of War, Mr [John Caldwell] Calhoun, lately appointed, & who is daily expected here, to digest a system of regulations, by my order, to be observed, in communicating the orders of the President, to the commanders of divisions, or any persons under them, at a distance from their Hd. Qrs. A few rules, will be sufficient for the purpose, & in them, the principle may be laid down, that, as a general rule, the order should go to the Commander of the division, and that in all cases, when deviated from, a copy should be sent at the same time, to him.[4] This will, I presume, terminate the affair, with perfect delicacy to you. No mention will be made of the affair, but it may be understood, that the case was held in view, & with sentiments of, delicacy, & regard, for you. If on seeing what is done, you are satisfied, nothing more need be said on the subject, unless indeed you may be disposed to intimate it. I shall do for you, what I should wish, to have done, for myself, in such a case. I need not add, my most earnest wish, that you may remain in the public service, at least as long as I do. with great respect and sincere regards yours

James Monroe

ALS, DLC (23). Published in Bassett, 2:336–37.

1. The annual message of December 2 appears in *Annals of Congress,* 15th Cong., 2nd sess., pp. 12–19.

2. See above, AJ to Monroe, October 22. George Graham had sent Jackson an extract of the order on February 1 (above). For John Rhea's efforts at mediation of the dispute, see Rhea to AJ, November 27.

3. See above, Monroe to AJ, October 5.

4. Calhoun (1782–1850; Yale 1804) took up his duties as secretary of war on December 8. For his subsequent order regarding the chain of command, see Calhoun to AJ, December 29.

To Winfield Scott

Head Quarters
Div: of the South
Nashville Decr. 3d. 1817

Sir

I have been absent from this place a considerable time rendering the last friendly office I could to a particular friend whose eyes I closed on the 20th. Ult owing to this, your letter of the 4th. Octr. was not recd. until the first inst.[1]

Upon the rect. of the anonymous Communication made me from New york I hastened to lay it before you;[2] that course was suggested to me by the respect I felt for you as a man & a *Soldier*; & that you might have it in your power to answer how far you had been guilty of so base & inexcusable conduct—Independent of the Services you have rendered your Country, the Circumstance of your wearing the badge and Insignia of a Soldier, led me to the conclusion that I was addressing a Gentleman, with these feelings you were written to, & had an idea been for a moment entertained that you would have descended from the high & dignified Character of a Majr. Genl. of the U. S. Army & used so approbrious & insolent language as you have done, rest assured, I should have viewed you as rather too contemptible to have held any Converse with you on the subject. If you have lived in the World thus long in entire ignorance of the obligation and Duties honor impose, you are indeed past the time of learning, & surely he must be ignorant of them, who seems so little under their influence.

Pray Sir, does your recollection serve. In what School of Philosophy were you taught that to a Letter enquiring into the nature of a supposed injury, & clothed in language decorous & unexceptionable, an answer should be given couched [in pompous][3] insolence & bullying expression—I had hoped what was charged upon you by an anonymous correspondent was unfounded. I had hoped so from a belief that Genl. Scott was a Soldier & a Gentleman but when I see those statements doubly confirmed by his own words, it becomes a matter of enquiry how far a man of honorable feelings can reconcile them to himself, or longer set up a claim to that character, are you ignorant Sir that had my order at which your refined Judgement is so exceedingly touched been made the subject of enquiry, you might from your standing not from your Character be made one of my Judges. How very proper then was it, thus situated & without a Knowledge of any of the attendant circumstances for you to have prejudged the whole matter, this at different times & in the circle of your friends you could do, and yet had I been arraigned & you detailed as one of my Judges with the designs of an assassin lurking under a fair exterior, you would have approached the Holy Sanctuary of Justice. Is conduct like this congenial with that high sense of dignity which should be seated in a Soldier's Bosom? Is it due from a Brother Officer to assail in the dark the reputation of an other & stab him at a moment when he cannot expect it? I might insult an honorable man by questions such as these, but shall not expect they will harrow up one who must be dead to all those feelings which are the true Characteristic of a Gentleman

In terms polite as I was capable of noting, I asked you if my informant had stated truly if you were the author of the Publication and remarks charged against you & to what extent. a reference to your Letter without any comment of mine will inform how far you have preserved a similar course—how little of the Gentleman & how much of the ⟨bullying⟩ hectoring bully you have manifested. If nothing else would, the Epauletts which grace your shoulders should have dictated to you a different course and have admonished you that however small might have been your respect for an other, respect for yourself should have taught you the necessity of replying at least mildly to the enquiries I suggested; and more especially should you have done this when your own convictions must have fixed you as guilty of the abominable Crime of Detraction, of slandering & behind his back a brother officer. But not content with answering what was proposed, your overweaning vanity has led you to make an offering of your advice. Believe me Sir, it is not in my power to render you my thanks. I think too highly of myself to suppose that I stand at all in need of your admonitions, & to light of you to appreciate them as useful; for good advice I am always thankful, but can never fail to spurn it when I know it to flow from an incompetent or corrupt source. The breast where base & guilty passions dwell is not the place to look for virtue, or any thing that leads to virtue. My notions Sir are not those now taught in modern Schools & in fashionable high life; they were imbibed in ancient days; and hitherto have & yet bear *me* to the *conclusion* that he who can wantonly outrage the feelings of an other, who without Cause can extend injury where none is due, is Capable of any Crime however detestable in its nature, & will not fail to commit it whenever imposed by necessity—

I shall not stoop Sir, to a justification of my Order before you, or to notice the weakness & absurdity of your Tinsel Rhetoric, it may be quite conclusive with yourself: and I have no disposition to attempt convincing you that your Ingenuity is not as profound as you have imagined it. To my

Govmt. whenever it may please, I hold myself liable to answer, & to produce the reasons which prompted me to the cause I took; & to the intermeddling Pimps & Spies of the War Deptt. who are in the garb of Gentlemen, I hold myself responsible for any grievance they may labor under on my acct. with which you have my permission to number yourself—For what I have said I offer no apology—you have deserved it all & more were it necessary to say more—I will barely remark in Conclusion that if you feel yourself aggrieved at what is here said, any Communication from you will reach me safely at this place[4]—I have the honor to be very respectfully Yr. Obt. Serv.

Sigd.) Andrew Jackson

Copies, THi (5-1153), TMM (5-1156), NWM (mAJs). Published in 1819 and 1828 newspapers and in Bassett, 2:338–39 (from Parton, 2:378).

1. See above, Scott to AJ, October 4.
2. See above, Unknown to AJ, August 14; and AJ to Scott, September 8.
3. Bracketed words from other copies.
4. For Scott's reply, declining to duel, see Scott to AJ, January 2, 1818.

To Richard Butler

Nashville Decbr. 6th 1817.

Dr Sir

Being absent for some time attending on my sick friend Major John Hutchings whose eyes I closed on the 20th. ult I did not reach Nashville untill the 1rst. Instant, which will account for your not receiving at an earlier period my answer to your very friendly letter of the 28th. of Sept. which is now before me.[1]

In the request you make you shall be gratified with much pleasure on my part, and you may say to Mr [William Edward] West, that if he comes to this country, I will be happy to see him at my house, where he shall be made as comfortable as I can make him untill the work is compleated, & If I should go on to the lower Country I shall notify him, that he may take it on my passage.[2]

Mr Earl an exellent artist, has lately taken a likeness of me which is thought to be striking and well executed, This Mr. E intends exhibitting in New orleans on its way to paris to be engraved[3]—I have said to Mr Earl, that I will sit for Mr West and for Mr West alone—That if any benefit can result, It shall, to him & Mr. W. alone—It is very Probable I shall have to go on to the city this winter—I have never sought to make enemies, but it appears I have some of high standing whom I never saw—I have long wished for retirement, I had a hope after my many Privations, and watchfull nights that I would have been permitted to have retired, to have regained a broken constitution, and this without any attempt either at my charector or honor—but this appears not to be the case—and I never will retire untill I can do it with honor—I obtained the hatred & hidden enmity of Mr Crawford, about the cherokee treaty, and the Presidential election[4]—at the moment he knew I was about to retire from the army—he interfered improperly with my Topographical staff, ⟨and expressly⟩ in open violation of express law, I remonstrated against it without effect, which gave rise to my order of the 22nd. of april last—Thus has the thing rested—and now rests waiting for Mr Munroe's letter—In the mean time a *great* general in the East, has been acting the Pimp & spy of Mr. C has been secretly arainging me & my order, no doubt to make an unfavourable impression on the publick mind[5]—I have *unrobed him*—you will know more of this hereafter—

Present Mrs. Jackson & myself affectionately to your lady,[6] and accept. of our best wishes for your Indivial happiness & believe me to be with sincere friendship—yr mo. ob. serv.

Andrew Jackson

ALS, LU (5-1165). Butler (1777–1820), Robert Butler's cousin, was a Louisiana planter.

1. Not found.

2. West wished to finance study in Europe by making a portrait of Jackson to be engraved and sold by subscription. His portrait of Jackson has not been found.

3. Ralph E. W. Earl had come to Nashville in February to paint the general. He recorded executing nine Jackson portraits in 1817; the painting indicated here has not been identified. Earl is not known to have exhibited in New Orleans before 1821, when he showed a full-length Jackson portrait previously displayed at his Nashville Museum.

4. The March 22, 1816, Cherokee treaty negotiated at Washington had aroused much protest in Tennessee, and Jackson publicly criticized the treaty, which Crawford staunchly defended. See above, AJ to Crawford, June 4, 1816. Crawford had briefly contested the presidential candidacy of James Monroe, whom Jackson supported.

5. Winfield Scott.

6. In 1799, Richard Butler had married Margaret Farar (d. 1820) of Adams County, Mississippi Territory.

To William Berkeley Lewis

Nashville Decbr. 8th. 1817.

Dr. Sir

Yours of the 1rst. Instant from Knoxville is Just to hand. I have duly noted its contents—and have barely to observe, that the rumor stated, is a mere pretext, to cover his real cowardice—and as such circulated by his friends to keep up appearences—you may have observed in his address, that he says I insulted him at Neworleans—now Sir when a military man can pockett an insult for two years before he complains, and then only to the Publick, without ⟨even⟩ calling on the person offending for redress—you may allways set it down such generals, are not dangerous, and that they would ruther spill quarts of Ink, than gills of blood—such you may rely on it, is general John Adair[1]

His publication is too contemptable for me to notice—and after he has complained of insult, without possessing the magnanimity to call for redress—I cannot as a brave man—probe the Poltroon farther—

I would be happy to hear from you whilst at the city[2]—it is more than probable, you can give me some information on the subject of the feelings & intention of Mr Munroe, as it respects my order of the 22nd. of april wishing as I do to retire as early as I can I am desirous of having this thing ⟨do⟩ finally acted on—

I returned to this place on the 1rst Instant, after closing the eyes of my friend and Nephew Major John Hutchings on the 20th. ult, in him I lost a faithfull & Valuable friend, I did my duty—but I could not save him—and we are directed to "weep not for the dead but for the living."[3] I must as far as I can Philosophise, adopt the text—and attend to the education of his dear little son—

we have nothing new here, all your friends well—

wishing you health and a speedy return to your family & friends I am yrs. respectfully

Andrew Jackson

P.S. Since writing the foregoing, yours of Novbr. 26th is recd.,[4] for which I thank you—you will see the ground I have taken—After his remark of insult in his adress—& not calling for redress—after submitting to be charge with unblushing falshoods, and proving them on him—without disgracing myself as I brave man—I could not do more—If I was to charge him with lying it would only be repeating the charge I have made & be introducing a black guard scene in reply—that his adress shows he does not mean fighting—and I have no doubt if he was challenged, he would shield himself under the duelling laws of Ky.[5]—you may assure Mr Munroe if an opportunity offers, that my friendship remains unabated for him & let the business Terminate as it may[6]—It will have no effect upon that friendship—differrence of opinion with me you know can exist without any diminution of friendship—There is one fact I wish Mr Munroe to know—that Mr Wm H Crawford, whatever his pretensions are, is not his friend—and facts can be produced on this head—I know he is my enemy—& I also know he is a base man—A.J—

P.S. Write me on recpt of this[7]—A.J.

ALS, NNPM (5-1169).

1. Lewis's letter has not been found. The rumor discussed was probably the report that John Adair had killed Jackson in a duel. The address was Adair's October 21 letter to the public on the Kentucky troops controversy.

2. Lewis was in Washington.

3. A paraphrase, not a direct quote, of Luke 23:28.

4. Letter not found.

5. By an act of February 4, 1812, the Kentucky legislature required that all officers of the Commonwealth take an oath that they had not, since the passage of the act, directly or in-

directly issued, carried, or accepted a challenge to a duel and that they would not do so while in office. The anti-dueling oath applied to Adair, a representative from Mercer County to the state legislature in 1817.

6. The controversy over Jackson's April 22 Division Order.

7. Lewis responded to AJ's letter on January 13, 1818.

To George Graham [John Caldwell Calhoun]

Hd. Qrs. Dn. of the South
Nashville 16th. Decr. 1817

Sir

I have the honor to enclose you copies of two letters from General Gaines, delivered me yesterday by express.[1]

I am in hopes that this check to the Savages, may incline them to peace; should it not, and their hostility continue, the protection of our citizens will require that the Wolf be struck in his den, for, rest assured, if ever the Indians find out that the territorial boundery of Spain is to be a sanctuary, their murders will be multiplied to a degree that our citizens on the southern frontier cannot bear. Spain is bound by treaties to keep the Indians, within her territory, at peace with us,[2] having failed to do this, necessity will justify the measure, after giving her due notice, to follow the marauders and punish them in their retreat. The War Hatchet having been raised, unless the Indians sue for peace, your frontier cannot be protected without entering their country: from long experience this result has been fully established. I enclose you a copy of Capt. [Lewis B.] Willis' report &c. &c[3]

I have this moment received your communication of the 26th. Ult. with its inclosures, which are noted & will be *duly* attended to.[4] I am Sir most Respy. Yo. Very Obt. St.

Andrew Jackson
Major Genl Comdg.

LS in James M. Glassell's hand, DNA-RG 107 (M221-78); Extracts, DNA-RG 46 (5-1177), DNA-RG 233 (5-1178). Published in Bassett, 2:340 (extract).

1. See Edmund P. Gaines to AJ, November 9, and, above, 21.

2. See the fifth article of the Treaty of San Lorenzo, October 27, 1795.

3. See Willis to AJ, December 4. Willis, of Virginia, was a captain in the 8th Infantry.

4. See Graham to AJ, November 26, discussing the payment of troops. For Jackson's action, see Robert Butler's division order, December 18, requiring strict enforcement of a March 4 division order that had made it "the special duty of commanding officers, to arrest every paymaster failing to make his payments in due time, unless he can make manifest good cause for delay" (Adjutant General's Order Book, DNA-RG 98).

To James Monroe

(Private) Nashville Decbr. 20th. 1817.

Dr. Sir

I have the pleasure to acknowledge the receipt of your favour of the 2nd instant, with your message to congress enclosed for which accept my thanks.[1]

The prosperous state of our country & particularly our finance, so near the close of an expensive war, must be a source of great gratification to every true american—and profitting from experience, will enable the Executive goverment, with the aid of congress to place the whole country in a state of defence, which will command Justice and respect from all nations & thereby perpetuate the blessings of peace.

I have read with great attention your letter. The plan proposed fully meets my approbation, for I see in it that magnanimity of conduct only to be met with in great & good minds—and also a system that will produce subordination & harmony, without which an army cannot be beneficial or effective—Whenever an officer is responsible for the defence of a country or place, his means never ought to be taken from him or directed without his knowledge

I had determined to retire from service, the moment I could with propriety & honor. but I have determined, since the receipt of your letter not to resign untill I can have the pleasure of seeing you, & untill you make the southern tower, you contemplated next Spring, & in which I intend doing myself the pleasure of accompanying you.

It is my wish to retire from publick life, for I am advancing to that age which makes retirement desireable, but as long as I can be really serviceable to my country and there remains any prospect of my services being wanted I will not retire, more particularly, as it is your wish I should not. I am sir with great respect & sincere friendship. yr mo. ob. serv.

Andrew Jackson

ALS, NN (5-1193); ALS copy, DLC (23). Published in Bassett, 2:340–41 (from ALS copy).

1. See above, Monroe to AJ, December 2.

From John Caldwell Calhoun

Department of War
Decr. 26th. 1817

Sir,

You will repair, with as little delay as practicable, to Fort Scott and assume the immediate command of the Forces in that Section of the Southern Division.

The increasing display of hostile intentions, by the Seminole Indians, may render it necessary to concentrate all the contiguous and disposable force of your Division, upon that quarter. The regular force now there is about Eight hundred Strong; and one thousand militia of the State of Georgia are called into Service. General Gaines estimates the Strength of the Indians at two thousand seven hundred. Should you be of opinion that our numbers are too Small to beat the Enemy, you will call on the Executives of adjacent States for Such an additional militia force as you may deem requisite.

General Gaines had been orderred early in last month to repair to Amelia Island. It is presumed that he has, therefore, relinquished the command at Fort Scott. Subsequent orders have been given to General Gaines, (copies of which will be furnished you) advising him that you would be directed to take command, and directing him to re-assume, should he deem the public interest to require it, the command at Fort Scott, until you Should arrive there. If, however, the General Should have progressed to Florida before these Subsequent orders may have reached him, he was instructed to penetrate to the Seminole Towns, through the Floridas, provided, the Strength of his command, at Amelia, would justify his engaging in offensive operations.[1]

With this view you may be prepared to concentrate your forces and to adopt the necessary measures to terminate a conflict which it has ever been the desire of the President, from considerations of humanity, to avoid; but which is now made necessary by their Settled hostilities. With great respect I have the honor to be, Sir, Your obedient, humble Servant

J. C. Calhoun

LS and Copy, DLC (23); LC, DNA-RG 107 (M6-9); Copy, DNA-RG 75 (M271-2); Copy and Extract, DNA-RG 46 (5-1198, -1207); Copies and Extract, DNA-RG 233 (5-1200, -1203, -1208). Published in Bassett, 2:341–42. LS endorsed as received January 11 and answered January 12, 1818. The DLC copy and one of the RG 233 copies are in James C. Bronaugh's hand and certified by him; the RG 46 copy is in Richard K. Call's hand and certified by him.

1. See George Graham to Edmund P. Gaines, November 12; and Calhoun to Gaines, December 26, both DLC-23. Acting on behalf of the republics of Venezuela, New Granada,

Mexico, and Rio de la Plata, Gregor MacGregor (1786–1845) had seized Amelia Island in June, and another filibuster Louis-Michel Aury (c1788–1821) had taken control in the name of Mexico in September. The United States military expedition against the resulting colony of pirates and slave traders seized control of the island on December 23.

1818

The rising hostilities along the Georgia-Florida border reinforced Jackson's long-standing belief that Spanish possession of Florida posed an unacceptable hazard to the security of the southern frontier, and in the letter below, he sought covert authority to occupy Spanish Florida. No reply has been found, but on January 30 Monroe directed Secretary of War John C. Calhoun to instruct Jackson "not to attack any post occupied by Spanish troops, from the possibility, that it might bring the allied powers on us" (DNA-RG 107, M221-79). While Monroe's instructions responded directly to news sent by Jackson to Calhoun on January 12, his precautionary directive may also have been influenced by Jackson's January 6 letter below, which he should have received by late January. Calhoun, however, apparently failed to issue any new order to restrain Jackson, and when Jackson's letter came to public attention in 1830 and 1831, none of the principals referred to Monroe's directive.

Jackson's letter became public after Crawfordites, hoping for a rapprochement with Jackson and attempting to undermine Vice-President Calhoun, reopened discussion of the roles played by Calhoun and William H. Crawford during the July 1818 cabinet discussions of Jackson's Florida invasion. Crawford claimed (to John Forsyth, April 30, 1830) that the letter had been shown to the cabinet and that he had then concluded that the general had taken the administration's failure to respond as approval. Calhoun, Crawford asserted, had urged punishing Jackson for his unauthorized Florida adventure. Crawford's statement was obviously self-serving, and Calhoun's denial that the letter had been produced for the cabinet was supported by the others present, but Crawford's assertions precipitated a rift between Jackson and Calhoun. When Jackson formally inquired regarding Calhoun's position at the 1818 meetings, Calhoun recognized the underlying charge that he had opposed Jackson in the cabinet while allowing a belief that Jackson had his support. He replied by insisting that the general had had ample reason to know that the administration thought he had exceeded his authority. The question of whether Jackson's "Rhea letter" had been answered thus became critical.

None of the recollections of the 1830s were consistent with Monroe's January 30 note being a reply to Jackson's letter. Monroe asserted that he had been sick when he received the letter and that after showing it to Calhoun and Crawford, who told him it was about Florida and would require *an answer, he laid the letter aside and forgot it until after the invasion was over. Calhoun, who published Monroe's statement (*United States' Telegraph, *February 17, 1831), supported Monroe's recollection. Conversely, Jackson stated in letters (see AJ to Richard G. Dunlap, July 18, 1831) and in an exposition prepared but not published at the time (Thomas Hart Benton,* Thirty Years' View . . . *[2 vols.; New York, 1856], 1:169–80) that John Rhea had written him conveying the president's approval of the invasion. Rhea's letter, received near Hartford, Georgia, in mid-February had, he claimed, been destroyed in 1819 at the president's request, again conveyed through Rhea.*

The case for the existence of a Rhea document relies ultimately on Jackson's credibility. The corroborating testimony he obtained from John Overton and from a nearly senile and obviously eager to please Rhea was weak, and he apparently did not seek or obtain support from former military associates who might have seen Rhea's letter. Although one might wonder how Monroe, who had been secretary of war when Jackson first invaded Pensacola in 1814, could have forgotten a letter from Jackson about Florida, especially after those he consulted agreed it would require an answer, there is no independent evidence to suggest that the president approved the invasion. To the contrary, Monroe's public stance in 1818, echoed in letters to former presidents Thomas Jefferson and James Madison, was that Jackson had exceeded his authority, and, as a matter of fact, Jackson did not claim presidential sanction for the invasion at the time. Yet Jackson seemingly never doubted that he had the administration's support, and, having promised that he would not "implicate" the government, he would not have revealed government directives if they had been sent. It is also possible that Rhea might have misunderstood Monroe and sent an approval that the president did not intend or that Jackson could have misconstrued a letter on some other subject into approval for action against Spanish Florida. Precisely because Monroe's approval, if given, was intended to be secret, the existence or non-existence of Rhea's letter can probably never be established with certainty.

To James Monroe

Hd. Qrs. S. Div.
Confidential Nashville 6th. Jany. 1818

Sir

A few days since I received a letter from the Secy of War of the 17th. Ult. with enclosures.[1] Your order of the 16th. Ult. through him to Brevet Majr. Genl. Gaines to enter the Territory of Spain & chastise the Ruthless Savages who have been depredating on the property & lives of our citizens, will meet not only the approbation of your country but the approbation of Heaven: Will you however permit me to suggest the catastrophe that might ensue by Genl. Gaines' compliance with the last clause of your order:[2] Suppose the case that the Indians are beaten, they take refuge either in Pensacola or St. Augustine, which open their gates to them; to profit by his victory General Gaines pursues the fugitives, & has to halt before the Garrison until he can communicate with his Government; in the mean time the Militia grow restless, and he is left to defend himself by the regulars; The enemy, with the aid of their Spanish friends, & Woodbine's British Partizans, or, if you please, with Aury's force, attacks him, what may not be the result? defeat & massacre; Permit me to remark, that the arms of the United States must be carried to any point within the limits of East Florida, where an Enemy is permitted & protected or disgrace attends.

The Executive Government have ordered (and, as I conceive, very properly) Amelia Island to be taken possession of;[3] this order ought to be carried into execution at all hazards, and, simultaneously, the whole of East Florida seized & held as an indemnity for the outrages of Spain upon the property of our citizens: this done, it puts all opposition down, secures to our Citizens a compleat indemnity, & saves us from a War with Great Britain, or some of the Continental Powers combined with Spain; this can be done without implicating the Government; let it be signifyed to me through any channel,[4] (say Mr. J. Rhea) that the possession of the Floridas would be desirable to the United States, & in sixty days it will be accomplished.

The Order being given for the possession of Amelia Island it ought to be executed, or our enemies, internal and external will use it to the disadvantage of our Government. If our troops enter the Territory of Spain in pursuit of our Indian Enemy all opposition that they meet with must be put down or we will be involved in danger & disgrace I have the honor to be very Respy. Yo. Mo. Obt. St.

Andrew Jackson

LS in James M. Glassell's hand, NN (5-1231); Copy certified by Andrew Jackson, Jr., DLC (23). Published in Bassett, 2:345–46. Monroe's AN filed with the LS reads: "Jany 6. 1818. He objects to last clause in Genl. Gaines's instructions, not to attack spanish posts—

proposes an understanding thro' Mr Rhea—I was sick, when I recd. it, and did not read it, till after rect. of Letters by Mr Hambly Expld. in my letter to him of Decr 21. Hearing afterwards, that such understanding, was imputed to me, I asked Mr Rhea, if any thing, had ever passd between him & me, He declard that he had never heard of the subject before. I knew the suggestion to be false, but having not read the letter, & it being possible, that Mr Rhea might have been written to, & have spoken to me, by distant allusion, to the object, to which I might have innocently given, from a desire to acquire Florida, a reply, from which he might have inferrd, a sanction, not contemplated, I was glad to find, that nothing of the kind, had occurrd."

1. See John C. Calhoun to AJ, December 17, 1817.
2. Calhoun's order to Gaines, December 16 (DLC-23), authorized him to attack Indians within Spanish territory "unless they shelter themselves under a Spanish port. In the last event, you will immediately notify this department."
3. See the correspondence enclosed with George Graham to AJ, November 13.

4. The certified copy in Jackson's papers indicates a marginal notation here: "Mr. J Rhea's letter in answer is burnt this 12th. of April 1818 [1819]. A.J." The notation on the copy is not in Jackson's hand.

Authorized by Calhoun's directive of December 26, 1817 (above), to call out militia for a Seminole campaign, Jackson chose instead to construct a reliable corps of Tennessee volunteers by asking officers who had served under him in 1814–15 to assemble troops. Congressional critics later contended that in doing so he usurped the powers of Congress by raising an army without authorization (see Abner Lacock's report to the Senate, February 24, 1819, ASP, Military Affairs, *1:740, and Henry R. Storrs's report to the House, February 28, 1820,* ibid., *2:99–103). In reply, Jackson argued that the volunteers were the functional equivalent of militia, raised in accordance with the laws of Tennessee and previous military practice. The need for haste in emergency conditions justified the manner of his call for troops (see "Strictures on Mr. Lacock's Report on the Seminole War," in Washington* National Intelligencer, *March 9, 1819, and Jackson's memorial to the Senate, February 23, 1820,* Annals of Congress, *15th Cong., 2nd sess., Appendix, pp. 2320–24).*

To Robert Henry Dyer et al.

(Copy) Head quarters Division of the South
(Circular) Nashville Jan 11th. 1819 [1818]—
Sir

The Seminole Indians have raised the war hatchet. They have stained our land with the blood of our Citizens; their war spirit must be put down; and they taught to know that their safety depends upon the friendship and protection of the U States. To accomplish this the aid of one Regiment of mounted Gun men, of one thousand strong, completely armed and equiped, and to serve during the Campaign is asked from West Tennessee: can you raise them and be ready for the Field in ten days? If you can your General who led you to victory on the plains of Talledega, Emuckfau, and Tahopk,[1] asks you to accompany him to the heart of the Seminole Towns, and there aid in giving peace and safety to the Southern Frontier. An answer is expected in five days, and it is anticipated that the number required is now ready. This is a private appeal to the patriotism of West Tennessee, and is not to appear in a Newspaper. If the Regiment is raised and marched all expenses for expresses shall be paid. By the return of the express you are expected to give your opinion of the probability of the result; that preparations may be made accordingly. Col. R. H. Dyer, Col. [John H.] Gibson, Col. [Thomas] Williamson, Col. George Eliott, Maj William Mitchell, Maj John Smith of Montgomery County, Col. [William] Martin of Williamson, and Capt. F[rancis S.]. Ellis of Dixon county have alone been addressed on this subject.[2] The grade of the Officers to be determined by themselves or the Platoon Officers of the Regiment. The Officers raising Companies to command them. Up on further reflection, it is requested that those Officers named above and all such as can raise a Company will meet me at this place on the 19th of the present month. punctuality in this is much desired; and it is further requested that all those Officers who have served in the late war, will be confidentially notified of the forgoing. I have the honour to be &c

A Jackson
Maj General Comd.

True Copy
R[ichard] K[eith] Call[3]
A D Camp

Copy, DNA-RG 46 (5-1242). Published in *ASP, Military Affairs,* 1:767. The Senate copy, made by Richard K. Call in 1819, was submitted with James Monroe's annual message, December 7, 1819, and is misdated. The letter was also widely published in 1819 newspapers as part of the "Strictures" on the Lacock report. Those publications quote an unlocated copy certified by James C. Bronaugh and correctly dated 1818. Dyer (c1774–1826), of Rutherford County, had served as a colonel of Tennessee volunteers in the Creek and New Orleans campaigns and would again serve as colonel of the 1st Regiment in the 1818 Florida campaign.

1. Jackson's soldiers had defeated hostile Creek forces in battles at Talladega, November 9, 1813, Emuckfau Creek, January 22, 1814, and Tohopeka (Horseshoe Bend), March 27, 1814.

2. All the addressees had served as officers during the Creek War. In the 1818 campaign, Gibson (d. 1823), of Rutherford County, and Mitchell, of White County, served as lieutenant colonels of the 1st Regiment of Tennessee volunteers; Williamson (1767–1825), of Davidson County, and Elliott (c1781–1861), of Sumner County, as colonel and lieutenant colonel of the 2nd Regiment; and Martin (1781–1843) and Ellis, as majors of the 2nd Regiment. Smith's 1818 service, if any, has not been verified.

3. Call (1792–1862) was appointed as one of Jackson's aides, May 7, 1818.

To John Coffee

Hermitage Janry 14th. 1818

Dr. Genl

I am ordered forthwith to repair to Ft. Scott assume the command, concentrate the forces, & call on the adjacent states for such auxiliary force as may be necessary to give peace & security to our Southern frontier—I have made an appeal to your Vollunteer Brigade through the officers that commanded the Regts. for one thousand mounted Gunmen[1]—& flatter myself, that twelve hundred will be found ready—the first question asked me was if you would command, I answered I could not say, but supposed from your official situation you could not go,[2] but that I knew you would if you could—The officers are to meet me next Monday the 19th. instant at Nashville, to report to me whether two Regts. can be raised—at which time and place, I have great solicitude to meet you—not that I expect you can go, or that I could ask you under existing circumstances to go, notwithstanding nothing could be more pleasing than to have you with me, but I do know under existing circumstances it would be too great a Sacrafice of interest for to leave your official duties—But I want to see you there on private business, and that your presence may inspire them with their former Patriotism—If I can get 1200 mounted gunmen from Tennessee with my regular force—If they Georgians should mutiny, I can put it down, & drive into the Gulf all the Indians and adherents be them, who they may—

I shall leave home on sunday, leave Nashville on Tuesday or thursday, & I wish to see you & James Jackson together, before I go—My absence will form a good pretext to try the sincerity of my Madison friends—In all which, if any benefit can result, I mean you & James to be equally benefitted—& I think it can be managed to benefit to all[3]—I wish to see you on the subject of our friend Jack Hutchings Estate—I wish aid given to Mrs. Hutchings & Christopher to buy the adjoining fraction—Christopher with Major George Martins note that can be discounted—against the sale can make his first payment[4]—I will endorse it—or if Mr. J. Jackson will, I will indemnify him—This If I have the pleasure of seeing you we can have eranged—I have not heard from the Gasgonading Genl Scott—I am advised by letter from Newyork that my letter was handed him on the 22nd of last month—If he intends adressing me, I will certainly hear from him by next Tuesday[5] If you can come down on Saturday evening next or meet me in Nashville on Monday next, I will be much gratified—with compliments to Polly and the family[6] I am yours sincerely

Andrew Jackson

P. S. I have got my young friend William Donelson to go up to your house with this letter in hopes he may find you returned from Huntsville[7] A. J.

ALS, THi (5-1281). Published in Bassett, 2:348–49 (extract).

1. See above, John C. Calhoun to AJ, December 26, 1817, and AJ to Robert H. Dyer et al., January 11.

2. Coffee was surveyor general for northern Alabama Territory.

3. When Jackson met with Coffee and James Jackson in late January, he authorized them to represent his interests at the upcoming Alabama land sales at Huntsville. See AJ to Coffee, January 27; and James Jackson to AJ, February 12, below.

4. Christopher Hutchings (c1783–1854), John's brother, made the indicated purchase at the February land sales (see Coffee to AJ, February 12). Martin's note has not been found.

5. See above AJ to Winfield Scott, December 3, 1817. The letter from New York has not been found. James M. Glassell delivered Scott's January 2 reply to Jackson on January 30.

6. Coffee's wife Mary Donelson Coffee and their three children Mary Donelson (1812–39), John Donelson (1815–37), and Elizabeth Graves Coffee (1817–38).

7. William Donelson (1795–1864) was Jackson's nephew and Coffee's brother-in-law. Coffee had left for Huntsville on January 2.

To Edmund Pendleton Gaines

Head Quarters Divn South
Nashville 20 Janry. 1818

Sir

I have received orders from the War Dept to assume the immediate command of the Troops assembling on the Southern Frontier & shall leave this on the 22d for Fort Hawkins—[1]

Two Regts of mounted Volunteers will rendevous on the 31st instt at Fayetteville, Tennessee, & move by forced marches the most direct route, via Fort Jackson to Fort Scott—Major [Alexander Campbell Wilder] Fanning is dispatched to Fort Hawkins to purchase, in the event of their being no Qr Master in that neighbourhood the necessary supplies of forage & provisions, to facilitate the movements of these Troops & to have the said supplies deposited at the most convenient points to intercept them on their march—[2]

Enclosed is a copy of instructions sent to the comd. officer of the Georgia Militia, issued on the presumption of your having left that Frontier for Amelia[3]—Should you however have returned & resumed the command; I most particularly enjoin upon you not to hazard a general engagement with the Seminoles unless with such a force as will ensure a decisive victory. The lives of our citizens are too precious to be wantonly exposed in an unequal conflict with Savages. You will therefore have your Forces prepared to march at a moments warning. As soon as reinforced by the Tennessee Volunteers, our strength will be sufficient to inflict, and speedily, merited chastisement on the deluded Savages—Let your supplies be abundant; I would not wish my movements retarded an hour on that account—If there is the least suspicion of the contractors failing, issue the necessary orders to the Qr Master to supply all deficiencies. your most obt serv

Andrew Jackson
Major Genl Comdg.

I have advanced Major Fanning 2000 dollars all that could be spared from the funds in my hands. he will therefore have demands on the Qr Master in your department for any deficiency—

LS in James Gadsden's hand, DNA-RG 94 (M566-105); Copy, DNA-RG 98 (5-1319). LS endorsed, "Recd. at 3. P. M. feby. 1. and answd. at the time."

1. See above, John C. Calhoun to AJ, December 26, 1817.

2. See James M. Glassell to Robert H. Dyer and Thomas Williamson, January 19, and AJ to Arthur P. Hayne, January 21. The order to Fanning has not been found. Fanning (d. 1846;

Military Academy 1812) was an artillery captain, breveted major for gallantry at the defense of Fort Erie during the War of 1812.

3. See AJ to Thomas Glascock, January 20. Glascock (1790–1841), of Richmond County, later represented Georgia in Congress, 1835–39.

To John Caldwell Calhoun

Huntsville Alab. Territory
Janry. 27. 1818—

Sir—

I arrived here last night on my journey to the Frontier of Georgia—In passing through Tennessee it gave me pleasure to dis-cover that my appeal had not been ineffectual, and that Volunteers were flocking to the standard of their country, with that patriotic zeal which has uniformly characterised the Citizens of that state. There is no doubt that Two full Regiments will rendezvous & be mustered into service at Fayetteville by the 1st of February, & thrice that number might be assembled if called for. The only difficulty has been the want of arms, & repeated applications have been made to me for the loan of government muskets—The arms which had been distributed to the militia for their services the last War have already disappeared; Many of them have been injured by neglect, but the greater portion have been sacrificed for a mere pittance, and carried from the state; possibly now in the hands of those very savages, who have been excited to war against us. This fact will prove the impolicy of relying in time of necessity upon such a distribution of arms. The only certain dependance, is upon well stored arsenals, judiciously located, from whence arms may be withdrawn in time of War, & on the return of peace be restored & repaired for future occasions—These reflections have again recalled to my mind, what I have so repeatedly recommended; The necessity of a national Depot, with an Armory, Foundery, & every facility for fabricating of Weapons of War: being established in the South West & induced me to suggest it as a proper period for obtaining the necessary appropriations. The survey of the land on Shoal Creek, reserved for this object was forwarded you some weeks since, and I hope that through your influence some progress may be made this session of Congress towards the accomplishment of an Establishment, important as intimately connected with the permanent defence of the South Western Frontier of our country[1]—If the Government is not disposed to incure the expense, or may be opposed to the erection of a National Foundery & armory, the benefits to be derived from such establishments may be obtained by an indirec*[t]* mode—Individuals in this country are willing to organise a company, with adequate funds for the erection of a Foundery capable of casting every species of ordnance, & an armory for the fabrication of the various smaller weapons of War, if such an encouragement could be given by our Government as would justify the undertaking—This has been suggested from understanding that a Foundery was commenced some time since by a company on the North river, under a promise that a certain proportion of the heavy ordnance for the Army & navy should be cast by them—A similar offer to Individuals at the West would be gladly embraced; It would be expected however that Government would dispose of, or lease for a term of years the reservation of lands on Shoal creek—It may be observed however that what is profitable to Individuals, must be equally so to the Nation, independant of the advantages of having a complete controul over the whole establishment—I can add nothing to what I have already written on this subject; I have only to hope that our Government may view it in the same important light, it has struck me & that an early opportunity *[wi]*ll be embraced to form a permanent National Foundery & Armory adequate to the supply of our South Western states, with all the necessary implements of War without being dependant upon foreign, or Atlanti*[c]* work shops—

The Individuals who have offered to make *[the]* establishment I speak of, would depend altogether on the lands now owned & reserved by Government in Shoal Creek—and if not to be purchased or leased could not undertake the erecting of the necessary foundary workshops &c with respect Your most obt Servt

Andrew Jackson

LS in James Gadsden's hand, MiU-C (5-1340). Published in Bassett, 2:350–51. Endorsed by Calhoun: "Zeal of the Tennesse voluteers merits the thanks of the nation. The establisht of the armory considered impt as soon the population resouces of that partir portion of the country will adt. and it has been recomd. to the land committee of the Senate to make the reservation."

1. See AJ to Calhoun, December 30, 1817. On February 4, Calhoun endorsed the Shoal Creek reservation in a letter to Jeremiah Morrow, chairman of the Senate Committee on Public Lands, but the Senate failed to act on the matter.

To William Rabun

Head Quarters Fort Hawkins
12 oclock Febr. 10. 1818

Sir—

Your letter of the 9th. Instt. has just been handed me.[1] It gives me pleasure to learn that all necessary arrangements have been made for assembling Four Battalions of Infantry at Hartford by the 15th instt—

The requisition made on you in my communication of the 12t. ulto—was altogether conditional, and to be complied with only in the event of General Gains' not having made a previous call upon you—It is of little consequence therefore which of the requisitions has been complied with, so long as the competent number of Georgia Militia are assembled in time to commence active & efficient operations against the Disturbers of our Frontier—[2]

It has caused me much pain to discover the publicity which has been given by the Journalists of this State to all communications from the Army—& I have to request that you will make use of your influence to check for a time this general practice—You will readily perceive the propriety of my request—Whatever is to be effected against the Seminoles must be done secretely & expeditiously; They doubtless have their emissaries amongst us, & if all our movements and intentions are made public, we are ourselves defeating the very objects we wish to effect—Surely our citizens can restrain their curiosity, or are willing to remain ignorant for a time of facts, when necessary for the general good—with respect your Most Obt Servt

Andrew Jackson
Major Genl Comdg.

LS in James Gadsden's hand, G-Ar (6-0011). Rabun (1771–1819) was governor of Georgia.
1. See Rabun to AJ, February 9.
2. See AJ to Rabun, January 12.

From John Henry Eaton

Nashville Feby 12th. 1818

Dear General

I had the pleasure yesterday of receiving your letter of the 5th. with its enclosures.[1] Scotts production is indeed of a non-descript character; & while it operates (as it must) prejudicially to him in the opinion of others, must have a tendency even to humble his own conception of himself whenever in future he shall advert to it. It is due from every man before he acts to weigh the *why* & *wherefore* of his course; had the general done this in the first instance he would have been relieved from his present dilemma & spared the excitement under which he seems to labour The course you have adopted I greatly commend. He has thrown himself on your mercy, & to say more would be error: trust him therefore untill the next war, when he says he will disprove by his conduct the epithet of coward should it be cast against him. His fears must have gone ahead of his judgment in supposing that you would have made any such public denunciation against him; for if any thing like a triumph had been sought after his letter in answer to yours was ample enough without any public exposition of the affair. Never will he shew your letter to any man of judgment & reflection, & tell him ⟨of⟩ the whole affair, but it will have a tendency materially to injure him; & yet by way of comfort & satisfaction to you, he says, but one of his staff has yet seen it, nor shall see it if you desire it to be burned. He must certainly be deffficient in correct judgment—blind to consequences & ignorant of what may seriously affect a soldiers honor. The best thing he can do, will be to let the matter sleep and from respect for the services he has heretofore rendered his country I hope this will be the case—He conjectures yr anonimous correspondent to be one, "who once essayed to raise himself above the highest in our American sphere." To whom is this allusion? either I suppose to [DeWitt] Clinton who sought the Presidential chair not long since; or [Aaron] Burr: doubtless it is to one or the other; which tho, or whom is I presume not material.[2]

Genl. Coffee & James Jackson are yet at Huntsville attending the sales: I will shew them the *Letter* on their return here; they will peruse it with much pleasure. The lands are said to have sold very high: some reports (for we have nothing official) state the average sale at 25 & 30 an acre.

I have just returnd from Winchester, whither I went to attend on the suit relative to the land you sold [William] Finch—The suit was dismissed by the plff; & I scarcly think it will be again commenced[3]

Letters from Fayettville say that the number of troops will meet your expectations. Col. Hayne is I understand well approved-of.

We have no news. Our town is still, & free of any thing to talk about. The conjecture that you are moving against Florida & the part the govt. should take with the patriots is the principle theme of our knowing ones. On this subject I fully expect Mr Clay will get shipwrecked. How a man of his *suspected* knowlege can think it right to jorpadise the liberties of his own people, for the sake of those who have not intelligence to live under any form of free goverment is indeed strange; it may gratify disappointed ambition; but cannot be sanctioned by correct policy. In such a contest we would risk too much—Happy ourselves & free, we should not so far regard that of others as to stake our all upon the issue. In such a contest the people will never unite, & ruin must result to the party that shall cause it. Clays sympathy is the offspring of his disappointment. He is seeking to rally what strength he can against the administration. The Aurora Enquirer & his own dear bantling the Reporter have enlisted under him their influence will be with him, & may perhaps raise a storm which Mr. Munroe will not be able to weather: I trust tho there will sufficent virtue be found amongst our people *[to]* put down every scheme, that seeks success through the ruin of the country.[4] But you have no time for reading like this. I have trespassed on yr patience too far—excuse it

When a leisure moment occurs it will afford me pleasure to hear from you. Your friends are well I am respectfully Yours—

Jno H. Eaton

ALS, DLC (24).

1. See AJ to Eaton, February 5.

2. See above, AJ to Winfield Scott, December 3, 1817; and Scott to AJ, January 2. Clinton (1769–1828) was the unsuccessful candidate of the Peace Party for president in 1812; Burr (1756–1836) tied with Thomas Jefferson in the electoral vote for president in the 1800 elec-

tion, but became vice-president when the House elected Jefferson. Scott alleged that Clinton was responsible for the anonymous letter.

3. Jackson and John Hutchings sold Finch (d. c1824), of Bourbon County, Kentucky, 1,000 acres along the Elk River for $1,500 in 1809. The suit has not been identified.

4. Clay had hoped to become secretary of state in the Monroe administration, but the position was offered to John Q. Adams. In a speech in the House on December 3, 1817, Clay charged that administration policies had favored the Spanish government in its conflict with the Spanish American "patriots" and moved that a committee inquire into provisions which would insure United States neutrality (*Annals of Congress,* 15th Cong., 1st sess., pp. 401–404). Eaton was referring to the Philadelphia *Aurora and General Advertiser,* the *Richmond Enquirer,* and the Lexington *Kentucky Reporter.*

As peace returned to the nation in 1815, Jackson's thoughts turned to the survey and settlement of the lands he had obtained for the United States at the Treaty of Fort Jackson. In doing all that he could to prod the government toward a rapid sale of the lands in what became Alabama, Jackson pursued what he saw as the best interests of both the nation and his friends and neighbors in Tennessee. Only settlement of the interior could control the Indian threat in the Southeast and secure the vital gulf ports against the foreign danger that Jackson had so narrowly turned aside in 1814–15. At the same time, the new lands, especially those in northern Alabama, opened magnificent investment opportunities to well-placed Tennesseans, and Jackson was not shy about pressing the claims of his friends for posts that would be important in the development of the new territory. Jackson clearly foresaw the Alabama land boom of 1817–19 and expected Tennessee to profit from it.

Jackson's expectations in regard to personal profit are, however, less easily established, and the extent of Jackson's activity in land speculation is still more obscure. His late-1816 venture with John Hutchings at Melton's Bluff testifies to an early interest in the acquisition of Alabama lands, and his correspondence with Daniel Parker shortly after demonstrates his interest in profiting by helping others to speculate as well. Arthur P. Hayne, whose duties as inspector general were arranged to facilitate attendance, kept Jackson informed of activities at the first sale of new lands at Milledgeville in August 1817, and when Jackson left for the Seminole campaign in January 1818, he arranged for James Jackson and John Coffee to act as his agents at the upcoming Huntsville land sales. Nonetheless, Jackson's recorded purchases are few. He never obtained more than an Indian title to the Melton's Bluff plantation, although he later bought three lots in Marathon, the town platted on the site. He moved his operation from Melton's Bluff to land purchased near Evans Spring in Lauderdale County, and at the same March 1818 sale, he acquired section 15 of township 3, range 12 west, about a mile south, for his ward Andrew J. Hutchings. In July he purchased several lots in the town of Florence, newly founded by the Cypress Land Company. When others at the November 1818 sale honored his services by refusing to bid against him, Jackson obtained a section near Big Spring in Franklin (now Colbert) County at minimum price. Records of Jackson's involvement in speculative ventures consist of the ownership of one share of Marathon stock and eight shares in the Cypress Land Company and a March 2, 1818, agreement by which Jackson associated with four other Tennesseans to purchase lands for three Philadelphia investors. Since Coffee acted for Jackson in both the Cypress and Philadelphia agreements, the general's actual activity in these investments is concealed. It remains possible that some of Hayne's entries at Milledgeville or some of the extensive entries by Coffee and James Jackson at Huntsville were made for the general, as James Gadsden purchased Florence lots to be divided with Jackson and James C. Bronaugh and James Jackson purchased the section for Andrew J. Hutchings, but nothing has been found which would establish that others purchased for Jackson lands beyond the tracts listed above, just as nothing has been found to show that Jackson acted as agent for Parker or others. The surviving evidence shows that Jackson was highly interested in the development of Alabama and that he was at least a minor participant in the land boom in which many of his closest colleagues were deeply involved, but little more.

From James Jackson

Dittoes Landing 12th. Feby. 1818

Dear Genl,

Genl. Coffee & myself came down this evening to see our friends in Camp & as it is more in his way to give you the Army News; refer to his letter & I must give some account of the Land sales.[1] you recollect [Thomas] Bibb & [Waddy] Tait called on us directly We got to Huntsville & some conversation occured relative to a Company that was then forming; by Invitation I attended one of their meetings where the terms of assosiation were discused & their views were in part made known.[2] I say in part, because it appeared to me there was a wheel within a wheel, or in other words a plott within a Plott. It was proposed to take in the persons who possessed funds, by the strength of which all other purchasers (or as they called them sharp shooter & quarter section men) were to be beaten fairly out of market, the Lands gotten for little or nothing—the company was then to have a second sale, by way of dividing the property It was proposed that Cash should be paid for all that any individual might purchase over and above the amt. of his Capital & whatever his proportion of proffits might be. It was afterwards so arranged that a short Credit was to be given on the excess purchased over the individuals Capital & proffit: I declined having any thing to do with them first because there was too much illiberality in the rich combining to push out of market those who were unfortunate enough not to have *[. . .]* funds, second because I dislike those large combinations and thirdly because I had no confidence in the greater part of those conserned: On Coffee & myself declineing to have any thing to do with them, they became very shy & distant with us & tawlked very big. I told them sharp shooters were hard to beat & that they would see what great things their mamoth Company (by some called Yazo Company) would effect. The first land offered was a fraction adjoining old Captn [Dabney] Morriss' Land on the Madison County line. I run him to 24$ from where We took a fair start. the next, a fraction adjoining Doctor [James] Manning I run to $36 ℔ acre, the people acted with great unanimity against them & wound up the sales of the good Limestone Lands at $78 ℔ Acre the Lands rose from the commencement in the first range on Madison County Line to the Close of sales of the fourth range which took all or very nearly all the good Lands, a large portion of which was sold at from $30 to 50$ ℔ Acre.[3] The handsomest game of sink pocket you ever seen was played on them & you never seen a set of great purs proud gentry so compleatly foiled, vexed & mad. This company was composed of people of Madison County, Kentucky, Virginia & Georgia, Not a man that Tennessee Claims belonged to them & Captn Ben Jones the only man that had even resided there lately.[4] I should not be surprised if old Morris [already?] abandoned his great commercial plans & returned to old Virginia compleatly disapointed: I got into two pretty high bargains in course of operations, a quarter section at $ 40 ℔ Acre (for which have *[. . .]* Cost) *[. . .]* one half of Bibbs Farm at $70 dollars ℔ acre Colonel [Robert] Weakly was my partner in the purchase of Bibbs quarter[5]—the people were highly delited at his [loosing] his farm—

A Company of Tennessee men, 20 in number, bought a Town site at or near the mouth of Limestone & Land adjoining amounting to fifty thousand dollars Genl. Coffee will enclose you one of our advertisements[6] We did not attempt to purchase any land in your name. We found those pretended friends so extremely selfish & hipocritical that Coffee & myself would not risk using your name with them, altho old Judge [Obadiah] Jones proposed it[7]—I told the Judge in my opinion the mamoth company did not possess [liberality?] enough to enable the object to be effected—

Colonel [Andrew] Hynes this day applyed to me about your farm & would I think purchase it payable on what he calls Government terms—one fourth down ¼ in two ¼ in three & ¼ in four years, with interest on the last three payments, but the great price lands have sold at here must effect the price in Tennessee & would not think of doing any thing with him untill I hear from you[8]—The sales will close on Saturday next two townships in the sixth range is yet to sell, after that is done will visit the Bluff & write you the situation of things there—I have sent for my Fellows and directed my women, boys & Girls to be left & hope your Cotton will be gotten out before I'll want them We have nothing new that is interesting since you left us—Josiah Nichol resigned his situation in the Nashville

Bank and [Stephen] Cantrell has been elected President in his stead[9]—The Directors of the United States Bank have determined to establish a Branch in Nashvill in defiance of the Law of the State[10]—I forgot to tell you that, the mamoth Company has got very little good Land, the Company price being limited, but each individual having a right to withdraw his funds to pay for any Lands ⟨bought⟩ they might purchase over the Company Limits, a large portion of them have withdrawn their funds in that way & the Company will in a few days die a natural death—I think you have a fine set of fellows here & hope Tennessee will find her character supported by them with you at their head sincerely yours

James Jackson

ALS, ICHi (6-0018). The manuscript has been torn lengthwise and mended. Ditto's Landing was located on the north bank of the Tennessee River about ten miles south of Huntsville.

1. See John Coffee to AJ, February 12.

2. Bibb (1784–1839), a younger brother of territorial governor William W. Bibb, moved to Huntsville in 1816 and served as Alabama governor, 1820–21. Tate (1786–1864), who married a sister of Thomas Bibb's wife, was a Huntsville doctor.

3. Morris, from Richmond, Virginia, purchased two fractional sections in township 4, range 1 west for $24.25 per acre. He became a trustee of the Cypress Land Company. Manning, who married another sister of Thomas Bibb's wife, was a Huntsville resident and large land owner. According to later testimony by John Coffee, opposition to the company was led by Coffee, the receiver John Brahan, and the register John Read. Brahan's purchases contributed to his later default. See *ASP, Public Lands,* 7:548–49.

4. Probably Benjamin Brauch Jones (c1792–1830), most likely the captain who served in the 24th Infantry under Jackson's command in 1814 and 1815. He represented Lawrence County at the 1823 session of the Alabama house.

5. Weakley (1764–1845), from Nashville, was a former congressman. Bibb's farm was in township 4, range 3 west.

6. In his letter of February 12, Coffee enclosed an advertisement for the town of Cotton Port.

7. Jones (1763–1825) had been appointed a U.S. judge for Mississippi Territory in 1810, and, taking up residence in Madison County, he served until 1819.

8. Hynes (1785–1845), a Nashville merchant and manufacturer, had served as Jackson's aide on the Natchez expedition and later as the state's adjutant general. The terms suggested correspond to those offered by the land sale act of May 10, 1800 (2 *U.S. Statutes at Large* 73–78 at 74), and subsequent sales.

9. Nichol (1772–1833) and Cantrell (1783–1854) were Nashville merchants and bankers. Cantrell also served at times as mayor.

10. By an act of November 22, 1817, the state legislature had assessed a prohibitive tax of $50,000 per year on the operation within Tennessee of any bank, or branch, not chartered by the state.

To John Caldwell Calhoun

Head Quarters Divisi South
Hartford Georgia
Febr. 14 1818—

Sir.

I arrived at this place on the evening of the 12th. & here met with General Gaines. From a letter received from the Governor of Georgia advising of the movement of the Militia from the several counties to the designated point of rendezvous, as well as the punctuality with which the Troops have assembled here under General Gaines' requisition, has induced a hope that I shall be enabled to make a prompt & speedy march for the relief of Fort Scott—[1]

I enclose you a Copy of a letter from Col. B[enjamin] G[rayson] Orr to Capt [Otho W.] Callis Contractors Agent at Fort Hawkins. From the sum with which he states to have furnished his Agents in this Country, you can judge how far efficient means have been adopted to ensure the necessary supplies to the Troops heretofore in service, as well as those summouned to the field under the late requisition[2]—The mode of provisioning an Army by contract is not adapted to the prompt & efficient movement of Troops—It may answer in time of profound peace where a failure or delay cannot produce any serious ill consequences—But where Active operations are necessary, & success dependant on prompt & quick movements There is no dependance to be placed on the Contractor. His views are purely mercenary & where the supplies will not ensure him a profit, he hesitates not on a failure, never regarding how far it may defeat the best devised plans of the Commander in Chief—Experience has confirmed me in this opinion & the recent failure has prompted me again to express it—

The plan which has been adopted to procure the necessary supplies for the Army, to transport them to Fort Scott, & the quantity otherwise ordered to that point, will I hope relieve me from any embarrassment on that account, untill a decisive blow has been struck upon the enemy.[3] I have been so frequently embarrassed from the failures of Contractors that I cannot but express a hope that some other more efficient & certain mode of supplying our Army may be adopted—Such a Plan as will render those charged with the execution of so important a trust responsible to military authority, & exposed to severe & merited chastisement, whenever defaulters, at the discretion of a Court Martial—

Since my arrival in this State, various accusations on respectible authority, have been made against General [David Brydie] Mitchell the Agent for the Creek Nation[4]—It is alledged in the first instance that he has used his influence in preventing the Creek Indians from joining General Gaines;

That he was induced to this act to assist himself & others in smuggling into this country a large number of Affrican Negroes which they had purchased at Amelia Island; That upwards of one hundred have been carried to the Agency, part of which have been seized by the officer of the Customs, but that a large number have by the Agents written pasport been carried to some point unknown. That thirty were transported from the Agency On the day the custom house officer arrived there & I am this day informed that upwards of one hundred Affrican Negroes, some time since, passed Mr Barnets on the Flint river bound to the Agency[5]—The Creek Indians complain that the General has retained in his hands the greater part of the Eighty five thousand dollars, appropriated by Congress to indemnify the friendly part of the nation for the depredations committed on them by the Red Sticks[6]—They further state that he has paid off the Indians for their military services in goods instead of in cash; That he has established a large store and Tavern within the nation & that he has taken into his possession all the Ferries at which the most extravagant tolls are exacted—Col [David] Brearly has exhibited to me a copy of the pasport given by Genrl Mitchell as Agent & has stated to me the fact of having seen several of the Affricans, mentioned above, in the possession of Genrl. Mitchell & further confirmed the statement of thirty having been run from the Agency the night of the arrival of Capt [McQueen] McIntosh the custom officer, but by whom run is not ascertained—[7]

I have thought it my duty to communicate these statements for the information of the Executive that such an order may be taken on the subject as comports with the character of our country & which justice to the Creek nation may demand—The Testimony of Col Brearly will throw great light on the subject if required—with respect your most ob Sert

Andrew Jackson
Major Genl commdg.

LS in James Gadsden's hand, DNA-RG 107 (M221-78); Copy, DNA-RG 59 (6-0022); Extracts, THi (mAJs), DNA-RG 233 (6-0027, -0031), DNA-RG 98 (6-0041), DNA-RG 46 (6-0035), NHi (6-0038). Published in Bassett, 2:354–55 (extract). The THi extract bears an ANS by Jackson discussing his actions following Calhoun's response to the charges against David B. Mitchell.

1. See William Rabun to AJ, February 9.

2. See Benjamin G. Orr to Otho W. Callis, January 26, DLC (24). Callis (d. 1831), from Virginia, had served as an infantry officer before resigning his commission in May 1817. Orr (c1763–1822), Washington mayor as well as contractor for Jackson's troops, reported sending $12,500 to Georgia in December and January to purchase supplies. Orr's failures as contractor were the subject of a Senate investigation in March (see *SDoc* 136, 15th Cong., 1st sess., Serial 3).

3. For Jackson's supply arrangements, see above, AJ to Edmund P. Gaines, January 20; Gaines to AJ, February 1; George Gibson to AJ, February 2; and William A. Trimble to AJ, February 4.

4. Mitchell (1766–1837) had resigned as governor of Georgia, November 4, 1817, to

take the appointment as Creek agent. He was removed from office in 1821 in consequence of the charges of complicity in slave smuggling. See AJ to John Clark, April 20, 1819, below.

5. Almost certainly the English trader Timothy Barnard or one of his many part-Creek sons, who lived south of the Creek Agency on the Flint River.

6. "An Act for the relief of certain Creek Indians," March 3, 1817 (6 *U.S. Statutes at Large* 191).

7. For the charges made by Brearley (1786–1837), a colonel in the 7th Infantry and later Cherokee agent in Arkansas, see Statement of Brearley et al., February 10–11. For a copy of the passport issued by Mitchell, January 28, see DNA-RG 75 (M271-2). McIntosh (d. 1819), surveyor and Inspector of the Revenue for Darien, Georgia, seized eighty-eight slaves near the Creek Agency in early February.

From Hopony and Echofixeca

Hopony place Ketchefonguy
March 13 1818

Sir,

I recieved your note from my friend and now give him an answer to it. It was respecting some Beef cattle & I am sorry it was not in my power to send more & better. The time of gathering the cattle has not yet come which is the reason of my not sending more. but should you want any more in a little time from this I shall be glad to supply you I have a large quantity of Stock which I shall be glad at any time to sell but could not now not having sufficient notice.[1]

I have a large parcel neart for[t] Early and the Cuseater's on there march down to the army have killed a good many[2] I cannot tell the reason why the ⟨the whites⟩ my white friends pass through the country and buy my produce without injuring me & when our own people pass through they trespass upon our rights now I wish you to enquire of them wether they done it through necessity or not if through necessity that you would make some provision for the payment of the same One of the Chehaw men was taken sick at fort Scott and one of the same family returned home with him On their march back they were met by the Cuseter's who took their guns from them and abusid them very much I wish my guns to be found and returned again to one of the same family now in company with Mr Lewis.[3]

I am anxious to move to the Chehaw town as I fear to stay here being close to the edge of the Hostile Indians and move there for Safety.[4]

I also wish to know of you if those Indian's who have done no mischief will be permitted to return to me as I know some have not done any mischief I do not want any to return who have ever fired a single gun at the white men and hope you will not have the life of those taken who has not done any mischief I present this to my friends General Jackson & Genl. Gains Your friends

his
Hopony X
mark
his
Echofixeca X
mark

LS by proxy, DLC (24). Endorsed as received March 23. Hopony (Opony; Ochacona Tustonaky; d. 1823) was the chief of a Creek (Ocmulgee) town east of the Flint River, apparently near the mouth of Kinchafoonee Creek. Warriors from his village were reputed to be active in depredations against Georgia settlements, and he had joined several hostile chiefs in signing a power of attorney for Alexander Arbuthnot in June 1817. Echofixeca, a distant relative of the Seminole chief Bowlegs, has not been further identified

1. Note not found. See receipt of William Triplett, March 25, for cattle purchased from Hopony for Edmund P. Gaines's troops.

2. Fort Early was located on the left bank of the Flint River in Crisp County, Georgia. Cusseta was a lower Creek town on the Chattahoochie River near Fort Mitchell, Alabama.

3. The Indians have not been identified. Lewis may have been Kendal Lewis, Creek interpreter on the 1816 Negro Fort expedition and assistant commissary for the Creek troops during the Seminole campaign.

4. On April 22, the Georgia militia, ordered by Governor William Rabun to destroy Hopony's town, instead attacked Chehaw, a friendly village west of the Flint River in its fork with Muckalee Creek in Lee County. The resultant massacre became a matter of controversy between Jackson and Rabun. See AJ to Chehaw Indians and to Rabun (below), both May 7. Hopony escaped the militia and subsequently established a new village along the Tolopchopko or Peace River east of Tampa Bay in Florida.

To Rachel Jackson

Fort Gadsden March 26th. 1818
East side of the appelachecola, where
the Negro Ft formerly stood.

My Love

No opportunity of writing you has occurred since I left Hartford, Georgia, untill now, nor have I heard from you, since I left that place untill yesterday, & that through a note from Doctor [Jabez Wiggins] Heustis, now at Ft Scot Sixty miles in the rear, adressed to Colo Butler who says he saw you, Mrs. Butler & Colo Hays family on the 8th. ult all well, this gave me much pleasure, as I suppose, if the dear little fellows the two Andrew had not been well you would have named it, or that he would have heard it.[1] Untill a few days past we have experienced bad roads, high waters, & constant rain, with the dreary prospects of great scarcity of provisions, the supplies ordered from New orleans, having been detained by adverse winds. This situation is changed, and the prospect of plenty is ours, Colo [George] Gibson with Capt [Isaac] McKeever comdg the armed vessells reached me last evening,[2] several of his vessells laden with supplies are in the bay, part of which I have recd, and the vessells separated in the gale are daily ariving, to detail to you our march from Hartford to this place, and the various incidents that has occurred, would occupy more time & space, than the limits of a letter will allow, time will only permit me to say to you, that scarcity of supplies from the commencement of our march, from the neglect of those who Genl Gains had charged with forwarding them began to shew itself, I had confidence in the exertion of Colo. Gibson who was charged with forwarding the supplies from N. orleans, on these, altho far in advance I depended, and I was determined to endeavour to reach them, trusting to the deity to aid my exertions, and supply the means to allay hunger, and preserve the health of my troops, untill I could meet them. dispatches, arrived from the commanding officer of Ft Scott, informing of the great scarcity there, and of his determination to abandon that post in a few days if supplies did not reach him, this occasioned Genl Gains to set out for that post,[3] to reach it in time to prevent such a disgracefull catastrophy & which would have threw some dificulty in the way in prosecuting the campaign, he got shipwrecked decending the river flint, lost his asst adjt. Genl & two soldiers drowned, and joined me six days after—nearly exausted with hunger and cold, having lost all his cloathing & baggage,[4] in the mean time I was endeavouring to push on the Georgia Brigade to cover & protect my supplies expected in the Bay & river appelachecola, that was threatened to be arrested by the enemy, I reached Ft Early where I expected & was promised supplies,[5] here I found half a pint of corn & half a pint of flower pr man, to ration my troops, through a wilderness of upwards of sixty miles, with various large water courses unusually high to pass, I recollected how the Isarelites of old had been fed in the wilderness, encouraged my men, had the pittance of bread stuff Issued, (I had hoggs on foot with me) ordered the line of march to be taken up, crossed the flint to draw what supplies I could from the Indians, altho detained many days making bridges, I reached Ft Scott on the night of the 9th. instant, the troops in good health not having lost one man by sickness or any other casualty—at Ft Scott I found a few poor Beeves which added to the scanty supply of Pork I had on hand would ration my men for three days, and one quart of corn pr man, on this I determined to look in to the bay for the supplies, and on the 10th. marched for this place, god favoured my exertions, I have met them, built a garrison for their reception & safety and march this day to reach the enemy, & endeavour with the smiles of heaven to put a speedy end to the campaign, this will be much facilitated by the cooperation of the navy commanded by that valuable officer Capt McKeever who is now here, and has readily agreed to cooperate with me, this will ensure me supplies along the coast, & capture such of the enemy who may attempt to make their Escape to the smaller Ilands bordering on our coasts. At Ft Scott I expected to meet the Volunteers from Tennessee, in this I was disappointed, I had caused supplies to be laid in for them at Ft Mitchell and advised them of a supply of corn at Ft Gains. Colo. Hayne recd. my despatch & the supplies at Ft Mitchel, with my instructions to pass by Ft Gains to Ft Scott, the idea of starvation had spread far & wide, and a panic was every where, he was told by officers of high grade that no supplies could be had at Ft Gains, if he advanced to Ft Scott he would starve, he changed his rout by Georgia, where the frontier has been drained of supplies, and where they will experience great scarcity. I hear the Tennesseens are in the wilderness and I hope will join me to day or tomorrow, But how grating to their feelings—how grating to mine, that those brave men, who have marched so far, should be thrown in the rear by false statements, by men of high grade in the army, whose duty it was to have urged them on to have saved the supplies coming by water & on which the safety of the army, & the future progress of the campaign rested, but an enquiry has been entered into, which will bring to light those who have been & are to blame for our scarcity and the change of rout by Colo. Hayne—was the Tennesseens up, I, under present circumstances, would be contented.[6]

I with my whole staff & army enjoy good health Shew this to Colo. Hays, & present him my best wishes. Tell Rachel B[utler] that her Colo. is remarkable well, kiss my two little fellows for me, and tell them papa is well—accept of my prayers for your health and happiness untill I return, day begins to appear, I must prepare the Troops for a march. I must bid you for the present adieu. I shall write you the first opportunity. May god bless you. I salute you with an affectionate farewell. I am your affectionate Husband

Andrew Jackson

P. S. we have taken a few prisoners, Genl McIntosh commanding the friendly creeks, who was ordered to pass down & reconnoitre the right bank of the appelachicola reports to me on the 19th. that he has without the fire of a gun captured of the red ground chiefs party 180 weomen & children & 53 warriors, With all their cattle & supplies the red ground chief with thirty warriors making their Escape on horseback—Ten of the warriors, after having surrendered, attempted to make their Escape, he killed fourteen in all of warriors has been killed.[7] I have reached this point without the least interruption from the enemy, we have obtained from them a small supply of corn on our march, which was much wanted

P. S. Capt John Gordon has joined me, on his way he overtook the Tennesseens when they took the rout to Georgia he shaped his course to me braving all dangers, the gods preserved him

ALS, MH-H (6-0173).

1. Note not found. Heustis (1784–1841), who later published studies of yellow fever,

served as an army surgeon from 1814 to 1819. The two Andrews were Andrew Jackson, Jr., and Andrew Jackson Hutchings.

2. Gibson (1783–1861), of Pennsylvania, was quartermaster general at New Orleans. McKeever (d. 1856) was a U.S. navy lieutenant.

3. See Mathew Arbuckle to Edmund P. Gaines, February 15, and Gaines to AJ, February 22. Arbuckle (1776–1851), a career army officer from Virginia and colonel of the 7th Infantry, was commander at Fort Scott.

4. Gaines's assistant adjutant general was Clinton Wright, son of Robert Wright, a former senator, congressman, and governor of Maryland. Gaines himself had been rumored to be drowned.

5. Gaines wrote Jackson, February 1 and 5, that he had ordered supplies to Fort Early.

6. See AJ to Arthur P. Hayne, February 11; Hayne to AJ, March 9, 19. Jackson blamed David Brearley for misadvising the Tennessee troops and charged him with unmilitary conduct, but Brearley's court-martial refused to consider the charge, agreeing with Brearley that giving advice when solicited could not constitute a military offense.

7. See McIntosh to AJ, March 16 and 19. Red Ground was an Alabama Indian village, formerly located near the present site of Montgomery, but at this time on the west side of the Chattahoochee River near the Florida border. By 1823, when he signed the Treaty of Moultrie Creek, the Red Ground Chief (Conchatee Micco) had become friendly to the United States.

To Francisco Caso y Luengo

Head Quarters Divis of the South
Before St Marks.
6 ⟨March⟩ April 1818.

Sir—

To chastise a Savage foe, who combined with a lawless band of Negro Brigands, have for some time past been carrying on a cruel & unprovoked war against the Citizens of the U States; has compelled The President to direct me to march my army into Florida—I have penetrated to the Mekasukian Towns & reduced them to ashes. In these Towns I found every indication of a hostile spirit—On a red pole in the center of the Council houses of Kenhagees Town more than fifty fresh scalps of all ages from the Infant to the aged matron, were found suspended—In addition to this upwards of three hundred old scalps were found in the dwellings of the different Chiefs settled on the Mekasuky pond[1]—Those Barbarians who escaped death have fled—From information communicated by the Governor of Pensacola to Two of my Captains, Gordon and Call, I was induced to believe that they had fled to St Marks for protection. The Governor stated that the Indians & Negroes had demanded of you large supplies of munitions of war, with a threat in the event of a refusal, of taking possession of your fortress. He further expressed an apprehension that from your defenceless state, They were already in possession of St Marks[2]—The Wife of Chenubbee, a noted chief, now a prisoner in my camp informs me that the Hostile Indians & Negroes obtained their supply of amunition from St Marks[3]—To prevent the recurrance of so gross a violation of neutrality & to exclude our savage Enemies from so strong a hold as St Marks I deem it expedient to garrison that fortress with American Troops untill the close of the present war—This measure is justifiable on that universal principal of self defence & cannot but be satisfactory, under existing circumstances to his Catholic Majesty the King of Spain—Under existing treaties between our two governments, The King of Spain is bound to preserve in peace with the Citizens of the U States not only his own subjects, but all Indian Tribes residing within his territory[4]—When called upon to fulfil that part of the treaty in relation to a savage tribe who have long depredated with impunity the American frontier, incompetency is alledged, with an acknowledgement that the same tribe have acted in open hostility to the laws, & invaded the rights of the subjects of his Catholic Majesty—As a mutual Enemy therefore it is expected that every facility will be afforded by the Agents of the King of Spain to chastise these lawless & inhuman savages—In this light is the possession of St Marks by the American forces to be viewed—I came not as the Enemy but as the Friend of Spain. Spanish rights, and property will be respected; The property & rights of Spanish Subjects will be guaranteed them; An Inventory of all public property, munitions of war &c shall be made out & certified by an Officer appointed by each of us, and a receipt given for the same to be accounted for to his Catholic Majesty by the U States[5]—The subject of my possession of the garrison of St Marks, will be referred to our respective governments for an Amicable adjustment—

Some Armed vessels of the U States are in the Bay of St Marks; with whom I wish to communicate: You will I trust furnish me with a small vessel to convey a letter, as well as some sick & wounded that are with me—[6]

As our mutual savage Enemies are concentrating their forces near or on the Sewaney, an early & prompt answer is requested to this letter, with an english translation, as neither myself or staff are acquainted with the Spanish[7]—I have the honor to be with great respect your Most obt Servt.

This will be handed you by my aid de camp Lt James Gadsden, by whom an answer is expected I have the honor to be with great respect your Most obt Servt

Andrew Jackson
Major Genl Comdg.

LS in James Gadsden's hand and Translation, SpSAG (6-0189, -0193); Copies, DNA-RG 46 (6-0196), DNA-RG 84 (6-0200), DNA-RG 94 (6-0202), DNA-RG 233 (6-0205, -0209, -0213). Published in *ASP, Military Affairs,* 1:704–705. Caso y Luengo (b. c1761), who had served in Spain's Louisiana Infantry since 1785, commanded Spanish forces at Fort St. Marks.

1. Kenhajee (King Hadjo, Cappachimico), the leading Mikasuki chief, was reported killed in the attack on his village on April 1, but he fled with his tribe. In November, he promised to gather his people, return to the village, and live in peace with the United States (see Alexander C. W. Fanning to Edmund P. Gaines, November 27, *ASP, Military Affairs,* 1:752).

2. Richard K. Call heard of José Masot's apprehensions about Fort St. Marks when he went to Pensacola in February to negotiate regarding the passage of supplies for Fort Crawford

(see *ASP, Military Affairs,* 1:751). He likely reported the conversation when he joined Jackson at Fort Gadsden in March. John Gordon carried Jackson's March 26 letter to Masot and may have returned with a verbal report by this time, although Masot did not officially respond until April 15.

3. Chennabee was a Fowltown chief most noted as the captor in December 1817 of Indian traders Edmund Doyle and William Hambly. His wife has not been identified.

4. See Article 5 of the Treaty of San Lorenzo, October 27, 1795.

5. See the reports of ordnance and of provisions and hospital stores at St. Marks, both April 7, DLC (69).

6. The schooners *Thomas Shields, James Lawrence,* and *Peacock,* carrying supplies for Jackson's army, arrived off St. Marks on April 2. The letter has not been found.

7. For Caso y Luengo's reply, see below.

From Francisco Caso y Luengo

Fort St. Marks April 7th. 1818—

Dear Sir,

Being made to understand altho with difficulty the contents of the letter with which your Excellency honored me yesterday evening, which was delivered me by your Aid De Camp James Gadsden,[1] I manifest to you the satisfaction the result of your expedition against Mickasuckey has given me, which could not be expected otherwise from the superior tallents, and active disposition of your Excellency, to which must be attributed the success, on which I return you my congratulations. My Chief the Governor of Pensacola had very good reasons for mentioning to your Captns. Gordon & Call [(]what you expressed in yours of yesterday) His fear [for] the fate of this Fort, menaced by Indians & negroes for some months past, and particularly since they have been deceived in not obtaining powder & balls which they have repeatedly solicited, and which they had thought themselves entitled to from the continual practice of yearly supplies. This is a proof of how groundless is the report of the wife of the Chief Chenabbee, who stated that the Indians have been supplied with amunition from this Fort which has not been the case since I was advised to keep a strict & perfect neutrality; no one better than the bearer of this Wm. Hambley who has interpreted for me various times the solicitations of many Indian chiefs in this neighborhood can testify;[2] he can also explain to you any opinion which you may have formed on this subject, he can inform you of my often advising them to avoid their present destruction. This being now complete, and no motive remaining to fear an insult to this fort from these barbarians & negroes I beg of your Excellency leave to state to you what difficulties I should involve myself in with my Government if I were to conform with what your Excellency proposes to Garrison this post with United States troops without first receiving orders to that effect which I shall immediately solicit as soon as an opportunity offers which I cannot doubt one moment would be refused as I know with what zeal she would wish to comply with the stipulated treaty with the United States. until such time I hope your

Excellency will desist from your intention, and be firmly persuaded of the good fellowship & harmony which will reign betwen this garrison & whatever troops you may think proper or convenient to leave in this vicinity, who may assist me in the defence of this Fort, or any unforseen event. The sick your Excellency has sent in, are lodged in the royal hospital, and are supplied with every necessary which our present circumstances will admit of—I hope Your Excellency may have further oc̨casions wherein I may be enabled to shew the good will I have to serve you. I hope your Excy. will pardon my not answering yours as soon as desired for reasons which I suppose have been given you by your Aid De Camp, nor for furnishing you with an English translation to this as there is no one in this Fort who is capable thereof, but the bearer of this Wm. Hambley, has promised to translate it for you in the best manner he is capable of God preserve your Excell: many years is the wish of you obt. Svt.

signed. Franco. Caso y Luengo

Translation, DLC (24); ALS and Translations, DNA-RG 94 (6-0253, -0256, -0259); ALS copy, SpSAG (6-0251); Translations, DNA-RG 46 (6-0265), DNA-RG 233 (6-0268, -0274, -0281). Published in Bassett, 2:356–57. For a transcription of the Spanish ALS, see Appendix.

1. See above.

2. Hambly, an Indian trader associated with the firm of John Forbes and Company, had served British Colonel Edward Nicolls as an interpreter during the War of 1812, but the Seminoles now perceived him as an ally of the Americans. Along with fellow trader Edmund Doyle (d. 1831), he was seized in December and threatened with death. The Indians delivered the two men to St. Marks in February after Caso y Luengo apparently agreed to hold them as prisoners. Hambly and Doyle subsequently testified that the Indians had been welcomed at St. Marks, but Indian acquisition of arms was not discussed in their letter of May 2 or Hambly's deposition of July 24 (*ASP, Military Affairs*, 1:716). Hambly's later career included service as Creek interpreter at Fort Mitchell in the 1820s.

To John Caldwell Calhoun

Head Quarters Divis South
Camp near St Marks
8 April 1818

Sir—

I wrote you from Fort Gadsden, communicating the embarrasments under which I had laboured previous to my arrival at that post; and my determination, being then in a situation to commence active operations, to penetrate immediately into the center of the Seminole Towns[1]—My army marched on the 26 ulto, and on the 1s of April was reinforced by the friendly Creek warriors under Genl McIntosh, and a detachment of Tennessee Volunteers commanded by Col Elliott; On the same day a mile and a half in advance of the Mekasukian villages, a small party of hostile Indians were discovered, judiciously located on a point of land projecting into an extensive marshy pond; the positio*[ns]*, designated, as since understood, for the concentrating of the negro, and Indian forces to give us battle—They maintained for a short period a spirited attack from my advanced spy companies, but fled and dispersed in every direction upon comming in contact with my flank columns, and discovering a movement to encircle them—The pursuit was continued through the Mekasukian Towns untill night compelled me to encamp my army[2]—The next day detatchments were sent out in every direction to reconnoitre the country; secure all supplies found; and reduce to ashes the villages—This duty was executed to my satisfaction: nearly Three hundred houses were consumed; and the greatest abundance of corn cattle &c brought in. Every indication of a hostile spirit was found in the habitations of the Chiefs: In the Council houses of Kenhajee's Town, The King of the Mekasukians, more than fifty fresh scalps were found, and in the center of the public square, The old red Stick's standard, *a red Pole,* was erected, crowned with scalps recognised by the hair, as torn from the heads of the unfortunate companions of Scott—

As I had reason to believe that a portion of the hostile Indians had fled to St Marks, I directed my march towards that fortress—As advised, I found that the Indians and negroes combined had demanded t*[he]* surrender of that work; The Spanish garrison was too weak to defend it, and there were circumstances reported, producing a strong conviction in my mind that if not instigated by the Spanish authorities, the Indians had received the means of carrying on the war from that quarter: Foreign agents who have been long practiseing their intrigues, and villanies in this country had free access into the Fort—St. Marks was necessary as a depot to ensure success to my operations—These considerations determined me to occupy it with an American force—An Inventory of the Spanish property, munitions of war &c has been taken and receipted for;[3] Personal rights and private property has been respected, & The Commandant and garrison furnished with transportation to Pensacola—My correspondence with the Spanish commandant, the evidences under which I acted, and a detailed account of my operations will be furnished you as early as practicable[4]—Success depends upon the rapidity of my movements, and tomorrow I shall march for the Sewaney river, the destroying the establishments on which, will, in my opinion, put a final close to this savage war Capt McKever of the navy cruising at my request on this coast, has been fortunate enough in securing [Josiah] Francis or Hillis Hajo, The great prophet, and Homattlemico an old red stick[5]—They visited his vessels under an impression they were English, from whom as they stated supplies of munitions of war &c under late promises, were expected—Abuthnot, a Scotch man and suspected as one of the Instigators of this savage war, was found in St. Marks. He is in confinement untill evidences of his guilt can be collected—with respect Your mo ob Sert

Andrew Jackson
Major Genl comdg.

LS in James Gadsden's hand, DNA-RG 107 (M221-78); Copies, DNA-RG 46 (6-0308), DNA-RG 84 (6-0313), DNA-RG 233 (6-0316, -0322, -0326). Published in Bassett, 2:358–59.

1. See AJ to Calhoun, March 25.

2. For detailed reports of the skirmish, see William Brady, Robert F. Crittenden, and Thomas Glascock to Robert Butler, all April 4, DLC (24); and Alexander Dunlap to [Butler], April 4, DLC (69).

3. See the reports of ordnance and of provisions and hospital stores at St. Marks, both April 7, DLC (69).

4. See AJ to Calhoun, May 5, below.

5. Francis, a war chief of the Alabama or Holy Ground tribe, had been one of the principal Creek leaders during the 1813–14 Creek War. Homathlemico (Neamathla Micco), of Autosse (Atasi), was also a Red Stick chief and reputedly a leader of the attack on Lieutenant Scott's boat. The men were captured on April 3, and on April 8, Jackson ordered both hanged.

To Rachel Jackson

26 miles in advance of St Marks on my march to
the Indian & Negro Towns on Suwaney
April 10th. 1818—

My Love

I wrote you on the 8th. from St Marks by the way of Neworleans, which I hope will reach you[1]—having an opportunity direct to Georgia, I cannot forego the pleasure of dropping you a line, and enclose you a letter recd. from Major Thomas Claibourn who is now member in congress—It affords such prospects of relief to Mrs. Caffery & Mrs. Hays in procuring a permanant settlement of land, and aiding Mrs. Hutchings in paying *[for]* what she has Bought[2]—This although I a*[m at]* present immured in a savage wilderness, aff*[ords m]*e much pleasure, I wish you to commu*[nicate th]*e contents to all concerned. The ballance of the Tennessee Vollunteers are near me, Colo. Elliott with about 400 having joined me on the 1rst. a few hours before the affair at the Mickesukey Towns—I hope in a few days to Break down the hostile savages & Negroes in this quarter & give peace to our frontier—It appears that the hand of offended daiety is stretched forth against the exc[i]ters of this cruel war, amonghst those killed in Battle & that has fell into our hands, five of the worst has fallen the 6th. Arbuthnot a Scotchman in irons I had Francis the prophet & Ho'Emattie'micko hung on the 8th. sixty men weoman & children on that day surrendered, I am in persuit of the fugatives I do not believe they will give us Battle—adieu my love & kiss my son & little charge for me

A. Jackson

ALS, MH-H (6-0344).

1. See AJ to Rachel Jackson, April 8.

2. Enclosure not found. On January 27 Claiborne had presented to Congress Jackson's remonstrance requesting that the heirs of John Donelson (c1718–86) be granted 10,000 acres

in the "Big Bend" of the Tennessee River as compensation for the survey work on which Donelson was engaged at his death. The matter was referred to a select committee of which Claiborne was a member, and he reported a bill "for the benefit of Thomas Carr and others" on February 9, when it was read twice and committed. Claiborne evidently wrote optimistically regarding the bill's prospects, but it was laid on the table, April 13. Similar bills were presented to subsequent Congresses until an act of May 24, 1824, authorized the Donelson heirs and their associated petitioners to claim 5,000 acres of public lands in Alabama or Mississippi (6 *U.S. Statutes at Large* 313). Regarding Catherine D. Hutchings's recent purchase, see above, AJ to John Coffee, January 14.

To United States Troops near Suwannee River

Adjutant Generals Office—
Head Quarters Division of the South
Camp near Swuaney—15th. April 1818—

General Order

Tomorrow we meet the enemy. The accompanying plan and explanation of attack on the negroes and Bowlegs Towns at Swuaney is given to the Army for their information and Goverment.[1] It has been adopted under the persuasion that if founded on correct information, and adhered to, it will close the campaign.

This General however expects that in the execution of this plan, no man will so far lose sight of the boasted character of a soldier, as to wilfully destroy the women and children, but to recollect we war with savages who have without mercy torn the locks from the head of the aged matron down to the infant babe. These are the wretches who should feel the avenging rod.

The troops and Indian warriors are forbidden to touch any of the supplies in the enemy's towns, until the action shall have closed; when they will be collected, and an equal distribution made. Such horses as may be taken from the enemy will be held subject to the use of the Army for the wounded, and such other distribution as the good of the service may require.

The General expresses, to the Officers and soldiers of the different species of troops under his command his entire confidence that they will perform their duty, in a manner to realize the expectations of their country.

By Order—(Signed) Robert Butler
Adj Genl

The Officers of the day will instruct their several guards not to permit any of the regulars, volunteers, or Militia Troops, to pass the chain, unless in detachments, and under an Officer.

By Order—(Signed) Robert Butler
Adj Genl

LC, DNA-RG 98 (mAJs).

1. The plan of attack has not been found. Bowlegs (Boleck; Islapao paya; d. c1820) was a brother of the Seminole chief King Payne (d. 1812) and an uncle of later chiefs Micanopy and Billy Bowlegs. By some reports Bowlegs was recognized as the principal Seminole chief at this time; certainly he was chief of a number of towns in the neighborhood of the Suwannee River. The town attacked by Jackson's troops on April 16 was probably Suwannee Old Town on the river's west bank in present-day Dixie County, Florida.

To John Caldwell Calhoun

Hd. Quarters Divn. of the South
Bowleg's Town, Suwaney River,
20th Apl. 1818

Sir

My last communication, dated Camp before St Marks 8th. Apl. and those to which it referred, advised you of my movements and opperations up to that date, and, as I then advised you, I marched from that place on the morning of the 9th.[1]—On the evening of the 10th. I was joined by the rear of the Tennessee Volunteers, also by the Indians under Genl. McIntosh, whom I had left at Mickasuky to scour the country around that place. Altho' the weather has been dry & pleasant, & the waters had subsided in a great degree, our march might be said to have been through water which kept the infantry wet to the middle, & the depth of the swamps added to the want of forrage occasioned the horses to give out daily in great numbers.

On the morning of the 12th near Econfinnah or natural bridge a party of Indians were discovered on the margin of a swamp and attack'd by Genl. McIntosh & about 50 Tennessee Volunteers, who routed them, killing 37 warriors & capturing six men & 97 women & children, also recapturing a white woman who had been taken at the massacree of Scott, the friendly Indians also took some horses & about 500 head of Cattle from the Enemy who proved to be [Peter] McQueen's party. Upon the application of an old woman of the Prisoners I agreed that if McQueen was tied and carried to the commandant of St. Marks her people should be received in peace, carried to the upper tribes of the Creek nation & there provisioned until they could raise their own crops, she appeared much pleased with those terms, and I set her at liberty with written instructions to the Commandant of St. Marks to that effect; Having received no farther intelligence from McQueen I am induced to believe the old woman has complied with her part of the obligation.[2]

From St Marks I marched with 8 days rations, those that joined me having but five, this was done under the expectation of reaching this place in that time founded upon the report of my faithfull Indian Guide, which I should have accomplished but for the poverty of my horses & the continued sheets of water through which we had to pass. On the morning of the 15th my scouts overtook a small party of Indians killing one man & capturing the residue consisting of one man & woman & two children, and on that evening I encamped, as my guide supposed, within 12 miles of Suwaney. I marched very early on the 16th. under the hope of being able to encompass & attack the Indian & negro Towns by one O'clock P. M. but much to my regret, at 3 Oclock, & after marching 16 miles we reached a remarkable pond which my guide recollected & reported to be distant six miles from the object of my march; here I should have halted for the night had not six mounted Indians, (supposed to be spies) who were discovered, have effected their escape, this determined me to attempt by a forced movement to prevent the removal of their effects &, if possible, themselves from crossing the river, for my rations being out it was all important to secure their supplies for the subsistence of my troops. Accordingly my lines of attack were instantly formed & put in motion, and about sunset my left flank column composed of the 2d. Regt. of Ten. Volunteers commanded by Col. Williamson & a part of the friendly Indians under Col. [Noble] Kanard[3] having approached the left flank of the centre town & commenced their attack, caused me to quicken the pace of the centre composed of the regulars, Geo. Militia, and my volunteer Kentucky & Tennessee Guards, in order to press the enemy in his centre whilst the right column composed of the 1st. Regt. of Ten. Vol. under Col. Dyer & a part of the friendly Indians headed by Genl. McIntosh, who had preceeded me were endeavoring to turn his left & cut off his retreat to the river; they however, having been previously informed of our force, by a precipitate retreat soon crossed the river, where it is believed Col. Kanard with his Indians did him considerable injury. Nine negroes & two Indians were found dead & two negro men made prisoners on the 17th. Foraging parties were sent out who found a considerable quantity of corn & some cattle, on the 18th. having obtained some small craft I ordered Genl. Gaines across the river with a strong detacht. & two days provision to pursue the enemy; the precipitancy of their flight was soon discovered by the great quantity of goods, corn &c. strewed through the swamps & convinced Genl. Gaines that pursuit was in vain; nine Indian & five negro prisoners were taken by our Indians; the evidence of the haste with which the enemy had fled induced the General to confine his reconoisance to search for cattle & horses, both of which were much wanted by the army. About 30 head of Cattle were procured, but from the reports accompanying Genl. Gaines, which in due time will be forwarded to you, and the disobedience of his orders by the Indians, not one pound was brought into camp.[4]

As soon as time will permit, I shall forward you a detailed account of the various little affairs with the enemy, accompanied with reports of the commanding officers of detachments suffice it for the present to add that every officer & soldier under my command when danger appeared shewed a steady firmness which convinced me that in the event of a stubborn conflict they would have realized the best hopes of their country and General.[5]

I believe I may say that the destruction of this place with the possession of St. Marks, having on the night of the 18th captured the late Lieut [Robert Christie] Ambrister of the British Marine Corps, and, as represented by Arbuthnot, successor to Woodbine will end the Indian War for the present, & should it be renewed, the position taken, which ought to be held, will enable a small party to put it down promptly.[6]

I shall order or, take myself a reconnoisance west of the Appalachicola at Pensacola point, where I am informed, there are a few red sticks assembled, who are fed & supplied by the Governor of Pensacola. My health being impaired, as soon as this duty is performed, the positions taken, well garrisoned, & security given to the southern frontiers, (if the Government have not active employ for me) I shall return to Nashville to regain my health. The health of the troops is much impaired, & I have ordered the Georgia troops to Hartford, to be mustered, paid & discharged, the General having communicated his wishes & that of his troops to be ordered directly there and reporting that they have a plenty of Corn and Beef to subsist them to that point.[7] I have written to the Governor of Georgia to obtain, from the state, the necessary funds to pay Genl. Glascock's Brigade when discharged, and that the Government will promptly refund it: I am compell'd to this mode to have them promptly paid, Mr. [John Benjamin] Hogan the Pay Master of the 7th. Inf. (for whom I recd. from Mr. [Robert] Brent, an enclosure said to contain $50,000) not having reached me.[8]

From the information received from Ambrister & a Mr. [Peter B.] Cook who was captured with him, that A. Arbuthnots schooner was at the mouth of this river preparing to sail for the Bay of Tampa, my A. D. Camp, Lt. Gadsden volunteered his services with a small detachment to descend the river and capture her; the importance of this vessel to transport my sick to St. Marks as well as to destroy the means used by the enemy, induced me to grant his request; he sailed yesterday & I expected to have heard from him this morning. I only await his report to take up the line of march on my return to St. Marks; The Georgia Brigade, by whom I send this, being about to march compells me to close it without the report of Lt Gadsden.[9] I have the honor to be Very Respy. Yo. Mo. Obt. St.

Andrew Jackson
Major Genl Comdg

LS in James M. Glassell's hand, THi (6-0405); Copies, DNA-RG 46 (6-0412), DNA-RG 233 (6-0425, -0433, -0441). Published in Bassett, 2:360–63.

1. See above.

2. For a detailed report of the battle near the Econfina River in Taylor County, see James L. Bell to Robert Butler, April 12, DLC (24). McQueen (d. c1820), the son of a Scots trader and a Tallassee woman, had been one of the earliest and most adamant of the hostile chiefs during the Creek War. Jackson's order regarding the woman has not been found.

3. Kennard, a Hitchiti chief and signer of the Treaty of Fort Jackson, was made a major

of the Creek troops in the Seminole campaign. Jackson promoted him to colonel for his conduct in the April 12 battle.

4. See Edmund P. Gaines to AJ, April 20.

5. See Robert Butler to Daniel Parker, May 3. The words "to add" and "every" were inserted by AJ.

6. Ambrister (c1797–1818), from the Bahamas, had been a midshipman in the British navy before serving as a lieutenant under Edward Nicolls in the British Gulf campaign of 1814–15.

7. See Thomas Glascock to AJ, April 18; General order, April 20. The words "frontiers" and "is" were inserted AJ.

8. See AJ to William Rabun, April 20; Robert Brent to AJ, March 6. Hogan (1787–1845) left the army in 1821 and moved to Alabama, where he served in the state legislature, 1829–35 and 1841, as emigrating agent for the Creek Indians, 1835–36, and as brigadier general of Alabama volunteer troops during the 1836 Seminole campaign. Jackson appointed him as collector of customs at Mobile in 1836. Brent (1764–1819) was paymaster general of the army.

9. Gadsden's report has not been found. He captured the *Chance* and sailed it to Fort St. Marks, arriving April 25. Cook, recently dismissed as Alexander Arbuthnot's clerk, was the chief witness at Arbuthnot's trial. Later reports from Nassau questioning Cook's credibility asserted that he had been convicted of embezzlement there, before Arbuthnot gave him a second chance. It also appears that Cook testified while in fear for his life. On May 13 he enlisted in the U.S. army "entirely against my own will," because he "supposed that if I did not Enlist that I should have the same fate of Ambrister and others." He deserted on July 10, apparently attempting to rejoin the Seminoles, but was recaptured. He was tried in October and sentenced to death, but President Monroe pardoned him (probably to avoid further inflaming British feelings about the executions of their citizens), and he served until June 1820 when he furnished a substitute and was discharged (see *Richmond Enquirer*, September 29; Record of the court-martial of Cook and others, September 9–October 30, and Proclamation pardoning Cook, December 22, Court-martial Case Files, S-8, DNA-RG 153).

*Perhaps because of concern about British reaction, the executions of Alexander Arbuthnot and Robert C. Ambrister, reported in the letter below, became one of the most significant subjects of the later congressional inquiry into the Seminole campaign. Indeed, the House majority report of January 12, 1819, which opened the debate, confined itself to a disapproval of the proceedings in the trial and execution of the two men (*Annals of Congress, *15th Cong., 2nd sess., pp. 515–18).*

For the most part congressional critics of the executions chose not to debate the guilt or innocence of Arbuthnot and Ambrister. Instead they challenged the court's jurisdiction—denying that the men's offenses were cognizable by court-martial; the rules of evidence used—complaining about the court's use of hearsay testimony; and the procedures followed—criticizing Jackson's decision to execute Ambrister in the face of a court recommendation for less severe punishment. As a result, the debate followed an ambiguity, present in both Jackson's reports and the court proceedings, as to whether the court was a "Special Court" or a "Court martial." Jackson, more interested in the "awfull example" the executions might provide to those who would incite Indian hostilities, had, no doubt, given little consideration to such legal distinctions, but he and congres-

sional defenders later argued that by associating with lawless pirates, banditti, and Indians, the two men forfeited rights and became subject to summary execution under the laws of nature and nations. Since, therefore, the court summoned by Jackson was merely advisory, criticisms of its irregularities as a court-martial were irrelevant.

To John Caldwell Calhoun

Head Quarters Division of the South—
Fort Gadsden
⟨4⟩ 5th May 1818

Sir

I returned to this post with my army on the evening of the 2d instant, and embrace an early opportunity of furnishing you a detailed report of my operations to the east of the Apalachacola River—In the several communications addressed you from Hartford, Fort Scott, and this place, I have stated the condition of the Army on my assuming the immediate command; The embarrassments occasioned from the want of provisions; The privations of my Troops on their march from the frontiers of Georgia; and the circumstances which compelled me to move directly down the apalachacola river to meet with and protect the expected supplies from New Orleans. These were received on the 25t. March and on the next day I was prepared for active operations. For a detailed account of my movements from that period to this day, you are respectfully referred to the report prepared by my Adjt General, accompanied with Capt Hugh Young's Topographical sketch of the route and distance performed[1]—This has been principally a war of movements: The Enemy cut off from their strong holds, or deceived in the promised foreign aid have uniformly avoided a general engagement—Their resistance has generally been feeble, and in the partial rencounters into which they seem to have been involuntarily forced; The Regulars, Volunteers, & Militia under my command realised my expectations; Every privation, fatigue, and exposure was encountered with the spirit of soldiers, and danger was met with a degree of fortutide calculated to strengthen the confidence I had reposed in them—

On the commencement of my operations I was strongly impressed with a belief that this Indian War had been excited by some unprincipled Foreign, or private Agents—The Outlaws of the old red stick party had been too severely convinced, and the Seminoles were too weak in numbers to believe, that they could possibly alone maintain a war with even partial success against the United States. Firmly convinced therefore that succor had been promised from some quarter, or that they had been deluded into a belief that America dare not violate the neutrality of Spain by penetrating to their Towns, I early determined to ascertain these facts, and so direct my movements as to undeceive the Indians. After the destruction of the Mekasukian villages I marched direct for St Marks: The correspondence between myself and the Spanish commandant in which I demanded the occupancy of that Fortress with an American Garrison, accompanies this.[2] It had been reported to me direct from the Governor of Pensacola that the Indians and Negroes unfriendly to the United States, had demanded of the commandant of St Marks a supply of amunition, munitions of war &c, threatning in the event of a non compliance to take possession of the Fort. The Spanish Commandant acknowledged the defenceless state of his fortress and his inability to defend it, and the Governor of Pensacola expressed similar apprehensions. The Spanish Agents throughout the Floridas had uniformly disavowed having any connection with the Indians, and acknowledged the obligations of his catholic Majesty under existing treaties to restrain their outrages against the Citizens of the United States—

Indeed they declaired that the Seminole Indians were viewed as alike hostile to the Spanish government, & that the will remained, though the power was wanting to inflict merited chastisement on this lawless Tribe—It was therefore to be supposed that the American Army impelled by the immutable laws of self defence to penetrate the territory of his Catholic Majesty, to fight his battles, and even to relieve from a cruel bondage some of his own subjects, would have been received as allies, hailed as deliverers, and every facility afforded to them to terminate speedily and successfully this savage war—Fort St Marks could not be maintained by the Spanish force garrisoning it—The Indians & Negroes viewed it as an asylum if driven from their Towns, and were preparing to occupy it in this event. It was necessary to anticipate their movements, independant of the position being deemed essential as a depot on which the success of my future operations measurly depended—In the spirit of Friendship therefore I demanded its surrender to the Army of the U States untill the close of the Seminole War—The Spanish Commandant required time to reflect, it was granted; a negotiation ensued, and an effort made to protract it to an unreasonable length. In the conversations between my Aid de camp Lt Gadsden and the Spanish Commandant circumstances transpired convicting him of a disposition to favour the Indians, and of having taken an active part in aiding and abetting them in this war—I hesitated therefore no longer, and as I could not be received in friendship I entered the Fort by violence—Two light Companies of the 7t. Regt Infantry and one of the 4t. under the Command of Major Twigs was ordered to advance, lower the Spanish colors, and hoist the Star Spangled banner on the ramparts of Fort St Marks—The order was executed promptly, no resistance attempted on the part of the Spanish garrison—

The duplicity of the Spanish Commandant of St Marks in professing friendship towards the United States while he was actually aiding and supplying her savage enemies; Throwing open the gates of his garrison to their free access—Appropriating the King's stores to their use, issuing amunition and munition of war to them, and knowingly purchasing of them property plundered from the Citizens of the U States is clearly evinced by the documents accompanying my correspondence—[3]

In Fort St Marks as an inmate in the family of the Spanish Commandant an Englishman by the name of Abuthnot was found—Unable satisfactorily to explain the objects of his visiting this country, and their being a combination of circumstances to justify a suspicion that his views were not honest, he was ordered in close confinement—The capture of his Schooner near the mouth of Suwaney river by my aid de camp Mr Gadsden, and the papers found on board unvailed his corrupt transactions as well as those of a Capt Armbrister, late of the British Colonial Marine Corps, taken as a prisoner near Bowlegs Town—These Individuals were tried under my orders by a Special Court of Select officers—legally convicted as exciters of this Savage and Negro War, legally condemned, and most justly punished for their iniquities. The proceedings of the Court martial in this case, with the volume of Testimony justifying their condemnation, presents scenes of wickedness, corruption, and barbarity at which the heart sickens and in which in this enlightened age it ought not scarcely to be believed that a Christian Nation would have participated, and yet The British government is involved in the agency[4]—If Arbuthnot and Armbrister are not convicted as the authorised Agents of Great Britain there is no room to doubt but that that Government had a knowledge of their assumed character—and was well advised of the measures which they had adopted to excite the Negroes & Indians in East Florida to war against the U States—I hope the execution of these Two unprincipled villains will prove an awfull example to the world, and convince the Government of Great Britain as well as her subjects that certain, if slow retribution awaits those uncristian wretches who by false promises delude & excite a Indian tribe to all the horrid deeds of savage war—

Previous to my leaving Fort Gadsden, I had occasion to address a communication to the Governor of Pensacola on the subject of permitting supplies to pass up the Escambia river to Fort Crawford—This letter with a second from St Marks on the subject of some U S cloathing shiped in a vessel in the employ of the Spanish Government to that post I now enclose, with his reply—The Governor of Pensacola's refusal of my demand, cannot but be viewed as evincing an hostile feeling on his part particularly in connection with some circumstances reported to me from the most unquestionable authority—It has been stated that the Indians at war with the U States have free access into Pensacola; That they are kept advised from that quarter of all our movements; that they are supplied from thence with amunition & munitions of war, & that they are now collecting in large bodies to the amount of 4 or 500 warriors in that city; That inroads from thence have lately been made on the Alabama, in one of which 18 setlers fell by the tomahawk—[5]

These statements compell me to make a movement to the West of the

Apalachacola and should they prove correct Pensacola must be occupied with an American force—The Governor treated according to his deserts or as policy may dictate. I shall leave strong garrisons in Fort St Marks, Fort Gadsden, and Fort Scott, and in Pensacola should it become necessary to possess it—It becomes my duty to state it as my confirmed opinion, that so long as Spain has not the power, or will to enforce the treaties by which she is solemnly bound to preserve the Indians within her territory at peace with the U States, no security can be given to our Southern frontier without occupying a cordon of Posts along the Sea Shore—The Moment the American Army retires from Florida, The War hatchet will be again raised, & the same scenes of indiscriminate murder with which our frontier setlers have been visited, will be repeated. So long as the Indians within the territory of Spain are exposed to the delusions of false prophets, and the poison of foreign intrigue; so long as they can receive amunition, munitions of war &c from pretended Traders, or Spanish commandants it will be impossible to restrain their outrages—The burning of their Towns, the destroying of their stock and provisions will produce but temporary embarrassments—Resupplied by Spanish Authorities they may concentrate, or disperse at will, and keep up a lasting predatory warfare against the Frontiers of the U States, as expensive as harrassing to her Troops—The Savages therefore must be made dependant on us, & cannot be kept at peace without persuaded of the certainty of chastisement being inflicted on the commission of the first offence—

I trust therefore that the measures which have been persued will meet with the approbation of the President of the U States. They have been adopted in pursuance of your instructions, under a firm conviction that they alone were calculated to ensure "Peace and security to the southern frontier of Georgia"—[6]

The Army will move on the 7t. from hence, crossing the Apalachacola river at the Ochesee bluff, about 30 miles above—with respect Your Most obt Sert

Andrew Jackson
Major Genl Comdg.

LS in James Gadsden's hand, DNA-RG 107 (M221-78); Copies, DNA-RG 46 (6-0592), DNA-RG 84 (6-0605), DNA-RG 233 (6-0609, -0617, -0629). Published in Bassett, 2:365–68. Registered as received in September 1818.

1. See Robert Butler to Daniel Parker, May 3; Hugh Young to AJ, May 5. See also Young's "Map of the Seat of War in East Florida during the Seminole Campaign," DNA-RG 77 (see Illustrations for an adaptation of the Young map).

2. See Francisco Caso y Luengo to AJ, April 7; AJ to Caso y Luengo, April 6 and 7.

3. See William Hambly and Edmund Doyle to AJ, May 2; David E. Twiggs to AJ, James Gadsden to AJ, Andrew F. Fraser and Daniel E. Sullivan to AJ, and Jacob R. Brooks and Peter Cone to AJ, all May 3.

4. See record of the courts-martial of Alexander Arbuthnot and Robert C. Ambrister, April 26–28.

5. See AJ to José Masot, March 25, April 27; Masot to AJ, April 15. According to Robert Butler's testimony in 1819, Jackson's information re Indian activity at Pensacola came from a letter written to Edmund Doyle; his information about murders near the Sepulga River on the Federal Road in Alabama came from letters (not found) brought from Fort Montgomery by John B. Hogan (see AJ to Calhoun, February 5, 1819).

6. The source of AJ's quotation has not been established.

Jackson's march into Florida with federal troops and militia and volunteers from Georgia, Tennessee, and Kentucky left a portion of the frontier settlements in Alabama Territory and southern Georgia open to continuing depredations. To protect these outposts, Governors William W. Bibb of Alabama and William Rabun of Georgia ordered out troops for local defense.

Rabun's order of April 14 gave command of the Georgia expedition against the reputedly hostile villages of chiefs Hopony and Phelemme near the Flint River to Obed Wright (b. c1788), from Chatham County, who had remained behind ill when the company of Georgia militia that he captained was called out to support the army's invasion of Amelia Island. Wright left Hartford on April 21, with about 270 men including a small detachment from Fort Early. Hearing that Hopony had removed to the Chehaw village, the Georgia troops destroyed that village on the following day.

When Jackson received Thomas Glascock's letter telling of the massacre of the Indians, he was outraged. He immediately ordered the arrest of Wright, fired an angry protest to Governor Rabun, and sought to conciliate the Chehaws lest they become a new threat to the peace of the frontier. Georgia newspapers were soon engaged in a lively controversy over Wright's actions, as his officers disputed the picture delineated in Glascock's letter and in Creek agent David B. Mitchell's protest to the governor, but Jackson, who had obtained supplies and warriors from the village, never deviated from his initial outrage, which went beyond Wright to include the governor's usurpation, as Jackson contended, of federal military authority. The war department, drawn into the affair by Jackson's inquiry as to whether Wright should be tried by civil or military authority, found itself fielding complaints from both the governor and the general.

Governor Rabun was sufficiently angered by the affair to devote almost half of his annual message to the legislature on November 2 to a discussion of it. Congress requested information on the matter for consideration in its investigation of the Seminole campaign. Meanwhile Wright, who was arrested by Jackson's order, freed under habeas corpus, and rearrested by the governor, escaped his confinement on June 27 and reportedly made his way through St. Augustine to Havana.

To William Rabun

On March toward Pensacola 7 miles
advanced of Fort Gadsden
May 7th. 1818.

Sir,

I have this moment received by express the letter of General Glascock a copy of which is enclosed, detailing the base, cowardly and inhuman attack, on the old woman and men of the chehaw village, whilst the warriors of that *village* was with me fighting the battles of our *country* against the common enemy, and at a time too when undoubted testimony had been obtained and was in my possession and also, in possession of Genl. Glascock, of their innocence of the charge of killing [Thomas] Leigh & the other Georgian at Cedar Creek.[1]

That a Govenor of a state should assume the right to make war against an Indian tribe in perfect peace with and under the protection of the U. States, is assuming a responsibility, that I trust you will be able to excuse to the Government of the U. States, to which you will have to answer, and through which I had so recently passed, promising the aged that remained at home my protection and taking the warriors with me on the campaign is as unwarantable as Strange—But it is still more Strange that there could exist within the U. States, a cowardly monster in human Shape, that could violate the Sanctity of a flag, when borne by any person, but more particularly when in the hands of a Superanuated Indian chief worn down with age.[2] Such base cowardice and murderous conduct as this transaction affords, has not its paralel in history and should meet with its merited punishment.

You Sir as Governor of a State within my military Division have no right to give a Military order, whilst I am in the field,[3] and this being an open and violent infringement of the treaty with the creek Indians, Captain Wright must be prosecuted and punished for this outragous murder, and I have ordered him to be arrested and confined in Irons untill the pleasure of the President is known upon the Subject. If he has left Hartford before my order reaches, I call upon you as Govr. of Georgia to aid in carrying into effect my order for his arrest and confinement, which I trust will be afforded, and Captain Wright brought to condign punishment for this unprecedented murder.[4] It is strange that this hero had not followed the trail of the murderers of your citizens, it would have led him to the Mickasooky, where we found the *bleeding Scalps of Your citizens,* but there might have been more danger in this; than attacking a village containing a few superanuated woman and men, and a few young woman without arms or protectors. This act will to the last ages fix a Stain upon the character of Georgia. I have the honor to be with due Respect Yr. Mot. Obt Sert—

(Signed) Andrew Jackson
Major Genl. Comg

Copies, DNA-RG 107 (M221-78, -79), DNA-RG 59 (6-0677), DNA-RG 75 (M271-2), DNA-RG 233 (6-0680). Published in contemporary newspapers and in Bassett, 2:369–70. The M221-78 copy was forwarded by Jackson to Calhoun, May 7; the M221-79 copy was forwarded by Rabun to Calhoun, June 1. There are no significant differences between the two copies.

1. See Thomas Glascock to AJ, April 30. On January 22, Leigh, an assistant wagon master, and Samuel Loftis, a member of the Georgia militia, were killed by Indians on Cedar Creek, seven miles east of the Flint River. In April Jackson's troops had found Leigh's wallet in Kenhajee's town.

2. Howard, an uncle of William McIntosh and a chief, had been shot in the attack, even though he was reportedly displaying a white flag.

3. In a March 6, 1824, editorial arguing that Jackson lacked the qualifications to be president, the *Richmond Enquirer* excerpted this letter, highlighting the first clause of this paragraph to show that he would not respect states rights. The *Enquirer* specifically asked "what would be the situation of the southern states, if in the midst of an insurrection they were compelled to wait, until the commanding officer of the U. States should please to issue his order for ensuring their safety?"

4. Jackson was referring to the Treaty of Fort Jackson, August 1814. In his reply, June 2, Rabun took exception to Jackson's contention that the governor lacked authority to give a military order, and in announcing that he had arrested Wright, Rabun made it clear that he did so on his own authority, not in response to Jackson's directive.

From José Masot

(Translated copy) Pensacola, 18th. May, 1818.

Most Excellent Sir,

On the 10th instant, I received your Excellency's letter of the 27th. of April last, informing me that some articles of the clothing used by the Troops of the United States, and supposed to be part of those taken in the boat in which Lieutt. Scott and his escort were so inhumanly murdered, were found in a small schooner, despatched from this port for that of Apalache, with provisions.[1]

Your Excellency inquires of me, in what manner these articles came into my possession; and you farther state that you feel yourself obliged to inform me, that the documents and other proofs found on St. Juan;[2] the detention of American cattle, found in St Marks; and the correspondence carried on between this post and the hostile Indians; are sufficient to create a belief that they were armed and excited to this cruel war against the United States by the Spanish officers.

Your Excellency adds that there exist positive proofs, that the Indians were supplied with Munitions by the last commander of St. Marks; and you conclude by saying, that an asylum has been granted here to the persons and property of the Indians, who are enemies of the United States and fugitives from the American Territory; and that these proceedings, and the refusing to allow the passage of provisions for your Troops, prove the unjust conduct of the Spanish Agents in the Floridas.

I shall answer the charges alleged, in their proper order, with candour, and without evasion, or reservation.

The first complaint made by your Excellency, is relative to the articles of clothing found on board the Schooner Maria, and which have been detained, on the supposition, that they are the property of the United States.

Part of these articles, as is proved by copy, No 1, were purchased at New Orleans, in the month of May, last year; part came from the Havanna; and part were purchased in this place.[3] All this is established. The charge is, of course, done away; and your Excellency's question is satisfactorily answered.

The succeeding one is more serious, and relates to the course observed, of late, by the Governor of St. Marks.

I immediately required of him an account of his conduct, and he made me the communication found in copy, No. 2.[4] However, as your Excellency affirms that you possess positive proofs of the misconduct of this officer, I must, as a necessary consequence, entreat you to submit them to me, that the fact being established, I may inflict on him deserved punishment. I assure your Excellency, with the sincerity natural to me, that he has acted in entire opposition to his instructions, and that if your Excellency will transmit me the proofs I request, he shall be brought before a council of war, and punished with all the severity his transgressions deserve; but your Excellency will be just enough to allow, that the Spanish Government cannot be responsible for the misconduct of its agents, when it neither upholds them therein, nor suffers their malepractices, being ascertained, to pass unpunished.

The last complaints of your Excellency have a personal and direct application to myself, and are relative to the asylum granted to the persons and property of the fugitive Indians; and to the passage of provisions up the Escambia.

It is easy for me to remove these charges, and, I think, your Excellency will be satisfied with a short and true relation of facts.

With respect to the Indians, your Excellency has assuredly been misinformed, as, although it is true, that some remained here, the greater part of them were women and children who procured a subsistence by furnishing the inhabitants with wood, fish, and other trifling objects, and were here, before the present war with the Seminoles. Others, now and then, assembled, on account of the war, but in very small numbers; as, when I had them collected in compliance with the proposition made by Major [White] Young, they, all together, amounted to eighty seven, and, assuredly, these few unarmed and miserable men were not hostile to the United States.[5] The continual passing of American citizens from the frontier to this people, who travelled alone and unarmed among them, without being, at any time, insulted or molested in their persons or property, is a proof of this

With respect to the passage of provisions up the Escambia, I have not hitherto prevented it; but, on the contrary, have facilitated it so far as I was able and my limited powers have permitted, even to the compromitting of myself, for, being only a subordinate officer, I could not consent to it as it is unauthorized, but I took the responsibility on myself, in consideration of existing circumstances; and so I stated to your Excellency, in my letter of the 15th. of last month, which I wrote to you by Major Perrault, and to which I refer you, in support of my assertion.[6] Now, that the free commerce of this people with those of the interior is declared admissible by higher authority; there will, in future, be no difficulty in allowing the Merchants to transport from hence to Fort Crawford, and other Forts on the frontier, as well by water as by land, whatever provisions and effects they may need or desire; by which means, these posts will readily be provisioned, and your Excellency will be satisfied.

I think, I have answered your Excellency's letter satisfactorily, and in a manner which can leave no doubt of the sincerity of my intentions, and which evinces my desire to contribute, so far as depends on me, to the good understanding existing between our respective Governments. God preserve your Excellency many years

(Signed) José Masot

Translation of LS, LS, and Translation of copy, DNA-RG 94 (mAJs); Copies, SpSAG (6-0720), Archivo Histórico Nacional, Madrid (mAJs), Archivo General de la Nacion Mexico (mAJs); Translations of LS, DNA-RG 233 (6-0733, -0742); Translations of copy, DNA-RG 59 (M116-4; mAJs), DNA-RG 46 (6-0723, -0727), DNA-RG 84 (6-0730), DNA-RG 233 (6-0739, -0755). Published in *ASP, Military Affairs,* 1:709 (translation of LS) and *ASP, Foreign Relations,* 4: 507–508, 564 (translations of copy). For a transcription of the Spanish LS, see Appendix.

1. See AJ to Masot, April 27. For the basis of Jackson's charge regarding the schooner *Maria,* see William Lindsay to AJ, April 27.

2. The Suwannee River.

3. See Benigno G. Calderon to Masot, May 18, and translation, DNA-RG 94 (6-0712; mAJs).

4. See Francisco Caso y Luengo to Masot, May 14, and translation, DNA-RG 94 (mAJs).

5. Youngs (d. 1822) served as an army captain, 1812–19, earning a rank of brevet major in 1814 for gallant conduct at Plattsburg. In April he led a punitive expedition from Fort Crawford into Florida after receiving news of an attack on a supply convoy (Eddy expedition) ascending the Escambia River. The eighty-seven Indians were Creeks who agreed to return to their Alabama villages. For a Spanish translation of Youngs's proposal, April 27, see Legajo 5562, Archivo Histórico Nacional, Madrid; see also Masot's replies, April 27 and 30, DNA-RG 94.

6. See Masot to AJ, April 15.

From José Masot

Protest

Pensacola 22 [23] May 1818

Having been informed of Your Excellency with the Troops under your command passing the Frontiers & entering the Territory of West Florida under my charge, against which proceedings I protest, as an infringement and insult offered to his King & Master, obliges me in his name to declair to your Excellency to leave the boundaries, and If you will proceed contrary to my expectations I will repulse you force to force. The results in this case will be an effusion of blood & will also disturb the present harmony existing betwixt our nations but as I will only oppose the insult of your approach I shall not consider myself the agressor. You will therefore be responsible before God & Men for the consequences & results of the same. God save your excellency many years,

Josse Massot

Translation in James Gadsden's hand and Copy of translation (both dated May 22), DLC (25); LS and Translations, DNA-RG 94 (6-0841, -0846, -0847, -0850); Translations, DNA-RG 233 (6-0854, -0857, -0860). The three different translations have been published in *ASP, Military Affairs,* 1:712; *ASP, Foreign Relations,* 4:567; and Bassett, 2:371 (dated May 22). For a transcript of the Spanish LS, see Appendix. Gadsden certified that a copy of this protest reached the American army "shortly after it had passed the Escambia river" (6-0845).

Upon receipt of Masot's protest above, Jackson immediately dispatched the following answer. James Gadsden, who carried the message, was unable to find Masot at Pensacola, however, as the Spanish governor had moved to the Barrancas. In consequence the letter was not delivered until after Jackson's troops had occupied the city on May 24.

To José Masot

Head Quarters Division of the South
On the line of March
May 23rd. 1818.

Sir,

The Southern Frontier of the U. States has for more than twelve months been exposed to all the horrors of a cruel and savage War—A party of outlaws and refugees from the Creek nation, negroes who have fled from their masters citizens of the U States and sought an asylum in Florida; and the Seminole Indians inhabiting the Territory of Spain all uniting have raised the Tomahawk & in the character of savage warfare have neither regarded sex or age helpless women have been massacred and the cradle crimsoned with the blood of innocence—The U. States true to their own engagements & confiding in the faith of Spain to enforce existing treaties never entertained a doubt but that these atrocities would early attract the attention of the Spanish Goverment & that speedy & effectual measures would have been adopted for their suppression—under this persuasion a cordon of military posts were established to give immediate protection to such of our Frontier settlers as were peculiarly exposed and strict injunctions issued to the American officers to respect the Territory of Spain, and not to attempt operations within its limits—These Instructions were most scrupulously observed, and notwithstanding the inactivity of the Americans Troops had encouraged the Indians to the more daring & outrageous acts of violence against our citizens—The Goverment of the U States was still disposed to respect the Territory of Spain & confide in the ability of the Spanish Goverment to execute existing Treaties until advised through you—that with every disposition the Spanish authorities had not the power of controuling the Indians in Florida—That their acts of late were viewed as equally hostile to ⟨Spain⟩ the Interest of Spain as those of the U States—That Spanish subjects were not exempted from the evils of which we complained, and that the negroe establishments in the Apalachicola & St Juan rivers were formed by British agents contrary to the will of Spain[1]—These representations determined the President of the U. States to adopt effectual measures to restore tranquility to the Southern Frontier of the American Republic & pursuant to His orders—justifiable by the immutable laws of self defence—I have penetrated into Florida—reduced to ashes the Seminole villages, destroyed their magazines of provisons beaten their warriors whenever they hazarded a contest dispersed some & expelled others across the river

In the course of my operations it became necessary to visit the Spanish Fortress of St. Marks—Entering the Territory of Spain to fight her Battles, to relieve fr[om] bondage her subjects & to chastise an Indian Tribe whom she acknowledged under existing treaties she was bound to preserve at peace with the U Sta[tes] I had every reason to expect that the American Army would have been received as Friends, and every facility afforded to insure success to operations so interesting to both Goverments—

My expectations have not been realised—It had been reported to me direct from you that Fort St. Marks had been threatened by the Indians & negroes and you expressed serious apprehensions from the weakness of the Garrison & defencless state of the work for its safety—From other sources to be relied on the same information had been furnished me[2]—It beca[me] necessary therefore to anticipate the movements of the Enemy and amicably to get possession of a work the dislodging the Enemy from which might have cost me much precious blood—

On entering St Marks evidence of the duplicity & unfriendly feelings of the commadant evinced itself—I found that the gates of his Fort had been thrown open to the avowed savage Enemies of the U. States—That councils of war had been permitted to be held within his own Quarters by the chiefs of warriors That the Spanish Store Houses had been appropriated to the use & were then filled with goods belonging to the hostile party—That Cattle knowingly plundered from the Citizens of the U. States had been contracted for & purchased by the Officers of the Garrison from the Spanish theieves—That foreign agents had free access within the walls of St

Marks—and a Mr. Arbuthnot condemned and executed as the instigator of this War—an inmate in the commandants family—

From this Fort was information afforded the Enemy of the Strength & movements of my army by the said Arbuthnot the date of departure of express noted by the Spanish commissary & ammunition—munitions of war & all necessary supplies furnished—

On my return from my operations East—your letter was received positively refusing to permit (unless exorbitant duties were paid) any provisions passing up to the American Fort on the Escambia[3]—connected with this strong indication of your unfriendly disposition on your part, I have from the most unquestionable authority that the city of Pensacola has for some months past been entirely under the controul of Indians That free ingress and egress is permitted to the avowed Savage Enemies of the U States—That supplies of ammunition munitions of war & provions have been received by them from thence—That on the 15th of April last there was no less than 500 Indians in Pensacola many of them known to be hostile to the U States, and who had but lately escaped my pursuit—The late massacre of 18 Individuals on the Federal road was comitted by Indians direct from their return to Pensacola who were receivd by you & transported across the Bay to elude the pursut of the American Troops The Americans returning—the savages were permitted to return—An Indian wounded in pursuit by a party for having killed a citizen of the U. S. was openly in the sight of many americans receivd by you & every comfort administered[4]—Such practices if authorisd by the King, would justify me in open hostilities—Disposed however to believe that it was one of the unauthorised acts of Agents—I deem it politic and necessary to occupy Pensacola—& the Barankas with an American Garrison until the Spanish Goverment can be advised of the circumstance, and have force sufficient to maintain & agents disposed to enfo[rce] existing Treaties

This is the third time that the American Troops have been compelled to enter Pensaco[la] from the same causes—Twice had the enemy been expelled & the place left in quiet possession of those who had permitted the irregular occupancy—This time it must be held until Spain has the power or will to maintain her neutrality—[5]

This is justifiable on the immutable principles of self defence—The Goverment of the U States is bo[u]nd to protect her citizens—but weak would be all her efforts & ineffectual the best advisd measures—if the Floridas are to be free to every enemy & on the pretext of policy or necessity Spanish Fortresses are to be opened to their use & every aid and comfort afforded—I have been explicit to preculde the necessity of a tedious negociation—My resolution is fixed—& I have strength enough to enforce it—My army now occupies the old Fort St Michael commanding Pensacola[6]—If the Town & Barancas are peacably surrendered an inventory of all the property, ammunition arms &c shall be taken by Officers appointed by both parties & the amount recd for by me—to be accountd for by the American Goverment The property of Spanish subjects shall be respected Their religion & Laws guarranteed to them—the civil goverment permitted to remain as now established subject to the controul of the military authority of the U States—The ingress and egress open to all individuals commerce free to the subjects of Spain as usual & the military furnished with transportation to Cuba—

If the peacable surrender be refused, I shall enter Pensacola by violence and assume the Goverment—until the transaction can be amicably adjusted by the Two Goverments—The military in thi[s] case must be treated as prisoners of war—The proof supporting the accusation against your official station will justify this procedure—In reply to your communication of the 22d Inst. I have only to observe that the cloathing detaind will be a subject for future friendly settlement How far the Indians permitted to remain in the neighborhood of Pensacola were friendly disposed to the Citizens of the U States is tested by the late massacre committed by them on the alabama.[7]

The Red Ground chiefs, Muldecoxy & Holmes avowedly hostile to the U States—were but lately seen in Pensacola and a body of Indians discerned a few days since in the vicinity of the Barancas in presence of several Spanish officers They & themselves have not delivrd themselves up & those red sticks who have surrended were not advised to this measure by you until intellygence of my movements had been receivd.[8]

By a reference to my communications of the 25th. March you will see how far I have been the egress or in the measure protested against[9]—You are there distinctly advised of the objects of my operations and that every attempt on your part to succour the Indians or prevent the passage of my provions in the Escambia would be viewed in no other light—than as hostile acts on your part—

You have done both, and exposed my Troops to the severest privations by the detention occasioned in the exactions of duties on my Provions' vessels in Pensacola—You have therefore been the agressor and the blood which may be shed by an useless resistance on your part to my demand, will rest on your head—Before God & man you will be responsible.

This will be handed you by my aid de Camp Captn. Gadsden, by whom an answer is expected.[10]

Signed Andrew Jackson
Majr. Genl. Commg.

Copies, DNA-RG 94 (6-0803), DNA-RG 46 (6-0784), DNA-RG 84 (6-0797), DNA-RG 233 (6-0813, -0821, -0829); Translations, SpSAG (6-0835), Archivo Histórico Nacional, Madrid (mAJs), Archivo General de la Nacion Mexico (mAJs). Published in *ASP, Military Affairs,* 1:712–13.

1. War department instructions as late as December 2, 1817, cautioned Edmund P. Gaines against crossing into Spanish territory, but on December 16, Secretary of War John C. Calhoun authorised Gaines to attack Indian towns in Florida (DLC-23). See also Calhoun to AJ, December 26, 1817 (above).

2. See above, AJ to Francisco Caso y Luengo, April 6.

3. See Masot to AJ, April 15.

4. In a series of attacks in March, hostile Indians killed a number of settlers about sixty-five miles east of Claiborne near the Federal Road, which ran from Fort Stoddert on the Mobile River to Fort Wilkinson near Milledgeville. The wounded Indian has not been identified.

5. Jackson was referring to his invasion of Pensacola in November 1814 and White Youngs's expedition to the outskirts of Pensacola in April.

6. The former British Fort George, Fort San Miguel was the main garrison at Pensacola.

7. See above, Masot to AJ, May 23.

8. Miccodoxy (Ou,ta,se,micco), chief of Etohussewakkes (Itahasiwaki), a town near Fort Gaines, was killed in July by the army's Indian auxiliaries. Holmes has not been identified further; William Hambly's deposition, June 2, asserted that Holmes was in Pensacola as late as May 22.

9. See AJ to Masot, March 25.

10. For Masot's reply, denying Jackson's charges, see Masot to AJ, May 24.

To [Luis Piernas]

Before Pensacola. May 24th. 1818.

Sir.

I am informed that you have orders to fire on my troops entering the City to procure supplies from an American vessel in the bay.[1]

I wish you to understand distinctly that if such orders are carried into effect, I will put to death every man found in arms. The regular Soldiers under your command must be placed under the direction and care of my troops until an answer is obtained from the Governor to my communications to prevent unpleasant occurences—[2]

Respectfully yrs. &c. &c. &c.
Andrew Jackson
M Genl. comdg.

LS copy in Robert Butler's hand, DLC (25). Published in Bassett 2:371. Piernas, the Spanish lieutenant colonel commanding at Pensacola, was a career soldier with thirty-eight years of service in the Louisiana Infantry.

1. Isaac McKeever, commanding the ketch *Surprise* mounting twelve guns, arrived at Pensacola, May 22, to provide naval support.

2. See above, AJ to José Masot, May 23; and AJ to Masot, May 24.

To José Masot

Head Quarters Division South Pensacola.
May 25 1818

Sir

The accusations against you are founded on the most unquestionable evidence. I have the certificate of Individuals who on the 23d Instant at or near the little bayou counted 17 Indians in company of several Spanish officers—[1]

I have only to repeat that the Barancas[2] must be occupied by an American garrison, and again to tender you the terms offered if aimacably surrendered. Resistance would be a wanton sacrifice of blood for which you & your garrison will have to atone. You cannot expect to defend yourself successfully, and the first shot from your Fort must draw down upon you the vengeance of an irritated Soldiery—I am well advised of your strength and cannot but remark on the inconsistency of ⟨permitting⟩ presuming yourself capable of resisting an army which has conquered the Indian Tribes too strong agreeably to your own acknowledgement to be controuled by you—If the force which you are now disposed wantonly to sacrifice had been wielded against the Seminoles The American Troops had never entered the Floridas[3]

I applaud your feeling as a Soldier in wishing to defend your Post, but where resistance is ineffectual & the opposing force overwhelming—The sacrifice of a few brave men is an act of wantonness for which the Commanding Officer must be accountable to his God—

Sn: And. Jackson
Mj G Comg

Copy in James Gadsden's hand, DLC (25); Copies, DNA-RG 46 (6-0924), DNA-RG 84 (6-0926), DNA-RG 94 (6-0928), DNA-RG 233 (6-0930, -0933, -0936); Translations, SpSAG (6-0937), Archivo Histórico Nacional, Madrid (mAJs), Archivo General de la Nacion Mexico (mAJs). Published in Bassett, 2:373–74.

1. See certificates of Richard Brickham and John Bonner, [May 25] (DLC-25).

2. Some translations in the Spanish archives read "las Florida" at this point, but the change was most likely a mistranscription, as other translations in the Spanish and Mexican archives have "las Barrancas."

3. For the terms offered, see above, AJ to Masot, May 23. Despite Jackson's warning, Masot chose to fight, and the fort was not occupied until 3 p.m. on May 28.

From John M. Davis

Fort Hawkins 30th. May 1818

Sir

By express I hasten to communicate to you, that in pursuance of your order to me of the 7th. Inst. I came up with Captain Obed Wright of the Georgia Militia, in Dublin on the 24th Inst. I arrested him, and brought him on with me as far as Milledgeville, where the civil authority interfered and discharged him. A copy of the proceedings is herewith enclosed to you—I also enclose you copies of my letters to the Secy. War, & Govr. of Georgia, together with a copy of your order to me (which you kept no copy of)—and a copy of Wright's arrest.[1]

So far as I have had an opportunity of discovering, the minds of the

Georgians is much agitated on this occation, and many of them warmly advocate Wright's conduct—I had to brook Several insults while I had him in custody—The General impression of the *rable* was that Wright would be delivered up to the Indians—The enlightened class new better, & said that you were incapable of doing Such an act—I did not let the court know the extent of my orders—I only shew my first order, which directs him to be delivered over to the military authority at Fort Hawkins there to be kept in close confinement untill the will of the President be known. The Govr. of Georgia is absent at present, whether he will on his return order him to be delivered over to me on my application, or not is uncertain, I dont expect he will.[2]

I deem it necessary & therefore have communicated the facts as herein related to the Secy. War, I have enclosed him a copy of the proceedings of the court, and a copy of Wrights arrest—and notified him that I have communicated the circumstance to you—I have the honor to be very Respectfully your Obt Sert—

Jno. M. Davis
Asst. Ins. Genl

ALS, DLC (25). Published in Bassett, 2:371 (extract). Davis (1783–1853) was at this time an assistant inspector general. He had previously served with Jackson in the New Orleans campaign, earning a brevet for gallant conduct, and AJ later appointed him marshal for the western district of Pennsylvania.

1. See Proceedings in the case of Obed Wright, May 28; and Davis to Wright, May 24, to William Rabun, May 29, and to John C. Calhoun, May 30, all DLC (25); AJ to Davis, May 7.

2. Only one order to Davis has been found. Davis may have intended reference to his authority to call on the governor of Georgia for aid, contained in Jackson's order of May 7.

To Rachel Jackson

Ft Montgomery, June 2nd. 1818

My Love

I reached here on last evening, on my return march with the Tennessee Troops, for Nashville having, I trust put an end to indian hostilities for the future, The Just Vengeance of heaven—having vissitted and punished with death, the exciters of the Indian war, and horrid massacre of our innocent weomen & children on the Southern frontier. I have destroyed the babylon of the South, the hot bed of the Indian war & depredations on our frontier, by taking St Marks & pensacola—which is now garrisoned by our Troops, and the american flag waving on their ramparts, we have Sufferred privation but we have met them like Soldiers. I march from here on the 4th. for Columbia, where I hope to reach by the 20 instant or 25. Should Colo. Hayne meet me there as I have ordered & requested to muster the Troops & close the accounts, created under his command I shall not be detained at Columbia more one day[1]—I would be happy to see you there provided the roads are good, otherwise meet me in Nashville on the 25th. instant—

I have been so much exposed wading waters that I have a bad cough, I am somewhat emaciated, but still able to march on foot 25 miles a day—our Troops are very healthy we have lost but three in Battle, one by Sickness, two by drownding, & one shot by accident in the whole campaign—providence has been with us, presiding over our destiny & guarding us from danger—

Kiss my Two little Andrews for me present me affectionately to all friends, & believe me to be your affectionate Husband.

Andrew Jackson

ALS, ViU (6-1011).

1. Order not found. Jackson reached Columbia on June 26 and ordered Hayne to discharge the troops at that time.

To James Monroe

(Private)

*[Hea]*d quarters *[Div]* of the South
Ft Montgomery June 2nd. 1818

Dr. Sir

I reached this place last evening with the Tennessee Volunteers & my guards on our return march to Tennessee, to have them mustered, paid & discharged after closing a fatigueing campaign, by hoisting the american Eagle over the Ramparts, of Ft. don Carlos de Barancas and Pensacola. This step became absolutely necessary to put down the Indian war, and give "peace & security" to our southern frontier, as you will see by the documents & certificates accompanying my letter of this date to the honourable Sec of war, to which I beg leave to refer you.[1] These documents plainly unfold the duplicity of the Governor, and his protest, accompanied with his boasted threat of opposing force to force in case I advanced, deserved a severer chastisement than he recd., but the humiliation he experienced after his boast of desperate resistance of being compelled to surrender to a batery of one 9 lb. & a 5 8/10 in. howitzer was a severe punishment to military feelings. The Judgt. displayed by my aid Capt Gadsden in selecting the Position, the daring courage of Gadsden, Capt Call my second aid & Capt Young supported by C. [George P.] Peters Lt [Henry H.] Menton & [James M.] Spencer struck the garrison with a panic,[2] and for its gallantry cannot be surpassed by any military act, recorded in history, and ⟨it⟩ there is not within my recollection an instance of a Position being taken & ground broke at the distance of 385 yards of a heavy battery and the Position held, untill the garrison surrendered, it was left for america to furnish the example of such determined bravery. and uropean Engineers will hear it as a fable, and declare it impossible. The fact exists, & will be acknowledged by all the garrison of Berancas.

The Possession of St Marks, Ft Gadsden, & Ft don carlos de Barancas, puts an end to all Indian wars ⟨fare⟩. These were the hot beds, and the Spanish officers & British agents excited the Indians to masacre & plunder to enrich their own coffers by purchasing the plundered property at a reduced price—I view the Possession of these points so Esential to the peace & security of our frontier, and the future wellfare of our country that I have directed my aid de camp Capt Gadsden to make a report of the aditional repairs necessary to those garrison to enable us to hold them, and as soon as I can spare him I intend to send him on to make to you a personal communication on this as well as other subjects closely connected with it & the peace & wellfare of our Goverment & country.[3] added to the importance of the position occupied by the late campaign, it is of great importance in another point of view, it has opened to our view a correct Topographical knowledge of a country hitherto unknown, and of which many eroneous opinions had been imbibed well calculated to deceive—for it is a fact, that no person to whom I applied knew any thing about this country, altho many professed an accurate knowledge of the whole—I say no except my faithfull Pilot [John] Blount, who accompanies Mr Hambly who will hand you this, he knew the country and rendered me important services as a guide, without him I could not have operated successfully, and have sent him to you & beg that he may be liberally rewarded for his attachment to the u states & faithfull services rendered, three of his clan accompanies him, who I also wish to receive the attention of the goverment. Blount ought to receive a pension, he has been stripped of all his property.[4] Mr Hambly has acted as my interpreter of the Spanish language & Linguister, he is a man of probity in whom confidence may be reposed, and from whom much usefull information may be obtained, he goes on with Blount at my request, as interpreter and I beg leave to request that he be kindly received & well paid by the Government—his friendship to the u states was the cause of the destruction of his property. I have caused every step I have marched to be measured & the course taken, so soon as leisure will permit, a correct plan of my various routs, accompanyed with the necessary remarks will be forwarded to the office of the sec of war, and will prove how eroneous the opinions of distance as well as the face of the country have been. ⟨of this country⟩[5]

Our marches have been fatigueing the privations great, the continued wading of the water & the swamps has first destroyed our horses, and in the next our shoes, the men are literarry barefoot and I think it but Just that the Goverment should give them a pair of shoes each which I am trying to obtain, and Justice requires that every horse that is lost be paid for by the Goverment. a great number of the horses that has gave out & are left will be regained by the Goverment. Indians have been employed to hunt & take care of them, sound policy as well as Justice require that the soldier receive pay for his horse These are the men who will defend your Eagles in the day of danger—These are the auxiliaries, that will aid in Possessing the goverment of Ft St augustine & Cuba, when thought necessary to be Possessed by the american republick. These are both Essential to the security of our southern frontier and to our commerce in a state of war, and can be taken by a Coup' de' Main whenever thought necessary.[6]

The reduced state of the 4th. & 7th. Infantry, the 4th. Betalion of artillery not being filled, the Posts being garrisoned by our Infantry has reduced our disposable force too small to hazard many excursions through our country in pursuit of the enemy—from the calm in *[the]* north, could not Genl [James] Miller of the 5th. Infa*[ntry]* be spared to the south.[7] This additional force with the 22 gun Briggs, would insure Ft St augusteen add another Regt. and one Frigate and I will insure you cuba in a few days. I am at present worn down with fatigue and by a bad cough with a pain in my left side which produced a spitting of blood, has reduced me to a skeleton. I must have rest, it is uncertain whether my constitution can be restored to stand the fatigues of another campaign—should I find it so I must tender my resignation. when I reach Nashville I will again write you, in the mean time permit me again to remark the importance of the Possession of Fts. St Marks, Gadsden & Barancas is to the peace & security of our southern frontier & to the growing greatness of our nation—the hords of negro Brigands must be drove from the bay of Tampee and Possess ourselves of it, this cutts off all excitement by foreign influence, by keeping from there all foreign agents. I shall be happy to hear from you, in all things, I have consulted publick good & the safety & security of our southern frontier. I have established ⟨that⟩ peace & safety, and hope the goverment will never yield it, should my acts meet your approbation it will be a source of great consolation to me, should it be disapproved, I have this consolation, that I exercised my best exertions & Judgt. and that sound national Policy will dictate holding Possession as long as we are a republick. you will excuse this scrall, I write in haste, & have no time to copy it. with a tender of my best wishes, I am respectfully your mo. ob. serv.

Andrew Jackson

ALS, NN (6-1014). Published in Bassett, 2:376–78.

1. See AJ to John C. Calhoun, June 2.

2. Peters (d. 1819; Military Academy 1808), Minton (d. 1820), and Spencer (d. 1829; Military Academy 1817) were officers in the corps of artillery. Other reports indicate that the fort offered "heavy" fire on May 26 and 27 (see AJ to Calhoun, June 2; and Isaac McKeever to Daniel T. Patterson, May 31, DNA-RG 45, M125-58).

3. See James Gadsden to AJ, August 1.

4. Blount (d. 1834) was a half-blooded chief of the Apalachicola (Tuckabatchie) Indians. According to newspaper reports, Blount and his two Indian companions Cochran, a full blood, and George McPherson, another half-blood, were satisfied by a government promise to pay reparations of less than $2,000 for depredations on their property.

5. See Hugh Young to AJ, May 5; and AJ to Calhoun, June 2.

6. The issue of compensation for horses lost in the Seminole campaign troubled Congress until 1824, when Jackson, as chairman of the Senate military affairs committee, reported a bill broadening earlier compensation laws, which passed in amended form (4 *U.S. Statutes at Large* 70).

7. Miller (1776–1851), who in May received a six-months furlough from his station in Boston, was not transferred. He became the first governor of Arkansas Territory in 1819.

From Christopher Vandeventer

Department of War, June 2d. 1818.

Sir,

Your letters of the 8th. of April, one without date from fort Gadsden, and of the 26th. of April, are received.[1]

The President of the United States, and the Secretary of War, are out of town. The former will return about the fifteenth instant, the latter not before the middle of next month. So soon as the President returns, your dispatches, together with your order to major Davis, commanding the arrest of capt. Wright, and a copy of your letter to the governor of Georgia, in relation to the horrid and atrocious destruction of the Chehaw village, will be laid before him.[2] In the mean time, I am advised to communicate the "opinion,["] that the trial of capt. Wright by court-martial, is decidedly preferable to a civil prosecution in the federal court, the latter being the mode suggested to this department by the agent of the Creek nation, as the one most agreeable to public opinion in Georgia. The trial by jury in the federal court, would be a mockery, because it is well known, that that court has refused cognizance of similar cases in the state of Georgia, on the ground that it does not possess jurisdiction. It is, therefore, left to you to institute such proceedings in the case as, in your judgment, you may deem best. Would it not be well to include in the arrest and trial, all officers of the grade of captain, who accompanied capt. Wright?[3] I have the honor to be, Your most Obt. Servant,

C. Vandeventer

LS and Copy, DLC (25); LC, DNA-RG 107 (M6-10); Extract, DNA-RG 233 (6-1018). Published in *ASP, Military Affairs,* 1:778 (extract).

1. See AJ to John C. Calhoun, April 8 (above), April 26, and [May 4].

2. See AJ to Calhoun, to John M. Davis, and above, to William Rabun, all May 7.

3. Jackson endorsed the LS, "Capt. Gadsden will please answer this letter, remarking that the reason why none but Capt. Wright was named in the order of arrest, was that none other of the officers names were known, & it is now submitted for consideration whether the orders of a superior officer, would not excuse, if not Justify, a subordinate officer in obaying an order of the superior, known to the inferior to be illegal. Inclose the report of Major Davis shewing Wrights liberation by habeus corpus Issued by three Justices of the peace &c, and Major Davis appeal to the governor, with the expression of my pointed disapprobation of this illegal interference of the civil with the military authority & express my firm hope that the Executive of the u states, will have a thorough investigation of this whole subject, that it is absolutely

necessary for the safety of our frontier, and that governor of states may be Taught to Know that it is Treason against our goverment to levy war against any tribe under the protection of the u states, and over which the sovereignity of the union extends—⟨as to⟩ The mode of trial recommended by the agent, is truly farcical & populartity of Georgia being the bases of the recommendation of his recommendation ought to be spurned by the goverment, when Justice to a much injured people require the exertion of energetic measures. A. J." See also James Gadsden to Calhoun, June 30.

From George Mercer Brooke

Fort. St. Carlos de Barrancas
2nd July 1818.

Dear. Genl.

In compliance with your wishes, and knowing your anxiety, to hear from this quarter, I proceed to lay before you the situation of affairs here. The Spaniards appeared, on our first taking possession, to be extremely dissatissfied, whither from the natural mortification, which a people, would feel, at being compelled to surrender their country, or the hostility, which they bear to the American Republic, it is difficult to decide; but I presume a little of both, has had its influence in forming their present disposition towards us. In some instances, a few ill disposed, and designing fellows, have added to their list of imaginary greevances, by circulating reports, that we intended to imprison and abuse, several of their citizens, but a better acquaintance with us, and a firm, and judicious conduct, on our part, has placed us in a fair, and honorable point of view. Every thing, therefore at this period of time, is perfectly quiet, and we go on as well, as the best regulated, but older governments can do. The Governor with all the troops have sailed for the Havanna and there stil remains, about one hundred and forty persons, belonging to the Civil department, who will be transported as soon as the vessels arrive. I do not believe many of the inhabitants will remove to the Havanna. Their prejudices in favor of a Royal master, must be very great indeed, which would induce them to leave their property, which had been just made valuable by our possession, and improving every day, in the price of sales. A good many speculators, as you would suppose have come into the market, and bought up all the reasonable priced lots, which they can at this moment, realize more than 50 pr Cent upon. We are under great anxiety, to hear what the President intends doing; whether to retain the country or not. If he should, I intend to commence improving the fortifications at this place immediately, and we shall want, as we now do very much, sixteen sea coast carriages for 24 pndrs., 10 truck wheel carriages for 24 pndrs on the upper work, one ten and half inch, and two nine inch, & 7/10 of an inch mortar beds; Also one carriage for an eight inch howitzer. We have tried all those mortars, and the howitzer with the shells rec'd here, and find them excellent, what the Spaniards could have been about, that they did not use them, is to me astonishing. I sent out some time since two parties, in search of indians, whom we were told, had been on St Rosa's island, and also a party of them, about twelve miles above the town at the mouth of the Escambia; of the first, we could discover none but very old signs, of the last, we were near catching them, as the sign was very fresh, and appeared to be about 20 in number. I believe that the Spaniard who gave the information, to me, sent them intelligence of our coming, so, that without being detected, he served both parties. from what I can learn the indians are almost reduced to a famine, but none of the hostiles, have yet come in. I heard from the Appalachicola yesterday, by one of our officers, who came with the sick, left, at Fort Gadsden by us. He states every thing as quiet, that about 100 warriors had returned to Mickasuckee, whom he supposed Genl. G would soon put to the route. The troops are sickly in that quarter: the U. S. brig of war Enterprize has just left this harbor, on a cruise, she had been in search of Woodbine's vessel, in Tampa bay, but did not meet with her;[1] He neither saw, or heard of any indians in the neighborhood of that place; only a few Spaniards, with some negroes, employed fishing.

Since taking possession of this harbor, three American vessels, laden in part with stores from the Havanna, have entered, without knowing the change of masters The two first Captain MCKeever seized, one with 19 and the other with six slaves. The third we took, having 85 negores, and a large quantity of sugar and coffee. All the negroes are owned in New orleans, we are informed, but I know not, that we shall be able to prove it. They have been sent to Mobile for trial.[2] Present me to Mrs. J. and the Gentlemen of your family and believe me to be Yr Most: Obt. Servant and friend

Geo. M. Brooke
Col. U. S. A

Col King took command at Pensacola on the 13th last month. and orderd me here, which is a most pleasant station.

ALS, ICHi (6-1099). Endorsed by AJ as received July 30. Brooke (d. 1851), of Virginia, entered the army in 1808 and became a career soldier, eventually reaching the rank of brevet major general. At this time he was a major with a brevet rank of colonel for distinguished service in the defense of Fort Erie.

1. Papers captured from Alexander Arbuthnot led Jackson to believe that a small ship carrying supplies to the hostile Indians would soon arrive at the mouth of the Suwannee River. On April 26 he wrote New Orleans naval commander Daniel T. Patterson to request that a vessel be sent to Tampa Bay to intercept the supply boat (letter not found). Patterson dispatched the *Enterprise,* a twelve-gun brig built in 1799 and enlarged to 165 tons in 1811. See Patterson to Benjamin W. Crowninshield, June 6, DNA-RG 45 (M125-58).

2. On June 18, Isaac McKeever captured the *Louisa* and *Merino,* and on June 24, Brooke captured the *Constitution.* The ships were seized under provisions of slave trading laws of May 10, 1800, and April 20, 1818, forbidding American vessels from carrying slaves between foreign ports (2 *U.S. Statutes at Large* 70–71; 3 *ibid.* 450–53). In 1824 litigation arising from the seizures reached the Supreme Court, which held that the non-American owners of

the slaves seized by Brooke could reclaim them (see *The Merino. The Constitution. The Louisa.*, 9 Wheaton 391–408).

To Isaac Shelby

Hermitage
7th. July 1818

Dear Sir

Your letter of the 27th. Ult. with its inclosures reached me on the 3rd. Inst.—the bad state of my health renders it impossible for me to state at what time I shall be able, with you, to hold the Chickasaw treaty. The importance of the Treaty to Kentucky & Tennessee will be a sufficient inducement to fix the period for the meeting, as early as possible.[1]

I have written this day to Major James Colbert Interpreter to the Nation, to meet me with the speaker, at the Tennessee river, on the 22nd. Inst. for the purpose of arranging the time & place of meeting:[2] should they fail to meet me as requested, I shall then adopt the plan recommended by you of sending a special messenger for that purpose, with instructions to prevail upon the Chiefs to fix the meeting at some point near Nashville. Indeed I anticipate great difficulty in getting the Chiefs to *[mee]*t us, as I have been informed that the Colberts are much opposed to holding any treaty or talk, and have declared that they will loose every drop of bl*[oo]*d in their veins, before they will yield to the United States another acre of Land; this I only consider as a declaration, without thought; but I know, that we shall be unable to effect any thing, until we silence their opposition & tha[t] of the Speaker of the Nation, & that can only be done, by some thing applied to their senses; and the small sum to which we are confined at once tells me, that without more ample powers & means nothing can be accomplished;[3] it will take at least Twenty five Thousand dollars to put to rest this strong opposition, but this once effected—our object is gained. The goods which have been sent to Chickasaw Bluff can not be converted to any benificial use, as they will be too distant from us; it is unaccountable that they should have been ordered to a place so very distant from any point, where the treaty can be held.[4]

So soon as I hear from Major Colbert I will write you the result—in the mean time I would beg leave to suggest to you the propriety of submitting to the President the expediency of leaving us f*[re]*e in our negotiations for this tract of country which is ⟨so⟩ important not only to the growing greatness of the west, but also to the strength & defence of the United States by allowing us to draw on the department for such sums as we may stipulate to give them in presents—to this I presume there can be no possible objection, unless they want confidence in us, & should that be the fact I wish to have no agency in the transaction. What is $20 or $30,000 or even $200,000 compared with the importance of this Territory so illegally withheld from our Citizens & so necessary in connecting the population of our western country?

So soon as my health will permit & a meeting of the chiefs can be obtained, I am willing to unite with you in making the effort, but without more ample means I am certain that we cannot succeed; the idea of an exchange for lands on the west side of the Mississippi cannot be realized—they set too high a price on their salt lick on Sandy to exchange it for any thing but money[5]—This they may be induced to do, when they are frankly told that under the Hopewell Treaty Congress have power to regulate all Indian concerns, & that to do justice to our own citizens an act will be passed authorising them to take possession of all the lands within the states of Tennessee & Kentucky. This was the language held out at the last Treaty, & which is no doubt perfectly understood by the Colberts, & is the ground upon which suitable presents will silence their opposition & no doubt secure the object which we have in view.[6] I have the honor to be, Sir, with great consideration & regard Yr. friend & obt. St.

Andrew Jackson

LS in James C. Bronaugh's hand, DLC (6-1108).

1. See Shelby to AJ, June 27.

2. Letter not found. Colbert (c1768–1842), a quarter Chickasaw, was half-brother to William, George, and Levi Colbert, important half-blooded Chickasaw chiefs. The Chickasaw speaker was Tishomingo. For Colbert's response, see Colbert to AJ, July 17.

3. Calhoun had authorized the commissioners to pay the chiefs "provided the whole amount drawn for, including your compensation, and that to your Secretary and Interpreters, does not exceed $4,500."

4. Calhoun had informed the commissioners that Superintendent of Indian Trade Thomas L. McKenney had been directed to forward $6,500 of goods for use at the treaty. The southernmost of three Chickasaw Bluffs along the Mississippi River in Tennessee was at the present site of Memphis.

5. By Article 4 of the 1818 treaty, the Chickasaws retained the salt lick on the Big Sandy branch of the Tennessee River as a reserve. The reserve was then leased to William B. Lewis in a transaction that led to rumors of corruption circulated by Jackson's enemies in 1819 and subsequent years. See AJ to Joseph McMinn, September 13, 1819, below.

6. By treaties signed at Hopewell in South Carolina, November 28, 1785, January 3 and January 10, 1786, the Cherokees, Choctaws, and Chickasaws had acknowledged themselves to be "under the protection of the United States of America." The most recent Chickasaw treaty had been negotiated by Jackson, David Meriwether, and Jesse Franklin in September 1816.

To William McIntosh

Head Quarters Division of the South
Nashville
8 July—1818

Friend and Brother

Shortly after the capture of Pensacola, I was taken very ill which prevented my writing you; I have continued indisposed ever since & on my return to Nashville was taken seriously ill. From this attack I have just recovered sufficiently to write you—

On my march from Fort Gadsden to Pensacola I received the disagreable intelligence of the wanton and outrageous attack by Capt Wright, commanding a detatchment of Georgia Militia, on the Chehaw Village—I immediately sent the Chehaws a talk which you have seen, and ordered Capt Wright to be apprehended & confined for trial.[1] Major Davis executed this order, arrested Capt Wright, and in passing through Milledgeville, Capt Wright was released from his confinement by the Civil Authority. I am awaiting the instructions of your Father the President of the United States on this subject.[2] That Capt Wright ought to be punished for this wanton outrage and murder all good men agree, and I have no doubt your Father the President of the U States will have ample justice done in this case—

I am just informed that a large portion of the Cattle you drove from the Seminole territory and which agreeably to my orders were to have been distributed amongst the Creek Nation to stock it, have been sold, and bought by young Mr [William Stephen] Mitchel Son of Genl Mitchel your Agent—[3]

If this is the fact it is not right, and the sale is illegal and void. You were in the service of the United States, and all the cattle taken from the Enemy was by law the property of the U States, and ought to have been delivered over to the Qr. Master General to be sold on public account—Knowing as I did that the upper Creeks were destitute of stock & their children in want of milk, I gave the order, that after my Army was rationed with beef, all the surplus cattle taken from the Enemy should be delivered over to you to be drove to your Nation, and there equally distributed—So anxious was I to have this effected that my orders were particular to preserve as many of the cows & calves as possible, that the Creek Nation might be again stocked, and our Indian children nourished with milk—My motives being humane & beneficial to those who have always been friendly to the U States, I had no doubt that the President would approve of my order—The sale of the cattle was not my intention & he cannot sanction it—You will therefore on the receipt of this call on the purchaser, receive the cattle & have them equally distributed to the Creek Nation agreeably to my order—or I will have them seized and delivered to the Quarter Master and sold for the benefit of the U States as the law directs—

I have written to Genl Mitchel on this subject & whose duty it is to see justice done to your Nation & that my orders be carried into effect—[4]

I have the pleasure to inform you that your father the President of the U States has ordered you & your warriors to be paid, and has placed funds in the hands of your Agent for this purpose—[5]

Mr Smith has not received the Cow, which My Friend the Mad Wolf neglected to deliver to the commanding officer at Fort Scott & which you promised should be left at the Agents—When Mr Smith applied at the Agency for the Cow he was answered that she was not there—You know the value I set on this cow for her blood, and how anxious I was to have it crossed with the English—I relied on your promise and was at considerable expense in employing Mr Smith to go, get her & deliver her at my house—I hope therefore you will have the Cow got and delivered to Major Alexr [L.] Lasley who has promised to bring her to Nashville for me—I rely on your promise to send me the Cow—[6]

I will expect to hear from you on the receipt of this letter Your Friend & Brother

Andrew Jackson
Major Genl Comdg.

LS in James Gadsden's hand, GU (6-1116); Extract, DNA-RG 107 (M221-78). The extract was enclosed by Jackson to John C. Calhoun, July 8.

1. See AJ to Chehaw Indians and to John M. Davis, both May 7. McIntosh had written Jackson on May 5 to request an investigation of the destruction of the Chehaw village.

2. See above, Christopher Vandeventer to AJ, June 2.

3. Mitchell (d. 1841; Franklin 1810), who served his father as an assistant agent, married McIntosh's eldest daughter on July 14. Jackson's order regarding cattle distribution has not been found; his information regarding sale of the cattle came from Benjamin F. Smith, June 30.

4. See AJ to David B. Mitchell, July 8. Jackson also wrote Calhoun on the subject, and following Calhoun's response, ordered seizure of the cattle that had been sold and their distribution among the Creeks. In November, sixty-nine cattle were returned to the Indians (see AJ to Calhoun, July 8; Calhoun to AJ, July 28; Robert Butler to Edmund P. Gaines, August 19; and Mathew Arbuckle to Creek chiefs, November 13, DNA-RG 94, M566-102).

5. The source of AJ's information has not been established.

6. Smith was probably Benjamin Fort Smith (1796–1841), later Chickasaw agent and Texas military hero. Mad Wolf (Yahau Haujo) was a chief of the Natchez Indians who served as one of Jackson's rangers in 1814 and as a captain of Creek troops in the Seminole campaign. Leslie (Lashley; Emauthlau Hautka) was the proprietor of Lashley's Fort at Talladega.

To Andrew Jackson Donelson

Head quarters D. of the South
July 14th. 1818

Dr. Andrew

I reached Nashville on the 29th. ult. in a bad state of health, much emaciated, I grew weak, but am again acquiring a little Strength, so that I can ⟨again⟩ attend to business. I am still much pestured with a bad cough and pain in my left side & breast, whether from the exposure, the complaint is fixed, the Doctor has not yet given me his opinion.

It is a long time since I have heard from you or Edward, the last letters I recd. was, when in the Seminole country.[1] I am anxious to hear from you both—The examination being over, I shall expect to hear how you have, & are progressing, and at what period of time you will finish your studies and the probability of your receiving an appointment in the line.

I trust I have given peace & security to the southern frontier so long as the goverment retains the positions I have occupied, which is all important to the security of the south. I have had an active campain, and what was to be expected, experienced many privations. I have traversed a country unexplored before by any but the Savage & wild beast, the importance of which was not known in the u states—but which will hereafter be duly appreciated & I have, and no doubt you have seen in the news papers, statements, of a differrence between Genl Scott & myself, which probable would end in a personal conflict—Whether these *little* publications are made by the instigation of Genl Scott or by some one else to impose upon the publick mind I know not, but to calm your mind on this subject, I have only to observe, that the last letter I recd from Genl Scott, has put an end to any personal conflict between him & myself, his religion & morallity, is opposed to such a mode of settling personal differrences, and after such a declaration, that he should be called on in that way by a brave man cannot be believed—Therefore these publications let them originate from what source the may are intended, to mislead the publick mind, by holding out an idea that it was expected I would challenge Genl Scott—This, if ever I had, had such intention, ⟨is known⟩ the humble, & extraordinary answer of Gen Scott to my letter has put to rest, and has shielded this, vain pompous nullity, from any personal conflict with me. I therefore hope that these publications will give you no uneasiness.[2]

I have no doubt but before this, you have heard of your grand fathers death, he, as I am informd, had a very painfull exit.[3] I shall expect to hear from you & Edward shortly, to whom present me affectionately, at the next vacation if convenient and you can obtain leave of absence I will be happy to see you. I shall write you again shortly, when it will be more in my power to give you a better account of my present dissease.[4] your aunt is at present in good health, altho she has not long since recovered from a severe attack of fever. They two Andrews are well, your aunt Together with my little son Joins in respects & best wishes to you, & to Edward to whom you are requested to present them.

I regret much my Dr. Andrew that you had not wrote more frequently to your grand father before his death. I am told he repined much at your silence and I beg of you to employ some of your leisure time in letting me know your progress and your wants, as *[far]* as I have the means all your real wants shall be supplied. I am my Dr Andrew *[your]* affectionate uncle

Andrew Jackson

ALS, DLC (6-1122). Published in Bassett, 2:381–82 (extract).

1. Letters not found.

2. See Winfield Scott to AJ, January 2. Newspapers throughout the nation reprinted an article from the *Savannah Republican*, June 1, stating that after concluding the Seminole campaign Jackson intended to journey to New York to challenge Scott.

3. Daniel Smith (1748–1818), guardian of Samuel Donelson's three sons, died on June 16.
4. See AJ to Donelson, August 3, below.

Reports that Jackson had captured Pensacola reached Washington by June 16; on July 8, Spanish minister Luis de Onís (c1769–1830; Salamanca), recently returned to Washington from his summer residence in Bristol, Pennsylvania, delivered a strongly worded protest demanding return of the Spanish posts and punishment of Jackson; but William Hambly, carrying Jackson's official dispatches on the subject, did not arrive until July 9, when he found James Monroe absent and hastened to Oak Hill, the President's estate near Aldie in Loudoun County, Virginia, approximately thirty-three miles from Washington (see ASP, Foreign Affairs, *4:496–97; AJ to Monroe, June 2, above, and to John C. Calhoun, June 2).*

*Monroe returned to Washington July 14, received Secretary of State John Q. Adams's report of the Spanish protest, and summoned a cabinet meeting for noon the next day to discuss Jackson's actions and to draft a response to the minister. According to Adams, cabinet discussions continued each day until July 21, with Adams mainly alone in support of Jackson's actions. On July 19 the cabinet modified Adams's draft for the letter to Onís to strike out "every part of the letter which imported a justification of Jackson's proceedings," but "determined that the President should write a friendly letter to Jackson" (*Memoirs of John Quincy Adams, *4:107–15).*

From James Monroe

Washington July 19. 1818

Dear Sir

I receiv'd lately your letter of June 2d. by Mr Hambly, at my farm in Loudoun, to which, I had retir'd, to await your report, & the return of our commissrs. from Buenos Ayres.[1] In reply to your letter I shall express myself with the freedom & candour which I have invariably used in my communications with you. I shall withhold nothing, in regard to your attack, of the Spanish posts, & occupancy of them, particularly Pensacola, which you ought to know, it being an occurrence, of the most delicate and interesting nature, & which, without a circumspect & cautious policy, looking to all the objects which claim attention, may produce, the most serious & unfavorable consequences. It is by a knowledge of all circumstances, and a comprehensive view of the whole subject, that the dangers to which this measure is exposed, may be avoided, and all the good which you have contemplated by it, as I trust, be fully realized.

In calling you into active service against the Seminoles, & communicating to you the orders which had been given just before, to General

Gaines, the views & intentions of the government, were fully disclosed in respect to the operations in Florida.[2] In transcending the limit prescribed by those orders, you acted on your own responsibility, on facts and circumstances, which were unknown to the government when the orders were given, many of which indeed occurr'd, afterwards, and which, you thought, imposed on you, the measure, as an act of patriotism, essential to the honor & interest of your country.

The UStates stand justified in ordering their troops into Florida in pursuit of their enemy. They have this right by the Law of nations, if the Seminoles were inhabitants of another country, & had enter'd Florida to elude our pursuit. Being inhabitants of Florida, with a species of sovereignity over that part of the territory, & a right to the soil, our right to give such an order, is the more complete, & unquestionable. It is not an act of hostility to Spain. It is the less so, because her govt. is bound by treaty, to restrain by force of arms, if necessary, the Indians there, from committing hostilities against the UStates.[3] But an order, by the government, to attack a Spanish post, would assume another character. It would authorise war, to which, by the principles of our constitution, the Executive is incompetent. Congress alone possess the power. I am aware that cases may occur, where the commanding general, acting on his own responsibility, may with safety pass this limit, & with essential advantage to his country. The officers & troops of the neutral power, forget the obligations, incident to their neutral character; they stimulate the enemy to make war; they furnish them with arms and munitions of war to carry it on; they take active part in other respects in their favor; they afford them an assylum on their retreat. The General obtaining victory, pursues them to this post, the gates, of which, are shut against him. He attacks and carries it, & rests on those acts for his justification. The affair is then brought before his government, by the power, whose post has been thus attacked & carried. If the government whose officer made the attack, had given an order for it, the officer would have no merit in it. He exercised no discretion, nor did he act on his own responsibility. The merit of the service, if there be any in it, would not be his. This is the ground on which this occurrence rests, as to the past. I will now look to the future.

The foreign govt. demands was this your act, did you authorise it? I did not, it was the act of the General. He perform'd it, for reasons, deemed by him sufficient, and on his own responsibility. I demand then the surrender of the posts, & his punishment. The posts will be evacuated, but to the criminal conduct of your officers, is the attack to be imputed. Their punishment will be demanded. The evidence justifying the conduct of the American general, and proving the misconduct of those officers will be embodied, to be laid before your sovereign, as the ground on which their punishment will be expected.

If the Executive refused to evacuate the posts, especially Pensacola, it would amount to a declaration of war, to which it is incompetent. It would be accused with usurping the authority of Congress, & giving a deep & fatal wound to the constitution. By charging the offense on the officers of Spain, we have taken the ground, which you have presented, & we look to you to support it. You must aid in procuring the documents necessary for this purpose. Those which you sent by Mr Hambly, were prepar'd in too much haste, & do not, I am satisfied, do justice to the cause. This must be attended to without delay.[4]

Should we hold the posts, it is impossible to calculate all the consequences likely to result from it. It is not improbable that war would immediately follow. Spain would be stimulated to declare it, and once declared, the adventurers of Britain & other countries, would under the Spanish flag, privateer on our commerce. The immense revenue, which we now receive, would be much diminished, as would be the profits of our valuable productions. The war would probably soon become general, and we do not forsee, that we should have a single power, in Europe on our side. Why risk these consequences? The events which have occurr'd in both the Floridas, shew the incompetency of Spain to maintain her authority in either, & the progress of the revolution in So. America, will require all her forces there. There is much reason to presume, that this act, will furnish a strong induc'ment to Spain, to cede the territory, provided we do not wound, too deeply, her pride, by holding it. If we hold the posts her govt. cannot treat with honor, which, by withdrawing the troops, we afford her an opportunity to do. The manner, in which, we propose to act, will exculpate you from censure, & promises to obtain, all the advantage, which you contemplated, from the measure, and possibly very soon. From a different course no advantage would be likely to result, and there would be great danger of extensive & serious injuries.

I shall communicate to you, in the confidence, in which I write this letter, a copy of the answ*[er]* which will be given to the Spanish minister, that you may see distinctly the ground on which we rest, in the expectation that you will give it all the support in your power. The answer will [be] drawn, on a view, and with attention, to the general interest of our country, & its relations with other powers.[5]

A charge will no doubt be made, of a breach of the constitution, and to such a charge the public feeling will be alive. It will be said that you have taken all power into your own hands, not from the Executive alone, but likewise from Congress. The distinction which I have made above, between the act of the general, & the act of the government, refutes that charge. This act, as to the general, will be right, if the facts on which he rests, made it a measure of necessity, & they be well proved. There is no war nor breach of the constitution, unless the govt. should refuse to give up the posts, in which event, should Spain embargo our vessels, and war follow, the charge of such breach, would be laid against the govt. with great force. The last imputation, to which, I would consent, justly to expose myself, is that of infringing a constitution, to the support of which on pure principles, my public life has been devoted. In this sentiment I am satisfied you fully concur.

Your letters to the dept. were written in haste, under the pressure of fatigue & infirmity, in a spirit of conscious rectitude, & in consequence with less attention, to some parts of their contents, than would otherwise have been bestowed on them. The passage, to which, I particularly allude, from memory, for I have not the letter before me, is that, in which you speak, of the incompetency of an imaginary boundary, to protect us against the enemy, being the ground on which you bottomed all your measures.[6] This is liable to the imputation that you took the Spanish posts, for that reason, as a measure of expedience, & not on account of the misconduct of the Spanish officers. The effect of this, and such passages, besides other objections, to them, would be to invalidate the ground on which you stand, and to furnish weapons to adversaries who would be glad to seize them. If you think proper to authorise the Secretary or myself to correct these passages it will be done with care, tho should you have copies, as I presume you have, you had better do it yourself.

The policy of Europe respecting So. America, is not yet settled. A congress of the allied powers, is to be held this year, Novr is spoken of, to decide that question. England proposes to restore the Colonies to Spain with a free trade & colonial govts. Russia is less favorable, as are all the others. We have a Russian document, written by order of the Emperor, as the basis of instructions, to his ministers at the several courts, speaking of the British proposition favorably, but stating that the question, must be considerd, & decided on, by the allies, & the result published, to produce, a moral effect, on the Colonies, on the failure of which, force, is spoken of. The settlement of the dispute, between Spain & Portugal, is made a preliminary. We partake in no councils, whose object is not, the complete independance of the Colonies. Intimations have been given us, that Spain is not unwilling, & is even preparing for war with the UStates, in the hope of making it general, & uniting Europe against us, & her Colonies, on the principle that she has no other hope of saving them. Her pertinacious refusal to cede the Floridas to us heretofore, tho' evidently her interest to do it, gives some colouring to the suggestion. If we engage in the war, it is of the highest importance, that our people be united, and with that view that Spain commence it, and above all, that the govt. be free from the charge of committing a breach of the constitution.[7]

I hope that you have recoverd your health. You see that the state of the world is unsettled, and that any future mov'ment is likely to be directed against us. There may be very important occasion for your services, which will be relied on. You must have the object in view, & be prepard to render them. with great respect & regard I am dear Sir your obt servt

James Monroe

Perhaps a copy may not be prepard in time to be forwarded, with this, of the letter to Mr Onis, but it will be deliver'd in that case, to the Secretary of war, & be forwarded by him, in my absence, it being my intention to go, without delay, to my farm in the country—Albemarle Virga.—[8]

ALS and Extract, DLC (71, 25); Copy, NcU (mAJs). Published in Bassett, 2:382–83 (extract).

1. See above. In late 1817 Monroe had dispatched Caesar A. Rodney (1772–1824), Theodorick Bland (1777–1846), and John Graham (1774–1820) to South America to gather information about the character and stability of the newly declared South American republics. Rodney and Graham landed at Norfolk on July 8, and Graham reached Washington, July 13.

2. See above, John C. Calhoun to AJ, December 26, 1817.

3. See Article 5 of the Treaty of San Lorenzo, October 27, 1795.

4. For Jackson's efforts to gather evidence, see AJ to Richard K. Call, August 5, and Hugh Young to AJ, October 12, both below.

5. See John Q. Adams to Luis de Onís, July 23, DLC (25).

6. See above, AJ to Monroe, June 2.

7. On February 26, George W. Erving, minister to Spain, had sent a copy of the Russian memorial of November 17, 1817, to Washington. The Russian proposals were not adopted at the Congress of Aix-la-Chappelle, which convened in late September.

8. On July 20, Monroe requested that Adams revise his letter to Onís. The letter was discussed again in cabinet meetings of July 20 and 21, prepared on July 22, and sent on July 23.

To James Colbert

Tennessee river mouth of Cypress
July 24th. 1818

Friend & Brother

I wrote you some time ago to meet me at this place with the Speaker of the nation & such other chiefs as you might think proper on the 22nd or 23rd. of this month explaining to you the object of the proposed meeting, that was, that Genl. Shelby & myself had been appointed by your father the President of the u states, to hold a treaty with the chiefs of your nation, for an exchange or purchase of the lands claimed by your nation, lying in the bounds of the state of Tennessee & Kentuckey for lands West of the Mississippi. you not having met me agreable to my request, has occasioned me to send you this by express, that I may have your written answer in which I ask you the reason why I have not heard from you.[1] I speak to the nation through you as its interpreter—Genl Shelby writes me he is verry infirm, and not able to go to your nation—Therefore we wish the chiefs of the nation to meet us in the neighbourhood of Nashville, or in the neighbourhood of this place.[2] Hearing that the agent has reached you I have wrote him on this subject. I informed you in my last that the sum due your nation by the stipulations in the last Treaty has been deposited in the Nashville Bank many months past, & if it has not been distributed amonghst your nation I have wrote the agent to have it done forthwith.[3] I have a great wish to see you. you know I am your friend & that of the nation, I never have told a red man a lie—I wish you to recollect what I said to you at the last Treaty, that all the lands claimed by your nation within the State of Tennessee, had been sold by the state of ⟨Tennessee⟩ North Carolina thirty odd years ago—and that they purchasers of this land who had paid their money to discharge the debt occasioned by the revolutionary war, had been & still was pressing your father the President for Possession of their land, that your father the President cannot keep them any longer out of Possession of their land, and that your father the President finding that next congress will pass a law authorising each individual who holds lands there to take Possession—has Instructed Genl Shelby & myself to hold a treaty and give you a Just compensation for it, in land west of the Mississippi, or in money.[4] I have only to repeat that this act of your father the President, shews how much he is your friend & with what paternal care he watches over your interest, for if Congress once passes the law authorising Each individual to take possession of their land, which will certainly be done, you then have to depend on the Justice of congress, and receive such compensation as congress may think proper to give you. It is that ample Justice be done you, and for these reasons we have been appointed to hold a Treaty with you before next congress, in all which you will discover the real friendship of your father the President of the u states. I am your friend & Brother

Andrew Jackson
Major Genl comdg.

Note. I added in conclusion the truth that the P. of the u. s. could not retain Possession any longer for them

ALS copy, DLC (25); Copy, NcD (6-1153).

1. Colbert had replied to Jackson's letter of July 7 (not found) on July 17, but Jackson had not yet received the response.

2. See Isaac Shelby to AJ, June 27.

3. Jackson's letter to Chickasaw agent Henry Sherburne, of July 24, has not been found. The Chickasaw treaty of September 20, 1816, guaranteed the tribe an annuity of $12,000 for ten years. On July 28, Sherburne indicated to Jackson that he had heard the money was at a Nashville bank, but that it had not been sent him for distribution.

4. On November 25, 1817, the Tennessee legislature adopted a memorial complaining that Chickasaw treaties had prevented individuals from occupying Tennessee lands granted by North Carolina in the 1780s and urging "that such steps may be taken as will remove those obstructions of those lands purchased by individuals under the laws of the state of North Carolina." The memorial was presented to the first session of the Fifteenth Congress, but a law passed April 4, 1818, specified that no titles should be perfected "for any land to which the Indian claim has not been previously extinguished" (Robert H. White et al., eds., *Messages of the Governors of Tennessee* . . . [10 vols. to date; Nashville, 1952–], 1:521–23; 3 *U.S. Statutes at Large* 416). Jackson apparently anticipated renewed consideration of the subject at the second session. Jackson's talk regarding Chickasaw claims in West Tennessee does not appear in records of the 1816 treaty. The treaty commissioners had been instructed to try to purchase the Chickasaw claim to lands in western Kentucky, but they reported that they had not thought it "prudent" to raise the issue (see William H. Crawford to AJ, David Meriwether, and Jesse Franklin, July 5, 1816; and above, AJ, Meriwether, and Franklin to Crawford, September 20, 1816).

To Richard Keith Call

Head Quarters D of the South
Nashville August 5th 1818.

Dr Capt.

We have nothing new here. I have received nothing Official from the government, either approbating or disapprobating my conduct in possessing myself of the Forts of St Marks and Barrancas—there has been some squibbing ⟨and a few disapprobating⟩ in the papers—some approbating and some disapprobating. On the 4th of July, in the toasts drank, there is a general display of approbation.[1]

From the silence of the Cabinet I am induced to belie*[ve]* they have become alarmed, and under a panic may be weak enough to order the withdrawal of our troops. Feeling as I do a conscious rectitude of having done my duty, and that every act of mine can be justified, under existing circumstances, by the law of nations I rest easy—Should the troops be with drawn we will soon see our frontier again deluged in blood, and Pensaa. garrisoned by Brittish troops, conjointly with Spanish, and to regain it will cost much blood and treasure. To be prepared at all points, I wish you to obtain all the proof you can of the Spanish Govenor at Pensacola, feeding the Indians, and furnishing them with the means of war—of his receiving the Indians after the 18 persons were killed on the Alabama, and Stokes' family near Ft Claiborne, and the Indians selling the plunder publicly in Pensacola—the Govenor sending them over the bay, on the approach, of Major Young and the friendly Choctaws, and bringing them back as soon as our troops had retired—his feeding them afterwards, and the Red Ground chief Holms, Miccadosy—being there with their warriors on the 23d of May, when I advanced, and the government, sending them over the bay, and at what time—and every circumstance that will show that the Spanish Govenor, aided, abetted, and excited the Indians to war against us.[2] From the silence, the Executive may attempt to throw all the responsibility on me—I am able to bear it—but I wish to be prepared. Col King—Col Brook, and the gentlemen of the 4th and the Artillery will I know aid you in this business to whom present me respectfully—

I wish you to answer this letter, and be ready to join me, you will receive an order shortly on this subject[3] I am Dr. Sir respectfully yr ob svt—

Andrew Jackson

Copy, FHi (6-1181). Published in Caroline May Brevard, *A History of Florida* (Deland, Fla., 1924), pp. 257–58.

1. For a sampling of the July 4 toasts from around the nation, see the Washington *National Intelligencer*, July 17, 20, 22, 27, 30, August 1, 5. A number of the toasts explicitly praised Jackson for his capture of Pensacola.

2. Call aided Hugh Young in obtaining depositions on these subjects at Pensacola in September (see Hugh Young to AJ, October 12, below). Around April 20, Stokes had been killed and his wife and daughters wounded by an Indian attack at their house about fifteen miles from Fort Claiborne.

3. Neither a subsequent order to Call nor a reply has been found.

To John Caldwell Calhoun

Head Quarters D. of the South
Nashville
August 10th. 1818

Sir

From the list of letters forwarded, I learned with extreme regret, that my communications from Fort Gadsden of the 1st. May with the accompanying documents had not reached you.[1]

The precaution I used of placing them in the hands of Major Davis Asst. Insp: Genl with instructions, that he should deliver them to the first safe Post Office in Georgia I had conceived, would have insured their safe arrival at your office.[2]

By Capt. Gadsden my Aid De Camp who will hand you this—you will receive duplicates of that dispatch and all other papers that have a bearing on the subject to which it related, which had not previously been forwarded.

Capt. Gadsden will likewise deliver you his report made in pursuance of my order, accompanied with the plans of the fortifications, thought necessary for the defence of the Floridas in connection with the line of defence on our Southern frontier.[3] This was done under the belief that Government will never jeopadize the safety of the Union or the security of our frontier by surrendering those Posts, unless upon a sure guarantee, agreeably to the stipulations of the articles of the capitulation, that will ensure permanent peace, tranquility & security to our Southern frontier.[4] It is believed that Spain can never furnish this guarantee; as long as there are Indians in Florida & it possessed by Spain—they will be excited to war & the indiscriminate murder of our citizens: by Foreign agents & Spanish officers—The conduct of Spain for the last six years fully proves this—It was under the belief that the Floridas would be held, that my orders to make the report, were given to Capt. Gadsden. To this I refer you its perusal will shew you, how important it is not only to the defence & security of the Frontier, but to the whole U. States—It points to our vulnerable points, & shews that our country can & was intended to be invaded during the last war from this quarter and that the attempt would have been made, had not the Creek Indians been subdued previous to the arrival of the British Troops—& afterwards their attempt to gain possession of Mobile Bay was frustrated by the repuls they met with at Fort Bowyer[5]—If possession is given of the points now occupied by our Troops and a war ensues, an attempt will no doubt be made to penetrate our Country by the Apelachecola, and by the aid of the Indians to reach the Mississippi at or above the Chickasaw Bluffs—should this be done with a formidable force in our unprepared state, it is highly probable that the Enemy might reach the Banks of the Mississippi; occupying these Posts will prevent the danger of such an occurance; surrender them, and I would not without a much stronger force hold myself responsible for the safety of my Division—but with those posts fortified as recommended, & with an effective force of five thousand men I pledge my life upon defending the Country from St. Marys west to the Barrataria, against all the machinations & attacks of the *Holy alliance,* & combined *Europe.*[6]

The erection of our fortifications under the eye of a skillful & confidential Engineer ought to employ our first attention. I am advised that Capt. Gadsden has been assigned to the superintendance of the works to be erected, the confidence in his talents & integrity is well reposed; but it cannot be expected that such talents as Capt. Gadsden possesses (which I must say are very important at present) can be retained and the flower of his life spent in the laborious superintendance of such works, with the responsibility for the trifleing pay & rank of Capt. of Engineers—something more adequate to such talents—such labor & responsibility must be given to obtain his services.

Col: A. P. Hayne has gone on to settle his accounts and resign his Staff appointment[7]—& here I must be permitted to observe, that the talents, enterprize & energy which Capt. Gadsden possesses are very important to the army & that to secure them to his country which may shortly require them I am induced to ask for him the appointment of *Inspector General* which will be vacated by the resignation of Col: Hayne—He is in every respect qualified to fill it—& in the event of war his value will be seen & his merits appreciated—

By Capt. Gadsden you will recieve some letters lately enclosed to me, detailing the information that the Spaniards at Fort St. Augustine were again exciting the Indians to war against us & a copy of my order to Genl. Gaines upon this subject.[8] It is what I expected and proves the necessity & sound policy of not only holding the Posts which we are now in possession of, but likewise of our possessing ourselves of Fort St. Augustine, this alone can ensure peace & security on our southern frontier.

It is alone, by a just & a bold course of conduct that we can expect to obtain & ensure respect from Europe & not by a timid, temporizing policy—the first commands admiration & esteem, the latter contempt; but from the composition of the present administration I can never for an instant suppose, that they will abandon rights or assume a timid & temporizing course of policy—I therefore conclude that the Posts will never be surrendered unless upon the terms agreed on in the capitulation—& then, it guaranteed that those terms will be punctually fulfilled; particularly when it is recollected that unless this is done, our frontier will be exposed to all the scenes of blood & massacre heretofore experienced—& to regain them will cost us much blood & treasure in the event of a war The security of the western States renders it necessary that they should be held—the voice of the people will demand it. But upon this, as well as every other subject, I refer you to Capt. Gadsden—Before I close this letter I must beg leave to call your attention to the unprepared state of our frontier, owing to my having no control over the Ordinance Department had I possessed the power, the necessary arrangements should have been made, to meet any event which might possibly occur—There is not a single piece of ordinance at Mobile fit for the field, their carriages are all out of repair, & when I sent Capt. [Abraham L.] Sands for the necessary train of Artillery to meet me at Pensacola, there was but one nine Pounder & one five & 8/10th. Inch Howitzer the carriages of which could convey them to me—I hope that all the field Artilly at Mobile may be forthwith ordered to be placed in a state of complete readiness for active operations in the field.[9] I have the honor Sir To be with gr. respect Yr. Mo. Obt. St.

Andrew Jackson
Major Genl comdg.

LS in James C. Bronaugh's hand, DNA-RG 107 (M221-78); Extract, DNA-RG 233 (6-1209). Published in *ASP, Military Affairs,* 1:744–45 (extract).

1. See Calhoun to AJ, July 21. No May 1 letter has been found; Jackson perhaps meant his May 5 letter to Calhoun.

2. See AJ to John M. Davis, May 7. Davis carried the packet to Fort Hawkins, where he gave the letters to John B. Hogan for mailing at Milledgeville, but the Milledgeville postmaster denied that Hogan delivered the package (see Charles Bullock to Walter Jones, September 3, and Jones to Abraham Bradley, Jr., September 4, DNA-RG 107, M222-20; Davis to AJ, September 9).

3. See James Gadsden to AJ, August 1.

4. Jackson had specified that restoration would be made only if Spain guaranteed to retain sufficient troops in the province to restrain Indian hostilities (see José Masot's proposals for the surrender of Pensacola with AJ's response, May 28; and AJ to Masot, May 23).

5. In September 1814 a British fleet supported by Indians and Marines attacked Fort Bowyer but were driven off with the loss of one ship.

6. The Holy Alliance, signed September 26, 1815, by Russia, Austria, and Prussia and eventually joined by all of Europe except Great Britain, Turkey, and the Papal States, merely bound the rulers to conduct themselves according to Christian principles. It was popularly confused with the Quadruple Alliance of victorious powers—Great Britain, Austria, Russia, and Prussia—to which Jackson probably refers here. Jackson pledged to defend the entire southern coast from St. Mary's River, which forms the Georgia-Florida border at the Atlantic Ocean, to Barataria Bay, south of New Orleans.

7. Hayne remained in the army until 1820.

8. When the president submitted an extract of this letter to Congress in November, it was stated that the enclosed letters had "been passed into the State Department, and cannot now be found," but see Gabriel W. Perpall to AJ, June 16; David E. Twiggs to Edmund P. Gaines, June 25 (DLC-25); and AJ to Gaines, August 7.

9. See Robert Butler to Sands, April 28. Sands (1782–1840; Military Academy 1809), of Connecticut, was officially promoted to captain of artillery in September.

To Isaac Shelby

Nashville august 11th. 1818.

Dr. Sir

I recd. by due course of mail, your last letter and would have replied to it on its receipt, but I was then awaiting the determination of the chikisaw Indians to whom I had written on the subject of meeting us in council on the subject of the treaty proposed to be holden with them. I have Just recd. their answer through James Colbert their interpreter, a copy of which I enclose you.[1]

They were very much opposed to meet us, they say, they have no lands either to exchange or sell, to which I frankly replied, that their father the President of the u states only asked them for the lands lying north of the southern boundary of the State of Tennessee, that these lands had been sold many years ago, to the citizens of the u states for a Valuable consideration, that the citizens of the u states had been kept out of Possession of those lands, for thirty odd years that the Indians might enjoy the benefit of the game, by hunting thereon—that now the game is destroyed, and it is of no further use to the Indians, they Individual who has Bought & paid for it demand possession of their land, and their father the President will be compelled to give it to them, if he refuses, congress will pass a law, authorising them to take Possession of it, that their father the President, foreseeing this, wishes as their friend to arange this business with them by treaty in which will be stipulated to be given them other lands, or a fair consideration for their claim in money—if they should refuse to meet us, and cede the land asked for on the terms proposed, that congress has the right under the Hopewell treaty by law to regulate all the concerns of the nation that it will exercise this right, on their refusal to treat with us, and take the land allowing the Indians such compensation for ther right of occupying this land as hunting ground as congress may deem Just & right—That their father the President as their friend, wishes that this stipulation should be made with the nation in open council by treaty, in which greater liberallity will be extended to them than they can expect from congress—This plain language of truth has brought them to their senses, and they have agreed to meet us on the 1rst. day of October next in the nation[2]

I tried to bring them near Nashville, then, to the Tennessee river, but all in Vain—they will not meet us at any other Point than within the nation—you being the first named in the commission, I have to ask you to give instructions what will be necessary to be ordered to the point of holding the treaty, as supplies for the commissioners, and the chiefs—and on the event that the contractor will not furnish the supplies, authority to engage some person to do it in whom we can confide—I am unadvised whether the contractor has an agent here, on whom a requisition can be made. If he has, I will find him out, and make a requisition on him for the necessary supplies[3]

I shall expect you at my house about the middle of September, where I shall calculate on your stay for several days, to rest and refresh yourself, from whence we will set out in due time, and by easy marches reach the place of meeting—from my house it is about two hundred miles. I have wrote to the agent to inform the chiefs we will meet them at the time and place appointed by themselves. to wit on the 1rst. day of October next.[4] Please inform me whether you intend bringing a secratary with you, or whether I shall secure one, Colo. Robert Butler my adjutant General will accompany us in that capacity if it meets your approbation.

I find with those Indians, in their present disposition, we will have to take a high and firm ground, or we will fail in success. we must speak to them in the language of truth—and endeavour to put to rest the oposition of the Colberts, by touching their interest, and feeding their avarice. The Subject is of great interests to our states, and the cession must be obtained if Possible, if not obtained, we must then appeal to the executive to refer it to Congress to whom strong remonstrances will be forwarded from this state, and I hope from yours, if the present spirit of the Indians are not checked, by some act of the goverment shewing them their real state of dependance, in a short time, no cession of land will be obtained from them—They Colberts say, they will part with their lands for the price the u. states gets for theirs.

These are high toned sentiments for an Indian and they must be taught to know that they do not Possess sovereignity, with the right of domain

I will thank you to write me as early after the receipt of this, as your convenience will permit. I am Dr. Sir with Sentiments of great respect yr mo. ob. Serv.

Andrew Jackson

P. S. my health is bad, I am much debilitated.

ALS, WHi (6-1217); Copy, T (6-1220). Published in Bassett, 2:387–88 (extract).

1. See Shelby to AJ, July 22; AJ to Colbert, August 4; Colbert to AJ, August 8.
2. See Colbert to AJ, July 17; and AJ to Colbert, July 24 (above) and August 4.
3. For reply, see Shelby to AJ, [cAugust 25].
4. Jackson's letter to Henry Sherburne has not been found.

Jackson drafted a broadly considered reply to James Monroe's letter of July 19 (above), in which he first argued that he was justified under his orders, then argued the strategic necessity of occupying Florida, and finally addressed Monroe's qualms about the constitutionality of the invasion by writing: "Here on your part is no exercise of power that belongs to con-

gress. war has not been declared; it is only the efect of war" (ALS draft dated August 1818, DLC-71). Jackson, however, apparently decided to shift his justification of the Florida campaign to a more narrowly legalistic question of the proper construction of orders following the arrival in Nashville of the July 27 issue of the Washington National Intelligencer, *containing an article regarding Monroe's decision to surrender the Spanish forts (republished without attribution in the* Nashville Clarion, *August 18). The article, drafted by William Wirt and based on extensive cabinet debate, included a discussion of four orders issued to "the American general," each of which barred him from attacking Spanish positions, noted that "no subsequent orders" had enlarged the general's authority, and stated that Jackson had attacked St. Marks and Pensacola "on his own responsibility, merely." Jackson held that the references to orders issued to Edmund P. Gaines before Jackson assumed command of the expedition misled readers regarding his authority, and he redrafted his letter to demonstrate that those earlier orders left him untrammeled.*

To James Monroe

Nashville August 19th. 1818

Dr. Sir

Your letter of the 19th. July apprising me of the course to be persued in relation to the Floridas, has been received.[1] In a future communication, it is my intention to submit my views of all the questions springing from the subject, with the fullness and candeur which the importance of the topic, and the part I have acted in it, demand. At present, I will confine myself to a consideration of a part of your letter which has a particular bearing on myself, and which seems to have originated in a misconception of the import of the order, under which I commenced the Seminole campaign. In making this examination, I will use all the freedom which is courted by your letter; and which I deem necessary to afford you a clear view of the construction which was given to the order and the motives under which I proceeded to execute its intentions.

It is stated in the second paragraph of your letter, that I *transcended the limits of my order,* and that I *acted on my own responsibility.*

To these two points I mean at present to confine myself. But before entering on the proof of their inapplicability to my acts in Florida, allow me fairly to state that the assumption of responsibility will never be shrunk from, when the Public interest can be thereby promoted. I have passed through difficulties and exposures for the honor & benefit of my country—and whenever still, for this purpose, it shall become necessary to assume a further liability, no scruple will be urged or felt. But when it shall be required of me to do so, and the result shall be danger and injury to that country, the inducement will be lost, and my consent will be wanting.

This principle is held to be incontrovertable—That an order generally, to perform a certain service, or effect a certain object, without any specification of the means to be adopted, or the limits to govern the executive officer—leaves an *entire discretion* with the officer as to the choice and application of means, but preserves the responsibility, for his acts in the authority from which the order emanated. under such an order *all the acts* of the inferior are the acts of the superior—and in no way can the subordinate officer be impeached for his measures, except on the score of deficiency in Judgtment and skill. It is also a gramatical truth that the limits of such an order cannot be *transcended* without an entire desertion of the objects it contemplated. For as long as the main legitimate design is kept in view the policy of the measures, adopted, to accomplish it, is alone to be considered. If these be adopted as the proper rules of construction, and we apply them to my order of Decbr 26th. 1817: it will be at once seen, that, both in discription, and operative, principle, they embrace that order exactly. The requisitions of the order are, for the comdg. Genl to assume the immediate command at Fort Scott—to concentrate all the contiguous and disposable force of the Division on that quarter, to call on the executives of adjacent states for an auxiliary militia force, and concludes with this general, comprehensive command—"with this view, you may be prepared to concentrate your forces, and adopt the necessary measures to terminate a conflict which it has ever been the desire of the President, from motives of humanity, to avoid, but which is now made necessary by their settled hostility."[2]

In no part of this document, is there a referrence to any previous order, either to myself, or another officer, with a view to point to me, the measures thought advisable, or the limits of my power in choosing and effecting them. It states that Genl Gains had been ordered to amelia Island; and then proceeds to inform me that "subsequent orders have been given ⟨him⟩ to Genl Gains (of which copies *will be* furnished you) that you would be directed to take the command, and directing him to reassume, should he deem the public interest to require it, the command at Fort Scott untill you should arive there"—lastly, it mentions that "he was instructed to penetrate the Seminole Towns through the floridas, provided the strength of his command at amelia, would Justify his engageing in offensive operations.[''] The principle determining the weight of *refferences,* in subsequent orders, to instructions previously given, is well settled. Such references are usually made with one of these two intentions—Either the order is given to a second officer, to effect a certain ⟨thing?⟩ purpose which was intended to be effected by another officer, and the instructions of the first are refered to as the guide of the second—or the order contains, and is designed for an extension of authority, and only refers to anterior communications to give a full view of what has been previously attempted and performed—In the first case, it is allways necessary to connect the different orders by a specific provision—that no doubt may exist as to the extent of the command; and thus, the several requisitions and instructions are amalgamated, and the limits of the agent plainly and securely established. In the second, no such provision is necessary—for an entire discretion in the choic and use of means being previously vested—the reference, if there be any, is only descriptive of the powers antecedently given and the results of measures attempted under such specified limitation—But admitting that on my order of Decbr 26th. 1817. there is such a reference as I contemplate in the first case—allow me to examine its charector and amount. It is stated, that "orders have been given to Genl Gains (copies of which will be furnished you)" but without affirming that they are to be considered as binding me, or—⟨or in any way binding me⟩ in any way connected with the comprehensive command that I should ["]terminate the Seminole conflict." on the contrary, so far are they from being designated as my guide and limit in entering Florida, that in stating their substance, in the ensuing sentance, no alusion whatever is made either to *means* or *limitation.*

How then can it be said, with propriety, that I have *transcended the limits* of *my orders* or *acted on my own responsibility*? My order was as comprehensive as it could be, and contained neither minute original instructions, or a reference to others, previously given, to guide and govern me. The fullest discretion was left with me in the selection and application of means to effect the specified, legitimate objects of the campaign; and for the exercise of a sound discretion, on principles of policy am I alone responsible—But allow me to repeat, that responsibility is not feared by me, if the general good requires its assumption, I never have shrunk from it, and never will—but against its imposition on me contrary to principle and without the prospect of any politic result, I must contend with all the feeling of a soldier and a citizen. Being advised that you are at your country seat in Loudon, where I expect this will reach you, I enclose you a copy of the order to me of the 26th. of Decbr. 1817. and copies of the orders to Genl Gains therein refered to; from a perusal of which, you will perceive, that the order to me, has no reference to those prohibitory orders to Genl Gains, that you have referred to.

It will afford me pleasure to aid the Goverment in procuring any testimony that may be necessary to prove the hostility of the officers of Spain, to the United States. I had supposed that the evidence furnished had established that fact—that the officers of Spain had Identified themselves with ⟨the⟩ our enemy, and that St Marks & Pensacola were under the compleat control of the Indians altho the Governor of Pensacola at least, had force sufficient to have controled the Indians had he choose to have used it in that way—For the purpose of procuring the necessary Evidence of the hostile acts, of the govr. of Pensacola, I dispatched Capt Young Top. Engineer, & as soon as obtained—will be furnished you. I trust on a view of all my communications (copies of which have been forwarded by Capt Gadsden) you will find that they do not bear the construction you have given them—They were written under bad health—great fatigue—& in haste.[3] My bad health continues, I labour under great bodily debility—accept assurances of my sincere reguard & Esteem; & am respectfuly, yr mo. ob. servt.

Andrew Jackson

ALS, NN (6-1247); ALS draft, LS draft (last page in AJ's hand), and Extract, DLC (71, 25); Copy, NcU (mAJs). Published in 1831 newspapers and in Bassett, 2:389–91 (from LS draft).

1. See above, Monroe to AJ, July 19.

2. See above, John C. Calhoun to AJ, December 26, 1817.

3. See above, AJ to Calhoun, August 10. For a report of Hugh Young's mission, see Young to AJ, October 12, below.

From George Mercer Brooke

Fort. St. Carlos de Barrancas
15th Septbr 1818

Dear. Genl.

I rec'd your favor of the 16th ultimo in due course of mail; and I regret to say, that since your departure, I have not rec'd one cent of cash. But I will most certainly, as soon as practicable, remit you the amnt. of Captain Phillips claim, by the first safe opportunity.[1] There is no circumstance more painfull than the owing of any debt, which it is not immediately in my power to discharge. I recollect too, with little satisfaction, that I have been extremely imprudent, and my conduct at Nashville occasions me frequently, moments of real anguish and I am almost afraid it produced opinions in some which my real character did not deserve. But I now say it with pleasure, there my wild oats are sown, and that the dissipation in which I engaged in Tennessee, exceeded greatly in its folly, that, of any period of my life. I have something coming from my fathers estate, and my oeconimy at this place will soon place me, in a better situation, than I have ever been before.

I am surprised you have not rec'd my letter written some time in June, and I regret it also, as you must have felt disappointment, in my not apparently, complying with your request.[2] I sent it to New Orleans, and directed it, by the way to Natchez. We have nothing new in this quarter. The indians I believe are broken down. I understand that two hundred delivered themselves (in one body) at Fort Gadsden some short time since. [Thomas H.] Boyle reported to me the other day in the absence of Col King.[3] He has not done a great deal. He burnt Holmes village, where he also destroyed a fine field of corn, and took, not far from it, eight Indians. They have been delivered at this place, and are confined in the calabooze. I thought it better, than to send them to Montgomery, as I was fearful, they might suffer a similar fate with those who were sent to Claiborne.[4] The massacre of prisoners who confide alone to your honor, deserves a more severe punishment, than the acts of a secret assassin. The Spaniards seem to be a little better satisfied than they were at first, and I believe they will petition Congress not to restore the country. Those who have gone to the Havanna, having sold out their property, at a very good advance, & the Spaniards now in possession are afraid of almost total ruin, in case of a restoration, as lots, would depreciate in price, to their value, in the worst of Spanish times. A schooner from the Havanna arrived yesterday and is now performing quarrantine. The captain of which, reports, they talk of nothing else but war there. They however know nothing more about it than we do. The cannot be much surprised at their gasconade, for they confine themselves pretty much to puffing. I hold them in less estimation for every valuable quality, which can adorn human nature, than any other nation of Christendom. They are the same from the times of Chatham to the present day.[5]

Governor Massot has not arrived at the havanna, he prefers Campeachy to which place he was carried by adverse currents. They have it reported at Cuba that he sold out to you, and he is now afraid to see the Captain Genl. This skipper of the vessel which is mentioned above, says, that the lower class of people are perfectly convinced of his being a traitor, and that it would be unsafe for him, to venture amongst them, at this time.[6]

I am happy to see that the Executive have approved of your conduct, although they intend to give back. I cannot understand exactly the conditions annexed, whether, they are to be simultaneous, with the restoration, or that it will be required of them, after they have been put in possession.[7] In case of the first, the province may be considered as virtually ours, or in the event of the last a great deal of time must elapse, as I suspect the Captain Genl would not receive the country, without special instructions from his Court. I expect Congress will make a good deal of noise about this business, and the party which has been forming (the head of it from Kentucky)[8] against the present administration, will make it a point to dissapprove, for the purpose of throwing all the odium possible on the Government and its officers. There can be no doubt but what many depositions can be obtained in this Town, of the Indians having been furnished with the munitions of war, by the resident Spanish authorities, and that it is their opinion, that they actually rec'd instructions to carry on the depredations they have committed. I am with great respect and friendship yr obt. Servt.

Geo. M. Brooke

ALS, DLC (25).

1. Letter not found; Phillips was possibly Joseph Philips (1784–1857), formerly an artillery captain from Nashville, who was at this time secretary of Illinois Territory and soon to become chief justice of the state.

2. Possibly Brooke to AJ, July 2, above.

3. For the official report of the Indian surrender in late August, see Edmund P. Gaines to AJ, September 16. Boyles (d. 1821), who had served as a spy for Jackson's 1814 Florida expedition, was authorised on May 31 to form a company of volunteers to search for hostile Indians between the Apalachicola and Escambia rivers.

4. On July 21 five captive Indians being transferred from Fort Claiborne to Fort Montgomery were seized by Alabama Territory citizens and put to death.

5. Probably a reference to Spain's alignment with France against Britain and her colonies during the Seven Years' War. William Pitt (1708–78), First Earl of Chatham, urged Britain to declare war on Spain in 1761, arguing that Spain's official neutrality masked her hostile cooperation with France.

6. José Masot's ships were forced to land on the Yucatan Peninsula for supplies. Subsequently captured by pirates, he did not arrive at Havana until December 6. In March 1819 he was placed under house arrest pending an investigation of the Pensacola surrender, but he died before a verdict was reached.

7. Brooke was referring to the July 27 Washington *National Intelligencer* announcement that the United States would surrender the Spanish forts, provided Spain would maintain sufficient military strength in Florida to control the Indians as required by Article 5 of the Treaty of San Lorenzo.

8. Henry Clay.

From James Gadsden

Washington Septr 28—18—

My Dear General

I returned to this city yesterday when your favr of the 8 Instt was handed me—The subjects in relation to the report of Genl Bernard, the selection of an Aid de Camp &c will be laid before the Secretary of War in a conversation which I propose to have with him this day—The President has not yet returned & the Secretary may feel delicate in deciding on those points—[1]

In a letter to you on my first arrival I detailed the motives of the Executive, as explained by Mr Calhoun, in relation to the Floridas[2]—I can say nothing more therefore on the subject untill another interview when I will endeavour to ascertain positively what are the private views of the administration; Whether to screen themselves &c by attempting the sacrifice of their best friend—I cannot myself but think the whole conduct of the Executive as mysterious, and characterised with a degree of indecision, & imbecility disgraceful to the Nation—Why the ambiguity? The People are in the dark, agitated by ten thousand different rumours & blinded [by] as many different beliefs—The manifesto of the President[3] has been misconstrued & dictated by every news Paper Editor & the only party I have found among the People who disapprove of your operations are those excited by your personal Enemies, and those who ⟨think⟩ have no opinion of their own but always going with the Executive, think that he disapproves; they therefore must—But there is no sentiment of this kind in the Cabinet, they secretly approve & do believe your operations were justified by the necessity of the case & the only ones calculated to put down the Indian Hostilities—But that fantom popularity, an ignis fatuus which will eternally lead its followers into the myres, has deluded the President—A bold & dignified stand would have secured all he wanted & made him the most popular Executive since Washington—For the People are with you—Your campaign is popular, but many of them are affraid to give vent to their feelings under a belief that it might be unfavourably received in the ⟨Great⟩ city—More of these speculations hereafter—Now for a little private business—I have received from Carolina 1/4 of Thirty thousand dollars to be invested in the company for the purchase of the York Bluff & adjacent lands—From my friends in New York I expect as much more by the 5 of October & Some Philedelphians have held out the wish of embarking if they can raise funds to overtake me in time at Nashville—I think therefore there will be no difficulty as to funds to effect our project & hope you have every thing arranged by my return—If you have Sell by all means my Stock in the Cypress company & the Lots at Florence[4]

⟨I am endeavouring to⟩

Col Haynes determination to remain in the Army has defeated my hope of joining you as Ins General—I shall make an effort however to rejoin you as Volunteer Aid de Camp, but I am affraid without success—At all events I shall leave this on the 5 of october for Nashville either as Aid de Camp—furloughed Officer—or humble Citizen—My respects to Mrs Jackson & staff your Friend

Gadsden

Major Eatons appointment I rejoice at—He will be a valuable Member in the Senate to the West this Cession[5]

ALS, DLC (25).

1. Letter not found. James Monroe returned from his Albemarle County estate on October 11. Gadsden was referring to "General Bernard's Report on the Defence of the Gulf of Mexico Frontier," December 23, 1817, DNA-RG 77.

2. Gadsden first arrived in Washington on August 28, but journeyed north to New York and New Haven, before returning to the capital. Letter not found.

3. Again, a reference to the July 27 announcement in the Washington *National Intelligencer* of the president's decision to surrender the Spanish forts.

4. The future site of York Bluff (New York) in fractional section 28, township 3, range 11 west, had been reserved by the government, but it was not yet surveyed. Jackson purchased the section directly south of the townsite at the November sales. York Bluff did not develop, and was soon succeeded by the neighboring town of Ococoposa (Tuscumbia). The Cypress Land Company was formed March 12, as an association of the Huntsville-based Bibb-Tate group of investors with a Nashville contingent, including Jackson but led by John Coffee and James Jackson, to profit by the sale of lots in the new town of Florence. The company held its first sale of lots, July 22–26.

5. Eaton had been named to fill the vacancy occasioned by the resignation of George W. Campbell, appointed minister to Russia.

From Hugh Young

Nashville Oct. 12. 1818.

Dear General

I reached this place on the evening of the 10th. in company with Capt. Call and Dr. Bell.[1] and am happy to be able to inform you, that I have succeeded in obtaining several valuable depositions, from respectable residents of Pensacola, fully proving the connection between the authorities at that place and the hostile Indians. Capt Call will submit them to you, and give you all the necessary information concerning the difficulties I encountered in procuring them, and the measures I was obliged to adopt before I suceeded. Mr. [Michael] McKenzie, Senior Justice of the peace in W. Florida, rendered me much assistance. He has also promised to send on other depositions; particularly Mr. Swiler's, proving the delivery of the *leaden aprons,* of the Cannon, to the Indians, and another respecting the period of Holmes' appearance in Pensacola before the siege. Respecting Holmes none of the witnesses examined could give me any *satisfactory* information.[2]

Capt. Call being able to give the fullest information concerning the detention of the provision Vessels, I thought it un necessary to take the deposition of any others.[3]

Gov. Bibb did not do me the honor to make any reply to my letter. Major Blue obtained the confession of an Hostile Indian, tried at Claiborne; but there is nothing important in it. Would not the confession of the Chiefs who have surrendered on the Apalachicola be of some importance? if so, Col Arbucle could easily obtain them.[4]

Hoping that the steps I have taken may meet your approbation, I remain Dear General, with great respect Your obt. Sert.

H. Young
Asst. Top. Eng.

Mr. Hambly arrived in Pensacola a short time before I left it. He begged to be respectfully remembered to you—H.Y.

ALS, DNA-RG 107 (M222-20).

1. Possibly Egbert H. Bell (d. 1821), a surgeon of the 8th Infantry, known to be at Nashville in October.

2. The depositions probably included those of Joachim Barelas, George Skeate, Charles LeJeune, and William Cooper, September 18; Carlos Baron, September 13; Sebastian Caro, September 7; José Esteeven Caro, September 10; Santiago Dauphin and Joseph Bonifay, September 19; and Pedro Senac, September 19 (see DNA-RG 107, M222-20). McKinsey, a former Mobile County Court clerk who moved to Pensacola in June, witnessed several depositions. Swiler's deposition has not been found, nor has he been identified.

3. Call had gone to Pensacola in February to negotiate passage for supply vessels destined

for Fort Crawford but detained at Pensacola. See his testimony in *ASP, Military Affairs,* 1:751.

4. Young's letter to William W. Bibb has not been found, but Bibb gave testimony in a letter to AJ, October 1. Blue was probably the chief who served as a major of the friendly Creek troops during the Seminole campaign, or possibly Uriah Blue (d. 1836), who had served under Jackson as a major of the 39th Infantry during the 1814–15 Gulf campaign. The confession has not been found, and the Indian has not been identified. Arbuckle, commanding at Fort Gadsden, had received the surrender of around two hundred Red Sticks in late August (see above, George M. Brooke to AJ, September 15).

Rachel Jackson to Andrew Jackson Donelson

Hermitage Oct 19. 1818.

Dear Andrew

I have long had it in contemplation to write to you. I feel so much interest for your welfare in every situation of your Journey through this variegated life. My dear young friend think not I flatter you when I tell you how gratifying it is to me that in all your deportment thus far you meet our highest expectations, and may you go on and prosper in every laudable undertaking is the sincere wish of a Second Mother. O Andrew death has made another demand. I have lost another favorite brother, your Uncle Severn Donelson. On earth he will be seen no more, forever he has finally bid adieu to all on earth, he died with the dropsy in the chest; has left seven small children The Lord giveth and the Lord taketh away, blessed be the name of the Lord.[1] My heart is sorrowful indeed, in less than three years we have lost three relatives—your grand father makes the fourth.[2] Your friends are all well at present as far as I know. Your Uncle Jackson has been from home going on five weeks. I hope he will be at home next week.

Permit me Andrew as a Mother to drop you a few hints. I am sincere I am in earnest, and I speak as one that has authority. That is, experience convinces me that pure and undefiled religion is the greatest treasure on earth, and that all the amiable qualities hang on this. You possess as many as any youth. Now, I, say, as the young man did in the gospel, what hinders me to be a Christian?[3] O let me tell you that this is all my real hopes of happiness. How beautiful it is in youth to approach the sacred ordinance. O how it adorns the person! but how much more his eternal glory. It will be a lamp to his feet and a light to his pathway;[4] I have had the symbols of the blody & the blood of the crucified Redeemer. What a privilege! O that my friends would fly to his expanded arms, imbibe His spirit, emulate His example, and obey his commands. I have so many things to say to you dear youth. Your happiness is near my heart. Let my advice be impressed on your heart Adieu. Let us often hear from you. I am looking for your Uncle next week, write to me & give my love to Edward B. tell Anthony to write: he has been, he tells me, to visit Edward at West Point. Farewell, dear nephew. May this God who holds the destinies of all men in his hands,

order your destiny happy in every sense of the word. Receive my blessing
Your affectionate aunt

Rachel Jackson

Copy, T (6-1372).

1. Donelson (1773–1818) died on October 17. He was survived by sons James Rucker (1805–29), John (b. c1807), Thomas Jefferson (1808–95), Samuel Rucker (b. c1811), and Alexander (1816–87), and daughters Rachel (1803–24) and Lucinda Rucker (1812–37). Rachel did not count Andrew Jackson, Jr., whom she and Jackson adopted, among Donelson's children. She was quoting Job 1:21.

2. Rachel was referring to the deaths of Severn Donelson, John Hutchings, John Samuel Donelson (1797–1817), and Daniel Smith.

3. Probably a reference to Matthew 19:16–23.

4. A paraphrase of Psalm 119:105.

To James Monroe

Head quarter D. of the South
Nashville Octbr. 30th. 1818

Sir

This will be handed you by Colo. Robert Butler Adjutant Genl of the Southern Division, and who acted as Secretary to the commission charged with holding a treaty with the chikisaw nation, who I beg leave to introduce to your personal knowledge as a good citizen & valuable officer who has served throughout the whole Southern campaigns in the late war, and accompanied me in the late campaign against the Seminoles, and to whom I beg leave to refer you for any information on the subject of the latter campaign

Governor Shelby & myself had the good fortune to conclude a treaty with the chikisaw nation of Indians on the 19th. instant, which with the accompanying documents will be handed you by Colo. Butler,[1] we deemed this instrument too valluable to be entrusted to the casualty of convayence by the mail, and hope that the allowance of pay as Secretary & his expence will be allowed him—by this treaty the Indians cede all claim or title to lands within the State of Tennessee & Kentuckey for the annuity of Twenty thousand dollars for fifteen years when the quantity & quality of this land is considered, the vast importance to the strength & defence of the northwest & south Eastern section of our country—added to the vast sum that it will bring into the treasury of the u states, I trust the price given will be viewed as a mere drop in the buckett, compared to the advantage of this cession—I have to refer you to our communations of this day, and to the documents thereto referred, for a detail of the whole proceedings, and to Colo. Butler the bearer hereof. I hasten to conclude by barely ⟨remarking⟩ Sugesting the propriety of an immediate election by the executive of the reserves, mentioned in our detailed report as the Individuals concerned

⟨will⟩ may have time to prepare to meet the bills, and Martin Colbert the trustee for the chiefs concerned, goes on to await the ratification of the treaty & if ratified goes on to Philadelphia to receive the goods—as to the vallue of the reserves, Mr George Graham, who called on us at the treaty with whom we advised on this subject can give you information[2]—I am with Sincere respect & Esteem yr. mo. obedient Servant

Andrew Jackson

P.S. On the 23rd instant I forwarded from Florence on my return to Nashville, the Testimony taken by Capt Young Topografical Engr. at Pensacola, they are full & Pointed, and I trust when added to the documents heretofore furnished will be conclusive[3]—I send duplicates by Doctor Brunaugh, least the originals might be lost on the way—A.J.

ALS, NN (6-1396).

1. See Chickasaw treaty, October 19; Confidential journal of Chickasaw negotiations, September 29–October 20; AJ and Isaac Shelby to John C. Calhoun, October 30.

2. Article 5 of the treaty confirmed reservations made in the 1816 Chickasaw treaty to George (north of the Tennessee River, around his ferry) and Levi Colbert (south of Cotton Gin Port in Mississippi). The reserves were then to be deeded to James Jackson in exchange for $20,000 in Philadelphia merchandise. In making the arrangement, which Jackson described as a way of bribing the Colberts without exceeding authorized expenditures, the commissioners gave the government an option to assume the deed by paying the $20,000 (see AJ to Thomas Kirkman, October 20). During the 1824 campaign, Jesse Benton alluded to the arrangement as an example of Jackson's corrupt use of position to assist his friends, a charge much elaborated by James Shelby in the 1828 campaign (Benton, *An Address to the People of the United States on the Presidential Election* [Nashville, 1824], p. 29; Shelby, *Chickasaw Treaty. An Attempt to Obtain the Testimony of James Jackson, Esq. to Prove the Connexion of Gen. Andrew Jackson with a Company of Land Speculators, While Acting as United States' Commissioner; and to Sustain the Statement on That Subject, of the Late Governor Shelby* [Lexington, 1828]). Martin Colbert (d. 1840) was Levi's eldest son.

3. See AJ to Calhoun, October 23.

To James Monroe

Hermitage November 15th. 1818

D. Sir

On my return from the Chickasaw treaty I found it necessary to pass by Melton's Bluff, where I had established some hands for the culture of cotton, hearing it had been laid out for a town and the lots sold, to have as much of my crop preserved as existing circumstances would permit.[1] From thence I took Huntsville in my rout and did not reach the Hermitage until the 12th. Instant and on the 13th. recd. your letter of the 20th. Ultimo. From an attentive perusal of which, I have concluded that you have not yet seen my dispatches from fort Gadsdone of the 5th. of May last, which, it is reported, reached the Department of War, by due course of mail, and owing to the negligence of the clerks was thrown aside as a bundle of Revolutionary and Pension claims.[2] This I sincerely regret as it would have brought to your view, the light in which I viewed my orders. The closing paragraph of that dispatch is in the following words—"I trust, therefore, that the measures which have been persued will meet with the approbation of the President of the U. States. *They have been adopted in persuance of your instructions* under a firm conviction that they alone were calculated to ensure peace and security to the Southern frontier of Georgia" The moment, therefore, that you assume the ground that I transcended my powers, the letter, refered to above, will at once unfold to your mind the view I had taken of them, and make manifest the difference of opinion that exist. Indeed there are no data, at present, upon which such a letter as you wish written to the Secretary of War, can be bottomed. I have no ground to believe that a difference of opinion exists between the Goverment and myself, relative to the powers given to me in my orders, unless I advert, either to your private and confidential letters, or the public prints, neither of which can be made the basis of an official communication to the Secretary of war. Had I ever, or were I now to view an official letter from the Secretary of war explanatory of the light in which it was intended, by the Goverment, that my orders should be viewed, I would with pleasure give *my understanding* of them.[3]

Here permit me to remark that I am well advised of the liberal and honorable sentiments of Mr. Calhoun. I have full confidence in them; and be assured that, on my part, nothing inconsistant with the pure principles of honor and friendship will be done calculated either to wound the feelings of Mr. Calhoun or yourself, or to injure your standing with the nation. Should circumstances make it necessary for me to enter into the defence of my conduct, on the Seminole campaign, it shall be bottomed upon the principles of truth and honor, and every thing extraneous or impertinent sedulously avoided. At the same time, however, that I am convinced of the honorable and liberal sentiments of Mr. Calhoun I am not insensible of the implacable hostility of Mr. Crawford towards me; nor have I any doubt of his hostility to you. I have lately been confidentially informed that a letter from him to Mr. Clay has been seen, proposing a coalition of interest against your next election.[4] As to myself I regard him not. I have for several years viewed him as a base unprincipled man—I have thus written him, and every day brings with it fresh proof that I have set a just estimate on his character. Indeed, I should not be surprised to learn that the intrigues of Mr. Crawford, (Mr. Calhoun being absent, at the time), occasioned my dispatches of the 5th. of May from Ft. Gadsdone, to be thrown aside as old papers, that they might not be seen until a determination, respecting the Floridas, should be made by the Executive. In this he would have the double object of injuring both you and myself in the estimation of our country; and to accomplish *an object* so desirable to himself and his colleagues, the injury, nay the *ruin,* of his country would interpose no barier.

If on the receipt of this you still think it necessary, and will direct Mr. Calhoun to write to me upon the subject of your letter, now before me, I will answer it as fully and as promptly as the nature of the case will admit of: In the mean time believe me to be, my dear sir, yours sincerely.

Andrew Jackson

LS, NN (6-1423); Copy and Extract, DLC (71, 38); Extract, NcU (mAJs). Published in Bassett, 6:468–69 (from copy). The LS and Copy are in the hand of William B. Lewis. The LS is accompanied by Monroe's endorsement: "He wishes the correspondence, explanatory of his views & of those of the govt., to take place, but expresses a desire that it may commence with the dept.—particularly confidential as to an Individual."

1. A sale of lots for the town of Marathon at Melton's Bluff (fractional sections 25 and 36, T3R7W, and sections 30 and 31, T3R6W) was held October 12. At that sale, AJ purchased a gin lot and others, paying $250 in scrip and $28.75 in cash.

2. See Monroe to AJ, October 20, and, above, AJ to John C. Calhoun, May 5. The source of Jackson's information regarding the misplacement is unknown. A post office investigation had been unable to confirm that the letters had left Georgia (see above, AJ to Calhoun, August 10). In early October the *Savannah Republican* reported that the dispatches had been found in the land office, where they had been misdelivered by the Washington post office, but the truth or falsity of that report or of the one that Jackson heard has not been established.

3. Monroe had suggested that Jackson write for the record an exposition of his understanding of his powers, to be answered "in a friendly manner" by Calhoun. For Monroe's response to Jackson's objections, see Monroe to AJ, December 21, below.

4. Jackson's informant was James Gadsden (see AJ to Gadsden, August 1, 1819, below). The William H. Crawford-Henry Clay letter has not been found.

From John Henry Eaton

Senate Chamber 20th. Nov. 1818

Sir

By Tuesdays mail I recvd. two letters from you dated at Florence; on the same day also was recvd the treaty lately concluded by you with the Indians. another Letter of the 30th. Octo was this day handed me[1]

I called upon the President to day: he having enquired after your health & if you were at Nashville at my departure gave an opportunity of speaking of the engagement on which you have lately been. It being however the first of the session and every member feeling it a duty to call on him occupies fully all the hours that the established etiquette of the day gives to the reception of visitors. I intend on tomorrow or next day again to call on him & will converse with them on the minor branches of the treaty referred to in your letter; as regards its outlines he stated that it had been effected on terms highly advantageous, & was much pleased at the result. How soon he may bring it up for ratification before the Senate rests with himself, when what can will be done towards its speedy passage—[2]

I wrote you a hasty scrawl a few days since enclosing the message of the President;[3] it is full upon the Florida question; and standing as a public &

official document before the world justifying & defending every thing done by you in that quarter, cannot on your part be considered otherwise than satisfactory & calculated to lull all the strong murmurings of your enemies. It is true he does not alledge that your orders prohibited the course you pursued; nor indeed could he go so far, after having ordered a redelivery of the Province in contravention of the treaty of Pensacola;[4] yet he declares it the only course you could have taken with a view to the object before you, founded in necessity and warranted by the outrages of the savages who were excited & urged on by the agents of Spain. The message certainly breaths strong hostility towards Spain; & points to rupture as strongly as the equivocal character of a modern state paper can. It is to me strange however if such be the end to which the President points, that he had not retained the posts untill the meeting of Congress, rather than to deliver them up, & then recommend a course which if adopted at once creates the necessity of retaking them

We have not yet gotten to business; a few days more will organise and arrange matters, and then something of bustle and noise may be expected. I am pursuaded so far as I have data on which to found an opinion that Congress will be disposed to go farther than the message has done in relation to Florida The affair will be brought up, & every thing in regard to it fully elicited; for it is a matter seemingly of general interest Such is my opinion at present, tho yr. experience in legislative matters is sufficent to assure you how little is to be relied on conjectures as to what a deliberative assembly may do

Your idea as regards appointing a surveyor & sectioning out the Chickasaw Country is one which I apprehend will not attach to the general govt. They are bound by their compact with NCarolina to extinguish her warrants on land fit for cultivation, whether Congress may not apportion first a part & not throw the whole Country open for this purpose is probable. Your opinion is that the Country heretofore reserved will be sufficent to satisfy all warrants; this however must be matter of uncertainty Untill then this fact be ascertained it would be unnecessary to lay off & to divide into sections a country which may be necessary to be opened for warrants. As regards ascertaining conflicting grants & laying the younger as near its culls as practacable would be perhaps taking away a right already secured by our laws of permitting warrant holders, (which they will be if their grants be vacated or lost) to lay them again where they please. I have not yet thought sufficently on the subject; what I state are but impressions; but it seems that the particulars in relation to entries & titles must be left to State regulations. I will bring the matter to the consideration of our Delegation & endeavour if possible to prescribe a plan by which frauds & litigation may be as far as possible prevented. It is a matter of great importance to our State, & I shall well ponder before I act—My difficulties at present are to know & understand how far Congress may act without infringing our State Soverignty; to this end a reference will be necessary to the compact & cession act.[5] Respectfully yours

Jno. H. Eaton

Col. Butler & Doc Bronaugh have just arrived

ALS, DLC (26). Published in Bassett, 2:401 (extract).

1. See Treaty ceding Chickasaw lands, October 19. Letters not found.

2. Monroe submitted the treaty to the Senate on November 30, and it was ratified on January 6, 1819.

3. Letter not found. Eaton had enclosed James Monroe's annual message, November 16 (*Annals of Congress,* 15th Cong., 2nd sess., pp. 11–18).

4. By "treaty of Pensacola" Eaton refers to the articles of capitulation for Fort Barrancas, negotiated by Jackson and José Masot, May 28.

5. See the act accepting North Carolina's cession of western lands, April 2, 1790 (1 *U.S. Statutes at Large* 106–109). See also the act authorizing Tennessee to issue grants, April 18, 1806 (2 *ibid.* 381–83).

To Isaac Shelby

Hermitage near Nashville
Novbr 24th. 1818

Dr. Sir

I reached home on the 12th instant, having gratified my friends in the A. Territory by the purchase of a Section of land South of the Tennessee on the military road between the river & big spring—This Section I bought at two dollars pr acre, no person bidding against me and as soon as bid off, hailed by the unanimous shouts of a numerous & mixed multitude[1]—This on the eve of my retireing from all Public appointment, I am ⟨say⟩ compelled to say was gratifying as it was an approval of my offical acts, and that too at a time when I was about to intermigle with them as a private citizen, and after they had full time to deliberate on all my official acts—

On the 20th the citizens of Nashvill & its vicinity gave myself & staff a Ball in commemoration of the late chikesaw Treaty where I had the pleasure to see your Portrait suspended at the head of the assembly room and I was gratified to find that Mr Earl had been so fortunate—for I can with truth say that there never came from the hands of an artist a better likeness.[2] I hope you reached home in good health, and has had a happy meeting with your family, finding them enjoying good health—

Present me to your son Major Thomas [Hart] Shelby respectfully, and altho unacquainted to your amiable lady & family,[3] & believe me to be with due respect & Esteem yr mo. ob. Serv.

Andrew Jackson

ALS, WHi (mAJs); Typed copy, ICU (6-1441). Published in Bassett, 2:401–402. ALS endorsed as answered December 14.

1. Jackson purchased section 33 in township 3 south, range 11 west. $2 per acre was the government's minimum price for purchases of public lands. Newspapers reporting the incident noted that second-rate land in the area went for as high as $83 per acre.

2. The ball, held at the Nashville Inn, was reported in the *Nashville Whig,* November 21. According to statements by the Shelby family in 1828, Jackson asked Shelby to sit for Ralph E. W. Earl during Shelby's stay at the Hermitage on his way to the Chickasaw meetings. On March 25, 1846, A. J. Smith wrote Andrew Jackson, Jr., concerning the portrait of Shelby, which Jackson had designated for the Shelby family (KyU).

3. Shelby (1789–1869), who had attended the Chickasaw negotiations, was the third son of Susannah Hart Shelby (1764–1833), who had married Isaac in 1783. During the 1828 presidential campaign, he charged that Jackson had paid too much for the Chickasaw lands (see *Truth's Advocate & Monthly Anti-Jackson Expositor,* August 1828, pp. 293–98).

To John Caldwell Calhoun

Head Quarters Div South
Nashville 28 Novr 1818

Sir

I enclose you a communication from General Ripley with my reply, as well as an answer of mine to a previous letter of his on the same subject[1]—I cannot but think that the alarms of the Louisianians are unfounded—Spain is at present too weak in the Texas, to effect any military projects against our territory from that quarter; and it would be the height of imprudence at present, to permit the occupancy of the Rio Hondo with an inconsiderable force, to attract our attention, from more important and vulnerable points[2]—The Spanish designs should be unmasked, before counter movements are attempted, in the mean while I shall keep my forces so disposed, that they may be concentrated to act with celerity and effect upon any point assailed—

I enclose you a copy of a letter from Col King, detailing a conflict between Captain Boyles of the Rangers & a detatchment of Hostile warriors[3]—The conduct of the Captain in this affair was meritorious, and I trust ere this he has recovered from his wound, and disappointed the hopes of the Warriors of the Choctawhatchy—A short time since every mail from the South reported the pleasing intelligence of the general submission of the Seminoles; the cause of the reassumption of hostilities is stated in the Colonels communication—The fact that the news of the restoration of Pensacola to Spain had revived their hopes and again excited them to war is an additional evidence of the propriety of my operations in The Floridas, and has confirmed me in my unalterable opinion that the Seminole conflict could not have been terminated by any other means than those adopted. My only apprehensions are that my operations were not sufficiently extensive to ensure permanent tranquility in the South—St Augustine is still in possession of the Spaniards, and the whole Peninsula is beyond the controul of our Garrisons—The situation of Florida in relation to our country is peculiar and demands the early attention of our Government—Bordering almost on the creek nation, and within the vicinity of the four southern Tribes of Indians, her territory will always prove an assylum to the disaffected and restless savage, as well as to a more dangerous population, unless some energetic government can be established to controul or exclude these Interlopers—The Savages & Negroes who have not submitted to our authority have fled east of the Suwaney river, and whether settled in the Alatchaway plains,[4] near St Augustine, or more southwardly we have yet to learn—Their force no doubt is too inconsiderable to create any serious disturbances with this country, but if unmolested they may acquire confidence with their strength, and prove a destructive Enemy to our Frontier settlers—They should be persued, before they recover from the panic of our last operations—I submit to your considerations Military operations for this Spring connected with the occupancy of the Bay of Tampea—The plan proposed is to embark from Fort Gadsden, or Pensacola 500 Regulars, for the Bay of Tampea, together with a force, say 150 or 200 men adequate to the maintaining of the work to be constructed at that point—Simultaneous with this movement, to push a force of 5 or 600 men up the St Johns, and occupy a position at or near the old Indian Town Pecolota:[5] This force as soon as strongly fortified, to be actively employed in scouring the country as far west as Sewaney forcing to, or receiving the, submission of the hostile Indians, who will be sent into the interior of the Creek nation—The Troops detatched to the Bay of Tampea—having constructed, and garrisoned a suitable work, having reconnoitered the neighbouring country, and destroyed woodbynes negro establishment, to march directly to the position occupied on the St Johns, deviating only where Indian villages or settlements (if there are any in the country) invite their attention—From the best information which I can collect, the march from Tampea to the point proposed on the St Johns, would not exceed 7 days—Each man from my own experience can march with 8 days rations on his back, which with due oeconomy will last twelve; time sufficient to perform the operation intended—The expence of the expedition would be trifling as it is proposed that none but Regulars should be employed; and the advantage to the nation incalculable, as finally crushing Savage hostilities in the south, and affording active service to some of our Regiments who have grown sluggish from the inactivity of garrison duties—with respect your ob Serv

Andrew Jackson
Major Genl Comdg.

LS in James Gadsden's hand, DNA-RG 107 (M221-81); Extract, DNA-RG 233 (7-0001). Published in *Calhoun Papers,* 3:312–14.

1. See Eleazar W. Ripley to AJ, October 31; AJ to Ripley, November 15 and 27.

2. On November 6, 1806, local army commanders James Wilkinson and Simon de Herrera agreed informally to regard the disputed area between the Sabine River and the Arroyo

Hondo, an effluent of the Red River near Natchitoches, as "Neutral Ground." A Spanish occupation of the Arroyo Hondo, as predicted by Ripley, would have violated that agreement.

3. See William King to AJ, October 15.

4. An area including the present Alachua County.

5. Picolata was the site of an abandoned Spanish fort on the St. John's River about twenty miles west of St. Augustine.

The replacement of Alden Partridge as superintendent at the United States Military Academy in July 1817 was not popular among the cadets. Among the reforms instituted by Sylvanus Thayer (1785–1872) was a significant increase in discipline, implemented by the new commandant of cadets, John Bliss (1787–1854). Bliss's rigorous treatment of the cadet corps during the summer encampment of 1818 created resentment, which was compounded when Thayer allowed Bliss to continue the daily instructions through the late fall. On November 22, Edward Lloyd Nicholson, a cadet from Maryland, misbehaved in the ranks during drill instruction. Bliss immediately ordered the cadet to his quarters, but Nicholson evidently did not react quickly enough and Bliss physically dragged the cadet out of the line, accompanied by a scolding. Two days later, a committee of five cadets, led by Thomas Ragland, protested Bliss's behavior, presenting Superintendent Thayer with a petition signed by 179 of the corps, including Andrew Jackson Donelson (see Donelson to AJ, November 23 and below, November 29). Thayer rejected the use of petitions from the corps as a proper method of remonstrance, but the committee returned on November 25 with formal charges against Bliss, whereupon Thayer dismissed the five from the corps. The cadets left, but not before procuring a letter of regret from 108 of their former classmates, again including Donelson. The controversy did not end then, however, and the five suspended cadets journeyed to Washington to take up their cause with the secretary of war and, eventually, Congress itself (see AJ to Donelson, January 31, 1819, and January 31, 1820, below).

From Andrew Jackson Donelson

West Point, Novemberth. 29th. 1818

Dear Uncle

Not being able to procure an entire copy of the papers, which may perhaps, better than my own report explain the cause of our discontent with the present commandant, I did not write as was promised last mail; and even now have not obtained what is of most consequence, a copy of charges against the above.[1]

Capt. John Bliss, to whom I allude, is the Commandant of cadets; Majr. Thayer the Superintendant of the Academy. Enclosed is a letter addressed to Thayer, by a committee on our behalf, which happily expresses my sentiments and feelings, as also the majority of the cadets. It was presented to him after an abrubt refusal to attend to or investigate in the least the subject of our complaint, though urged by three fourths of the corps.[2]

The warmth eagerness and earnest solicitations of the cadets, prevailed however so far as to excite his curiosity, and prompted him *not as an officer* but *privately* to scan over our grie[v]ances.

From ⟨the⟩ a tenacity of his duties as superintendant, he has withall, converted this sly glance, into a military arrest, and an immediate order from the post, the committe who had the honour to represent us; The commte., was composed of 5 cadets, Genuine in principle distinguished on the rolls of this Academy, and exemplary in military deportment.

By what rule of justice or Military law, Thayer, has been governed, you may perhaps say, but in the scanty limits of my mind, I could frame an inconsistency, which wonderfully accords with his movements; and differs from my idea of a good officer.

I hope however for the good of the ⟨family⟩ academy that Thayer may excuse himself before proper authority but I should be glad to see John, Bliss, for a day or so, converted into a man of feeling, and the definitions of honour and his duty, perfectly understood, and then feel, the weight of woe, which measures a violation of them, this should be my judgement and I think even the contents of the enclosed will convince you, that he is unfit for a Commandant of Gentlemen, or a company of soldiers I regret that I have not a copy of charges preferred against him by our committe; ⟨they were taken away by the committee,⟩ they have taken them away, and will urge them at Washington City[3] they were allowed to stay on West Point but 6 hours after Thayers order, not time enough to collect their clothes and even without money They were supplied by 5 or 6 cadets among the rest myself: I have borrowed here about 80 Dollars for their use, and called upon Mr. Kirkman for 150 $, subttracting 80 I shall [have] 70 for my own use, I think you will commend me for this;

I am determined Dear Uncle, never to brooke such insults as have been suffered by some of the cadets, either here or any where else, I think it therefore advisable that I should have your permission to resign, whenever it should be attempted, as resistance would be dismissal I remain forever your affectionate Nephew.

Cadet Andrew J. Donelson

ALS, DLC (71).

1. See Donelson to AJ, November 23. Although Donelson did not enclose the charges in this letter, he did enclose the certificates of cadets James T. Worthington, William E. Cruger, and Edward L. Nicholson, November 24, Westwood Lacey, November 26, and Edward L. Nicholson, November 27, all DLC (26), testifying to their maltreatment. For the charges, see *ASP, Military Affairs,* 2:13–14.

2. See Wilson M. C. Fairfax et al. to Sylvanus Thayer, [November 24], DLC (60). Bliss

was relieved of his duties at West Point in January, but he remained in the army until 1837, rising to lieutenant colonel.

3. The cadets brought their case before the department of war, which issued, December 9, an order for a court to inquire into the "transactions and disorders" that prompted their dismissal (see *ASP, Military Affairs,* 2:16–17, 20).

From Isaac Shelby

Travelers Rest near Danville
Decr. 8th. 1818

Dear Sir.

Your favour of the 29th. Ulto. has been duly recd. that of a former date has not come to hand[1]—I am pleased to learn that our treaty meets the approbation of the Secy. of War, who most probably speaks the sentiments of his *Chief*—should any difficulty occur in the Senate the whole deligation west of the Alligany ridge, will no doubt exert themselves to procure its confirmation

I regret to see it stated in the Newspapers that the Choctaw treaty failed—it is rumoured here that but little effort was used to effect it. we must ⟨must⟩ have some of their Country, and I shall not be Surprised if the Governmt. calls upon you next fall to Conclude a Treaty with that Tribe[2]—I have urged some of my friends in our Legislature to propose an amicable adjustment of the question as to Boundary between Tennessee & Kentucky.[3] I hope it will be done in that Spirit of Conciliation & affection which should always Characterise the proceedings of two states, so nearly allied in all respect as we are—it is a question that has long been at issue—it is my opinion the present moment is a fortunate one to renew the negociations, and I think it a Subject highly deserving the first Consideration of the two states.

I am glad to learn that your health is returning—you want rest—and your Country is in a Condition to afford it to you—if any occurrence should lead you to the blue Licks (which is evidently the best watering place in Kenty)—if you will do me the honour to call on me I will accompany you there.[4]

present my Cordial respects to your good Lady—to whose hospitality and politeness—I feel great obligation with Considerations of the highest Esteem and regard. I frankly Subscribe myself Your friend

Isaac Shelby

ALS, DLC (26). Travelers Rest was Shelby's plantation in Lincoln County, Kentucky, about seven miles south of Danville.

1. See AJ to Shelby, November 24 (above) and 29.

2. In May William Carroll, John McKee, and Daniel Burnet (1763–1827), a former territorial lieutenant governor from Claiborne County, Mississippi, were commissioned to negotiate for Choctaw lands in Mississippi. Carroll declined his commission, and when the other

commissioners met with the tribe in October they were unable to obtain a cession. As Shelby predicted, Jackson was commissioned in March 1819, along with McKee and Burnet, to renew negotiations.

3. By the North Carolina charter, as accepted by Virginia, the boundary between the two states, and hence their western neighbors Tennessee and Kentucky, was fixed along the latitude of 36° 30′. Inaccurate surveys, however, led to boundary disputes which the two parent states settled in 1790–91 by accepting Walker's Line, which ran several miles north of the official latitude by the time it reached Tennessee. When Tennessee repudiated Walker's Line in an 1803 dispute with Virginia, Kentucky reopened the boundary question, contending for a resurvey along the 36° 30′ line. Tennessee having failed to accept a compromise offered by the Kentucky legislature in 1816, Kentucky voted on January 30, 1818, to declare her southern boundary at 36° 30′, and a survey of that line between the Mississippi and Tennessee Rivers was undertaken in 1819. Soon after, the two states appointed commissioners, Felix Grundy and William L. Brown for Tennessee and John J. Crittenden and Robert Trimble for Kentucky, who reached an agreement February 2, 1820, confirming Walker's line to the Tennessee River and following the new Kentucky survey west from there to the Mississippi.

4. Blue Lick Springs was on the Licking River, about seven miles north of Carlisle in Nicholas County.

From Robert Butler

Washington City December 15th. 1818.

Dr. General,

I yesterday read your letter to Doctor Bronaugh with considerable interest, and we had previously determined that a state of things might exist here which would render your presence necessary[1]—we have much rumor that Georgia and New York have joined forces, and determined to injure the Administration if possible on the Florida Question—There has been much warmth already manifested, but I think it is now subsiding, on the documents being given to the world. If this attempt is made you are to be the wounded instrument on the occasion—This party is very few, and from the preparations making I think they will get lashed in the house beyond endurance.

It is desirable you should jump into the stage and come on for several reasons—

It is said Genl. Brown will be here, and much intrigue will be on foot in relation to the army.

The Chickesaw Treaty is still in the senate, and I learn there will be some opposition to it on two grounds 1st. with regard to paying for the relinquishment of lands for Kentucky, secondly, establishing the principle of suffering reservations, to be given in fee simple, thereby leaving open room for such stipulations in all future treaties—however futile their opinions are they have their supporters, but I fancy the think will be brought about without danger—[John Jordan] Crittenden Swears it shall go down and assigned a reason to me for delay which I think prudent—[2]

Agreeable to your note I shall not return until I see you here or learn that you will not come on, for however disagreeable it is to me to be separated from my little family, yet considerations growing out of your military reputation, would have induced me to remain even without your note—[3]

Please write me by return mail and present me affectionately to all friends—health accompany you adieu.

Robert Butler

ALS, DLC (26). Published in Heiskell, 3:146, and in Bassett, 2:403 (extract).

1. Letter not found. For contrary advice that Jackson should not visit Washington, see John H. Eaton to AJ, December 14.

2. Article 5 of the 1818 Chickasaw treaty converted three conditional reservations granted the Chickasaw nation by Article 4 of the 1816 treaty into fee simple grants to George and Levi Colbert and John McLeish (McClish). The rumored objections to the Chickasaw treaty, which had been submitted to the Senate on November 30, did not prevent its ratification on January 6, 1819. Crittenden (1786–1863) was the junior senator from Kentucky.

3. Not found.

From James Monroe

Washington Decr 21. 1818

Dear Sir

I recev'd your letter of Novr. 15. sometime past, and should have answer'd it sooner, but for the great pressure of business on me, proceeding from duties, connected with the measures of Congress.[1]

The step suggested in mine to you, of Octr 20th., will I am inclin'd to believe be unnecessary.[2] My sole object in it, was, to enable you, to place your view of the authority under which you acted in Florida, on the strongest ground possible, so as to do complete justice to yourself. I was persuaded, that you had not done yourself justice, in that respect, in your correspondence with the dept., & thought, that it would be better, that the explanation should commence with you, than be invited by the dept. It appear'd to me that that would be the most delicate course in regard to yourself. There is, it is true, nothing in the dept., to indicate a difference of opinion, between you & the Executive, respecting the import of your instructions, and for the reason, that it would have been difficult to have expressed that sentiment, without implying by it, a censure on your conduct, than which nothing could be more remote from our disposition or intention.

On receiving your communications by Mr. Hambly,[3] three objects, were preeminently in view, the first, to preserve the constitution from injury; the second, to deprive Spain & the allied powers, of any just cause of war; & the third, to improve the occurrence to the best advantage of the country, and of the honor of those engaged in it. In every step, which I have since taken, I have pursued these objects, with the utmost zeal, & according to my best judgment. In what concerns you personally, I have omitted nothing, in my power, to do you justice; nor shall I in the sequel of the business.[4]

On what ground you have form'd the opinion stated in your letter, respecting a certain gentleman, is unknown to me.[5] It is due to candour to state, that I have seen nothing, of that character myself; and that the decision of the administration, on the three great points above stated, respecting the course to be pursued by the administration, was unanimously concurrd in, and that I have good reason to believe, that it has been maintaind since, in every particular, by all, with perfect integrity.

It will be gratifying to you to know, that a letter of instructions has been drawn, by the Secretary of State, to our minister at Madrid in reply to the letter of Mr [José Garcia de Leon y] Pizarro, which has been published, in which, all the proceedings in Florida, & in regard to it, has been fully reviewd, & placd in a light which will I think be satisfactory to all. This letter will be reported to Congress, in a few days, & published of course.[6] with great respect & sincere regard I am dear sir yours

James Monroe

ALS and Extract, DLC (26); AL draft and Copy, NN (7-0069, -0065); Copy, NcU (mAJs). Published in 1831 newspapers and in Bassett, 2:404–405. The 1831 publications conclude with a paragraph absent from both the ALS and Monroe's copy but present in draft form among Monroe's papers. The paragraph reads: "On one circumstance it seems proper that I should now give you an explanation. Your letter of January 6 was received while I was seriously indisposed. Observing that it was from you, I handed it to Mr. Calhoun to read, after reading one or two lines, only, myself. The order to you to take command in that quarter had before then been issued. He remarked, after perusing the letter, that it was a confidential one, relating to Florida, which I must answer. I asked him if he had forwarded to you the orders of Gen. Gaines on that subject. He replied that he had. Your letter to me, with many others from friends, was put aside, in consequence of my indisposition and the great pressure on me at the time, and never recurred to until after my return from Loudoun, on the receipt of yours by Mr. Hambly, and then on the suggestion of Mr. Calhoun" (Washington *National Intelligencer,* February 9, 1831).

1. See above.
2. See Monroe to AJ, October 20.
3. See AJ to Monroe, June 2, above, and AJ to John C. Calhoun, June 2. Monroe's copy (NN) reads "Capt. Gadsden," as do the 1831 publications. See above, AJ to Calhoun, August 10, for the letter carried by James Gadsden.
4. Monroe's copy, reflecting an earlier draft, includes a passage marked for excision at this point:

"A strong disposition was manifested, by many of the members of Congress last session, to pa[ss] an act, to authorize the Executive, to take possession of Florida, & to hold it, subject to negotiation. I was consulted on the measure, & dissuaded them from it, in consideration of the danger to which it was exposd, of involving us, in a war with Spain & the allied powers. I think that the proof which is now in possession of the Government, is satisfactory, that the policy which was then, & has been since pursued, in regard to Florida, & to Spain & the colonies in South America, has contributed essentially, to produce the decision of the allies, at Aix la chapelle, not to interfere in favor of Spain, against the Colonies, or against us. By this policy we have lost nothing as by keeping the allies out of the quarrel, Florida, must soon be ours, & the colonies, must be independent, for if they cannot beat Spain, they do not deserve to be free. My candid opinion is, that your measures in Florida, have contributed much to shake that province, out of the hands of Spain, & connected with what has since followed to do it, with the approbation of the allies. This it is true is not yet done, but the result appears to be inevitable.

"altho I never meant to go farther in regard to Florida, than I have heretofore stated, or to imply such an intention"

5. See Jackson's criticism of William H. Crawford in his November 15 letter, above.

6. See John Q. Adams to George W. Erving, November 28, replying to Pizarro to Erving, July 26, August 6, 11, and 29 (*ASP, Foreign Relations,* 4:539–45, 518–19, 522–23). Adams's letter was submitted to the House of Representatives on December 28. Pizarro (1770–1835) served as Spanish foreign minister from October 1816 to September 1818.

On July 26, 1794, John Overton purchased from Elisha Rice a claim to 30,000 acres of Western District lands originally obtained from North Carolina by Elisha's brother John, Jackson obtaining a half interest in the purchase, pursuant to his May 12, 1794, partnership agreement with Overton. Included within the purchase was patent 283 for 5,000 acres at the Chickasaw Bluffs near the mouth of the Wolf River, and on July 3, 1797, Jackson conveyed half of his interest in that patent to Richard and Stephen Winchester, who then transferred their interest to their brothers James and William. Overton, Jackson, and the Winchesters were unable to confirm their claim, however, as the 1806 federal law authorizing Tennessee to confirm North Carolina patents had reserved most of West Tennessee, which was recognized as Chickasaw territory by the 1785 Hopewell Treaty, as a Congressional District not subject to state use (see above, AJ, David Meriwether, and Jesse Franklin to William H. Crawford, September 20, 1816, and AJ to James Monroe, March 4, 1817). With the appointments in May of Jackson and Isaac Shelby as commissioners to extinguish Chickasaw claims in the area, Overton saw the opportunity to capitalize on the long-held investment. By July, he was conferring with James Winchester to clarify titles preparatory to laying out a town on the tract. As the treaty was negotiated, Winchester and Overton continued to confer, firming plans for creation of the town that would become Memphis. Jackson's role in the speculation appears to have been peripheral—on December 12, he conveyed half of his remaining interest to Winchester, keeping only an eighth interest, and he does not appear to have joined in Winchester's and Overton's plans to visit the site.

From John Overton

Travellers Rest 21st Decr 1818

Dear Genl

Inclosed is a letter from Genl Winchester, as also copies of notices, to be signed by you, Genl Winchester and myself—I have written to Genl. W—a copy of which letter is inclosed for your inspection, a copy of this letter Genl W. has transmitted to his relations[1] But Genl W. upon the rect of my letter had informed them of the same thing—In the month of July last the heirs were applied to, to sell—their answer was that they expected a treaty, that they understood it was a good site for a town, observing at the same time that ⟨they had been⟩ propositions had been made to them the spring before—They refused to sell, alleging two reasons, one was that they did not know how much they were entitled to; the other was that they esteemed it very valuable

The notices, are so framed, that they can have no reason to complain hereafter, if they do not think proper to join us—and cannot hereafter allege fraud, concealment, or surprise

Genl Winchester has agreed to have the notices served, and returned—you will, if approved, sign them all. Examine the term of them, being all alike except that to [James] Campbell the father of two infant children. I cannot see any way that they can be included—their part must be laid off to itself, being incapable of giving assent—There is but one case agreeably to our Laws whereby the land of orphans can be alienated, and that is to pay debts—which must be made appear to the Court of the County where the land lies—upon which the Court makes an order of Sale, which cannot take place until twelve months after the order is made—and moreover the orphan must have a guardian, in this state, as it would seem from the law. You will readily perceive that this course cannot be taken. because 1t. The children have a father alive living in Baltimore, a man of property and of course, there are no debts of the mother to burthen the estate of the children, who are the heirs of the mother, as to this land. Beside if there were debts no sale could by any possibility take place under eighteen months—a delay too long for us, even if we should become the purchasers—Therefore, it is that we shall have to lay off the part of those two children to itself[2]

After signing the notices, transmit them, by the bearer Lucilius Winchester the son of the genl.[3]

It is possible, that the heirs may take it into their heads to sell to us—or to me as it was by my agent that a proposition was made to them in July last. If so, you will have an interest in it if you think proper—If they do not, all who are of age may join us in the town if they chuse; if not we will lay off our part to itself

My Nephew Mr Saml [Ragland] Overton Junr. will be in company with Mr W the bearer He is a young man of worth and talents, in whom I have the most perfect confidence. His health is weak and unable to undergo hardship, and wishes to procure some business which will enable him to live. It is thought probable, a land District will be laid off during the present Session of Congress in the lower part of Missouri or upper part of Louisiana, including the Red River Country—His disposition is to go to that Country. May I ask the favor of you genl to drop *[a li]*ne to Mr Eaton on this subject, requesting him, in case such an event should take place, to mention Mr. Overton to the President in your name, or with your recommendation. If any impropriety in this course, such other as you may think proper to adopt, of which you alone, can judge[4]

Should any thing occur to you respecting our Bluff business, let me know and I will meet you at any time in Town, and if that should not be convenient, will come up to your house; particularly after the first of January, when I shall have an overseer Very resply yr. friend

John Overton

Note. Do you observe ⟨that⟩ Winchesters letter, where he ⟨observes⟩ says Judge [John] Mc[Nairy] has a claim to the Bluff—*[It]* seems in reality a little strange that *[th]*e Judge is so often crossing peoples paths, both public and private. I suspect however, that W. has been erroneously informed, as I know to a Certainty that John Rices claim is indisputable and I sincerely believe we are the only rightful owners of that The matter, scarcely deserves notice[5] Take care of Winchesters letter, and copy J O

Let me know Genl by Return of Mr. O. or as soon as conv*[en]*ient, whether a Surv*[eyor]* must be Sent dow*[n]* to Survey & examine before, I go down in April—Note what W. say about it J O

It is also important, as Winchester mentions in his letter—that we Shd. execute an instrumt of writing vesting in an agent & agents power to proceed—with the town in case of any of our death, See Copy of my letter to Genl W.—Let me know yr mind on this point[6] J O

ALS, DLC (26). Overton (1766–1833), a Nashville lawyer, had long been Jackson's friend and partner in land speculations. Travellers' Rest was his plantation about five miles south of Nashville.

1. See James Winchester to Overton, December 17, and Overton to Winchester, November 10, both DLC (26). The copies of the notices have not been found.

2. Campbell (1770–1846), who had married Rebecca Winchester (1785–1812), a daughter of James Winchester's brother, William (1750–1812), had two children from the marriage, Mason (1810–69) and Mary (1811–35).

3. Lucilius Winchester (1803–33).

4. Arkansas Territory was separated from Missouri Territory by the act of March 2, 1819 (3 *U.S. Statutes at Large* 493–96). Jackson later recommended Samuel R. Overton (d. 1827), a son of John's brother Waller, for register in the territory (see AJ to James Monroe, March 14, 1820).

5. Nothing further has been found regarding any claim in the Memphis area by McNairy (1762–1837), federal judge for both districts of Tennessee, 1797–1833. Rice (d. 1792), the father of Joel Rice who represented Davidson County at the North Carolina convention that ratified the U.S. Constitution, had extensive land holdings in West Tennessee, much of which Jackson and Overton purchased.

6. Jackson's reply has not been found.

To Andrew Jackson Donelson

Hermitage Decbr. 28th 1818

Dr. Andrew

yours of the 23rd ult. reached me by due course of Mail, yours of the 29th. with the enclosures alluded to in your first reached me by last mail[1]

I have read them with great care and attentition & sincerely regret the occurrencies you have related. If they cadets who were the objects of abuse have acted toward the Drill officer with that becomming respect due from an inferior to his superior, then his conduct is unpardonable, and any punishment could not be too severe for such conduct so unbecoming a superior to an inferior, and so inconsistant with the feelings of a man of honour and a gentleman—If they cadets have acted disrespectfully towards him, it became his duty to have them arrested & regularly punished. Their conduct even then, could not have excused him from deviating from that rule of conduct, which decorum as well as law, has established as the guide to a superior officer, in his conduct towards his inferior, but the disrespect of the inferior to his superior & that personal, would in a great degree excuse, altho not Justify such conduct

They cadets certainly pursued in their application to Capt. Thayer (he being the commander of the Post) the proper & legal course for redress, and it is more than strange, his conduct, as you have related, I have read the adress with care, it is respectfull, and in all respects proper, the facts being true as stated—it was due from him as the superin[ten]dant, to hear the statement of grievances, and if substantiated, arrest the officer on the charges exhibitted, & refer him for trial to a courtmartial—The superintendants conduct in refusing to hear the complaint officially, was compelling they cadets to complain to his superior for redress, and I trust the President of the u states, has not forgot the law, or the duty he owes to Justice to pass such unheard of conduct over in silence. I hope he has, or will, order a prompt investigation of the whole cases, and if substantiated as presented to my view ⟨from⟩ by the vouchers you have forwarded me, there can be no doubt but the commadant of the cadets will be cashiered, or stricken from the Rolls of the army—& Capt Thayer reprimanded if not dismissed—

My dear nephew, I rejoice in the interest you have taken in aiding to procure redress for innocence unjustly injured, such acts are the buds of virtue and ought to be cherished, but it ought allways to be clearly shewn to you, that the subject of abuse is innocent, and the treatment unjust—When you clearly see this, it is your duty to aid injured innocence when & wheresoever you meet with it—But allways recollect, that there are a certain respect due to your superiors, that ought allways to be rendered, and he who witholds this Just respect from his superior, cannot be in the situation of innocence opressed, for the very act of witholding that, that is due to another, is criminal—

I really can see no ground or excuse for the conduct of Capt Thayer to the five young gentlemen who presented the adress. Their conduct therefore in proceeding to Washington to lay their complaint before the President was correct, your aiding them with the means under their circumstances—meets with my full approbation.

I am pleased with your feelings which you have expressed—whilst on the one hand, you sedulously avoid intentionally wounding any persons feeling, you are right never to permit your own to be insulted without redress, under a full persuasion from your uniform good conduct at every school you have been at, that those who would attempt to treat you as some others of the Cadets have been treated, would be void of propriety of conduct, and suffer death before you will dishonour, recollect the duty you owe to your superior & never forget to render it, & if ever a superior forgets what he owes to you, & to his station, & attempts to insult or malltreat you as ⟨it⟩ has been the case with others, you have my permission to resign—but if the superior attempts either to strike or kick you, put him to instant death the moment you receive either—never my son, outlive your honour—never do an act that will tarnish it—never deviate from a Just subordination to your superiors, never permit your feelings to be outraged with impunity—I shall be anxious to hear the fate of the committee who has gone to the city write me the history of the whole transaction, present me to Edward, and except of my prayers for your health & happiness & believe me to be your affectionate uncle.

Andrew Jackson

P.S. write me often & tell Edward to write me also—

ALS, DLC (7-0085).

1. See Donelson to AJ, November 23, and above, November 29.

To John Caldwell Calhoun

Nashville Decbr. 30th. 1818

Dr. Sir

Inclosed you will receive a written adress from James Pitchlynn a half breed son to Mr John Pitchlynn interpreter *[for]* the Choctaw nation of Indians.[1]

Mr James Pitchlynn is Just from his nation, and appears very anxious that an exchange of land should be effected by his nation for lands west of the Mississippi, and as you will see gives it as his opinion that it can be effected.

He informs me that there are upwards of three hundred choctaw Warriors with their families, that have crossed the M. River under the command of *[a choctaw chief c]*alled Capt. White, who *[have]* united their settlement with the quashatas & allabamians the whole under the command of Capt White—These choctaws with their friends in the nation are all axious for an Exchange[2]

Mr Pitchlynn has applied to me to submit to him in writting the terms on which the u states would exchange—I have answered him, I have no instructions from his father the President of the u states, that I would give him my opinion in writing, and that he must make it known to his nation merely as my opinion—I stated him as follows—[3]

That the u states will give them as much *[la]*nd west of the Mississippi river as his nation *[no]*w has East—that his father the President *[will]* allow them a fair consideration for *[all]* improvements, which adds real vallue to the land—and to the poor of the nation as a full compensation for their improvement, a gun, a Blankett, & a trapp—or in lieu of the latter a Kettle—That he would furnish them with provisions untill the could raise a crop, with Boats to pass their families & stock across the M. river—and powder & lead to last them the first year and if any remained on this side the M. they *[should be subje]*ct to the laws of th*[e]* u states. I have *[Told]* him to inform his *[na]*tion that congress has a bill now before them which I expect will pass into a law, preventing the choctaws from hunting west of the M. should they not agree to exchange their lands.[4] Mr P. appears fully to understand this, and asked me for authority & the means of bearing his expense to explore the west of the M, and to pass throug[h] his own nation, to explain the subject fully to them; & gives it as his opinion, that he can take more than half the nation with him across the M. I have answered him, I have no authority to grant his request, but would Submit his proposition to his father the President, and forward to him his answer, if he thought proper to give one.

Mr P. has requested me to make kn*[own]* to his father the P. u. states, that the ch*[octaws]* on the west under command of Capt White are solicitous for the exchange & ask that a Sub agent for them may be appointed to aid them in obtaining it. Should the Govr. think this advisable, I would recommend, that Mr P. be appointed interpreter to that part of the nation, he appears zealous in this thing, & I have no doubt but he will use his best exertions—& if one half goes, the whole nation will remove there are few indeed of the cho*[ctaws who]* remain to be controled by *[our laws, and]* I am informed that there are only those opposed to an exchange, who are making money on the Public road.[5]

Mr P. returns to day to his nation. I have promised ⟨him⟩ to transmit to him your answer. I am respectfully yr mo. ob. Serv.

Andrew Jackson

ALS, DNA-RG 107 (M221-81). Published in Bassett, 2:405–406. Missing letters and phrases supplied from Bassett.

1. See James Pitchlynn to AJ, [December]. James Pitchlynn (d. c1834), also an interpreter, reportedly lost his influence in the tribe as a result of his role in the negotiation of the 1820 Choctaw treaty.

2. The Alabama (Alibamu) and Coushatta (Koasati; Coosada) were members of the Creek Confederacy located near where the Tallapoosa and Coosa rivers join to form the Alabama. The Indians dispersed following the defeat of their French allies in 1763, with significant settlements along the Sabine and Red Rivers in Louisiana. White has not been identified further.

3. See AJ to James Pitchlynn, [December].

4. On November 20, Mississippi representative George Poindexter had asked that the Committee on Public Lands consider the matter. The committee reported a bill to that effect on December 1, but it did not pass (*Annals of Congress,* 15th Cong., 2nd sess., pp. 297, 336).

5. The road from Nashville to Natchez along the old Natchez Trace, in accordance with an 1801 treaty, ran through Choctaw lands in northern Mississippi.

1819

To John Coffee

January 4th. 1819. 8 oclock P M

Dr. Genl

I am Just returned from the moloncholy Task of paying the last tribute of respect to the mains of our friend Mrs. [Mary] Hamblin,[1] where the distress of the Husband & parents, were more acute & distressing than any thing I have ever seen—

I am off to the city on Thursday morning reguardless of any pecuniary loss that I may experience—advices of last evening state the British cock burn of conflagration memory with his train of Incendiaries, has invested the City, that he has brought over several members of Congress to his stander—that the shades of Arbuthnot & ambrister has excited the Negroes in Richmond to the indiscriminate Butchery of its citizens reguardless of ages & Sex, that Genl Scott aided by the Editor of the Enquirer Mr [Thomas] Richey has placed themselves at their head, and indiscriminate butchery is expected & on the last dates the capitol & presidents house were hourly expected to be burned. This being in my division, I make a sudden movement, to surprise the enemy & save the citidal—it being reported in Richmond that I am dead, I do not fear of surprising the enemy—& you make expect to hear that the law of retaliation is enforced—[2]

Can I ask you when you reach Florence & a leisure day will permit, to lay out my plantation near Florence for me—bring it as near the site for the dwelling house as you think right—I shall not be long gone, but in my absence instruct William [White] Crawford in those things that you think requires it—Shew him the place where to make little Andrew J. Hutchings plantation &c &c &c[3]—My waggon & two hands with salt pork &c will sett out on Thursday next—I will send him a pony & I think he will be able to superintend both farms the present year—another cannot be got, at any reasonable terms—In haste I am yrs respectfully

Andrew Jackson

ALS marked "private" and sent by William Donelson, Jr., DLC (7-0114).

1. Mary Hamblen (1799–1819), daughter of William (1756–1820) and Charity Dickinson Donelson (1778–1827), married Dr. John M. A. Hamblen in 1818. She died on January 3, apparently during childbirth, leaving an infant daughter, Mary Eliza Overton Hamblen.

2. The January 5 *Nashville Clarion* printed this rumor in language remarkably similar to Jackson's. British Admiral Sir George Cockburn (1772–1853), coordinator of the 1814 attack on Washington, was nowhere in the vicinity of North America in 1819, nor were Winfield Scott or Ritchie (1778–1854), editor of the *Richmond Enquirer,* involved in any revolutionary intrigue. Ritchie, however, was aligned politically with William H. Crawford, and Scott had been named by the Philadelphia *Aurora* as an instigator of public sentiment against Jackson's Florida actions. The rumor about Jackson's death was not repeated in the *Nashville Clarion.*

3. Jackson was closing down the Melton's Bluff plantation in Lawrence County and relocating his Alabama operations to the Evans Spring property in Lauderdale County, near land owned by his ward, Andrew J. Hutchings. Crawford, the son of Jackson's first cousin, James Crawford, Jr., managed both Lauderdale plantations from September 1818 through October 15, 1819, and returned as overseer at the Evans Spring site in late 1820, remaining until its sale the following year (see Account of Jackson's and Hutchings's joint ventures at Melton's Bluff, December 14, 1816). By 1830 Crawford had removed to Fayette County, Tennessee, where in 1832 he was colonel of militia (see Account with Crawford, October 28, and AJ to Nelson P. Jones, November 25, 1820, below).

After the president's November 1818 message to Congress endorsed Jackson's invasion of Florida, Speaker of the House Henry Clay, in temporary alliance with the forces of the treasury secretary William H. Crawford, spearheaded the congressional investigation of Jackson's conduct, attempting to eliminate a potential political rival in the West and to position himself as successor to James Monroe. Feelings in Congress ran high against the invasion, fanned by rumors circulated by Jackson's Tennessee opponents, particularly John Williams. Especially damaging were charges of Pensacola land speculation by Jackson's friends and alleged favoritism in the leasing of the 1818 Chickasaw salt lick reserve (see AJ to Thomas McCorry, March 8, to John Coffee, April 3, to Joseph McMinn, September 13, to John Brown, October 8, and Affidavit of Thomas Childress, January 12, 1820, all below). Not yet aware of Williams's activities, Jackson heeded Robert Butler's advice and traveled to Washington to defend his conduct in Florida (see above, Butler to AJ, December 15, 1818). Both houses of Congress planned investigations of the Florida invasion, but the Senate withheld its probe when it appeared that the House, under Clay's leadership, would censure the general. On January 12 the majority of the House Committee on Military Affairs condemned the executions of Arbuthnot and Ambrister while the committee chair Richard Mentor Johnson submitted a minority report commending Jackson's conduct. Georgia congressman Thomas Willis Cobb (1784–1830), an ally of Crawford, submitted additional condemnatory resolutions. The ensuing debate occupied official Washington until February 8. Clay's greatly anticipated January 20 speech to the House, while expressing personal respect for the general, attacked Jackson as the administration's standard bearer, criticizing not only the invasion of Florida but Jackson's alleged harsh treatment of the Creek Nation at the 1814 Treaty of Fort Jackson. Clay's fellow Kentuckian Richard

M. Johnson spoke immediately afterward, giving by all accounts the best defense of Jackson's conduct and turning the tide of debate in favor of the general and the administration. Moreover, Clay's support of the Creeks did not sit well with westerners, eliciting strong denunciations in the western press, which Jackson, after his arrival in Washington on January 23, was only too happy to abet. In the end, Clay's carefully orchestrated attack on the administration through Jackson failed, and the House exonerated Jackson on February 8, leaving the issue to Abner Lacock and his Senate committee (see Annals of Congress, *15th Cong., 2nd sess., pp. 631–74).*

To William Berkeley Lewis

City of Washington
Janry. 30th. 1819—

Dr. Sir

Inclosed you will find a pece adressed to the Honourable Mr Clay which I wish you to have republished, you will see him skinned, here & I hope you will roast him in the west—I have enclosed his speech to Colo. S[tockley] D[onelson] Hays. I wish you to see & read it, & if Mr Casedy can be got sober, I wish him to scorch him for his attack upon the Treaty of Fort Jackson—[1]

I find Mr Calhoun is sore from the remarks made by B. B. in the aurora, he has professed to be my friend, approves my conduct and that of the President—Mr Munroe, has told the members if an opportunity offers, to declare on the floor of Congress, in addition to what Mr Adams has said that he fully & warmly approves every act of mine from first to last of the Seminole campaign. Mr Lounds has made his speech to day, & has vented all his spleen against me and exonerated the President—Judge [Hugh] Nelson follows him & has given him the gaff untill It is believed he is sorry for his deception & versitility—It is said by all who heard Lounds that his speech has been the weakest thing that has appeared.[2] Judge Nelson will conclude his speech on Monday, will be followed by two gentlemen from Pensilvania [Henry] Baldwin & [John] Seargeant on the same side who I am told will be able & Severe—[George] Poindexter & [Thomas] Claibourn will conclude—both with severity[3]—Genl [Alexander] Smyth V[irginia] & [James] Talmage [Jr.] from Newyork has it is said made two of the most lucid speeches ever heard on the floor & [Philip Pendleton] Barbour V. one of the most logical—I will as they appear forward them—I have never been at the house, & I have declined all that hospitality offerred by the Mayor & the city and heads of Department untill the question is ended[4] There will be a vast majority I am Told in my favour, & I have seen a letter from Mr Jefferson fully approving all my conduct—and that of the President, & bestowing one of the handsomest compliments on Mr Adams letter ever penned—It is stated that Mr Loundes is allied to Mr Crawford—Mr Clay does not deny that there is a combination, but says that there is no *systematic* combination—he dares not deny that crawford wrote him on the subject—& you may occasionally probe him & Mr Crawford on this point—I enclose a letter for Mrs. J. please send it to her[5]—I am yours respectfully

Andrew Jackson

P. S. If you know B. B. Tell him to exonerate Mr Calhoun from a coalition with Mr Crawford present me to the ladies affectionately. I would be glad to hear from you—The combination formed was more extensive than I calculated on, but Mr Clay anxiety to crush the Executive through me has defeated them & it is recoiling on the heads of the Coalition—I was induced to believe from Colo Hayne & others here that Lounds would defend me, but his engagements to Crawford it is supposed, & the influence of Clay has pushed him to his political ruin for this is become a great party question & it will end in it—& must become the Touchstone of the election of the next President and the hypocracy & baseness of Clay in pretending friendship to me, & endeavouring to crush the executive through me maks me dispise the villain ⟨A. J.⟩ the whole K[entucky] delegation except clay I am told goes with me—& Clay is politically damd—& I have exposed the corespondance with Genl Scott & he is double damd.[6] it is fortunate I have come on—had I not things would not have been as they are—A. J. Let Mrs. J. have a perusal of the enclosed as soon as they are reprinted in the Whigg & Clarion for I wish both these papers to take up the subject warmly. A. J.

ALS, NN (7-0214). Published in Parton, 2:543–44. Endorsed by Lewis: "The articles signed B. B. referred to in this letter as having been published in the Phila. Aurora were written by the undersigned, ⟨and⟩ which was made known confidentially to the Genl. before he left home for Washington City—Copies of which have been preserved and filed with my papers WBL."

1. The article denouncing Clay's characterization of the Treaty of Fort Jackson was probably the piece signed "TENSAW," published in the *Nashville Whig,* March 13. Cassedy had already defended Jackson's conduct in Florida (see Augusta *Chronicle and Georgia Gazette,* June 13, 1818).

2. Lewis's letter, "B. B." appeared in the January 28 issue of the *Aurora* and claimed that Calhoun was "playing a double game" by pretending to support Jackson's conduct in Florida while actually opposing it; Lewis later retracted the criticism (see Parton, 3:313). James Monroe's approval was not nearly so unequivocal, for on February 7, he noted to James Madison that he supported the general despite Jackson's mistakes in judgment (Stanislaus Murray Hamilton, ed., *Writings of James Monroe* [7 vols.; New York, 1898–1903], 6:87–89; see also, Monroe to AJ, October 20, 1818). In his January 30 remarks South Carolina's William Lowndes maintained that the occupation of St. Marks and Pensacola was unconstitutional. Nelson (1768–1836; William and Mary 1780), former judge of the Virginia General Court, and at this time chairman of the House judiciary committee, began his address on January 30, concluding on February 1.

3. Baldwin (1780–1844; Yale 1797), who spoke on February 5, was appointed by Jackson to the U.S. Supreme Court in 1830. Sergeant (1779–1852; Princeton 1795) was a Federalist

representative; neither he nor Claiborne was recorded as speaking. Poindexter (1779–1853) had emigrated to Mississippi Territory from his native Virginia, and later was governor (1820–22) and senator; he spoke February 1–3.

4. Smyth (1765–1830), a brigadier general in the inspector general's office in 1812, served intermittently in Congress from 1808 until his death. Tallmadge (1778–1853), a brigadier general of New York militia in War of 1812, was serving his only term in Congress. Smyth and Tallmadge spoke on January 21 and 22–23, respectively. Barbour (1783–1841; William and Mary 1799) represented Virginia; in 1836 Jackson appointed him to the U.S. Supreme Court. Jackson declined an invitation from the secretary of state (see AJ to John Q. and Louisa Catherine Adams, January 25), and presumably one also from Benjamin G. Orr, mayor of Washington. He did relent in one instance, however, and dined with Secretary of War John C. Calhoun. After the House vote on February 8, Jackson also attended a reception at the White House and a dinner at Adams's residence.

5. Undoubtedly Monroe had shown Jackson letters from both former presidents Thomas Jefferson and James Madison giving general approbation of the administration's conduct in Florida, although Jefferson's January 18 letter (DLC-Jefferson Papers) was much more supportive than Madison's of November 28, 1818 (DLC-Madison Papers; see also Jefferson to AJ, November 22, below). Jefferson had termed Adams's letter to George W. Erving of November 28, 1818, one of the "most important" and "ablest compositions" he had ever seen. Regarding the purported letter from Crawford to Clay, see above, AJ to Monroe, November 15, 1818, and AJ to Gadsden, August 1, below. The enclosure was AJ to Rachel Jackson, January 30.

6. The controversy between Jackson and Winfield Scott had subsided during much of 1818, only to resume by the publication of an unsigned article by Scott printed in the August 10, 1818, *New-York Evening Post* (reprinted December 14), criticizing Jackson for executing Ambrister, and made known to Jackson in Thomas Claiborne's letter of December 23, 1818. Jackson undoubtedly came to Washington with manuscript copies of his correspondence with Scott (AJ to Scott, September 8; and above, December 3, 1817, Scott to AJ, October 4, 1817) which he circulated among friends and political allies. Scott, too, previously had shown the correspondence to friends. When Scott, who was in Richmond, became aware of Jackson's actions, he requested that Calhoun waive a February 1818 order prohibiting the publication of personal correspondence between army officers, but the secretary twice refused. This prompted Scott to prepare for private circulation a manuscript of the complete exchange, following Jackson's precedent and evading Calhoun's order. Almost immediately, and perhaps against Scott's wishes, newspapers began printing the correspondence, and it was issued in pamphlet form as *Correspondence between Major General Jackson, and Brevet Major General Scott.* On the matter, see also William O. Winston to AJ, May 12.

To Andrew Jackson Donelson

City of Washington
Janry 31st. 1819.

Dr. Andrew

I have no doubt ere this you have seen in the news papers announced my arival here, on the morning of the 23rd. instant, and I have no doubt but you have seen the discussion before Congress which brought me here—I fortunately arived here in time to explode one of the basest combinations ever formed, the object not to destroy me but the President of the u States, and to wound my reputation & feelings—The virtue of a majority will defeat these hellish Machinations, at the head of which is Mr Wm. H. Crawford & Mr Speaker Clay, ⟨whose⟩ the latters speech is in print, and noted by me for the purpose of commenting on it as soon as the debate is ended—and if necessary I shall await the 4th. of March next when Mr Clay has no congressional privileges to plead—My good friend Genl. Scott who has informed me that "he will not accept my challenge, perhaps on account of religious scruples &c &c"—is also believed to be in the combination[1]—I shall endeavour to see you at west Point before I return—I am truly happy to hear that harmony is restored at the accademy—I am much pressed with company, present me to Edward affectionately to Cadet [Nicholas P.] Eastling, & Mr [Richard C.] Cross—I will be happy to hear from you & those young Gentlemen on the receipt of this.[2] I shall write you again as soon as the debate before the house is ended in the mean time accept of an expression of my warmest friendship & Esteem. from your affectionate uncle

Andrew Jackson

P. S your aunt & little Andrew desired that I should present them to you affectionately. A. J.

ALS, DLC (7-0220). Published in Bassett, 2:408–409 (extract).

1. For Jackson's long-held notion of Scott's involvement with William H. Crawford, see above, AJ to Richard Butler, December 6, 1817; for Scott's declination of a duel, see Scott to AJ, January 2, 1818.

2. Jackson was alluding to the five cadets' dispute with John Bliss and Sylvanus Thayer (see above, Donelson to AJ, November 29, 1818). Secretary of War Calhoun had suggested the eventual reinstatement of the dismissed cadets, but compromise attempts failed, and courts-martial were ordered on March 9. Neither Eastland nor Cross (c1800–23), both from Tennessee, graduated from West Point. In 1821 Cross purchased Jackson's Evans Spring plantation in Lauderdale County, Alabama.

To Rachel Jackson

City of Washington
Janry [February] 6th. 1819.

My Love

I recd. your kind & affectionate letter of the 20th. ult.[1] & I sincerely regret to learn that you are indisposed—my health thank my god continues, probably the excitement of mind since I have been here, has kept me up—The Seminole war is still before the house, when a question may be taken I know not as I never have been in congress Hall since I have been here, nor do I mix with the members, determined that my enemies shall not have it to say that I attempted to influence their vote—the voic of the people begins to *[move, & have]* its eff*[ect]* here—I am told that there will be a great majority in my favour—and the insiduous Mr Clay will sink into that insignificance, that all those who abandon principle & Justice & would sacrafice their country for self agrandizement ought & will experience—[2]

I have bought a Negro girl recommended to me by Mrs. Peal of Philadelphia as honest & a good servant I send her to day to you by the mail stage—she carries a small quantity of wheat presented to me by a gentleman of this country that I wish carefully sown the instant it arrives—I send by the girl whose name is Sally a few carricatures, for the children—& to shew you the spirit of the times—& how Mr Richey conduct is appreciated[3]—let Stokely Hays have one of them—I shall return as soon as I can, in the mean time I have only to say to you take care of your health, & recollect that all earthly things are but baubles, compared to health—accept a reiteration of my sincere affection & believe me to be yr affectionate Husband

Andrew Jackson

ALS, MH-H (7-0243).

1. Not found.

2. The House debate on the Seminole War ended on February 8. In separate votes the chamber soundly defeated resolutions condemning the executions of Arbuthnot and Ambrister and one that called the Florida invasion unconstitutional.

3. The slave mentioned by Jackson may have been Big Sally (b. c1804) who had nine children in 1846. Mrs. Peal was possibly Hannah Moore (1755–1821), wife of Charles Willson Peale.

Rachel Jackson to Ralph Eleazar Whitesides Earl

Febary 23rd. 1819

Dear Sur I Send Sargent Day Down to Day See If Ther is aney Letters or papers from the Eastward I Cant help feeling so much anxiety but hope has supported So often and Still Does—

Let me as a real & Cincere Friend perswad you to try and reconcile this Solemn Dispensation for be asurd My Friend you have not to weep as those that have no hope—Angels wafted Her on their Celestial wings to that blooming garden of roses that have no thorns where Honey has no Sting,[1] Look forward to that happy period when we Shall meet all our Dear Friends in Heaven wher the parteing sigh will be no more be herd, all Tears will bee wiped from our Eyes. But Let us first Secur an interest in a Crucifyed redeemer. o My Friend Mr Earle thes is Sacred facts religion prepares for Life or Death I know you ar not fare from it for I Can Say with Truth that a more Correct young man I never knew therefore put your trust In the Lord he never will Desert nor forsak those that Chose him, think not this a gloomey subjec, oh. no—Its a ligt to my bath a Lamp to my feet—Come and See me as soon as Convenient. May the God fo all Comfort Speak Peac to your Heart and say my grace is sufficent for the Amen

R Jackson

ALS, DLC (26).

1. Sergeant Day, for whom Jackson paid tuition to William McKnight on May 11, 1818, has not been further identified. Jane Caffery Earl and her infant had died during childbirth on February 11.

A continuing interest among Americans about the newly acquired West, created by the 1804–1806 Lewis and Clark explorations, together with desires to protect American fur trade and limit British influence with northern Indians, prompted then secretary of war James Monroe in February 1815 to recommend the establishment of a line of army posts in the upper Mississippi River area. Jackson, too, feared British influence among the Indians, and the Convention of 1818, defining the border between the United States and British North America along the 49th parallel, apparently did not assuage his concerns (see above, AJ to George Graham, April 22, 1817, and AJ to Henry Atkinson, May 15, below). Only after John C. Calhoun assumed the war office did the government take action to secure the frontier. Modifying an earlier, more ambitious scheme, Calhoun planned three separate though related expeditions up the Missouri, up the Mississippi, and westward across land to Pike's Peak. At the same time Calhoun shifted the intended fortification on the Yellowstone southward to the Mandan Village, on the Missouri, north of present Bismarck, North Dakota (see Calhoun to AJ, March 17 and August 22, 1818). Although the upland site had been abandoned, contemporaries confused and conflated the three distinct expeditions with the name "Yellowstone." To supply the expeditions the government, under some political pressure, let contracts to former lieutenant colonel James Johnson (1774–1826), brother of Kentucky congressman Richard M. Johnson, a decision that proved ill-fated (see Richard M. Johnson to AJ, April 26, and AJ et al. to [James Monroe], July 5, both below). Calhoun had sought Jackson's recommendation for a commander (see Calhoun to AJ, December 28, 1818), and while Jackson was in Washington, the two agreed on Henry Atkinson to lead the Missouri expedition and to command the 9th Military Department. Atkinson (1782–1842), a North Carolina native, had joined the army in 1808, and was retained in 1815 as colonel of the 6th Infantry Regiment, due in some measure to the influence of his friend Winfield Scott. As major general of the Southern Division, Jackson oversaw Atkinson's progress.

From John Caldwell Calhoun

Department of War,
6th. March, 1819.

Sir,

You are already informed of the motives of the President, and of the arrangements which have been made to occupy in force the contemplated posts on the Missouri. It is believed, that our principal post ought to be at the Mandan Village, or in its' neighbourhood, and, for the present, no attempt ought to be made, until it is strongly occupied, to ascend the river to a more remote point. The Missouri there approaches nearest to the establishment of the Hudson Bay Company on Red River, and holds, in its descent to the Mississipi from that point, a more southerly direction, both of which will render the position permanently important.[1] You will, accordingly, give orders to render it, with the means which may be in possession of the detachment, as strong as practicable. Whether an attempt ought to be made to push our troops during the next summer, to this remote position, will depend on circumstances to be judged of by the officer charged with the command of the Department. Should it be deemed practicable, without exciting Indian hostilities, to occupy the position at so early a period as to afford time to render it sufficiently strong and to construct the necessary buildings to protect the troops against the inclemency of the winter in that high latitude, it ought to be attempted; but, should a contrary impression exist, some strong position less remote ought to be occupied. The Council Bluffs, or the Great Bend will probably afford such positions, and, as one or both of these will probably have to be permanently occupied in considerable force, the labour which may be bestowed to render the troops secure will not be lost. It is hoped and beleived, that, with proper caution, the contemplated movements may be made, without exciting Indian hostilities; yet, it will be necessary to be so prepared, at all times, should they be excited, as to experience no disaster. To effect these important objects, much will doubtless depend on the character of the officer charged with their execution. The selection of Coll. Atkinson has been made with much reflection. It is beleived, that he possesses all of the requisite qualities. You will, however, inculcate on him the necessity of the greatest caution and vigilance. No pains ought to be spared to conciliate the various Indian Tribes by kind treatment, and a proper distribution of presents. Govr. Clark will be directed to furnish the means of making the presents. Mr. [Benjamin] O. Fallon, the Agent for the Missouri, will accompany, or precede the expedition. He is represented as eminently qualified for this office. Major Long with his command, accompanied by several citizens eminent for scientific acquirements, will ascend the river, about the same time, in a Steam-boat of light draught, in order to acquire a more enlarged and accurate knowledge of the country between the Rocky Mountain and the Mississipi. You will give orders to afford to the expedition under him every aid and protection which may be practicable. Strict orders will also be given to treat with kindness and justice such citizens as may be permitted by the Government to carry on trade among the Indians.[2] Should the necessary protection be afforded to our traders, it will, in addition to the profits of the Fur Trade, afford the means of greatly extending our influence over the various tribes within our limits. I am with Sentiments of respect & esteem Yours &c

J. C. Calhoun

LS, DLC (26); LCs, DLC (7-0401), DNA-RG 107 (M6-10); Copy, NjMoHP (7-0405). Published in *Calhoun Papers,* 3:633–34.

1. The Hudson Bay Company maintained trading posts all along the Red River of the North, the most important of which was located near Pembina in present North Dakota.

2. The Great Bend, or Grand Detour, is south of present-day Pierre, South Dakota; the Council Bluffs, on the west bank of the Missouri River, near present Fort Calhoun, Nebraska, became the army's farthest outpost on the frontier. Jackson left orders in Washington for Atkinson and presumably for Long as well (see Robert Butler to Atkinson, March 7, and Atkinson to AJ, April 17; the orders for Long have not been found). O'Fallon (c1792–1843), Missouri Governor William Clark's nephew, had been employed previously as Indian agent along the Missouri River.

Jackson's triumph over his political adversaries in the House of Representatives was short-lived, for as the debate on the Florida business ended there, the Senate commenced its own investigation through a committee chaired by Pennsylvania's Abner Lacock, a Crawford ally, and including Georgia's John Forsyth, Rhode Island's James Burrill, Jr. (1772–1820; Brown 1788), New York's Rufus King (1755–1827; Harvard 1777) and John H. Eaton. Forsyth soon resigned from the Senate to accept appointment as minister to Spain, and his committee post went to Virginia's John Wayles Eppes (1773–1823; Hampden-Sydney 1786), another Crawford ally. On February 24 the committee majority (Eaton and King dissenting) issued a report that, according to the Washington National Intelligencer, *was in "decided reprehension" of Jackson and the invasion of Florida. Among other charges the report (rumored to have been written by either William H. Crawford or Henry Clay) condemned the Florida invasion as unconstitutional and the executions of Arbuthnot and Ambrister as unwarranted, and implied that Jackson was involved in Pensacola land speculation, which had induced him to invade that city (see John Jackson to AJ, April 5, AJ to John Coffee, April 3, to Joseph McMinn, September 13, and to William Williams, September 25, and Affidavit of Thomas Childress, January 12, 1820, all below). Jackson, returning to the capital from New York where he had gone on a tour, did not learn of the Lacock committee report until he arrived in Baltimore. After attending a public dinner he rode through the night and reached Washington early on March 2, the day the Lacock report appeared in print in the* National Intelligencer.

On March 9, the Jacksonian response (dated March 5) appeared also in the National Intelligencer, *as an unsigned article entitled "Strictures on Mr. Lacock's Report on the Seminole War." Written by two of Jackson's aides, probably James C. Bronaugh and Richard K. Call (who, together with Robert Butler and Richard I. Easter, had formed the general's party in the East), the "Strictures" denied all the committee's accusations and produced documents as proof. Jackson, convinced that Crawford had written the report, was most likely involved in preparation of the "Strictures," and certainly had access to the manuscript version, since his enclosure be-*

low to Thomas McCorry (1776–1835), a Knoxville alderman, preceded publication by a day. As the debate lingered, Jackson put aside plans for retirement and began assembling evidence for a more formal response (see AJ to William B. Lewis, March 26, and to John Clark, April 20, both below). The preparation of that rebuttal to the Lacock committee report, formally presented to the Senate on February 23, 1820, occupied much of Jackson's time for the remainder of the year.

To Thomas McCorry

City of Washington
March 8th. 1819

Dr. Sir

Herewith enclosed you will receive a copy of Genl Smyth speech & the reply to the report of the committe in the senate, which Report you will have seen published in the Intelligencer without the documents—it is stated by Genl [Montfort] Stokes & others that Colo. [John] Williams has been inveterate against me, doing all the injury he could under the rose[1]—I shall see him as I return as I expect to Tarry with you in Knoxville one day agreable to my promise, and spend that with my friends—I am happy to find that the public indignation high, with the wicked, unjust, & ungenerous attempt to persecute, me unheard in my defence—Mutilating, & witholding the evidence they themselves have taken, where it was calculated to do me Justice How Colo. Williams will Justify his conduct on this occasion to the state I cannot say when he himself, without authority raised & appointed his officers & marched a mounted volunteer corps into Georgia & into the Seminole Country.[2] Present me respectfully to Capt. Crowel[3] & believe me to be your friend sincerely

Andrew Jackson

P.S. I shall leave here tomorrow & write you on the way—A. J.

ALS, Anonymous (7-0416).

1. Alexander Smyth had defended Jackson's Florida actions on January 21. Stokes (1762–1842), a senator from North Carolina, had been a major general of that state's militia during the War of 1812. Williams (1778–1837) was U.S. senator from Tennessee, 1815–23; for his invasion of Florida in 1812–13, see Pleasant M. Miller to AJ, and Samuel Bunch to AJ, both September 23.

2. The Lacock committee report had also charged Jackson with the unauthorized use of state militia and the appointment of officers therein. See Robert Butler to Daniel Parker, January 28, and Robert H. Dyer to AJ, May 21. The reference to mutilated testimony is to the deposition of Robert Butler (cMarch 1), included without his corrections in the committee report, but printed as corrected in the "Strictures."

3. Not identified.

Rachel Jackson to William Davenport

Hermitage, March the 18th 1819

Dr Sur

I received your agreeable letter Febury 20 New York,[1] I am happy to find you have not forgoten your Tennessee Friends and I Can asure you that you ar in Their friendly recollections. I must repeate the thanks I ow you for writeing to me at the time you Did It was releiving my mind from Doubts and fears for the wellfare of my Dear Husband, I am indeed gratifyed at the attentions the Citizens of Philadelphia and New york have manifested towards the Genl in as much as the insidious base Enemies that Envy yes Even to Green Eyed jealosey what a Combination of villiney indeed I Did think hard, that after all All the Fatigues and hard ships of so many campaines after all araigned and Calld in question by a set of Reptiles—well Let us forgive them, how shall I relate the scenes of Sorrow I have Experienced since you Left us the Hand of Death has snatched of three members of my famaly o yes the blooming youth must yeld you knew them all My Brother Mrs Hamlin o my friend one that you so lately saw in the all Admireing Eyes of a fond Husband is gon into the gloomey Shades of Death yes our Jane is gon[2]—Dear Mr Earle how Cincerely I Sympathize with him Saint Paul says I would not have you sorrow as Those that have no hope our Friend must Mr Earle take hold of the promises the Lord says he will be with us in six troubles in seven he will not forsake us I hope those Dispensations will bee sanctifyed to us She seemed as if she slept in Jeasus and all those God will bring with him At His Comeing, in first Thesslonians iv Chapter 13 14 verses is the Text preached from at her funeral[3] Mrs Hamlins is not yet Celibrated She was in her 19th year—all those scenes of woe I have Experienced in the absence of him whome I should have Expected a word of Comfort, I am afraide I have tresspassed on the feelings of my Friend—The Miss Lewises ar as you left them and the Miss Hayses I made your compliments to Miss Hays I have not seen the rest. your Friends in Nashville are all well ecept Mrs [Elizabeth] Kingly. Their are none of your acquainteces Married eccep Capt [Benjamin Brauch] Jones and Miss [Elizabeth] Simes and Miss [Jane Martin] Childress to Mr [Samuel B.] Marshall[4] I have no more at present worth Communicating and beleive me your sincerre Friend

Racheal Jackson

P. S. give my compliment to all your Friends

ALS, PHi (7-0425). Davenport (d. 1858), a career army officer from Pennsylvania, had been in Nashville the previous March. On the trip north from Washington, Jackson apparently conferred with him.

1. Not found.

2. Severn Donelson, Mary Hamblen, and Jane Earl.

3. In addition to her reference to Thessalonians, Rachel's words of comfort derived from Job 5:19.

4. Probably Elizabeth Sims, who had married Phillip J. Scudder on January 21. Jones married Martha Haywood at Nashville in December 1818. Narcissa (b. c1795) and Elizabeth Hays (1805–41) were Rachel's nieces. Marshall, a volunteer aide to Jackson during the 1818 Florida invasion, wed Jane Martin Childress, daughter of John Childress, on December 31, 1818. Elizabeth Kingsley, a fellow Presbyterian, was the wife of Alpha Kingsley (c1779–1846), former army paymaster and justice of the peace for Davidson County. The "Miss Lewises" were likely daughters of Joel Lewis (1760–1816), a brother of William Terrell Lewis (1757–1813).

To William Berkeley Lewis

Knoxville March 26th. 1819.

Dr. Sir

I hope to reach home on the 1rst of april I have been recd here with the greatests mark of attention—& one of the most flattering adresses I have recd. any where, every citizen but the honourable senator was present greeting my return, & happy triumph over my enemies—he to whom has been traced all the hidden slander, of speculation &c &c was locked up in his house—I hope to reach home on the day named & I want to see you as early thereafter as it will be in your power to ride up. it is important to me that I see you—I am collecting materials for a respond to the report of the senate[1]—Major Eaton I expect will reach here to day & travel out with me—My staff except Doctor Brunaugh are all behind[2]—I am yrs respectfully

Andrew Jackson

ALS, NNPM (7-0422).

1. Both Enoch Powell and Hugh Lawson White delivered addresses to Jackson upon his arrival in Knoxville (see Powell to AJ, and White to AJ, both March 25, and AJ to John Coffee, April 3).

2. Jackson's staff—Robert Butler, Richard K. Call, and Richard I. Easter—all returned to Nashville in early April.

From Thomas Hill Williams

Washington
March 29. 1819

Dr Sir,

Early in the morning after the close of the Session, I went to Fredericksburgh, and being detained there by bad weather did not return to this place until you had left it. I was anxious to see you before your departure, because among other things I wished to have some conversation with you in relation to another attempt at negociation with the Choctaws.

The following plan has been agreed on, which I hope you will execute:

You are to be added to the former commission, in the place of Genl. Carroll who declined acting.

Col. McKee will be instructed to open a correspondence with you in relation to the prospects of resuming the negotiations with effect; leaving it with you to decide whether those prospects will warrant another attempt. By this mode we expect to avail ourselves of any favourable turn which has, or may take place in the minds of the Choctaws, and at the same time avoid the expense and vexation of an abortive attempt.[1]

Your toils have been great for several years past, and entitle you to repose: but I hope this business may be so conducted as to interfere but little with your plans in relation to private concerns. The people of Mississippi believe that you alone can succeed with the Choctaws, and will not be easy until an effort under your authority is made.[2]

The President leaves here tomorrow on his southern tour—accompanied by the Secretary of War. Mr. Poindexter and myself set out today for home via Pittsburgh. With great regard Yr Mo. Ob. Servt.

Tho H. Williams

ALS, DLC (26). Williams (1780–1840) was U.S. senator from Mississippi.

1. Under pressure from Mississippi residents, John C. Calhoun had reluctantly agreed on February 19 to make another attempt to negotiate with the Choctaws.

2. Although he had refused a similar request from the Georgia legislature to negotiate with the Cherokee Indians, Jackson accepted the commission to treat with the Choctaws in Mississippi (see Calhoun to AJ, March 29; and AJ to John McKee, April 22, below).

To John Coffee

Hermitage
April 3rd. 1819.

Dr. Genl

I reached home last evening in good health except a cold taken on my return Journey which has given me a cough which is a little troublesome—I had the good fortune to meet here my friends Mr James Jackson & Colo. [James W.] Sitler by the former I have an opportunity to send you this.[1]

I wrote you from the city enclosing you Genl Smyth speech & the Strictures on the report of the Senate on the Seminole war, from the failure of the mails I fear you have not recd. the pacage.[2] I have requested Mr Jackson to inquire at the Post office in Murfreesborough for it and if there, hand it you—the report of the Senate is one of the most wicked productions ever penned, by the hands of a wicked unprincipled man—it is believed & so said that it is penned by Mr Wm H Crawford, on the information of that hypocritical lying puppy Colo. John Williams who has lately become the corrispondant of Genl Cocke[3]

The Colos. conduct is well understood at Knoxville & occasioned, that friendly & polite attention that was bestowed upon me there—I was met by a citizen & military Escort at Capt [John] Kains & conducted to Knoxville, where the whole Town & vicinity was collected to receive me, when was delivered to me by Judge [Hugh Lawson] White an adress calculated to put Colo. Williams & all his adherents down—it is the best penned thing I ever saw, & shews his independance, his friendship, & his Justice[4]—I was invited to a public dinner, at which the toasts were such as to shew there entire disapprobation of every act of their Senator Colo. Williams, indeed the Citizens of Knoxville to form a resolution that the will instruct their representatives at the next assembly to request Colo. Williams to resign, not having represented them in the last Congress. Judge [Charles] Taitte from Georgia the particular friend of Crawford & Williams, was at Knoxville & invited to the dinner, during the whole of the drinking of the toasts, he was like a man sitting on a hot gridiron—Judge Taitte is mustered out of the Senate in Georgia, is on his way to allabama to get into office there.[5] I hope the good citizens of allabama will select men of more honesty & less hypocrisy than he, to fill their offices.

The report of the senate has & will have the effect to bring forth the full expression of public sentiment & in Virginia the Seminole question will change many of its representatives—in short it will ultimately have a good effect upon the nation, & put down Clay & Wm. H. Crawford. There is no papers that attempt to advocate the report but the Federal gazzett of Baltimore, the enquirer, & I am told by Mr Jackson the Reporter, the latter I expected, as it was under the influence of the hopocritical Clay.[6]

I shall be out as soon as I can, will you have the goodness to see William [White] Crawford, & say to him to write me, how he is getting on & be good enough to write me by Mr. J. how my business is progressing—If my lotts at Marathon could be sold, I should like it—My Journey altho a very pleasant one has been a very expensive one—and of course has infringed upon funds which I intended to have applied to the payment for my lands, & building—present me affectionately to Polly & believe me to be sincerely your friend.

Andrew Jackson

P. S. I wish you to guard the citizens against the appointment of Judge Taitte to any office he is sent by Mr Crawford, with a view to promote his views—& I trust the good sense of the people will frustrate his designs—A. J.

ALS, THi (7-0453).

1. Sittler (d. 1826) was a Nashville merchant and adjutant general of the West Tennessee militia during the Creek War.

2. Letter not found.

3. The correspondence between John Williams and John Cocke, both War of 1812 veterans, has not been found. Jackson's notion that William H. Crawford had written the Senate report was based upon James C. Bronaugh's observation of Abner Lacock's visit to Crawford's home immediately following the publication of the "Strictures" (see John H. Eaton to AJ, April 16, 1820).

4. Kain (c1759–1831), a prominent resident of Knox County, lived at "Trafalger," at Kains Bend on the Holston River. White (1773–1840), former state supreme court judge and president of the Bank of the State of Tennessee, was Williams's brother-in-law.

5. Tait (1768–1835), a former Georgia circuit court judge, had just completed ten years' service as U.S. senator; in 1820 Monroe appointed him federal district judge for Alabama.

6. Jackson was referring to the Baltimore *Federal Gazette,* the *Richmond Enquirer,* and the Lexington *Kentucky Reporter.*

From Isaac Lewis Baker

St. Mary's Attakapas La—
7th. Apl. 1819.

My Dear Genl.

Allow me to congratulate you on the discomfiture of your Enemies in congress and the testimonies of gratitude and approbation with which you were every where received in your late journey to the East. I rejoice in all this not only because it is highly honourable to you and the nation, & grateful to your feelings—but because it overturns the calculations and demolishes the hopes of certain cold blooded calculating scoundrels who were willing to sacrifice you and dishonour our country to answer their own factious purposes. In rear of all this comes the Spanish Treaty, evidently extorted by your opperations in Florida and adds much to the vast districts which you have already acquired.[1] Amidst all this cause of congratulation however I feel mortified at the conduct of our poor contemptible Senate. Their sins are however on record, as well as those of Robertson—[Étienne] Mazereau & [Fulwar] Skipwith & shall not be forgotten. Your friend Duncan has a desire to be our next governor and if we can completely get Robertson down will succeed—Should you make us a visit—this year (as it is said you will) your presence would be important to him and totally ruin Robertson who is hand & glove with the Algernon Sidney club—[2]

I have some prospect of visiting Tennessee & Ky—in the Summer but have so often made calculations of this kind only to be disappointed that I feel fearful I may not be able to accomplish my wish. My business—& care of a large family give me so much occupation—that I must not indulge my propensity for travelling unless I can in doing so make it turn to profit—

This state must become a very important one in a few years as we are daily receiving large accessions of rich, respectable inhabitants from Maryland Virginia & the Carolinas—I long to see the day when we can claim & enjoy the complete ascendancy over the French—who tho: in general an excellent well disposed people are too much under the influence of certain corrupt chieftains—who would do more honour to a gibbet than to the best and most responsible posts in the government—

My neighbour Mr. [Donelson] Caffery is very well—likewise his little wife.[3] Matrimony has made such a favorable change in his household & comforts that I feel much inclined to follow his example but in spite of all efforts get on with my old success—

Should your leisure permit it would afford me great satisfaction to hear from you. Have the kindness to present me respectfully to Mrs. Jackson & believe me your friend—& Obt. hl. St.

Isaac L. Baker

ALS, DLC (26). Endorsed as "private" and "answered 20th. July 19."

1. After long delays, Spain had finally signed the Adams-Onís Treaty on February 22.

2. Robertson was elected governor in 1820, serving until 1824, when he resigned to become federal district judge. "Algernon Sidney" was the pseudonym of Benjamin Watkins Leigh, a Virginia Republican and Thomas Ritchie's ally. Beginning on December 22, 1818, "Algernon Sidney" submitted five extremely anti-Jackson letters to the *Richmond Enquirer*, denouncing Jackson's suspension of the writ of habeas corpus in New Orleans in 1815, the 1818 invasion of Florida and the executions of Arbuthnot and Ambrister, as well as John Q. Adams's support for Jackson. Thus, Baker was probably referring to the similar views held by Robertson and "Algernon Sidney." Mazureau (1772–1849), a Napoleonic exile, had served as Louisiana's attorney general, arguing against Jackson during Jackson's 1815 trial for contempt of court. Skipwith (1765–1839), a native of Virginia and father-in-law of Robertson, had led the 1810 revolt in Spanish West Florida and served briefly as governor of the "West Florida Republic." Jackson did not visit Louisiana until 1821.

3. Caffery (1786–1835), Jackson's nephew, had married Lydia Murphy (1802–81) the previous year, and resided in St. Mary's parish, Louisiana (see Caffery to AJ, November 26, 1818).

To Willie Blount

Nashville April 8th. 1819

Dr. Sir

I have no doubt but you have seen the late Pamphlet written by Genl Cocke, and addressed to Major Eaton, in which he introduces you & me in not very respectfull terms—The slander of such a man is certainly a Eulogy on the virtues & merit of those he attacks—however as his intention is to advance himself, and thereby obtain a seat in congress in the room of Mr Wm [Grainger] Blount—& to injure the Election of Major Eaton an answer is proper to place this hypocritical pander before the publick in his true colours[1]—The object of this letter is to request your statement of his engagement to me to attend to the procuring for my branch of the army in East Tennessee Bread stuffs & sending them down Tennessee to Dittos landing or whereever else directed—and that on the subject of the 1500 men you were authorised by the Sec of War to bring into the field, he insisted on the right of the East end of the state having the whole of that requisition, when I on the other side claimed the right of one half this requisition from the west end as they were sure of receiving their pay at the end of the campaign or time of service—the Genl complains ⟨that it⟩ of this having been imposed upon him &c &c—I mean as Major Eaton does to unrobe him[2]—you cannot have forgotten how solicitous I was about breadstuffs, stating we had neither mills or wheat—and that we must depend on East Tennessee for bread stuff—that Genl Cock replied that he would attend to the obtaining & sending me breadstuff, which on Holston could be so Easily obtained—and see that they should be shipped down the river these necessary supplies—I hold his letter in answer to mine on the subject of supplies in which he says—one hundred & fifty barrells of flower is on float for me & 1000 barrells &c will soon follow, but he denies in his pamphlet that he had made any erangement with me on this subject—you must recollect this as well as his promise to heartily cooperate with me[3]—I am respectfully yr mo ob servt

Andrew Jackson

ALS, T (7-0467).

1. John Cocke's sixteen-page pamphlet was in the form of an open *Letter to the Honorable John H. Eaton. December 16, 1818* (Knoxville, 1819). Cocke disputed Reid and Eaton's *Life of Jackson* (1817), especially the treatment of provisioning the West Tennessee militia and terms of service of the state's militia, and called the work a "compound of abuse" (p. 15). Cocke asserted that Jackson's "tyrannical treatment" of his troops was the true cause of their dissatisfaction, and impugned Willie Blount's (1768–1835) honesty when the former governor suggested that the East Tennessee militia had been liable for more than three months' service.

2. John H. Eaton was preparing his pamphlet *To the Public* ([Nashville, 1819]), which responded to Cocke's criticism of Eaton's biography of Jackson and recalled Cocke's 1814 court-martial for incitement to desertion. In turn, Cocke answered with his open letter *To the Hon. John H. Eaton. June 26, 1819* (Knoxville, 1819). Jackson did not respond at this time directly to Cocke, but made his letterbooks available to Eaton (see Robert Butler to AJ, April 25, below).

3. For Cocke's promise, see Cocke to AJ, October 2, 1813. For Blount's response, see Blount to AJ, April 18, below.

From John McCrea

Philada. April 15. 1819

Dear Sir.

On my arrival from New York a few days since, our mutual friend John Jackson informed me that he had received a Letter from you offering to him and myself Four shares of Florence stock[1]—I had however, just before the receipt of your Letter received a communication from Pope & Hickman of Huntsville, agreeing to furnish me with 8 shares of that stock, in payment of a note of theirs recd by me from them while in Huntsville, this stock together with the eleven shares I had purchased of Dr. [Samuel] Brown while you were here exhausted all the means I could at present conveniently command. Had you but intimated while here a desire to part with any portion of your florence Stock It would have afforded me real pleasure to have had an opportunity of promoting your views, & which at that time would have been amply within my reach.[2]

I still continue to entertain the most favorable opinion of Florence, and the growing importance of the Country in its immediate vicinity. And tho' the prospects of the Cotton Planter are evidently at this moment somewhat clouded, from the extreme dullness of Cotton, generally in the European markets, arising from the extraordinary fiscal embarrassments of the trading part of the community in both France & England; I am, notwithstanding well satisfied, that Such an impetus has already been given to the settlement of the Lands in alabama on the Tennessee River, that nothing can permanently retard the growth of that section of our Country—It is true, cotton may not bear the price it has maintained for some years past, But let the price be what it may, it appears to me, as far as my observation has extended, that no where in the Carolinas or Georgia, can Labour be so profitably employed in the Culture of Cotton, as in Alabama—nor the health of your Stock so well preserved—and if this opinion is fully supported by experience—there is at any rate no danger to be apprehended that those who have emigrated from these states to the alabama, ⟨being⟩ are likely to retrace their steps-–But on the Contrary, a gradual accession of population, particularly if the Climate should prove healthy as the face of the Country becomes cleared—a consequence there is every natural reason to anticipate.

It would give me much satisfaction to have your opinion of the present prospects of Florence and of the Lands generally in Lauderdale County—whether you consider high or Low priced Lands in that County, are most likely to yield the possessor the best Interest. The great dullness which pervades our large commercial Cities at present, has given rise to an extensive disposition among the Citizens to remove their families where the difficulties of supporting them may be lessened & I have not a doubt but both Tennessee and Allabama will ere long number among her Citizens a large proportion of the present population of the altlantic sea Board—

Before this reaches you, you will no doubt have seen De Witt Clinton's denunciation of General Scott—had any thing more been wanting to have sealed the general's fading reputation, than the internal evidence contained in the very corrispondence he appears to have been so unaccountably solicitous to pass the eye of Public Scrutiny; Governor Clintons brief but pungent appeal makes sure his Bankrupt Fame. He mistook his man in assailing DeWitt. But this is not the first error of that kind he has committed.[3]

Be pleased to present my respects to your Lady; and my best wishes to the several members of your military family—Respectfully Your Obd. Servt

Jno. Mc.Crea

P. S You may recollect, I expressed to you while here, a desire to dispose of my 1/8 of the Pensacola speculation, provided a liberal price could be obtained on it. If you should hear of any person in Nashville desirous of purchasing a Share in that speculation, in a Credit of 2 years, have the goodness to inform me[4]

J. Mc.C

ALS, DLC (26). McCrea (d. c1867), a relative of John Jackson, was a Philadelphia merchant.

1. Letter not found. John Jackson (1773–1832), a brother of fellow merchants James and Washington Jackson, had remained in Philadelphia after immigrating from Ireland; he subsequently settled in Florence, Alabama.

2. Brown (1769–1830), brother of Kentucky Senator John and Louisiana Senator James Brown, was a member of the medical faculty at Transylvania University. Jackson's eight shares in the Cypress Land Company had been purchased for him by his agent James Jackson on April 7, 1818.

3. Winfield Scott's pamphlet, *Correspondence between Major General Jackson, and Brevet Major General Scott,* asserted that Clinton had instigated the anonymous letter detailing Scott's criticism of Jackson's Division Order of April 22, 1817 (see above, Unknown to AJ, August 14, 1817). Clinton publicly denied the charge on April 6 and termed Scott's conduct in the matter such "a total departure from honor and propriety, as to render him unworthy of the notice of a man who has any respect for himself" (*Richmond Enquirer,* April 13).

4. John Jackson, along with McCrea, James Jackson, Sr. and Jr., John Donelson, Jr. (1787–1840), John C. McLemore, Thomas Childress, and John H. Eaton had formed a Pensacola land speculation concern in the fall of 1817. In a February conversation with Secretary of State Adams, Jackson had specifically denied the rumor that he had taken Pensacola to secure his own financial interests in the venture. See the Deposition of John H. Eaton, [cFebruary 24] (*ASP, Military Affairs,* 1:751); John Jackson to AJ, April 5; and AJ to William Williams, September 25, below.

From Willie Blount

Bakerdon Apl. 18th. 1819

Dear Sir,

I have read Mr. [Charles Fenton] Mercer's speech on the Siminoles war[1]—He was pregnant with it a long time as it would seem from what he said before he was delivered of it—He was much pestered in his mind about your violation of the Constitution, as he supposed, so much so that he could not get a good night's sleep—poor man if he will read Alexr. Smyth's speech on that subject I think he may sleep soundly—did you hear whether or not he could take good sleep after he delivered his speech? it is a pitty the man could not get sleep what poor minded Bitches are Messrs Cobb & Clay—It appears that you have most clearly outpolled the Committees of the House and of the Senate—you have the People and the Government on your side & the Committees have Mr. Mercer and Mr. Lacock of writing memory on their side—The Floridas are at last ours and I should be glad to learn that the future Government of them was committed to your care until you could by your wholesome regulations purge out the evil weeds that have taken root & grown up there—I wish this most earnestly, and likewise for an extinguishment of the Chickasaw & Choctaw claim to a strip of Country on the East side of the Mississippi, wide enough for a string of Counties, at least, along that river, so that the upper and lower Country may be connected by a white population—I wish you would urge this Last point—now is the time, for that subject ought not to sleep[2]—I have not seen Genl. Cocke's Book nor did I know of its publication until the receipt of your letter[3]—I had heard that he was writing a Pamphlet—I believe that it was Job who exclaimed "Oh that mine enemy would write a Book"[4]—Tell Col. Robt. Hays I look towards him as usual—your friend

Willie Blount

ALS, DLC (26). Endorsed by Jackson: "Govr. W. Blounts Letter & certificate—to be filed A.J." Blount's certificate, also dated April 18, detailed John Cocke's arrangements for supplies to Jackson's forces prior to the Creek campaign of 1814. Bakerdon, Blount's home, was located in Montgomery County, near Clarksville, Tennessee.

1. Mercer (1778–1858; Princeton 1797), a Virginia lawyer and congressman, 1817–39, had attacked Jackson's invasion of Florida in the House on January 25–26.

2. Indian claims to land on the eastern bank of the Mississippi River were relinquished with the Choctaw cessions of 1820 and 1830 and the Chickasaw cession of 1832.

3. See above, AJ to Blount, April 8.

4. A reference to Job 31:35: "My desire is, that the Almighty would answer me, and that mine adversary had written a book."

Acting upon his conviction that William H. Crawford had authored the Lacock report, Jackson solicited information for a response to it and for an attack against the treasury secretary. In John Clark (1766–1832) Jackson found a ready collaborator, for Clark, having fought an inconclusive duel with Crawford in 1806, led the anti-Crawford faction in Georgia (see AJ to Clark, April 20, below). Indeed, Clark was already gathering evidence against David B. Mitchell, former governor and now Creek Indian agent and a Crawford ally, who had been implicated in an 1817–18 Amelia Island slave smuggling adventure (see above, AJ to John C. Calhoun, February 14, 1818). Clark's investigation suited Jackson well because Mitchell had joined the chorus of criticism over the invasion of Florida, and the comity of interest shared by Jackson and Clark soon sparked an exchange of information about Mitchell and the rumored split in the Monroe administration over the Florida invasion (see Clark to AJ, May 24, August 18, November 2 and 29; and AJ to Clark, July 13; and [September] 18, and January 6, 1820, below). The exchange also added a new dimension to Jackson's longstanding legal dispute with Andrew Erwin (1773–1834) of Bedford County, for Erwin, just arrived in Tennessee from Georgia and another Crawfordite, was also implicated in the slave smuggling enterprise. While Jackson compiled information about Crawford, Mitchell, and Erwin throughout the spring and summer, Tennessee politics heated up. Erwin and Jackson ally John H. Eaton, seeking election to a full U.S. Senate term, sparred in the public prints and very nearly fought a duel, adding fuel to the fire and confirming the enmity between Jackson and Erwin, a personal, legal, and political estrangement that would influence Tennessee politics for the remainder of Jackson's life (see AJ to William B. Lewis, August 17, to Richard K. Call, September 9, and to James Monroe, September 29, all below).

To John Clark

Nashville 20th Apl. 1819

Sir.

You will pardon the liberty I have taken in addressing you on so slight acquaintance, and permit me to hope that you will favour me with such facts as you may be in possession of, relative to the public or private Character of Wm. H. Crawford Esq now Secty. of the Treasury, Mr. Crawford having been long resident in your state, and having Commenced his political Career in it, induces the belief, That as his Theatre of Action must have been under your observation, you wo*[u]*ld be, consequently, better capable of affording me the information I desire, than any other gentleman I could apply to in Georgia. This Gentleman whilst he was charged with the superintendance of the department of war, having manifested as little respect for the feelings of officers, as he felt interest; or solicitude, for the respectability or prosperity of the Army, persued a course as unfriendly to the establishment as it was unbecoming & unworthy the man holding the power to controll the chanel of its existence, Such conduct naturally placed us at issue, in the process of which, he has swerved from that strictly honorable course which it is usual for one gentleman to observe towards another. I therefore feel myself at liberty to make such enquiries concerning him as may properly illucidate his Character. I shall Therefore Consider myself under many obligations to you, for such a statement as you feel at liberty to make. I have the honor to be Very respectfully your Obt. Servt.

Andrew Jackson

LS, TxU (7-0486); Draft with revisions by AJ, DLC (26). Published in Bassett, 2:146 (from draft). LS endorsed by Clark: "Taken out of the post office at Milledgeville 15th. May 1819 late in the evening by J—Clark."

To John McKee

Hermitage near Nashville
22d April 1819—

Sir

I have received a Commission from the President to hold in conjunction with yourself and Col Bernett a Treaty with the Chocktaws. It appears from the communication I have received that you are instructed to obtain the sence of the Nation whether or not they are disposed to treat and that the Treaty is not to be Ordered unless there is a probability of success.[1]

Permit me to suggest the propriety of making the following statement to the Chiefs of the Nation by way of preparing them for the Cession so important to themselves, to the People of the State of Mississippi and desireable to their friend and father the President of the United States. It is a fact and ought not to be withheld from them, as it will bring to their view their true Situation and open their Eyes to their own benefit and happiness. It is this that a Bill was reported at the last Session of Congress the object of which was to enforce the return of that part of the Nation, which has settled West of the River Mississippi, which Bill is suspended until the next meeting of Congress, for the purpose of obtaining the sens of the Nation whether a part or the whole of the Nation would agree to exchange the Land where they now live and cross and Settle with them what is ment by the whole is the great body of the Nation, who are not inclined to come under the immediate Laws of the United States, all that are ripe for Society, and wish it would be indulged with a reservation. should it appear that the Nation is opposed to the exchange of their present Situation, the next Congress will pass a law as I believe to bring back those now settled West of the Mississippi—this will place the Nation in an unpleasant Situation—for as soon as it is made known that the Chocktaw Nation has declined removing to this Country procured for them by the U States, the Whites will immediately Settle on it and the U States will be compelled to make Sail of it

What then will be the Situation of the Nation a vast portion of them will not labour, and they cannot support East of the River by hunting.

The Six Towns can not exist where they now are,[2] and the conciquence will be that necessity will compell them to separate, and some join one tribe and some an other, by which they will become extinct, and lost as a Nation.

Every friend to the wellfare of that Nation ought to advise them against a conduct which will lead to that event, now is the time and the only time the Government will have it in it power to make them happy by holding the Land West of the Mississippi for them and this can only be done be their consent to an exchange in whole or in part. Now the Government has it in its power to act liberally with them this is its wish

The instructions given me are ample, and if I act at all it will be with a view to the happiness of the Nation and the convenience of the State of Mississippi. every friend of the Nation must see the road to the perpetuation and happiness of the whole Nation in the place proposed, and the happiness of those who wish to remain by being secured in a reservation of Land where they now are, and protected by the Laws and becoming Citizens of the U. S.

If they exchange provisions will be made for their comfort until they are Settled in their new Country, and if a Treaty is held You may say to the Chiefs, that we are instructed not only to be liberal to the Nation but to them individually.

I would recommend should this meet Your approbation that You send it round to the Chiefs by Young Peachland eldest Son of the Interpreter to the Nation that he may explain it to the Chiefs and Warriors, for which Service if a Treaty is made he will be amply rewarded if the Nation does not treat You will have to Stipulate, as Agent that he will be paid for his trouble and expences. he has writen to me that he would be willing to undertake this Service[3] On the receipt of this pleas write me I am Respectfully Your Obt Servt

Andrew Jackson

LC in Richard K. Call's hand, DLC (63); Copies, DNA-RG 46 (7-0493), DNA-RG 75 (M271-2). Published in *ASP, Indian Affairs,* 2:229.

1. For the instructions, see John C. Calhoun to AJ, March 29. On the pending negotiations, see also above, Thomas H. Williams to AJ, March 29.
2. The Six Towns were located near present-day Garlandsville, in Jaspar County, Mississippi.
3. James Pitchlynn, interpreter, had written Jackson in [December] 1818 and again on March 18, 1819, reporting favorably on the prospects for Choctaw removal and offering his assistance, for proper compensation.

To Edmund Pendleton Gaines

Hermitage April 24th. 1819.

Dr Genl

Meeting with Capt Russell from Savanah Georgia I seize the opportunity to drop you a hasty line I wrote you by mail some few days ago, which I hope will reach you—[1]

I have no doubt you have seen the Report of the Committee of the Senate, attached to which is the affidavit of Genl Mitchell. This was a measure of the cunning Mr Wm H Crawford as intimated to me to attempt to throw a shade over your military charector & that of the executive, by endeavouring to throw the blame of the Seminole war on you—[2]

I intend putting in an answer to this report at the commencement of the next congress both full, free, & independant, in which I feel very much disposed fully to meet that attack on you as far as I can possess myself of the materials—the object of this letter is that you may forward to me any documents or affidavits, that you may think proper & be in possession of or can obtain, to that point. There is one fact, that is, that Genl Mitchell appointed his own son Brigade adjutant to McIntosh & commissioned him, himself[3]—I think Major Glassell ⟨to at my request⟩ took a copy of it at my request, for its novelty—by applying to Major Glassell, he can give you his recollection on this subject—present me respectfully Sir to Major Glassell, & say to him I had the pleasure of seeing his friends in Winchester who were all well—his uncle & aunt inquired very affectionately for him & express a desire for him to vissit them—

I shall expect to hear from you on the recpt of this—& Capt Russell has said to me he will have it carefully convayed to you. present Mrs. J. & myself respectfully to your Lady[4] & believe to be yr mo. ob. serv.

Andrew Jackson

ALS, DNA-RG 94 (7-0499).

1. Probably John M. Russell, who served during the War of 1812 and was discharged June 15, 1815. See AJ to Gaines, April 15.

2. In a deposition submitted to the Lacock committee on February 23, David B. Mitchell declared that Gaines's attack on Fowltown had precipitated the Seminole War. Moreover, Mitchell discounted the circumstances surrounding the attack, noting that "aggressions of this kind were as frequent on the part of whites, as on the part of the Indians" (*ASP, Military Affairs*, 1:748–50). In the fall Gaines wrote the secretary of war defending his conduct in the matter (see Gaines to John C. Calhoun, October 17).

3. William Stephen Mitchell.

4. In 1815 Gaines had married his second of three wives, Barbara Grainger Blount (c1792–1836), daughter of William and Mary Grainger Blount.

From Robert Butler

Nashville April 25th. 1819.

D. General,

I find from examination that there is no file of Papers from the Secretary of War in 1814 among your files in this office nor can I find any of your papers here relating to the Seminole War—Your letter Book which has the correspondence between you and General Scott is also not here; I therefore enclose you the letter of Mr. Shields—[1]

I would beg leave to recommend that your papers should be all collected together and properly arranged and to offer my services to aid in the execution of it: you will then be enabled to find at all times any papers you might desire—Those of the Creek War should be seperated from the official papers which has accrued since you joined service,[2] and those also separate which have grown out of your different Indian Treaties together with private correspondence—this will be no difficult task and I trust you will readily see the propriety of it—at present your papers are arranged some here, others at Nashville and many at your house—

I enclose you the account and receipt for the repairing of your carriage—[3]

Maj. Eaton sent for your letter Books on day before yesterday, and if you send for them I shall direct the boy to his office—[4]

I leave this letter open, expecting to hear from you—

The order and copy of the first proceedings of the court held in the 9th. M. Department is prepared agreeably to your instructions, and shall be fully acted on by tomorrows mail—[5]

Mr. James Jackson has not yet arrived, and I wish your advice whether to await his coming or run the risk of seeing him at Tennessee.

I find Mr. [William] Eastin is the second subscribing witness to the Colberts deed and I believe he is now in your neighborhood—if you see him please speak to him of the necessity for his accompanying me to Tennessee to prove that Deed—[6]

Capt Call has handed me your remarks on the subject of the *jumbled court martial*[7] they accord with my wishes and I will arrange the ballance to your satisfaction—

25th. April.

I enclose you a copy of Division Order and my letter to General Parker which will place you at rest (I fondly hope) on this disagreeable subject—

I have a wretched head ache this morning—else all well. Our love to Mrs. Jackson and believe me yours' &c.

Robert Butler

ALS, DLC (26).

1. The letterbook mentioned by Butler is not among Jackson's papers, although the correspondence with the war department during 1814 and that concerning the Seminoles in 1818 is present. Shields has not been identified.

2. Jackson had been commissioned major general in the U.S. Army on May 28, 1814.

3. Probably the account with Samuel Van Dyke Stout & Co., February 10.

4. John H. Eaton was preparing a response to John Cocke's pamphlet attack on *The Life of Jackson*. See above, AJ to Willie Blount, April 8.

5. The Division Order of April 24 regarded the court-martial of Stoughton Gantt and related to a jurisdictional question. Jackson (through Butler) maintained that because the order for the trial had originated with the war deparment, it, and not the Southern Division, should review the proceedings. On April 24 Butler directed the matter to the attention of Daniel Parker. For Parker's decision, see Parker to Butler, July 19, and Division Order, August 22.

6. The Colberts' deed has not been identified, but it probably related to Colbert's Reserve, secured in the 1818 Chickasaw treaty (see above, AJ to James Monroe, October 30, 1818). Eastin (1784–1829), a Nashville merchant, had married Rachel Donelson, Jackson's niece, in 1809. He had furnished supplies to the commissioners during the 1818 Chickasaw treaty

negotiations (see Contract with Eastin, August 30, and Memorandum by AJ and William B. Lewis re George and Levi Colbert, October 17, both 1818).

7. Jackson's remarks on the Stoughton Gantt court-martial have not been found.

The significant expansion enjoyed by the American economy after the War of 1812 came to a startling halt in 1818–19. Before the summer of 1818 banknotes of each branch of the second Bank of the United States had been honored by all the system's branch banks, functioning as a kind of national currency. Endeavoring to replenish its dwindling specie reserves, the Bank reversed policy in the summer of 1818 and began a credit contraction; consequently, no banknote was acceptable throughout the country. State and local banks refused other's notes, resulting in a specie shortage, severe discounting of some banknotes, and a financial panic that lasted in Tennessee and Kentucky until the mid-1820s. At the same time the international cotton market collapsed, and those Americans who had participated in the boom through overextension and speculation suddenly faced huge debts coming due with a shrinking money supply. In short, debtors engaged in a mad scramble to pay debts and stave off bankruptcy (see above, John McCrea to AJ, April 15).

James Johnson was no exception to this pattern. An army contractor of good reputation, he had just engaged to transport and supply the Missouri expedition, contracts amounting to more than $200,000. Unfortunately, as a result of his speculations Johnson's personal finances were overextended, and he found himself increasingly unable to meet his obligations. Acting as agent while his brother was in the West procuring supplies, Richard M. Johnson began drawing advances upon the expedition contracts, allowing him to deposit government funds in various banks so that local private debts might be paid with local notes. While these actions temporarily aided the Johnsons' personal finances, the Missouri expedition's supplies deteriorated in quality and quantity, setting the stage for a later government investigation.

From Richard Mentor Johnson

Great Crossings
26th. Aprile 1819

Dear Sir,

My Brother has left home for Louisville where he has 4 very good Steam Boats & many Small Craft for the Yellow Stone & St Anthony. The Splendour of this expedition & the importance of these distant military occupations have attracted the public attention, and I have often thought that your presence at the point from which the expedition would Set out, Bell

Fountaine, would have added importance to the enterprize; & your experience would have suggested many useful lessons.[1]

I expect all things will be concentrated by the middle of May, troops, munitions rations &c at Bell Fountain—my Brother Col James Johnson has the transportation of all these matters for the Government—My Brother has also the Supply of rations for the Orleans & adjacent Country under contract with Col Gipson,[2] & the deposits under that contract will devolve upon the agents of my Brother with my advice, and &c in his absence—The difficulty of the times as to the circulating medium of the Country is a good reason why the Govt should be liberal, in advances of money, to enable faithful men to perform their duty—the purchase for nearly the whole year must, in the western Country, be made in the winter & Spring, to leave nothing to hazard—I have explained these things to Col Gipson & have advised him, that I have been compelled to raise funds here by drawing Bills payable in Pha. & City of Washington between the 1st & 10th of June which if not met would be injurious to ⟨all⟩ my Brother & to the public service. I have very little doubt but what the advance of another quarter viz 35.000$ will be made as I have also written to Mr Calhoun; there is no danger, in making the advance, the provisions are chiefly provided, and the best Security is given for the true performance of the Contract

I feel great anxiety to prevent any inconvenience to us here on acct of the Bil*[ls]* to the army under your command as to *[good]* rations &c; one object of this letter is to r*[equ]*est you to drop Col Gipson a *[line]* calculated to put the advance out of doubt as you can Speak of the times & of the Standing & former punctuality of the Contractor for my Brother fed your army at orleans during the war west [William] Ward &c. & if you should write the Sec of war you might do some good by incidentally speaking of the necessity of a liberal support to those who risque so much in expense &c for the Cause of the Country.[3] Wishing you happiness, prosperity and Success I remain yours sincerely

Rh. M. Johnson

ALS, DLC (26). Published in *RegKyHi* 39(1941):37–38. Endorsed by AJ: "Capt Call will please prepare a letter to Colo Gibson barely stating to him the importance of the necessary supplies for the expedition & from the deranged state of the banks & commercial men in the west a liberal advance may be necessary, to enable the Supplies to be certainly forwarded—My army under the contract of Ward & Taylor, was well fed, Col James Johnston was one of the contractors & I have great confidence in him, that he will furnish if Gov. will afford him the funds—A.J."

1. James Johnson's decision to transport the Missouri expedition via steamboats proved disastrous. None of the four boats, the *Expedition, Jefferson, Johnson,* or *Calhoun,* were powerful enough to navigate the treacherous currents of the Missouri River, the *Calhoun* never ascending as far as St. Louis.

2. George Gibson had been appointed commissary general in April 1818.

3. For Jackson's recommendation of the advance, in line with the endorsement on this letter, see Jackson to Gibson, May 13; and AJ et al. to [James Monroe], July 5, below. Ward

(d. 1836) and Benjamin Taylor (1784–1850?) had been army contractors during the War of 1812. Ward had married the Johnsons' sister.

From James Gadsden

Mobile Point
3 May 1819

My Dear General

I have this moment received you letter of the 8th. Ulto[1]—The reception you met with from your fellow citizens on your return home was in unison with their feelings[2]—The gratitude of the American People is not to be questioned—They generally think, and feel correctly—their actions are the result of these unless misguided by designing demagogues—They have been with you, and will always honor and reverence the man whose life has been devoted to the interests and glory of their country—The attack made upon you in Congress was solely to forward private views; to strike at the Executive over your head; You might fall in the contest but they did not regard that so as their own ambition, was gratified—Had you split with the Executive your conduct would have been viewed in a different light by these consistent characters—But you were too honest to subserve their designs, therefore it was necessary to them that you should be crushed—They have been foiled, and the attempt in the Senate will doubtless meet with the same fate—Your Enemies however will be diligent during the recess of Congress; your Friends must be alike active to counteract their intrigues—Recollect there are two Senators to be chosen this fall from the new state of Alabama—This Country ought to be with you, and the People no doubt are, but honesty may be imposed upon by artifice, and Crawfords friends will doubtless attempt at Huntsville to secure the election of those who think & feel with them—Intimate this suspicion to Jackson, Coffee &c Your friends must not be luke-warm on the occasion—Could not Coffee go, he could doubtless be elected[3]—I wish I had but political influence enough, I do not aspire to political life, but it would gratify me to be in the Senate but for the session—On a subject in which recoil has been had to misrepresentations & gross falsehoods to support the charges, I think I could be eloquent—The facts would discomfort your vile Calumniators—

I have heard that Crawford was the author of the report in the Senate—It is in character. Too cowardly to meet an enemy in open combat, like a snake in the grass, he can throw his poison only from his concealment—I will write to my friend on the subject of the Confidential communication, and endeavour to obtain the document—[4]

I find myself in a dilemma since writing you from orleans, which may compel me to an act which may subject me to the charge of indecision—I have stated to you the embarrassments under which I labored in my first arrival in this country; produced by the contract system which may involve the government if persisted in in heavy lossesses—The Contractors were little qualified for what they had undertaken, the fulfilment of their contract was hazarded, unless a responsibility was assumed on my part, a responsibility which as I am informed can only be justified in the result—The Executive state that they have a confidence in me & whatever acts beyond the stipulations of the contract are necessary to its accomplishment they leave to my discretion—I have been compelled to assume responsibility, and have a reasonable hope that under the system established the works will now progress & be completed—If abandoned by me, My successor unwilling to hazard, may cause a failure, all of which will be thrown upon me. Would it be prudent therefore to risque the loss of reputation and to be exposed to censure, for an appointment which can not be more than a bare subsistence. I would wish your candid advice on the subject as well as your opinion whether a reputation would not be gained by the completion of the works in the Gulf—If so connected with the belief that my resignation at this period would embarrass the operations now in a train of successful result, I will bend my attention to that object—I am now comfortably situated at Mobile Point & the extra pay allowed me I find adequate to a respectable support—If you think I ought to continue in service untill the Gulf is fortified, I wish you to state to the President that I shall decline accepting the Appointment of Collector, stating candidly my motives for so doing, arrising from an anxiety of seeing these works completed, &c—[5]

Since my last I have reflected much on the subject of a narrative of your Campaigns—It is an undertaking I would be pleased with, though I could wish that the subject could fall into more abler hands—You will therefore act on this subject as in your own opinion is judicious—There are many Literary characters of Eminence in this country who would be gratified with the materials in your possession, & who would produce a work which would add to the literary reputation of the Country as it would faithfully record the splendid achievements of her Hero—Consult therefore with your friends, and make a selection of one who would do ample justice to the narrative—If you still wish me to undertake it, my efforts will be to the best of my abilities—I would not wish however under any circumstances to present to the world a hasty production—The subject requires a finished work, and would demand much time and reflection—A history cannot be written in a day, or accomplished as speedily as you achieve a victory—Remember Eatons & Reids work required nearly two years—Wirt was 4 years composing his life of Patric Henry and 9 in collecting materials[6]—I would endeavour to produce a finished work, and if the activity of your mind can await the slow progress of a dull genius your papers may be sent me as early as possible—I have now a snug box in Mobile Point, and at that retired spot will have all my hours, not devoted to Professional avocations, to myself—I shall make while in this country & as opportunities offer correct plans of the scene of your operations—I must be indebted to you however for a map of that part of the Country embraced between the Tennessee River & the junction of Coosa & Talapousa—

Do you intend visiting Washington next session of Congress, & if so will my presence be of any consequence to you—My absence from the Works would greatly embarrass operations, but I would not regard the consequences if I can be of any service to you—Notify me in time that I may make the necessary preparations—Why will you not take this route to the North, visit Louisiana & Mobile in October & take shipping from hence to some of our Atlantic cities—A sea voyage would benefit your health & this route would afford me an opportunity of seeing you & arranging matters & things—You might bring your papers with you—Let me know your decision on this subject as early as possible & address my letters hereafter to Mobile—

I shall leave this for my last visit to Orleans for this summer in 4 or 5 days, from whence I shall send you the deposition mentioned in my last[7] my respects to Mrs J—& your military family your Friend

Gadsden

ALS (postmarked Mobile, May 15 and 16), DLC (72). Published in Bassett, 6:472–73 (extract).

1. Not found.

2. Arriving at the Hermitage on the evening of April 2, Jackson was officially welcomed home in ceremonies on April 6. John Overton, speaking for the committee of welcome, assured Jackson of his neighbors' unfailing support and appreciation.

3. When Alabama's first legislature met in November, political control of the state was divided between the Georgia and Tennessee factions, the former composed mainly of allies of William H. Crawford. The Georgia faction secured the election of John W. Walker to one Senate seat and acquiesced in the selection of southern Alabama's William Rufus de Vane King to the other. Both men, however, were favorable to Jackson.

4. Gadsden was referring to Joseph G. Swift, whom he had served as aide before joining Jackson's staff in early 1816.

5. Gadsden was supervising the construction of Fort Morgan, the replacement for the inadequate Fort Bowyer. On Gadsden's declining the appointment as collector at Mobile Point, see Gadsden to AJ, November 8.

6. William Wirt, *Sketches of the Life and Character of Patrick Henry* (Philadelphia, 1817). Gadsden did not undertake a biography of Jackson at this time.

7. Gadsden was preparing his deposition supporting Jackson's actions in Florida.

From Andrew Jackson Donelson

West Point May th 5. 1819

Dear Uncle,

I have just seen in a paper from Nashville, mention of your return home and the welcome, which men of principle and open hearts, always display to long tried wrath, and injured virtue;

Encircled thus by your friends, while holding the social round, I have assured myself that the fatigues of your journey have vanished and that once again (in joyful bondage fill) you cheer the shades of hermitage with your presence;

I am sorry that I could not supply Col. [John Roger] Fenwick with a copy of the correspondence between Genl. Scott and yourself, as requested by you; having accidentally left Mr. Keen's without them, after twice writing I was answered that they were lost; but as they have been discussed in most of the papers they have certainly been read by Col. Fenwick and will not therefore much regret the loss of a copy.[1]

Anthony Butler wrote me that he was about to go to Princetown instead of Yale College, he mentioned not his reasons which I doubt not are good, and meet the approbation of his friends. He is in waiting at Elizabethtown N.J. for some arrangements previous to his entrance in Princetown.[2]

Edward & myself upon our return to West-Point, found ourselves a little in the rear of our class, and have not a moment to lose between this and the Examination which commences on the first of next month.[3] This Examination determines the merit and standing, and consequent rank in the army, of each cadet in the first class. The staff will say, but how far their decision is consistent with truth is the question to be solved, and if truly solved would in my opinion find in the composition of merit, (prejudice partiality and truth). I speak so, not that I am placed low, on their report to the Secretary of war, on the contrary my standing, was second in my class, and I shall always feel grateful to the staff for their instruction.

I might have been promoted next month if I had chosen but for reasons which I mentioned to you, and as you approved them, it was thought better to remain one year Longer, in which time I hope to acquire useful knowledge to learn the principles of war and Fortification.

As regards the pecuniary line Uncle, I propose paying my debts here, on the middle of June next, and having a sufficiency of funds by me, to enable me to give in New-York cash for such articles as are necessary instead of depending on a store here which is exhorbitant in its charges.

My debt next June will be near 200$ to pay this and keep out of debt next year I only wish 100 more; which will certainly supply me with all necessary articles next year If you agree to my proposition you will be good enough to tell me in your first letter.

I shall write you again on sunday untill then repeat my love to Aunt Jackson Andrew and all my relatives and accept the prayers, of a nephew who is at a loss for words to express his love and Gratitude to his Uncle Yr Ob St

Andrew J Donelson

ALS, DLC (72).

1. Fenwick (d. 1842), a native South Carolinian and lieutenant colonel of the 2d Artillery Regiment, was stationed in Boston. He and Jackson evidently had just missed seeing each

other in Washington, for Fenwick was there on January 19, Jackson arriving the 23rd. In June Fenwick served as president of the Board of Visitors of West Point, and he later commanded Edward G. W. Butler in the 4th Artillery Regiment. Keen has not been further identified.

2. See Anthony W. Butler to AJ, May 6.

3. Donelson, Edward G. W. Butler, and Anthony W. Butler had met with Jackson in February in New York City during the latter's eastern tour.

To Henry Atkinson

Head Quarters
Nashville 15th May 1819—

Sir

I do myself the pleasure of acknowleging the receipt of your communication of the 17th of April[1]

I am pleased to hear of the progressive State of the preparations for the expedition with which you have been charged, and flatter myself this will find you with your Command in St. Louis.

I[n] addition to the instructions already given for your government I deem it necessary only to recommend the strictest observance of *caution* and *vigilence* in ascending the Missouri. It may be necessary by acts of friendship to quiet the fears and conciliate the feelings as much as possible, but at the same time to Suffer no act or profession, on their part to put you for a moment off your Guard. the Treachery of the Indian character will never justify the reposing of confidence in their professions. be always prepared for defence and ready to inflict exemplary punishment on the offenders when necessary.

The British Traders will no doubt excite the Indians to hostility they ought in my opinion to be hung, where ever they are found among the Indian Tribes within our Territory a few examples would be sufficient and the Commanding Officer of the Troops is the proper authority to judge of their Guilt and Order their execution. But the over cautious policy of the Executive, has directed that they only be arrested and reported to him (as expressed in your Orders).[2] This instead of puting down the influence of British emmissaries I fear will have a different effect. I have the honour to be Very Respectfully Your Obt Servt

Andrew Jackson

LC in Richard K. Call's hand, DLC (63). Published in *Calhoun Papers,* 4:63.

1. See Atkinson to AJ, April 17.

2. John C. Calhoun's orders of March 27 directed Atkinson to exercise "sound discretion" and take "no decisive step" until his army posts were firmly established. Only then, after notice of a fixed time limit, ought Atkinson to "rigidly exclude" foreign traders (see above, Calhoun to AJ, March 6; Calhoun to Atkinson, March 27, DNA-RG 107, M6-10; and Robert Butler to Atkinson, March 7).

To Andrew Jackson Donelson

Hermitage May 17th. 1819.

Dr Andrew

I have been looking with some anxiety for some time for a letter from you, as yet I am without the receipt of one since I left you at Newyork— The only information I have recd from you since we parted was through a letter recd from Edward [G. W. Butler] dated the 11th. of last month.[1] I returned home in good health, but the various changes of weather, & the fatigue of the Journey shortly after my return brought on my old complaint, and a small exposure brought on one of the most violent attacks I ever experienced. Nothing but the skill of Doctors Brunaugh & [Samuel] Hogg[2] and their arduous attention saved me, from which I am so far recovered as to be able to walk [to] my room & write a little—I am very much debilatated.

I suppose in next month your examination comes on—the result I am anxious to hear—and if you wish to pay us a vissit draw on Mr Kirkman for such sum as will enable you to reach me—Should you be promoted and ordered to service I wish you to come on—as I am not desireous you should serve in a subordinate capacity in a state of peace—and I am unwilling you should serve in any other, than the Engineer corps—so soon as you compleat your study at the military academy, I wish you to read law, if that profession should be agreable to you—but when I see, or hear from you, I shall speak, or write you fully on this subject—

Your aunt enjoys good health—little Andrew I have with Doctor [James] Priestly—he is now at home sick with the Meazles, from which I hope he will soon recover—your Cousin Jane is no *more,* she died before my return—& her infant died also—The rest of your friends enjoy health—Daniel [Smith Donelson] is with Doctor Priestly, progressing in his studies well—and is a boy of fine promise—[3]

let me hear from you shortly, and if you have heard any thing of Antony W. Butler please inform me. I had a hope that he would repair to Yale College the day after I left him in Newyork. after my return I recd two letters dated in Newyork, calling on me for more funds—This extraordinary conduct of his, has occasioned me to lose all confidence in him—and knowing as I do that Colo. Richard Butler furnishes him with ample funds I did not comply with his request[4]—in fact the great expence of my Journey left me but little cash on hand—& I did not think it right to encourage his foolish extravagance.

I write to Edward by this mail[5]—your aunt Joins me in affection & good wishes to you—present us to Edward and believe me to be your affectionate uncle.

Andrew Jackson

ALS, DLC (7-0524).

1. Not found.

2. Hogg (1783–1842), a physician residing in Lebanon, Tennessee, had just retired from Congress after serving one term.

3. Donelson (1801–63; Military Academy 1825) was Andrew J. Donelson's brother, and Jackson's nephew. Priestley (c1751–1821), a native of Ireland, was an educator and former president of Cumberland College.

4. Only Anthony W. Butler's letter of March 10 has been found. On Jackson's agreement with Richard Butler, see AJ to Donelson, July 23, below.

5. Letter not found.

On March 30 President Monroe, with Secretary of War Calhoun acting as military adviser, began a four-month tour of the South and West. Like his 1817 New England trek, this trip combined an ostensible military inspection with a more political purpose. Although his course lay entirely in the Southern Division, Monroe intentionally excluded Jackson from the first half of the tour (see Monroe to [William H. Crawford, May 1819], DLC-Monroe Papers), no doubt reacting to the Florida controversy, the recent renewal of tension with Winfield Scott, and Jackson's well-known antagonism towards Georgia's William H. Crawford and Thomas Cobb. While in Georgia Major General Edmund P. Gaines joined the party, allowing Calhoun to return home to South Carolina. Monroe then relented and agreed to Jackson's inclusion on the second half of the tour. Gaines led the way for Monroe's advance into Tennessee, arriving at the Hermitage a few days before the president (see Gaines to AJ, May 16). Originally Jackson had planned to meet Monroe in Huntsville, Alabama, and accompany him to Nashville, but ill health intervened, and Jackson dispatched Richard I. Easter in his stead. Monroe arrived at the Hermitage on June 5, spending some time there before going to Nashville for its official greeting on June 9, accompanied by Jackson and elements of the Tennessee militia. Monroe stayed in Nashville until June 11, then returned to the Hermitage, remaining until the 14th when he and Jackson proceeded north to Louisville, Frankfort, and finally Lexington, where the party arrived on July 2.

To [James Monroe]

Lexington July 5th. 1819

Sir

The Military establishments on the Mississippi and Missourie have excited the deepest interest; and the feelings of an intelligent community give the highest evidence of the Vital importance of Success in the enterprize: we have no hesitation in saying that no measure has ever given stronger claims of confidence to the administration of the Genl. Govt. This enterprize so wise, so timely and politic must necessarily, in the commencement, create expenditures far beyond the control of any one individual in these times of great pecuniary distress and calamity; when Banks are closed against all kind of accomodation and individuals without means to lend—Under this view we most earnestly solicit the liberal aid and support of the Govt. in purchasing the means to effect the Object without injury or loss to the individual who has undertaken the transportation (Col. James Johnson) It was indispensible to employ a man in whom you could place confidence and we believe that Col. James Johnson is a man who deserves it.

The community have confidence in him, and he is now giving proof of his merit and energy, in the arrangement—

In fact he and his near relatives are all exclusively devoted to the accomplishment of the great Object and they have put to hazard their property and resources in the result;[1] Such exertions are worthy of support. And in the commencement the establishments are expensive; it must be recollected that every year, less expense will be incured, and to fail in this first assay, for want of the means, the British agents would feel, as if they had gained a triumph; Our Own Citizens would feel as if they had met with a defeat, most sensibly; Savage depredations might be excited by it; and it would take a Million of Dollars to reinstate it—It is expected that some disasters may happen; but a determined perseverance will effect the Object—With adequate means, we consider the establishments certain—No pecuniary consideration involved, in this subject, upon a basis of rational & reasonable calculation, can be compared with the great, & permanent advantages and blessings which will flow from it. We therefore recommend a determined perseverance; and the liberal support of men who, in the late war, and on all occasions, have manifested such entire devotion to the Country and we are of the opinion that the result will be glorious[2]—with sentiments of respect & esteem your ob Sets.

Isaac Shelby
Andrew Jackson
W[illiam] A[llen] Trimble
John T[homson] Mason Jr
Robert Wickliffe
James Morrison
W[illiam] T[aylor] Barry
Thos: Bodley

LS, DNA-RG 107 (M221-87); Copy endorsed by Monroe, "To Js. Monroe—July 5. 1819—Govr Shelby—Genl Jackson & others—" DLC (mAJs). Published in *Calhoun Papers,* 4:136–37. This letter, mistakenly identified as to John C. Calhoun, was delivered to Monroe by the signers while all were in Lexington, Kentucky. Monroe sent it to the secretary of war on the same day, and it was deposited in the war department records, thus accounting for its misattribution. Trimble (1786–1821), former lieutenant colonel of the 8th Infantry, resigned in early 1819 to become senator from Ohio. Mason (1787–1850), second son of former Virginia Senator Stevens Thomson Mason, nephew of George Mason, and brother-in-law of William T. Barry, was U.S. marshal for Kentucky. Wickliffe (1775–1859) was a lawyer and member of the Kentucky legislature. Morrison (1755–1823) was a Lexington merchant and army contractor. Barry (1784–1835), at this time a Kentucky state senator and a law professor at Transylvania University, was appointed postmaster general by Jackson in 1829. Bodley (d. 1833) served in the Kentucky militia during the War of 1812 and had been a Monroe elector in 1817.

1. Besides Richard M. Johnson acting as James Johnson's financial agent, brothers Joel, Henry, and Benjamin Johnson piloted three of the four steamboats built for the Missouri expedition. Subsequently, Richard and James Johnson mortgaged or deeded much of their land to their creditors in an effort to secure their debts.

2. This letter to Monroe, undoubtedly in response to Johnson's June 27 letter to Jackson, had its desired effect. Monroe ordered Calhoun to advance another $35,000 to James Johnson on the provisions contract and $57,500 upon transference to the United States of title to the four steamboats (see Monroe to Calhoun, July 5, *Calhoun Papers,* 4:135–36).

From Arthur Peronneau Hayne

Private

Philadelphia
7th. July 1819.

My Dear General,

I have the pleasure to inform you of my safe arrival in Philadelphia. I had the happiness to find my dear Wife & sweet Children in good health.

In my late Tour I visited the following Post's & Cant's. viz; Cantonment Mt. Pellier, Fort Montgomery, Mobile, Bay St. Louis, New-Orleans, Baton Rouge, Fort St. Philips, & the Harbor of Norfolk. In my next Winter's Tour I shall visit the Harbor of Charleston, Savannah, Amelia Island & the Appalachicola. So soon as I get over my fatigues I shall write you fully.[1]

I have forwarded to Nashville to my Brother, Coll. Robert Y[oung] Hayne, a letter of introduction to you. About a Twelve month ago he was so unfortunate as to lose his Wife. He is travelling for his health & will remain a few days in the Vicinity of Nashville. My Brother entertains the highest respect & admiration for yr character; & I feel no hesitation in saying, that you will find my Brother a young man of distinguished Talent's & the highest Integrity of character. Altho' my Junior by four years, he has already filled all of the distinguished Offices in the State of South-Carolina, & is at present the Attorney General of that State. If I was addressing any one else, I might be accused of Vanity, but I talk to you upon paper, as if I was present with you. I will not therefore apologize.[2]

Since Mr. [Langdon] Cheves has been at the head of the U.S. Bank, he has pursued a bold & manly policy.[3] He stands high in Phila. & his modesty & comdg. Talents are highly appreciated. The times are dreadful & dishonesty almost universal. Some of the public Officers in the U.S. Bank at *Baltimore,* also some of the Officers in the City Bank, have lately exhibited a degree of moral depravity that is without parallel. They have absolutely gone so far, as to rob the Vaults of the Bank, & for which some of them are to be tried. Mr. [James A.] Buchannan, the partner of Genl S[amuel] Smith & President of the U.S. Bank at Baltimore, & who has always been pronounced the most profound Merchant in our Country & a man heretofore of unimpeachable Integrity of Character, stands first in this Black Catalogue of Fraud. Genl. Smith has acted honestly & honorably. Buchannan sails from Baltimore shortly to pass the remainder of his life at Leghorn.[4]

I shall very shortly set about my Confidential Report.[5]

Frances & myself beg to be remembered most affectionately to Mrs. Jackson, to whom we both owe, as well as to yourself, more than we can ever repay, & for her's & yr happiness we both feell the liveliest interest. Martha-Ann & my sweet little babe[6] send Mrs J. yrself & Andrew each a Kiss. My Children ever surpass my most sanguine expectations. My means are moderate on the subject of wealth, & in the restoration to my family, the every wish of my heart is realised. I am yr faithful & affectionate friend.

A. P. Hayne

ALS, DLC (27).

1. Hayne began his inspection of the Southern Division in March (see Hayne to AJ, March 6). Cantonment Montpelier, built in 1817, lay about seven miles northeast of Fort Montgomery in Baldwin County, Alabama. Fort St. Philip was an old Spanish fort, reconstructed 1808–10, on the east bank of the Mississippi River, about seventy miles below New Orleans.

2. Robert Y. Hayne (1791–1839) had been married to Frances Henrietta Pinckney (c1790–1818), daughter of Charles Pinckney. See AJ to Robert Y. Hayne, October 2, below; and Robert Y. Hayne to AJ, November 10.

3. Cheves (1776–1857), a former South Carolina congressman and teacher of Robert Y. Hayne, became president of the Bank of the United States in March 1819. He continued the policy of credit contraction begun by his predecessor William Jones.

4. Scandal broke out in April and May with the revelation of the malfeasance of Buchanan (1768–1840), president of the Baltimore branch of the Bank of the United States, and its cashier James W. McCulloch. Buchanan, a long-time partner of Smith (1752–1839), then a Maryland congressman, and McCulloch used millions of dollars of bank funds for private speculation in bank stock. Although no blame attached to Smith, the scandal destroyed the firm of Smith & Buchanan and Smith's personal fortune. Trials in 1821 and 1823, however, failed to convict Buchanan. The City Bank of Baltimore also closed at this time.

5. For Hayne's report on his inspection of the military readiness of the Southern Division, see his Confidential report, [October].

6. Elizabeth Hayne was born the preceding February.

To Andrew Jackson Donelson

Hermitage July 23rd. 1819.

Dr. Andrew

The president reached me whilst recovering from a severe illness; before he proceeded on his tour, having regained my strength, duty combined with inclination, urged me to escort him through the north western part of my Division, from which Tour, I have Just returned & recd. your letter of the 25th. ult.[1]

I regret that Mr Kirkman found it inconvenient to furnish you with the funds you wanted, as from the great pressure of the times & our banks having suspended Specie payments it is dificult to procure Eastern paper—in fact I have been trying to obtain some to remit you & as yet have entirely failed.[2]

I beg of you not to form too hasty an opinion of Mr Kirkman refusal—at the time your letter reached him he was much pressed—Sixty odd thousand dollars of bills from Nashville & Huntsville & their vicinities, that he had recd in payment, was protested—on this sum he had calculated to close his business in Philadelphia preparatory to his moving to Nashville with his family in Sept. next—The protest & nonpayment of these bills placed him under pressures, that he did not foresee, and for which he had to resort to every source to raise this amount—& had he not been firm in his situation, this would have occasioned him to have stopped payment, altho he has in bank at Nashville upwards of $40,000 in cash—but his funds were wanted in Philadelphia—Therefore this circumstance put it out of his power to advance in Philadelphia for money in Nashville where he had a superabundance lying idle & of no use to him—from these circumstances you will readily find a cause for the refusal by Mr K in the case you have named, as well as in your own—in short my dear young friend there never was such a pressure—houses breaking—banks suspending payment—& all confidence between man & man destroyed—& how to remit to you at present I cannot see, but in a short time I hope to procure the means, that will enable me to send you the amount you stand in need of, in the mean time if you can obtain an advance there for a draft on me, notify me thereof & your draft will be honoured at sight. on the receipt of this write me whether you can raise the amount you want by a draft on me payable in Nashville—in the mean time I shall be endeavouring to procure a draft or Eastern bills to remit you, if you cannot get the amount for a draft on me.

I have recd. a letter from Antony dated at yale college.[3] I am happy he has at last gone there, his breach of promise to me, his stay in Newyork, and his extravagance, under his circumstances, displeased me very much—for having violated his word pledged to me has destroyed all confidence or reliance in his promises, and untill I find he has reformed, I cannot have confidence in his word—when a youth becomes so far lost to propriety, as to forfeight his word to his friend, he is on the road to ruin—I hope he has reformed—it will be a source of great pleasure to me to find that he really has—he has called on me for funds, he well knows—& so it was clearly understood—that his cousin Richard was to finish his education—& I was with the Little funds in my hands to finish Edwards—the whole amount of the two sons were *$1400* This you know is a sum in the support & education of two youths is soon expended—out of this sum I advanced the mother *$200* now when his cousin furnis*[hed]* him so bountifully—that he should draw on *[me]* for funds to buy watches, when the wants of his Mother, the pittance that was in my hands & Edwards education to compleat is such an act of wanton extravagance that has hurt me much—I have not wrote him yet, altho I mean to do it, & in such terms as I hope will bring him to his Senses & induce him to attend to his Studies, and in such away as he ought—his conduct to his friend & patron Colo. Richard Butler has been unpardonable—write me on the rcpt of this. I write by this mail to Edward.[4] your friends are all well & your aunt & Andrew Joins me in love to you—In haste I am your affectionate uncle—

Andrew Jackson

ALS, DLC (7-0585).

1. Not found.

2. Once the Bank of the United States began demanding specie payments, local banks especially in the West quickly depleted their meager reserves. Deprived of specie and left with rapidly depreciating local bank notes that eastern banks no longer honored, westerners had to acquire eastern bank notes to discharge eastern debts (see AJ to Donelson, August 6, and above, Richard M. Johnson to AJ, April 26).

3. See Anthony W. Butler to AJ, May 6.

4. Letter not found.

To Eleazar Wheelock Ripley

Head Quarters
Nashville 31st July 1819—

Sir

Your Letter of the 12th Inst has been received[1] and it would have afforded me much pleasure to have found from its perusial conclusive testimony of the correctness of ordering a road to be opened from the Bay of St Louis to intersect the Military road, at a time when it was believed by Myself and the Government that all the Troops under your command that could be spared from other necessary duties were employed on the Military Road.

That every disposable Soldier would have been engaged in completing this Road I had a right to expect, both from my Letters of the 15th and 27th. of November last as well as from your letter of the 1st of May[2]

I have read your Letter with attention but Shall come to no conclusion on the Subject until I have received the Report you have promised me of Lieuts [Jeremiah] Yancey and [Isaac E.] Craig,[3] and Your own report with which I shall expect, You to furnish me with a plan of the Road you have been cuting, connecting with the rout up the Chatahoola River, then the portage over Land to Pearl River. In the mean time I will barely observe from my Person knowledge of that Country (having explored it with an eye to its defence) I have no doubt but the most certain, the expeditious and the least expencive mode of Supplying the Detachment with Provisions will be to transport it from Cheffontie a long the road which has been cut, while the Troops are progressing to wards the Tombigbee a Depot should be established on that River at the Point where it will be intersected by the Military road and from thence they may draw their supplies as soon as they are within Striking distance.[4] It appears to me that if the expence and Labour bestowed in opening this cross road had been employed on the Military road it would ere this been nearly completed. I cannot imagine how the transportation of Supplies for the Troops along the road they are cuting can interfere with the progress of their Work. the Quarter Masters and Commissaries Departments are bound for their conveyance, and the Teams employed with the Troops are competant to their removal from Camp to Camp this can be done with little inconvenience as the camps are so seldome removed

When you reflect Sir that this road was commenced in the Summer of 1817 and yet progressed not more than from fifty to Seventy miles You must expect the Government will require a satisfactory report of the cause from which this extraordinary delay has Originated, and for this purpose you have been called on repeatedly for special report on the Subject. Be assured Sir it will afford me much satisfaction to find that your rangements for supplying the Troops with Provision were judiciously made, and that the opening of a road from the Bay of St. Louis to intersect the Military road was best calculated to promote the Public Service, though none of the reasons which you have given for its commencement, from the evidence now before me are satisfactory, for I can discover no reason why either the Troops or their Supplies should pass by the way of Shieldsbourough to the Military road[5] and it appears evident to me that all the Sufferings and privations of the Troops has originated from a deviation from the System of supplying them along the road they are cuting, and along which every Detachment should have marched intended to reenforce the Party.

I sincerely regret that you have not sent on your report as required by the Orders of my Adjt. General that I might Learn, what number of Troops are employed on the Military road.[6] I regret to find that in Aprile & May there was not more than 50 Soldiers capable of performing labour, and this from the want of Shoes which might have been drawn at any time from the Depot at New Orleans, and I still more regret Sir that on the 13th Inst. this small number of men Should be in a state of starvation, and for a Subsistence compelled to depredate on the cornfields of the Neighbouring Farmers, what has become of the 30,000 Rations ordered on the 29th of may certainly transportation might have been procured for its conveyance up the Military road before the 13th Inst. there must be neglect some where or a want of supplis would not have been experienced by this Small detachment within 70 or eighty miles of New Orleans Untill I receive your promised report I shall give no other opinion than the one above stated with regard to the diferent routs you have mentioned for supplying the Troops but I hope some expeditious mode has been adopted for supplying their immediate wants, and that you have not depended on the experiment of the Chathoola for their first supply. As soon as practicable I shall expect to receive from you a report, showing the number of men at present employed on the military Road, what numbers there have been at different times since its commencement how many miles of the road is completed, the time you commenced the Cross road, and the number of men you have employed on it.

It is necessary that the utility of this road be plainly manifested, as it appears on the 12th Inst you Ordered an aditional force for its completion, in direct violation of my repeated Orders, directing all the disposable force to be employed on the Military Road I am Sir Very Respectfully Your Obt. Servt

(Signed) Andrew Jackson

LC in Richard K. Call's hand, DLC (63); Copy also in Call's hand, DNA-RG 107 (M221-86).

1. See Ripley to AJ, July 12.

2. See AJ to Ripley, November 15 and 27, 1818, and Ripley to Robert Butler, May 1. Public pressure for the road's completion was also increasing at this time (see "C" to AJ, June 17).

3. Yancey (d. 1829) and Craig (d. 1819) were 1st lieutenants of the 8th Infantry, and had reported to Ripley their agreement with his management of the military road's construction.

4. Catahoula Creek and Tchefuncta River run parallel to the Pearl River, east and west respectively.

5. Shieldsborough was an earlier name for Bay of St. Louis.

6. See Butler's orders to Ripley to report the progress on the military road, April 8, 16, May 12, June 6, and July 16.

To James Gadsden

Hermitage August 1rst 1819

Dr. Gadsden

On last evening I recd. your letter of the 6th. of July in answer to mine by Major Armstrong. I have wrote you often since that time, I might say, every week that I was able to write—I adressed several via New-orleans, and some direct to Mobile.

I wrote you last on the 29th. ult. on the subject of your funds in the Nashville Bank and the dificulty there is ⟨was appeared⟩ in getting them transferred to Neworleans & the City of Washington[1]—I have the promise of both the banks to let me have all orleans paper that they can get—and if I cannot get the whole I will send you a draft on Mr [Bernard de] Marigne & Mr Livingston retaining the amount of the draft in bonds untill I am notified of it being paid—I am in hopes in a few days we will be able in this way to get you to Neworleans, the amount of your Bill forwarded in my favour on the Nashville Bank. Times are dreadfull here confidence entirely destroyed, specie payments suspended, and no foreign notes to be got—and upwards of six hundred suits returnable to our last County Court in Davidson—however you are safe, your money is in bank & I will endeavour to have it out in some way that will answer your wishes.[2]

I ⟨found your⟩ knew you would be astonished⟨ment⟩ at that part of my letter that related to Genl Swift—that you may form your own ideas from facts I enclose you a confidential statement of them substantially as the took place. I was aware that it would astonish you, I knew how much confidence you had in the Genl.[3] I had you know the same exalted opinion of him—and when I wrote you on this subject it was to bring to your View, the weakness of human nature, the depravity of man that you might be allways on your guard. let me assure you, I applaud you for your principle, it is the only correct one to be persued, never abandon a good opinion you have formed of any man unless on the most stuborn proof—but Sir in the mean time it is prudent, to View facts, and consider of them well—If the Genl as he says was your informant, ⟨and⟩ he had read the letter, ⟨made use of the language⟩ declared the ⟨first⟩ statement true, his attempt to give it a different coulouring ⟨that it was⟩ at the time he did, endeavouring to change it to a mere letter of introduction when he knew & had said differently, is positive proof of his ⟨tripping, and⟩ want of stability, firmness, & integrity—I have no objections when you meet with Genl Swift that you shew him the enclosed confidential statement for his own ⟨perusal⟩ use & his own eye I trust he will have the candeur to acknowledge the statement I have made to be substantially correct.

I see from your letter that business will compell you on to the city this fall that you wish to be on before congress meets although I am very anxious to go on to Congress unless I can sell some of my out ⟨property⟩ lands so as to aid me in funds to meet the payment for my farm, lotts &c &c, in & near Florence, & to aid my pay & emolument for travelling expences, I cannot, proceed—I sett out in a few days, to sell my farm near florence if I can,[4] if I should I will desend the Mississippi & pass round by water & Touch at Mobile Point for you But my Dear young friend, I cannot under uncertainties request you to pospone your Journey to the city—I would advise you to proceed when your business calls—advising me when you will be at the city to which place I will write you My ultimate determination—being determined to leave the army the moment the business in the Senate is acted on, I do not wish to create debts, that I am unable to meet—Mrs. J. Joins me in good wishes. I am your friend sincerely

Andrew Jackson

ENCLOSURE: CONFIDENTIAL NOTE

Confidential—I thought it a duty I owed to Mr Munroe to put him on his guard as it respected Crawford—I wrote him[5] ⟨confidentially,⟩ that I was informed confidentially, that Mr Wm. H Crawford had written a letter to

Mr Clay the object of which was to form a combination and opposition against Mr Munroes reelection that I could vouch for the veracity of my confidential informant—but from whom my informant obtained his information I knew not, (you recollect you gave me no name) all that my informant stated to me was, that his informant was of high Charactor, & standing in the united States. When I reached Washington this thing was spoken of in confidential circles[6]—on my arival at the city amonghst the number of my friends Genl Swift waited upon me with his usual friendship & Frankness. I was happy to see him, for as you know I had the most exalted opinion of him. a few evenings after Genl Swift called to see me again & Spent the evening, in the course of the evening he asked to have some private conversation with me I shewed him to my bed room—as soon as we were alone, he introduced the subject of Mr Wm H Crawfords letter to Clay, and observed that he felt much interested in knowing who was my informant, and if I would disclose it to him in the strictest confidence I would lay him under obligations—Knowing the confidence you had in Genl Swift—having equal confidence in him myself, & finding from his declarations that he was materially interested to know, under the strictest confidence I gave him you as my informant—the Genl smiled & observed (here I will give you his words) "he has not treated me generously—but it is true I am the man I saw the letter & read it"—I instantly replied, Sir you are not to charge my informant with ungenerous treatment, let it be remembered that ⟨my⟩ I have informed you & now repeat it that my informant gave me no name from whom he derived his information—but told me it was from a gentleman of high standing & respectability & if any person is to blame for speaking of it, it is me. The Genl then repeated it is me, I saw & read the letter but ⟨that⟩ as Mr Crawford & himself had been at war, but had buried the Hatchett, he hoped it would not be stirred unless some grand political purpose could be effected by it.[7] I told him I had named to Mr Munroe that Mr Crawford had written such a letter, I had stated it to some others, but as he had requested it, I should not bring it before the public unless I thought I could effect some public good by it. here for the present the conversation ended, and the Genl left me. a ⟨few days⟩ day or two after I waited on the President, during my vissit, the subject of the letter to Clay introduced, ⟨the conversation, and⟩ Mr Munroe told me, that he had a conversation with Mr Crawford on that subject and that he had denied positively ever writing such a letter and also Mr Crawford said that he ⟨or any other person⟩ situated as he was, holding an office under Mr Munroe must be a Villain ⟨who⟩ if he would attempt to intrigue & to form a combination to defeat his election—I looked sternly at Mr Munroe & replied, say to Mr Wm H Crawford from me that he is a Villain, and that he dare not put his pen to paper and sign his name to the declaration that he never wrote such a letter to Mr Clay, if he does say to him from me, if I do not prove it upon him, I will apologise to him in every gazzett in the U States: he replied, you rest upon Genl Swift to prove this,

⟨to⟩ be careful⟨ly⟩ least when it comes to the test, ⟨if⟩ he does not deceive you—that he does not trip—I replied on my informants veracity I was ready to risk my life, who was his I did not know he told me he was a man of high standing & respectability, whether it was Genl Swift or not I did not know, but tripping was out of the question with me, no man should do it—& I would thank him to say from me to Mr Crawford that he was the very villain he had described himself to be, that I had such confidence in my informant that I repeated, that Mr. C. durst not put his pen to paper & deny the charge & sign it, if he did I pledged myself to prove the fact upon him, & if I failed, I pledged myself to apologise to him in every gazzett in the U States—from the Presidents, I went to the Sec of War—there being alone, the conversation turned on the subject. Mr Calhoun stated that Mr Crawford denied writing such a letter—I replied to him in the same way I had to Mr Munroe, requesting the Sec of war to give Mr Crawford the information of my declarations—

The night following Genl Swift waited upon me & asked to have some private conversation, I shewed him into my bed chamber—as soon as alone, he introduced the subject of the letter & said he had waited upon me to have some conversation, fearing that I had not fully comprehended him—I replied I could not mistake him, that I understood him to say that he was your informant, that it was true, that he had seen & read the letter—the Genl replied that was true, but I had not taken up a proper idea of the tenor of that letter, that it was merely a letter of introduction from Mr Crawford ⟨to⟩ in favour of a gentleman from North Carolina to Mr Clay and there was nothing else contained in it ⟨relating to a combination or the next election for President⟩ I felt ⟨a little⟩ roused, and observed Sir it is strange that a mere letter of introduction could inspire you with ideas of combinations at the next presidential election—and if you are the informant of my confidential friend ⟨account⟩ explain to me Sir for the expressions then used if the letter as you now say was a mere letter of introduction, my friend said to me that his informant observed to him, that this letter from Mr. C. to Clay was the first evidence to him, that Mr Wm H Crawford was one of the greatest Villains & rascals that ever disgraced human nature, that holding an office under Mr Munroe & intriguing against him was the highest evidence of his corruption & baseness. Genl Swift paused for at least a minute without reply—& when he broke silence asked me if there was no way to bring about a reconciliation between Mr Crawford and myself—I told him there was none, that I knew him to be a Villain—that I had made it a rule through life never to take a rascal by the hand knowing him to be such—that I never gave my hand where my heart could not go also—believing as I did of Mr Crawford I never would take him by the hand, that I did not know who was the informant of my confidential friend, but If Mr Crawford would deny the fact of writing the letter the object of which was to form a combination against Mr. M. election & that if I did not prove it upon him I would apologise to him in every gazzett—

we parted & here this thing has rested, ever since—Shortly after this the vote was taken in the house of representatives on the Seminole question, I had recd. many pressing invitations to vissit Baltimore Philadelphia, New-york & Boston, intending to go as far as west point if I found the vote of the house of representatives put an end to a further investigation in the Senate. I sent for a member of the committee in the Senate who informed me that the committee in the Senate would not stir the thing as he believed any further[8]—I prepared to proceed to the Eastward—when I returned to Baltimore on the Sunday evening before the rise of Congress I met the report of the Senate, I was engaged to dine with the Citizens on Monday; at 8 oclock in the evening, I took the stage for the city and reached there the next morning half after three—where I was informed that the report of the committee was written by Mr Crawford, which I verily believe, and that after I had left the city for the Eastward Genl Swift & Mr Crawford had been very intimate often together, and on the most friendly footing—When I left the City Genl S. was to have ⟨been on⟩ overtaken us in a few days—I am of the opinion that all my conversation was detailed to Mr Crawford—& finding I would not be friends with him, he drew the report & urged his tools to report it to the Senate. The information of their intimacy and being frequently together, is from undoubted authority. but this intimacy alone would have created no unfavourable opinion of the Genl—but his avowal of being your author, having read the letter & declaring it was true—& then attempting to say it was a mere letter of introduction, combined with the intimacy—⟨afterwards—& which you will see from the whole statement⟩ afterwards & Crawford drawing the report, during this intimacy induced me as well as a number of my friends to form unfavourable opinion of him knowing your unlimited confidence in him, as a man of honor & probity—I named the circumstances, that you, at least, might be on your guard It is also stated that on another occasion he has tripped—your friend Sincerely

Andrew Jackson

ALS copy, DLC (27). Published in Bassett, 2:421–24.

1. See Gadsden to AJ, July 6. The bearer of Jackson's letter to Gadsden was possibly Francis Wells Armstrong (1783–1835), who had resigned from the army in 1817 after relocating to Tennessee from his native Virginia. In 1831 Jackson appointed him Choctaw agent. None of Jackson's letters to Gadsden, referred to above, have been found.

2. Marigny (1785–1868), a long-time member of the Louisiana legislature, had contracted, through Edward Livingston, for Jackson to purchase for him a pair of carriage horses.

3. For further discussion of Swift and the Jackson-Crawford dispute, see above, Gadsden to AJ, May 3.

4. Jackson did not sell his Evans Spring plantation until September 1821.

5. See above, AJ to James Monroe, November 15, 1818.

6. Jackson had discussed the purported Crawford letter with John Q. Adams. See above, AJ to William B. Lewis, January 30.

7. The "war" between Swift and Crawford probably related to Crawford's efforts, when secretary of war, to appoint French engineer Simon Bernard to the Army, in effect supplanting

Swift's role as chief engineer. Upon becoming president Monroe confirmed Swift's position, but Swift was never happy with the arrangement and resigned in November 1818, accepting the lucrative appointment as surveyor and inspector of revenue at the port of New York. His ill feelings towards Crawford may have prompted him to circulate the story of a Crawford-Clay alliance.

8. Probably John H. Eaton.

Agreement with Malachi Nicholson

August 12th 1819—

Articles of agreement made & concluded this 12th day August 1819 between Andrew Jackson Guardian of Andrew Jackson Hutchinson of the one part and Malachi Nicholson of ⟨the⟩ Lauderdale County of the Other part, witnesseth, That the said Malachi has this day agreed, with the said Andrew, that he will take possession of the plantation and Negroes belonging to the said Andrew Jackson Hutchins minor, situate lying & being in Lauderdale County, on the 15th of October next in the capacity of an Overseer, and continue thereon in said capacity until the 1st day of January 1820, and Superintend said farm and negroes in an industrious carefull manner, planting as much cotton as his hands can pick out and clearing as much ground as the hands can clear, & planting it in corn potatoes &c &c. taking care of the Stock of Horses Hoggs and cattle, Keeping the farming Tools in good order and in all things conducting himself as a carefull industrious Overseer, For Which services the said Andrew Jackson guardian for the said A J. Hutchins does agree & bind himself to pay to the said Malachi the Sum of two Hundred & fifty Dollars in Cash & furnish him Eight Hundred Weight of pork, & Seven barrels of Corn for bread for himself & family. In testimony whereof we bind ourselves our heirs Executors & administrators for the faithfull performance of the above agreement and hereunto Set our hands and Seals the day & date above written

Malachi Nicholson
Andrew Jackson

Witness Richd. Rapier[1]

I certify that the agreement Contemplated and made between the within Subscribed parties was intended to bind the Said Overseer Nicholson to continue in the Service of the Said Andrew Jackson Guardian of A J. Hutchins until the 1st day of Jany 1821 instead of 1820 as expressd. within making One year two months & a half—[2]

Richard Rapier

R[ichard] I[vy] Easter[3]

ADS in Nicholson's hand, also signed by AJ, THi (7-0603). Nicholson remained as overseer for Andrew J. Hutchings until his death in the fall of 1825.

1. Rapier (d. 1826) had recently moved from Nashville to Florence, where he traded under the name Rapier & Simpson.

2. The preceding paragraph is in Richard I. Easter's hand.

3. Easter (d. 1825), a Georgia native, served in the army during the War of 1812, rejoined in 1818, and became Jackson's aide later that year. He attained the rank of captain but problems with his accounts as a quartermaster lingered years after his 1821 resignation. He subsequently read law with John Overton and moved to Florida where he and Richard K. Call opened a law office. See AJ to John Clark, [September] 18, and to George Gibson, January 3, 1820, both below.

From John McKee

French Camp Choctaw Nation
Aug. 13 1819.

Sir,

I have the honor to enclose a copy of an address from the Council of the Nation to the President which speaks for itself[1]

I had the fullest confidence before the council convened that the Six Towns at last would accede to the wishes of the Government. At a council in their own District at which Messrs. [John] Pitchlynn & [Edmond] Folsom & [Middleton] Mackay were present they expressed an unequivocal desire to cross the Mississippi, but a few halfbreeds with but little claim to distinction have by their exertions and misrepresentations of the country on Red River alarmed many of the Indians who were disposed to migrate, into an opinion that the country affords neither soil water nor game. These men are now exerting themselves to raise a party to go on to Washington The Chiefs asked pecuniary aid from me which I refused on the ground of a letter from the Department of war directing me to inform the Chiefs that such a visit was deemed useless and expensive and therefore to be discouraged.[2] They are no*[w endeavoring]* to raise the means amongst themselves for the journey—*[The party, as far as I can learn, will consist]* of the three Great Medal chiefs *[(if Puchshunnubby can be prevailed on to go)]* Jesse Brashears, Alexr. Hamilton *[Benjamin James, Levi Perry & David Folsom,*[3] *and perhaps]* some others, *[of these the two latter only have any weight in the nation If they go I will also be there if possible—They speak of starting about the last of September and I can scarcely expect to obtain permission by that time. It is due to J Pitchlynn Sen E Folsom and M Mackay to say that they have exerted themselves with zeal and industry to accomplish the object of the Government and are sorely mortified at the failure.*[4] *I have the honor to be with sincere respect & esteem Sir, your obedient Servant*

(Signed) Jno McKee]

AL fragment, DLC (75); Copies, DNA-RG 75 (M271-2), DNA-RG 46 (7-0605). Published in *ASP, Indian Affairs,* 2:230. Bracketed material supplied from the copy in DNA-RG 75.

1. See the Council of the Choctaw Nation to James Monroe, August 12 (DLC-27).
2. Pitchlynn, Folsom, and Mackay were all Choctaw interpreters.
3. The system of Medal Chiefs was imposed in the eighteenth century by the French, who gave medals to the Indian leaders they wished to deal with, creating a Choctaw hierarchy. At this time, Pushmataha (c1765–1824), Mushulatubbe (d. 1835), and Apuckshunnubbe (c1739–1824) were the three principal or Medal Chiefs, ruling, respectively, the Southern, Northeastern, and Western Districts of the nation. Jesse Brashears, possibly a mixed-blood son of Turner Brashears, signed the 1820 Treaty of Doaks's Stand. Alexander Hamilton was the mixed-blood ward of William P. Anderson (see Pushmataha et al. to AJ, October 19, 1820). Benjamin James and Levi Perry were mixed-bloods, the latter being a prominent chief. David Folsom (1791–1847), brother of Edmond, became an important chief in 1827 when he deposed Mushulatubbe.
4. See AJ to Calhoun, August 24.

John H. Eaton's 1818 ad interim Senate appointment would last until the Tennessee legislature elected a permanent successor to George W. Campbell, who had been appointed minister to Russia. But the legislative and congressional campaigns preceding the August 5 and 6 elections revealed that national political alignments had become enmeshed in local politics, and the newly elected legislature, meeting in September, would determine Eaton's personal political future as well as reflect the strength of William H. Crawford's forces in Tennessee.

During the summer Eaton had published a handbill (only an extract has been found in the Milledgeville Georgia Journal, *November 23) that castigated Georgia politicians in general and Andrew Erwin, the former Augusta, Georgia, merchant, Jackson's political opponent, and defendant in a lawsuit arising out of land speculation along the Duck River, in particular. In a series of published exchanges (many of which have not been found), a piece published over Erwin's name attacked Eaton, Jenkin Whiteside (1772–1822), and James Jackson, partners with Andrew Jackson in* Jackson *v.* Erwin *(see AJ to William B. Lewis, August 17, and to James Jackson, August 25, both below).*

It is unclear whether Eaton regarded the Erwin piece (printed in the Shelbyville Tennessee Herald *on August 14—no copy found) or another statement as an affront to his honor, but by early September the senator had challenged Erwin and selected Richard K. Call as his second, prompting Jackson himself to take an active interest in the prospective duel (see AJ to Call, September 9, below, and James C. Bronaugh to AJ, [cSeptember 12]).*

To William Berkeley Lewis

(Private) August 17th. 1819

Sir

I had on yesterday a great desire to se you as I returned through Town—I there saw an answer of Andrew Irwin to Major Eatons hand bill—in which I am introduced—& the Salt Spring reserved for the use of the Chikesaw Nation—on this subject I wish to see you. If you can come up I will be glad to see you—& if you can procure *[it]* bring up one of those papers it will b*[e]* well—in due time I shall attend to this Mr Irwin in proper manner—I have been very wantonly assailed. I shall wait with patience to the proper time—In the mean while I mean to make a report to the Govr that will bring the treaty before the assembly, where its benefits & reserves will be duly considered[1]—I wish to see you between this & Saturday—I am yrs. respectfully

Andrew Jackson

ALS sent "pr boy," NNPM (7-0613).

1. For a discussion of the salt lick controversy, see AJ to Joseph McMinn, August 25, and September 13 (below).

The controversy arising out of the Allison land claim along the Duck River (see Jackson, *2:62–63, 296–97) had entered a new phase when Jackson filed suit on July 8, 1814, claiming the entire 85,000 acres. Jackson asserted a right, transferred to him by the heirs of David Allison (d. 1798), to redeem title to the land by paying off the balance of the original debt (plus interest) owed to Philadelphia merchant Norton Pryor; to do so, he entered into a financial agreement with Jenkin Whiteside and James Jackson, dividing the claim among the three (see Deed of release, August 3, 1812; Articles of agreement, January 9, 1813; and AJ to John Overton, December 9, 1821). Jackson's claim, if allowed, would have negated all sales and rentals in the tracts and created economic chaos for Andrew Erwin, a chief speculator in the area, and all those who had acquired land through him. Erwin was, therefore, the major defendant in the lawsuit, and had submitted his formal answer on March 7, 1817. Whiteside, acting as Jackson's attorney, had filed an amended bill of complaint on June 12, 1819, adding additional defendants to the action and asserting that Erwin, among others, knew at the time of his purchase that his title was questionable. It is unclear whether the amended bill prompted Erwin's newspaper attack in the August 14 Shelbyville* Tennessee Herald *(not extant), but Jackson's strong reaction (see above, AJ to William B. Lewis, August 17) undoubtedly prompted Jackson to retell the entire story of the Allison land controversy. In turn, Whiteside and James Jackson used the following letter in preparing their newspaper response for the September 4* Nashville Whig.

To James Jackson

Hermitage August 25th. 1819

Dr. Sir

To enable you & Mr Whitesides to give a true statement of facts, if deemed necessary I make the following—about the year 1794 or 1795, having purchased in partnership with John Overton Esqr 25000 acres of land, this land was sold by Major [James] Grant as agent to David Allison—on a credit for which his notes were taken at Philadelphia—The part due me was laid out in merchandize—Allison was then in good credit—I had scarcely reached home when I was notified that Allison had failed & to prepare to cover my endorsement I sold my Store then in Nashville to Colo Elijah Robertson for thirty three thousand acres of land or thereabout—proceeded to Knoxville, and sold this land to Colo James Stuart of Jonesborough at one quarter dollar pr acre, & took a draft on Govr. Wm Blount then residing in Philadelphia for the amount—proceeded on to Philadelphia, where I found Blount Equally involved with Allison in distress & with great dificulty, got up the paper I had endorsed—& was compelled in closing this disasterous business, to take D. Allisons paper for the amount due me—Thus David Allison became indebted to me—the land I sold Stuart to enable him to take up his paper I had endorsed is now worth at least $200000—D. Allison died in Philadelphia Jail as it was thought insolvant In his life time he had morgaged the 85,000 acres of land on Duck River to Norton Prior to secure the payment of a debt—that in the latter end of the year 1799, or early in the year 1800 Joseph Anderson as agent for Norton Prior, came to an agreement with me to have the morgage prosecuted to a foreclosure in the name of Norton Prior against the heirs & devisees of David Allison, for which I was to have a part of his proportion of the land—this suit by the instructions of Jos. Anderson was to be instituted & prosecuted in the Federal court at Nashville—I not then being a practising lawyer, but engaged in public life a Judge of the Supreme Court—employed John Overton to originate & prosecute the same which he did agreable to the instructions given by Jos. Anderson to a decree—and the Tittles under the decree, was made agreable to the written instructions given me by Joseph Anderson—The part of the land Deeded to me by the marshal, I sold believing it to be a good tittle—being present when Thos. Blount signed the Deed for the same to David Allison, and I never once thought of a defect in the decree, for the want of Jurisdiction in the court. I was not present when the decree was entered up—and the cause having been prosecuted agreably to the instructions of Judge Anderson in the Federal court[1]—I never once thought on the subject—Untill after I had sold the land, George W. Campbell came to me in Nashville I think in the year 1810 or 1811, and told me he had been examining the proceedings in that suit and the sale under the decree was a nulity the court not having Jurisdiction—Having sold & made a general warrantee, I became alarmed and knowing that Jenkin Whitesides was interested under the marshals sale I immediately went to Mr J Whitesides and informed him of Mr. Campbells opinion—Mr Whitesides replied that he knew that, and that he had informed Mr Irwin that the heirs of David Allison had it in their power at any time to redeem but Mr Irwin & himself was of opinion that the debt was so great that they heirs never would be able to redeem—I told Mr Whitesides I had never sold any land but what I thought the title was a good one—that I would not rest my title on such a foundation—that David Allison was indebted to me in the sum of about $20,000—and that if the heirs could redeem, I would endeavour to secure my debt and those honest men to whom I had sold when I thought my title was good I prosecuted a suit by J[ohn] Dickeson on one hand to Judgt—against the heirs of David Allison I proceeded to Georgia carrying with me the record met William Allison who was present when I last settled with his brother David knew the Justice of my claim & how much I had sufferred in sacrafice of property by him he convened the heirs who readily agreed to transfer me all their right to any property within the State of Tennessee that they were invested with by descent as heirs of David Allison and executed a Deed to me and I executed to them a release against the debt—This is a conscise statement of the facts—you know the ballance—I enclose you a copy of the record which I have procured accidentily since I saw you—it proves what Judge Overton states that he alone prosecuted the suit in the name of Norton Prior as council alone—and is full proof that Irwin in his answer has stated & swore to a falshood, when he states that this suit was prosecuted by whitesides[2]—& this ought to be stated in a clear manner—that the people might see, that a man who would swore to a falshood, proven as such by record would state any thing—to benefit himself—in time I will hunt up all the papers on this subject, but being so long engaged in public business, my papers are so numerous & disorted that it is hard to find any particular one—I shall see you on Saturday—I am your respectfully—

Andrew Jackson

ALS draft, DLC (72). Published in Bassett, 2:427–28.

1. Grant, a resident of Knox County, also acted as an agent for William Blount and was involved in Blount's 1796 filibustering scheme against Spanish Florida. Robertson (1744–97) and James Stuart (1751–c1816) served in the Tennessee legislature; William Blount (1749–1800) had been governor of the Southwest Territory and U.S. senator, replaced by Joseph Inslee Anderson. Thomas Blount (1759–1812), brother of William, was a North Carolina congressman. The bulk of the land sold by Jackson to Stuart in 1796 was on the Duck River (see *Jackson,* 1:88–89, 441). As payment for arranging the federal lawsuit foreclosing the Allison mortgage, Jackson received 10,000 acres of the Duck River lands.

2. Overton and Whiteside had each purchased 2,500 acres from Jackson's portion of the land. In his March 7, 1817, answer, Erwin contended that in early 1807 Jackson had assured

him there was no equitable redemption possible by the Allison heirs and encouraged him to buy the land. Erwin alleged that Whiteside had also advised him that his purchase was "perfectly safe." The lawsuit prosecuted to judgment by Dickinson (1781–1815) was possibly *AJ* v. *John Allison et al.,* December 17, 1810. Both Dickinson and Jenkin Whiteside were Jackson's attorneys in the later Erwin suit. The enclosed record was for *Norton Pryor* v. *John Allison et al.* (U.S. District Court, West Tennessee, Minute Book A, pp. 364–67, M1213-1).

To George Gibson

Hermitage Sept. 7th. 1819.

My Dear Colo.

Your letter of the 18th. ult reached me by due course of mail it found me flat upon my back, and yesterday was the first day in twelve that I could sit up long anough to write a letter, this will account for this delay in my answer, indeed I have recd others from you which I have not answered.[1] Those frequent attacks, give me so little time to attend to the various official duties that crowd upon me when able to attend to business that I find no leisure.

The novelty of the information contained in your letter has produced some serious deliberation with me. it is this—is it possible that this man under all circumstances would have the audacity to place his name before Mr Munroe for appointment, unless he is supported by part of the Executive branches who would communicate to him that his application would be heard—What must my feelings be with reguard to Mr Munroe, and the Estimation of the Public generally with reguard to his professions of friendship towards me if he would under existing circumstances even condescend to read it—It is impossible that Mr Munroe can appoint him, it is impossible that he can act with such duplicity but should I be disappointed, in this & Leacock appointed paymaster General, which I will never believe untill I see it officially announced, the whole american nation shall soon hear of the perfidy & treachery as it respects myself.[2]

I have never believed that Spain would ratify the treaty—I do not believe she will now—I hope I may be mistaken but I allways thought it was a stroke of policy to gain time and possession of her strong posts again—I know Mr Munroe was allways sanguine that it would be ratified. Should a war grow out of this thing—nothing my Dear Colo would give me as much pleasure—& nothing more confidence than to have you with me—But were you to see how much I am emaciated, you would scarcly believe I could ever again take the field—however excitement has kept me alive & it might raise me quickly to the necessary strength; I am beginning to eat with a good a*[ppe]*tite—four days I lived on water gru*[el]*—I am much debilitated—I will thank you for a line when you have leisure I am with great respect yr friend sincerely

Andrew Jackson

ALS, MiDbEI (7-0642).

1. See Gibson to AJ, August 18; see also Gibson to AJ, August 2.

2. Gibson had reported that Abner Lacock and Nathan Towson were candidates for paymaster general of the army; Towson was appointed.

To Richard Keith Call

Hermitage Sept 9th 1819

Captain Call.

In prosecuting the business you have taken charge of, for your friend Major Eaton, you must steadily keep in mind that the *man* you have to deal with is unprincipled, you will be guarded in all your acts, have every thing in writting, and hold no conversation with him unless in the presence of some confidential person of good character, he is mean and artful. It is possible from what I think of the man, that he will propose Riffles or muskets.[1] These are not weapons of gentlemen—and cannot and ought not to be yielded to. Pistols are the universal weapons (with one solitary exception) of fire arms gentlemen use—These or swords, ought to be selected, and as neither of those concerned are in the habit of using swords—the offending party will make choice of this weapon—The next choice in the opponent is distance—ten paces is the longest—and *altho* the defendant may choose as far as ten paces, still if the offended is not as good a shot as the defendant, custom and justice will bring them to a distance that will put them on a perfect equality Position—to prevent accident—let them keep their pistols suspended until after the word fire is given.[2] The first rule is to let each man fire when he pleases, so that he fires one minute or two after the word. Charge your friend to preserve his fire, keeping his *teeth firmly* clenched, and *his fingers* in a position that if fired on and *hit,* his fire may not be extorted—Some times when the distance is long it is agreed, that both or either may advance and fire. If this arrangement is made, charge your friend to preserve his fire, until he shoots his antagonist through the *brain,* for if he fires and does not kill his antagonist, he leaves himself fully in his power. Have every rule written down and signed by his friend, receive none but written answers, and all open, that you may inspect and see that they are decorous, for this is the friends duty to see that no paper that comes through him, ought to contain indecorous expressions. I have been always of an opinion that a *base man* can never *act bravely.* The attack upon Major E. was in the first place wanton, then throwing the authorship on a *diminutive blackguard printer,* that no one could notice, only with a cudgel—shows a meanness and cowardice, with all his boasted courage, that induces me to believe that he will not fight.[3] It may be—he may rather select me—as he may think that I will have nothing to do with him—and in this way get off—should he—(by way of example sake) just close with him—I then have a right to choice of distance—take him at seven feet—placed *back to back*—pistols suspended—until after the word fire—and I will soon put an end to this troublesome scoundrel—it is possible from what I have heard—that he may attempt to take this ground—and I charge you agree on my part without hesitation—he is a man I cannot challenge—but if a villain will run from one danger and hold out ideas of bravery—they ought always to be taken in. I pledge myself on the foregoing terms—if my pistol fires—I kill him—

A.J.

Copy, FHi (7-0651). Published in *The Collector* (April 1902):73–74 (7-0648).

1. Arrangements for the duel between John H. Eaton and Andrew Erwin had proceeded sporadically throughout August and September. Rumors in Shelbyville confirmed that Erwin, the challenged party, would select rifles or muskets. Eaton, however, was unskilled with these weapons.

2. The questions of weapons and the distance between the duelists eventually were submitted to the arbitration of William Carroll and William White, who decided each point in Erwin's favor; see James C. Bronaugh to AJ, [cSeptember 12].

3. Boyd McNairy acted as Erwin's second. The admission by Shelbyville *Tennessee Herald* editor Theodorick F. Bradford that he, rather than Erwin, had authored the offending attack against Eaton, apparently allowed both principals a graceful exit from their confrontation. The *Nashville Whig* of September 25 printed an announcement dated the previous day of the amicable settlement of the disagreement. See also Memorandum of a conversation between James L. Armstrong and Theodorick F. Bradford, September 26.

On November 30, 1818, the president submitted for ratification the Chickasaw Treaty negotiated the previous month by Jackson and Isaac Shelby. During the closed debate Tennessee Senator John Williams, Jackson's political opponent, circulated the rumor that the treaty's reservation of a salt lick along the Big Sandy branch of the Tennessee River had been either directly for Jackson's benefit or for that of a near relative (see AJ to William Williams, September 25, below; see also AJ to Joseph McMinn, August 20, Depositions of William B. Lewis, August 20, Richard K. Call, August 25, and Richard I. Easter, August 27, Robert Butler to AJ, August 23, and James C. Bronaugh to AJ, August 26). In truth, Jackson's friend William B. Lewis, present during the negotiations, had leased the salt lick from the Chickasaws, although apparently without Jackson's knowledge. The resulting embarrassment prompted the Senate to request the appointment of new commissioners whose sole objective would be the cession of the salt lick reserve. Although the president appointed John Overton, Newton Cannon, and Robert Weakley in February, the salt lick was not ceded to the United States until 1834.

Jackson paid little attention to the matter until Andrew Erwin's August 14 newspaper attack in the Shelbyville Tennessee Herald *(see above, AJ to Lewis, August 17). Almost immediately Jackson gathered his aides and advisors together at the Hermitage in order to prepare a report to the Ten-*

nessee legislature attesting to his disinterestedness regarding the salt lick reserve. The report (no version found), sent to Joseph McMinn about August 25, did not end the controversy, and Jackson seriously considered an addendum on the salt lick to his answer to the Lacock committee report (see AJ to John H. Eaton, November 29, below). The Nashville Whig *of December 22 printed several of the supporting depositions, attesting to Jackson's innocence. There the matter rested until Jesse Benton reopened the question in his 1824 anti-Jackson campaign pamphlet,* An Address to the People of the United States on the Presidential Election.

To Joseph McMinn

Private Hermitage 13th. Sept 1819

Sir

Your Letter of the 9th Int with its enclosure has been receved.[1] Your Idea that a submission of the secret Journal to the Legislature might be improper upon reflection meets my approbation. Secrecy was imposed on the Senate of the US by the President from an apprehension that its publicity might endanger the lives of certain chiefs; & on this a/c it yet continues necessary still to preserve that secrecy

I have altered the report heretofore made to you & request by the altered copy now returned to you, that you will cause the orriginal to be corrected.[2]

⟨Still⟩ you are at liberty should you in the progress of matters deem it advisable, to submit the secret Journal to any particular member or members that you might think could be safely confided in; or should their be a committee appointed on this Chickasaw business, to them, if you think proper, you can present it in confidence ⟨They however⟩ it is yielded, to be used as your own *safe discretion* may consider best

I shall be in Murfreesborough on Sunday night or Monday[3]—My old friend Colo [Robert] Hay[s] is about breathing his last, my attention is due to him—I am in haste your respectfully

A.J.

LS copy in John H. Eaton's hand with endorsement "Private" and final paragraph by AJ, DLC (27). Published in Bassett, 2:428–29 (extract).

1. See McMinn to AJ, September 9.

2. When McMinn submitted Jackson's report to the legislature on September 23 (together with a report of commissioners John Overton and Robert Weakley, and a letter from John Williams, none of which have been found), that body appointed a joint committee to investigate the matter. Although no record of the committee's decision has been found, the legislature's attitude may be inferred from two other actions: a series of resolutions (November 22) commending Jackson and Gaines for their actions in Florida, and a law prohibiting anyone from claiming land under the state's control that contained salt licks or springs.

3. Jackson attended the meeting of the Tennessee House on September 21, the second day of the legislative session.

To Andrew Jackson Donelson

Hermitage Sept. 17th. 1819

Dr. Andrew

Shortly after my last to you[1] in which I enclosed one hundred dollars, I was taken very ill & confined to my bed for ten days, on my recovery my attention was drew to the dying bed of Colo. Robert Hays, whose eyes I closed on the 14 & buried him on the 15th. instant.

I am fearfull my letter with the *$100* has not reached you, or I would have been in recpt of your letter acknowledging it.

I am waiting to hear from you before I attempt to make any farther remittance Eastern paper is not to be obtained here & there is no such thing as obtaining a draft on Philadelphia or Newyork—the merchants are offering as high as 13 percent premium, for Eastern paper or good drafts to make remittance with—even at this premium they cannot be had, I have got one hundred dollars which I mean to send you by mail as soon as I am advised that the other has reached you

I have recd a statement of the case of the cadets, & the committee of five who were selected to make known their grievances—I have gave it a carefull examination & perusal, and am happy to have it in my power to say that their conduct fully meets my approbation. They have displayed in the course of their procedure, a manly honourable feeling, with talents, which reflects upon them great credit. I regret much that when the court decided that it had not Jurisdiction, that it had not expressed their opinion of the honourable & proper conduct of the Cadets on this ocasion This I think was due to them, & would have operated as a salve to their feelings.[2]

Present me affectionately to Edward [G. W. Butler] My hand shakes from debility—& I cannot write with facility—I am anxious to hear from you both, & can find no excuse for your silence only that I see you are on duty in the field, and that you have been in the city of N. York. My letters may have reached West Point in your absence.

I think the treaty with Spain will not be ratified, whether war may grow out of it or not rest with the constituted authorities I suppose it will be regretted by them that the strong fortresses were so suddenly delivered to Spain, that will cost us much blood & treasure to regain them—I remonstrated with the executive on this subject, pointing out all the inconvenience that would result from this measure, and bringing to view the treachery of Spain all without effect[3]—if the treaty with Spain is not ratified, there is no honourable course for our Goverment but war—negotiation is at an end—& on the event of war we have again to reduce the Barancas & St Marks.

If war should result, it may afford a theatre for young enterprising men, should we be blessed with peace, I wish you out of the army untill you acquire a profession—I mean to resign in all December next, unless something intervenes that would make it dishonourable to withdraw, my health is gone, my constitution I fear will never bear up under another campaign—but should I take the field I shall want you with me—that under my eye you may gain a little experience when I retire I wish you as shortly thereafter to vissit me—& if you have finished your course of study at the military academy to resign. I have but one wish & that is to live untill I see you fairly in life as a professional man—

The distressed state of the mercantile world has introduced its effects every where—money has disappeared & brought the great mass of mankind into distress, from which there is no escape but ⟨by⟩ from industry *[& eco]*nomy;

I wish you to write me your w*[ishes]* as it respects your future course of study & of life—& when you think you can vissit me. your aunt & little Andrew requests to be affectionately named to you—all your friends enjoy health.

Accept my best wishes for your health & happiness & believe me to be your affectionate uncle & friend.

Andrew Jackson

ALS, DLC (7-0667).

1. See AJ to Donelson, August 6.

2. After Jackson had met the dismissed cadets in January, they were ordered to New York to await court-martial, but on May 29 the court refused to decide the case, claiming lack of jurisdiction (see Case file of Thomas Ragland et al., Court-Martial Case Files, Records of the Office of the Judge Advocate General, DNA-RG 153). The document concerning their case to which Jackson refers has not been identified, but the five cadets sent a memorial to the president sometime in August 1819 summarizing their situation and asking for a decision. It is possible that Jackson received a copy. Although Attorney General William Wirt concluded in late August that West Point cadets were subject to the military code, when the court reconvened in October it adhered to its disclaimer of jurisdiction (see above, AJ to Donelson, January 31).

3. See above, AJ to John C. Calhoun, August 10 and November 28, 1818; and to James Monroe, August 10 and December 7, 1818.

To John Clark

Nashville
August [September] 18th. 1819.

Dr Sir

I have the pleasure to acknowledge the recpt of your letter of the 18th ult.[1] it reached me in due course of mail, and found me Just recovering from a severe attack of sickness—By my aid de camp Capt Easter I should have wrote you—but the attention due to a dying friend prevented me—

but Capt Easter was charged to wait upon you, present my respects, and inform you the cause of the delay in my answer, which I hope he has done.[2]

I feel much indebted to you for the facts communicated, they shall be used with discretion, and I shall wait with anxiety for the recpt of the information promised and the copy of the pamphlet[3]—I send enclosed to your adress to Milledgeville a pamphlet lately published by a Citizen of Tennessee on the Seminole war[4]—It gives a condensed view of the documents that enables the reader to form a correct Judgt. for himself, the manner in which the official documents were published by Congress was intended by the opposition that they should not be understood, and the publick are indebted to Mr Adams Sec of State for the arangement of them as far as he had it in his power at the day he wrote to Mr Irwin our minister[5]—But I think this pamphlet by a citizen of Tennessee has placed the subject fairly before the public, and has aded a number of documents that was not before the public world before and places the wickedness of the majority of the committee who made the report to the Senate at the close of Congress in its true light.[6]

If any of the printers at Milledgeville would reprint the pamphlet ⟨there⟩ for the perquisites of the sale thereof, I know it would be gratefull to the author as well as myself—I believe it would open the eyes of the whole state of the abominable intrigue of Crawford, Clay, Cobb & Co, to sacrafice the man & men who had given peace to their butchered borders, from the ruthless hand of the savage to agrandize themselves—they Junto will be Hurled to ther native dung hill, nev*[er]* to rise again—

on the receipt of this I will be happy to hear from you, & receive your op*[inion]* of the merits of the pamphlet sent you I am Dr Sir with great respect yr mo. ob. serv

Andrew Jack*[son]*

ALS, TxU (7-0616). Postmarked "Sept 20." The reference to the death of Robert Hays suggests that this letter was actually written in September.

1. See Clark to AJ, August 18, 1819.

2. Richard I. Easter, ordered to Washington via Georgia to settle his accounts with the war department, left in early September, but failed to meet Clark (see Robert Butler to Daniel Parker, August 17, to Easter, August 22, and Easter to AJ, September 30).

3. Clark's letter of August 18, as well as an earlier one of May 24, reported William H. Crawford's revelation of the cabinet's division over Jackson's invasion of Florida in 1818 and over Jackson's arrest for insubordination. Additionally, Clark relayed rumors of the involvement of Crawford and David B. Mitchell in slave smuggling. Clark was preparing *Considerations on the Purity of the Principles of William H. Crawford, Esq. . . .* (Augusta, Ga., [1820]). See above, AJ to Clark, April 20; see also Clark to AJ, May 23, 1820, and AJ to Clark, November 23, 1820.

4. The pamphlet by "A Citizen of Tennessee" [John Overton], was *A Vindication of the Measures of the President and His Commanding Generals . . .* (Nashville), published in mid-September. Overton had also penned newspaper articles under the name "Aristides" defending Jackson's conduct (see *Nashville Whig*, January 16 and 30).

5. Adams defended Jackson in his letter to George W. Erving, then minister to Spain, November 28, 1818 (see above, James Monroe to AJ, December 21, 1818).

6. The pamphlet printed 41 documents in an appendix, many of which Jackson had solicited from interested parties throughout the spring and summer (see Joseph McMinn to AJ, April 6; Easter to AJ, April 21; Robert H. Dyer to AJ, May 21; Deposition of Arthur P. Hayne, June 12; Deposition of James Gadsden, June 30; Deposition of James C. Bronaugh, July 29; and Deposition of Richard K. Call, July 30).

From James Houston

Maryville Septr 24th 1819

Dear sir,

I have in Possession two negroes a son & daughter of old Peter that I am informed you own[1] the Girl has three verry likely children one Girl & two boys. Mr Saml Miller told me that you wanted the family all together & had authorised him to purchaise mine. My object is humanity & accomodation. If you still retain the idea of bringing the family together & appoint any Agent in this place you may have my negroes at a fair price[2] I am sir with sentiments of Respect yours &c

James Houston

ALS, DLC (27). Published in Bassett, 2:430. Endorsed by AJ: "Mr James Houstons letter to be answered on the subject of Peters children—answered 7th octbr. 1819." Houston (1757–c1830), a first cousin once removed of Samuel Houston, was a life-long resident of Maryville, representing Blount County in the first state legislature.

1. Old Peter has not been identified; his two children were Betsy (b. c1797) and Bob (b. c1801).

2. Samuel Miller has not been identified. Jackson's reply of October 7 (not found), evidently authorized Houston to secure an estimate of the slaves' value, which for Betsy (and her three children) and Bob was $1800 (see Houston to AJ, November 7). Jackson's endorsement on the November 7 letter is as follows: "answered 3rd Decbr that if funds could be raised I would take them—an answer final as soon as I could hear from Florence." The December 3 letter has not been found, nor is it known whether Jackson reunited this slave family.

To William Williams

Sept. 25th. 1819.

Dr. Sir

Having made a report to the Governor concerning the Chikesaw treaty & the reservation of the salt spring; accompanying the same with documents to shew that the statement made by Colo. John Williams in the Senate of the u States were false, malicious, and without the slitest foundation

This report is laid before the assembly, & in conjunction with a communication that I am Just informed Colo. Williams has made to the assembly through the Governor may lead to some discussion, I take the liberty for your information, to state his conduct in the last Congress, referring you to Doctor Hogg & Major Eaton for the truth of this statement[1]—I have no doubt but you have seen the report of the Committee of the Senate with its accompanying documents, as I am informed & believe Colo. John Williams gave to the members on that committee information that I was one of the company who had invested large sums in the purchase of real property in Pensacola, and in order to enhance the vallue of my Property, And without any real necessity, in open violation of the constitution, had marched my army there & seized the place—to Establish this fact my staff were summoned, before said committee, and Colo Butler interr*[o]*gated by them on this head—finding themselves disappointed and being informed by Major Eaton one of the committee, that they were badly informed that it was Mr James Jackson of Nashville that he ⟨Major Eaton⟩ was one of the company & he did know I had no interest in the purchase nor was I one of the company, nor had I ever been—[2]

On that committee was Mr Laccock, Mr. Burrill Major Forsythe—Mr King of Newyork, & Major Eaton—the three first named were for making an unfavourable report, respecting me, they two latter were opposed to such report, Major Forsythe was appointed minister to Spain, and left the committee precisely divided on this question

Colo. Williams Knowing that Mr King of Newyork was opposed to the wicked designs against me—in order to gain him over, and poison his mind against me, communicates to him in confidence, that I had made the reservation of the salt lick in the chikesaw treaty for my self, and that the Ink had not dried on the treaty before I had obtained a lease for it—This came to the ears of Doctor Hogg, who made it known to Major Eaton who adressed a Note to Mr King on the subject which he handed to him in the Senate chamber—Mr King after reading the note said the information was communicated in confidence, he would see the Gentleman and give him an answer—Mr King stepped to Colo. Williams Took him by the arm walked him across the room and after conversing some time, returned & said to Major Eaton, the Gentleman who gave the information requested him to say, that he hoped there would be no fuss made about this thing, that he was mistaken, that it was not Genl Jackson that had leased the lick, but a near relation of ⟨mine⟩ his—I ought to have remarked that when Mr King first spoke of it he said he had been informed by a member of congress from Tennessee—Altho Colo. Williams did know as well as I did that Major Lewis was no relation of mine—still he made this Statement altho he knew it to be false, to carry with it the Idea that if I had not procured it for myself, that I had for my relation—When he did know I had not a relation in america except by marriage.[3]

Colo. Williams being here disappointed—& the house of representatives in congress having approved by a large majority my conduct on the Seminole campaign. This combination of enemies of their country, composed of Clay, Crawford, Williams & Co—fell to work to devise something that would if possible counteract the vote of the house of representatives in Congress. The committee of the Senate was Sugested, but to enable it to act another member must be added who would foster their views, & make such a report as would be acceptable to the combination—Mr Laccock made the motion that a member should be added to fill the place of Mr Forsythe—they had the member Selected, Mr. Epps—This motion was opposed by Mr King and Major Eaton—the question was carried by a majority of one vote—when Mr Eppes was nominated by Mr Laccock, and Mr [Jeremiah] Morrow by Mr King—and Mr Epps was elected by a majority of one vote, Mr Williams voting for Mr Eppes[4]—In the mean time as I am informed Mr Wm H Crawford was engaged drawing up the report on the information of Colo. Williams—which was approved by Mr Epps, as he says without examination—This gives a clue to its varying from the testimony as the object of Crawford & Williams was reguardless of the means employed if they could to Tarnish my reputation by the report. I make this Statement to you that the assembly may Judge at a proper time, how far such conduct of Mr Williams their Senator is consistant with their Ideas of Justice & propriety, and at a proper period as soon as the election for Senator is over that the assembly if it chooses may employ a corrective.[5] The statement in my report as far as it relates to the information given by Colo. Williams to Colo. King of my having reserved & leased the salt lick my self is set forth in the precise words given by Mr King to Major Eaton, & from him to me—Therefore Major Eaton I refer to, & Doctor Hogg can give a full detail of the Colo. Conduct on the subject of the chikesaw treaty—When you come to Contrast the chikesaw treaty with the late Cherokee, which Colo. Williams advised and has so loudly extolled for its benefits—you will find, 1rst. that 12 miles Square (worth at least a million) is reserved to be sold for the benefit of that part of the cherokee nation remaining East of the Mississippi (as a dower I suppose to keep them here) many other reservations of iron works &c &c—and twenty one six hundred & forty acres of land within the State of Tennessee long since Known to be patented by Colo. Williams[6]—why then has the Colo vociferated so loudly against the reservation of the *bubble—the salt lick*—and extolled the other—because he expected he could injure me thereby—and it is believed that many of his friends (not relations) are interested, and that the reservations was the property of those he wished to injure—Such as Capt Thos. N[orris] Clark, Mr McCampbell &c &c—I am Told that he has in his communication complained that the commissioners has not in the terms of the reservation secured the public against the high prices of salt, inasmuch as they commissioners has only extended the limitation of the price of salt within the reservation—Is it Possible that this Senator is so *profoundly ignorant* as not to know that the commissioners has no power to controll the price of salt beyond the limits of the reservation nor is it believed that the President & Congress have this right—if they have, how *criminally remiss* in his duty to the interest of the Public has Colo. Williams been in not regulating the price of salt made at the u States Saline, and other places, and why did not the Colo. attach a

⟨line or⟩ clause to the ratification of the chikesaw treaty regulating the price of the salt made at this lick every where it was transported to; if Congress had such power; and surely it will not be contended by Colo. Williams that the President can, (under the treaty making power) delegate to commissioners, greater powers than both he & Congress can exercise under the constitution. I have barely made this remarks that you may fully understand, Colo. Williams conduct, and give you a clue to the object of Colo. Williams views in his communication to your body through the Govr. He wishes to injure the Election of Major Eato*[n]* knowing that my answer to the report of the Senate will bring out things unpleasant to himself, and he wishes to avoid the comments that will be made by Major Eaton on that subject, & to have one chosen whose disposition he can wield to his own *views*.[7] I am sir respectfully yr mo. ob. servt.

Andrew Jackson

ALS, THi (7-0681). Transmitted by "Colo. Edward Ward." Published in Bassett, 2:430–32. Williams (1776–1862), a Nashville lawyer, represented Davidson County in the state legislature, 1819–21, and served on the joint committee investigating the Chickasaw salt lick reserve.

1. John Williams's letter has not been found.

2. John H. Eaton had testified before the Lacock committee that he, together with James Jackson and the general's nephew John Donelson, Jr., among others, had purchased lots in Pensacola during the fall of 1817. Eaton maintained, however, that the general was not involved directly or indirectly in the activity (see above, John McCrea to AJ, April 15; Depositions of Eaton, [cFebruary 24], *ASP, Military Affairs,* 1:751, and of Robert Butler, [cMarch 1] and March 3; and Deposition of Thomas Childress, January 12, 1820, below).

3. Jackson's disclaimer of relations "except by marriage" is curious. While most of those he considered family were kin of his wife, Jackson was also related to William W. Crawford (the overseer for Andrew J. Hutchings's Alabama plantation) and Andrew Jackson Crawford, sons of James Crawford, Jr. (d. 1816), his first cousin, with whom he had had land dealings. James Crawford, Jr., was the son of Jenny Hutchinson Crawford, the sister of Jackson's mother. See AJ to John Coffee, January 4 (above), and William McCully to AJ, September 29, 1821; AJ to Andrew J. Crawford, May 1, 1833; and [James Crawford] to AJ, [n.d.] (DLC-60).

4. After a lengthy debate in which Eaton attempted to prevent the substitution appointment (thereby deadlocking the committee), the Senate elected John Wayles Eppes to the vacancy, Morrow (1771–1852) of Ohio voting against.

5. Eppes's addition to the committee only a week before it issued its report, together with his opposition to the invasion of Florida, greatly angered Jackson, and in an incident denied in 1828 by pro-Jackson forces, only the intervention of Commodore Stephen Decatur in early March 1819 prevented the general from carrying out a threat to cut off Eppes's ear. Reportedly, John Williams took the threat so seriously that he armed himself to protect his Virginia colleague from an anticipated assault, and Ninian Edwards of Illinois had feared that Jackson would follow Eppes home after Congress adjourned in order to challenge him.

6. John C. Calhoun concluded a treaty with the Cherokee Nation on February 27, in Washington, D.C. The first article reserved a twelve-square-mile tract in northern Alabama Territory, southeast of Huntsville, for a Cherokee school fund. Thirty-one separate, 640-acre reserves were made in the treaty's third article, of which twenty lay within Tennessee.

7. Williams had generally favored the terms of the Cherokee treaty negotiated by Calhoun, and introduced the resolution for ratification. Clark, a resident of Kingston, was an old friend and sometime business partner of Jackson's. Jackson possibly referred to John McCampbell

(d. c1821), who had served as U.S. district attorney for East Tennessee from 1810. The United States Saline, located between the mouths of the Wabash and Saline rivers in present Gallatin County, Illinois, supplied salt for the upper Ohio River valley, including western Tennessee. Although Article 4 of the 1818 Chickasaw treaty set the price of salt from the reserve at $1.00 per bushel of 50 pounds, that price applied only within the four-square-mile reserve itself. William B. Lewis's lease of the salt lick, and subsequent control of the price of salt, was Williams's stated reason for opposition in a letter to John Overton of January 15 (THi). Jackson was undoubtedly correct, however, in viewing Williams's opposition as potentially damaging to Eaton's political fortune, as the legislature also was preparing at this time to elect a permanent successor to George W. Campbell's senate seat.

On September 24 John H. Eaton and Andrew Erwin settled their dispute and called off their duel, but the settlement did not calm Jackson's anger toward his Shelbyville nemesis, for Jackson had learned that Erwin was seeking the federal marshal's post for West Tennessee (see James C. Bronough to AJ, cSeptember 12). Fearing the appointment of a Crawfordite and personal enemy, Jackson sought to kill Erwin's chances by informing the president about Erwin's involvement in the David B. Mitchell slave smuggling incident (see above, AJ to John Clark, April 20; Clark to AJ, August 18; and AJ to James Monroe, September 29, below).

But the Erwin family's involvement in slave smuggling may have been more extensive than even Jackson suspected. John Clark's investigation of Mitchell, aimed at embarrassing Mitchell's patron William H. Crawford, eventually revealed the indirect connection of Andrew Erwin, his son and partner James (1796–1851), and their joint partner Jared Ellison Groce (1782–1836) in the nefarious business. In August 1817 James Erwin, managing the Savannah firm of Erwin, Groce & Company, lent $25,000 dollars to William Bowen, Mitchell's employee at the Creek Agency, supposedly for the purchase of coffee and sugar at the Spanish-patriot-controlled Amelia Island. Instead, Bowen bought about one hundred African slaves captured from the Spanish ship Isabelita *and declared forfeit by the island's rump government. Violating federal law, Bowen brought the slaves into the United States, housing them with Mitchell's approval at the Creek Agency from December 1817 until early February 1818. At that time Groce, acting on directions from Andrew Erwin, went to the Agency to secure the $25,000 debt, and ended up taking forty-seven of the Africans with him to Alabama as a "mortgage." On the way, he was intercepted by the inspector of the revenue from Darien, Georgia, arrested, and the slaves seized; the ensuing court battles over ownership of the Africans lingered into the 1820s, rising as high as the U.S. Supreme Court. Perhaps not coincidentally, the Erwins' merchant business in Georgia collapsed just a month later in March 1818, and Andrew Erwin and his family relocated to Shelbyville, Tennessee, in April. Although the Erwins and Groce constantly maintained their innocence, Attorney General William Wirt's 1821 report concluded otherwise, leading to Mitchell's dismissal as Creek agent* *and labeling Groce (who emigrated to Texas in 1822) as a direct and the Erwins as indirect collaborators in the smuggling adventure. Brought to full light in 1822 when Wirt's report was published, the slave smuggling charge followed Andrew Erwin throughout the remainder of his life. An 1823 request to Wirt for review and exoneration of the Erwins was refused, and when the charge surfaced again in 1828 in the pro-Jackson Washington* United States' Telegraph, *it prompted Andrew Erwin to take the lead in the Tennessee opposition to Jackson's presidential candidacy.*

Jackson's letter to Monroe, below, marked the first time that Jackson escalated his heretofore personal and legal conflict with Erwin to the national political arena, confirming a rift that divided Tennessee politics for the next fifteen years.

To James Monroe

Hermitage Near Nashville
(Private) Sept. 29th 1819.

Sir

In my last to you on the subject of a fit person to fill the office of Marshall of west Tennessee,[1] I stated that as Early as I could I would enclose you a copy of a letter from a Gentleman of high standing in the State of Georgia—In compliance with that promise I herewith enclose a copy of that letter. I trust it will aid you, in forming a correct opinion of things as they *are* and give a clue by which the person combinding to violate the laws of the united States, by the purchase of african slaves at amelia Island and introducing them into the united States may be discovered. I have no doubt but the public weal requires that this subject should be investigated, that an end may be put to such violent outrages of the law and morallity & officers of the Government if concerned in this inhuman & illegal traffic may be dismissed from office & legally punished. you will see that the writer permits the letter to be used as my discretion may direct. I submit it to you for your information & to be used as you may Judge right in bringing to light this transaction.[2]

In addition to the information which the copy of the letter enclosed will furnish, which is marked no 1—I am advised by a Gentleman who wishes his name not to be mentioned that by calling on Colo. Gideon Morgan of the cherokee Nation & Colo. Andrew Erwin now of this state & who is now a candidate for the Marshalls office for West Tennessee, will prove positively that Genl Mitchell did purchase by his agent who he had furnished with funds for that purpose a large number of african Negroes at amelia Island, which were brought through the Indian Country to the agency. My informant states that care must be taken, in putting the Interrogatories so that the witnesses Colo. Morgan & Erwin may not object, as the answers might implicate themselves, they both being engaged in the purchase of africans at amelia Island at or about that time, Mr Gross was the partner of Colo. Erwin about that time & it was to this same Mr Gross that the agent Genl Mitchell gave the passport under which he proceeded to carry his Negroes through the Creek nation to the Allabama Territory.

I would here remark that the deposition of Genl David Merryweather of Georgia might throw some light on this subject, disclosing the manner & under what circumstances the agency was given to Govr. Mitchel by Wm H. Crawford then Sec of War. I will here give you a substantial detail of the circumstances as related by Genl Merryweather to myself & staff at the cherokee treaty in 1817. as far as my recollection serves me it was as follows—"That Wm H Crawford met with him in the fall 1816 in the state of Georgia, and recommended him to accept of the agency to the creek nation—the Genl replied he had determined to retire from public life—Mr. C replied that this office would enable him to educate the younger branch of his family without infringing on his little Estate &c &c &c—the Genl observed that he would reflect on the subject and advise him of his ultimate determination—Genl Mitchell then Govr. of Georgia met with Genl Merryweather Joined his solicitations to that of Mr Crawford that he would accept the agency & urging the same reasons why he should accept as Mr Crawford had done—Genl Merryweather replied he would think on the subject, consult his family and then determine on the subject—after consulting with his family, he determined he would accept the appointment and wrote accordingly to Mr Crawford that he had concluded to accept the appointment of agent &c &c In the mean time Congress had passed a law appropriating $85,000 to pay the friendly Creeks for the depredations committed on them by the red sticks, which was to pass through the hand of the agent, and be distributed by him—on the receipt of Genl Merryweathers letter Mr Crawford replied expressing great regret that his letter had not reached him sooner as three days (or thereabout) before its receipt he had filled up an appointmt. for & forwarded it to Genl Mitchell then Govr of Georgia—Whether Govr Mitchell was an applicant for said office is not known, suffice it to know that he resigned & accepted the appointment, & recd. the $85.000, of which there is so much said both by the Indians & whites, and if rumor is true was a fund from which the store was Established in the nation and so many african negroes were bought—The statement of Colo. Brearly to me at Ft Hawkins was full on these points—I enclose a copy of the memorandum then made. I saw Colo. Brearly last Spring at Trenton—I then asked him how it happened that he had not in his Depositions spoke to all the points named to me at Ft Hawkins, he replied the Interrogatories did not require him & he did not believe he was bound to answer beyond them—but if I required he would forward to me his deposition embracing all these points in his relation to me & staff on the 10th. & 11th. February 1818—I therefore enclose it, that Colo. Brearly may be interrogated on those points his Deposition does not include[3]—I do think this is a subject that ought to be investigated—

From the Gentleman who has recommended Colo Gideon Morgan & Andrew Erwin to be interrogated &c &c—I learn that there are letters in the possession of a Gentleman of high standing in this state, that if I can get them will unfold compleatly the combination of Crawford, Clay, Cobb, Williams & Co the extent & precise views of the combination. I have no doubt but I can prove, notwithstanding Mr C. pledge to you & the declaration of the baseness of the man that could thus act, that he Mr Crawford is this base man having been guilty of this base act—I named to you that Doctor Hogg stated to me at next Congress there would be a caucus to endeavour to raise Crawford up again—Colo. John Williams silently & under the rose has been at work for a long time—he has been using this same Andrew Erwin as a tool—Colo Cannon in this way was brought forward & has been elected—& Colo. Erwin is now in the same way endeavouring to get the Marshalls office. the cunning of Colo A. Erwin aided & abetted by Mr [Henry] Crabb atto. Genl of the u States for West Tennessee, produced the plan of Silently applying to the members of the Legislature for a recommendation many of whom before it was known publickly ⟨had⟩ it being presented had signed it, as soon as it was known a counter recommendation for Genl [Robert] Purdy was set on foot, and a majority of the Legislature that would sign for Either signed the recommendation for Genl Purdy, one of the members as soon as he heard Genl Purdy was a candidate went to Colo A. Erwin and had his named erased from his paper—with such unprincipled men it is hard to compete—and let me say to you again *that the old leaven is not dead, it only Sleepeth.*[4] It is true I believe that the Junto cannot make much head against you—But should you appoint Colo Andrew Erwin, a Bankrupt Merchant, a man with out principle, and a tool to your enemies—believe me when I tell you, it will arouse the feelings of the people of the west part of Tennessee against you, lessen your popularity, and the appointment of Erwin will strengthen your enemies. I have used candeur in my former letters to you, and I hope this will reach you before you make the appointment of Marshall—Capt [Samuel B.] Marshall is a high minded honest and honourable man—Genl Purdy has great claims from length of Service, he is honest, poor & unencumbered, Mr [Thomas H.] Fletcher is a broken merchant, high toned Federalist & supported Cannons election—Doctor [Roger B.] Sappington is a honest Republican, poor and whether involved in the prevailing wreck I cannot say[5]—Colo. A. Erwin is a Bankrupt both in property & Charector, and strongly attached to your worst enemies, and in the man no confidence ought to be reposed out of these you can make a good choice that will give satisfaction to the State, and security to the honest creditors of other states. Present me respectfully to your lady & family, and believe me to be respectfully yr mo. ob. serv.

Andrew Jackson

ALS, NN (7-0689); ALS draft, DLC (27). Published in Bassett, 2:433–37.

1. John Childress, marshall for West Tennessee since 1803, had died on September 10. See AJ to Monroe, September 10 and 22.

2. Jackson enclosed John Clark to AJ, August 18.

3. Jackson was referring to the act for the relief of certain Creek Indians, March 3, 1817 (6 *U.S. Statutes at Large* 191). The enclosure was the Statement of David Brearley, February 10, 1818. See also the interrogatories and reply, enclosed in Edmund P. Gaines to AJ, November 20, 1818.

4. The "Gentleman of high standing" has not been identified. Crabb (1793–1827) was U.S. district attorney for West Tennessee from 1818 until 1827, when he was appointed to the state supreme court. Purdy (d. 1831) received Monroe's appointment as district marshal, serving until his death. Andrew Erwin's son John Patton Erwin (1795–1857) had married John Williams's sister Fanny in 1815. Newton Cannon had been elected to Congress the previous month, representing Davidson County. Jackson's reference, also made in his letter to Monroe of September 13, was probably to 1 Corinthians 5:8, "Therefore, let us keep the feast, not with old leaven, neither with the leaven of malice and wickedness, but with the unleavened bread of sincerite and trueth."

5. Marshall was the son-in-law of Childress and the administrator of Childress's estate; Jackson appointed him marshal in 1831. Fletcher (1792–1845), a Nashville merchant until the Panic of 1819, became a lawyer, serving in the Tennessee legislature, and as secretary of state, 1830–32. Sappington (d. c1824), the son of Dr. Mark Sappington, was one of four brothers trained in medicine. Sappington also was actively involved in horse breeding and racing.

To Robert Young Hayne

Hermitage near Nashville
Octb. 2nd. 1819

Dear Colo.

I had the pleasure of receiving your much Esteemed favour of the 13th. ult. from Lexington Ky. and much regret the misfortune of our friend Doctor Simmons, but am much gratified to learn that he is fast recovering of the injury he received.[1]

I anticipated your dislike to the society of the Shakers—reason revolts at such an asociation, and it is evident that the god who rules the universe never intended to put an end to the world of mankind, in that way.[2]

I sincerely regret, the malancholoy information you have recd from Charleston, which hasten your departure from Kentuckey, as you had found some gratification from vissitting the mamouth cave. I am certain you would have been much gratified with a vissit to the big bone & mud licks, but certainly you are right to hasten to the superintendance of those dear relatives, & friends that look to you in time of peril[3]—I trust Sir that you will find them protected & preserved by the great *I am*—who is able to give health in the greatest perils, and protect from the greatest calamities. I have Just heard from our friend Colo A. P. Hayne[4]—he does not enjoy as good health as I could wish him, but his amiable little family are well, his eldest daughter had been a little unwell but has recovered. I would to god he could enjoy as much good health & happiness as I wish him.

By the mail that carries this I send you a pamphlet on the Seminole war, "*By a citizen of Tennessee*" I wish you to read it with attention, and give me your opinion of its merits or demerits. Should your Judgt. approve, and any printer in the city of Charleston will republish it, for the sale thereof, it will be gratefying not only to the author but myself, it is the only way that the public can become acquainted with the facts, and the wikedness of the triumvirate of the committee of the Senate, who composed the majority thereof & made the report.

I am informed & believe that Wm H. Crawford wrote the report on the information of Colo. John Williams Senator from Tennessee and, ⟨accounts⟩, the committee of the Senate reported it without the examination or consideration—and in part accounts for the gross falshoods it contains, it was the intention of the grand mover behind the scene that this report should counteract the vote of the house of representatives in congress—and the Junto was in hopes it never would be investigated, but if there is any Justice or Virtue in the Senate of the u States, (and I trust there is) I will have it brought up at the next session of Congress. I will present such a case before them by proof, that Justice to injured innocence will compell them to act. Present me respectfully to Doctor Simmons, & be pleased to let him have a perusal of the pamphlet—Mrs. J. Joins me in good wishes to you & Doctor Simmons and believe me to be with sincere reguard your mo. ob. Servt.

Andrew Jackson

ALS, NcD (7-0698).

1. Letter not found. Possibly William H. Simmons, a Charleston native, who moved to St. Augustine, Florida, in mid-1821 and served on the territorial legislative council, 1823–24. See Hayne to AJ, November 10.

2. Jackson and President Monroe had visited the Shaker settlement at South Union, Kentucky, in mid-June while on their way to Lexington.

3. An outbreak of yellow fever prompted Hayne's abrupt return to Charleston. Mammoth Cave is located approximately 28 miles east-northeast of Bowling Green, Kentucky; Big Bone Lick, in Boone County, northern Kentucky, is famous for its deposits of mammoth fossils. Mudlick is located in Monroe County, Kentucky.

4. Letter not found.

To John Brown (1779–1843)

Hermitage near Nashville
Octbr. 8th 1819.

Dr. Sir

Yours of the 25th. ult is Just received[1] and that you may correct the Egregious Error which you have fallen into I hasten to reply—I well recollect on my return from the city last spring the conversation that Took place between you & myself relative to the conduct of Colo. John William towards me, during the last session of congress, and I also recollect your wishes as well as desire expressed of bringing about ⟨friendship⟩ a reconciliation between us—to which I ⟨reiterated⟩ as well recollect I replied that his late as well as former conduct towards me required explanation & reparation his late attempt in the Senate to injure me, by secretly diseminating the basest falshoods, (that I had reserved the salt spring in the late chikesaw purchase for myself & had leased it before the Ink was dry upon the treaty &c &c)—& that I was engaged in large speculations in Pensacola—&c &c which he intended as a vital stab to my reputation ⟨and that friendship never could exist or be restored untill and⟩ notwithstanding at my age I had a wish to be in friendship with all the world—⟨still⟩ I never could be friendly with Colo. Williams untill a full explanation and compleat satisfaction for the injury he had attempted to do me during the last session of congress was made—I cannot forsee from the conversation that passed between us how you have fell into the Error you have done and which you have expressed when you say in your letter that my reply was that you might say to Colo. Williams I had no wish to remain unfriendly with him—unless you mean to convay the Idea, that I was axiously waiting, a fit opportunity to have the necessary explanation with him, and thereby put an end to the differrence that existed between us ⟨by his accusations, injuries various attemps secretly to injure me by circulating the basest falshoods⟩ If this is your meaning, you might have inferred it from our conversation, but that I did, or ever intended to say to you that I was willing to become friends with Colo. Williams without his first making a satisfactory explanation of ⟨the⟩ and attonement for his conduct in the various attempts it is alledged he has made to injure me is incorrect—

⟨And⟩ As I allways despised duplicity in others and never have practised it myself I have to request that you, without delay make known to Colo. Williams this mistake you have fell into and & explain to him that I never can become friendly with him, untill this explanation does take plaice; that had it not have been for the *cry of the military power bearing down the civil,* even where a military man is only defending himself this explanation would have been long since called for, and if Colo. Williams will say to me senatorial priviledges aside, ⟨we will soon be friends⟩ we will soon put an end to our dispute I will place before him ⟨the information of⟩ the injuries he has attempted to heap upon me, and the attonement necessary to made, provided he admits the facts, or I ⟨am able to⟩ substantiating them—should he refuse to do this I may ⟨be must⟩ yet a little be compelled to bear with the injury untill I can with honor retire ⟨from my office⟩ to private life & lay down my commission—Then having all the rights of a citizen, I can ⟨a right to⟩ protect my reputation without the *cry of military usurpation*—I have to ⟨ask of you⟩ repeat the request that you without delay, ⟨to⟩ make known to Colo. Williams the mistake you have been under in the communication you have made to him as detailed in your letter of the 25th. of Sept. last as I do positively deny having ever gave you such authority—

Blessed is the peace maker, but even in the terms of the Scriptures, where one injureth another he must make reparation before forgiveness & friendship can be restored—and I sincerely regret ⟨without applying bad motives to you that you⟩ that your zeal to restore friendship should have ⟨fallen⟩ lead you into so great a mistake as the one commented on—I am with due respect yr mo. ob. Serv.

Andrew Jackson

P.S. I shall expect to hear from you on the recpt of this, & that you have ⟨have corrected the mistake with⟩ made the communication requested to Colo. Williams—[2]

ALS draft, DLC (27). Published in Bassett, 2:437–38. Brown, a resident of Kingston and the sheriff of Roane County, had commanded East Tennessee militia units during the War of 1812.

1. See Brown to AJ, September 25.

2. Brown subsequently apologized for misunderstanding Jackson's intention (see Brown to AJ, October 16).

From John Overton

Travellers Rest 21st October 1819

Dear Genl.

Meeting with Dinwiddie yesterday on his way to Huntsville I have thought it probable you would be there, and therefore take the liberty of asking you to do me a favor

Capt Brahan owes me $792.50 on a note payl. in the Huntsville Bank—Will you take it over and lodge it in Bank, and let Brahan know it is there. The breaking of people in our Town, has left me Scarce of money, and obliges me to look for the collection of this note

Please tell Brahan of this, and *[of]* my necessity

If he *[ca]*nnot pay, probably he may w*[ant]* me to take a Negroe boy or two—The money wd suit me best, but will take one or two likely healthy boys of 12 or 13 years of age at such price as you may think they are worth in Cash, and as you would trade for yourself[1]

I left Murfreesbo yesterday Every thing is going on well—The resolutions I saw and approve of them—passed unanimously in the H. R, and will so pass in the Senate—probably with an absentee—but that you nor I care nothing about[2] Resply yrs. &c

J*[o]*hn Overton

ALS, THi (7-0721). Sent by "Mr Lawrence."

1. Jackson left the following day for northern Alabama and an inspection tour of the military road. See Bill of Sale of John Brahan to Overton, November 9.

2. On October 16 the Tennessee House of Representatives passed five resolutions commending Jackson, Edmund P. Gaines and the 1818 invasion of Florida, voting a sword of honor to the two generals, and instructing Tennessee's senators to oppose any congressional measure critical of the Florida enterprise. The Senate agreed to all except the resolution of instruction, and on November 22 the House acceded.

From Thomas Jefferson

Monticello Nov. 22. [1819]

Th: Jefferson returns his thanks to General Jackson for the copy he has been so good as to send him of the Vindication of the proceedings in the Seminole war.[1] if doubts on these proceedings have existed in candid minds this able vindication can scarcely fail to remove them. in addition to what had before been laid before the public, it brings forward some new views, and new facts also, of great weight. on the whole he cannot doubt but that the gratitude of his country for former atchievements will be fortified by these new proofs of the salutary energies of their great benefactor. he salutes the General with assurances of his constant & affectionate attachment & high respect.

AL, NjP (7-0878); AL copy, DLC (mAJs); Copy (dated 1820), DLC (7-0880). Published in *Pittsburgh Mercury,* July 24, 1827.

1. *A Vindication of the Measures of the President and His Commanding Generals,* by [John Overton]. See above, AJ to John Clark, [September] 18; and AJ to William B. Lewis, January 25.

The Adams-Onís Treaty, signed on February 22 and ratified by the Senate on February 24, required the United States and Spain to exchange ratifications within six months. As the August 22 deadline approached, it became apparent that Spanish ratification would be delayed. The cession of American claims to Texas had already prompted criticism from some west-

erners (see AJ to John C. Calhoun, July 24), and although he supported the treaty, Jackson was not sanguine about Spanish intentions (see AJ to Calhoun, August 24, and above, to George Gibson, September 7, and to Andrew J. Donelson, September 17). President Monroe, barely rested from his four-month tour of the South and West, returned to Washington in August to meet with his cabinet advisers, and on August 23 Secretary of State John Q. Adams advised the American ministers in Europe that the United States considered Spain in breach of its obligation to ratify and would, with the concurrence of Congress, immediately occupy the Floridas. When Spain had not ratified nor responded to the American dispatch by November, Monroe and the cabinet, preparing the annual message to Congress, agreed to ask for authorization to take possession of the Floridas (see below, James Monroe to AJ, December 12), and chief clerk Christopher Vandeventer, acting secretary of war, began issuing the necessary orders.

From Christopher Vandeventer

(Confidential)

Department of War,
22d. Novemr. 1819.

Sir,

The return of the Secretary of War, to, the seat of government being delayed by his illness,[1] the President directs me to say to you, that it is possible a rapid military movement, will be ordered upon Florida soon after the meeting of Congress. Preparatory to which, he directs that you hold the troops under your command in readiness for such service.

Should the movement be sanctioned by Congress, the Light Artillery and 2d. Regiment of Infantry will be marched from the North Division; the former may be embarked at Boston; and the latter, now at Sackett's Harbor and Plattsburg, may be concentrated at New York for embarkation, at the shortest notice. It may, therefore, enter into your views of operation, to concentrate the disposable force of the South Division, upon some point near the Alabama, and leave the reduction of East Florida, to the troops which may reinforce your Command from the North Division.

Believing such a disposition would facilitate successful operations in that quarter, with the least delay, after the final order for the occupancy of Florida may be given, orders have been transmitted to Major Genl. Gaines, to move the troops of the 4th. & 7th. regiments of Infantry, now at Trader's Hill and Vicinity, to the respective Head Quarters of their regiments, unless, in his opinion, powerful reasons forbid it, before the arrival of the reinforcements from the North.

A copy of this letter, with corresponding orders, have been forwarded to Generals Brown and Gaines, to enable them to effect the preparatory measures contemplated in this arrangement. The final order for a movement will be determined by intelligence from the American Minister at Madrid, which is daily expected by the return of the Hornet.[2] I have the honor to be Your most Obt. Servt.

C. Vandeventer
Chief Clerk

LS, DLC (28); LC and Copies, DNA-RG 107 (M7-1, M222-1, 7-0883, -0885, mAJs); Copies, DNA-RG 94 (7-0888, -0892). Published in *Calhoun Papers,* 4:426–27.

1. John C. Calhoun had left Washington for South Carolina in late September. On his return trip in November he suffered an attack of bilious fever which, turning into a "typhus type," nearly killed him. He did not reach Washington until about December 6 and did not resume full duties until the twentieth of that month.

2. Traders Hill is located on the St. Marys River in Charlton County, Georgia. Dispatches from John Forsyth and other American ministers in Europe arrived in Washington on November 25. The combined import of this intelligence caused Monroe to alter his request for authority to occupy Florida, making it contingent upon the arrival of a new Spanish minister sent to discuss problems and seek clarification of the Adams-Onís Treaty. Vandeventer enclosed copies of his letters to Edmund P. Gaines and to Jacob J. Brown, both November 22. The sloop-of-war *Hornet,* a 440-ton, 18-gun vessel built in 1805, was lost off Tampico in 1829.

To John Henry Eaton

Nashville Novbr. 29th. 1819

Dr. Sir

This will be handed you by Doctor Brunaugh who will also hand you my answer to the report of a majority of the Senate on the *Seminole War,* with such documents as is thought relevant to that subject.[1]

You will find by way of postscript to my answer the Subject of the reserve, & lease of the Salt spring noticed. and the certificates of Doctor Brunaugh & Capts Call, Easter, the stament of Colo. Butler, & Major Wm. B. Lewis—& the certificates of [George] Bell, [Boyd] McNairy & Capt [Thomas] Eastland forwarded with the other Documents. Although the majority of the committee, does not notice this subject in the report, still, as it originated, ⟨in and⟩ with one of the Senators, and communicated to Mr King one of the committee, as it is believed to poison his mind against me, and to procure if possible his vote of censure, well knowing that he approbated the measures adopted in the prosecution of the Seminole War, and particularly as the committee have arraigned my motives as a public officer—I have thought it proper to lay these documents before the Senate—however you will see, that, it is annexed to the answer on a seperate sheet, that if you & my friends should think it improper to be annexed that it can be seperated, and the P. S. used as a preface to the publication of the documents as you may Judge best—or used in any way that you and my friends may think proper so that Congress may see them & Judge of the motives and actions of Colo. John Williams & others.[2] There can be no question but it is proper that the Senate & house of representatives should see them & the world in some shape or other—in this, thing there was much depravity & malevolence in its author, that the world ought to see—so soon as I can with propriety, The honourable member shall be accountable to me, but in the mean time the Senate & house of representatives ought to be informed on this subject.

I wish you to Consult Mr Crittendon & others that you may have confidence in on this subject; what you may do will be approved by me—[3]

My friend Judge Overton has thought it improper that I should condecend to put in an answer at all—I have thought differrently, believing, when ever ⟨a⟩ this subject is touched, it ought to be fully and effectually answered so that the weakest capacity that reads may understand—The answer is drew with Christian mildness, brings before the reader the facts, and a referrence to the documents prove them—The letter recommended by Judge Overton as a Substitute and herewith enclosed may serve the learned, and the man of research, but would not be understood or perhaps read but by few—I there fore prefer the answer But enclose the letter for your and Mr Crittendons consideration & determination—being on the ground you can better Judge.

I send on the documents eranged to be annexed to and presented with the answer as lettered—unless upon reading the answer another erangement should be preferred.

Should it so happen that you Should prefer the letter to the President of the Senate then a different erangement of the documents will be necessary, and a republication of the pamphlet[4] corrected and amended by such aditions from my answer as you may think proper to select particularly, that part that relates to the execution of Arbuthnot and ambrister & the right of the state to organize and officer its own Militia, to satisfy any call made upon it by the Executive of the United States. I send on an abstract,[5] and erangement of the documents made out by Judge Overton, for this purpose I send on the letter & the erangement by the Judge, from the respect I have for his Judgt. knowing him to be actuated from the purests motives of friendship, more than with an expectation that the course he recommends will be preferred by you & Mr Crittendon in preferrence to my answer, as many of my friends agree that the answer ought to be preferred. But on this as on every other thing appurtaining to this unpleasant business I leave to your & my friends Judgtment, after having expressed my opinion on the subject—let all your deliberations be founded on this—that I fear not investigation, but court it, wherever it is necessary for the understanding of the nation—

I have wrote to Mr Crittendon a short note.[6] I wish him to present the answer for this reason only—that it is known that you and myself are friendly, and he being from another state, it will have a much better impress upon the Senate and the nation—There is one part of the answer not accompanied with documents, that is the stoppage of the amelia at Pensacola and another provision Vessell at the Barancas, which made her Escape.[7] These facts can be Established by Colo. Gibson who is in the city and who I wish to be in interrogated on this subject should it be found necessary indeed, his statement of this part I would advise to be taken and appended to the answer before it is presented. Permit me to suggest for your consideration & that of Mr. Crittendon, that when the answer with the Documents are presented to the senate, that it be moved to refer them to a select committee, to whom shall be referred the report of *the Majority* of the committee of the senate on the Seminole war of the 24th. of February 1819—⟨By this order,⟩ and that it be printed for the use of the members &c—

By this order the whole will undergo, a full investigation and the answer & acompanying documents be placed before the nation—If it could be done, as many copies might be ordered as was of the report—This would only be Justice to me and to the nation—

you will have seen by the Georgia Journal that Genl Clark is elected Governor, and Genl Mitchell is under the Hackle for smuggling affrican slaves. The documents published, and others in the hands of the Executive must lead to an official investigation of his conduct & dismissal[8]—The Election of Clark shews that Wm H Crawford has politically fallen never to rise again—& his quondam friend Colo. Andrew Irwin & his sateletes in Bedford has failed in all their attempts for offices both from the President and state Legislature.[9] I have no time to give you any of the news of the place, but all friends *living* are well. I am yrs respectfully

Andrew Jackson

P.S. I find in several of the printed documents errors which, has been corrected in copying you will have the printing (if done) from the manuscrip, in my letter to the sec of War Dated Washington city, I find a great error, which changes the sense & fact, in the 40th. line of said letter as printed in the pamphlet I find it printed, thus "to Pensacola," read instead thereof "toward Pensacola"[10]—I note this as you will find in my communication to the sec of war from Ft Gadsden[11] detailing the information enemerated in the above letter, that I give that as my reason for marching in person towards Pensacola A.J—

ALS copy, DLC (28). Published in Bassett, 2:443–46.

1. Jackson's original draft of the memorial has not been found. A revised version was submitted to the Senate on February 23, 1820.

2. See AJ to Joseph McMinn, August 25, and, above, to William Williams, September 25. The postscript referred to is the fragmentary statement on the Salt Lick Reserve [1819–20]. The other enclosures included James C. Bronaugh to AJ, August 26; Deposition of Richard K. Call, August 25; Deposition of Richard I. Easter, August 27; Statement of Robert Butler, March 3; Deposition of William B. Lewis, August 20; Deposition of George Bell, Boyd McNairy and Thomas Eastland, August 23. Bell, a Nashville merchant, was a brother-in-law of McNairy (1785–1859; Pennsylvania 1805), a Nashville physician and youngest brother of

Judge John McNairy. Eastland lived near Old Stone Fort, near Manchester in Coffee County, where he operated a tavern and distillery.

3. Jackson was apparently unaware of Crittenden's resignation from the Senate in March.

4. John Overton had contended that his newspaper articles defending Jackson (signed as "Aristides") and the pamphlet *A Vindication of the Measures of the President and His Commanding Generals* were sufficient answer to the Lacock committee report. The letter to Vice-President Daniel D. Tompkins, phrased as an alternative to the memorial, may be that of [cJan] 1820.

5. Not found.

6. Not found.

7. The *Amelia,* a thirty-two-ton public transport schooner built about 1812, had been detained by Spanish authorities at Pensacola in May 1818 and prevented from ascending the Escambia River to deliver its supplies to American troops at Fort Crawford. The other vessel has not been identified.

8. John Clark had been elected governor of Georgia after the death of William Rabun. Accusations of David B. Mitchell's involvement in slave smuggling appeared in the Milledgeville *Georgia Journal* in October and November 1819. Jackson had enclosed a copy of Clark's letter of August 18, 1819, to James Monroe on September 29. See above, AJ to Clark, [September] 18; see also Clark to AJ, November 2 and 29.

9. Jackson was referring to Erwin's candidacy for marshal of West Tennessee, Erwin having been recommended for the post by John Cocke. John Atkinson was elected to the state senate, and Joseph Brittain and John Tillman were elected state representatives from Bedford County.

10. See AJ to John C. Calhoun, February 5.

11. See above, AJ to Calhoun, May 5, 1818.

To James Monroe

Nashville Novbr. 29th. 1819

Dr. Sir

This will be handed you by Doctor Brunaugh of my staff, who takes the city in his rout on his Tour to vissit and inspect the posts of Norfolk—Charleston, Neworleans &c &c, by whom I forward my answer to the report of the committee of the Senate with such documents as I have thought relevant to the subject, which will I trust convince every mind that in prosecuting the Seminole war I have neither infringed the perogative of the states, nor the constitution and laws of the united States; but that the measures adopted, were the only means, to give a permanant & honourable peace to our country, with security to our borders.

When I take a review of the conduct of the opposition, and reflect upon the means used by some Senators, combined with the information & belief that Mr Wm H. Crawford drafted that vindictive, false, and malevolent report, I sicken at the Idea of continuing in office with those men in power, who when I am risqueing my life, & sufferring every privation to promote the best interests of my country—they are employed inventing plans, to injure my reputation These men cannot injure me. But it is more than ⟨there⟩ ought to Exist, that when I ought to have a little rest and respite from business, to indulge in attention to health and the restoration of an impaired constitution that I should be compelled to refute the slanders of such men, be laboriously engaged for a longer time, than I was employed in giving peace and security to our borders. Such scenes as these must be irksome to every honest man and make him lament the depravity of human nature.

I cannot bare the idea of abandoning you, so long as you may think my services may be necessary for my country—and this I never will do, without your consent But my constitution is so much impaired that I am fearfull it never will permit me to prosecute another Campaign with vigor and effect—added to this, Candeur compells me to state, that my private concerns requires my attention—I cannot attend to them as long as in the army without affording my enemies ground for clamouring against me and I cannot ask a furlough from you, for if granted, it would afford ample ground for clamour & censure against you Therefore so soon as it will meet your convenience, & in your opinion my services can be dispensed with, I hope you will signify it to me, that I may tender to you my resignation. I will barely add that there are many dependants upon me, whose education it becomes necessary to attend to which I cannot do so long as I remain in public life

Permit me to bring to your view, the letter of Colo. Robert Butler which I handed to you at the city last spring, with a request that you would decide upon the grievance complained of. I have wrote you once upon this subject a*[nd]* recd your answer that you would attend *[to it]* when a leisure moment would offer—I have now to request, that you will have the goodness to enclose me Colo. Butlers letter with any decision you may have come to, on his case submitted—[1]

With a tender of Mrs. J. & my best wishes to your amiable lady and family, and with a request that you accept our best wishes for your health and happiness beleve me to be with due respect yr mo. ob. servt.

Andrew Jackson

ALS, NN (7-0899); Copy in Anthony Palmer's hand, DLC (72). ALS endorsed "abuse of WHC"; Copy endorsed by AJ: "making known my wish to resign so soon as my services can be dispensed with & a request that he may advise me thereof that I may tender my resignation—."

1. See Robert Butler to AJ, January 30. Neither a letter from Jackson nor one from Monroe addressing Butler's complaint about his brevet rank has been found, nor did Monroe return Butler's January 30 letter to Jackson.

To John Caldwell Calhoun

Head Quarters
Nashville 11th. Decr 1819

Sir

Your Letter of the 27th. ult with its enclosure has been this moment received[1] it contents have been duely noted and will be promptly attended to. Orders have been issued to carry in to effect the preparatory measures; and I would suggest the propriety of having water Transportation to convey the 7th. Regiment to any point which circumstancies may require. I have requested Commodore Patterson confidentially to have in readiness such Armed force as may be competent to protect such Transportation if ordered by the proper Department.[2]

Should it be true that St. Augustine has been reenforced by 1200 Troops, it would be risquing too much to attempt its reduction with the Regiment of Light Artillery and the 2d Regiment of Infantry only. If that Fortress is not or should not in the interim be reenforced, those two Regiments might be competent to its reduction. But it would be hazarding too much in my opinion to make the attack calculating on a cooperation from the Troops under my command; when we consider that the Barrancas has been greatly strengthened and that the Troops at Pensacola and Barrancas are estimated by report at 2000 and which can be reenforced in five or six days from the Havanah[3]

There can be no doubt but a simultaneous attack on both Pensacola and St Augustine with competent force would facilitate the opperations but if any doubt should exist as to the competency of the force it will be better to concentrate our whole force and reduce the different Posts in detail; and in that event I would reduce the Barrancas and Pensacola first, which would give security to Mobile and its dependencies. next St. Marks which would insure the nutrality of the Indians and with the whole force combined reduce St. Augustine. The probability is that on the reduction of the other posts St. Augustine would surrender. On the plan of concentrating the whole force the Light Artilery and 2d. Regt. of Infantry might be landed at Blakely on the Mobile, and from thence march direct to Barrancas, as to the point of general Rendzvous, as circumstancies may require. I have taken correct measures to ascertain the strength of the forces at Pensacola and Barrancas.

The disposable force of my Division you will learn by reference to the Report of my Adjt. General[4] and in calculating, its eficient strength in the Field, I would suggest that its aggregate numbers should be reduced ⟨one⟩ at least one forth

As the Quarter Master and Commissary Generals are located at Washington City, I have to request that on the determination of the President ample funds may be forwarded for the Transportation and support of the Army, and that orders be given to each Department to make the necessary arrangement for carrying promptly in to effect the object of the Government. I am induced to make this request in order to obviate the inconvenience and privations attendant on an expedition insufficiently equiped and to which my Army has been exposed on every Campaign, which I have had the honor to command I am very Respectfully your Obt Servt

(Signed) A. Jackson
M G Comd.

LC in Richard K. Call's hand, DLC (63). Published in *Calhoun Papers,* 4:477–78.

1. See above, Christopher Vandeventer to AJ, November 22.

2. See Richard K. Call to Edmund P. Gaines, December 11; see also, Call to James B. Many, December 12, and to John Symington, December 13; and AJ to James Monroe, December 10. The letter to Daniel T. Patterson has not been found.

3. Reports of the reinforcement of the Barrancas and Pensacola arrived in November (see Elbert Woodward to AJ, November 3, and Gaines to AJ, November 7). No report concerning St. Augustine has been found.

4. Robert Butler's report, dated October 31, has not been found, but see AJ to Calhoun, January 10, 1820.

From John Henry Eaton

Washington City
Dec. 25. 1819

Dr Genl.

This day was recd. your Letter of the 10 Int. To the several matters it refers you will find my answer in a letter addressed to you a few days ago.[1] Your memorial ⟨will be⟩ is now transcribing & will be finished by Doc. Bronaugh to day. You will pardon the liberty I have taken in interfering with it when I assure you that your views are nothing infringed upon. The phraseology in many places the gramatical construction in others could not be amended without transcribing; while in some places I have made it to speak a language *demanding* justice & right, not asking for favour and courtesy. I have done nothing that you will not be completely satisfied with when you shall come to see it. One material fact is adverted to to wit a Letter from Secty war to the chairman of the Comitte of ways & means dated April 1818 asking for an additional sum of 90.000 & giving as a reason that 1200 mounted gun men instead of militia were called out; this goes at once to assail the report which charges that they knew nothing about these troops, & that they were Volunteers untill they saw the pay roll[2]

The Seminole house bill is for the present postponed but will shortly be again taken up. Upon this argument genl. Smith of Baltimore came to me,

& inquired if you had communed with the governor about the Volunteers—did the governor agree to it; & how were the troop organised and commissioned. I gave him full information on the several points, and he shortly afterwards got up & made a full & satisfactory speech upon these points only. Several who heard it, admitted that he had placed the matter in a new & satisfactory point of view different from what had before been understood[3]—when yr. memorial shall become public all these matters will appear in a different light to minds not prejudiced or heretofore committed; let me therefore suggest to you that any further defence is unnecessary. The one you will have presented is full able & satisfactory. The spirit & moderation in which it is written will give you a triumph over your enemies such as they do not look for; while its facts & arguments will cause all who are free from prejudice at once to understand in a way different from what they have done.

I begin to fear that Mr. Monroe is to be jeopardised by his Spanish affairs; and that the Ho of Rep will not support him. Forsyth is the subject of general derision His correspondence is laughed at for its weakness, & purile spirit: & already is it doubted if the Ho of Rep will support their Executive in his measures.[4] I am far from bei*[ng]* satisfied that on the score of policy we should e*[ngage?]* in war or by seising Florida hazzard its consequences; but the dignity & char*[acter]* of the Country is at stake, & every consideration oug*[ht]* perhaps to yield to this. Foreign interference should *[at an?]*y rate weigh nothing with the determination of Congress

I want the Senate to be full before yr. memorial is produced. two from Maryland, one from Louisiana & Kentucky & N. York & are yet absent & some are gone home. Johston of Louia. sailed from New Orleans nearly forty days ago; fears are entertained for his safety[5]

(He has arrived)

Our Treasury deficiency is placed at 5. millions which you will find is charged to the Army. It is rumored that Calhoun & Mr. C. will squabble about the business[6]

Present me if you please to Mrs. Jackson: If Capt Call is with you say to him I should be glad to hear from him truly yr friend

J. H. Eaton

Often as you have leasure write me, I will do the same

ALS, DLC (28). Published in Bassett, 2:449 (extract).

1. Neither Jackson's letter of December 10 nor the response from Eaton has been found.

2. John C. Calhoun wrote William Lowndes on April 13, 1818, advising him of increased costs in the Florida campaign due to the use of mounted troops rather than state militia (*Calhoun Papers*, 2:244). The Lacock committee had charged Jackson with usurpation of power by raising the mounted gunmen without legislative authorization.

3. On December 21 the House began consideration of a bill compensating army officers for personal losses sustained during the invasion of Florida. Debate soon focused on the legality of the invasion and the manner that officers had been commissioned in the mounted

volunteer troops employed by Jackson (see Robert Butler to Daniel Parker, January 28). Samuel Smith chaired the House Committee on Ways and Means and defended Jackson's call for volunteers, arguing the necessity for a speedy response to the Florida situation. The House postponed consideration of the bill until January 19, 1820, when it was rejected.

4. The president's annual message of December 7 included documents relating to the Florida treaty, among which was John Forsyth's curt note of June 21 to the interim Spanish foreign minister, reacting to the delay in ratification. The House foreign affairs committee did not consider the president's request for discretionary authority to occupy Florida until March, after the debate upon the admission of Missouri. At that time William Lowndes reported a bill that would have required occupation.

5. William Pinkney and Edward Lloyd of Maryland, Henry Johnson (1783–1864) of Louisiana, Rufus King of New York, and Richard M. Johnson of Kentucky all took their seats later in the session.

6. William H. Crawford submitted the treasury report on December 10. Although the report itself made no specific recommendation about a reduction in expenditures, the treasury secretary's allies in the House soon focused upon the war department budget, seeking to trim expenditures and, not incidentally, the political fortunes of Calhoun, Crawford's potential rival. See below, George Gibson to AJ, February 14, 1820, and Eaton to AJ, March 11, 1820.

1820

From George Gibson

Washington Jany 3. 1820

Dear General

Yours of the 13th Decr Reached me two days since.[1]

The ordnance at Mobile is Reported unfit for Service, but in the Event of operations in that quarter Battering Guns will be Sent Round or transported from above; and I hope you will order a Sufficient Number of large Howitzers. The Dons do not like shells and by throwing them frequently it distracts them & gives time & security to the working parties. Congress is getting in better humour than at first. I never witnessed that body so restless at the Commencement of a Session and it is dificult to account for it—I beleive the Two Mr C.s are the prime movers.[2]

I am told that your Enemies are delighted at the idea of your sending in a Memorial to the Senate—they will, when it is Read, be greatly disappointed for it is very different from what they Expect—Your friends are only waiting for the Senator from New York & those from Maryland—the one from N York will be appointed to day by the Legislature of that State.[3] Doctr Bronaugh is in Loudon but Returns tomorrow[4]—Capt. Easter is here busy with his accounts and will in all probability leave us for Richmond in a week.[5] Present me in affectionate terms to Mrs Jackson & beleive me Sincerely Yours

Geo Gibson

ALS, DLC (28).

1. Letter not found.

2. A reference to William H. Crawford and Henry Clay.

3. Although the faction-torn Republicans controlled the New York legislature, they distrusted one another more than a resurgent Federalism, and reelected Rufus King to the U.S. Senate. Edward Lloyd (1779–1834), newly elected senator from Maryland, had taken his seat on December 27, 1819; William Pinkney (1764–1822), elected to fill the place of the deceased Alexander C. Hanson, took his seat on January 4.

4. James C. Bronaugh's family resided in Loudoun County, Virginia.

5. Richard I. Easter's problems with his army account as assistant quartermaster general began almost six months earlier when, as he prepared to resign, the war department noted a substantial imbalance (see Daniel Parker to AJ, July 16, Robert Butler to Easter, August 22, and Easter to AJ, November 25, all 1819). In February John C. Calhoun informed Jackson

that Easter owed the army almost $22,000 (see John C. Calhoun to AJ, February 17, AJ to Calhoun, March 9, and to Gibson, March 15).

To John Clark

Nashville Janry. 6th 1820

Dear Sir

I have the pleasure to acknowledge the receipt of your kind letter of the 29th. of Novbr. last, and sincerely thank you for the Trouble you have taken to have the pamphlet republished in numbers in the chronicle—To the Editors of which, when an opportunity offers have the goodness to present my acknowledgements—[1]

Having laboured from my youth to Establish a charector founded upon uprightness of conduct in every station that it has been my fate to fill, by the unsolicited voice of my Country, the only solicitude I had upon the subject was that I should not be deprived of that charector, by the falshood of a conspiracy, formed by designing Demagogues, of which I found William H. Crawford the chief, surrounded by his Minnions, Clay, Cobb, & Co—who he wielded with the dexterity that a shewman does his puppets, to exalt himself by prostrating the Executive through me, and thereby raise himself to the Presidential chair, and his minions to office, by which Mr Speaker Clay might become secratary of state, and his other minions to distinguished offices—*Like lucifer they have politically fallen never to rise again.*

I would have been gratified to have recd. your pamphlet before I sent on my answer to the false & wicked report of a majority of the Committee of the Senate of the united States. It might have assumed a differrent charector in some respects. But I hope to receive it in due time for other valuable purposes[2]—I intend Sir when leisure will permit to annalise the speach of Mr Cobb on the Seminole question, in which the certificate of Doctor [Thomas] Moor can be introduced to advantage and will bring out Mr Crawford when I am prepared to bring him before the public in a manner which I know he dreads & must feel[3]—or if he should come forward before the public in any other way he shall be duly noticed—I have had a wish for some time to retire—my official duties, impair my health and does not afford leisure for attention to ⟨my health⟩ its restoration, or any other business that require attention. I had a hope that the moment had arived when I gave peace to our borders, and Terminated the Seminole war—But the perfidy of Spain encouraged by the Debates in last congress & calculating upon a continued support from that body Ferdinand has had the Temerity to withold his signature from the Treaty, and from information, ⟨from⟩ your Frontier, may be again involved in an Indian & Spanish war—The Floridas will have again to be occupied by our Troops, or our Frontier deludged in Blood, under these circumstances I am requested not to resign—[4]

I have allways viewed my services to belong to my country, when it was thought it could be beneficial—altho' enfeebled, with a broken constitution, that requires rest—under these circumstances I cannot withdraw—But will lend my feeble aid in again giving security to our borders; This Sir may afford me an opportunity of seeing you & my friends in Georgia, which will afford me much pleasure, & which I will view as one of the happiest occurrences of my life.

I hope & Trust that the movement of our Troops from Traders Hill to Ft Scott will keep down the hostile spirit of the Indians on your Frontier—untill Congress acts upon the subject, I trust that the Representatives in congress from Georgia, (altho some of them are in a dilemma)—will act with promptness, to prevent the savage Tomhawk from desolating your Frontier; again, excited by Spanish perfidy. Should the representatives in congress not do their duty in ordering a speedy remedy to prevent Indian outrage upon your borders, I trust that the good people of Georgia will exercise their right by witholding their suffrages from such unworthy servants. I know the President will act with promptness, and energy as far as he has the power and be assured as far as I am authorised nothing shall be witheld from the defence of your frontier.

I have only to remark, that every preparatory measure is adopted, to act, when authorised, with effect, and I am well aware that Genl Gains feels every disposition to render every secur*[i]*t*[y]* in his power to your state.

I thank you for the certificate of Docto*[r]* Moor, you had before forwarded a copy. I named to you in a former letter, that I had given it a proper direction.[5]

The late investigation of the agent, Genl Mitchells conduct in his illicit conduct in smugling african slaves cannot fail to bring the subject before congress and the President—Should it fail to produce an investigation of his conduct, one thing is certain, the omission will be noticed by the people—There is not a shade of doubt left of his guilt[6]—Accept assurances of my Esteem & respect, & believe me to be yr mo. ob. serv.

Andrew Jackson

ALS, CtY (7-0977).

1. The pamphlet was John Overton's *A Vindication of the Measures of the President and His Commanding Generals* (see Clark to AJ, November 29, 1819). The *Augusta Chronicle and Georgia Gazette,* edited by John E. Kean, Benjamin T. Duyckinck, and John K. M. Charlton, had reprinted Overton's pamphlet in November and December 1819.

2. Clark's *Considerations on the Purity of the Principles of William H. Crawford* did not appear until May 1820 (see Clark to AJ, May 23, and AJ to Clark, June 21 and November 23).

3. Thomas W. Cobb spoke against Jackson during the House debates on January 18, 1819. Moore was a brother-in-law of Fleming and Seaton Grantland, editors of the Milledgeville *Georgia Journal,* which had first published the rumor about the cabinet's division over the Florida invasion. Moore's statement (enclosed in Clark to AJ, November 2 and 29, 1819) recounted a conversation reported to him involving William H. Crawford and Cobb in which

Moore understood Crawford to have instigated the report of the division in the cabinet over Jackson's invasion of Florida and possible arrest (see AJ to Clark, November 23, 1819).

4. See James Monroe to AJ, December 12, 1819.

5. Jackson had forwarded a copy of Moore's statement to James Monroe on November 22, 1819.

6. See above, AJ to Monroe, September 29, and to John H. Eaton, November 29, both 1819.

Affidavit of Thomas Childress

State of Alabama
[January 12, 1820]

Being informed that Col Wm P[reston] Anderson[1] by the instigation of the enemies of Genl. A. Jackson or through his own wicked intentions has obtained a copy or copies of Letters given to Capt John Donelson addressed to the Govr. of Pensacola: And as I conceive intends to make some use of them derogatory to the Character and standing of the said Genl A Jackson: Therefore that justice may be done to the said Genl A Jackson I. Thomas Childress being one of the original partners in the purchase of some Lotts in the Town of Pensacola and some lands in the neighbourhood there of made by Capt. John Donelson in the winter 1818 do Solemnly depose and say that I never heard or understood: nor do I believe that the said Genl. A. Jackson was at that time or, has he been at any time Since either directly or indirectly interested in Said purchase: and that such letters were given through friendly motives and not, pecuniary as, the said, Col Anderson would wish to represent: Sworn to, and, subscribed before me this 12th. day of January 1820.

Hugh Campbell J. P[2] Tho. Childress

ADS endorsed by Richard K. Call, DLC (28). Childress, a brother of John, was a founder of the Nashville Female Academy. He later removed to Florence, Alabama.

1. Anderson (c1776–1831), former friend and aide-de-camp to Jackson and colonel of the 24th Infantry Regiment, was estranged from Jackson, presumably over Jackson's dispute with Anderson's father-in-law, John Adair.

2. The letter of introduction by Jackson to then Florida governor José Masot in late 1817 or early 1818 has not been found, but John Donelson (1787–1840) also denied any pecuniary involvement by Jackson in Pensacola speculation (see depositions of Donelson, January 13, James Jackson, Jr., January 12, and John Jackson, January 13). Anderson did not publicly break with Jackson until the 1828 presidential campaign. The charges about Jackson's Pensacola speculation, first raised in the 1819 Lacock committee report, were repeated in 1824 by Jesse Benton. Benton reported that the Pensacola speculators purchased 220 town lots and 1,300 acres of land one mile outside town. Campbell was a resident of Florence, Alabama.

From John Caldwell Calhoun

War Dept
Private 23d. Jany. 1820
Dear Sir,

I have received your private letter in relation to your Nephew Cadet Andrew J Donelson, now at West Point.[1] Under existing regulations, the regular examination will take place in June, at which time, your Nephew will be entitled to promotion, and if you would permit me to offer my advice, I would suggest it as the most advisable for him to remain till that time, unless Congress should authorise military operations against Florida previous to that period: Your Nephew Stands very high, and will, if he continues till the regular examination, be placed, in all probability, among the first of the Cadets, which will give him the right to select the corps in which he may choose to serve. Should he leave the academy before the examination, he will loose this advantage. The advantage of making a campaign under your immediate observation, should Congress authorise operations this Spring, would doubtless much more than counter ballance that, which I have stated; but, if they should not, I think you would find the course, which I have suggested, as the most advisable. If, however, you should still be ⟨of⟩ desirous of his return to Tennessee in April, I will with pleasure grant the permission which you request.

I entirely agree with you, as to the importance of Cuba to our country. It is, in my opinion, not only the first commercial and military position in the world, but is the Key stone of our Union. No American statesman ought ever to withdraw his eye from it; and the greatest calamity ought to be endured by us, rather than it should pass into the hands of England. That she desires it, and would seize it, if a fair opportunity presented itself, I cannot doubt; and that, such an event would endanger our union, is to me very manifest. These are my fixed opinions. Should our relation with Spain end in a rupture, we ought to be prepared immediately, at the very commencement of the hostilities, to seize on it, and to hold it for ever. On the contrary, I think there are strong reasons, why we ought, at first, to limit our operations to Florida, and rest there for the present, unless Spain should choose to come to a rupture with us; or that the designs of England on ⟨it,⟩ Cuba should become sufficiently manifest.[2]

Congress has not evinced so much feeling on these important points, as I expected. The subject of Florida appears for the present to sleep, tho' I can not doubt, that, before the termination of the session, they will authorise the President to occupy it.[3] With sentiment of Sincere esteem & respect I am sir

J. C. Calhoun

ALS, DLC (28). Published in Bassett, 3:11–12.

1. Not found.

2. For similar statements re Cuba, see [Thomas Sydney Jesup? to AJ], November 7, 1819; John H. Eaton to AJ, January 13; and AJ to George Gibson, February 1, below.

3. See above, Eaton to AJ, December 25, 1819, and Calhoun to AJ, March 15, below.

From James Jackson Hanna

Portsmouth Jany. 30th. 1820

Dr Sir

I fear our detention in this country has been a Serious inconvenience to you and my Mother. We have used every exertion, but have been So unfortunate; as to take the Wrong course & go to places Where few Negroes Were for Sale, & difficult to purchase. Had one of us come on here at first, & the other gone to the Eastern Shore of Maryland, We Should have been at home before this. I left Mr Clay about three Weeks ago at Plymouth N.C. & yesterday received a letter from him Stating, he had done nothing Since I left him.[1] I expect him here every day. Since My Arrival here I have purchased five fellows for you viz Ned at $450. Tom $455. Argyle $450. Titus $460. & Ned $475 Some of them are better bargains than others: but I dont consider any of them bad ones, they are all very likely and under 24 years of Age, except Titus, Who is 30, but is a very large Strong likely fellow & represented to be very trusty. Ned, the highest priced one is an uncommon likely fellow about 22 years of Age, & Was Supplied With his blankets & Winter clothing. Tom, I was rather taken in With. I examined him While Standing: & after having paid the Money, & gotten the bill of Sale, I was told he had a little halt in his Walk, occasioned by a hurt in his hip in his youth, Which has Made one leg a little longer than the other. The defect is only in appearance I think he Will Make as good a field Negroe as any I have purchased. He has got about Sense enough to do What he is told, & Strength enough to do any thing.[2]

When Mr C. arrives I Will get him to go to the Eastern Shore, & if there are as many Negroes for Sale, there, as has been represented to Me, We may calculate on getting home about the 20th March. Please Give My respects to Mrs Jackson & Allow Me to call Myself your Friend & obt Servt.

Jas. J. Hanna

ALS, DLC (28). Published in Bassett, 3:12–13. Endorsed by AJ: "Mr Jas Hannas. letter 30th. January 1820—on the subject of the purchase of Negroes, five bot their names & prices as stated in the memorandum Book A.J." Hanna (1800–67) was the son of James (d. 1817) and Sarah Jackson Hanna (c1769–1843), former residents of Nashville. After her merchant husband's death, Sarah Hanna and her brother James Jackson acted as executors of the estate, and by 1821 she had removed to Florence, Alabama (see James Jackson to AJ, November 19, 1821). In 1836 Sarah and family moved to Thibodeaux Parish, Louisiana, where she died.

1. Clay has not been identified.

2. See Account with William Cumming for purchase of Tom, January 18; Bill of sale for Ned from David Bell, February 18. A slave named Tom ran away to Virginia where he was retrieved in March 1821 (see Account for advertising for runaway slave, [February 1821]; Account with Hanna for recapture of Tom, [February 1821]; Account with Hanna for trip to Virginia, [March 1821]; and James Jackson to AJ, May 28, 1821; see also Hanna to AJ, March 1, 1821, discussing the sale of the runaway slave Ned, possibly one of those purchased in 1820). Slaves with the names mentioned above were at the Hermitage in 1829, after which time Argyle and Titus disappear from the plantation records. Tom and two Neds are included in the 1846 inventory.

To Andrew Jackson Donelson

January 31rst 1820, Hermitage

Dear Andrew

I have the pleasure to acknowledge the recpt of your letter of the 4th. instant.[1]

I am pleased that the Pamphlet which I directed to be forwarded to you & Edward, has reached you, and it confirmed you in the opinion you had formed, that I had not deviated either from the path of honor, nor infringed the constitution or laws of my country—[2]

Let me assure you my young friend that I have sufferred too many privations in my youth for the Establishment of that happy constitution, & form of goverment, under which we live ever to violate its provisions, unless when dire necessity compells me; and then only to preserve my country, & the constitution with it.

I hope ere long you will see my answer to the report of the triumvirate of the committe of the Senate made at the close of the last session of Congress, with the documents appended. This I trust will bring fully before the nation the Seminole campaign—& Convince it, how wiked have been the combination of Crawford, Clay, Cobb & Co—with their *little* satellites—towit, [Henry Randolph] Storrs of Newyork & [James] Johnston of Virginia with their associates,[3] to prostrate me and through me the administration, reguardless of the means they employed—I trust these Demagogues has stumbled in the Pitt they had prepared for me—

I am in possession of the memorial and documents accompanying it, presented to Congess by they five Cadets who formed the committee &c &c &c I have read it with much attention, and do assure you that it is with heart felt pleasure, I pronounce my full approbation to the whole conduct & procedings of those young Gentlemen. They have been cruelly treated, but if there is any Justice or Maninimity remaining in congress; which I trust there are, that body will duly appreciate, their talents & propriety of conduct, and as far as the power exists, will do them Justice.

I am certain from my knowledge of Mr Monroe, that he must have been much imposed on, by false information or that censure in his general order would never have been pronounced.[4]

I am sure he will take on early opportunity, on a fit occasion to restore the feelings of those amiable & intelligent youths.

I have wrote the Sec of war requesting that you have an examination on the first of april next—as soon as I receive his answer I will advise you thereof—[5]

I have been confined with a bad cough and violent pains—I am now up, altho neither free from cough or pain, but greatly relieved.

Present Mrs. J. & myself to Edward say to him, I shall write him shortly—your friends & his are all well—say to him I shall be happy to hear from him by letter & how Antony is and whether he is at yale College.[6]

your aunt, & Andrew Joins me in our best wishes for your health & happiness, we hope to see you in the Spring—believe me to be your affectionate uncle

Andrew Jackson

P.S. In my last I advised you I had wrote Mr [Joshua] Baker to meet him at Washington[7] A.J.

ALS, DLC (7-1018).

1. Not found.

2. Probably John Overton's *A Vindication of the Measures of the President and His Commanding Generals.*

3. Storrs (1787–1837; Yale 1804) was a Federalist congressman, serving intermittently, 1817–31. Johnson (d. 1825; William and Mary c1795) served 1813–20. In December 1819 Storrs had reopened the debate concerning Jackson's invasion of Florida by inquiring if any money had been spent by the army for unauthorized activity; on February 28 a committee chaired by Storrs condemned Jackson for raising troops without authorization. Similarly, Johnson opposed indemnifying losses sustained by troops in the 1818 invasion, suggesting that they had been illegally called into service.

4. When the courts-martial refused jurisdiction of their cases, the five dismissed cadets submitted a memorial, dated December 20, 1819, to Congress on December 27, 1819 (see *ASP, Military Affairs,* 2:5–30). James Monroe's censure was included in a general order by Adjutant General Daniel Parker, November 10, 1819, which disapproved the refusal of jurisdiction, but lifted the cadets' suspensions and approved their return to West Point. Unsatisfied, the cadets resigned shortly thereafter.

5. See above, John C. Calhoun to AJ, January 23.

6. No letter to Edward G. W. Butler has been found for this period.

7. Baker (1799–1885; Military Academy 1819), the brother of Isaac L., had been Donelson's roommate at West Point. He resigned from the army in 1820, and later served briefly as governor of Louisiana (see AJ to Donelson, August 6, 1819, to Donelson, and to James Monroe, both December 30, 1819).

To George Gibson

Nashville, Feb. 1, 1820.

Dear Colonel:

I received your esteemed favour of the 12th inst.[1] I am much gratified to see that our chief has so handsomely acquitted himself in his report on the Yellow Stone Expedition—he has put down our little crowing cock of Tennessee and his resolutions. This little crowing Cock is only a tool to other greater Cocks in the back ground, he has always and will ever be a tool, and a feeble one to would-be great men.[2]

I really hope that Mr. [Rufus] King is elected, not on my own account alone, but because I think on all occasions he will consult the public good, and preserve as far as he can the National character.

If it is really the fear of expense that induces the National Legislature to bear with the insults and injuries from Spain, request the Sec. of War to assure that honorable body, that if it will authorize the measure, the Floridas shall be in possession of the United States in three months from the date of the notification of the act, the Government paying for the powder and the transportation of the troops and their necessary supplies of provisions and munitions of war. This I will pledge myself for, with my own strength in my own division, and if the Congress should will it, with the regulars alone, and the necessary equipment and Naval aid, Cuba, in six months. Not with a view of Conquest, but to be held by the United States until Europe guarantees the possession to Spain, and that it shall not pass from her to any maritime power of Europe, without the full consent of America and the European powers.[3]

Does Congress believe that it is consulting the feelings of the American nation, when it is bearing with the perfidy and insults of Spain—from a fear of the holy alliance, or can it believe that the American people will bear a state of vassalage in disguise, more than a disclosed state of slavery, and are we thus to be humbled, and by our conduct declare to the world "Do as you please, we will submit to any disgrace you please to inflict upon us, before we will risque our popularity by imposing a tax upon the people to raise the necessary funds to preserve our national independence."

Believe me, sir, the people in the west are prepared to live free or die in the last ditch. They are prepared to surrender the last cent, before they will surrender their independence and those who brude over the national purse and are ready to part with their independence, rather than pay a lot for its support badly calculate on the feeling of the people of the west.

I am anxious to see my answer before the Senate—as soon as presented my dear sir, advise me of the result. Altho' regardless of the result, still I cannot but feel a little anxiety until I hear that it is before that body, and whether the Senate will give it to the nation. Should it not, I hope some of my friends will have it printed and circulated, at least 500 or one thousand copies, for which I will pay if it takes the last dollar I have.

Mrs. J. joins me in prayers for your health and happiness and believe me to be your friend sincerely.

Andrew Jackson.

Printed, *The Collector* (May 1909), pp. 74–75 (7-1022).

1. Letter not found.

2. John Cocke's resolutions questioning the goals and costs of the Missouri expedition were part of a larger campaign by forces loyal to William H. Crawford to reduce war department expenditures and thereby diminish the stature of John C. Calhoun, Crawford's potential rival for the 1824 presidential nomination. Calhoun's December 29, 1819, report defended the importance of the Missouri expedition and the fortifications in the West (see AJ to George Gibson, March 15, and to Calhoun, August 9; see also *Calhoun Papers,* 4:519–24).

3. See above, Calhoun to AJ, January 23.

To John Coffee

Hermitage Febry 23rd. 1820

Dr. Genl

I have recd a letter from Mr James Jackson advising me that you had been very much indisposed but had recovered your health,[1] you must be more carefull than heretofore, your constitution like mine is much imp*[aire]*d & we *[must be patient]* that it will be *[. . .]* exposure—we must content ourselves with things as they are, wind up our worldly concerns, & take care of our health.

I have heard nothing from Congress lately the Misouri question has occupied all their attention, ⟨of late⟩, at length is determined in the Senate by a great majority against the restrictions[2]—Congress may now begin to do something for the National benefit, as yet they have done nothing, but spend the public money in useless debate.

In passing from Franklin court I called at Judge Overtons, when he presented me with the enclosed papers & a warrant to transfer—as these papers may be of use to you I enclose them, that you may either file or destroy them.[3]

Mrs. J. Joins me in good wishes for your health & that of your family—present us to Polly & the children & believe me to be respectfully your friend—

Andrew Jackson

P.S. I have endeavoured to see Joe Smith but as yet I am disappointed—Mr [Thomas] Washington has not returned[4]—A.J—

ALS fragments, Mrs. H. A. Brewer (mAJs).

1. Not found.

2. Controversy over Missouri's admission to the Union first surfaced in February 1819 when an attempt was made to prohibit slavery, but the House and the Senate failed to agree on the question and the bill died when Congress adjourned on March 3. When Congress met in December 1819, the question of Missouri's admission was further complicated by Maine's application for admission. On February 1 the Senate had defeated 27 to 16 an attempt to restrict slavery; the question of Missouri's admission was not finally settled until 1821 (*Annals of Congress,* 16th Cong., 1st sess., p. 359; see George Gibson to AJ, February 14; and AJ to James Monroe, January 1, 1821).

3. Not identified.

4. Joseph Dickson Smith (d. c1823) was the son of Bennett Smith. The elder Smith, maternal grandfather of Jackson's ward Andrew J. Hutchings, was contemplating a lawsuit against John Hutchings's estate, of which Coffee, Jackson, and Stockley D. Hutchings were executors (see Coffee to AJ, January 12; and AJ to Coffee, December 13, below). Washington (1788–1863), long-time head of the Nashville bar and a native of Brunswick County, Virginia, was Jackson's attorney in the lawsuit with Bennett Smith.

To Return Jonathan Meigs (1740–1823)

Head quarters Nashville
February 28th. 1820

Dr Sir

Last evening was handed me by Mr [James Glasgow] Williams, your letter of the 17th Instant with the several letters & the affidavit of Mr [Thomas Carmichael] Hindman, referred to.[1]

I have adressed a letter to Mr. [Abner] Underwood.[2] I hope it will have the effect of putting down any contemplated hostility. I have no knowledge of the man, but Judging of him from his conduct & letters, I would conclude that he is more a man of words, than action—and his view is to alarm the Indians into a compliance by his threats.

I have forwarded by Mr Williams a notification to the Intruders, requiring all those not holding permission from the agent forthwith to remove from the lands reserved to the cherokee nation of Indians or they will be removed by the first day of April next by military authority and all intruders found within the reservation aforesaid, with their stock, will be arrested and delivered over to the civil authority to be dealt with as the law directs[3]—I will thank you to give this publicity throughout the nation, it may have the effect of inducing all to remove without military coercion

By a confidential order from the President of the u states through the sec of war, I have been some time since, ordered to have all the force in my Division concentrated at certain points[4]—and I have no troops within three hundred miles of the cherokee nation, and without permission I cannot withdraw them from the Points they now occupy—I am forbidden to employ Militia on any occasion—Therefore all I have in my power is for the present to talk big, which may counteract the proceedings of Mr Underwood, and induce Those turbulent spirits to withdraw themselves from the nation.

I shall write the sec of war on the subject for instructions, you will please to notify me of the names of the intruders & the parts of the nation they are settled,[5] it will be well to let the Indians distinctly understand, that no whiteman will be permitted to remain in the nation without your permit. I am sir very respectully yr mo ob servt

Andrew Jackson

ALS copy, DLC (28).

1. See Meigs to AJ, February 17. Williams, a native North Carolinian, was the son of Joseph McMinn's third wife, Nancy Williams, and served as Cherokee sub-agent until August 1832. In 1821 Williams's drunkenness prompted Richard K. Call to request his removal, but Meigs's intervention dissuaded Calhoun. Hindman (1792–1856), of Rhea County, had served in the 39th Infantry during the War of 1812. In later years he relocated to Alabama and thence to Mississippi, establishing a large plantation near Ripley. The papers transmitted by Williams included Abner Underwood to George Lowery, February 6, Meigs to Underwood, February 10, Underwood to Meigs, February 14, and the depositon of Hindman, February 16, all DLC-28.

2. See AJ to Abner Underwood, February 26. Underwood has not been further identified.

3. See Order for the removal of intruders from Cherokee lands, February 26.

4. See above, Christopher Vandeventer to AJ, November 22, 1819.

5. See AJ to John C. Calhoun, February 28, and Meigs to AJ, March 13.

Debate on the admission of Missouri and Maine had preoccupied the Senate from the beginning of its session in December 1819 until mid-February 1820, delaying the submission of Jackson's formal answer to the Lacock committee report. In the interim, John H. Eaton, Rufus King (who submitted the document to the Senate on February 23, 1820), and William Pinkney took considerable care to revise the language of the memorial, trimming provocative phrases, so that it might put the controversy surrounding Jackson and the Florida invasion to rest (see above, Eaton to AJ, December 25; and AJ to Eaton, December 28, both 1819; Eaton to AJ, January 13, February 23, March 11, below, and March 15). Jackson's memorial, designed to be his definitive rebuttal to the attacks upon his conduct in Florida, served merely as his longest statement on the controversy (see above, AJ to Andrew J. Donelson, January 31; and AJ to Unknown, April 3). Contrary to James Parton's suggestion, Henry Lee (1787–1837) did not author Jackson's memorial. In 1830, however, Lee did agree to write a defense of the Seminole campaign and, as a result of the 1831 break between Jackson and then Vice-President John C. Calhoun, aided Jackson in preparing a response to Calhoun, an answer that evidently was never issued.

From John Henry Eaton

Washington City
March. 11. 1820

Dear Genl.

In my letter a few days ago,[1] I promised that shortly thereafter I would again write you. Your memorial was at that time postponed that gentlemen might have an opportunity to examine and see how far it would appear to them palatable and how far the language might be considered decorous; as you will have perceived by the news papers it was shortly afterward called up, but interrupted upon the discussion by the *slave bill* which had been returned to us from the House of Representatives. That being disposed of, the memorial was again adverted to by Mr. King, and after about six or eight speeches, and divers animadversions on the character of the Report of last year, and after the acrimony & severity of your memorial had been descanted upon & defended, it was ordered to be printed.

The advocates and the opposers you will have seen in the Intelligincer: amongst the number was Mr. Pinkney who advocated the memorial.[2] He said it was true that it did not, as regarded the Committee speak in laudatory phrase, or in suppliant style, nor would such language have been worthy of yourself: that it was a manly argumentative and dignified appeal, and a bold and free examination of an *Indictment* prepared at last Session, and was drawn in a style & manner suited to the cause that produced it. He said it was a duty the Senate owed, after what had heretofore transpired, to give under their sanction publicity to the memorial, and by this official act to ward off assault from one whose reputation and character was the property of the nation, and ought to be so considered It must be to you a matter highly satisfactory, that men so eminently distinguished, and at the same time so competent to judge as King and Pinkney are discovered to be approvers of your course and conduct in the Seme. war men who being almost strangers to you, can feel no other impulse than that which reason sanctions. The opposition to printing was so feebly maintained, and the strength of argument and numbers being on the side of the memorial, that in the end, before the discussion had closed, opposition was withdrawn, & six hundred copies were ordered to be printed: so soon as they are finished I will send you one

You will remember I stated to you, that Doct Bronaugh and myself had transcribed and made some changes in the memorial[3] After this it was handed over to Mr. Pinkney and to Mr. King who had desired to see it. They proposed, after having examined it, that some alteration or changes should be made in the first pages; and particularly desired that the sentences which alledged that you had "*understood*" the report had not been drawn by any of the Committee should be crossed out, & not printed. They said that any thing the memorial might contain, directly personal would in coming before the public prove injurious, not beneficial to the end, which ought to be the only one intended to be answered, (to wit) the placing the report of the Senate properly before the public. I at first refused, but on a second interview with them on the subject, this was my reply; that you would I well knew be satisfied with any freedom or course your friends might deem advisable and if they would state their opinions in writing, to be sent to you, & thereby unite with me in the responsibility I would consent to the alterations proposed. Accordingly they were made; and when you shall see the memorial I am persuaded that in what has been done, there is nothing to which you will object. I will enclose you the writing referred to as the basis of what was done, when next I write; it is not at hand or it would be now forwarded.[4] The memorial will I expect be printed in eight or ten days hence

Andrew Jackson

James Monroe

John Caldwell Calhoun

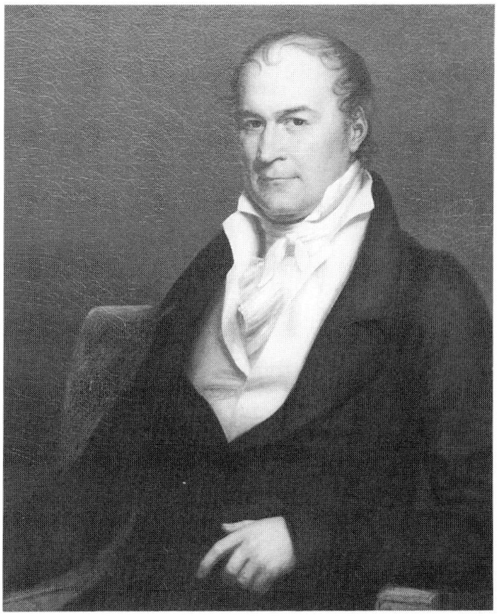

William Harris Crawford

James Gadsden

Richard Keith Call

James Craine Bronaugh

Stockley Donelson Hays

Jacob Jennings Brown

George Gibson

Edmund Pendleton Gaines

Eleazar Wheelock Ripley

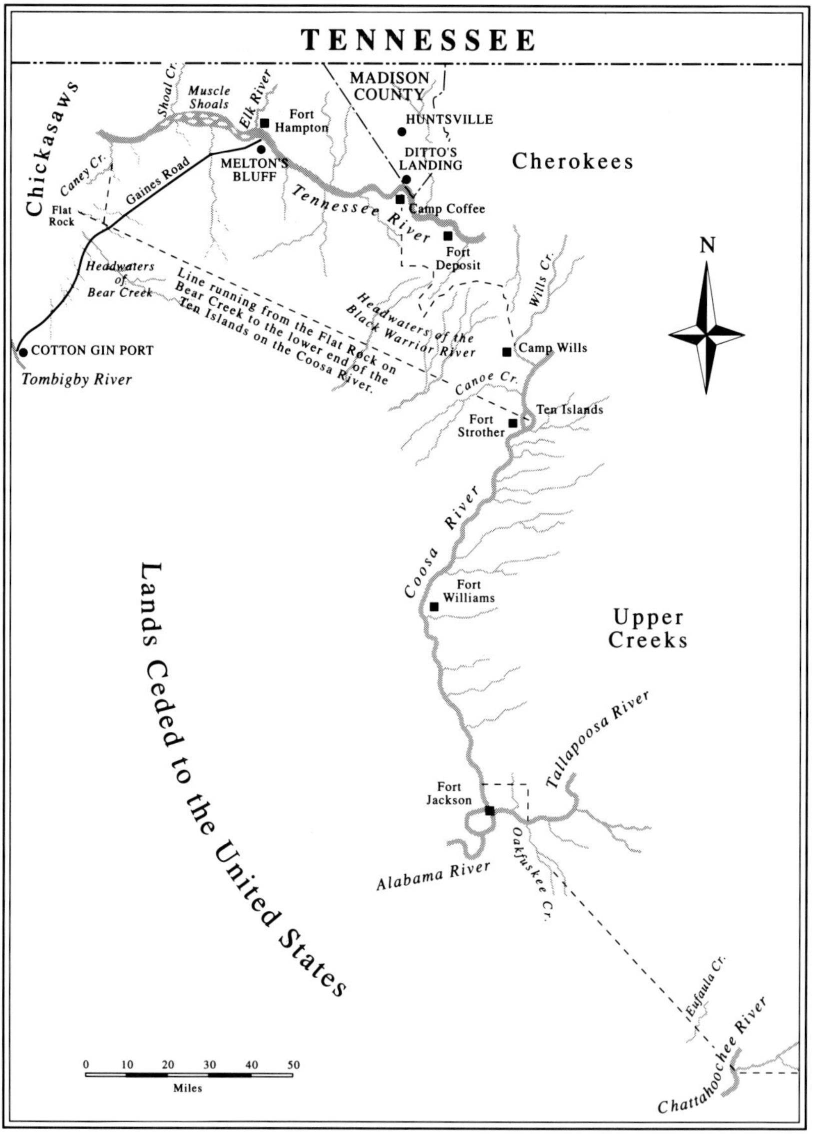

SURVEY OF CREEK TREATY, WITH CHICKASAW AND CHEROKEE BOUNDARIES, [1817]

John Adair

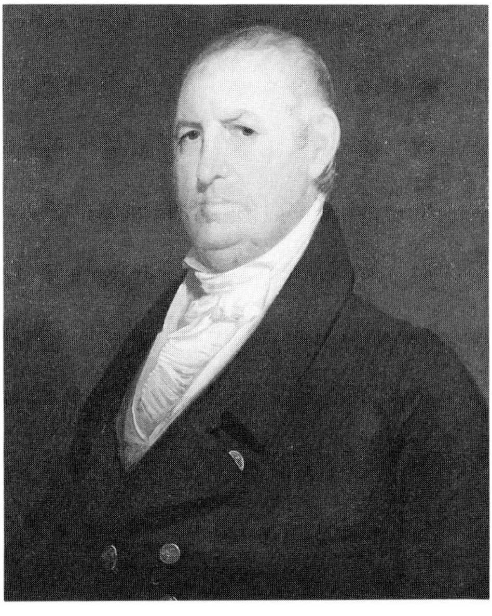

Isaac Shelby

Winfield Scott

Stephen Harriman Long

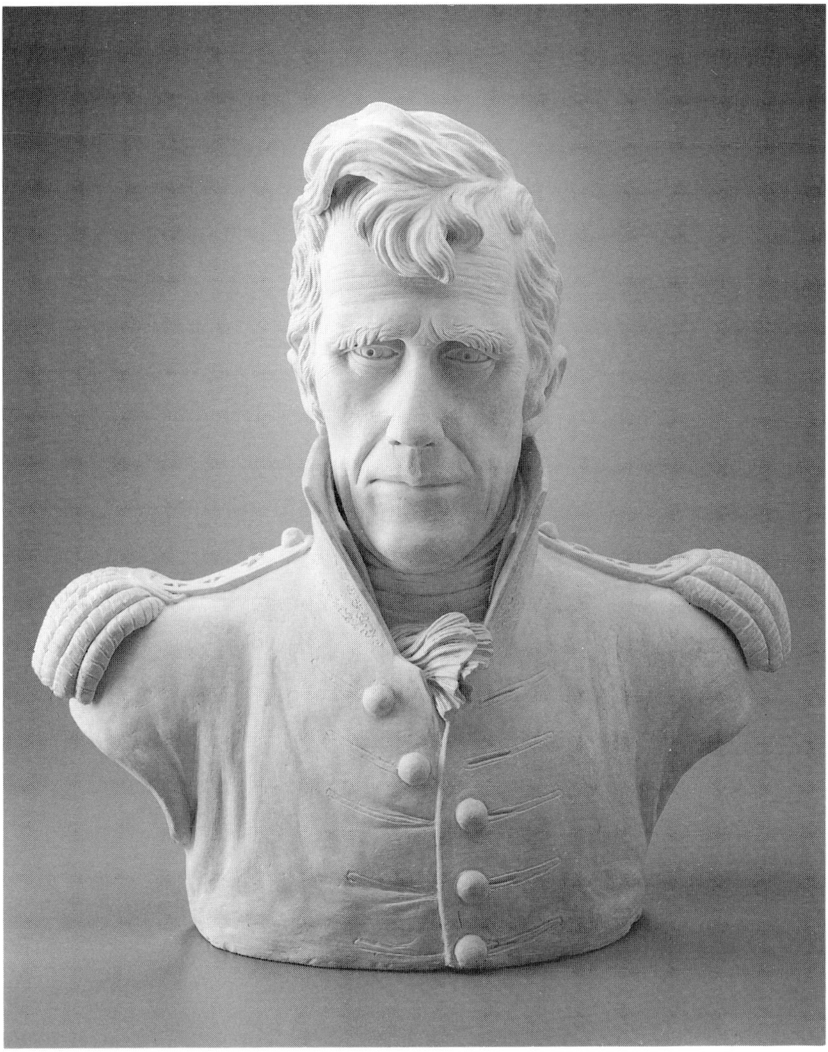

Andrew Jackson

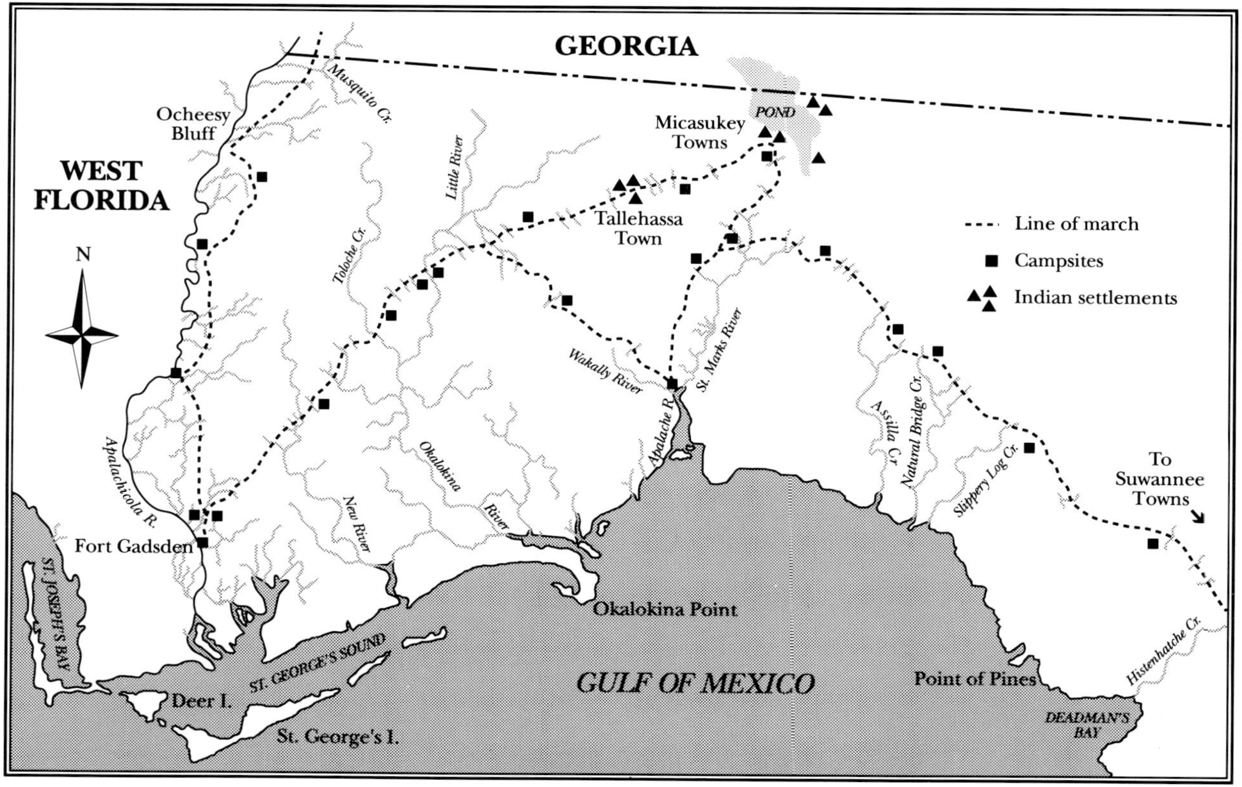

THE SEMINOLE CAMPAIGN IN EAST FLORIDA, 1818

"American Justice!! or The Ferocious Yankee Genl. Jack's Reward for Butchering Two British Subjects!!!"

Pushmataha

Colonel William McIntosh

Abner Lacock

Rufus King

David Brydie Mitchell

John Clark

Rachel Jackson

Andrew Jackson

Those gentlemen and others warmly your friends are opposed to any further examination of this subject. There is no way to reach it but by reference of the whole matter again to a committee, and they say that this ought not to be done—that the Report of last year is duly appreciated every where, & is without any [of] the effects in relation to you, that you conjecture to have been produced; that the Senate never made the report theirs by *adoption,* or did more than to direct, as a matter ordinarily usual, its printing: and that your memorial which is as full and satisfactory as any report that could be made, being also by the Senate ordered to be printed, is making the reparation commessurate with the injustice. They say, it is not an answer and defence published by yourself, & therefore a private matter; but a reply presented to the Senate, who by the order made for its publication, sanction your opinions, as much as they, by ordering the publication of the report, give *it* sanction; and that, hence, the whole matter stands as tho the Senate never had acted on it as the opinions of three men. Added to all this a great majority concur with you, that it is a business with which the Senate had, and ought to have had nothing to do, & that a sacrafice of this opinion would be contained, in pressing the enquiry again. Such being the opinions of those whose frendship is unquestionable gives additional weight. Of the good wishes of him who is principal actor in this business the presenter of the memorial you have heretofore had evidence[5]—that of Mr. Pinkney is no less than his

A further objection however to the referrence is this, that (for you know they are chosen in the Senate by ballot) an unfavourably disposed committee might be selected. It is very easy in a body of 40, for 12 or 15 men acting in concert to appoint a committee of their own: their own ballots would be certain, while the scattering votes, of those unapprised of the scheme might effect the purpose: true a similar concert by a majority might defeat it, but then here is the objection; you have presented the memorial, & stirred the investigation, and for your friends under such circumstances to attempt any concert of the kind would afford room for recrimination & censure to you; having a regard for your honor & feelings they could not venture upon such a course; and not to do so, but to trust the matter to those ⟨who⟩ inimically disposed, would be to venture at great hazard, in pursuit of an unprofitable result, and to afford an opportunity for the venting of any lurking spleen. Your memorial having been printed by order of, and bearing with it the sanction, of the Senate, is as full a report as *any Committee* could give however favourably disposed

Besides, the opinions entertained my many, that the Senate, have not, & never should have entertained jurisdiction, as you have well argued, would render an attempt to recommit the enquiry hazardous; & should it be made & fail of success it might produce an injurious effect Upon the whole therefore, your friends have come to this conclusion, that the "strong spirited & dignified" appeal you have made through the Senate, and by them under a feeble opposition ordered to be printed, will effectually put the "Lacock

Report" to rest, and ought forever to quiet your feelings upon the subject. My desire to consult and to pursue your own wishes upon this subject would be sufficient to attempt the reference but your frends deeming a different course advisable and proper, renders it prudent to forbear any further attempt; especially too as public opinion is now decidedly with you The Committee on foreign relations in the Ho Rep, yesterday made report authorising the President to take possession of E & W. Florida.[6] Mr. Forsyth's correspondence in addition to what you have seen was yesterday laid before both houses. His remonstrance as he calls it to the Spanish Secy. of State, was refused & sent back as highly offensive, he informs Mr Secty Adams that he shall retire from Madrid into France. Doubtless he has left the Spanish Court[7]

Some of our profound politicians have shewn a great knowlege of the situation of the affair of their Country, & if clothed with sensibility must feel a little mortified. A reference to the Intelligencer of yesterday will shew them debating on the reduction of the army & navy, & urging it as necessary, when lo, on the very next day, out comes a report for active measures of a unlike nature, which points to the necessity of an increase, instead of a diminution.[8]

In the progress of my horse bill for the relief of the Volunteers it has been urged that they were paid for clothing. There is an old law, during the war which directs volunteers tendering their services for one year, & accepted of by the President to be supplied or paid for clothing; but this law is obsolete, & at any rate applied not to the Seminole volunteers who were to have the same pay &c as had been given to the Militia during the war, which was $6.^{66}/_{100}$ under the act of 1795 in lieu of every thing. Pray did they receive cloathing, & was it by your orders?[9]

The President says he has recd your letter[10] He said he wanted to have with me some conversation in relation to it, but it being a levee evening & much crowded no opportunity was then had. He desired me to say to you, that he had been so taken up with the deep agitations here the (Missouri bill), that he did not [have] time but that he would shortly write to you. The agitation was indeed great I assure you—dissolution of the Union had become quite a familiar subject. By the compromise however restricting slavery north of the 36½ degrees we ended this unpleasant question. Of this the Southern people are complaining, but they ought not, for it has preserved peace dissipated angry feelings, & dispelled appearances which seemed dark & horrible & threating to the interest & harmony of the nation. The constitution has not been surrendered by this peace offering, for it only applies while a territory; when it is admitted congress hold the power & right to legislate, & not when they shall become States

I fear I have tired you so good night Present me respectfully to Mrs Jackson & to my friend Capt Call Yours truly

J. H Eaton

ALS, DLC (28). Published in Bassett, 3:15–18.

1. Possibly Eaton to AJ, February 23.

2. Senators Freeman Walker (1780–1827), Samuel Whittlesey Dana (1760–1830; Yale 1775), and James Burrill, Jr., initially opposed the memorial because of its strong language. Eaton, Pinkney, King, James Jefferson Wilson (1775–1824), David Lawrence Morril (1772–1849), James Lanman (1767–1841; Yale 1788), and William Smith (1762–1840) all favored the memorial; it appeared on March 20 (see George Gibson to AJ, March 20).

3. See above, Eaton to AJ, December 25, 1819.

4. The statement by King and Pinkney, enclosed in Eaton to AJ, March 15, read in part that with the alterations suggested the "Facts & Reasons in vindication of the General, which the memorial contains, will be more likely to have their proper Effect."

5. King had opposed the Lacock committee report while sitting on the committee, and had also reported John Williams's anti-Jackson activities (see above, AJ to William Williams, September 25, 1819).

6. The House foreign relations committee, chaired by William Lowndes, reported the bill on March 9 (see John C. Calhoun to AJ, March 15, below).

7. John Forsyth's correspondence as minister to Spain, communicated to Congress on March 9, appeared in the Washington *National Intelligencer* on March 13 and 14.

8. On March 8 Tennessee congressman Newton Cannon proposed reducing the army to half its level of 10,000 enlisted men (see Washington *National Intelligencer*, March 10).

9. Eaton's proposed bill would have compensated soldiers for horses lost during the Seminole campaign. Although the measure passed the Senate on March 20, it lost in the House (*Annals of Congress*, 16th Cong., 1st sess., pp. 22–23, 526–27, 1862). Clothing had been furnished by the government under the militia law of February 6, 1812 (2 *U.S. Statutes at Large* 676–77; for the act of 1795, see 1 *ibid.* 408–409). Jackson's reply has not been found.

10. Probably AJ to James Monroe, January 15.

To George Gibson

Hermitage March 15th. 1820

Dr. Colo.

This is my birth day, but I am so aflicted with pains, that I have some doubts whether I ought or ought not to rejoice, that I was born—or at least whether it would not have been better for me to have not lived to see the 15th of March 1820—but I co[n]clude, that it is best, as it is the lords will that I am here.

Last mail brought me intelligence that my answer to the report of the Committee of the senate was presented by Mr King of Newyork on the 23rd ult.[1] I hope it will be given publicity by the senate & take the same range as the report to which it is an answer. If this is done & no more, I will be gratified—as I did believe it was due to the nation, that the falshood *[& wick]*edness of the report, should be made known to the people of the u States—This being done I am reguardless what may ⟨be the other⟩ result from it—When I review my whole public conduct I am content with it, my conscience are calm—and I am reguardless of the frowns of the *base* part of my country—I have allways had the support of the virtuous and brave, I am therefore content.

you know my *[sincere hope to retire]* as soon as this question is finally acted on I wish to forward my resignation—I am somewhat bound to remain untill the Florida question is acted on by Congress—I do not wish to retire, so long as Mr Munroe does believe that I can be usefull to my Country. But it does appear to me that from the palsied state of Congress, that nothing efectual will be done this session—and of course my remaining in the army can produce no good—perhaps congress may Legislate me out—Should this be the case I am content, it will save me the trouble of resigning, and be a beacon hereafter for all military men to look at; and warn them of the uncertain tenure upon which those men who risque their lives, their health & constitutions hol*[d]* their office in a government like ours.[2]

The Spaniards are strongly fortifying the Barancas, & have Erected a batery with 14 heavy guns on the spot occupied by our 9lb. battery in 1818. which communicates with the Barancas by a covert way—and rumor states the have means to blow it up, if attempted to be stormed—The Governor of Pensacola has withdrew from St Marks one half of its garrison, from all which I should not suppose that Spain has any intention of delivering up the floridas peaceably—or ratifying the treaty. Nor do I believe their *Minister* will be here before next august, and then only to procrastinate & deceive.[3]

If Congress has lost all sight of our national charector, and future peace & happiness, it is time that the people should take a view of our real situation, of which I have but little doubt they will in a short time.

I will ⟨greatly⟩ thank you if the Seminole question should be debated in the Senate to send me a paper that contains the debate—

Mrs J. begs to be remembered to you, so does Capt Call—I have not heard from Capt Easter since he left the city—and regret to learn from the sec of war, that he has not settled up his accounts, and that there is a ballance standing against him of upwards of $21.000 This was the first intimation to me, that he owed the government—his letter to me from the city was quite different from this.[4] I still hope he will be able to account, and shew he has acted as an honest & honourable man—Should he not, my mortification will be great as he was, when I took him into my family, altho a stranger, recommended to me as a young man of worth & honesty—I have directed Capt Call to write him to come on here—Where the sec of war expects he is, obtaining vouchers to close his accpts. I will as soon as he arives, & obtains his vouchers, order him to the city to close his accounts—how mortifying it must be to him, as well as to myself should he become a public defaulter. accept assurances of my sincere friendship & Esteem & believe me to be yr mo. ob. Servt.

Andrew Jackson

ALS, THer (7-1045).

1. Probably John H. Eaton to AJ, February 23.
2. A reference to the campaign to reduce war department expenditures.

3. See the report of James Gadsden, February 6. The new Spanish minister to the United States, General Francisco Dionisio Vives, arrived in Washington in April.

4. See Calhoun to AJ, February 17; AJ to Calhoun, March 9; and Richard I. Easter to AJ, November 25, 1819.

From John Caldwell Calhoun

Department of war,
15th. March, 1820.

Sir,

I enclose the report of the committee of Foreign relations of the House of Representatives to whom was referred that portion of the Presidents message which relates to our Spanish affairs. You will perceive on its' perusal that it takes strong grounds; which, I hope, will be supported by Congress. I would have transmitted it to you immediately, but was desirous to learn what would be its' probable fate. The general impression is, that it will not be adopted, and that nothing will be done by Congress in relation to it this session; and I am myself inclined to think it is very doubtful as to what will be done. In this state of uncertainty the President is of the opinion, that it would be improper to take any military measure now, in contemplation of the passage of the bill reported by the committee, which would involve any considerable expense; and he is the more confirmed in this opinion from the belief that the season will be too far advanced to operate in Florida until the fall, even should the bill be taken up and passed without delay, which will not be the fact. There is an additional reason for not incurring further expenses until the passage of the bill becomes certain, which ought to have much weight, I mean the amount which it is proposed to appropriate for the Military service of the year. Each head of appropriation has been reduced to its' lowest amount, and it will require much economy and good management to meet the ordinary expenditure of the year. You will accordingly take no measure, in the present state of the business, which will much increase the expence of your division. Whenever the fate of the bill and report can be ascertained, you will be informed, and will receive further instructions.[1] I received yesterday a copy of your letter to Coll. Atkinson,[2] and I take a pleasure in saying that he well deserves the approbation which you have expressed of his conduct. I have the honor to be, Your most obedt. Servt.

J C. Calhoun

LS, DLC (28); LC, DNA-RG 107 (M6-11). Published in *Calhoun Papers,* 4:715–16.

1. The enclosed report of March 9, no longer found in Jackson's papers, accompanied a bill that would have "authorized and required" the president to occupy Florida (*Annals of Congress,* 16th Cong., 1st sess., pp. 1618–20). In a March 27 message to Congress James Monroe suggested postponing the occupation of Florida, citing the continued friendly influences of Russia, England and France, and Spanish internal upheaval as reasons for forebear-

ance. For the secretary's efforts to reduce expenditures in the war department, see Calhoun to Samuel Smith, February 5 (*Calhoun Papers,* 4:638–41).

2. See AJ to Henry Atkinson, February 27. The depressed economic condition of the country prompted Congress to reduce war department appropriations to a minimum. Although the Senate attempted to restore funds for the completion of the Missouri expedition to the Mandan Village, it eventually acceded to the reduction, ending the enterprise. The army manned the outpost at Council Bluffs, however, until 1827. Calhoun informed Jackson of the suspension of the expedition on April 13.

To Andrew Jackson Donelson

[April 16, 1820]

Dear Andrew

The bearer Mr Abram [Poindexter] Maury [Jr.] having obtained a warrant to enter the military academy, was good enough to give me a call to aford me an opportunity of writing to you.[1]

Mr. Maury is the son of Major Abram Maury of franklin, a Gentleman of good Standing in our country—he is a respectable youth, of good education, and respectable connections—and as such I introduce him to you, and request, that you will make him known as such, to the Cadets—and Teachers and particularly to young Mr Baker your room mate to whom I have not time to write.

Some weeks since I wrote you & enclosed you a post note for five hundred dollars to enable you, to pay off all demands, and transportation to me[2]—I hope it has reached you in safety—however from the late roberies committed on the mail, I have had some fear on this head—I took the precaution to write you by the same mail, by the post rout through Kentucky, giving you the No. mark & date &c &c of the post notes if taken from the mail that you might immediately write to the cashier of the Bank, and stop payment of it—I am anxious to receive a letter from you advising me of its being to hand.[3]

I, together with your friends are anxiously waiting for the time of your vissit to us, all desirous to see you—I calculate on your reaching here in all the month of June

I have the unpleasant task of informing you, that we are again covered with mourning. your Uncle William Donelson is no more—he departed this life on the 13th. instant—a better man never lived, nor one more regretted by his neighbours.

You will have seen that the long looked for minister of Spain has reached the city of Washington on the 9th of april—We will either have a long negotiation—or a speedy possession of the Floridas—

Having got nearly through the Seminole war, (except what is due to Mr Storrs' wicked, and false report, to the house of representatives, which will receive its exposure in due time) I have wrote to the President, for permission to resign—as soon as congress rises[4]—I hope you have seen my memorial and answer to the report of the triumvirate of the senate of the last year—I am gratified, that it gives my friends general satisfaction, and even draws from my enemies there approbation. How disgracefull to our nation—that select committees of Congress have become the hotbeds of falsehood & calumny to serve the views of party, regardless of the means they employ. for my own part I am regardless of their wicked attempts—I am aware that truth is mighty & will ultimately prevail.

The Misouri question so called, has agitated the public mind—and what I sincerely regret & never expected—but what now I see, will be the entering wedge to separate the union. it is even more wicked, it will excite those who is the subject of discussion to insinuation & masacre—it is a question of political asscendency, and power, and the Eastern interest are determined to succeed regardless of the consequences, th*[e]* constitution or our national happiness they will find the southern & western states equally resolved to support their constitutional rights—I hope I may not live to see the evills that must grow out of this wicked design of Demagogues, who talk about humanity, but whose sole object is self agrandisement regardless of the happiness of the nation.

I shall expect to see you soon—your friends are all well, your aunt & Andrew Joins me in love to you—I am affectionately yrs

Andrew Jackson

ALS, DLC (7-1073). Published in Bassett, 3:20–21 (extract).

1. Maury (1801–48) left West Point the following year and returned to Tennessee. Later he served several terms as a Tennessee legislator.

2. See AJ to Donelson, March 21.

3. See AJ to Donelson, May 6, below.

4. Jackson refrained from a public response to Henry Storrs's report (see AJ to Unknown, April 3, and Eaton to AJ, April 16). On Jackson's contemplated resignation, see AJ to James Monroe, April 15.

To Andrew Jackson Donelson

Hermitage May 6th. 1820

Dr. Andrew

Your letter of the 15th. ult. is this moment to hand,[1] and I am happy to learn that the remittance I made you, reached you in safety.

On the subject of my opinion of the Corps I would advise you to enter—I have to remark, that from the Sec of wars letter to me,[2] he advances it as one reason for his advice that you should remain untill June, that on that event, you would have a right to select the Corps, you would desire to be attached to—whether this was from the report of your merit to him I cannot say, but he was pleased to make mention of you in very flattering terms. I therefore recommend to you to select the Engineer corps, if this should be practicable I could assign serious reasons for this advice, and from the letter of the Sec of war, I have no doubt but your acquirements, merit the distinction of this corps—But should it not be practicable to make this Selection, I would recommend you to choose the corps of artillery—in the infantry, in the Southern Division there would be more rapid promotion in the line—but if peace continues, I have no idea of you wasting the prime of your life in the army, when you could employ time much better for yourself and country in the pursuit of the study of law & civil Goverment and when your country became involved in war, or Demagogues arose, to trample under foot our constitution & our laws, that you may be prepared to resist them; both in the councils, & in the field—Therefore promotion in the line in a state of peace is of no consequence. When war arise—when our rights are endangered, it is then, that talents are sought for & men are promoted who are capable of wielding our armies for our countries defence—in times of peace, it is the *drones* who eat the honey, & men of merit & capability, are hunted down to make way for the drones to eat the honey—

I leave it to yourself, as to your stay with the Cadets during the period of their encampment, barely remarking, that my wish is that you may gain all experience in military matters that opportunity may afford—it is certain I am anxious to see you, but that anxiety will bend to your benefit. I this day write to the sec of war, on the subject of your being permitted to vissit me,[3] & if attached to the Engineer or any other corps, that you may be ordered to my Division, when I have much to say to you, that I cannot write.

Present me to Edward affectionately and say to him, if he has any desire to vissit this country before he is of age I will write to the sec of war & endeavour to obtain him permission. your aunt Joins me in our usual good wishes for your health & happiness—Andrew is at school with Doctor Priestly—I am your affectionate uncle

Andrew Jackson

P.S. say to Edward I have named him also in my letter to the sec of war & hope it will have its effect—I have asked for him what I have conceived would result to his benefit—as I have done for you—A. J.

ALS and Typed copy, DLC (7-1086, -1090).

1. Not found.
2. See John C. Calhoun to AJ, January 23.
3. Not found.

To John Caldwell Calhoun

Nashville 17th May 1820

Sir.

Having received information that the Military Road is complete[1] I have determined to leave this today with a view to examine it, and to take such further measures for its improvement as seem to be necessary on an examin*[ation]* of its present State. I shall on my arrival at the encampment of the Troops operating on the northern end, direct, That they return for the purpose of repairing Certain Bridges and Cosways that have been injured or destroyed, and for the Shrubing the road which is rendered indispensable. A detachment from the Command to which this duty will be assignd, will be employed in removing from the Cherokee Lands all intruders.[2]

Contemplating an absence of two or three weeks I have deemed it necessary to advise you of my departure and that arrangements are made for the prompt receipt of any thing of which you may deem it necessary to have me advised. I have the honor to be your very obt. Hbe. Servt.

Andrew Jackson

LS, DNA-RG 107 (M221-89).

1. In a letter not found, Duncan L. Clinch had informed Jackson of the military road's completion, which was fortuitous, as Secretary of War Calhoun had just written Jackson that budgetary contraints would force suspension of the project (see Richard K. Call to Daniel Bissell, May 22, and John C. Calhoun to AJ, May 16).

2. After completing his inspection of the military road, Jackson continued through the southern portion of the Cherokee and Creek nations, arriving in early June in Wilkes County, Georgia, where he obtained from David Allison's heirs a duplicate of the deed of release to the Allison lands in Tennessee. On his return to Tennessee, Jackson stopped at Florence, Alabama, before reaching Nashville on June 18.

From Edward George Washington Butler

West Point June 5th. 1820
Military Academy

My Dear General

I have this moment received your letter of the 17th. Ult.[1] and should have delayed answering it untill day after tomorrow, in consequence of my examination which commences this afternoon, But the great disappointment which the non-receipt of the money has occasioned me; and the mortification which I feel at the idea of calling on you for money which was not in your possession, and of receiving at different times sums of money not my own, has induced me to answer it immediately, and as an appology for the great inconvenience which I must have occasioned you, to plead my entire ignorance of the state of my property; and more particularly of the funds remaining in your hands.[2] I was under the impression that they must have been nearly exausted, yet was in hopes there was still enough remaining to pay off my debts, and furnish me with the cloathing necessary to enter the army. As I am now unavoidably in debt, and as I have excited expectations in my creditors which it would be dishonorable to disappoint, I am reduced to the disagreeable necessity of requesting that you will, (if not attended with too much inconvenience) remit me the sum which I required, and I shall make it my business to visit you for the purpose of adjusting all matters of estate, and of securing to you, my part thereof, which I trust will at least be aequivolent to the reqrd amount.

I wrote you a few days since advising you of the receipt of your last and also repeating my request.[3] I am unable to express the gratitude which I feel for your continued acts of kindness to me, both in an official and private capacity. Mr. Calhoun is expected here the 1st. of next month, when I suppose he will inform me of the result of your request. Genrl.'s. Brown & Jessup arrived here on saturday evening. I received a letter from Mr. Bell a few days since appologising the inactive part which he has taken with respect to my mother. I am induced to believe she has but little to expect from that quarter, and so soon as I become stationary I am determined she shall have a proportion of my pay.[4]

Messrs. Donelson & Maury are extremely well and request to be remembered. Mr. D. will I have no doubt, be able to give you in a few days, a gratifying account of the result of his exam*[ina]*tion. Be pleased to write me on the receipt of this. Remember me most affectionately to Mrs. Jackson, Andrew, Col. S. D. Hays & family, and believe me Dear General Ever Yours

E. G. W. Butler

ALS, DLC (29).

1. Not found.

2. On April 27 Butler had requested $500 to pay for a uniform and debts. Jackson had sent small sums of money for Butler and his brother Anthony Wayne in his letters to Andrew J. Donelson, February 29 (above) and March 21; he also made Edward advances of $100 in April and $40 in August (see Memorandum of accounts between Edward G. W. Butler and AJ, [August 7]).

3. Letters not found.

4. In 1817 Robert Bell had arranged for Jackson, controlling the estate of Edward Butler, to pay taxes on land near Pittsburgh, Pennsylvania, for Isabella Butler Vinson, Butler's mother and Bell's mother-in-law (see above, AJ to Vinson, May 9; and Bell to AJ, October 21, both 1817; and Memorandum of accounts between Edward G. W. Butler and AJ, [August 7]).

From John Rodgers, Sr.

Spadru Bayou Arkansas—
June 7. 1820—

Sir,

In consequence of promises made to us at Highwassee; by Yourself and the other commissioners, I removed to this country, where I have been since, awaiting their fullfilment—The promise that we should have a factory has been complied with—perhaps you do not know it, but I assure you it is ⟨this⟩ true, that no other promise made at that time has been complied with The high Standing, and character of the Commissioners precluded the possibility of doubt that their promises would ⟨not⟩ be promptly fullfilled—We were promised bread for the first year after our arrival here—we came calculating to find it—but there was none—The sufferings and privations we had to contend with in consequence of this failure are better felt than described—hunger, sickness, and in some instances death has been the fatal consequence—We were promised that the white intruders on our land Should be removed by the government—but Our Agent has stated he had no orders from Government to remove them—as also does Major [William] Bradford—We were also told that no white people Should Settle between Arkansas & White river, to the west of us—White people have, and Still are Settling there.[1] I can not suppose Sir these things are to be attributed to You—and the very high esteem I have for You Sir, induces me to trouble you on this occasion—I am an old man now, and ⟨to be c⟩ disappointments affect me more Sensibly than if I were young, and could move about with entire ease—and I therefore Soliscit the favour to be informed whether you think the promises made at Highwassee will be complied with—as these promises alone induced me to come here. Until those promises are complied with, I can⟨t⟩ not ask or recommend my friends to follow me—My health is better than when you saw me for which I am thankfull to providence—With Sentiments of real esteem I remain Sir, Your friend & obdt.

John Rodgers Senir

ALS, DNA-RG 107 (M221-89). Endorsed by AJ: "Mr. John Rodgers who handed this, and as agent for the Arkansa Cherokees, wisshes it to be made known to the President of the U States, that the Arkansa cherokees claim, all the cherokee land, watered by the waters of the Tennessee river, and will claim from the Govrt. of the u. States, an equal quantity of land on the Arkansa, agreable to the Terms of the treaty of 1817—& wish their bounds to be laid off by the u States, that intrusions by the Whites May be put an end to—the Arkansa cherokees complain of injustice done them by the last treaty & are disatisfied with it. A.J." Rodgers (b. c1749), an Englishman, had married Elizabeth Emory, a mixed-blood; they had five children, including John Rogers, Jr. (1776–1846), an important Western Cherokee chief. Rodgers, Sr., was an influential leader of the nation, and had been involved in the assassination of Doublehead in 1807. Spadre Bayou, the site of the U.S. Indian Trading Factory, is located in present-day Johnson County, Arkansas; the factory operated until 1822.

1. For a further description of the Arkansas Cherokees' conditions, see William Bradford to AJ, December 7, 1819. Bradford (c1771–1826), a veteran of the War of 1812, was commander at Fort Smith, Arkansas Territory.

From Richard Keith Call

Huntsville 8th July 1820

Dear General

I arrived here last Night, where I found Col Williams the Sub Agent with a Small Guard, and three Prisoners arrested on the Indian Land. I have been compelled to remain here to day in order to dispose of the Prisoners. They have been brought before Judge [Clement Comer] Clay and two of them have entered in to a recognisance to appear before the District Court to be held at Cahaba in July 1821 their securities are bound in the sum of $1000 for their attendance. One of the Prisoners being unable to obtain security and the Circuit Judge not having the Power to commit him, I have found it necessary to send him to Nashville to appear before Judge McNary who is the neares Officer of the Government who has the power of commiting him.[1]

The Marshall of this State has lately been nominated, and not having yet received his commission, has not commenced the duties of his office.[2] I shall not be enabled therefore to comply with that part of your Order, which directs that the Prisoners arrested and the Property seized shall be delivered to the marshall of the State within whoes Territorial limits such arrests and seizures shall be mad.[3] On examination I find that the non-intercourse Law of 1802 directs that the Intruders who shall be arrested on the Indian Land, shall at their request be carried before the nearest Judge of the Circuite or Supreme Court, and be held to Bail provided they can give sufficient Security, and where the Prisoner cannot or will not give the requisite security the officer by whom he has been arrested may send him before a Judge of the Supreme Court of either of the three adjoining States. under this authority I feel myself at liberty in the present case to send the Prisoner either to Nashville or Cahaba, and have prefered sending him to the former. The Guard which has charge of the Prisoner is acquainted with all the circumstancies of his Guilt and will be enabled to give the necessary testimony to commit him.[4]

Col Williams informs me that great opposition has been threatened, and in some instance's offered by the Intruders. his Party was fired on a cross the River at Nickajack and near that place his Camp which was guarded by two men while the rest were on duty at a short distance was attacked by two or three white men and one of the Indians ⟨was⟩ severely wounded. At Crow Town Island in the Tennessee River[5] there is a large improvement made by the Intruders, and at the time the Cherokee Ligt Horse arrived at that point there were 70 armed men assembled for the purpose of defending it. The Greater part of those men I am informed reside within the Limits of Tennessee but had crossed over and offered their services to the Intruders. The party under the Command of Col. Williams being too small to oppose this Lawless multitude was compelled to pass on and leave them unmolested, and I have been informed that they have all dispursed except those who own the property on the Island. The Cherokee Ligt Horse are encamped on the Creek Path about 10 miles from Paces, where I suppose the regulars will have arrived by tomorrow morning, at which time I expect to join them. After breaking up the settlement on the Creek Path I shall proceed to Wills Creek, and thence up the Coossee to the Chata Hoochee, and along the Frontier of Georgia and Tennessee, where I am told there are a great number of Intruders all of whom threaten the most violent opposition to the Indian Light Horse, such is the threats of one party and the fears of the other that I shall be compelled to accompany the Indians quite around the Nation. I fear General it will be extremely inconvenient for the regular Troops under my command to march in to the Creek Country after performing their duties in the Cherokee Nation. Their services will be required at all points, the Indians are affraid to act without them, the Intruders will all fly at the approach of the regulars, they will not dare to oppose them but I am apprehensive if the Indians go alone they may suffer considerably. I shall therefore unless I receive your orders to the contrary, continue with the Indians until all the Intruders are removed and their Settlements destroyed. in doing this I shall have to pas from the Chata Hoochee over to the Tennessee, as the intermediate space between the two Rivers is thickly inhabited by the Intruders. And from the Tennessee River ⟨to⟩ it will be more inconvenient for my Troops to march to the High Tower trace on the Creek boundary, than it will be for ⟨Those⟩ the Detachment which you contemplate ordering to remove the Intruders from the other part of the Creek Nation. I shall expect to receive your instructions on this Subject—if you have any wish whatever for me to go on the Creek Boundary, as far as the Alcova River, I will go with much pleasure as soon as my presence can be dispenced with in the Cherokee Country.[6] It will be necessary for me at any rate before I can go to Break up the Settlement on Crow Island. (While I am with the Troops I am convinced there will be no opposition, but I should not wish to leave the nation, until all the duties for which we entered it have been performed) I have directed Mr Henderson[7] who has charge of the Prisoner, and who will deliver you this letter to call on you for any communication which you may wish to make. I shall take command of the Regulars and Indians tomorrow and move on with the greatest despatch until ⟨all⟩ our duties are accomplished.

You will not I presume hold the Chocktaw Treaty until the latter part of Sept or the 1st of November. pleas inform me on this subject, as I am extremely anxious to join you previous to your departure, and I know not how long I may be detained ⟨in⟩ among the Indians in this Country Pleas present me Respectfully to Mrs Jackson And believe me General most affectionately yours

R. K. Call
A De Cam

ALS, DLC (29).

1. Clay (1789–1866; East Tennessee 1807) was a member of the Alabama state circuit court, later serving as governor and U.S. senator. The prisoners have not been identified.

2. David Files (d. 1820) had been confirmed in May as marshal for Alabama, but apparently never took up his duties.

3. See AJ to Call, July 1.

4. Reference is to section sixteen of the act to regulate trade and intercourse with the Indian tribes, and to preserve peace on the frontier, enacted March 30, 1802 (2 *U.S. Statutes at Large* 144–45; see also section four of the 1816 supplemental act, 3 *ibid.* 333).

5. Crow Town Island, lies in the Tennessee River, approximately two miles northeast of Wannville, Jackson County, Alabama.

6. Paces, probably a roadhouse, lay about fifteen miles south of the Tennessee River, along the road from Huntsville to the headwaters of the Black Warrior River (see Call to Return J. Meigs, June 28). Once in Georgia and contrary to Jackson's orders of July 1, Call planned to sweep northward toward the Georgia-Tennessee border, removing intruders from Cherokee lands, rather than move southeast along the High Tower Path, roughly the boundary in 1820 between Cherokee and Creek lands, running from just south of Alpharetta to the Apalacee River at High Shoals, Georgia. The Alcova (also Alcovy) River flows southward, through Gwinnett and Newton counties, Georgia. Jackson agreed with Call's decision, and ordered Edmund P. Gaines to remove intruders from the Creek lands (see AJ to Call, July 31, below).

7. Not further identified.

To George Gibson

Hermitage July 10th. 1820

Dear Sir

I have the pleasure to acknowledge the recpt of your letter of the 19th. ult. with its enclosure, for which I thank you.[1]

I am Looking for Capt Gadsden daily as by his last to me he has promised to take this in his rout to Washington.[2]

Since my last letter to you, I have recd. a letter from Mr Monroe, and has had an interview with Major Eaton.[3]

Mr Monroes letter is frank, friendly, and explanatory of our relations with Spain and places every thing before me that may grow out of this, as well as the present disturbed state of Europe, and sugests, that good may result to our country by my remaining in service a little longer. This added to the communication made me through Major Eaton, has induced me to pospone my determination of retireing from service for the present, untill our affairs with Spain is brought to a close believing it to be my duty, to lay aside my private views, for public good—But believe me my Dr Sir that my patriotism had a hard struggle, for the first time in my life, to conquer my inclination for retirement. I will hold on as long as it is believed either my services or name can be serviceable to my Country, or at least untill I see what course will be adopted by Congress at their next Session with regard to Spain. This honourable body will at their next Session, I have no doubt, reduce at least the staff of the army, and then I can retire by legislative approbation. This my present determination will cause me as well as my staff (who had all determined to go out with me) some expence & trouble—we have all made erangements to go out—we have now to make new erangements to stay in—I have wrote to my friend Colo. Hayne who had forwarded his resignation to me, to forward with my own—what may be his conclusion on receiving my letter I cannot say—he has seated himself upon his farm, with a view to private life.[4] Mrs. J. has Just recd a letter from Mrs. Hayne—the family enjoy good health.[5]

Capt Easter lies very sick at present, he is prostrate, cannot move himself without assistance—whether he will get over it, is doubtfull—

Mrs. Jackson renews with me, our best wishes for your health and happiness, & believe me to be your friend sincerely—

Andrew Jackson

ALS, NN (7-1145).

1. See Gibson to AJ, June 19. The enclosure has not been identified.

2. Possibly James Gadsden to AJ, April 30.

3. Jackson's last letter to Gibson was probably that of April 15 (not found). See James Monroe to AJ, May 23. John H. Eaton had returned to Tennessee after the close of Congress in May.

4. See Arthur P. Hayne to AJ, June 10. AJ's letter to Hayne, relating his decision to remain in the army, has not been found. Hayne's resignation was accepted on September 20. His farm was located on the west bank of the Alabama River, in Autauga County, Alabama.

5. Not found.

As the financial crisis of 1819 deepened, appeals for debtor relief prompted Governor Joseph McMinn to call a special session of the Tennessee legislature for June 26, 1820. Former Tennessee congressman Felix Grundy (1777–1840), a leader of the relief movement representing Davidson County in the legislature, proposed as centerpiece legislation the creation of a state loan office, empowered to issue new notes that debtors might use to pay off their creditors. Not surprisingly, the Blount-Overton faction, which controlled the state's banking system, opposed the loan office, and included in their number Hugh Lawson White, president of Knoxville's Bank of the State of Tennessee, John Overton, head of the Knoxville bank's Nashville branch, Pleasant M. Miller, and William B. Lewis. That faction's opposition pushed Grundy, at least temporarily, into the waiting arms of the anti-Overton alliance, headed by Andrew Erwin and John Williams. Jackson, later the perceived leader of national reform, was himself a member of the Blount-Overton faction and resolutely opposed relief in gen-

eral and the loan office proposal in particular, leading the Davidson County protest (see Memorial of citizens of Davidson County, July 15; and AJ to Lewis, July 16, below). Yet in the exchange of letters with Lewis, below, Jackson revealed a general antagonism to banks that went beyond opposition to merely one proposal, suggesting his later campaign against the Second Bank of the United States. More immediately the political divisions arising from the loan office debate set the lines for the next gubernatorial election. William Carroll, a War of 1812 hero and a failed Nashville merchant, led the forces for relief, championed by the Erwin group, and Edward Ward (d. c1837), Jackson's friend and neighbor, carried the Blount-Overton faction's banner. When the 1821 elections were over, not only had Carroll won the governor's chair, but Andrew Erwin himself was elected to the Tennessee legislature.

From William Berkeley Lewis

Nashville July 15th. 1820

D. Genl.

Your letter of this Inst. has been recd. I have both seen, and read with attention, the law, or Bill, now before the Legislature, authorising the establishment of a Loan Office; and altho I think it a dangerous experiment, and that by passing it we will be hazarding much, yet I hope, and am inclined to think, it will not be fraught with such consequences as your lively interest for the prosperity of the State, have induced you to believe. There is no essential difference between that Office and the Banks, and if it is unconstitutional to establish the former it was equally so to have incorporated the latter. As to the constitutionality of either, I do not pretend to be a competent judge; but if it is so, every state in the Union have equally violated the Constitution of the U. States.[1]

I think it impossible to arrest the progress of the Bill; at the time I was in Murfresborough I thought there was a large majority in favour of ⟨the⟩ establishing a Loan Office. I do not pretend to know what are the sentiments of the people in the State generally, but I am inclined to think there is a considerable majority in favour of the measure in this place and its vicinity. There will be no way of getting rid of it until the next Legislature sits, by which time the voice of the people can be collected, and the law, if it should be the will of the people, I have no doubt will then be repealed. My plan would have been to consolidate the State and Nashville Banks, the State to have taken a million of Stock, and then to have authorised the Bank to issue, in addition to what they now have out, the sum intended by this Bill to be thrown into circulation. They could also have reserved to the Legislature the right of appointing 8 out of 15 Directors, and inspecting, by committee, the Books of the Bank. This would have enabled the Banks to resume specie payments.[2] The Specie in the vaults of the State and Nashville Banks amount to nearly Six hundred thousand Dollars; add to this $250,000 the Sum that will probably be recd. from the sales of public lands, and it would amount to a sum fully adequate to the redemption of the Bank notes with Specie. If this plan had been adopted we would then have but one description of paper currency in the State: the institution would have been placed upon a solid foundation and under the direction and controul of the people themselves, and would have created a reserve to the State of 75 or 80 thousand Dollars per annum—a sum amply sufficient not only to have defrayed the expenses of the Goverment, but likewise to have opened in a few years all of our most important navigable rivers. As this could not be done at this session of the Legislature, ⟨and⟩, should this ⟨law⟩ Bill pass, I am in hopes, if nothing better can be done, that the Loan office and all the Banks will be consolidated at its next session ⟨of the Legislature⟩. I do not know what better can be done, in as much as we have the Banks and cannot now well get rid of them.

The members of the Legislature, I am told, and particularly some of your warmest friends, think your remarks about them, when in Murfresborough, were very harsh. Members of Assembly, acting under the sanctity of an Oath do not like to be told that by voting for certain measures they have been guilty of perjury.[3] Such harshness my dear General, is calculated to do yourself an injury without producing the desired good. Mildness universally has a much more salutary effect; ⟨than warmth⟩ it often convinces the understanding without wounding the feelings. Your enemies will, and are already giving a high colouring to the observations you made in Murfresboro. the other day.[4] These remarks are made in the Spirit of friendship, and I flatter myself they will be recd. in the same way. With sentiments of esteem, I am sincerely yours

W B Lewis

ALS, NN (7-1154). Published in *New York Public Library Bulletin,* 4 (1900):188–89.

1. See AJ to Lewis, July 15.

2. The Nashville Bank was controlled by the Blount-Overton faction and included Stephen Cantrell as its president and John H. Eaton and Lewis among its directors. Only the bank in Knoxville, operating in the relatively prosperous eastern portion of the state, continued to redeem its notes in specie.

3. Jackson denounced the loan office bill while visiting Murfreesboro on July 12, and repeated the accusation of perjury in his letter to John Coffee of July 19: "When I found corruption such as this at work to silence opposition to such a corrupt, base, wicked and unconstitutional law, I felt every virtuous spark in my system in a flame, and I stared villany in the face, and lashed corruption—brought to their view the solemn oath they had taken, and if they passed the law they would be pronounced perjured by every honest man in the nation" (see also the Memorial of citizens of Davidson County, July 15).

4. When the Memorial of citizens of Davidson County was presented on July 17, state senators Adam Huntsman and David Wallace vehemently protested Jackson's earlier Murfreesboro remarks as "a direct and unwarrantable attack upon the dignity of the Senate," and the memorial as "dictatorial, indecorous and intemperate" (*Journal of the Tennessee*

Senate, 13th General Assembly, 2nd sess., pp. 87–89). Reports that Jackson had authored the memorial were later denied (*Nashville Gazette,* September 9).

To William Berkeley Lewis

July 16th, 1820

Dr. Major

I have this moment recd your letter in answer to my note yesterday, and inclose you a copy of the remonstrance unanimously agreed to by every man who was present,[1] the notice was short & limitted to a small circle, but the collection was as large as the number of citizens contained within the limits would permit, and a unamous voice of those collected shews how unpopular the thing really is, and from what I learn in the lower end of the county of Sumner, the collection was much greater, but the result I have not heard, but it is believed they would be unanimous[2]—from this I have no doubt but it could be arrested provided the voice of the people as far as it could be obtained, was obtained & forwarded to the legislature—for if it goes into a law & should be repealed at next Session of which I have no doubt, it will produce injurious effects to all those who in the mean time get into their hands these Bills of credit or if you please Treasury notes. you will see my opinion as far as it is detailed in the remonstrance—I will therefore confine my remarks in reply to that part of your letter where you state "That you can see no essential differrence, between the Bill authorising, or creating a loan office & the laws Establishing differrent Banks"—you know my opion as to the Banks, that is, that the Constitution of our State, as well as the Constitution of the United States prohibited the Establishment of Banks in any state—and that such a thing as loan offices by a State for the purpose of creating a fund out of the property of the State for the payment of individual debts certainly is a power not granted by any provisions of the State constitution, and is unheard of, ⟨by⟩ and prohibited by the principles of general Justice to the people: if even the constitution would permit it. But Sir the 10 Section of the 1st Art of the Federal constitution is positive & is explicit & when you read the debates in the convention will find that it was introduced to prevent a state Legislature from passing ⟨the⟩ such Bills, as the loan office Bill under consideration—when we view the Bill & its details it violates every principle of our own constitution—I wish you to turn to the 4 Sec of the 10 article, The first & 2 Sec of the IX article; and the Seventeenth art of the Bill of rights, and then take into view the X sec of the 1st art of the Federal constitution, and answer me whether any man who is capable of reflection, & who will reflect can believe that the Bill under consideration is not a palpable violation of the constitution that we have sworn to support—and particularly those who framed it and is now on the assembly—and who laboured with me to have our constitution so worded as to prevent future Legislatures in times of Corruption to pass Such laws as the one under consideration[3]—I know I was warm at Murfreesborough. It is my foible on Such Topics to get two warm & I often regret it: but Sir it is time for every man who wishes to perpetuate the constituted goverment of our choice to Speak out—when the modern Doctrine is; because I steal my neibours horse, it Justifies my Neighbour to steal yours; or in other words: because we have once violated our constitution, and other States has also; it will Justify us in going on & violating it still until it is entirly destroyed—for permit me to ask what law cannot our Legislature pass, and not Justify it, if it can pass the present—is there any more express provisions in the constitution than those which this law positively oppose, and the same reasons would be as good to Justify the assembly against any other, as the present, that is to say, that we had violated it in other parts, other states had also; therefore we might go on—In fact Sir if this Bill passes, constitutions, or oaths to Support them give no security to the rights of they Citizens—and I for one would be of opinion—hereafter that no oaths ought to be administered, for they are no security, and I am free to repeat, that every man who votes for this bill after mature deliberation does violate his oaths prescribed under the constitution for let me draw your attention to the oath of a Legislature in adition to his oaths to support the constitution in the 9th. article, & the 4th. Section of the 10 art. & then the Bill of rights—

I agree with you that mild reasoning is the best at all times as long as there is hopes that reasoning will prevail, but when all hope of this is lost, ⟨then⟩ and the dearest rights secured to the Citizen under the constitution is about to be violated, Strong and candid language is the only alternative for the citizens to use & *it will be heard,* & if I do not Judge badly from the times—that the Majority of the people will arise in their Strength & put down this Loan office Bill & if attempted to be taxed to the Banks they will be both put down—and let me assure you that the only way that the friends of the Bank can keep them in existance is to unite & put a Stop to the loan office law, which will create a necessity (perhaps) in the minds of the people, for their existance a while longer—I am informed that Mr [William Little] Brown in the Senate has obtained an amendment to the bill in the Senate[4]—that body is still wavering; a strong remonstrance from Davidson with that of Sumner & Rutherford, would stop its ⟨there⟩ passage, when, by eranging *matter* might enable the Banks to lend more relief than this wicked law will do to the distressed—for in my opinion it will relieve none—the notes must depreciate, its credit will sink, & the farmers will not receive it—it will destroy our credit abroad. No merchant, will be creditted abroad & every cent of current money will be shut up, this law destroying all confidence at home between man & man. When I see you I will give you a clue to part of my warmth—and I will Just add here, when I am told, you must be silent on this unconstitutional law, or when your friends election comes on I will even contrary to the solem oath I have taken, and contrary to my own opinion, I will vote against him—Sir Such corruption I hope will allways arouse my feelings—and you will see in the remonstrance, their oath spread before them, this they know will go to the wor[l]d and if they act corruptly they good people will be able the better to Judge of their corruption—and Sir I find at least with the people it has had a good effect, I know human nature so well, that I do know it has & will have its effects upon the religious & moral part of mankind—The violation of the constitution is so manifest & palbable that all honest men must see it, who are not led a stray by interest & their Judgts swayed thereby—I wish you to hand the enclosed when read to Colo. Stockly Hays, should you approve the remonstrance you can—aid in such way as you think best to procure signatures to it so as to reach Murfreesborough by the next mail—I am induced to believe that the loan office bill will not pass finally before next week, and I do believe that signature respectable in character and numbers will prevent its passage[5]—Capt Easter is very ill. I cannot say whether I can be down tomorrow or not, I have to be at court to transact some business as one of the executors of Wm Donelson deceased, when I will see you—The mist will soon blow over at Murfreesborough, and calm reflection will produce differrent results than is expected about the loan office bill but be this as it may, it will as long as I live meet my opposition—I am Dr Sir yours respectully

Andrew Jackson

P.S. I write in haste to send it by the boy that carries our remonstrance to send by this days mail from Nashville to Murfreesborough—

ALS, NN (7-1162). Published in *New York Public Library Bulletin,* 4 (1900):189–91.

1. See above, Lewis to AJ, July 15. Jackson enclosed a copy of the Memorial of citizens of Davidson County, July 15; William Williams presented the memorial to the state house of representatives on July 17.

2. Other meetings protesting the loan office bill had been scheduled for Sumner and Wilson counties, and the grand jury of Dixon County adopted resolutions opposing the bill and sent them to the legislature (see AJ to Lewis, July 15).

3. Jackson was probably referring to the *Journal, Acts and Proceedings of the Convention, Assembled at Philadelphia* . . . (Boston, 1819), published according to a congressional resolution of March 27, 1818. Article I, Section 10 of the U. S. Constitution prohibits states from issuing legal tender. The first and second sections of Article IX of the Tennessee constitution describe the oath for state officers; the fourth section of Article X makes the rights listed in the state bill of rights inviolate; and Article XVII of the bill of rights prohibits taking property without due course of law, undoubtedly meaning to Jackson that the issuance of loan office notes would "take" the debt owed to creditors in return for near-worthless inflated paper. Only two members of the state constitutional convention of 1796 were members of the legislature in 1820: John Clack (1757–1833), representing Giles County in the state house, who opposed the loan office bill; and Edward Douglass, Jr. (1745–1825), representing Sumner County in the state senate, who favored the measure. Governor Joseph McMinn, who had proposed the loan office scheme in his opening message, was also a member of the constitutional convention.

4. Brown (1789–1830), a South Carolina native and Clarksville lawyer, was serving his only term in the senate. He subsequently relocated to Nashville, joining Ephraim H. Foster in a law practice, and sat on the state supreme court, 1822–24. Brown's amendment, adopted

on July 18, changed the proposed institution from a loan office to a new state bank, thereby meeting the constitutional objection raised by Jackson and the Davidson County memorial.

5. The legislature passed the bill creating the Bank of the State of Tennessee on July 26, but an attempt to win over opponents by appointing John H. Eaton and William L. Brown directors of the new bank was unavailing, and Jackson remained firmly opposed to the enterprise (see AJ to John C. Calhoun, August 5, and Pleasant M. Miller to AJ, August 9).

To John Caldwell Calhoun

(Private)

Head Quarters
Division of the South,
Nashville July 24th 1820

Sir

Your General order of June 14th 1820 has just reached me; I have directed it to be promulgated to my Division—[1]

Will you permit me to draw your attention to this order, and request you maturely to deliberate on it. Compare it with the rules and regulations under which the Soldier is enlisted, And the rights and emoluments Secured to him under his compact to Serve the U. States by which is Secured to him, his monthly pay & rations[2]—let me then presume to ask you to Compare the law with the General order of the 14th of June last And then conclude whether any power exists, Competent to take from the Soldier, *Eighty five Cents out of every hundred of his pay* for the purpose of buying *Seeds utensils* &c &c for the Cultivation of "wheat and other component parts of the Ration" When by the terms of his compact the Goverment is bound to furnish the Soldier rations at its own expence—As far as I have been Conversant with the law Martial, And the rules and regulations for the Government of the Army, it does not appear to me that there is any power Competant to retain the Soldiers pay, Save that of a Court martial, and then only for the Commission of a Crime, recognised as Such by the rules and regulations for the Government of the Army.

The order for the Cultivations of Gardens was for the Comfort & health of the Troops; The order for the Cultivation of wheat, is Considered for the benefit of the Government, by saving them the expence of *Component parts of the ration* by the labour of the Soldiery, hence it would Seem to me but Justice, that the Seed, utensils & farming tools Should be laid in by the Goverment, and not taken from the Pittance of the Soldiers pay. I really cannot believe that any power exists of applying the pay of the Soldier to the purpose of farming utensils and Seed for the benefit of the Goverment. ¿How will the Commanding officer collect this from the Soldier; Suppose this order a violation of the compact under which the Soldier was enlisted—how will the officer Justify himself in laying his hand upon Eighty five Cents out of every hundred of the Soldiers pay to purchase "wheat, Seed-Corn, axes, wedges[''] &c &c to Carry on farming for the benefit of the United States—Suppose the Soldier appeals to the law for redress, to recover ⟨his⟩ pay; will not the law of the land afford him relief from this order; Nay further, may it not lead to Serious discussions in Courts martial, and may not the Soldier, after being thus deprived of his pay Contrary to the terms of his enlistment, on the charge of Desertion, with great force alledge in his defence, that the Goverment has violated the Contract with him when enlisted, and from that moment he was disolved from his enlistment & Cannot Justly be punished for leaving the Service, & may it not happen, that officers acting under oath may incline to this opinion, and at once, by their decision absolve all those (whose pay has been thus applied) from the obligation of their enlistment.

Be assured that these remarks are made with the most friendly views, to draw your close attention to the order and its consequences, believing that you have not well considered the Subject before the order was Issued[3]—I am Sir with great respect yr. mo. ob. Servt.

Andrew Jackson

LC, DLC (63). Published in Bassett, 3:29–30.

1. The order of June 14 limited the government expense for the cultivation of gardens at permanent garrisons (see Division Adjutant General Order Book, DNA-RG 98).

2. Jackson was referring to the *Articles of War, Military Laws, and Rules and Regulations for the Army of the United States* ([Washington], 1817), pp. 37–38, which describe a soldier's pay and ration.

3. In his reply of August 10, Calhoun assured Jackson that the department only intended to limit the initial cost of gardening and reminded Jackson that this expense was not, strictly speaking, part of the soldier's ration.

To Richard Keith Call

Hermitage July 31rst. 1820.

Dr. Capt.

I recd. yours of the 23rd Instant from Lasleys last night—I regret to learn the outrageous conduct of some of the Citizens of Allabama on the property of Tomeson & others—the course you have recommended is highly proper and is fully approved[1]—I wrote you by Joseph Elliot on the 29th. and Some time before through Colo Meigs[2]—I hope these will reach you in due time In those I have directed you to Issue an order to Genl Gains to order a Detachment forthwith to remove the intruders from the creek land, and instructed you to give him the same orders under which you are now acting[3]—if those letters has not reached you, you will on the receipt of this Issue the necessary orders to Genl Gains, and continue yourself with the Detachment of u states Troops & Light horse clear round the cherokee country, and terminate your duty below Lowries ferry on the north side of the Tennessee removing all intruders on indian land, as well from reservations under the treaty of 1817 Designated by the written certificate of

Colo Meigs agent as other Indian land, that Colo. Meigs may by his written requisition require you—[4]

I recd. a communication from the Sec of war last evening enclosing me the commission to hold the treaty with the choctaws—the time is left to us—I have wrote Genl [Thomas] Hinds, as to the appointment of time and left him to say after the 15th. of Sept. next to the first of October[5] you will calculate to be here at least by the 15th. of Sept, Capt Easter is still confined & will resign as soon as he gets up—The Dept. has notified him that a Suit will be the consequence, & of course an arrest—Therefore the only alternative as I believe of relieving me from the delicate situation in which I am placed, as well as himself will be his resignation—[6]

I am much pressed with business—keep no copies of my letters to you, I name this that you for your safety as well mine preserve the originals—Mrs. J Joins me in good wishes to you, and are anxious for your return—I am Dear Call your friend sincerely

Andrew Jackson

ALS, NjMoHP (7-1180); Copy fragment, FHi (mAJs).

1. See Call to AJ, July 23. The Cherokees later granted Thomason (not further identified) permission to complete his harvest before removal, but whites outside of the nation despoiled his crops.

2. Neither letter found. Elliot has not been further identified.

3. See AJ to Call, July 1.

4. Lowry's Ferry was located at the junction of Battle Creek and the Tennessee River, in southwestern Marion County, Tennessee. See Call to Edmund P. Gaines, August 19.

5. See John C. Calhoun to AJ, July 12. Jackson's letter to Thomas Hinds (1780–1840), brevet brigadier general for gallantry during the Battle of New Orleans, has not been found.

6. Calhoun granted Richard I. Easter additional time to settle his accounts, and, as Jackson predicted, Easter resigned from the army in February 1821 (see Calhoun to AJ, July 31, and Easter to AJ, February 28, 1821).

Although attempts in 1818 and 1819 had failed to arrange an exchange of Choctaw holdings in Mississippi for land in the Arkansas Territory (see above, Thomas H. Williams, March 29, AJ to John McKee, April 22, and McKee to AJ, August 13, all 1819), pressure from Mississippi's congressional delegation, increased white settlement, and indications that some Choctaw chiefs and warriors were now willing to accept exchange had led to the appointment of Jackson and Thomas Hinds as commissioners to negotiate the cession of Choctaw land in central Mississippi. Jackson arrived at the treaty ground on September 28, and Hinds joined him a day later. Ultimately the commissioners were successful, and the Treaty of Doak's Stand, signed on October 18, secured Choctaw acceptance of exchange and removal.

To John Caldwell Calhoun

Nashville August 2nd. 1820

Dear Sir

I have the honour to acknowledge the recpt of your letter of the 12th. ult. accompanied with a commission to myself and Genl Hinds, with Instructions for holding a treaty with the choctaw nation of Indians

Genl Thomas Hinds being at Beard*[stown]* Kentuckey, by yesterdays mail I adressed him on the subject of this communications—& requested him to state what time would be convenient for him to attend to his duty[1] I have sugested to him that as early a period as will promise supplies of corn in the nation will be the 20th. of Sept, and from that to the first of October will be a proper time to convene the nation—as the huntsmen & warriors of the Nation generally set out on their fall hunts About the Middle of October. It will be necessary to have the funds here as early as possible, that part may be placed in the hands of those who may undertake to furnish the supplies for the Indians during the conferrence—I have some time since wrote to Colo Mckee the agent, to furnish me with a Statement of the probable amount of rations that will be daily required to be Issued, which I expect to receive in a few days, and which will be a guide to the commissioners in making the contract for supplies.[2] I observe in looking over the circular & letter of Instructions, that there is not any thing said on the subject of reservations It strikes me that reservations will have to be made to some of the half breeds who have a wish to remain, before their consent can be obtained—But if made that the limitation of right ought to be so long as the actually resided thereon, or their descendants, that the fee simple ought not to be granted, but that the right should accrue to the United States so soon as the reservee removed from the land—I bearly name this to bring the subject *[to]* your view, that on this point we may receive instructions.[3]

I expect to hear from Genl Hinds in the space of Eight days when you will be advised of the time the Indians will be convened[4]—In the mean time you may make the erangements for forwarding the funds, calculating on the assemblage of the Indians, sometime between the 20th. Sept and first of October, this will enable us to close the conferrence, and forward the result to you early after the meeting of Congress, and leave me free for any other duty, that may arise out of the proceedings of congress, relative to our affairs with Spain—Should not the new Goverment be disposed to act Justly toward us. I am Sir very respectfully your. mo. ob. servt.

Andrew Jackson

ALS, DNA-RG 107 (M221-89); LC, DLC (63).

1. See Calhoun to AJ, July 12. Jackson's letter to Hinds has not been found.

2. See AJ to John McKee, July 21; McKee's response has not been found. On August 5 Jackson informed Calhoun that the discount rates in Nashville and Huntsville made it advisable that the $20,000 allotted for the negotiations be drawn upon the bank at Natchez, which redeemed its notes in specie, and passed current in the Choctaw Nation. The war department agreed, and a warrant issued on August 25 (see Christopher Vandeventer to AJ, August 21, and William Lee to AJ, August 25). Jackson and Hinds ultimately awarded the contract for rations to William Eastin and William B. Lewis (see Memorandum of contract, August 31, and AJ to Rachel Jackson, September 30, below).

3. Calhoun's instructions of July 12 left the terms of the proposed Choctaw cession "entirely to your sound discretion."

4. Jackson and Hinds informed Calhoun on August 7 that they planned to begin negotiations on the first Monday in October.

Traditional American antipathy towards a peacetime standing army, declining revenues, and the recognition by potential rivals of John C. Calhoun's rising political fortunes led Congress to reduce appropriations for fortifications, clothing, and the Missouri expedition. On May 11 the House of Representatives took the next logical step and called for reducing the army from 10,000 to 6,000 enlisted men (see above, AJ to George Gibson, February 1, and John H. Eaton to AJ, March 11; see also AJ to Calhoun, January 27, and to Henry Atkinson, June 26). On July 21, Calhoun began soliciting advice from the army's field commanders about the prospective reduction; Jackson's response follows, below. Both Jackson's proposal and the plan finally submitted by Calhoun in December were less drastic than the reduction adopted by Congress in March 1821 (see Calhoun to AJ, December 16, and 3 U.S. Statutes at Large *615–16).*

To John Caldwell Calhoun

Head Quarters
Nashville 9 August 1820.

Sir.

I have now the honor of forwarding you in detail my ideas on the subject of the resolve of Congress for the reduction of the Army—

Considering the Extent of the sea coast frontier of the United States, the number of permanent defences now constructing,[1] and the additional number that will be necessary before security can be given to our exposed commercial Towns, and capacious estuaries; the Extent of our inland frontier bordering on a jealous commercial rivall, as well as suspicious, if not dangerous savage tribes, A frontier extending with a growing, enterprising & restless population: it would appear that the present Military Establishment was not even adequate to the objects for which it was retained, & that so far from a reduction, both policy, and sound judgement would enforce the propriety of a gradual annual increase—To preserve our permanent defences; to protect our sea coast frontier from insult, to overawe savage neighbours, check their maraudings, and ensure their respect for the American republic by the existence of a positive force always prepared to inflict chastisement on the commission of the first outrage; and finally to retain the seeds of Military science & tactics by those to whom it becomes a profession seems to be the objects for which even in time of profound peace a Military establishment becomes necessary—It would be wiser to annihilate the Army entirely than to retain a force inadequate to the objects for which it should be appointed—Even under the present establishment, the extent of our frontier, the number of posts to be garrisoned, & the number of public works progressing by the labor of soldiers, has rendered the concentration of a force adequate to the forming of a camp of instruction impracticable, while the greater part of the Army has been detached, and divided into seperate command of companies & company drills alone attended to—To comport however with the views of the resolve of Congress, & in a manner least detrimental to the public interest, I now submit a plan of reduction of the Army to the number contemplated, retaining the skelleton of a force, the body of which may be filled up or reduced as the Exigencies of the case may require—

It does not appear that the Ordnance or purchasing departments are to be effected by the Resolve of Congress—There are other departments that cannot without serious injury to the public be greatly reduced; but should rather be firmly established & perfectly organised with a view to a state of peace as well as war—Of these are the Engineer, Quartermasters & Commissariats Departments—

The Engineer Corps should be composed of Officers of no ordinary merit & talents—To be a skilfull Engineer requires long practise, severe discipline of mind; and a rare combination of talents & acquirements—Individuals every way qualified to the discharge of duties so arduous & responsible as those devolving on an Engineer, cannot be retained permanently in the service of Government without compensation adequate to their support & rank equal to their merit—The number of fortifications now constructing, the additional number necessary, the public works for internal improvements contemplated, all requiring the direction of Skilful Engineers, seem to urge the necessity of an increase of the number & rank of the Officers of the Engineer Corps; and an addition to their compensation equal at least to that allowed the members of the Ordnance Department—

The Topographical Corps is alike important—To the mariner accurate charts of our sea coast are greatly needed; while correct military surveys of our frontiers & country at large will be indispensable to the success of all defensive operations in time of invasion—This is a work of many years and can only be effectually accomplished by a Corps of skilful Topographers, adapted in its organisation to the objects to be effected, & controuled by an experienced & energetic head—The present Corps is defective in its organisation; it has no Chief held responsible for its duties; while its officers occasionally compose a part of the Staff of our Generals, and again are subject to the orders of Every department—

The Quartermasters & Commissariats Departments To these departments are confided the quartering, and transporting of Troops, the transporting of provisions, & military Stores; the purchasing of forage, fuel, provisions, and all other articles or supplies not appertaining to other departments—On them devolves duties of a complicated & important character; ultimately connected with the efficiency of Corps, and the success of all operations in the field—In times of peace alone can judicious selection of officers be made; & the officers acquire that experience which will ensure certainty to the supplies of the Army; & economy in the expenditures: and at that period alone can these Departments receive that organisation which may be adapted to a state of war—It is in these departments that the most profligate waste of public property & the grossest misapplication of pecuniary expenditures may take place from inexperience, or want of integrity, and it can only be guarded against by establishments of high minded regular Officers, controuled by an able, vigilant, and virtuous Chief—To the temporary appointments of Qr Masters; & Commissaries of subsistence accompanying Militia Corps called into service for a short period, pecuniary disbursements of public funds should never be confided, & it is all important that the Quartermasters & Commissariats departments should receive such an organisation as may be adapted to any occasion, & confine to the regular officers of experience, bound under responsibilities, for all expenditures appertaining to these departments—

The plan submitted is herewith enclosed, and marked A[2]—I am very respectfully your Most Obt Servt

Andrew Jackson

LS in James Gadsden's hand, DNA-RG 107 (M221-89); LC (dated August 11), DLC (63); Copy, DLC (7-1191). Published in *Calhoun Papers,* 5:317–19.

1. Fortifications then under construction throughout the United States included Fort Diamond on Long Island, New York; Fort Pea Patch, on the Delaware River; Fort Washington on the Potomac River; Fort Monroe at Old Point Comfort, Virginia; Fort Calhoun at Rip Rap Shoals, Virginia; Mobile Point and Dauphin Island in Mobile Bay, Alabama; and the Rigolets, in Louisiana.

2. Jackson's plan would have established the engineer, topographical, medical, quartermaster, and commissary departments as outlined above. Combat forces would be led by one major general, headquartered in Washington, who would command one rifle, two artillery, and six infantry regiments.

To John Caldwell Calhoun

Head quarters Division of the South
Nashville Sept. 2nd. 1820—

Sir

I have Just recd the enclosed letter from John Rogers the Deputy from the Arkansa cherokees, to the cherokees on Tennessee river & now there, and hasten to lay it before you, believing with proper caution the information it contains may prove beneficial in laying the ground work, of which, the whole Georgia claim may be obtained from the cherokees.[1] This Summer as I passed through the lower part of that nation, I was informed by a half Breed Riley, that the opinion now expressed by Rogers was prevalent amonghst the indians in that part of the nation, and Hicks and others threatened with death for deceiving them[2]—I have now but little doubt, that a large portion of the real Indians wish to pass to the Arkansa if they had the means—Might it not have a good effect to have this inquired into and the real fact obtained—and if found true, could it not be carried into effect without much expence to the u. States, except the transportation and provisioning them—Let a confidential agent who will act impartially be appointed to go through the nation, and enroll all Indians who wants to pass to the arkansaw and when enrolled take their relinquishment of all their claim to land where they now live—as soon as this is done, let congress provide the means for transporting & provisioning them, and pass a law providing that land shall be laid out for them adjoining the bounds of the cherokees on arkansas, and that a like portion of their land here, shall be surrendered to the State of Georgia adjoining the settled parts thereof. There can be no question but congress has the right to Legislate on this Subject—The policy of treating with Indian tribes within the Jurisdiction of the united States and acknowledging its sovereignity, could only have arisen at a time when the arm of Goverment was too weak to execute any law passed for the regulation of the Indian tribes within our Territorial limits—To treat with Indians acknowledging our sovereignity, and situate within our declared Territorial limits as a nation ⟨was⟩ has allways appeared very absurd to me; now when more Justice can be done the Indians by Legislation than by treaties, and the arm of Goverment is sufficiently strong to carry into effect any law that Congress may deem necessary and proper to pass for the welfare & happiness of the Indian and for the convenience and benefit of the u. states—It appears to me that it is high time to do away the farce of treating with Indian tribes. Should it be the fact that the wish of the large mass of the cherokees on this side the M. river are ripe for emigration, it opens a fair field for Legislative interference by Congress, by which Justice can be done the Indians, and the pledge of the union to Georgia, ⟨carried into⟩ to extinguish the Indian title fulfilled. These are a few hasty hints for your consideration—I have heretofore submitted to Mr Monroe my ideas more fully.[3] I am Sir with Sincere respect yr mo ob servt

Andrew Jackson

ALS, DNA-RG 75 (M271-3); LC, DLC (63). Published in Bassett, 3:31–32 (from LC).

1. See Rogers, [Jr.], to AJ, [August 17], in which Rogers detailed the divisions between the eastern and western Cherokees and his belief that many more of the nation would emigrate to Arkansas if the government provided the necessary aid.

2. See above, AJ to Calhoun, May 17. Rogers asserted that the eastern Cherokee chiefs had misled the nation when they maintained that the 1819 treaty negotiated at Washington had superceded the 1817 treaty negotiated by Jackson. Riley was possibly John Riley (1796–1820), son of the white interpreter Samuel.

3. Georgia's cession of its western lands in 1802 was conditioned upon the federal government extinguishing Indian land claims within the state's boundaries. For a fuller exposition of Jackson's views, see above, AJ to James Monroe, March 4, 1817.

From Cary Nicholas

Nashville 14th. September 1820

Sir.

I have the honor to report that on Tuesday the 12th. Inst.—I received from T[homas] T[udor] Tucker Esqr. Treasurer of the United States—A Dft. for funds, of which the accompanying is a copy.[1] The funds are to meet my Estimate for May & June current—towards my disbursements for the District of which I am Paymaster. The amount of the dft is equal to the amount of my Estimate, but dificient in specie value by—from twelve to fifteen percentum against Nashville currency—& Nashville currency is the only kind of money the Nashville Bank will pay.[2]

Already two officers—Col. Butler A. G. & Doc. Bronaugh A. S. G. have declared they will not receive this money from me, & I have now in my office demands from a gentleman at Louisville Kentucky—which are suspended & he advised that I can only pay in depreciated paper.

I report, in compliance with my duty under specific instructions, from the Chief of my Department.[3] Respectfully

C. Nicholas
Batln P. Mr.

ALS, DNA-RG 107 (M221-89). Nicholas (1786–1829), a Kentucky native, served as battalion paymaster, 1817–21, thereafter removing to Florida where he edited the Pensacola *Floridian* and served as postmaster.

1. Tucker (1745–1828) had served in the first two congresses and was appointed Treasurer of the United States by Thomas Jefferson, a post he retained until his death. The enclosure has not been identified.

2. Depreciated currency had created similar problems with pay for troops working on the military road (see Nicholas to AJ, February 25).

3. See AJ to John C. Calhoun, September 15; Calhoun to AJ, October 4; and Robert Butler to AJ, January 15, 1821. Paymaster General Nathan Towson's instructions have not been found.

To Rachel Jackson

Choctaw Treaty Ground
Sept. 30th. 1820

My Love

I reached this place two days since, & would have wrote you by the last mail, but the want of paper, and the mail passing Just as I had arived prevented me. This moment the waggons has arived, and affords the facility of writing you by the mail that passes during this night.

We experienced several days rain on our Journey, hither—and from the exposure, I have caught a slight cold which has fell upon my bowels & threaten a return of my old complaint. perhaps it may in some degree, be ascribed to the water, which has been both scarce and bad in many places, but here we are blessed with as good water as the climate can afford, and I cherish a hope that I may Escape a serious attack of my old complaint.

Genl Hinds Joined me last evening, and brings me the pleasing intelligence, that your sister [Mary Donelson] Caffery is in good health, that Sophia [Caffery Van Dorn] has presented Mr. [Peter Aaron] Vandorin with a fine son, and him & Mr [Abraham] Green will be up here in a few days to spend some days with us[1]—The Indians are collecting & I hope we will not be detained as long as I expected—but in a few days I will be able to form a better Judgt. on this point. Andrew [Jackson Donelson] is well—Doctor [William Edward] Butler & Mr Eastin are both here & in heath—which you will please to communicate to our friends—[2]

Andrew Joins me in the affectionate good wishes to you & our two little Andrews,[3] to whom present us affectionately, as well as to all our friends and accept for yourself my warmest prays for your health & happiness untill I return, & believe me to be your affectionate Husband

Andrew Jackson

ALS, MH-H (7-1364). The Choctaw Treaty Ground, or Doak's Stand, was located on the Natchez Trace, near the Pearl River, in the southeast corner of present Madison County, Mississippi.

1. Mary Donelson Caffery (c1756–1823) resided at Port Gibson, Mississippi. In 1811 her daughter, Sophia (b. 1792), had married Van Dorn (1773–1837; Princeton 1795), who witnessed the Treaty of Doak's Stand and would, in 1821, help to lay out the new Mississippi capital of Jackson in the ceded territory; their son, Earl (1820–63), was born on September 17. Green had married Eliza "Betsy" Caffery (c1784–1823), another daughter of Mary, in 1801.

2. Donelson had been appointed aide-de-camp on September 20, in place of Richard I.

Easter. Butler (1790–1882) and his brother Robert had married sisters Martha T. (1790–1857) and Rachel Hays, Jackson's nieces.

3. Andrew Jackson, Jr., and Andrew J. Hutchings.

To Choctaw Indians

(Copy.)

Choctaw Treaty Ground,
October 3rd. 1820.

Friends & Brothers of the Choctaw Nation;

Your father the President of the United States has been informed, that many of your nation have crossed the Mississippi, and that a number of others desire to remove. He has, therefore, appointed the undersigned Commissioners, to convene the head men and warriors of his Choctaw children, and when assembled in a general council, to deliver to them a friendly talk. He also desires to hear the wishes of your nation, and in treaty to do such things as will most promote the happiness and prosperity of all his Choctaw children.

With these instructions, we made known to the nation, through your agent, Colo. John McKee, that a general meeting of the chiefs, head men and warriors was requested and expected at Doake's stand, in said nation, on the 1st day of October, 1820.[1] On that day, the undersigned attended at this place, and expected, that the chiefs, head men and warriors of the Choctaw nation were on the road to the treaty grounds to meet us in council, and listen to the talk of their father the President of the United States. This is the third day we have waited to see you. Only about sixty chiefs and warriors have attended; and we are informed, that not more than one hundred are expected. We are told, that the chiefs and warriors have been advised by some bad men, to stay away from the council, and not come forward to hear the talk of your father the President of the United States. We have also learnt with much pain, that many threats have been made, declaring that any one should be put to death who attends the treaty, and consents to sell or exchange any part of the Choctaw land. Fear not those threats. The arm of your father the President is strong, and will protect the poor Indian from the threats of the white man and half breed, who are growing rich by their labor. They make slaves of the poor Indians, and are indifferent to their happiness. They care not whether the poor perish, or are lost to the nation, if they can grow rich by their labor, and by living on the main roads through the country.

Many of your poor Indian brothers have gone over the Mississippi. It is represented to your father the President, that a number more wish to go to that country. He has, at much expence, purchased it for you. He invites you to come forward, and tell him your mind freely, and without fear. You shall not be injured. He will protect you. Those who choose to move beyond the Mississippi, there is a good country for a small part of their lands here. Those who wish to stay and cultivate the earth, your father the President wants to remain here. He therefore, desires to see you all at this place, so that each may make a choice freely, and all be happy. You are all interested, and must be heard. As the friends and brothers of the white people, you cannot refuse to listen to the council and advice of your father the President of the United States. As soon as you all assemble at this place, we will deliver his friendly talk to his Choctaw children. If you will not come and hear it, he may never speak to you again.

This talk is sent to you by your friends and our friends, Edward Folsome and Middleton Mackey, by whom you will send us an answer, informing us whether you will or will not attend at the treaty, and hear the talk of your father the President of the United States.

We are your friends & Brothers,

(Signed) Andrew Jackson,
Tho: Hinds.

Copy in Samuel R. Overton's hand, DNA-RG 75 (T494-1); Copy, DNA-RG 46 (7-1380). Published in *ASP, Indian Affairs,* 2:234–35. Overton had been appointed secretary to the commissioners on August 24.

1. See AJ to John McKee, July 21 and August 24, and Memorandum on Choctaw negotiations, August 8.

To John Caldwell Calhoun

Choctaw Treaty Ground
Octbr. 11th. 1820.

Sir

We arrived ⟨here⟩ on this ground on the first of this month; being ⟨previously⟩ in the neighbourhood of Mr [William] Dokes a few days, we soon found but few of the chiefs and half-breeds were about to convene, and those ready to tell us that they had neither land to sell or exchange. We were informed that the great Mingo Puchenube had directed his chiefs and warriors to bring with them provisions for four days. This chief on the third inst arrived—When he was asked by the commissioners his reasons for such conduct—he answered because he did not intend to grant any thing asked of his nation by the United States—he was then asked if he knew what would be asked by the United States—he replied he did not A talk was then given him which is detailed on the journals and in which he is distinctly told that we have come to speak to the whole nation and not to a few, and we would remain until they could be collected, runners were accordingly dispatched to collect the body of the nation.[1] A few days after a deserter from the United States army was discovered in the nation married to the Grand daughter of Puchenube—he was arrested as a deserter, and proof of the fact obtained—as soon as this was made known great interest was expressed by the chief and his clan, to get him relieved, by furnishing a substitute—I hesitated on subject, knowing its tendency as a bad precedent in the army—But being advised that it would greatly soften the temper of the chief, and knowing that much good would result from it, should the great chief be thereby brought to hear and adopt our talk; I agreed if a good substitute could be produced, young healthy and stout, I would take him and release the other—the substitute was brought examined and received and the soldier named Welch, released. This made the old chief very friendly—and he has been intimate and friendly ever since. I trust my conduct in this particular may be approved, as the service by the exchange is much benefitted and the release of the soldier Welch, may contribute greatly to bring the old chief and his clan over to hear and adopt our talks. The application of the mother was an affectionate one, which was supported by many of the chiefs and the agent—By not granting it, I would have added weight to the opposition—By granting it many are brought over, who were much opposed to the treaty, and those too whose interest will be much effected by it, being situated within the bounds of the country we wish to obtain—finding the moment a favorable one, as soon as Welch was released, we assembled the chiefs and warriors who were present and read them our talk. To day they go into council, and as soon as the others arrive, we have told the chiefs now here, we will read our talk to them—then we will keep them employed until the whole is assembled, when we will press them for a favourable answer.[2] I am Sir with great respect your. most. ob. Servt.

Andrew Jackson

LS in the hand of Andrew J. Donelson, DNA-RG 107 (M221-89). Published in Anna Lewis, *Chief Pushmataha, American Patriot* (New York, 1959), pp. 144–46.

1. Both Apuckshunnubbe and Pushmataha arrived on October 3. The third principal chief, Mushulatubbe, arrived on October 6 (see Journal of the Choctaw negotiations, August 24–November 10). Doak operated an inn ("Doak's Stand") at the Choctaw treaty ground, 1812–22.

2. The war department later approved Jackson's decision regarding Welch, not further identified (see Calhoun to AJ, November 6).

To Choctaw Indians

Choctaw Treaty Ground,
October 17th. 1820

Friends and Brothers;

Your father the President of the United States has already delivered two talks to your nation.[1] He has endeavored to explain to you your interests, and induce you to promote them. Your welfare and happiness are his grand objects. To advance your civilization, and to preserve and perpetuate you as a nation, are considerations dear to his heart. The first, he is desirous to accomplish, by establishing and fostering your schools. The second, by ceding you a country beyond the Mississippi, where all who have gone over and wish to remove, may be collected together upon land of their own. Here, also, he wishes to settle all those who will not work, but are straggling about in every direction, so as to preserve them as a part of your nation. These are the friendly and humane views of your father the President of the United States, and he is determined to effect them. If the nation here, are so lost to humanity, as to abandon those who have gone and settled over the Mississippi, it is a circumstance of great regret. Your father the President will not permit them to be lost. He could not have anticipated, that any great and good chief and warrior would consent to consign his friends and brothers to misery and destruction, when they might preserve them by exchanging a small part of their land, which they can conveniently spare. The friend of such a measure, is the enemy of your happiness, and unworthy of the Indian character. He must be destitute of all magnimity and virtue, and should not preside over the councils of your nation. It is the duty of every good and wise chief and warrior to make individual sacrifices for the benefit of all his people. He should not be governed by his own private convenience, or that of a small part of his nation. No other course can promote the welfare and happiness of any people. If the Choctaw children of your father the President, will adopt the measures here recommended, they will be happy; if they should not, they may be lost forever.

We have been sent here by your father the President, to explain these things to the Chiefs, headmen and warriors of this nation. These are the valuable objects which Mr. Jefferson promised you and was desirous to accomplish.[2] You have been requested to listen well, and avoid the counsel of bad men. All we wish, is, that you should secure your own happiness. If you will not hear, and be advised by your father the President of the United States, you must suffer the consequences. He is resolved to preserve and protect his Choctaw children beyond the Mississippi. If you reject his friendly proposals, he will treat with them for the accomplishment of this humane object. They are ready to negociate with us, and will receive us with open arms. If you will permit the obstinacy and folly of a few amongst you, to work your own destruction, you cannot hereafter complain.

Such conduct on your part, will force your father the President to adopt the course above mentioned; or Congress, at their approaching session, will take the business into their own hands. By the treaty of Hopewill, they have a right to manage the affairs of this nation; and they will do so, if compelled by the obstinacy of your chiefs, and the wickedness of your advisers.[3] It will be the last time a talk will ever be delivered by your father the President, to his Choctaw children, on this side of the Mississippi. You are advised to beware. This is the second time we have met you in council, and the patience of your father the President may be exhausted.[4] He has heretofore treated you as friends and brothers. He has protected you, and more than once saved your nation. During the late war, he took you by the hand as beloved children, and defended you from your and his enemies. Had he failed at New Orleans, your nation would have been destroyed. Be careful you do not forfeit his friendship and regard. He does not ask you for favors, but only for what is just and reasonable, and for your good. If you refuse it, you must submit to the consequences. Your evil advisers may rely upon it, that they will suffer for their folly. They are now offered reservations and other advantages; but hereafter their interests will not be consulted, only as they are connected with that of the great body of the nation. This is the last attempt, we repeat it, that will be made to treat on this side of the Mississippi. When so many advantages are offered you, and they are rejected, it will be hereafter useless. If evil counsel is permitted to prevail amongst you, your nation must be discarded from the friendship and protection of their white brothers. It is painful to your father the President to do so; but necessity will compell him, and that too at a time, when your people are weakened by emigration, and more than ever require his fatherly advice and assistance.

Your father the President offers you every advantage, and again wishes to preserve and perpetuate you as a nation. The chain which unites his white and Choctaw children will then be brightened. He wishes to treat with you upon terms that will accommodate those living here. He obliges himself to endow your schools, and to provide for the happiness of all. If he is compelled to treat with those beyond the Mississippi, in an exchange of land, he will insist upon acre for acre, and the country here may be cut up, so as to interfere with your schools, as well as the great body of the nation. All the advantages now proposed, may be lost forever. We may no longer be friends and brothers, and the Choctaw name here be irrecoverably lost.

Let us entreat you to avoid bad counsellors. Remember that your nation was in great danger of being governed by the advice of wicked men on two former occasions. When two of your Choctaw brothers were taken prisoner by the British, during the late war, they were sent amongst you with a talk, which you heard. They also brought with them, as presents, twelve bundles of good and war hatchets, which were distributed in this nation. Your father the President then interposed. He destroyed the enemy, and saved your people. When General Jackson was at Mobile, he sent you a talk, as his friends and brothers. afterwards, a Spanish agent paid you a visit, and as he was informed, spoiled this talk. As soon as he received this intelligence, General Jackson immediately dispatched the bearer back again, and directed him to say to the Red Fort, a chief of the Six Towns, that unless he and his warriors joined him within a given time, he should find him and his army in his town in a few days. This chief was told, that he must take sides either for or against us. He heard General Jackson's talk; joined him within the time mentioned. He held his father the President fast by the hand, and by our united efforts the enemy was conquered, and your nation saved a second time.[5] General Jackson has come a third time to preserve you, and he will do so, if you will listen to the talk of your father the President of the United States. Are you unmindful of all these things, and of what your father the President has done for you? Pause before you decide. Frown upon evil counsellors, and consult your best interests, and all will be well. Otherwise no foresight can calculate your distresses. Your father the President will not be trifled with, and put at defiance. A heavy cloud may burst upon you, and you may be without friends to counsel or protect you. The chain which has hitherto united us may be broken. Listen well, and then determine. Your existence as a nation, is in your own hands.

The project of a treaty delivered to you on yesterday, contains the basis of every thing necessary for the permanent happiness of your nation. It is such a treaty, as all real friends to your nation will say, it is your interest to make, and by which your welfare and prosperity will be secured forever. Have the pegs driven down, and the lines distinctly marked, as proposed, so that they never can be altered until you request it yourselves, or until you are advanced to that state of civilization, when the land will be apportioned out to each family or individual in the nation. Hear and listen well. Decide for the happiness of all your people, and let not a few obstinate and wicked men destroy your welfare and security. We have labored hard to convince you of your real interests. We hope you will see them as we do, and adopt the treaty proposed, an outline of which has been submitted to you, in order that it may be frequently read to you, and you might understand its objects. Should you reject it, it will be a source of great regret, as it may be a measure fatal to your nation.[6]

(Signed) Andrew Jackson.
Thomas Hinds.

Copy in Samuel R. Overton's hand, DNA-RG 75 (T494-1); Copy, DNA-RG 46 (mAJs). Published in *ASP, Indian Affairs,* 2:239–40.

1. See AJ and Thomas Hinds to Choctaw Indians, October 10 and 13.

2. Thomas Jefferson had addressed visiting Choctaw delegations twice, in December 1803 and again in March 1805, promising government aid as the Choctaws developed a more agrarian culture.

3. The 1786 Treaty of Hopewell placed the Choctaw Nation under the protection of the United States.

4. A reference to the failed negotiations of October 1818. See Isaac Shelby to AJ, December 4, 1818.

5. The commissioners' October 13 proposal pledged the proceeds of the sale of one township of ceded land for a Choctaw school fund. The specific British attempt to recruit Choctaws during the War of 1812 has not been identified, but in July and August of 1814 George Woodbine, a British army officer stationed in Pensacola, was actively engaged in recruiting both hostile and friendly Indians to the British cause (see *Jackson,* 3:111–12, 122–23). On the Spanish attempt to win over the Choctaws, see Joseph Carson to AJ, August 29, John McKee to AJ, September 13, AJ to McKee, September 15, James E. Dinkins to AJ, September 30, and AJ to McKee, October 19, all 1814.

6. The draft treaty has not been found. The council remained divided when Apuckshun-

nubbe abruptly declared his unalterable opposition to removal and left the treaty ground. Jackson and Hinds intervened one last time, reminding the nation that recalcitrant chiefs might be deposed, whereupon the council accepted the treaty and sought the removal of Apuckshunnubbe (see Journal of the Choctaw negotiations, August 24–November 10, and Pushmataha et al. to AJ and Hinds, October 20). Unfortunately, the Arkansas land ceded to the Choctaws was already being settled by whites, prompting much protest against the treaty and leading to the treaty of 1825, which revised the boundary of the Choctaw's Arkansas land.

*Corporal punishment was a long-standing tradition in the American army, approved and ordered by Jackson throughout his military career. Although Congress had forbidden flogging in 1812, the Rules and Articles of War did not generally ban corporal punishment but in several instances specifically authorized it, and Article 20 gave wide discretion to courts-martial in punishing desertion (*2 U.S. Statutes at Large *359–72, 735). As a result some forms of physical punishment were tolerated, chiefly branding, cropping of the ears, and beating with a flat stick (called "cobbing" and ordered by Jackson during his Florida invasion; see General Order, May 8, 1818). In his report, below, Stockley D. Hays, the Southern Division judge advocate, recommended a strict interpretation of the Rules and Articles of War. In contradistinction to common practice, Hays argued that punishments not specifically authorized were illegal. Jackson concurred with Hays's strict interpretation, and expanded upon it in his December 8 letter to Henry Atkinson (below), in stark contrast to his own past conduct and his continuing personal support for William King, who had been suspended from the army for five years for ordering deserters shot on sight (see AJ to King, November 29, below).*

From Stockley Donelson Hays

Judge Advocates office S. Division
Nashville.
Novr. 12th. 1820—

Sir,

I have the honor herewith to send for your investigation the proceedings of a General Court Martial, convened at the Bay of St. Louis, under department order of date 18th. July 1820, of which Capt. William Davanport 8th. Infy. was president—

In the examination of these proceedings I fear you will find much to censure—In the several cases, of Martin Thorning, Charles Perine, William Smith, William Wilson, John Apple, Lewis Doteridge & Sergt. William Church, found Guilty of Desertion—The Court have sentenced them to be branded with the letter D on the Cheek & some other, but milder punishment—In the cases of Thos McNally and John Cummings Private Soldiers, found Guilty of Desertion—The Court have sentenced them not only to be Branded with the Letter D. but to be cropped and drummed out of service all of which punishments, are ⟨equally⟩ ignominious ⟨and illegal and⟩ impolitic—& illegal[1]—To wear the indelible and legible marks of infamy is certainly ignominious—to exercise an arbitrary power to a cruel extent not sanctioned by law, in a Government like ours must be impolitic, and that this proceedure of the Court, is illegal, you no doubt will believe. But should you entertain any doubt on the Subject, I beg leave to refer you to the rules & articles of War, the only source from whence Courts Martial derive any authority to punish⟨ment⟩ soldiers at all—On a carefull examination of those Rules & Articles, you will find such punishment no where authorised nor any where enumerated—But the Congress in distributing punishment to enumerated offences, refers them often times to the sound discretion of the trying Court—and the Courts Martial in the exercise of this discretion, should be limited to the punishments enumerated & recognised by the law from whence they derive their authority, viz the Rules & articles of War—If on examination of ⟨those rules & articles⟩ them, we can no where find, this description of punishment under consideration, mentioned, or in any wise authorised—the conclusion is inevitable; that the ⟨exercise⟩ infliction of them, is contrary to law—and an arbitrary assumption of power; which should not be permitted, in a country, justly proud of its civil & religious liberties—⟨The only assylum from oppression⟩—where too every injury, has its appropated remedy and every crime its enumerated & known punishment—⟨the only assylum from oppression—⟩

The commanding officer Brevt. Brigr Genl. Daniel Bissell in acting on the proceedings of the Court, disapproves their sentence in the cases above mentioned on the ground (as it seems) of their impolicy alone; leaving the question of their legallity or illegality totally out of view; But in the exercise of his authority as Commanding Genl departs as widely from his duty, in my opinion as the Court did from theirs whose sentence he disapproves ⟨and from theirs—⟩ He disapproves the sentence of the Court—This he had a right to do; But he does not stop here—He orders, a distinct and totally different kind of punishment to be inflicted—by what he calls a commutation of punishment, and directs *his sentence* to be carried into immediate effect—Thus assuming to himself the authority which the law gives to the Court exclusively—

A Comdg officer in acting on the sentence of a Court Martial, may disapprove the whole proceedings or a part and order the residue to be carried into effect—He may approve the whole and remit the punishment or any part of it—But he can in nowise alter the nature or kind of punishment assessed by the Court nor commute it, for a different Kind—He may lessen the degree of punishment; But in no case can he increase it—[2]

I have thought it my duty to make this communication, on account of the gross error in the sentence of the Court as well as in the conduct of the Genl in acting on their proceedings—

Was this case to remain unnoticed and uncorrected, it would operate as an example in future; be made use of as a pretext, nay perhaps quoted hereafter as authority, both by Courts & Comdg officers, to the great injury of the army—Very respy. I have the honor to be yr obt st

S. D. Hays J. A. D.

ALS draft, DLC (29); LS copy in Robert Butler's hand, DNA-RG 153 (7-1407).

1. All of the men named above served in the 8th Infantry. In addition to branding and cropping, the "milder punishment" referred to by Hays consisted of wearing an iron collar while at hard labor.

2. Bissell (d. 1833), a Connecticut native, had taken command of the 8th Military Department upon Eleazar W. Ripley's resignation, and was discharged in 1821. Bissell had substituted hard labor and docking of pay for sentences of corporal punishment and dismissal. Jackson endorsed Hays's view (see AJ to John C. Calhoun, November 30).

To Nelson P. Jones

⟨Hermitage⟩
Nashville Novbr. 25th. 1820

Sir

When I returned home from Nashville and the day after I left you, Mr. Sanders informed me, that from a conversation he had with you that you had stated that you were only to deliver me the amount of cotton shipped last year, instead of the amount raised—and that Toll was to be deducted as it was last year as he understood you—I told him he must have mistaken you—But to put disputation on this subject beyond reach I enclose this letter to Genl Coffee with a request that he deliver it to you & read the contract to you least you may have taken up improper Ideas of it—without prefacing any thing that lead to it—our contract as I understood it is This "That you deliver to me as much seed cotton as was raised on the plantation last year as good & merchantable as is raised on the place this year—that This should be assertained first by the Ginners recpt—who ginned the cotton last year—If that could not be obtained, Then by the shippers recpt—That this cotton should be ginned by my Ginn, & Bailed by you with the hands on the place I finding rope & linnen."[1]

Surely such a preposterous Idea cannot have been taken up, that I was to pay toll at my own ginn for ginning and bailing and my own hands to aid in doing This labour—

The contract ⟨I thought was⟩ is well expressed & as I thought as well understood—that I was to receve the full amount raised on the place last year & that was to be weighed in the seed & whatever it produces is to be Bailed for me—Why the Ginners recpt was first named, was for this purpose to shew the whole crop raised, which if obtained, would prevent the calculation & the addition of the Toll deducted last year, and the amount reserved for the supply of the two farms for spinning to cloath the negroes with—It being (as you acknowledged yourself) such a liberal proposition on my part, and as you have often expressed since such a beneficial contract on your part, ⟨that⟩ I am confident Sanders has mistaken you. But to prevent any ⟨Jawing⟩ misunderstanding or dispute I have wrote this & requested Genl Coffee to hand it to you & to read the contract again to you—When you are ready to commence ginning my cotton—Genl Coffee will attend & see the Seed cotton weighed—and after weighed It will be ginned immediately & Bailed. without interfering with any other cotton.[2] I am yrs respectfully

Andrew Jackson

ALS copy, DLC (72). Jones, formerly of Abbeville County, South Carolina, had moved to Davidson County in 1818 and temporarily resided near the Hermitage. In December 1819 he and Jackson contracted to farm Jackson's Evans Spring plantation, where he relocated. In partnership with John Donelson (1787–1840) and David Love, Jones purchased a 1,452 acre tract in Lauderdale County in 1824.

1. Jackson was quoting from his agreement with Jones, November 4. While returning to Nashville after completing the Choctaw treaty negotiations, Jackson stopped at Florence, Alabama, and dissolved his partnership with him. Sanders was probably Harrison Saunders, Jackson's overseer at the Hermitage. The letter to John Coffee has not been found.

2. See AJ to Coffee, December 13, below, and February 6, 1821.

To William King

Head quarters D. of the South
Nashville Novbr 29th. 1820—

Dr. Sir

I have the pleasure to acknowledge the receipt of your letter of the 30th. ult, it reached me by yesterdays mail & I hasten to answer it. On the recpt of your letter of the 11th. of June last, I enclosed it to the adjutant Genl of Division Colo. Butler making inquiry of him whether the order "*for shooting Deserters,*" Issued as therein stated had ever come to his office—to which he replied as you will see by the enclosed, a ⟨duplicate⟩ copy of which I ⟨enclosed⟩ sent to you under date of the 4th. of august—I regret that letter ⟨did⟩ has not reached you.[1]

When I first saw it announced in the papers that you had ordered a deserter to be shot and that it was carried into effect with the cruelty as stated in the reports ⟨&c &c⟩ I took the liberty to ⟨give it the positive⟩ contradict⟨ion⟩ it—nor was I informed of the fact of such an order untill a verry short time previous to your arrest—when ⟨it⟩ your arrest was announced to me by the Department of War, at the Instance of Major Hogan, and on charges & Specifications exhibitted by him whilst he was under arrest by your order I adressed a letter to the Sec of War on that subject; ⟨to him⟩ that letter will shew my feelings toward you as an officer.[2]

When I saw my approbatory letter of your conduct whilst in command at Pensacola produced upon your trial, as approving ⟨that⟩ the order for shooting deserters which I had never seen Justice to my self, ⟨having your trial⟩ Justice to truth compelled me, to adress the note I did to Sec of war—But that note did not carry with it the Idea that such a report ⟨never⟩ had not been made out by you, but that it never had reached me—⟨when my letter re⟩ There is no letter of mine wrote upon this unpleasant, & to you unfortunate subject that can be Tortured to ⟨mean⟩ shew that I did not at all times view you a valluable officer, and your military conduct as far as I was informed of it, met my approbation—you ⟨yet⟩ know me not; if you have taken up an Idea—that I ever abandon ⟨a M⟩ an officer of merit when ⟨his⟩ he is surrounded with dificulty or misfortune—Then is the time I will support him as far as truth & Justice will authorise me.[3]

I have enclosed you here the note of Colo. Butler which will prove to you, that your order for "shooting Deserters," never came to his office and permit me to assure you that there was no act of mine, ⟨that can be shewn⟩ that was unfriendly to you, and it will give me pleasure to see you restored to your command—with sentiments of personal friendship, Mrs. J. Joins me in good wishes to you and your lady, and believe me to be very respectfully yr mo ob Servt

Andrew Jackson

P.S. present me to Lt [John] Hull say to him I feel pleasure that his ⟨is⟩ sword is restored to him, & I trust that his prudence & good conduct will enable him to wear it long, with honor to himself & benefit to his country[4]—A. J.

ALS draft, T (8-0001).

1. Letters not found. The enclosure was Robert Butler to AJ, August 3.

2. See AJ to John C. Calhoun, September 7, 1819. Jackson probably learned of King's order to shoot deserters from the Lexington *Kentucky Reporter,* July 7, 1819. Adjutant General Daniel Parker ordered King's court-martial on August 10, 1819; King was convicted on December 8, 1819, and suspended from the service (see Records of the court-martial of William King, DNA-RG 153, mAJs).

3. See AJ to Calhoun, December 28, 1819. The court-martial record contains Jackson's letter to King of April 13, 1819, in which Jackson gave his "entire approbation" to King's conduct while commanding American troops in Florida. The record also reveals that King defended his actions on the ground that his superiors (Edmund P. Gaines and Jackson) had known of his order to shoot deserters (a point investigated by the House of Representatives in December 1820; see *ASP, Military Affairs,* 2:198–99).

4. King's wife has not been identified. Hull, a native of Kentucky and 1st lieutenant of the 4th Infantry, had been court-martialed for fighting and was to be dismissed from the service,

but President Monroe reinstated him (see Hull to AJ, October 15, and AJ to Calhoun, October 16).

To Henry Atkinson

Division of the South
Head Quarters
Nashville Decbr 8th 1820

Sir

Your letters of the 14th and 17th ultimo have been recd., with the report of Capt. [Alphonso] Wetmore Paymaster of the 6th Infantry; all of which are duly noted.[1]

I regret with yourself, that a milder course had not been pursued by Col. [Talbot] Chambers, towards the two deserters. I have no doubt, (as you express) but Col Chambers was actuated by the purest principles, and that he believed the course taken was the only one, by which Desertion could be effectually prevented.[2] But the law positively forbids the infliction of corporeal punishment. The Legislative authority enacting, has limited our duties expressly, to the execution of the Laws. As the act complained of has only come to your knowledge unofficially, and has long since been committed, I approve of your determination to await the orders of the Secy. of War, And as you have not informed me whether you have made report of the case to the Secy of War, I shall enclose him an extract of your letter of the 17th, and also await his instructions. I have long since urged the propriety of the President of the U. States, issuing a Genl order, prohibiting in all cases corporeal punishment from being awarded by Courts-Martial. This would put a stop to the difficulties which have heretofore attached to Courts, awarding corporeal or unusual punishments.[3]

The report of Capt Wetmore, exhibiting the disposition of funds in his hands, is satisfactory and from his good character, I have no doubt but the public mony in his care will be well applied, and the Troops punctually paid—I am with great respect your Mo Obt servant.

(Signed) Andrew Jackson

LC in Andrew J. Donelson's hand, DLC (63).

1. See Atkinson to AJ, November 14 and 17. Wetmore (d. 1849), a Connecticut native, served in the army 1812–33. His report (not found) concerned the large amount of unexpended funds for the period April through July.

2. Atkinson had reported on November 17 that in June 1819 Chambers, colonel of the Rifle Regiment, had ordered the ears cropped of two soldiers attached to the Missouri expedition, that Chambers had not acted from malicious intent, but that "the punishments are past and cannot be recalled."

3. See AJ to John C. Calhoun, December 8. Calhoun had already ordered Chambers to be court-martialed; the trial took place the following May. Chambers was found guilty and suspended for one month, a sentence that Calhoun found inadequate to the offense, but which

the president confirmed (see Calhoun to AJ, January 21, 1821, and AJ to Calhoun, February 8, 1821).

From James Gadsden

Mobile 8 Decr 1820

My Dear General

I arrived here last evening after a tedious, & solitary ride—

It gives me pleasure to state that the Contractors for Dauphin Island & the Rigolets are progressing with some degree of success: though not with the rapidity desirable—It is an object however under existing circumstances to secure the completion of the works although attended with much delay & many Embarrassments—I wish it was in my power to report as favourably of Mobile Point. All operations appear measurably to be suspended at that place & the Contractor but a few removes from actual failure—I suppose we shall have to remain quiet spectators of events untill the time limited for the completion of his contract expires, and the Government can progress itself—This will not be untill July next—

The Presidents Message has just reached us—It appears not to satisfy expectations—The Florida question remains still in an uncertain, unsettled state—On the subject of deficiency in revenue nothing is said: & still less of the army or navy—In short we find no measures recommended: & every step which may be taken left at the option & on the responsibility of Congress—[1]

The Election for Speaker appears to have been contested; and it is with regret that I perceive in the contest the commencement of Northern against Southern Interests—The Triumph of the Northern candidate in this instance, will not it is hoped encourage the Northern Members to revive the Missouri question—The feelings of the South & west are too much excited on that subject: & a revival of it in the house may result unhappily—It will most unquestionably give a direction to the party feelings in this Country; which may tend to results of a most calamitous character to this Country—There are no parties more to be deprecated in this country than those which depend upon sectional interests. Once excite a belief that the interest of the North or atlantic states, are in opposition to those of the West; and we strike the first & most effectual blow at the union of the states. We are now in the full tide of successful experiment; free & strong at home; and respected abroad—We weaken the first; and most unquestionably loose the second by seperation—[2]

My best respects to Mrs Jackson & your family generally Your friend

Gadsden

ALS, DLC (29). In October Gadsden had been appointed colonel and inspector general of the Southern Division, replacing Arthur P. Hayne.

1. For James Monroe's annual message, dated November 14, see *Annals of Congress,* 16th Cong., 2nd sess., pp. 11–17.

2. On November 15 John W. Taylor (1784–1854; Union 1803) of New York, a leader of the antislavery forces during the previous winter's Missouri debate, was elected speaker of the House on the twenty-second ballot. Missouri's admission to the Union again became a controversy when the territory sought approval of a constitution which barred free blacks and mulattoes from entering the state (see AJ to Monroe, January 1, 1821).

Sometime before 1817, Bennett Smith, a prominent Rutherford County lawyer and brother of South Carolina Senator William Smith, sold a family of slaves to his son Joseph Dickson Smith for approximately $1,700. The elder Smith conditioned the sale upon his son-in-law, John Hutchings, becoming security for the bond, and also suggested that Joseph give Hutchings a mortgage on the slaves as an indemnity. After Hutchings's death in November 1817, Joseph D. Smith sold the slaves to Gilbert Gray Washington (d. c1847), brother of Thomas and a Davidson County lawyer. In 1819 Bennett Smith announced his intention to collect the debt from Hutchings's estate (in effect, from his grandson, Andrew J. Hutchings), and successfully sued John Hutchings's executors (Jackson, John Coffee, and Stockley D. Hutchings) in Madison County, Alabama (see Coffee to AJ, January 12; and Deposition of Coffee, August 5, 1822; and Bennett Smith to Minor & Taylor, January 1, 1821, THi). Jackson, who as guardian of Andrew J. Hutchings controlled the paid-over assets of the estate, consulted with Coffee on how best to respond to the judgment. The legal maneuvering, which continued until a compromise settlement in 1824, centered on how best to obtain equitable relief against the Alabama judgment, thereby protecting the interests of young Hutchings against the claims of his grandfather.

To John Coffee

Nashville Decbr. 13th. 1820—

Dr. Genl

I have this moment recd yours of the 9th. Instant, and have to thank you for your kind attention to my business with that *fiend* Jones, and I hope I will now get Clear of him without much more Injury, and when that time arives I will rejoice. I find from Will Crawfords letter that he wanted to put on me all the Frostbit corn, from Mr James Jacksons letter, that he denied it to you—I think with you that William had better remain untill the crop is gathered & divided, and indeed then I would believe ⟨him⟩ Jones not to be too good after you weigh the cotton, that he would cabbage unless he was overlooked—however, I think to get clear of him any how is a blessing.[1]

I have at length obtained an interview with Mr Whiteside & Major

Washington The latter has entered into an article with me which is left in the hands of Thos. Washington Esqr for safe keeping, that we Jointly defend the suit, brought by Bennet Smith against the Executors of J. Hutchings Deceased, at our Joint expence prosecute a Bill in chancery at our Joint expence, and if Smith ultimately succeeds G. G. Washington is to keep the Estate indamfied, I thought this better for the child than to run the risque & expence of recovering the negroes in a distant country where the dificulty of Identifying them was great, and Washington having purchased them by & with the knowledge of old Smith might ultimately turn the child back on him for a recovery—The old Gentleman Bennett has on the 2nd of this month adressed me a long letter on the subject, in which he makes two precious statements—the first is his acknowledgement that you frequently pressed him to bring suit against his son on the note or that he would not have yet sued &c second that by his will, he has released & given to his sons all debts due by them to him by note &c &c. This at once is an acknowledgement, aded to his not suing his son, that he never intended making his son liable on the note that he has brought suit vs the executors. This Whitesides believes is a strong point in equity.[2]

The course recommended by Whitesides is, first to reverse the Judgt in Allabama, and as soon as that is done; to file a bill against him in this state, and for this purpose I enclose a copy of the errors assigned, or to be assigned & made out by Whitesides memorandom which is enclosed with his note of directions as to the record, how it is to be made out after the writ of error is obtained—I would advise you to get Mr Coulter, and William S[avin] Fulton to draw out the errors assigned from the memorandom of Mr Whitesides enclosed—The copy enclosed of the record will be sufficient, for the purpose of founding a petition for the writ of Error, and as soon as the writ is granted a compleat copy of the record must be had, Just as it exists in the clerks office—I wish the copy of the record I enclose you to be preserved. Mr Whitesides is of the opinion that nothing can be levied on by the present Execution, unless such property that is found in the actual possession of the Executors, therefore at next court, unless we can reverse the Judgt, the plaintiff will try by Scire facias, or Motion, to have an execution against the Executors. I wish you to keep an account of the amt of fees promised to the Lawyers that you may employ in this case, as Washington & myself are bound to pay them. Should security be required, for the costs of the writ of Error Mr James Jackson will become security on application—I would thank you to send me a copy of the laws of your Judicial System. I want them for Mr. Whitesides, if we fail to reverse the Judgt, we must be prepared with a Bill of injunction in your state, preparatory to this it is necessary that he should read & Know your rules of court when he draws the bill. If it should become necessary I will come out. I have but little doubt if we can reverse the Judgt. in allabama, file a bill here that we will obtain a perpetual Injunction. as soon as you receive this & see Coulter & Fulton, be pleased to write me whether the circuit

Judge, or the clerk has the right to grant the writ of Error—& in what court the writ will be made returnable.[3] I am Dr. Sir with sincere respect your mo. ob. Servt.

Andrew Jackson

P. S. Say to Mr J. Jackson I have recd his letter but have not time to write at present present me to him respectfully & our best wishes to your lady & family

ALS, THi (8-0021).

1. Neither Coffee's letter of December 9, nor the letters from James Jackson and William W. Crawford have been found. Jackson had terminated his overseer agreement with Jones (see above, AJ to Nelson P. Jones, November 25).

2. Smith's letter of December 2 has not been found (see Deposition of Coffee, August 5, 1822).

3. Probably George Coalter, a former Kentucky militia officer, who had moved to Florence before 1820. Fulton (1795–1844), a Maryland native, had served as Jackson's private secretary during the invasion of Florida in 1818 and settled in Florence in 1820. Jackson appointed Fulton secretary of Arkansas Territory in 1829 and governor in 1835. The enclosures have not been found.

It was not unusual for Jackson to develop paternal feelings for members of his military family, and no where was this more evident than during the long and stormy courtship between Richard K. Call and Mary Letitia Kirkman (1801–36). The following two letters reveal Jackson as conciliator and matchmaker, roles he continued to play until Call and Kirkman married in July 1824 at the Hermitage.

To Ellen Jackson Kirkman

Hermitage December 16th 1820

Dr Madam;

I have received your note of yesterday, and would cheerfully drop the subject forever, was it not that justice has not been altogether measured to me in your statement, and as I have ever, so do I wish, to receive and mete justice to all and on these terms live in friendship with you and your family—Your note of Tuesday night I did not receive until just before I left Town on Wednesday, and in the midst of business, and on the moment of leaving town I gave it a hasty answer.[1] Permit me to bring to your view how the conversation of Tuesday was introduced. I ask you, was it not by yourself in the presence of Mary, when your mind was in a very purturbed state. I endeavored to calm your mind, for I found in the presence of your daughter the subject must be both unpleasant and improper—You still pressed the subject, I observed as I had done on a former occasion to you, that I knew not whether any engagement existed between Mary & Capt ——, but that it had become a Town talk that Capt —— had in a tavern declared the engagement with Mary and his certainty of success—this should have been in the presence of Mr Patterson, whom I told you, had been called on by Capt ——, and, Mr P. had positively denied it in the presence of Doctr Bronaugh, and then told you, that such things would lead to consequences very unpleasant—for I knew so much of the honorable feelings of Capt that if he could find out the author of this falsehood, and slander of your daughter, he would chastise him, and I recommended and seriously so, that less talk should be had upon this delicate subject and less Town tales listened to. I was in hopes that here the conversation would have ended, particularly in the hearing of your daughter—it was still urged, and the Capt the subject of abuse. I then observed, would it add to your peace of mind if Capt should leave the state if it would, I would pledge my honor he would do it, that I had before pledged my honor that he never would attempt, even if any engagements existed, to run away with your daughter; that I had fully and confidentially given my disapprobation of run-away matches, an[d] enumerated to you an unhappy instance that I still much regretted. You still pressed the subject, and began to speak in the most light, bitter and disrespectful manner of Capt —— the feelings of justice would not permit me to be silent—I again as I had before, stated to you that at the tender age of Eighteen, he had joined me, that from his uniform, upright and honorable conduct, he had endeared himself to me and to the whole Army, that there was not a stain or spot upon his character, that you might appeal to every officer in the Army and every Citizen who Knew him for the reality of his good character, even to your Brother James, to verify my statement of his character: But you do me injustice when you say, that I said, that several Gentlemen of considerable standing would freely give their daughters to Capt. ——, and on that subject that I referred you to your Brother James, and that I did not instance any case when the name of Crawford was named. I did instance a case when Mr Cross was married—when you charged men with mercenary views, I knew you wronged him[2]—I did say, and now repeat that I do know several Gentlemen of fortune and standing in society, that would freely give their daughters to Capt ——, I did say this, in reply to your attack upon his mercenary views, his character and standing, but you do me injustice when you ascribe this to my desire to thwart your influence over your daughter—That I knew him to be a man of honor and character, the extract of the Capt —— letter which I now enclose you proves the high estimation in which I held him as a man of honor & propriety, to be true.[3] I hail the event with ⟨your⟩ pleasure, as it will give peace to your mind and to that of your family, and the society in which we dwell—And I do hope when you read the extract of the letter that I enclose from Capt —— to me, you will find realized all my declarations with respect to the honor and proper conduct of Capt ——, and will hereafter do him and his reputation justice—Recollect that the greatest compliment a Gentleman can bestow upon the merits and accomplishments of a young lady, is by bestowing upon her his affection, and the greatest magnanimity that can be displayed is to withdraw for the happiness of others

It is true that I did say that Capt —— was a match for any man's or merchants daughter in America, who made choice of him, both as it respects his family, connections, and his own propriety of conduct—I did, and do believe that the son of Majr [William] Call who fought and atchieved the liberties we enjoy, who was of the first families of Virginia, who had sacrificed his property and his private interests in procuring the boon and blessing of liberty, that his son who had braved every danger to support and preserve our independence, and who had supported an unblemished character, was an equal of any mans daughter in America[4]—I think as still—And it will give me great pleasure that your amiable daughter move more to your inclination, and to her individual happiness, and when this happens I will rejoice in your prosperity and happiness and that of your amiable daughter. I therefore now trust and hope that you will do justice to Capt —— who has shewn the utmost magnanimity on this occasion; and permit me to cherish a friendship for him which I know he merits, and do me the Justice to believe that I had no agency in bringing about an engagement which I never knew existed, until I received the letter an extract of which I now enclose you, and the determination therein expressed. I will guarantee its performance by Capt Call—Therefore as all things have thus happily terminated, my hopes are, that tranquillity and friendship will again be restored and established

Copy, THi (8-0025). Kirkman (1774–1850), a native of County Monaghan, Ireland, and sister of James, John, and Washington Jackson, had married Thomas Kirkman, of County Cork, Ireland; they moved to Nashville about 1807.

1. Neither Kirkman's letters of December 12 and 15 nor Jackson's answer have been found.

2. Patterson has not been identified. Crawford and Cross may have been William W. Crawford and Richard C. Cross.

3. The enclosed extract has not been found.

4. William Call had owned a plantation near Petersburg, Virginia, before the Revolution; he removed his family to Mecklenburg County of that state after Richard Keith's birth in 1792, and died soon thereafter.

To Richard Keith Call

[cDecember 16, 1820]

*[Dr Ca]*ll

I recd yours of the 15th instant by Doctor B*[ronaugh a]*t the same time recd. a note from our mutual *[frie]*nd Mrs. Kirkman.[1] I am delighted with the honoura*[bility a]*nd magnimity of your conduct on this ocasion *[and]* if the parents of Mary, can distinguish and *[d]*ecently appreciate, nobleness of Soul and actio*[n they]* must appreciate their daughters conduct & *[he]*r noble sacrafice of feeling, & affection for th*[eir hap]*piness—how sordid must be the soul whi*[ch wou]*ld prefer riches, to worth, the atosnation [ostentation?] of Man *[beca]*use he possessed wealth, to a noble, generous, & *[di]*sinterested, lover, who alone appreciated the worth of the person beloved; how lost to the real happiness of a *[d]*aughter, must they be, who alone views riches as t*[he]* only qualification, of the man, they wish to unite a daughter to. your conduct is fully appr*[obated]* by me, and it is the only one that a high min*[ded hon]*ourable man, should have adopted—the sacraf*[ice neces]*sary is not a voluntary one, it is one that is *[poi]*nted out by filial duty and shews the virtue *[of]* her soul—it is a sacrafice proper, and I have *[no]* doubt but the proper one, even she looks forward to both your happiness. I have wrote to *[Mrs]* E. Kirkman in answer to her note, and enclos*[ed her]* an extract of your letter.[2] I trust & hope sh*[e will]* refrain from persecuting you, and that he*[r standi]*ng in society will be restored—I am yours w*[ith sincere]* reguard & Esteem

Andrew Jackson

ALS fragment, TNJ (7-1371).

1. Neither letter found.
2. See above, AJ to Ellen J. Kirkman, December 16.

To John Caldwell Calhoun

Division of the South
Head Quarters Nashville
December 21st. 1820

Sir

Your's of the 25th ulto. is just recd, with its enclosures; I have duly noted the contents and ordered Brevet Brigd Genl Bissell by a confidential officer, to have a site for a Fortification on the Sabine selected and the country explored, and to report to me whether all the protection now afforded to the frontier by the Garrison at Natchitoches cannot be equally secured by advancing the Garrison of Nats. to a point on or near the Sabine river.[1]

There cannot exist any serious apprehension of an invasion of the Spaniards in that quarter whatever may be apprehended from their exciting the Indians to depredation on our frontier, and, as I believe, the only thing to be guarded against in that quarter, is Indian depredation.

If we do not possess the Floridas, I have supposed we would take possession of Texas and extend our Garrisons to our Territorial Limits; by which we would overawe the Indians under Spanish influence, and form a Cordon of Posts from the Mandan Villages south west to the Rio Grand or Del Norte, or at least as far West as Galvestown and direct to the Mandan Village. This I should suppose (if our Treaty with Spain is not ratified and we abandon the possession of the Floridas, and continue our claim over Texas), would be a thing necessarily following the abandonment of the principles contained in our Treaty with Spain. I must confess that I am one of those who believed, and still believes, that our Treaty with Spain as it respected our limits and the possession of the Floridas, was a good one—Texas for the present we could well do without—But without the Floridas our lower country cannot be made secure, and our Navy cannot afford protection to it in time of War. The idea of invading our Territory through the province of Texas, is to me absurd. Should it be attempted, a vigilant General with a competent force and transportation concentrated at New Orleans, could cut the Invaders in the rear and destroy or capture the whole. No military man would hazard such a step with a view to conquer New Orleans—one fourth his force in his front could bury him in the passes and defiles through which he would be compelled to advance. I therefore never had any apprehensions of an invasion from that quarter; but still have ordered the enquiry and a Topographical view of the country, and as soon as I receive the report, I shall act on the subject and make report thereof to you.[2] Should we not have use for our military forces to occupy the Floridas, a Garrison on or near the Sabine will be useful to Keep down the hostile spirit of the Indians.

I contemplate either visitting the posts in my Division this spring, or causing my Aid de Camp, Lt. Donelson of the Engineer Corps to do so, and report to me their condition—

I wrote you sometime since, on the subject of obtaining a warrant for Daniel S Donelson to enter the Military Academy.[3] I see there will be attempts by some members of Congress to put it down—These cannot be the sentiments of any who really wish us an Independent nation—And I have always thought, that they only originated with members riding the *little pony* of popularity, or with fools who really did not understand the first principles of our Government. I see it is alledged that the wealthy alone have been instructed at West Point;[4] as far as the youths from this state have been admitted this is not true, and as it respects the young Gentleman I have named, he is an orphan and without means of his own to finish his education. I wish him to finish his education at the Military Academy. He is a fine material for a military man—large, portly, and a good constitution—If he cannot be admitted I wish to know it, that I may send him to Yale College—I am Sir, with great respect yr Mo Obt servant.

Andrew Jackson
Major Genl Comdg.

LS in Andrew J. Donelson's hand and Copy, DNA-RG 107 (M221-89); LC, DLC (63). Published in Bassett, 3:35 (extract from LS).

1. See Calhoun to AJ, November 25.

2. See Andrew J. Donelson to Daniel Bissell, December 15 and 20; and AJ to Calhoun, April 10, 1821.

3. On January 13, 1821, Calhoun reported that Daniel S. Donelson's application was on file with the war department. Donelson was appointed in March and entered the Academy in July 1821 (see Calhoun to AJ, March 7, 1821).

4. In March, during the preceding congressional session, Newton Cannon had alleged that the Military Academy was "for the benefit of a few favorites of the most wealthy of our country," and on December 5, at the present session, Cannon introduced a resolution inquiring into the Academy's costs. Later, on January 15, 1821, he sought an investigation of the quality of the cadets at West Point (*Annals of Congress,* 16th Cong., 1st sess., p. 1599; *ibid.,* 16th Cong., 2nd sess., pp. 502–503, 712–13).

Appendix

TRANSCRIPTIONS PREPARED BY JESÚS F. DE LA TEJA

From Mauricio de Zuñiga

Panzacola 26 de Mayo de 1816.

Exmo. Señor.

El 24 del corriente puso en mis manos el Capitan Amelung del 1er. Regimiento de los E.U. la carta de V.E. fechada en Washington, territorio del Misisipi, a 23 de Abril proximo pasado, en la qual despues de enterarme del encargo que le ha confiado su Gobierno acerca de hacerme saber qe. el Fuerte de Negros eregido durante la ultima guerra con la Gran Bretaña cerca de la juncion de los Rios Chatahouche y Flint, ha sido reforzado y se halla en la actualidad ocupado con mas de 250 negros, de los quales muchos fueron substraidos por seduccion del Servicio de sus amos, ciudadanos de los E.U. y que todos estan bien armados, provistos, y disciplinados, hace varias y prudentes reflexiones acerca de los graves perjuicios que pueden resultar de la tolerancia de semejante establecimiento, no solo á los circunvecinos en la perturbacion de la Paz de la Nacion, sino tambien á la buena armonia que felizmente reina entre nuestros respectivos Gobiernos: Discurre sobre lo que corresponde hacer á la autoridad Española para poner termino á un mal de naturaleza tan grave en el modo que prescriben los principios de buena feé que son el fundamento de la amistosa vecindad entre las Naciones: Explica lo que este Gobierno se halla en el caso de hacer inmediatamente, sin lo qual se verá impelido el suyo á executarlo en obsequio de la seguridad de los Habitantes de los E.U. y termina pidiendome que en respuesta á su Carta le exponga, si dicho Fuerte ha sido construido pr. el Gobierno Español, ó si los negros que lo guarnecen son considerados vasallos de S.M.C. y no habiendolo sido por la autoridad Española, por la qual, y por que orden fué establecido.

En su respuesta dire á V.E. con aquella verdad que es propia de un oficial de honor, en cuya clase me considero, que habiendo llegado á esta Plaza casi á fines del mes de Marzo anterior, e instruidome de lo que V.E. se sirve participarme, en lo que solo hay la diferencia de que el Fuerte, en lugar de hallarse en el parage que lo situa se encuentra en la orilla oriental del Apalachicola como á distancia de quince millas de su desembocadero ó desague en el Mar, no perdi tiempo en proponer á mi Capitan General los medios que me parecieron aproposito, tanto para poner á los habitantes de la jurisdiccion de mi mando al abrigo de los daños atrazos y perjuicios que se les han seguido y estan siguiendo de semejante establecimto. como para evitar continuasen experimentandolos los Ciudadanos Americanos é Yndios Amigos de su vecindad. No he recivido aun la respuesta, y en su virtud V.E. que sabe el punto hasta donde llegan los limites de las facultades de un oficial subordinado, no puede extrañar le manifieste, qe. aunque mi modo de pensar coincide enteramente con el Suyo sobre el particular de desaloxar á los negros del Fuerte, ocuparlo con tropas Españolas, ó inutilizarlo y entregar á los legitimos dueños los Negros que puedan recogerse, no podré operar mientras no reciba las ordenes de mi Capitan General, y los auxilios convenientes y necesarios para proceder á la empresa con moral seguridad de conseguir el fin. Me persuado á que la resolucion de dicho Gefe no puede tardar, y si fuere la de autorizarme á obrar, viva V.E. cierto y persuadido no perdere instante en poner de mi parte los medios mas eficaces para cortar de raiz un mal que al par de los que V.E. indica en su carta, los ocasiona gravisimos á los habitantes de esta jurisdiccion vasallos de mi Soberano, cuyo bien y tranquilidad es mi obligacion proteger y conservar.

Con esta exposicion podria considerar enteramente contestada su citada Carta, pues se deja conocer que pensando como V.E. piensa con respecto á la necesidad de destruir los Negros el Fuerte de Apalachicola, ocupado por ellos, no fué construido por disposicion del Gobierno Español, y que los Negros aunque en la parte perteneciente á Habitantes de esta jurisdiccion, y como entes racionales sean vasallos del Rey mi Amo, los considero en la Clase de Ynsurgentes ó levantados contra la autoridad, no solo de S.M.C. sino tambien de los propietarios de cuyo servicio se han substraido; unos por la seduccion del Coronel Yngles Eduardo Nicolls, el Mayor Woodbain y sus Agentes; y otros por su inclinacion á la desercion: Pero como V.E. manifiesta deseo particular de que en caso de no haber sido construido el Fuerte por autoridad Española, le diga por qual, y de que orden, no tengo embarazo en satisfacer su curiosidad diciendole que segun he sabido desde mi llegada á esta Plaza dicho Fuerte y otro cerca de la confluencia de los Rios Chatahouche y Flint, que parece no existe ya fueron construidos por orden del citado Coronel Nicolls. No asegurare lo executase autorizado por su Gobierno, pero si que se procedio á artillarlo municionarlo y aprovisionarlo por disposicion del Contra Almirante Malcom y que quando el Coronel Nicolls y tropas de su destacamento, concluida la Expedicion contra la Luisiana, se retiraron de aquel punto, dejó Ordenes á los Negros en todo contrarias al incontestable derecho de Soberania que el Rey mi Señor exerce desde la linea de los treinta y un grados de latitud N. acia el S. De todas estas acciones han dado parte mis antecesores en este Gobierno á las autoridades de que depende pa. que se reclame por quien corresponda la satisfaccion que exige la violacion.

Creo haber satisfecho á la Carta de V.E. en terminos que no podra dudar de lo sincero de mis intenciones en favor de la Causa comun á los Habitantes Americanos y Españoles, y de que mi actual inaccion no procede de falta de voluntad tambien me lisongeo que en el interin que mi Capitan General decida, no se dará por el Gobierno de los E.U. ni por V.E. paso alguno que perjudique la Soberania del Rey mi Amo en el Distrito de Apalachicola dependiente de la jurisdiccion de este Gobierno, y por ultimo concluyo asegurando a V.E. me servira de particular satisfaccion encontrar ocaciones en que acreditarle que mis deseos, á mas de contribuir en quanto de mi dependa á cimentar la buena armonia existente entre nuestros respectivos Gobiernos, se extienden á probar á V.E. el alto concepto que tengo formado de sus virtudes, y talento militar.

Dios guarde á V.E. muchos años.

Mauricio Zuñiga

LS, DNA-RG 94 (mAJs).

From Francisco Caso y Luengo

Sn. Marcos de Apalache 7 de Abril de 1818.

Exmo. Sor.

Mui Señor mio: Hecho cargo aunque con suma dificultad del contenido de la carta conque V.E. me honrró la tarde de ayer, y me entregó su Edecan el Cavro. James Gadston, manifestaré á V.E. la satisfacion que me ha causado saver el resultado de su expedicion contra Micusuque, que no devia dudarse de los superiores talentos, y acertadas disposiciones de V.E., á quien por ello tributo la mui gustosa enhorabuena.

Efectivamente tuvo razon mi Gefe el Govor. de Panzacola de decir á los Sres. Capitanes Gorden, y Call lo que V.E. se sirvio expresarme, y de temer la suerte de este Fuerte, amenazado por los Yndios y Negros de algunos meses á esta parte, y principalmente despues de desengañados de obtener la polvora, y balas, que tan repetidamente han solicitado, y á que se creian acrehedores por la practica, que havia de subministrarseles anualmente. Esto prueba el ningun fundamento conque la muger del Gefe Chinape ha dicho que en este Fuerte seles ha subministrado municiones desde que seme previno, y propuse guardar la mas perfecta neutralidad. Nadie mejor que el portador de esta Dn. Guillermo Hambly, como que me interpretó varias veces la solicitud de los varios Gefes Indios, que me rodeaban podrá desimpresionar á V.E. de qualquier concepto que en esta parte haya podido formarse, y de los consejos que siempre les di para qe. evitasen la destruccion, que han experimentado, y prevení desde los principios.

Verificada esta, y sin motibo yá para temer sea insultado el fuerte por estos barbaros, y los negros, pido á V.E. me permita le haga presente lo comprometido que quedaria con mi Gobierno, si desde luego me conformase con lo que V.E. me propone de guarnecer este Fuerte con tropas de los Estados Unidos, sin antes recibir sus ordenes: Estas solicitaré inmediatamente, que seme proporcione ocasion, y no dudo un momento seme dará como tán celoso mi Gobierno de cumplir lo estipulado con el de los E.U. En el interin, espero merecer á V.E. desistirá de su intento, firmemente persuadido de la buena fee, y armonia que reinará entre esta guarnicion y qualesquier tropa, que V.E. tuviese por conveniente dexar en estas cercanias, que podran ayudarme á la defensa del Fuerte en qualquier evento inesperado.

Quedan en este Rl. Hospital los enfermos que V.E. há remitido: Seles facilitará aquellos auxilios, que las circunstancias permiten; y Yo con deseos de que V.E. me proporcione otras ocasiones enque poder acreditarle lo que me asisten de complacerle.

Espero dispensará V.E. no haya contextado con la brevedad que me pedia por las rasones, que le habrá manifestado el Sor. su Edecan. No acompaño la traduccion de esta en idioma Ingles, como lo desea V.E. porq. no hay en el Fuerte quien esté en el caso de hacerlo, pero el referido Dn. Guillermo Hambly se propone traducirla á V.E. del mejor modo que le sea posible.

Nro. Sor. gue. á V.E. muchos años como selo supco. Exmo. Sor. BlM. de V.E. su mas atto. y Segro. Servor.

Franco. Caso y Luengo

ALS, DNA-RG 94 (6-0253).

From José Masot

Panzacola 18 de Mayo de 1818

Exmo. Señor

El 10 del corrte. recibi la carta de V.E. de 27 Abril popo. en la qual me dice que en una pequeña goleta despachada de este Puerto para el de Apalache con proviciones, se encontró algunas prendas de vestuario del que usan las tropas de los Estados Unidos, que supone ser parte de las tomadas en el bote en qe. tan inhumanamte. fue muerto el Tente. Scot con su escolta; preguntandome V.E. de que modo vine a hallarme posesor de estas prendas: prosigue manifestandome, que siente estar obligado a decirme que de los papeles, y otras pruebas adquiridas en Sn. Juan de la cantidad de ganado Americano encontrado en Sn. Marcos; y que la correspondencia que se seguia entre aquel puesto y los Yndios hostiles son motivos suficientes para creer que fueron armados y exitados pr. los oficiales Españoles a esta cruel guerra contra los E. Unidos: añade V.E. que existen pruevas positivas de que los Yndios fueron socorridos de municiones pr. el ultimo comandante de Sn. Marcos: y finaliza expresandome, que aqui se ha dado asilo a las personas y propiedades de los Yndios enemigos de los E. Unidos, fugitivos del territorio Americano; que estos hechos y el de haberse negado el pase de viveres para sus tropas, prueba la conducta injusta de los Agentes Españoles en las Floridas.

A los cargos referidos, contestaré pr. su orden con franqueza, sin circumloquio, ni reserva.

La primera quexa formada pr. V.E. es relativa a las prendas de vestuario hallado a bordo de la Goleta Maria, y han sido detenidos en el supuesto de que pertenecian a los E. Unidos. Parte de esas prendas, segun se comprueva, por la copia No. 1 fueron compradas en Nueva Orleans en el mes de Mayo popo. año, parte procedente de la Habana y parte comprada en esta Plaza; todo queda acreditado, de consiguiente desvanecido el cargo, y satisfecha la pregunta de V.E.

La segunda es mas grave, y es relativa a la conducta observada en estos ultimos tiempos por el comandte. de Sn. Marcos: pedi la inmediatamente cuenta de ella y me expresó lo que aparece de la copia No. 2; pero como quiera que V.E. asienta que posede pruevas positivas de la mala conducta de este oficial en su consequencia no puedo menos de suplicarle me las subministre para qe. comprovada pueda imponersele el condigno castigo; asegurando a V.E. con aquella sinceridad que me es propia; que ha obrado en un todo contrario a sus instrucciones y que pasandome V.E. las pruevas que solicito, sera puesto en mi consejo de Guerra y castigado con toda la severidad que merezcan sus excesos; mas la justificacion de V.E. conocera que el Gobierno Español no puede ser responsable de la mala conducta de sus agentes, no sosteniendolos ni tolerando sus faltas quando se compruevan.

Las demas quexas de V.E. se dirigen personal y peculiarmente contra mi y son relativas al asilo dado a las personas y propiedades de los Yndios fugitivos, y pase de viveres pr. el Escambia. Facil me es, el desvanecerlas y creo quedara V.E. satisfecho con una suscinta y verdadera relacion de los hechos Respecto á los Yndios, Seguramente ha sido V.E. mal informado, porque, efectivamente aunque aqui permanecian algunos, la mayor parte mugeres y niños, que para subsistir proveian a este pueblo de leña, pesca y otros menudencias y existian antes de la actual guerra con los Seminoles, tal vez con motivo de ella se agregarian otros, pero en muy corto numero, pues quando los hize recoger adhiriendo a lo propuesto pr. el mayor Youngs, entre todos se reunieron ochenta y siete y seguramente los pocos hombres que habia desarmados y miserables no eran hostiles a los Estados Unidos sea prueva de ello el continuo transito de los ciudadanos Americanos de la frontera a este pueblo, que solos y sin armas viajavan entre ellos, sin que jamas hayan sido insultados, ó molestados en sus personas ni propiedades.

En quanto al pase de viveres pr. el Escambia no lo he privado antes al contrario facilitado en quanto he podido y me lo han permitido mis cortas facultades aun comprometiendome pues como subordinado no podia consentirlo, por no estar declarado, pero lo tome sobre mi en vista de las circunstancias y asi lo expresé á V.E. en carta del 15 del mes popo. que le escribí pr. el Mayor Perault a cuyo contenido me refiero; mas declarado actualmente por la superioridad el libre comercio de este Pueblo con los del interior, en lo succesivo no habra dificultad para que sus comerciantes conduscan desde aqui al Fuerte Crawford ú otros de la frontera tanto pr. agua como pr. tierra, quantas proviciones y efectos sean necesarios y quieran con lo que quedaran facilmente provistos esos Puestos y complacido V.E.

Creo haber satisfecho a la carta de V.E. en termino que no podra dudar de lo sincero de mis intenciones y comprobado que mis deseos son de contribuir en quanto de mi dependa a conservar la buena armonia existente entre nuestros respectivos Gobiernos.

Dios Guarde a V.E. muchos años

José Masot

LS, DNA-RG 94 (mAJs).

From José Masot

Panzacola 23 de Mayo de 1818.

Habiendo llegado a mi noticia haver V. con las tropas de su mando pasado las fronteras, y hallarse en el Territorio de esta Provincia de la Florida Occidentl. de mi cargo, de cuyo proceder protexto solemnemente el agravio hecho a mi Soberano, exhortando y requiriendo a V en su nombre Salga de el; pues de lo contrario y si continuase V. en sus agreciones, rechazaré la fuerza por la fuerza.

Las resultas sin duda seran en este caso haya efucion de sangre, y tambien que se perturbe la buena harmonia que hasta ahora ha reinado entre nuestra naciones respectivas; mas como el que repulse el insulto jamas se le tuvo pr. agresor, quedará V. responsable delante de Dios y de los hombres de todas las conseqüencias funestas que resulten.

Dios Guarde a V. muchos años.

José Masot

LS, DNA-RG 94 (6-0841).

Calendar, 1816–1820

1816

Jan 1	From George Croghan (enclosure: Petition recommending Benjamin F. Harney for surgeon, Dec 13, 1815, DNA-RG 107, M221-70). ALS with ANS by AJ recommending appointment of Enoch Humphrey as ordnance officer, DLC (20); ALS draft, DLC (4-1314). Requests instructions on confirming Charles Wollstonecraft as ordnance officer.
Jan 1	Account with United States for pay and subsistence. DS, DNA-RG 217 (4-1316). Runs to April 30.
Jan 2	To John Reid. Photocopy of ALS, InU-Li (4-1319). *Cincinnati Commercial Gazette,* Jan 13, 1883 (extract). Commiserates on the illness of Reid's sister, Maria Cabell.
Jan 2	To John Reid. ADS, DLC (69). Furloughs him to June 1.
Jan 4	From Edward Livingston. ALS, DLC (15). Bassett, 2:224–25 (extract). Discusses New Orleans citizens' high regard for AJ and urges him to use his influence in Washington to expedite payment of discharged soldiers.
Jan 4	From Edward Livingston. ALS, DLC (20); AL draft, NjP (mAJs). Requests information regarding Michael Reynolds's claim that Livingston authorized two cannon for Barataria without AJ's order.
Jan 5	From David C. Ker. ALS, DLC (15). Requests support of claim for compensation as acting apothecary general.
Jan 5	Robert Butler to Thomas Sidney Jesup. ALS, DLC (mAJs). In AJ's name orders Jesup to report for duty at New Orleans.
Jan 6	From Jacob Jennings Brown. ALS, DLC (20); LC, DLC (4-1320). Expresses hope to meet AJ in Washington.
Jan 8	From Daniel Bissell (enclosures: Statements of Alexander McNair, Jan 5, DLC-20; of Abraham Stewart, Nov 5, and Stewart to Bissell, Nov 7, 1815, DLC-19). ALS, ICHi (4-1321); ALS draft, DNA-RG 107 (M221-101). Requests copy of charges against him.
Jan 10	From Thomas M. Winn. ALS, DLC (20). Requests assistance in securing a transfer for his son, Charles.
Jan 12	From William Harris Crawford. ALS, DLC (20). Introduces James Gadsden of the corps of engineers.
Jan 12	From Edward Mitchell (enclosure: Statement of Turner Brashears, Dec 12, 1815). ALS, DLC (20). Requests settlement of his wife's wages for teaching spinning and weaving at the Choctaw Agency.

Jan 12	Bank book of James Jackson with AJ entries. AD, Mrs. Uhland O. Redd (4-1325). Runs to December 31, 1818.	
Jan 14	From Clabon Harris. ALS, DLC (20). Protests presidential order removing settlers from public lands in Mississippi Territory.	
Jan 15	*To John Reid.*	3
Jan 15	From Daniel Bissell (enclosures: Robert C. Nicholas, d. 1836, to Bissell, Feb 1, Oct 31, 1814, DLC-8, -13; Bissell to Nicholas, Nov 15, 1814, DLC-14). ALS, DLC (20). Defends himself against charges of Nicholas.	
Jan 15	From George Bomford. ALS, DLC (20). Seeks information on Mississippi Territory lands.	
Jan 15	Decision in *Alexander Richardson* v. *Executors of William T. Lewis*. Copy, TNDa (4-1363).	
Jan 17	From William Harris Crawford (enclosure: David R. Williams to AJ, Dec 22, 1815). ALS, DLC (20). Acknowledges recommendation of John Reid for a staff appointment.	
Jan 18	Decision in *Administrators of Matthew Brooks* v. *Executors of William T. Lewis*. Copy, TNDa (mAJs).	
Jan 19	From Charles Slocum. ALS, DLC (20). Resigns as surgeon's mate.	
Jan 20	From George Argenbright. ALS, DLC (20). Requests endorsement of claim against the quartermaster department.	
Jan 20	From Henry Conway. ALS, DLC (20). Requests transfer to the 8th Infantry in St. Louis.	
Jan 20	From William Lewis Lovely. ALS, DLC (20). Urges AJ to send troops to the Cherokee Agency in Arkansas.	
Jan 21	From John Coffee. ALS, DLC (20). Bassett, 2:225 (extract). Discusses Creek cession survey.	
Jan 23	To James Brown (1766–1835). ALS draft, DLC (20). Discusses the importance of proper military facilities in the South and asks him to urge the secretary of war to send a military engineer to New Orleans.	
Jan 23	To John Reid. ALS, DLC (71). Describes trip from Virginia to Tennessee.	
Jan 23	To Thomas Adams Smith. LC, DLC (62). Grants furlough.	
Jan 24	*From Arthur Peronneau Hayne.*	5
Jan 26	From Thomas C. Clarke. ALS, DLC (20). Requests discharge of his nephew.	
Jan 26	From Elisha T. Hall (enclosure: George Croghan to Hall, Oct 17, 1815, DLC-68). LS, DLC (20). Requests order to proceed to Washington.	
Jan 27	From William Harris Crawford (enclosure: Proclamation of December 12, 1815, *Nashville Whig*, Feb 21). LCs, DNA-RG 107 (M6-8), DNA-RG 75 (M21-11); Copy, DNA-RG 46 (4-1364); Extracts, DLC (20), DNA-RG 217 (4-1366). Bassett, 2:227–28. Orders removal of intruders from Indian lands.	
Jan 29	From William Harris Crawford. LS, DLC (20); LC, DNA-RG 107 (M6-8). Authorizes suspension of squatter removal from Giles and Maury counties.	
Jan 30	Account with W. H. Quarles for board and lodging in White Plains, Tennessee. ADS, DLC (69).	

Feb 1	From John A. Rogers. ALS, DLC (20). Reports that claims on the quartermaster department have not been paid.	
Feb 2	*To John Coffee.*	6
Feb 2	To William Harris Crawford (enclosures: Edmund P. Gaines to Harry Toulmin, Sept 4; Toulmin to Gaines, Nov 6, both DNA-RG 107, M221-70; Gaines to AJ, Dec 17; Thomas A. Smith to AJ, Dec 25, all 1815). LS, DNA-RG 107 (M221-70); LC, DLC (62). Announces his arrival in Nashville and plans to inspect the southwest frontier; discusses release of William Johnston, a military prisoner, by civil authority.	
Feb 2	To Thomas Adams Smith. LC, DLC (62). Condemns discharging military prisoners by writ of habeas corpus; orders him to prepare for establishment of posts from St. Louis to Prairie du Chien.	
Feb 2	From Thomas Langford Butler (enclosure: Certificate of Thomas L. Harman, Feb 2). ALS, DLC (20). Discusses his reinstatement in the army and settlement of AJ's account in New Orleans.	
Feb 2	From George Croghan (enclosure: James B. Many to Croghan, Jan 13, DLC-20; Memorial of Anatole Peychaud et al., Jan 31, DNA-RG 94, M566-89). LS, DLC (20); ALS copy, DLC (4-1376). Transmits report on 7th Military Department artillery and memorial in behalf of Josiah Leach.	
Feb 2	From Edward Livingston. ALS, DLC (71). Offers to buy thirty slaves from AJ.	
[cFeb 2]	To John Overton. ALS, THi (4-1380). Reports arrival home and requests a visit.	
Feb 3	To Daniel Bissell. LC, DLC (62). Advises that he will be court-martialed on charges brought by Robert C. Nicholas (d. 1836).	
Feb 3	To Robert Carter Nicholas (d. 1836). LC, DLC (62). Advises that he will be court-martialed on charges brought by Daniel Bissell.	
Feb 3	From Thomas Adams Smith. LS, DNA-RG 94 (M566-91); LC (dated Feb 4), MoHi (4-1382). Reports that he has retained Joseph Philips in service.	
Feb 4	To Alexander James Dallas. LC, DLC (62). Reports death of John Reid; recommends appointments of George Smith as register and John Coffee as receiver of public monies for Creek cession land.	
Feb 4	From Thomas Adams Smith. LC, MoHi (4-1384). Discusses prospects of Indian war on the upper Mississippi.	
Feb 6	From Henry Snyder, George Jones, and T. Simpson. ALS, DLC (20). Inform AJ of election as honorary member of the Jackson Beneficial Institution of Pennsylvania.	
Feb 8	*To Nathan Reid, Jr.*	8
Feb 8	From John M. Armstrong. ALS, DLC (20). Seeks authority to raise men to accompany John Coffee's survey party.	
Feb 8	From John Coffee. ALS, DLC (20, mAJs). Bassett, 2:228–29 (extract). Discusses survey of Creek cession.	
Feb 8	From Abram Maury. ALS, DLC (20). Inquires about John Reid's papers and asks AJ to recommend author to complete Reid's biography of AJ.	
Feb 9	To Thomas G. Holmes. ALS, DLC (20). Explains that confusion over agents has delayed delivery of Holmes's slaves to Mobile.	

Feb 9	To William Walton Morris. ALS copy, DLC (20). Bassett, 2:229–30. Comments on dismissal of Morris's nephew, Charles H. Roberts, for dueling and reports referral of a request for reinstatement to William H. Crawford.	
Feb 9	To David Rogerson Williams. ALS copy, DLC (62). Bassett, 2:229. Thanks him for copies of South Carolina resolutions of December 15, 1815.	
Feb 10	To William Harris Crawford (enclosure: Petition recommending Benjamin F. Harney for surgeon, Dec 13, 1815). LS, DNA-RG 107 (M221-70). Discusses arrangements for courts-martial of Daniel Bissell and Robert C. Nicholas (d. 1836); urges clarification of brevet rank.	
Feb 10	From Joseph Jones Monroe. ALS, DLC (20). Offers to finish Reid's biography of AJ.	
Feb 11	*To William Harris Crawford.*	10
Feb 11	From Thomas Adams Smith. ALS, DLC (20); LC, MoHi (4-1389). Reports on efforts to establish military posts on the upper Mississippi.	
Feb 12	From Wigton King. ALS with AJ endorsement to retain letter pending an interview with Cocke, DLC (20); Copy, DNA-RG 75 (M271-1). Complains that Chickasaw agent William Cocke is unpopular and dishonest.	
Feb 12	From William Lindsay. ALS, DLC (20). Reports organization of artillery units at Charleston and requests transfer to Norfolk.	
Feb 12	Robert Butler to Thomas Adams Smith. ALS, DLC (20). Grants permission to move depot from Fort Bellefontaine.	
Feb 13	To John M. Armstrong. LC, DLC (62). Authorizes twenty-five mounted volunteers for Coffee's survey team.	
Feb 13	To John Coffee (enclosures: AJ to John M. Armstrong, Feb 13; AJ to Coffee, Feb 13). LS, THi (4-1392); ALS draft, DLC (20). Bassett, 2:231–33 (extract). States urgency of running cession line and reports that he has warned George Colbert against interference by the Chickasaws.	
Feb 13	To John Coffee. LS, THi (4-1396); LC, DLC (62). Authorizes a guard for survey party.	
Feb 13	*To John Coffee.*	11
Feb 13	*To George Colbert.*	13
Feb 13	To William Harris Crawford (enclosure: John Coffee to AJ, Feb 8). LS, AMobM (4-1402); LC, DLC (62). Reports authorization of John M. Armstrong's volunteers.	
Feb 13	To Joseph McMinn. AN, THi (4-1406). Expresses regret on missing McMinn in Nashville and invites him to the Hermitage.	
Feb 13	From Daniel Parker. ALS, DLC (20). Forwards letter (not identified) mistakenly directed to him.	
Feb 15	From Thomas Emmerson. ALS, DLC (20). Requests discharge of Mitchel Childress.	
Feb 16	From Edmund Pendleton Gaines. ALS and LS duplicate, DLC (69). Reports on the strength and location of units under his command.	
Feb 17	From Abram Maury. ALS, DLC (20). Bassett, 2:234 (extract). Discusses completion of Reid biography.	

Feb 17 From John Miller. ALS, DLC (20). Offers to supply saltpeter to the ordnance department.

Feb 18 To Robert Butler. LC, DLC (62); Extract, DLC (mAJs). Relays decision that George Croghan, not Thomas S. Jesup, will command the 8th Military Department in Daniel Bissell's absence.

Feb 18 From George Washington Campbell (enclosure: James Madison to Congress, Jan 18, *ASP, Indian Affairs,* 2:26). ALS, DLC (20). Discusses federal response to Creek donation of land to AJ, the claims of John Donelson's heirs, removal of intruders from public lands, and factionalism in the Republican party.

Feb 18 From John Coffee. ALS, DLC (20). Discusses Creek cession survey.

Feb 18 From Thomas Adams Smith (enclosures: Joseph Selden to Smith, Nov 28; Affidavits of David Riddle, Nov 27, Wilie J. Gordon, Nov 29, George P. Peters, Nov 27, William S. Hamilton, Dec 1; Hamilton to Smith, Nov 27, all 1815). LS, DNA-RG 107 (M221-70). Encloses details of charges against Hamilton.

Feb 18 Robert Butler to Thomas Sidney Jesup. ALS, DLC (mAJs). Reports AJ's action regarding Jesup's brevet rank.

Feb 19 To William Harris Crawford. LS, DNA-RG 107 (M221-70); LC, DLC (62). Reports that influenza outbreak has delayed tour of southern defenses; requests settlement of quartermaster accounts in Tennessee.

Feb 19 Check to Pritchett & Shall for $686.60. ADS, DLC (20).

Feb 19 From Pritchett & Shall (enclosures: Accounts with Pritchett & Shall, May 23, 1815, and with Thomas Yeatman, Jan 22, 1815). ALS, DLC (20). Acknowledge receipt of check for $686.60.

Feb 20 From Edmund Pendleton Gaines (enclosure: Statement of Ned, Feb 20). ALS and Copy, DLC (20). Reports murder of Daniel Johnston and McGaskey near Fort Claiborne; encloses description of Negro Fort.

Feb 21 To John Coffee. ALS, THi (4-1408). Advises on survey lines and describes influenza epidemic in Nashville.

Feb 21 To James Monroe (enclosure: Report of I. Bolen, n.d.). Copy, DNA-RG 59 (M179-33). Bassett, 6:458. Announces the arrival of James Gadsden.

Feb 21 From Jack Ferrell Ross. ALS, DLC (20). Requests furlough.

Feb 22 To Francis Wells Armstrong. Copy, DLC (20). Orders him to transport public property in Knoxville to the assistant commissary general in New Orleans.

Feb 22 Account with Pritchett & Shall for Edward G. W. Butler's clothing. AD, DLC (69). Runs to August 11.

Feb 24 To Donelson Caffery. ALS, MiU-C (4-1410). Discusses family affairs and upcoming visit to New Orleans.

Feb 24 Check to Sanders & Sewell for $57.08½. ADS, DLC (20).

Feb 24 Account with James Condon for servant's clothing, with receipt, April 23, 1817. ADS, DLC (22).

Feb 26 From Robert Breckinridge McAfee. ALS, DLC (71). Requests information and papers for *History of the Late War in the Western Country* (Lexington, Ky., 1816).

Feb 26 Checks to self for $9,677 and $2,000. DS, DLC (20).

Feb 27	To William Harris Crawford. LS, DNA-RG 94 (M566-90). Recommends Joseph J. Miles for army appointment.	
Feb 28	Plat of survey for 640 acres in Wilson County. Copy, TLWil (4-1412).	
March 1	From George Colbert. ALS, DLC (20). Bassett, 2:234. Thanks AJ for informing him that John Coffee is running the cession line.	
March 3	From R. H. Macpherson. ALS, DLC (20). Offers to export wines for AJ directly from Madeira.	
March 6	From Charles Kavanaugh. ALS, DLC (20). Complains of his replacement as sutler at Fort Jackson.	
March 7	From Abiel Wilson. ALS, DNA-RG 94 (M566-93). Requests aid in securing military reappointment.	
March 8	From William Harris Crawford. LS, DLC (20); LC, DNA-RG 107 (M6-8). Bassett, 2:235. Advises AJ to concentrate troops in the southwest in case of war with Spain and reports that Cherokee delegates are in Washington to secure boundary adjustments.	
March 11	From George Buchanan and Benjamin S. Smoot. ALS, DLC (20). New Orleans *Louisiana Gazette,* April 4. On behalf of the citizens of St. Stephens, Mississippi Territory, thank AJ for his leadership during the war.	
March 11	To George Buchanan and Benjamin S. Smoot. AL draft, DLC (59). New Orleans *Louisiana Gazette,* April 4. Thanks citizens for reception.	
March 11	From Walter Bourke. ALS, DLC (20). Requests restoration to rank as captain or appointment as sutler.	
March 12	To Edmund Pendleton Gaines. Copies, DNA-RG 107 (M221-69, -70). Details the disposition of troops along the Florida border.	
March 12	From Robert Butler. ALS, DLC (20). Reports on the health of AJ's family and slaves.	
March 12	From William Harris Crawford (enclosure: General order, March 6, DLC-20). LS, DLC (20); LC, DNA-RG 107 (M6-8). Discusses brevet rank and authorizes suspension of intruder removal.	
March 12	From Edmund Pendleton Gaines. LS, DLC (20). Reports efforts to apprehend the murderers of Johnston and McGaskey near Fort Claiborne.	
March 13	*To Rachel Jackson.*	14
March 15	To William Harris Crawford. LS, DNA-RG 107 (M221-70). Reports on efforts to capture murderers in Mississippi Territory.	
March 15	To [Henry Snyder, George Jones, and T. Simpson]. Draft by James Gadsden, DLC (20). Thanks them for election to membership in the Jackson Beneficial Institution of Pennsylvania.	
March 15	From William Harris Crawford. LS, DLC (20); LC, DNA-RG 107 (M6-8). Announces that Eleazar W. Ripley will be transferred to the Southern Division.	
March 15	*From William Harris Crawford.*	15
March 15	From Edmund Pendleton Gaines (enclosures: Joseph W. Allston, Presly Scurlock, and Stephen M. Ingersoll to Gaines, March 8, DLC-69; Micajah Crupper and Allston to Gaines, March 8; Ingersoll to Gaines, March 9; George Birch, Ingersoll, and Scurlock to Gaines, March 10). LS, DLC (20). Complains of fraud by food contractors.	

March 19 From Robert Butler. ALS, DLC (20). Discusses Thomas A. Smith's command; reports death of Joshua Baker (c1762–1816).

March 20 From Edmund Pendleton Gaines. ALS, DLC (20); Copy lacking postscript, DNA-RG 107 (M221-70); Extract, DNA-RG 233 (4-1415). *HRDoc* 122, 15th Cong., 2nd sess. (Serial 22), pp. 16–17 (extract). Recommends erection of a fort on the Chattahoochee River near the Florida border.

March 21 From William Harris Crawford (enclosure: James Monroe to Crawford, March 21, DLC-20). LS, DLC (20); LC, DNA-RG 107 (M6-8). Requests furlough for Monroe's nephew, Lieutenant James Monroe.

March 21 From Benjamin Hawkins. ALS, DLC (20). Clement L. Grant, ed., *Letters, Journals, and Writings of Benjamin Hawkins* (2 vols.; Savannah, Ga., 1980), 2:778. Discusses the Creek delegation headed to Washington and payments to Creeks.

March 22 From William Starks et al. ALS, DLC (20). Petition for help in obtaining pay for service in the war.

March 24 From James Monroe. ALS, DLC (20). Laments death of John Reid and reports on relations with Spain.

March 25 To William Harris Crawford (enclosure: Thomas A. Smith to AJ, Feb 4). LC, DLC (4-1416). Reports on inspection tour.

March [25] From William Cocke. ALS, DLC (20). Requests removal of squatters from Chickasaw lands.

March 26 From Francis Barbin de Bellevue. ALS, DLC (20). Requests court-martial.

March 26 From Robert Butler (enclosures: William H. Crawford to AJ, March 8; General order, March 6). ALS, DLC (20). Forwards war department communications; discusses courts-martial; reports on continuing influenza epidemic in Davidson County.

March 26 From Jean Cherbonnier. ALS, DLC (20). Expresses gratitude for and admiration of AJ's defense of New Orleans.

March 26 From Waddy Vine Cobbs. ALS, DLC (20). Requests transfer to the 1st Infantry.

March 26 From Thomas Carmichael Hindman. ALS, DLC (20). Requests transfer to the 8th Infantry.

March 27 To William Harris Crawford. LS, NjP (4-1418). Approves transfers of Cobbs and Hindman.

March 27 From George Croghan. ALS, DLC (20). Approves transfers of Cobbs and Hindman.

March 27 *From Arthur Peronneau Hayne.* 17

March 27 Isaac Lewis Baker to William Starks et al. ALS copy, DLC (20). Promises pay shortly.

March 28 To Robert Butler. ALS, DLC (20). Forwards approval of William Ligon's resignation.

March 28 To William Harris Crawford (enclosures: Recommendation of Thomas P. Chapman by Thomas L. Butler, Feb 26, DNA-RG 94, M566-86; Report by William S. Hamilton, Jan 20; Thomas A. Smith to AJ, Feb 3). LS, DNA-RG 94 (M566-89). Discusses the William Bradford-Joseph Selden quarrel over seniority and the retention of Joseph Philips in service.

March 28	From William Christy. ALS, DLC (20). Requests permission to settle 1st Infantry paymaster accounts in Washington.
March 29	To William Harris Crawford (enclosure: Thomas A. Smith to AJ, Feb 18). LS, DNA-RG 107 (M221-70). Urges early decision in the William Bradford-Joseph Selden dispute.
March 29	From George Croghan. ALS, DLC (20). Disapproves William Christy's request to travel to Washington.
March 29	From Joseph McMinn. ALS, DLC (20). Discusses survey of the Creek cession lands and settlement of pay due Tennessee troops.
March 29	Order for the court-martial of Francis Barbin de Bellevue. Copy, DLC (20).
March 30	From George Farragut. ALS, DLC (20). *American Historical Review,* 9(1903–1904):767. Reports that he has settled near Pascagoula, Mississippi Territory.
March 31	From Thomas S. Rogers. ALS, DLC (20). Requests transfer to the 1st Infantry.
April 1	From Jacob Jennings Brown. ALS, DLC (20); LC, DLC (4-1419). Requests assignment of Loring Austin as his aide-de-camp.
April 1	Change of venue to Smith County Circuit Court in *Alfred M. Douglass, executor* v. *Jackson & Hutchings*. Copy, TGSum (4-1432).
April 1	Case file, with decisions and change of venue to Smith County Circuit Court in *Jackson & Hutchings* v. *Benjamin Rawlings*. Copies, TGSum (5-0001).
April 2	From Isaac Lewis Baker (enclosure: Thomas S. Rogers to AJ, March 31). ALS, DLC (20). Requests a transfer for Rogers; discusses personal business.
April 5	To William Harris Crawford (enclosure: James B. Many and Enoch Humphrey to AJ, April 5). Abstract, DNA-RG 107 (M22-8). Encloses letter.
April 5	From Samuel Acre. ALS, DLC (20). Requests letters of introduction to AJ's friends in New Orleans; reports on attempts to recover AJ's lost sword.
April 5	From James B. Many and Enoch Humphrey. LS, DNA-RG 94 (M566-83). Recommend Michael Walsh for an army vacancy.
April 7	From Robert Butler (enclosure: William H. Crawford to AJ, March 12). ALS, DLC (20). Forwards war department communications and explains his non-action regarding suspension of intruder removal; objects to the diversion of officers to the Bissell and Nicholas courts-martial.
April 7	From Daniel Carmick. LS, DLC (20). Requests a second court-martial of Francis Barbin de Bellevue.
April 8	To Edmund Pendleton Gaines. Copy, DNA-RG 107 (M221-70); Extract, DNA-RG 233 (5-0025). Bassett, 2:238–39 (extract). Demands that Indians guilty of Fort Claiborne murders be punished; asserts the necessity of destroying Negro Fort.
April 8	To Edward Livingston. LS, NjP (mAJs). Introduces Samuel Acre.
April 8	From George Croghan. ALS with AJ endorsement, DLC (20); ALS copy, DLC (mAJs). Approves furlough for William O. Butler.
April 8	Order convening second court-martial for Francis Barbin de Bellevue. Copy, DLC (20).

April 11 — To William Harris Crawford. Abstract, DNA-RG 107 (M22-8). Discusses defense of the southern frontier and disposition of troops.

April 11 — Jean Pierre Thibault to George Croghan. ALS with ANS by AJ approving, DLC (20). Submits resignation.

April 12 — To William Harris Crawford. LS, DNA-RG 153 (5-0029). Forwards proceedings of Andrew Ross's court-martial and recommends pardon.

April 12 — From George Croghan. ALS, DLC (20). Retracts decision on William Christy's trip to Washington.

April 12 — From Thomas Freeman. ALS, DLC (20). Outlines itinerary of the Creek survey party and offers to employ some of the Donelsons.

April 13 — To John Coffee. ALS, THi (5-0032). Criticizes Cherokee claim to Creek cession lands.

April 13 — From George Graham (enclosures: Contracts with Ward & Johnson, Jan 15, Barclay H. McGhee, Feb 15, Charles Tyler, Feb 26, and William Morrison, April 3, all DLC-69). LC, DNA-RG 107 (M6-8). Forwards rations contracts.

April 14 — From William Charles Cole Claiborne. LS with AJ endorsement accepting claim, DLC (20); LC, Ms-Ar (mAJs). Dunbar Rowland, ed., *Official Letter Books of W. C. C. Claiborne, 1801–1816* (6 vols.; Jackson, Miss., 1917), 6:399–400. Claims muskets from discharged militia for Louisiana.

April 15 — To William Harris Crawford. Abstract, DNA-RG 107 (M22-8). Transmits statement of Southern Division strength.

April 15 — To Unknown. LS, LNHiC (5-0037). Introduces Henri de Saint Gême.

April 15 — From James B. Many. ALS, DLC (20). Recommends furlough for Abraham L. Sands.

April 15 — Order to paymaster to settle accounts of Jean Joseph Amable Humbert's legion. LS, DNA-RG 94 (5-0035).

April 16 — *From Big Warrior.* 19

April 17 — From James Johnson. ALS, DLC (20). *RegKyHi,* 35(1937):313–15. Defends conduct as supplier for Fort Jackson.

April 18 — From Daniel Appling. ALS, DLC (20). Resigns commission.

April 18 — From George Croghan. ALS, DLC (20). Recommends promotions in the 1st Infantry.

April 18 — From Edmund Pendleton Gaines (enclosure: Big Warrior to AJ, April 16). ALS, DLC (20). Bassett, 2:240 (extract). Reports deployment of troops along the Chattahoochee and Apalachicola rivers and efforts to apprehend murderers of Johnston and McGaskey.

April 18 — From Joseph Woodruff. ALS, DLC (20). Requests appointment to the quartermaster or commissary department.

April 19 — To William Harris Crawford. LS, DNA-RG 107 (M221-70); Extract, DNA-RG 156 (mAJs). Reports on inspection of posts in Louisiana and offers recommendations for strengthening the lower Mississippi defenses.

April 19 — To Edward Livingston. ALS, NjP (mAJs). Bassett, 6:459. Asks Livingston to transmit evidence of Spanish intrigue.

April 19 — General order by James Gadsden directing troop movements and authorizing furlough for George Croghan. DS, DLC (mAJs).

April 21	From Edmund Pendleton Gaines (enclosures: James E. Dinkins to Gaines, April 19; William H. Crawford to William Barnett, Benjamin Hawkins, and Gaines, March 14). ALS, DLC (20). Encloses letters discussing supplies at Fort Jackson and survey of the Creek cession boundary line.	
April 21	*From Benjamin Hawkins.*	21
April 22	To [Robert Butler]. Extract, Anderson Galleries (March 1913), Item 591 (5-0039). States that if Indian war should break out, Butler will accompany him to the northwest.	
April 22	To John Hutchings. ALS, THi (5-0040). Bassett, 2:241. Discusses negotiations for purchase of Louisiana coastal property, most likely a sugar plantation from Washington Jackson.	
April 23	To William Harris Crawford. LS, THi (5-0042). Reports recommending furlough for James Monroe's nephew.	
April 23	*To [Mauricio de Zuñiga].*	22
April 23	*From Abner Lawson Duncan.*	23
April 23	Isaac Lewis Baker to Ferdinand Louis Amelung. Copies, DNA-RG 107 (M221-70), DNA-RG 233 (mAJs). *HRDoc* 122, 15th Cong., 2nd sess. (Serial 22), p. 7. Instructs him on confidential mission to Pensacola.	
April 24	*To William Harris Crawford.*	25
April 24	To William Harris Crawford. LS, DNA-RG 107 (M221-70). Announces that he is sending James Gadsden to Washington with report on defense of the lower Mississippi.	
April 24	To George Croghan. LS, DLC (75). Discusses troop disposition in anticipation of an attack on Negro Fort.	
April 26	From Daniel Rawlings. ALS, DLC (20). Requests payment for a horse.	
April 26	From Little Prince. Copy, DNA-RG 107 (M221-69). Complains about forts under construction along the Chattahoochee; requests permission for Indians to subdue Negro Fort.	
April 27	From William Bradford. ALS, DLC (20). Requests furlough.	
April 27	From John Tinley. ALS, DLC (20). Accuses John Trimble of misappropriating public property at Tellico Garrison.	
April 27	*Rachel Jackson to Sophia Thorpe Reid.*	27
April 30	From George Croghan (enclosures: Nathaniel Smith to Croghan, April 7; Charles Slocum to Croghan, April 16; Departmental orders, April 23, all DLC-20). ALS, DLC (20); ALS copy, DLC (5-0070). Discusses appointments and troop dispositions of 8th Military Department.	
April 30	From Benjamin Franklin Harney. ALS, DLC (20). Inquires about his commission as surgeon of the 1st Infantry.	
May 2	From George Croghan. ALS, DLC (20). Reports inability to identify "Capt. Emulung," to whom AJ had enclosed an order.	
May 2	From Enoch Humphrey. ALS, DLC (20). Discusses transfer of funds from an 1814 recruiting account to bounties for new artillery recruits.	
May 5	Robert Butler to Jean Pierre Thibault. LC, DNA-RG 98 (4-0129). Accepts resignation.	
May 6	From Daniel Parker. LS, DLC (20); LC, DNA-RG 94 (M565-5).	

Advises that the war department knows nothing of William O. Allen's whereabouts; reports that James C. Bronaugh has been assigned as surgeon at AJ's headquarters.

May 7 From William Harris Crawford (to AJ and to Jacob J. Brown). LCs, DNA-RG 107 (M6-9), DNA-RG 98 (mAJs). Authorizes extra liquor ration for troops on fatigue duty.

May 8 To Jacob Jennings Brown. LC, DLC (5-0072). Assigns Loring Austin to Brown's command.

May 8 To John Coffee. ALS, THi (5-0073). Reports his arrival in Nashville and disappointment over concessions to the Cherokees in the March 22 treaty.

May 8 To William Harris Crawford. Abstract, DNA-RG 107 (M22-8). Requests a statement of Cherokee spoliation claims.

May 8 To James Monroe. LS, DLC (5-0075). Requests appointment of John Coffee as receiver of public money for Creek cession lands and discusses intrigue of Spanish officials in New Orleans.

May 10 From James Gadsden (enclosure: Report on fortifications, DNA-RG 77, mAJs). ALS, DLC (20). Encloses report; discusses levee break and flood in New Orleans.

May 12 To William Harris Crawford (enclosures: AJ to Edmund P. Gaines, April 8, and to Mauricio de Zuñiga, April 23; Isaac L. Baker to Ferdinand L. Amelung, April 23). LS, DNA-RG 107 (M221-70); Copy, DNA-RG 233 (5-0078). *HRDoc* 122, 15th Cong., 2nd sess. (Serial 22), p. 6 (extract). Forwards letters.

May 12 *To James Monroe.* 28

May 13 From George Croghan. ALS, DLC (20); ALS draft, DLC (5-0083). Denies furlough for Lieutenant James Monroe; discusses preparations to turn over his command to Thomas S. Jesup.

May 14 *From Edmund Pendleton Gaines.* 30

May 15 To George Croghan. LS, DLC (75). Explains confusion over Amelung's name.

May 15 From Edmund Pendleton Gaines (enclosure: James McDonald to Gaines, May 2). ALS, DLC (20). Reports that accusations against paymaster John H. Mallory were unfounded.

May 15 From Jack Ferrell Ross. ALS, DLC (20). Explains that illness prevents his return from furlough.

May 16 To William Harris Crawford. Extract, Thomas Madigan Catalog 55 (1929), Item 69 (5-0085); Abstract, DNA-RG 107 (M22-8). Requests payment of supernumerary officers attached to Coffee's brigade in 1814.

May 16 From Thomas Carmichael Hindman. ALS, DLC (20). Requests statement regarding public property allegedly given Hindman by John Williams.

May 18 From Edmund Pendleton Gaines (enclosures: Duncan L. Clinch to Gaines, May 7 and 9; Gaines to James McDonald, April 29 and 30; Gaines to Clinch, April 28; Gaines to David E. Twiggs, May 6, all DLC-20). ALS, DLC (20); Extracts, DNA-RG 107 (M221-70). Discusses alleged cattle stealing by Indians and failure to take Negro Fort.

May 18	Isaac Lewis Baker to Robert Searcy. Printed, *Nashville Whig,* May 14 (mAJs). Orders payment for military service to original warrant holders before paying merchants and others.	
May 20	From David Burwell. ALS, DLC (20). Requests information on Mobile.	
May 20	From William Harris Crawford. LS, DLC (20); LC, DNA-RG 107 (M6-9). Announces that Congress has authorized recruitment and that Simon Bernard will direct the rebuilding of fortifications.	
May 20	*From William Harris Crawford.*	32
May 21	From William Harris Crawford. LS, DLC (20); LC, DNA-RG 75 (M15-3). Approves measures taken to capture the murderers of Johnston and McGaskey, but disapproves restrictions on friendly Creeks.	
May 21	From William Harris Crawford. LS, DLC (20); LC, DNA-RG 107 (M6-9). States that despite AJ's objections, Eleazar W. Ripley will be assigned to the Southern Division.	
May 22	From George Croghan. ALS with ANS by AJ approving transfers, DLC (20); ALS draft, DLC (5-0086). Reports that Amelung will not return from Pensacola before May 30; requests transfers of George W. Boyd and Fernando Gayoso de Lemos.	
May 22	Robert Butler to Daniel Appling. LC, DNA-RG 98 (4-0127). Accepts resignation.	
May 23	From David Brydie Mitchell (enclosure: Georgia resolutions, Dec 15, 1815). LC, G-Ar (5-0090). *Nashville Whig,* June 11. Congratulates AJ on his victories during the war.	
[May 23]	Record of abatement in *David Cummins* v. *Executors of William T. Lewis.* Copies, TNDa (5-0088).	
May 24	From William Harris Crawford. LC, DNA-RG 75 (M15-3). Discusses Cherokee claims to Creek cession lands.	
May 27	From Edmund Pendleton Gaines (enclosures: Statement of Samuel Acre, May 26; Gaines to David B. Mitchell, May 24; Thomas Freeman to Gaines, May 23; Gaines to [Duncan L. Clinch], May 23; Gaines to George Croghan, May 23, all DNA-RG 107, M221-70). ALS, DNA-RG 107 (M221-70); Copy lacking postscript, DLC (20). Discusses Indian hostilities near the Apalachicola River and his response.	
May 27	From Joseph McMinn. Extract, DLC (20). Protests Cherokee claims to land ceded by the Creeks and requests AJ's intervention with President James Madison.	
[May 27]	From Joseph McMinn. Extract, DLC (20). Discusses a conversation with Return J. Meigs concerning Cherokee negotiations in Washington; stresses need to extinguish Cherokee claims north of the Tennessee River.	
May 28	From William O. Winston. ALS, DLC (20). Announces his appointment as judge advocate for the Southern Division.	
May 29	From Leroy Pope. ALS with AJ endorsement, DLC (20). Protests Cherokee negotiations in Washington.	
May 30	*To James Gadsden.*	34

May 30	From Fernando Gayoso de Lemos. ALS, DLC (20). Resigns commission.	
May 31	From Richard H. Fenner. ADS, DLC (69). Certifies Jack F. Ross's ill health.	
May 31	From Arthur Peronneau Hayne. ALS, DLC (20). Expresses pleasure that John H. Eaton will finish Reid's biography of AJ; complains about Creek cession boundary.	
May 31	From Daniel Parker. LS duplicate with ANS by AJ ordering implementation, DLC (20); LC, DNA-RG 94 (M565-5). Instructs on recruiting service.	
May 31	Receipts from John Phillips for slaves captured by Indians and now returned to their masters. AD by AJ signed by Phillips, DLC (20).	
June 2	To William Harris Crawford (enclosures: Edmund P. Gaines to AJ, May 18; Gaines to James McDonald, April 30; Duncan L. Clinch to Gaines, May 7 and 9). LS, DNA-RG 107 (M221-70). Stresses need for action against marauding Indians at junction of Flint and Chattahoochee rivers.	
June 2	From Isaac Lewis Baker (enclosure: Baker to John A. Allen, May 27). ALS, DNA-RG 107 (M221-70). Discusses squatter removal from Chickasaw lands.	
June 2	Invoice from Horatio Cleland for a bonnet. AD, DLC (22). Receipted paid November 19.	
June 3	To William Harris Crawford (enclosure: Isaac L. Baker to AJ, June 2). ALS, DNA-RG 107 (M221-70). Reports decision to use volunteer militia to remove squatters from Chickasaw lands.	
June 3	From Edmund Pendleton Gaines. ALS, DLC (20); Copy, DNA-RG 107 (M221-70). Reports on Indian raids and apprehension of the Indian murderers.	
June 3	Record of abatement in *Thaddeus Holt* v. *Andrew Jackson* (debt). Copies, TNDa (5-0121).	
June 4	To Richard Butler. ALS, LU (5-0131). Announces John H. Eaton's decision to finish biography of AJ.	
June 4	*To William Harris Crawford.*	36
June 4	*From Ferdinand Louis Amelung with enclosure.*	39
June 4	From William Harris Crawford. LS, TKL (5-0144). Notifies AJ of his appointment with David Meriwether and Jesse Franklin as commissioner to negotiate Chickasaw treaty.	
June 4	From George Croghan (enclosure: Departmental orders, June 3). ALS, DLC (20). Reports Amelung's return from Pensacola and argues against war with the Seminoles.	
June 4	From John Gordon. ALS, DLC (20). Estimates manpower and equipment needed to survey military road from Nashville to New Orleans.	
June 6	From Thomas Sidney Jesup (enclosure: Charles Wollstonecraft to Jesup, June 6, DNA-RG 107, M221-70). LC, NcD (5-0148); Copy, DNA-RG 107 (M221-70). Reports assumption of command in the 8th Military Department; complains of war department's insensitivity to the need for funds.	
June 7	From William Harris Crawford. LS and Copy, DLC (20, mAJs); LC, DNA-RG 107 (M6-9). Complains about George Croghan's failure to	

secure accounting for medical supplies received from Christopher Backus.

June 8 — From John A. Allen. ALS with AJ endorsement, DLC (20); Copy, DNA-RG 107 (M221-70). Reports on destruction of squatter improvements on Chickasaw lands.

June 8 — From Isaac Lewis Baker. ALS, DLC (20). Resigns as aide and requests permission to settle his accounts.

June 8 — From Robert Butler (enclosure: Edward Livingston to AJ, Jan 4). ALS, NjP (mAJs). Reports no recollection of passport granted by Livingston to Ellis P. Bean.

June 9 — *To William Harris Crawford.* 43

June 9 — To Edward Livingston (enclosure: Robert Butler to AJ, June 8). ALS, NjP (mAJs). Reports no recollection of the Ellis P. Bean passport.

June 9 — From Abner Lawson Duncan. ALS, DLC (20). Reports obstacles to concluding the purchase of a Louisiana plantation for AJ, most likely the Houmas grant.

June 10 — To William Harris Crawford. ALS, THi (5-0150). Introduces Isaac L. Baker.

June 10 — To William Harris Crawford (enclosure: Joseph McMinn to AJ, May 27). Copy, DNA-RG 46 (5-0152). Bassett 2:243–46. Complains that land cessions to the Cherokees obstruct southern military security.

June 10 — To William Harris Crawford. Abstract, DNA-RG 107 (M22-9). Discusses the recruiting service.

June 10 — Robert Butler to Daniel Parker. ALS, DNA-RG 94 (M566-87); LC, DNA-RG 98 (4-0129). Submits AJ's recruiting plan.

June 11 — From William Harris Crawford. LS, DLC (20); LC, DNA-RG 107 (M6-9). Reports no provision for payment of supernumerary officers attached to Coffee's brigade in 1814.

June 11 — From James Gadsden. ALS, DLC (20). Reports his arrival in New York and advises that the building of fortifications in the South will be delayed pending the arrival of Simon Bernard.

June 12 — From William Bradford (enclosure: General order, March 6). ALS, DLC (20). Reports that war department has ruled in his favor in the seniority dispute with Joseph Selden.

June 12 — From William Cocke. ALS, DLC (20). Reports need of troops to remove intruders from Chickasaw lands.

June 12 — Toast at public dinner honoring Thomas Hinds: "James Monroe, our next President." Printed, *Nashville Whig,* June 18 (mAJs).

June 13 — To William Harris Crawford (enclosure: Edmund P. Gaines to AJ, May 27). ALS, DNA-RG 107 (M221-70). Discusses Gaines's arrest.

June 13 — From Thomas Sidney Jesup. ALS and Extract, DLC (20, mAJs); LC, NcD (5-0164). Reports movement of troops and matériel in his department.

June 13 — Lonsford M. Bramlitt to William Harris Crawford (enclosure: James Kimbro to Crawford, June 13). ALS with endorsement by Crawford directing transmittal to AJ, DLC (20). Supports petition for clear title to land purchased in Indian territory.

June 13 — Check to John Hall for $166.40. ADS, DLC (20).

June 15 To William Harris Crawford (enclosure: Mauricio de Zuñiga to AJ, May 26; Ferdinand L. Amelung to AJ, June 4; Isaac L. Baker to Amelung, and AJ to Zuñiga, April 23). ALS, DNA-RG 107 (M221-70); Copies, DNA-RG 46 (5-0168), DNA-RG 233 (5-0166). *ASP, Foreign Relations,* 4:557. Declares that an attack on Negro Fort would not damage relations with Spain.

June 15 From William Harris Crawford (to AJ, David Meriwether, and Jesse Franklin). LS, DLC (21); LC, DNA-RG 75 (M15-3). Sets September 1 for commencement of Chickasaw negotiations.

June 15 From David Walker. ALS, DLC (21). Requests loan of a cannon for a militia demonstration in Russellville, Kentucky.

June 16 *To William Harris Crawford.* 45

June 17 From David McClellan. ALS, DLC (21). Requests permission to open a sutler's stand at Fort Hampton.

June 17 From Return Jonathan Meigs, 1740-1823 (enclosures: Meigs to intruders on Indian lands in North Carolina, Georgia, and South Carolina, June 17, and in Tennessee and Mississippi Territory, June 14, DNA-RG 75, M208-7). ALS, DLC (21); ALS copy, DNA-RG 75 (M208-7). Requests a detachment to preserve order during payment of the Cherokee annuity.

June 17 Deed for town lot 4 in Gallatin to John H. Bowen from AJ and John Hutchings. Copy, TGSum (5-0169).

June 17 Deed for town lots 5 and 6 in Gallatin to Robert Desha and Anthony B. Shelby from AJ and Hutchings. Copy, TGSum (5-0170).

June 18 To William Harris Crawford (enclosures: John A. Allen to AJ, June 8; George Croghan's order, June 3, DLC-20). LS, DNA-RG 107 (M221-70). Encloses report on Indian land intruders and order appointing Charles Wollstonecraft quartermaster.

June 18 To William Harris Crawford. LS, DNA-RG 94 (5-0172). Informs Crawford that he has previously reported recruiting plans.

June 18 From James Monroe. ALS, DLC (21). Expresses support for payment of John Coffee's supernumerary officers and survey crews.

June 19 From William Harris Crawford (enclosure: Creek-Cherokee agreement, Aug 9, 1814, DNA-RG 75, M208-6). LC, DNA-RG 75 (M15-3); Copies, DNA-RG 46 (5-0180), DNA-RG 233 (5-0174). *ASP, Indian Affairs,* 2:112. Rejects AJ's argument that concessions to the Cherokees present a danger to the defense of the southwest; writes that the United States will pursue a similar policy of justice and "liberal compensation" with the Chickasaws.

June 19 From Andrew Hynes. ALS, DLC (21). Relays solicitation of the St. Andrew's Society of Baltimore for AJ's membership; reports rumor in Philadelphia that AJ will move to Louisiana.

June 20 To William Harris Crawford (enclosures: Edmund P. Gaines to AJ, June 3; Charles Wollstonecraft to Thomas S. Jesup, and Jesup to AJ, June 6). LS, DNA-RG 107 (M221-70). Deplores the lack of funds for his division.

June 20 From James Cage. ALS, NcD (5-0183). Reports murder of a wagoner on Cherokee lands in East Tennessee.

June 21 From George Graham. LS, DLC (21); LC, DNA-RG 107 (M6-9). Announces that $15,000 will be issued for the quartermaster account.

June 21	Case file of *Executors of William T. Lewis* v. *Thomas J. Campbell and Carlisle Humphreys*. Copies, T (5-0187). Runs through 1818.	
June 23	*To Nathan Reid.*	47
June 24	To William Harris Crawford. LS, DLC (5-0236). Discusses difficulty in obtaining a qualified surveyor for the military road through Mississippi Territory.	
June 25	To Return Jonathan Meigs (1740–1823). Extract, Ernest D. North Catalog 16 (1909), Item 267 (5-0243). Pledges forces to remove intruders from Cherokee lands.	
June 25	From Thomas Sidney Jesup (enclosure: Jesup to William H. Crawford, June 19, DLC-21). ALS, DLC (21); LC, NcD (5-0240). States that he has appealed directly to Crawford for funds.	
June 25	From Thomas Sidney Jesup. Extract, PCarlMH (mAJs). Relays confidential information on British agents' collusion with hostile Florida Indians.	
June 25	From Tobias Lear. ALS, DLC (21); LC, DNA-RG 217 (5-0242). Transmits $15,000 warrant for quartermaster's use.	
June 25	Account with James B. Houston for making and repairing furniture. ADS, DLC (69). Receipted paid November 14.	
June 25	Deed to Thomas Norris Clark for 1,000 acres in Rhea County. Copy, TDRh (5-0238).	
June 27	From Joseph McMinn. ALS, DLC (21). Reports two murders in the Cherokee territory; discusses protest of Cherokee treaty.	
June 27	Robert Butler to Thomas Sidney Jesup (enclosure: Division order, June 27, DNA-RG 98, mAJs). ALS, DLC (mAJs). Grants post commanders power to regulate contractors and supply provisions.	
June 27	William Orlando Butler to Thomas Sidney Jesup. ALS, DLC (mAJs). Announces that eased relations with the Spanish in Florida and Indians in Georgia will allow cancellation of scheduled troop transfer.	
June 28	Jonathan S. Cool to Daniel Parker (referred to AJ). ALS with ANS by AJ to accept Cool's resignation, DLC (21). Solicits reassignment or dismissal.	
June 28	Check to Robert Bell for $236. DS, DLC (21).	
June 29	To William Harris Crawford. Extract, Stan. V. Henkels Catalog 1439 (1930), Item 62 (5-0244). Insists on payment of supernumerary officers attached to Coffee's brigade in 1814.	
June 29	From James Gadsden. ALS, DLC (21). Complains again about the hiring of French engineers; maintains that recent land concessions to the Cherokees were improper.	
June 29	From Joseph McMinn. ALS, DLC (21). Reports arrest of Cherokees accused of murder.	
June 29	From Eleazar Wheelock Ripley. ALS, DLC (21). Reports that his transfer to AJ's command will be delayed by Edmund P. Gaines's court-martial in New York City.	
June 29	Order from William Eastin to pay $150 for Nashville Bank stock. ADS, DLC (21).	
June	Decision in *Executors of William T. Lewis* v. *William Ball and Green McCafferty* (debt). Copy, TPGil (mAJs).	
July 1	*From William Harris Crawford.*	48

July 1 From William Harris Crawford. LS, DLC (21); LC, DNA-RG 107 (M6-9). Orders removal of barracks and Indian factory from private land in Natchitoches.

July 1 Account with United States for pay and subsistence for self and servants. DS, DNA-RG 217 (5-0251). Runs to September 30.

July 2 From James Gadsden. ALS, DLC (21). Reports Crawford's acceptance of the plan of defense for the Southern Division; discusses Cherokee depredation claims.

July 2 From Thomas Sidney Jesup (enclosures: Charles Wollstonecraft to Jesup, June 26; Edward Livingston to Wollstonecraft, June 27; Rowland Craig to Wollstonecraft, June 28, all DLC-21). AL, DLC (21); LC, NcD (5-0254); Extract, DNA-RG 107 (M221-70). Encloses quartermaster report and again complains about lack of funds.

July 2 From Louis Winston (enclosures: Wigton King to Levi Colbert, Feb 7, 1815; Permits for Thomas Redus by George W. Sevier, Nov 24, 1811, and Richard Sparks, Jan 11, 1814; Bond of Redus et al., Dec 26, 1814). ALS, DNA-RG 75 (5-0256). Requests exemption of seven families from removal from Chickasaw lands by virtue of special permits granted in 1814.

July 3 From William Bradford. ALS, DLC (21). Forwards resignation (not found) of Wilie J. Gordon.

July 3 From John Brandt (enclosure: Rowland Craig certificate, June 29). LS, DLC (21). Defends his handling of military stores against accusations of Charles Wollstonecraft.

July 3 From James Monroe. ALS with AJ endorsement, DLC (21). Reports the president's opinion that government documents supplied to Arsène L. Latour for a second edition (not found) of his *Historical Memoir of the War in West Florida and Louisiana in 1814–15* show the legitimacy of AJ's 1814 invasion of Pensacola.

July 3 Check to Richard Rapier for $29. DS, DLC (21).

July 4 To William Harris Crawford (enclosures: Louis Winston to AJ, July 2; James Cage to AJ, June 20). LS, T (5-0260). Discusses removal of intruders and the apprehension of murderers in East Tennessee.

July 5 From William Harris Crawford (enclosure: Abstract of Cherokee spoliation claims, DLC-69). LS, DLC (21); LC, DNA-RG 75 (M15-3). Agrees to forward information on Cherokee claims requested in AJ's letter of May 8.

July 5 From William Harris Crawford. LC, DNA-RG 75 (M15-3); Copy, DNA-RG 46 (5-0262). *ASP, Indian Affairs,* 2:102. Orders suspension of squatter removal on lands between the Cherokee line and the Tennessee River pending the Chickasaw negotiations.

July 5 From William Harris Crawford (to AJ, David Meriwether, and Jesse Franklin). LS, NNMAI (5-0263); LC, DNA-RG 75 (M15-3); Copies, DNA-RG 11 (M668-4), DNA-RG 46 (5-0274). *ASP, Indian Affairs,* 2:100–102. Issues detailed instructions for the Chickasaw negotiations.

July 5 From William Harris Crawford (to AJ, David Meriwether, and Jesse Franklin; enclosures: Affidavits of William James, May 10, DLC-4, Hardy Perry, May 7, and James Gunn, May 10, both DLC-20). LS,

	NNMAI (5-0283); LC, DNA-RG 75 (M15-3); Copies, DNA-RG 11 (M668-4), DNA-RG 46 (5-0287). *ASP, Indian Affairs,* 2:102. Gives additional instructions for treaty negotiations.	
July 5	From Return Jonathan Meigs, 1740–1823 (enclosure: Deposition of John Holshousen, June 24). ALS, DLC (21). Columbia (Tenn.) *Chronicle,* Aug 1 (extract). Discusses the pending trial of the Cherokee murderers.	
July 6	From John Brandt (enclosure: Edward Livingston certificate, July 2). ALS, DLC (21). Encloses certificate concerning dispute over quartermaster stores.	
July 6	From Return Jonathan Meigs (1740–1823). ALS, DLC (21); Copy, THi (5-0289). Reports instructions to negotiate with Cherokees for lands north of the Tennessee River and suggests that AJ write to Chiefs Richard Brown and John Lowry.	
July 6	Check to John C. Hicks for $12. ADS, DLC (21).	
July 7	To Joseph and Moses Norvell. Printed, Columbia (Tenn.) *Chronicle,* Aug 1 (5-0293). Sends Return J. Meigs's letter of July 5 for publication.	
July 8	From Tobias Lear (enclosure: Lear to John Hutchings, July 8, DLC-21). LS, DLC (21); LC, DNA-RG 217 (5-0294). Requests enclosure forwarded.	
July 8	From Thomas Adams Smith. ALS, DLC (21); Copy, DNA-RG 107 (M222-19). Reports on inspection of posts from St. Louis to Prairie du Chien.	
July 8	From Thomas Adams Smith. ALS, DLC (21). Asks that Angus L. Langham be allowed to take Willoughby Morgan's place on a court-martial.	
July 8	Accounts with Hewlett & Harper for horse tack, runs to May 24, 1817, AD, DLC (69); from Richard B. Owen for blacksmithing, runs to March 11, 1817, ADS, DLC (22).	
July 8	Check to Jenkin Whiteside for $2,000. ADS, DLC (21).	
July 9	To Abner Lawson Duncan. ALS draft, DLC (21). Relates decision not to purchase land in Louisiana.	
July 9	*To James Monroe.*	50
July 9	From William Cocke. ALS, DLC (21). Defends operation of the Chickasaw agency against charges of corruption, favoritism, and drunkenness.	
July 9	From William Harris Crawford. LC, DNA-RG 107 (M7-1); Copy, DLC (21). Orders AJ not to move the post from Natchitoches to the Sabine River until boundary negotiations with Spain have been concluded.	
July 9	From Thomas Sidney Jesup (enclosure: Jesup to William H. Crawford, July 8, DLC-21). ALS, DLC (21); LC, NcD (5-0295). Requests transfer of the balance of the ordnance department account to the quartermaster.	
July 9	From Daniel Parker (to AJ and Jacob J. Brown). Copies, DNA-RG 107 (M222-19), DLC (23). Inquires about routing of general orders.	
July 9	Endorsement by AJ, William Carroll, and James Trimble of Thomas Washington (1788–1863) and James Stewart as agents to settle	

claims against the federal government. Printed, *Nashville Whig*, July 9 (mAJs).

July 9 — Account with David Irwin for fabric and hardware. ADS, DLC (23). Runs to August 29, 1817.

July 10 — From Hypolite Dumas (enclosure: Answer to charges, July 6, by George W. Boyd, n.d.). ALS, DLC (21). Responds to allegations.

July 11 — From George Graham. LS, DLC (21); LC, DNA-RG 107 (M6-9). Clarifies procedures for issuing rations; authorizes surveyor for military road.

July 11 — From Arthur Peronneau Hayne. ALS, DLC (21). Discusses arrangements for publishing the Reid-Eaton biography in Philadelphia.

July 11 — Account from Henry Terrass for pastries and liquors. ADS, DLC (69). Runs to July 31.

[July 11] — Certification of service of Archibald Potter. ADS, Greensboro (NC) Historical Museum (5-0300).

July 12 — Receipt to U.S. treasurer Thomas Tudor Tucker for two treasury drafts. Copy, DLC (21).

July 13 — To William Harris Crawford. Abstract, DNA-RG 107 (M22-9). Recommends Thomas G. Bradford as pension commissioner.

July 13 — From Thomas Adams Smith (enclosures: Richard Graham to Smith, June 23; Edmund Shipp to William S. Hamilton and to William Lawrence, June 23). ALS with ANS by AJ approving Smith's orders and directing copies sent to the war department, DLC (21). Reports arrangements for command of the 9th Department in Smith's absence.

July 15 — Check to John Caffery for $124. ADS, DLC (21).

July 16 — From Robert Brent (enclosure: Brent to Joseph McMinn, July 16). LC, DNA-RG 99 (5-0303). Sends copy of a letter relating to pay of Tennessee troops.

July 16 — From George Graham. LS, DLC (21); LC, DNA-RG 107 (M6-9). States that AJ's letter of June 29 will be forwarded to Crawford.

July 16 — From Tobias Lear. LS, DLC (21); LC, DNA-RG 217 (5-0304). Reports forwarding $10,000 for the quartermaster account.

July 16 — From James McDonald. ALS, DLC (21). Discusses defenses along Florida border.

July 17 — To William Harris Crawford (enclosure: Thomas S. Jesup to AJ, July 2). LS, DNA-RG 107 (M221-70). Again recommends a new post on the Sabine River; discusses funds for the quartermaster department and recruitment.

July 17 — To Thomas Sidney Jesup. LS, NcD (5-0307). Discusses storage of quartermaster supplies.

July 17 — James McDonald to Robert Butler (enclosure: Stephen M. Ingersoll to McDonald, June 14). ALS with AJ endorsement accepting resignation, DLC (21). Sends resignation of surgeon's mate and requests replacement.

July 18 — From Thomas Johnson. ALS, DLC (21). Asks that AJ help secure a pension for James Royel.

July 18 — From John S. Richardson, Thomas Bennett, and Thomas Lee. LS and Copy, DLC (21). Inform AJ that "the Ladies of South Carolina" wish to present him a silver vase.

July 18 — From James Riddle. ALS with AJ endorsement, DLC (21). Sends AJ a pair of military boots.

July 18 — From William O. Winston. ALS with AJ endorsement ordering him to Nashville for court-martial, DLC (21). Explains delay in reporting to headquarters.

July 18 — Order to Howell Tatum to pay account of Mrs. Anne Jones. ADS, Roy W. Breault (mAJs).

July 19 — To John Coffee (enclosure: AJ to Richard Brown, [July 19]). ALS, THi (5-0312). Bassett, 2:253–54. Requests his assistance in persuading Cherokees to sell their disputed lands.

July 19 — To William Harris Crawford. Copy, DNA-RG 46 (5-0316). *ASP, Indian Affairs,* 2:103. Discusses arrangements for treaty negotiations with Chickasaws and Cherokees.

July 19 — Order to William Berkeley Lewis to pay account of James Tatum. ADS, NjP (5-0310).

[July 19] — To Richard Brown. AL (signature removed), InU-Li (4-1368). Urges Brown to influence Cherokees to sell their claims to lands south of the Tennessee River.

July 20 — To William Harris Crawford. Copy, DNA-RG 46 (5-0317). *ASP, Indian Affairs,* 2:103. Requests guidance on funding for treaty negotiations.

July 20 — From Robert Davis. ALS, DNA-RG 94 (5-0318). Seeks assistance in securing his pay.

July 20 — From John McKee. ALS with abstract of reply, DLC (21). Advises that Choctaw negotiations will be difficult because of the government's delay in paying them for war service.

July 20 — From Daniel Parker (enclosure: General order, July 20, DNA-RG 98, mAJs). LS, DLC (21); LC, DNA-RG 94 (M565-5). Informs AJ that William Lindsay will replace George Croghan on the court-martial in Nashville.

July 20 — Commission of AJ, David Meriwether, and Jesse Franklin to negotiate with the Chickasaws and Cherokees. DS by James Madison, DLC (21); Copy, DNA-RG 59 (5-0320).

July 20 — Account with William Berkeley Lewis for food, drink, and wood. AD, DLC (22). Runs to December 27.

July 21 — *To John Coffee.* 52

July 21 — From Edmund Pendleton Gaines (enclosures: Duncan L. Clinch to Gaines, June 12, DLC-20; Clinch to Gaines, June 14; John Machesney to Gaines, June 30; Gaines to Big Warrior, July 15). ALS, DLC (21). Discusses arrangements for department during his absence; reports that William McIntosh with a band of 600 warriors will attack Negro Fort.

July 22 — From William Cocke. ALS, DLC (21). Announces that he will arrange supplies for the treaty meetings.

July 22 — From George Croghan. ALS, DLC (21); AL draft, DLC (5-0325). Reports that he has been ordered to the Edmund P. Gaines court-martial in New York.

July 22 — From James McDonald. LS, DLC (21). Requests permission to hire Indians to aid in tracking down renegades; complains about lack of funds for supplies and pay.

July 22	From James B. Many. ALS with AJ endorsement referring matter to Edmund P. Gaines, DLC (21). Sends charges against Andrew Ross and requests court-martial in New Orleans.
July 22	Thomas Adams Smith to Robert Butler (enclosures: Francis S. Belton to Willoughby Morgan, April 13; Morgan to [Smith], July 5). LS, DNA-RG 107 (M221-72). Requests that AJ block transfer of Rifle Regiment detachment to 5th Infantry.
July 22	Account with Robert Smiley for tailoring. ADS, DLC (21). Runs to August 18.
July 24	To William Harris Crawford. LS, DNA-RG 107 (M221-70). Bassett, 2:255–56. Condemns Cherokee spoliation claims as fraudulent; announces that he will invite several Creek chiefs to testify at the Chickasaw meetings re cession boundaries.
July 24	*To Isaac Thomas.* 54
July 24	From John Coffee. ALS, DLC (21). Reports his itinerary in the Cherokee country.
July 24	From Kinchen T. Wilkinson. ALS, DLC (21). Claims that AJ is indebted to Elizabeth Wilkinson's estate.
July 24	Robert Butler to Daniel Parker. ALS, DNA-RG 94 (M566-87); LC, DNA-RG 98 (4-0135). Encloses division orders on recruiting.
July 25	From John A. Allen. ALS, DLC (21). Reports expedition to remove intruders from Indian lands and destroy improvements.
July 25	From Joseph McMinn. ALS, DLC (21). Expresses hope that AJ will be able to negotiate Cherokee land cessions; announces that he has appointed John Williams to superintend future purchases of Cherokee lands.
July 25	From William MacRea. ALS, DLC (21). States his desire to remain at his post in Norfolk.
July 25	From Daniel Parker (to AJ and Jacob J. Brown). LC, DNA-RG 94 (M565-5). Orders that recruitment of deserters from foreign armies cease.
July 25	Robert Butler to Eleazar Wheelock Ripley. LC, DNA-RG 98 (4-0135). Provides details on Ripley's new command.
July 25	Order on Nashville Bank for payment of $246 to William Green. ANS, DLC (69).
July 26	To John Coffee. ALS, THi (5-0327). Bassett, 2:256. Argues that Cherokee claims for wartime damages are fraudulent and asks Coffee to warn the chiefs to sign a new treaty before an investigation revokes the claims.
July 26	From Howell Tatum. Copy, DLC (21). Denies validity of Cherokees' spoliation claims.
July 27	To Tobias Lear. LS, NN (5-0330). Encloses Thomas Carson's account (not found) for transporting troops in 1815.
July 27	To James Monroe. ALS, DLC (5-0331). Requests copy of Monroe's letter of October 21, 1814, for the Reid-Eaton biography.
July 27	From William Cocke. LS, DLC (21). Requests authority to contract with George Colbert to supply the treaty meetings.
July 28	To John A. Allen. ALS, DNA-RG 217 (5-0335). Orders discharge of men detailed to remove intruders.

July 28	From Mathew F. Degraffenried. ALS, DLC (21). Requests furlough extension.
July 28	Duncan Lamont Clinch to Robert Butler. ALS, DLC (21). Reports destruction of Negro Fort.
July 30	To George Graham. LS, DNA-RG 107 (M221-70). Acknowledges receipt of $10,000 draft for Jesup's quartermaster department.
July 30	To Thomas Sidney Jesup. LS, NcD (5-0338). Informs him of $10,000 deposit in the Louisiana Bank.
July 30	From George Bomford. LS, DLC (21); LC, DNA-RG 156 (5-0336). Agrees with AJ's recommendation of Baton Rouge as site for ordnance depot.
July 30	From William Cocke. ALS, DLC (21). Reports that George Colbert will deliver flour to the Chickasaw treaty ground.
July 30	From Joseph McMinn. ALS, DLC (21). Reports failure to conclude an agreement for Cherokee lands north of the Tennessee River.
July 31	To William Harris Crawford (enclosures: Edmund Shipp to William S. Hamilton, June 23; Shipp to William Lawrence, June 26). LS, DNA-RG 107 (M221-70). Forwards Thomas A. Smith's orders encouraging peaceful relations with the Indians.
July 31	Robert Butler to Mathew F. Degraffenried. LC, DNA-RG 98 (4-0136). Grants furlough extension.
July	To [James B. Many, William Lindsay, and William McRea?]. Extract, Goodspeed's Catalog 369 (1943), Item 1121 (mAJs); Abstract, *The Month at Goodspeed's,* 18(1946):83 (5-0245). Discusses artillery recruiting in the Southern Division.
July	Account with William Berkeley Lewis for grain. AD, DLC (69). Runs to December 6.
Aug 1	From Robert Evans. ALS endorsed by AJ agreeing to request, DLC (21). Requests assistance in securing pay for blacksmithing at Fort Williams.
Aug 1	James Gadsden to Thomas Sidney Jesup. ALS, DLC (mAJs). Urges vigilance in light of buildup of Spanish troops in Cuba.
Aug 2	To [Robert Brent] (enclosure: Robert Davis to AJ, July 20). Extract, J. Fricelli Associates Catalog 17 (1977), Item 67 (5-0340). Encloses letter for Brent's action.
Aug 2	Duncan Lamont Clinch to Robert Butler (enclosures: Articles of agreement, July 18, DLC-21; Inventory of stores captured at Negro Fort, July 28, DLC-69). Copy, DNA-RG 94 (mAJs). *Niles' Register,* Nov 20, 1819. Reports on destruction of Negro Fort.
Aug 2	Check to self for $120. DS, DLC (21).
Aug 3	From William Cocke. ALS, DLC (21). Suggests that George Colbert be allowed to supply corn, beef, and potatoes for the treaty meetings.
Aug 3	From George Graham. LS, NNMAI (5-0341); LC, DNA-RG 107 (M6-9). Sends a certified copy of Crawford to AJ, July 1, which AJ had returned for signature.
Aug 3	From Tobias Lear. LS, DLC (21); LC, DNA-RG 217 (5-0342). Acknowledges AJ's receipt for $4,000.
Aug 4	Robert Butler to Jonathan S. Cool. LC, DNA-RG 98 (4-0137). Accepts resignation.

Aug 5	From Alexander Fulton Cochrane. ALS, DLC (21). Explains his delay in reporting for duty at Nashville.	
Aug 5	From George Graham. LS, NNMAI (5-0343); LS duplicate, DLC (21); LC, DNA-RG 75 (M15-3); Copy, DNA-RG 46 (5-0345). *ASP, Indian Affairs,* 2:103. Discusses arrangements for treaty negotiations.	
Aug 6	To William Harris Crawford. Abstract, Parke-Bernet Catalog (May 1957), Item 181 (5-0346); Abstract, DNA-RG 107 (M22-9). Transmits muster roll of John A. Allen's volunteer company.	
Aug 6	From George Croghan. ALS, DLC (21). Expresses outrage over William H. Crawford's remarks on arrest of Christopher Backus.	
Aug 6	From Joseph McMinn. ALS, DLC (21). *American Historical Magazine,* 8(1903):382 (extract). Reports that Cherokees decline to sell their lands; asks that AJ accept commission to negotiate on behalf of Tennessee.	
Aug 6	From Return Jonathan Meigs (1740–1823). ALS, DLC (21); Copy, DNA-RG 75 (M208-7). Discusses Cherokee refusal to sell land.	
Aug 6	Account from Thomas Ramsey & Co. for general merchandise. ADS, DLC (22). Runs to December 21.	
Aug 6	Robert Butler to William O. Winston. LC, DNA-RG 98 (4-0137). Requires his immediate presence at headquarters.	
Aug 7	*From Return Jonathan Meigs (1740–1823).*	55
Aug 8	From Patrick Carey. ALS, DLC (21). Requests payment for publication of courts-martial in the Rogersville *Gazette.*	
Aug 8	From Moses Harlan. ALS, DLC (21). Requests discharges for his sons, Harman and Thomas.	
Aug 8	From Return Jonathan Meigs (1740–1823). ALS, DLC (21); Copies, DNA-RG 46 (5-0348), DNA-RG 75 (M208-7). *ASP, Indian Affairs,* 2:113. Disagrees with AJ's objections to the late convention with Cherokees and rejects the argument that charges of depredation tarnish the reputation of AJ's army.	
Aug 8	Account with Thomas H. Fletcher for cloth goods. ADS, DLC (21). Runs to September 26.	
Aug 9	From George Graham (enclosure: Commission, July 20). LS, NNMAI (5-0350); LC, DNA-RG 75 (M15-3). Forwards commission to negotiate with Chickasaws and Cherokees.	
Aug 9	From Daniel Parker (enclosures: Edmund P. Gaines to Rider H. Winder, July 18, DNA-RG 94, M566-88; Parker to James Madison, Aug 5). LC, DNA-RG 94 (M565-5). States that witnesses from AJ's division will be required to attend Gaines's court-martial in New York.	
Aug 10	From Thomas L. Harman. ALS, DLC (21). Acknowledges treasury draft for $10,000.	
Aug 10	From Thomas Hinds. ALS, DLC (21). Forwards a sketch of the war service of his Mississippi dragoons.	
Aug 12	To Joseph McMinn. Copy, T (5-0352). *American Historical Magazine,* 8(1903):383. Agrees to negotiate for Tennessee with the Chickasaws and Cherokees.	
Aug 12	To John S. Richardson, Thomas Bennett, and Thomas Lee. Printed, *Lynchburg* (Va.) *Press,* Sept 26 (mAJs). Promises to notify them of	

his availability to receive the silver vase from the ladies of South Carolina after he returns from the Chickasaw negotiations.

Aug 12 From Thomas Sidney Jesup (enclosures: William C. C. Claiborne to Jesup, Aug 4; Jesup to Claiborne, Aug 10, both DLC-21). LS and Copy, DLC (21, mAJs); LC, NcD (mAJs). Forwards Claiborne's letter asking vigilance against privateers fitting out under Mexican flags.

Aug 12 From Tobias Lear. LC, DNA-RG 217 (5-0351). Informs AJ that he will be reimbursed for settlement of Thomas Carson's account.

Aug 12 From Samuel A. Storrow. ALS, DLC (21). Requests exchange of posts with a judge advocate in AJ's division.

Aug 12 From Isaac Thomas. ALS, DLC (21). Agrees that Cherokee compensation was excessive but claims that congressional action was not intended as an insult to AJ's troops.

Aug 12 Robert Butler to Daniel Parker. ALS, DNA-RG 94 (M566-87); LC, DNA-RG 98 (4-0137). Reports on disposition of troops and explains his failure to route properly an order through Parker's office.

Aug 12 Check to Kinchen T. Wilkinson for $72. ADS, DLC (21).

Aug 12 Receipt from Thomas B. Craighead for payment of tuition for Edward G. W. Butler. ADS, DLC (21).

Aug 13 Account with Berryhill & McKee for shoes, trimmings, and Bibles. ADS, DLC (22). Runs to January 9, 1818.

Aug 14 To William Orlando Butler. Copies, NcD (5-0353), DNA-RG 46 (5-0356). *ASP, Indian Affairs,* 2:119–20. Appoints him assistant topographical engineer to survey the military road from Nashville to New Orleans and Mobile.

Aug 14 From James Monroe. ALS, DLC (21). Encloses copy of his letter of October 21, 1814, for use in Reid-Eaton biography; discusses Spanish concerns about U.S. citizens aiding South American rebels.

Aug 14 From Joseph B. Porter. ALS, DLC (21). Reports giving a statement on Cherokee claims to Washington L. Hannum.

Aug 15 From George Graham. LS, DLC (21); LC, DNA-RG 107 (M6-9). Authorizes appointee of AJ's choice for military road surveyor.

Aug 15 From Polk & Walker. ALS, DLC (21). Ask if they are the sole suppliers for the Chickasaw and Cherokee treaty meetings.

Aug 16 Land grants: #9547 for 102 acres in Rutherford County; #9548 for 266 acres in Bedford County. Copies, T (5-0359, -0360).

Aug 17 From Thomas Sidney Jesup. ALS, DLC (21); LC, NcD (5-0361). Encloses duplicate receipts (not found) for $10,000 for quartermaster department.

Aug 17 Account with John Hutchings for goods and services furnished for treaty negotiations with Chickasaws. Copy with AJ endorsement, DLC (69). Runs to January 6, 1817.

Aug 18 To William Harris Crawford (enclosures: AJ to John Hutchings, Aug 18; AJ to William O. Butler, Aug 14). LS, MiU-C (5-0363); Copy, DNA-RG 46 (5-0366). *ASP, Indian Affairs,* 2:120–21. Reports appointments of John Hutchings to furnish provisions for the treaty negotiations and William O. Butler as surveyor for the military road.

Aug 18	To John Hutchings. Copies, DNA-RG 46 (5-0370), Anonymous (5-0367). *ASP, Indian Affairs,* 2:120. Asks him to serve as supply agent.
Aug 18	From John Allcorn. Copy, DLC (21). Insists that Cherokee claims are highly exaggerated.
Aug 18	From Thomas Norris Clark. ALS, DLC (21). Requests a land title to settle a law suit.
Aug 18	From Thomas Sidney Jesup. LS and Copies, DLC (21, mAJs); Extract, DNA-RG 107 (M222-19). Reports on Florida defenses.
Aug 18	Check to John Hutchings for $500. ADS, DLC (21).
Aug 18	Land grant #9564 for 54 acres in Bedford County. Copy, T (5-0362).
[cAug] 18	From John W. N. A. Smith. ADS, DLC (22). Denies legitimacy of Cherokee claims.
Aug 19	To James Gadsden. Copies, DLC (62), DNA-RG 11 (M668-4), NcU (5-0435). Appoints him secretary for the treaty negotiations.
Aug 19	*From Return Jonathan Meigs (1740–1823).* 58
Aug 19	Checks to Edward George Washington Butler for $203.20, ADS; to Robert Butler for $319.49, ADS; to Pritchett & Shall for $162.35, ADS; to Robert Smiley for $49.50, ADS; to self for $100, DS, all DLC (21).
Aug 19	Journal of treaty proceedings with Chickasaws and Cherokees. Copies, DLC (62, runs to Oct 4), NcU (5-0372, runs to Sept 20), DNA-RG 11 (M668-4, runs to Oct 4).
Aug 20	Check to self for $1,000. DS, DLC (21).
Aug 21	From Thomas Sidney Jesup. ALS and Copy, DLC (21, mAJs); LC, NcD (5-0436). Sends more evidence that Spanish are preparing to attack New Orleans, discusses his defensive preparations, and repeats his proposal to attack Cuba.
Aug 22	From Joseph B. Porter. ALS, DLC (21). Discounts Cherokee claims, based on information obtained during 1806 road survey.
Aug 22	From James Standifer (enclosure: Certificate of Return J. Meigs, 1740–1823, Aug 21, DLC-21). ALS, TNJ (5-0441). As attorney for seven Cherokees, asks pay for services rendered after their discharge in 1814.
[cAug 22]	William McIntosh to Cherokees. LS addressed to AJ, NNMAI (5-0439). States Creek position regarding disputed boundary.
Aug 24	Check to James Jackson for $1,000. DS by proxy, DLC (21).
Aug 26	From Matthew Lyon. ALS, DLC (21). Asks AJ's opinion of his enclosed article (not found) on concessions to Indians; relates a discussion with James Madison on Indian affairs.
Aug 28	From William Hall. Copy endorsed by Henry L. Douglass and David Humphreys, DLC (21). Certifies that West Tennessee troops under his command took no goods from Cherokees without just compensation.
Aug 29	From John Coffee. ALS, T (5-0443). Sends papers (not identified) regarding Creek boundaries and relates that he will not attend the Chickasaw meetings.

Aug 29	Daniel Parker to Isaac Lewis Baker. ALS, DLC (21). Requests that he consult with AJ and John Coffee regarding investments in Mississippi Territory lands.
Aug 30	To Big Warrior. Copies, DLC (62), DNA-RG 11 (M668-4), NcU (5-0444). Chastises him for not bringing a Creek delegation to the Chickasaw negotiations.
Aug 30	From Joseph McMinn. LS, DLC (21). Bassett, 2:256–58. Instructs AJ on purchase of Chickasaw lands.
Aug 30	From Return Jonathan Meigs, 1740–1823 (enclosure: Meigs to John Armstrong, May 5, 1814, DLC-10). ALS, DLC (21); AL draft (dated Aug 29), DNA-RG 75 (M208-7). Encloses copy of letter regarding Cherokee spoliations and again declares their legitimacy.
Aug 30	Commission of AJ as agent of Tennessee to negotiate release of Cherokee and Chickasaw claims to land north of the Tennessee River. ADS by William Alexander for Joseph McMinn, DLC (21).
Aug 31	To John Coffee. ALS, THi (5-0447). Reports arrival at Chickasaw treaty ground and discusses pending talks.
Aug 31	Check to "AB" for $50 in silver. DS, DLC (21).
[cAug 31]	From Joseph McMinn. LS, DLC (23). Offers advice on Cherokee negotiations.
[cAug 31]	From Joseph McMinn. LS, DLC (23). Describes his failed negotiations with Cherokees.
Sept 1	From William O. Winston. ALS, DLC (21). Requests posting as judge advocate in South Carolina or Georgia so that he can tend to his law practice.
Sept 2	From William Harris Crawford (enclosure: Isaac L. Baker to Crawford, Aug 31, DLC-21). LS, DLC (21); Copy, DNA-RG 107 (M6-9). Recommends approval of Baker's request for a six-month furlough.
Sept 2	From Joseph McMinn. ALS, DLC (21). Bassett, 2:258. Urges AJ to treat for Chickasaw lands.
Sept 3	From Lewis Evans. ALS, DLC (21). Requests certification of his claim for timber destroyed in 1814.
Sept 4	To William Harris Crawford (from AJ and David Meriwether). Copies, DLC (62), NcU (5-0450), DNA-RG 11 (M668-4). Discuss treaty negotiations.
Sept 5	To Robert Butler. ALS, DLC (21). Bassett, 2:259 (extract). Requests Coffee's papers concerning Creek boundaries; relates that his thoughts are occupied in an effort to "disappoint the *would be President*," Crawford.
Sept 5	From Abner Lawson Duncan. ALS, DLC (21). Recommends retention of Charles Wollstonecraft as quartermaster in New Orleans.
Sept 5	From Thomas Sidney Jesup. ALS, DLC (21). Recommends Wollstonecraft's retention; relays confidential information that Spain is negotiating transfer of Cuba and Florida to Great Britain.
Sept 6	To James Brown (1766–1835). Extract, Forest H. Sweet Catalog 2 (1924), Item 10 (5-0453). Bassett, 2:259 (extract). Relates that his dispute with Judge Dominick A. Hall is ended.
Sept 6	To Duncan Lamont Clinch. Printed, Washington *National*

Intelligencer, April 27, 1819 (5-0454). Acknowledges report on the destruction of Negro Fort and orders him to demand the release of slaves captured by the Seminoles.

Sept 6 *To Thomas Sidney Jesup.* 60

Sept 6 From William Orlando Butler. ALS, DLC (21). Discusses survey of the military road from Columbia to the Tennessee River.

Sept 6 From Joseph McMinn. ALS, DLC (21). Explains his response to a report of the killing of two Cherokees.

Sept 6 Certification of Lewis Lafloeur's service in the Creek War. DS, THi (5-0457).

Sept 7 *To William Harris Crawford.* 60

Sept 7 From Clinton Wright. ALS, DLC (21). Defends his reputation against an attack by James V. Ball.

Sept 8 To Chickasaw, Choctaw, and Cherokee Indians (delivered by AJ on behalf of himself and David Meriwether). Copies, DLC (62), DNA-RG 11 (M668-4), NcU (5-0464). States that the meeting is to establish boundaries between their tribes, the Creeks, and the United States.

Sept 9 From Thomas Sidney Jesup (enclosures: Charles Wollstonecraft to Jesup, Aug 17, Sept 5, both DLC-21; Wollstonecraft's statement of disbursements, Sept 7; and Estimates of quartermaster expenditures for August and September, all DLC-69). ALS and Extract, DLC (21, mAJs); LC, NcD (5-0466). Encloses quartermaster reports and discusses defenses around New Orleans.

Sept 9 James Bankhead to Robert Butler. ALS with AJ endorsement ordering conformity with divisional general order, DLC (21). Requests permission to remain at present station.

Sept 10 From William Harris Crawford (to AJ, David Meriwether, and Jesse Franklin; enclosure: Return J. Meigs, 1740–1823, to Crawford, Aug 19, DLC-21). LC, DNA-RG 75 (M15-3); Copy, DNA-RG 46 (5-0468). *ASP, Indian Affairs,* 2:103–104. Requires them to define lines to be run by Creek survey commissioners.

Sept 11 From Thomas Sidney Jesup. ALS and Copy, DLC (21, mAJs); LC, NcD (5-0469). *Nashville Whig,* Sept 24. Reports the capture of *USS Firebrand* by a Spanish squadron.

Sept 11 From Richard Bland Lee. ALS with AN by AJ to obtain and forward muster rolls, DLC (21); LC, DNA-RG 217 (5-0471). In order to expedite claims processing, requests a list of militia and volunteer officers who served with AJ in the war.

Sept 12 To Chickasaw, Choctaw, and Cherokee Indians (from AJ and David Meriwether). Copies, DLC (62), DNA-RG 11 (M668-4), NcU (5-0473). Urge Cherokees and Chickasaws to relinquish their claims along the Tennessee River.

Sept 12 To Rachel Jackson. ALS, PPRF (5-0480). *History of America in Documents,* Part 2 (Philadelphia, 1950), p. 81 (extract). Announces that "we will this day make our ultimate propositions to the cherokees and chickesaws."

Sept 12 From William Harris Crawford (to AJ, David Meriwether, and Jesse Franklin; enclosure: Crawford to William Clark, Ninian Edwards, and René A. Chouteau, May 27, *ASP, Indian Affairs,*

2:125). LC, DNA-RG 75 (M15-3); Copies, DNA-RG 46 (5-0477). *ASP, Indian Affairs,* 2:104, 125. Sends documents to aid in securing Cherokee cessions in Georgia.

Sept 14 Draft treaty with the Cherokees. Copies, DLC (62), NcU (5-0414). *ASP, Indian Affairs,* 2:92.

Sept 15 To Joseph McMinn. Copy, T (5-0483). *American Historical Magazine,* 8(1903):386–87. Reports that the Cherokees will yield their claim only to lands south of the Tennessee River.

Sept 18 *To Rachel Jackson.* 62

Sept 18 From Daniel Parker. ALS with AJ endorsement, DLC (21). Sends a sample land patent form for soldiers' bounties.

Sept 19 *To John Coffee.* 63

Sept 19 From Tobias Lear. ALS with AJ endorsement, DLC (21); LC, DNA-RG 217 (5-0493). Announces forwarding of $10,000 for the quartermaster's account.

Sept 20 *To William Harris Crawford (from AJ, David Meriwether, and Jesse Franklin).* 65

Sept 20 To William Harris Crawford (from AJ, David Meriwether, and Jesse Franklin). Abstract, DNA-RG 107 (M22-9). Report payment of $1,000 each to Tishomingo and four members of the Colbert family.

Sept 20 Check to Thomas Eastland for $200. ADS, DLC (21).

Sept 20 Chickasaw Treaty signed by AJ, David Meriwether, Jesse Franklin, and twenty-three Chickasaws; signed by James Madison, December 30. DS, DNA-RG 11 (M668-4); Copies, DLC (62), NcU (4-0419). *ASP, Indian Affairs,* 2:92–93.

[cSept 20] From James Colbert and Turner Brashears (to AJ, David Meriwether, and Jesse Franklin). Copy, DNA-RG 46 (5-0449). *ASP, Indian Affairs,* 2:105–106. Request salary increase as interpreters to compensate for entertainment of guests.

Sept 21 Check to James Jackson for $1,250. DS by proxy, DLC (21).

Sept 23 From Thomas Sidney Jesup (enclosure: Inventory of medicines at New Orleans, May 7, DLC-69). LS, DLC (21). Encloses an inventory of hospital stores on hand when George Croghan arrested Christopher Backus.

Sept 24 From William Harris Crawford. LC, DNA-RG 107 (M6-9); Copy, DNA-RG 233 (5-0516). *ASP, Military Affairs,* 4:627. Announces appropriation of $10,000 for two military roads in the South.

Sept 25 From Joseph McMinn. ALS, DLC (21). Relates news he has heard about treaty negotiations.

Sept 27 From William Harris Crawford. LS duplicate, DLC (21); LS copy, DLC (5-0518); LC, DNA-RG 107 (M7-1); Extract, DNA-RG 46 (5-0522). *ASP, Military Affairs,* 1:764–65 (extract). Discounts Thomas S. Jesup's alarm about war with Spain.

Sept 27 From Return Jonathan Meigs (1740–1823). LS copy, DNA-RG 75 (M208-7). Supports Cherokee claims to lands in northern Mississippi Territory.

Sept 30 From John C. Kouns. ALS, DNA-RG 94 (M566-89). Resigns commission.

[Sept] Summary of John L. Allen's military service in support of his bid for election as colonel of the 19th Regiment, Tennessee militia. Printed, *Nashville Whig,* Nov 12 (mAJs).

Oct 1 Account with United States for pay and subsistence. DS, DNA-RG 217 (5-0524). Runs through October 31.

Oct 2 From William Harris Crawford. LC, DNA-RG 107 (M7-1); Copy, DNA-RG 46 (5-0527). *ASP, Military Affairs,* 1:764. Reasserts the view that war with Spain is improbable, but orders reinforcement of southern defenses as planned.

Oct 3 From Tobias Lear. LS, DLC (21); LC, DNA-RG 217 (5-0529). Advises that $5,000 is being forwarded for the Indian department account.

Oct 4 To Cherokee Indians (from AJ and David Meriwether). Copies, DLC (62), DNA-RG 11 (M668-4). Present treaty of September 14 for ratification.

Oct 4 To William Harris Crawford (from AJ and David Meriwether). LS and Copy, DNA-RG 11 (M668-4), Copy, DLC (62). *Nashville Whig,* Jan 8, 1817 (extract). Report presentation of treaty to the Cherokees; advise that some chiefs have discussed exchanging their lands for territory west of the Mississippi.

Oct 4 From William Harris Crawford. LS, DLC (21); LC, DNA-RG 107 (M6-9). Informs AJ that a warrant for $10,000 has been issued for the quartermaster department.

Oct 4 From Samuel Hawkins. ALS with note signed by Big Warrior and William McIntosh and AJ endorsement to forward to secretary of war, DNA-RG 107 (M221-60). Seeks return of Robert Grierson's twelve slaves, seized by Cherokees during the Creek war.

Oct 4 Cherokee Treaty signed by AJ, David Meriwether, and nine Cherokee chiefs. DS, DNA-RG 11 (M668-4). Approved by James Madison, December 30.

Oct 4 Certification of services rendered by William McIntosh and sixty warriors during the Creek War. DS, DNA-RG 94 (5-0530).

Oct 5 Account with William Lientz for shoes and boots. ADS, DLC (22). Runs to March 11, 1817.

Oct 6 From James Brown (1766–1835). ALS, DLC (21). *Louisiana Historical Quarterly,* 20(1937):87–88. Disparages William C. C. Claiborne, his opponent for U.S. Senate from Louisiana.

Oct 6 From William Orlando Butler. LS, DNA-RG 107 (M221-74). Reports abandoning the survey of the military road because of poor health, bad weather, and inadequate supplies.

Oct 8 From William Southerland Hamilton. ALS, DLC (21). Requests furlough.

Oct 8 From Tobias Lear. ALS with AJ endorsement regarding receipt, DLC (21); LC, DNA-RG 217 (5-0533). Advises that $10,000 is being forwarded for the quartermaster department.

Oct 8 Order for the removal of white intruders from Cherokee lands within thirty days. Printed, Washington *National Intelligencer,* Nov 28 (5-0532).

[cOct 10] Certification of Andrew Hynes's service as aide, 1812–13. DS, DNA-RG 94 (5-0669).

Oct 11	From [Jesse Franklin]. AL with AJ endorsement, DLC (21). Approves the Chickasaw and Cherokee treaties.	
Oct 14	Check to self for $50. DS, DLC (21).	
Oct 15	From George Bomford. ALS, DLC (21). Seeks advice on the establishment of military depots along the Mississippi River.	
Oct 15	Receipt from William Hume for tuition of Andrew Jackson, Jr., at the grammar school, Cumberland College, Nashville. ADS, THi (5-0534).	
Oct 16	To Joseph McMinn. Printed, *American Historical Magazine,* 8(1903):387–88 (5-0536). Announces signing of treaties with the Cherokees and Chickasaws.	
Oct 17	Price quotation from McKiernan & Stout for a new carriage. ADS with AJ endorsement agreeing to exchange old carriage for new with additional payment, DLC (69).	
[Oct 17]	Approval of bond for U.S. storekeeper, Howell Tatum. DS, DNA-RG 107 (M221-69).	
Oct 18	To William Harris Crawford. LS, TNJ (5-0538); Copy, DNA-RG 46 (5-0542). *ASP, Indian Affairs,* 2:107–108. Reports settlement of Chickasaw-Cherokee boundary dispute and anticipates Cherokee cession of eastern lands.	
Oct 18	To William Harris Crawford (enclosure: William O. Butler to AJ, Oct 6). LS, DNA-RG 107 (M221-74). Discusses prospects of war with Spain and preparations to defend the Gulf Coast.	
Oct 19	From William Cocke. ALS with draft of reply, DLC (21). Requests payment to John Hutchings for supplies furnished at Chickasaw Council House.	
Oct 19	Checks to James Jackson for $3,000, DS; to [?] Natt for $5.25, ADS, DLC (21).	
Oct 20	From Thomas Adams Smith. ALS with AJ endorsement, DLC (21). Advises on deployment of troops during his absence.	
Oct 21	From Joseph McMinn. ALS, DLC (21). Compliments AJ on treaties and reports meeting with Cherokee chiefs in Knoxville to discuss additional land exchanges.	
Oct 22	To James Riddle. Printed, Salem (Mass.) *Essex Register,* July 2, 1827 (5-0544). Thanks him for boots.	
Oct 22	Robert Butler to Robert Houston. LC, DNA-RG 98 (4-0147). Orders removal of intruders from Cherokee lands north of the Tennessee River.	
Oct 23	*To James Monroe.*	69
Oct 23	Check to James Camp for $300. DS, DLC (21).	
Oct 24	*To Edward Livingston.*	71
Oct 24	From James Brown (1766–1835). ALS with AJ endorsement, DLC (21). *Louisiana Historical Quarterly,* 20(1937):88–89. Requests help in settling accounts in New Orleans for transport of men and supplies in 1815.	
Oct 24	Check to Robert Butler for $4,000. ADS, DLC (21).	
Oct 25	From Joseph McMinn. ALS, DLC (21). Advises that the war department has instructed him to prepare the Tennessee militia for mobilization.	

Oct 25 From Joseph Woodruff. ALS, DLC (21). Requests support for his continuation as paymaster at Charleston.

Oct 25 Check to Alpha Kingsley for $1,200. ADS, DLC (21).

Oct 26 From George Graham (to AJ and David Meriwether). LC, DNA-RG 75 (M15-3); Copies, DLC (21), DNA-RG 46 (5-0549). *ASP, Indian Affairs,* 2:108. Relays president's approval of the treaty negotiations and his willingness to receive Cherokees' proposal for an exchange of lands.

Oct 26 James McMillan Glassell to Robert Butler. ALS, DLC (21). Accepts appointment as aide-de-camp to AJ.

Oct 28 From Duncan Lamont Clinch. ALS, DLC (21). Discusses attempts to recover slaves from Seminoles and renegade Creeks.

Oct 28 From Thomas Sidney Jesup. ALS, DLC (21); LC, NcD (5-0550). Complains about supplies sent by the apothecary general.

Oct 28 From Joseph Watson (enclosures: Certificates of Daniel Miltenberger, n.d., Basile Demazelliere, April 3, 1815, and Jacques P. Villeré, Aug 20, DNA-RG 15, mAJs). ALS, DLC (21). Requests certification of signatures for pension application of Alexis Andry.

Oct 28 Robert Butler to Thomas Adams Smith. LC, DNA-RG 98 (4-0149). Authorizes him to settle accounts in Washington.

Oct 29 To William Cocke. ALS draft (endorsed on Cocke to AJ, Oct 19), DLC (21). Explains settlement of account with John Hutchings.

Oct 29 From Robert Carter Nicholas (d. 1836). ALS, DNA-RG 107 (M221-70). Complains about his court-martial.

Oct 30 To George Graham. Abstract, DNA-RG 107 (M22-9). Transmits Robert C. Nicholas to AJ, October 29.

Oct 30 To Robert Carter Nicholas (d. 1836). Extract, John Heise Catalog 7245 (1922), Item 224 (mAJs). Reports that Nicholas's court-martial proceedings have been sent to Washington and that he will forward Nicholas's objections as well.

Oct 30 From Peter Hagner. ALS, DLC (21); LC, DNA-RG 217 (5-0551). Acknowledges receipts from Thomas S. Jesup and George Gibson for $10,000 each.

Oct 31 From George Graham (enclosure: Luis de Onís to James Monroe, Oct 17, DLC-21). LS, DLC (21); LC, DNA-RG 107 (M7-1); AL draft, DNA-RG 107 (5-0552). Encloses extract discussing the *USS Firebrand* seizure.

Oct 31 From George Graham. LS, DLC (21); LC, DNA-RG 75 (M15-3); Copy, DNA-RG 46 (5-0557). *ASP, Indian Affairs,* 2:108. Reports that AJ will be remitted an additional $3,000 for expenses of the treaty negotiations.

Oct 31 From William Martin (1765–1846). Copy, DLC (21). Recounts Tennessee troops' appropriation of Cherokee property in 1813 and 1814.

Oct 31 Check to George Mayfield for $150. DS, DLC (21).

Oct 31 Approval of sentence in the court-martial of William Oliver Allen. DS by Robert Butler, DNA-RG 153 (mAJs).

Nov 1 To [George Bomford]. AL draft, DLC (21). Suggests Muscle Shoals as site for an ordnance depot.

Nov 1	Account with United States for pay and subsistence. DS, DNA-RG 217 (5-0561). Runs to May 31, 1817.	
Nov 2	From Peter Hagner. ALS, DLC (21); LC, DNA-RG 217 (5-0563). Informs AJ of the remittance of $3,000 for the Indian department.	
Nov 3	From Newton Cannon. ALS, DLC (21). Defends his actions in Congress on Cherokee spoliation claims and alleges that AJ exaggerates the insult to his army's reputation.	
Nov 4	From George Graham. LS fragment with AN fragment by AJ directing orders to seize rafts, DLC (75); LC, DNA-RG 107 (M6-9). Orders interception of timber illegally cut on the public lands and shipped on western rivers.	
Nov 4	From Jacob Tipton. ALS, DLC (21). Requests information regarding United States arms supplied to Tennessee.	
Nov 5	*From George Graham.*	72
Nov 6	To Newton Cannon. ALS draft, DLC (21). Bassett, 6:460–61. Chides him for failure to examine and question the Cherokee claims accounts.	
Nov 6	From Isaac Lewis Baker. ALS, DLC (21). Reports on crops and health in Louisiana, his law study, and the Senate election; recommends James Collins for officer's commission.	
[Nov] 6	To Thomas Sidney Jesup. LS, NcD (5-0146). Reports departure of George Gibson for New Orleans with $20,000 for the quartermaster account.	
Nov 7	From George Graham. LS with AJ endorsement, DLC (21); LC, DNA-RG 75 (M15-3); Copy, DNA-RG 46 (5-0568). *ASP, Indian Affairs,* 2:108. Relays the president's order to continue removing intruders from the lands north of Tennessee River.	
Nov 7	From George Graham. LS with AJ endorsement, DLC (21); LC, DNA-RG 107 (M6-9). Advises that he has ordered a warrant for $15,000 for the quartermaster department.	
Nov 7	From Peter Hagner. ALS, DLC (21); LC, DNA-RG 217 (5-0569). Advises of transmittal of $15,000 draft.	
Nov 7	From Edward Livingston. ALS with AJ endorsement re answer, DLC (21). Bassett, 2:263 (extract). Discusses the *USS Firebrand* affair and enthusiasm in Louisiana for the liberation of Mexico.	
Nov 8	From Thomas P. Carnes. ALS with AJ endorsement directing a reply, DLC (21). Requests assistance in securing compensation for Robert Grierson's slaves seized by Cherokee John Walker.	
Nov 8	From Thomas C. Clarke. ALS, DLC (21). Asks help in settling a disputed claim for a slave.	
Nov 8	From Alexander McCoy. ALS with AJ endorsement, DLC (21). Asks help in securing payment for one of Grierson's slaves that McCoy bought and John Walker later seized.	
Nov 12	To William Harris Crawford (enclosures: Certificates of Reuben McCoy, Oct 6, and John K. Wynne, July 31, both DLC-21; Return J. Meigs, 1740–1823, to John Armstrong, May 5, 1814, DLC-10; Howell Tatum to AJ, July 26; John Allcorn to AJ, Aug 18; William Hall to AJ, Aug 28; William Martin, 1765–1846, to AJ, Oct 31). Copy, DLC (21). Transmits affidavits defending the Tennessee militia against Cherokee claims.	

Nov 12 To [George Graham] (enclosure: Samuel Hawkins to AJ, Oct 4). LS, DNA-RG 107 (M221-60). Endorses the claim of Robert Grierson's heirs for compensation for slaves.

Nov 12 To [George Graham]. LS, TNJ (5-0570); Copy, DNA-RG 46 (5-0578); Extract, DNA-RG 11 (M668-4). *ASP, Indian Affairs,* 2:117. Transmits Cherokee treaty and his account for expenses; urges Muscle Shoals as site for ordnance depot.

Nov 12 *To James Monroe.* 73

Nov 12 From Peter Hagner. ALS, DLC (21); LC, DNA-RG 217 (5-0583). Asks for statement of Southern Division accounts.

Nov 13 To [George Graham]. Abstract, DNA-RG 107 (M22-9). Expresses gratitude for the president's satisfaction with the Chickasaw and Cherokee treaties.

Nov 14 From John Henry Eaton. ALS fragment, DLC (75). Discusses publication of AJ's biography.

Nov 14 From William Martin (1765–1846). ALS, DLC (21). Asks help in securing military pay of his deceased brother, Patrick H. Martin.

Nov 14 From E. D. Morrison. ALS, DNA-RG 45 (M124-77). Requests a major's commission.

Nov 15 To William Martin (1765–1846). Photocopy of ALS, TU (mAJs). Discusses status of land claim in Congress and Patrick H. Martin's back pay.

Nov 15 From Duncan Lamont Clinch. ALS, DLC (22). Relates rumor that the war department will suppress his report of Negro Fort's destruction; requests a court of inquiry to clarify his orders to enter Florida.

Nov 16 To William Harris Crawford [George Graham]. Copy, DNA-RG 107 (M222-19); Extract, DNA-RG 46 (5-0584). Discusses military road.

Nov 16 Account with Isaac L. Crow for beef and eggs. ADS, DLC (22). Runs to January 4, 1817.

Nov 17 From James Gadsden. ALS with AJ endorsement, DLC (22). Reports on trip to Washington with the Indian treaties.

Nov 18 From Robert Brent. ALS, DLC (22). Discusses distribution of duties among Southern Division paymasters.

Nov 18 Account of Rachel Jackson with Crockett & Adams for linen and a trunk. ADS by Joseph Anderson, DLC (22).

[cNov 19] To George Washington Martin. ANS, DLC (22). Requests him to deliver payment to McKiernan & Stout for a carriage; with receipt of McKiernan & Stout, November 19.

Nov 22 Deed from David Melton for Melton's Bluff. AD in AJ's hand, signed by Melton, DLC (22).

Nov 22 Bills of sale from Eliza Melton to AJ and John Hutchings for a slave, Jenny; from Nancy Melton, for her farm and a slave, Jame. AD by AJ signed by Eliza and Nancy Melton, DLC (22).

Nov 22 Account with Nathaniel Peck for carpentry. ADS, DLC (22).

Nov 26 From [Leroy Pope]. AL with AJ endorsement for removal of Taylor, DLC (22). Complains of Abner Taylor, who operates an unlicensed ferry below Muscle Shoals.

Nov 27	From Arthur Peronneau Hayne. ALS, DLC (22). Describes growth of St. Stephens, Mississippi Territory.
Nov 29	From Hugh Young. ALS with AJ endorsement, DLC (22). Reports on status of the military road.
Nov 30	From David Meriwether. ALS, DLC (22). Credits success of recent treaty negotiations to harmony of AJ and himself.
Nov 30	Deed to John Donelson (1755–1830) for 640 acres in Wilson County. DS endorsed by AJ, Mrs. W. R. Stevens (mAJs).
Nov	From Nicholas Girod (enclosure: James Brown to AJ, Oct 24). ALS, DNA-RG 217 (5-0558). Requests expeditious payment of New Orleans transport claims.
Nov	Record of abatement in *State of Tennessee* v. *Robert Searcy* (AJ surety). Copy, TNDa (mAJs).
Dec 2	From Thomas Sidney Jesup. LC, NcD (5-0588). Expands his complaint about quality of hospital stores supplied by Apothecary General Francis Le Baron.
Dec 3	To George Graham. Photocopy of LS, T (5-0589). Announces his return from a trip to the Tennessee River and Huntsville; acknowledges receipt of funds for the Southern Division.
Dec 3	Receipt from Thomas Harlin for payment for wood. AD by AJ signed by Harlin, DLC (22).
Dec 4	To George Graham. ALS, DNA-RG 107 (M222-19). Reports issuance of orders for the arrest of timber poachers on public lands.
Dec 4	To Peter Hagner (enclosure: Nicholas Girod to AJ, Nov). LS, THi (5-0593). Requests settlement of account for drays, carts, and labor commandeered for the defense of New Orleans.
Dec 4	From George Graham. LS with AJ endorsement calendaring receipt and summarizing contents, DLC (22); LC, DNA-RG 75 (M15-3); Copy, DNA-RG 46 (5-0590). *ASP, Indian Affairs,* 2:122–23. Agrees that Mississippi Territory lands should be quickly opened to settlement and approves Muscle Shoals as site for ordnance depot.
Dec 4	From George Graham. LS with AJ memorandum of letter to James Colbert re gift, DLC (22); LC, DNA-RG 75 (M15-3); Copy, DNA-RG 46 (5-0592). *ASP, Indian Affairs,* 2:109. Acknowledges receipt of Indian treaties and accounts delivered by James Gadsden; authorizes additional $500 gift to Tishomingo.
Dec 4	From Hugh Young. ALS, DLC (22). Reports progress of the military road survey.
Dec 5	To Edward Livingston. ALS, NjP (mAJs). Bassett, 6:461–62. Opines that there will be war with Spain; encloses another copy of his inscription for the Jean François Vallée miniature.
Dec 5	From James Titus (enclosure: Census of Mississippi Territory, 1816, DLC-59). ALS, DLC (22). Reports on sentiment in Mississippi Territory for admission to the Union and his opposition to the division of the territory.
Dec 6	Robert Butler to Robert Brent. LS, DNA-RG 99 (mAJs). Discusses assignments of Southern Division paymasters.
Dec 7	From Daniel Parker. ALS, DLC (22). Transmits the president's order for Robert C. Nicholas (d. 1836) to resume his duties.

Dec 7	Account with A[lfred] Osborn[e] & [John] Gardner for tailoring. AD, DLC (22).
Dec 7	Statement of Jeremiah Doxey's services as an express rider. DS, T (5-0597).
Dec 8	From Edmund Pendleton Gaines. ALS, DLC (22). Thanks AJ for support during his court-martial.
Dec 9	To Daniel Parker. ALS, PHi (5-0598). Offers to undertake contracts to purchase land in newly ceded territory; recommends John Coffee for surveyorship.
Dec 9	From Eleazar Wheelock Ripley. ALS, DLC (22). Announces arrival at New Orleans.
Dec 10	To Daniel Parker (enclosures: Certificates of Daniel Miltenberger, n.d., Basile Demazelliere, April 3, 1815, and Jacques P. Villeré, Aug 20, DNA-RG 15, mAJs, with AJ's certification of signatures, Dec 10). Copy, DLC (22). Forwards papers.
Dec 10	Account with Thomas J. Read & Co. for ribbon. ADS, DLC (30). Runs to April 14, 1821.
Dec 10	Certification of signatures of Jacques P. Villeré and Pierre Lacoste on documents supporting pension application of Alexis Andry. ADS, DNA-RG 15 (mAJs); Copy, DLC (22).
Dec 11	To George Graham. LS, DNA-RG 107 (M221-74). Bassett, 2:265 (extract). Reports ordering officers in his command to refrain from provoking war with Spain; discusses removal of intruders from public lands.
Dec 11	From Peter Hagner. LC, DNA-RG 217 (5-0601). Transmits statement (not found) of AJ's account.
Dec 13	Disapproval of sentence in court-martial of Robert Goode. DS by Robert Butler, DNA-RG 153 (mAJs).
Dec 14	From James Monroe. ALS and Copy certified by Andrew J. Donelson and with ANS from John H. Eaton to Gales & Seaton, DLC (22); ALS draft and Copies, DLC (5-0615). Washington *National Intelligencer,* May 12, 1824. Bassett, 2:266–70. Congratulates AJ on the Chickasaw and Cherokee treaties; disagrees with AJ's recommendation on nonpartisan appointments; describes new arrangements for military and naval engineering under Simon Bernard.
Dec 14	Accounts of Jackson's and Hutchings's joint ventures in farming at Melton's Bluff and elsewhere in northern Mississippi Territory (now Alabama). AD, THi (5-0602). Run to October 25, 1827.
Dec 14	Bill of sale from Zachariah Betts for a slave, Penny. ADS, DLC (22).
Dec 15	From George Gibson (enclosure: William H. Crawford to Gibson, Oct 21, DLC-21). ALS, DLC (22). Discusses disposition of the army's storehouses, supplies, and land in New Orleans; predicts that AJ will soon add Florida to the Union.
Dec 17	To George Gibson. ALS, DNA-RG 217 (5-0631). Orders compensation to Maunsel White for cotton seized in defense of New Orleans.
Dec 17	From James Benton. ALS, DLC (22). Arranges payment of rent for land leased from AJ.

Dec 18 From Peter Hagner. ALS, DLC (22); LC, DNA-RG 217 (5-0632). Reports arrival of Robert Butler's receipt for $5,000.

[Dec] 19 From William Cocke. ALS, DNA-RG 107 (M221-68). Explains delay in appointing Chickasaws to aid in running treaty line.

Dec 20 From Thomas Bibb. ALS, DLC (22). Requests postponement of removal of intruders from public lands pending action on protests.

Dec 20 From George Graham (enclosures: Graham to Joseph Hopkinson, Nov 25; Hopkinson to Graham, Dec 9, both DLC-22). LS, DLC (22); LC, DNA-RG 107 (M6-9). Reports delay in procuring AJ's gold medal voted by Congress.

Dec 20 From Peter Hagner. ALS, DLC (22); LC, DNA-RG 217 (5-0633). Instructs AJ on submitting claims for expenses of treaty negotiations.

Dec 20 From Peter Hagner. ALS, DLC (22); LC, DNA-RG 217 (5-0634). Acknowledges receipt of transport compensation claims from New Orleans citizens.

Dec 21 To George Graham. Copy, DNA-RG 46 (5-0635). *ASP, Indian Affairs,* 2:123. Restates his opinion that newly ceded lands in Mississippi Territory should be quickly opened to settlement and says that survey of the military road will now proceed.

Dec 21 To George Graham. LS, DNA-RG 107 (M221-74). Suggests that additional payment to Tishomingo be made secretly; discusses settlement of other accounts.

Dec 21 From Eleazar Wheelock Ripley (enclosure: Charles Morris to Ripley, Dec 11, DLC-22). ALS, DLC (22); Extract, DNA-RG 107 (M221-73). Reports on his command at New Orleans.

Dec 21 From Dominique Salle, Joseph Pulaski Kennedy, and John Elliott (enclosures: Affidavit of John Albey; Map of Mobile; Indictment of George P. Peters). LS, DLC (22). *TPUS,* 18:25–30. Complain of army-constructed fence blocking main road to Mobile.

Dec 22 *To George Washington Campbell.* 75

Dec 22 From Hugh Young. ALS, DLC (22). Reports on road survey.

Dec 24 James McMillan Glassell to Peter Hagner. ALS, DNA-RG 107 (mAJs). Acknowledges receipt of November 2 letter to AJ.

Dec 26 *To John Coffee.* 77

Dec 26 James McMillan Glassell to Duncan Lamont Clinch. Printed, Savannah *Georgian,* April 19, 1819 (mAJs). States AJ's approval of Clinch's conduct in destruction of Negro Fort.

Dec 27 To George Washington Martin. Photocopy of ADS, MsSM (5-0643). Empowers him to conduct transactions in Mississippi Territory land on AJ's behalf.

Dec 27 To Daniel Parker. ALS, PHi (5-0646). Introduces George W. Martin, who is empowered to conduct transactions in Mississippi Territory land for AJ and Parker.

Dec 27 From George Washington Campbell. AL draft, DLC (5-0639). Bassett, 2:271 (extract). Discusses relations with Spain and the effort to secure compensation for services performed by John Donelson (c1718–86); mentions an unidentified request AJ made in regard to Lyncoya.

Dec 28 From George Graham. LS, DLC (22); LCs, DNA-RG 107 (M6-9),

DNA-RG 75 (M15-3, 5-0647). Gives additional instructions on removal of intruders from reserved Indian lands.

Dec 29 From John Coffee. ALS, DLC (22). Reports completion of Chickasaw boundary survey; urges leniency in enforcing intruder removal.

[1816] To William Harris Crawford. Extract, Goodspeed's Catalog 369 (1943), Item 1120 (4-1313). Sends certain material to be "laid before the President of the United States—for his inspection and consideration."

1817

Jan 6 *To George Graham.* 79

Jan 6 *To James Monroe.* 80

Jan 6 From Daniel Parker. ALS, DLC (22). Discusses proposed speculation in Alabama lands.

Jan 6 From Robert Searcy. ALS, DLC (22). Explains that the paymaster general has instructed him to pay the Tennessee militia, but forbidden him from paying U.S. Army troops.

Jan 6 Robert Butler to Edmund Pendleton Gaines. LC, DNA-RG 98 (mAJs); Copy, DNA-RG 107 (M221-77). Orders him to establish headquarters near Fort Montgomery.

Jan 7 To [George Gibson]. Abstract, Stan. V. Henkels Catalog (Nov 22, 1932), Item 41 (5-0666). Issues an order concerning the quartermaster department.

Jan 8 Certification regarding transportation of West Tennessee volunteers in 1812 and 1813. DS, DNA-RG 94 (mAJs).

Jan 9 To George Graham (enclosure: Abraham Wendell to Graham, Jan 6, DNA-RG 94, M566-101). LS, NjP (5-0667). Encloses transfer request and complains of policy re appointment of infantry and artillery officers.

Jan 9 To George Graham. Abstract, DNA-RG 107 (M22-10). Requests appointment of a paymaster for the Southern Division.

Jan 10 To James Monroe. ALS, NN (5-0677). Introduces George W. Martin.

Jan 10 To James Monroe. ALS, MB (5-0678). Introduces Anthony Butler.

Jan 10 From Arthur Peronneau Hayne. ALS, DLC (22). Discusses plans to summer in Nashville, the possibility of war with Spain, and Alabama lands.

Jan 10 From Samuel Houston. ALS, DNA-RG 94 (5-0674). Amelia W. Williams and Eugene C. Barker, eds., *Writings of Sam Houston* (8 vols.; Austin, Texas, 1938–43), 1:7–8. Requests correction of the date of his promotion to 2nd lieutenant.

Jan 10 *From Joseph McMinn.* 83

Jan 11 From Peter Hagner. ALS, DLC (22); LC, DNA-RG 217 (5-0679). Acknowledges receipt of AJ's claim for services as Indian treaty commissioner.

Jan 12 To Samuel Carswell. ALS, PHC (5-0683). Introduces John H. Eaton, who is in Philadelphia to superintend the printing of AJ's biography.

Jan 12 To Andrew Jackson Donelson. AN, DLC (5-0685). Encloses a letter of credit.

Jan 12 To George Graham (enclosure: Samuel Houston to AJ, Jan 10). LS, DNA-RG 94 (5-0686). Supports Houston's request for a corrected date of promotion.

Jan 12 To James Monroe. ALS, NN (5-0689). Seeks appointment of Andrew J. Donelson to West Point.

Jan 12 To Alden Partridge. ALS, CSmH (5-0691). *Huntington Library Bulletin,* 3(1933):118. Introduces Andrew J. Donelson and recommends Edward G. W. Butler.

Jan 12 *To Joseph Gardner Swift.* 83

Jan 12 To John Payne Todd. ALS, NHi (5-0694); Photocopy of ALS, DLC (71). Introduces John H. Eaton.

Jan 12 From William Orlando Butler. ALS with AJ endorsement, ICHi (5-0680); Typed copy, DLC (71). Requests order to travel to Washington to settle his accounts.

Jan 13 From George Graham. LS, DLC (22); LC, DNA-RG 75 (M15-4); Copy, DNA-RG 59 (M179-36). *TPUS,* 18:16. Orders AJ to support the efforts of local marshals to remove squatters from Indian lands.

Jan 13 From George Graham. LS, DLC (22); LC, DNA-RG 75 (M15-4); Copy, DNA-RG 46 (5-0696). *ASP, Indian Affairs,* 2:140. Authorizes purchase of two reservations granted to Cherokees by 1806 treaty.

Jan 14 *To George Graham.* 84

Jan 14 From George Gibson. ALS, DLC (22). Acknowledges receipt of treasury funds; discusses land titles near New Orleans; reports likelihood of attack on Pensacola by American mercenaries.

Jan 15 From William Cocke. LS, Douglas Crowder (5-0704). Requests compensation for service in early 1814 and for provisions furnished troops returning from New Orleans in 1815.

Jan 15 Deed to William Lyon quieting title to 100 acres in Knox County for $1. Copy, TKKn (5-0707).

Jan 17 From Benjamin Grayson Orr. ALS with AJ endorsement, DLC (22). Discusses plans to fulfill contract for Southern Division troops.

Jan 19 To George Graham (enclosure: Robert D. Richardson to Jehiel Brooks, Nov 20, 1816, DNA-RG 94, M566-86). LS, DNA-RG 107 (M221-74). Reports intention to select site for a new armory; requests that new paymaster be given funds to pay army officers.

Jan 19–29 From Hugh Young. ALS with AJ endorsement, DLC (22). Discusses difficulties in surveying for a military road in Mississippi Territory.

Jan 20 From Richard Mentor Johnson. ALS with AJ endorsement, DLC (22). *RegKyHi,* 39(1941):25–26. Complains of the behavior of the new army contractor, Benjamin G. Orr.

Jan 20 From William Wilson. ALS and Copy, DNA-RG 153 (5-0709, -0710). Requests court of enquiry to investigate his prosecution of charges against John Henderson.

Jan 21 Robert Butler to Samuel Houston. ALS, DLC (22). Authorizes Houston to open and forward mail addressed to AJ and to Butler.

Jan 21 *Robert Butler to William King.* 86

Jan 22 From William Lee. ALS, DLC (22); LC, DNA-RG 217 (5-0712). Acknowledges receipt of AJ's accounts.

Jan 23	From George Graham (enclosure: Contract with Benjamin G. Orr, Nov 21, 1816, DLC-69). LS, DLC (22); LC, DNA-RG 107 (M6-9). Encloses contract for supply of troops in Mississippi Territory and Louisiana.	
Jan 23	Account with Marshall & Watkins for hearth rug. ADS, DLC (22). Paid January 23.	
Jan 23	William Lee to James McMillan Glassell. ALS with AJ endorsement, DLC (22); LC, DNA-RG 217 (mAJs). Acknowledges letter regarding AJ's accounts.	
Jan 24	From Big Warrior. LS by proxy with AN by AJ directing a letter to Thomas C. Clarke, DLC (22). Requests return of a slave.	
Jan 25	From George Graham (enclosures: William Gibson to David B. Mitchell, Jan 4; Mitchell to Graham, Jan 13, both DLC-22). LS, DLC (22); LC, DNA-RG 107 (M6-9). Requests information regarding deployment of troops along the Georgia frontier.	
Jan 27	From Abner Lawson Duncan. ALS, DLC (22). Requests help in collecting an 1811 judgment against Thomas James.	
Jan 27	Record of pleas and judgment against Thomas Crutcher, AJ, and Alfred Balch in the case of *David Cummins* v. *Executors of William Terrell Lewis*. Copy, TNDa (5-0713).	
Jan 31	From James B. Many. ALS, DLC (22). Requests the transfer of Thomas J. Beall to his battalion.	
Feb 1	*From George Graham.*	86
Feb 2	From Albert Vickrey. ALS, DLC (22). Requests aid in securing pay for services during the War of 1812.	
Feb 4	*From John Henry Eaton.*	87
Feb 4	William MacRea to Robert Butler (enclosure: William Wilson to AJ, Jan 20). ALS with AN by AJ ordering court-martial of Wilson, DNA-RG 94 (M566-101). Encloses letter.	
Feb 7	From William Lee. LC, DNA-RG 217 (5-0721). Renders a new balance for AJ's accounts with the U.S. treasury.	
Feb 8	From Edmund Pendleton Gaines (enclosures: David B. Mitchell to Gaines and Gaines to Mitchell, Feb 5). ALS, DLC (22). Reports ordering an artillery company to the Georgia frontier to stop Seminole hostilities.	
Feb 10	*From Daniel Parker.*	89
[Feb 10]	Notice of delinquent taxes for 1815 owed by AJ and Samuel Donelson for 178 acres of land on Pond Lick Creek in Wilson County. Printed, *Knoxville Gazette,* April 3 (mAJs).	
Feb 12	To George Graham (enclosure: Report of Shoal Creek survey, Feb 4, M221-73). LS, DNA-RG 107 (M221-73); Copy, DNA-RG 46 (5-0722). Recommends site for a foundry and armory.	
Feb 12	From James Johnson. ALS, DLC (22). *RegKyHi,* 35(1937):317–18. Recounts problems faced in fulfilling his contract to supply AJ's troops.	
Feb 14	From Edmund Pendleton Gaines (enclosure: Richard M. Sands to [Gaines], Feb 2). ALS, DLC (22). Stresses need for army officers to remain neutral in regard to rumored filibustering expedition against Pensacola.	

Feb 14	James McMillan Glassell to George Graham. ALS, DNA-RG 107 (M221-73). Discusses disposition of troops.
Feb 15	From Moses H. Elliott. ALS, ICHi (5-0726). Explains his delay in reporting for duty.
Feb 15	Robert Butler to Edmund Pendleton Gaines. LC, DNA-RG 98 (mAJs). Orders movement of artillery company from Charleston to Fort Scott.
Feb 15	Robert Butler to Robert Houston. LC, DNA-RG 98 (mAJs). Orders removal of intruders from Indian land north of the Tennessee River.
Feb 16	Receipt from Wood Jones for payment for shoes. ADS, DLC (22).
Feb 17	To George Graham. LS, DLC (71); Copy, DNA-RG 46 (5-0728). Discusses ownership of 1806 Cherokee treaty reserves and asks alteration of instructions regarding their purchase.
Feb 17	Robert Butler to Moses H. Elliott. LC, DNA-RG 98 (mAJs). Orders him to Fort Montgomery.
Feb 18	To [Thomas] Beale. ALS draft, DLC (22). Acknowledges letter (not found) announcing gift of a sword; discusses value of new military road and proposed armory to security of the Gulf Coast.
Feb 18	From [George Washington Campbell]. AN draft, DLC (5-0734). *Southern Historical Society Papers,* 9(1881):41. Declines to engage agent to secure passage of a law.
Feb 18	From John Adems Paxton. ALS, DLC (22). Poses questions about the Mississippi Territory for his gazetteer.
Feb 21	From George Graham (enclosures: Marquis de Lafayette to James Madison and to William H. Crawford, Nov 11, 1815, DLC-19; Regulation establishing a board of engineers, n.d., DLC-22). LS, DLC (22); LC, DNA-RG 107 (M6-9). Introduces Simon Bernard.
Feb 21	Account with Bedford & Co. for flour. AD, DLC (22).
Feb 23	To Samuel Carswell. Extract, Charles Hamilton Catalog 117 (Jan 18, 1979), Item 110 (5-0735). Introduces Andrew J. Donelson and recommends him for temporary employment pending his enrollment at West Point.
Feb 23	To Andrew Jackson Donelson. ALS, DLC (5-0736). Advises him to hire a tutor before he enrolls at West Point.
Feb 23	To Thomas Kirkman. ALS, Clyde de L. Ryals (mAJs). Asks Kirkman to supply Andrew J. Donelson.
Feb 24	*To Andrew Jackson Donelson.* 91
Feb 25	From Thomas C. Clarke. ALS, DLC (22). Requests permission to delay returning a slave claimed by Big Warrior.
Feb 26	To George Graham. LS, DNA-RG 107 (M221-74); Copy, NN (5-0743). Renews objection to the transfer of Stephen H. Long.
Feb 28	To Mary Smith Donelson Sanders. ALS, THi (5-0747). Discusses his efforts to settle Andrew J. Donelson at West Point.
Feb 28	From Eleazar Wheelock Ripley. ALS, DLC (22). Proposes to deploy troops around New Orleans in a way to prevent smugglers and to inhibit sickness.
March 1	From Richard Brown. LS by proxy with ANS by AJ directing order to Robert Houston, DLC (22). Asks AJ to appoint Thomas Austin to burn the homes of squatters but to preserve the fencing on Brown's land.

March 1 From James Monroe. ALS, DLC (22). Bassett, 2:276–77. Discusses cabinet appointments and particularly that of secretary of war, for which AJ and Isaac Shelby were candidates.

March 4 *To James Monroe.* 93

March 4 Memoranda by James Monroe containing abstracts of selected correspondence with AJ from March 4, 1817, to July 26, 1822. AD, DLC (5-0770).

March 6 From Edmund Pendleton Gaines. ALS, DLC (22). Reports scarcity of provisions and destitution of settlers in Mississippi Territory; relays rumor that the Spanish have asked Seminoles to help defend Pensacola from mercenaries.

March 8 Account with Hai Metcalfe for bricks and labor, with receipt for payment April 1. ADS with ANS by AJ directing James Jackson to pay the account, DLC (22).

March 10 William Allen Trimble to Eleazar Wheelock Ripley. Copy endorsed by AJ to order investigation and arrest of Spanish agent, DLC (22). Warns of activities of a Spanish agent among southwestern Indians.

March 11 *To William W. Worsley and Thomas Smith.* 100

March 12 Hermitage farm journal and account book. AD, THer (mAJs). Runs to 1832.

March 14 From Hugh Young. ALS, DLC (22); Extract, DNA-RG 107 (M221-74). Reports completion of survey of military road to Madisonville, Louisiana.

March 17 From William Wade (enclosure: Plan of works proposed for Baton Rouge, DLC-69). ALS, DLC (22). Submits plans for fort and ordnance depot.

March 17 Francis Wells Armstrong to David Brearley. ALS, ICHi (5-0779). Submits his resignation from the army for AJ's approval.

March 18 *To James Monroe.* 102

March 20 *From John Henry Eaton.* 103

March 20 From George Gibson (enclosures: Estimates of expenditures in the quartermaster's department for 1817, DLC-69). ALS with ANS by AJ directing letter approving Gibson's conduct, DLC (22). Defends himself against charges of irregularity in the quartermaster department of the Southern Division.

March 22 From James Gadsden. ALS, DLC (22). Reports his arrival at New Orleans and discusses a recent assault on a British ship.

March 22 From George Graham. LS, DLC (22); LC and Extract, DNA-RG 75 (M15-4, M208-7); Copy and Extract, DNA-RG 46 (5-0785, -0787). *ASP, Indian Affairs,* 2:141. Discusses proposed negotiation for Cherokee lands; explains congressional inaction on reservation of lands for a new armory.

March 22 From William W. Worsley and Thomas Smith (enclosure: Editorial from Lexington *Kentucky Reporter,* March 21). ALS, InU-Li (5-0789). Lexington *Kentucky Reporter,* April 23. Apologize for misattribution to AJ of quotation re Kentucky militia at New Orleans; decline to reprint AJ's 1815 letter to John Adair.

March 25 From George Graham. LS, DLC (22); LC, DNA-RG 75 (M15-4); Copy, DNA-RG 46 (5-0793). *ASP, Indian Affairs,* 2:141.

Countermands his suggestion that AJ postpone Cherokee negotiations.

March 25 From Return Jonathan Meigs (1740–1823). ALS, DLC (22); ALS copy, DNA-75 (M208-7). Reports notifying Cherokees of May 1 conference.

March 27 To James McMillan Glassell. AN, DLC (22). Requests news from Nashville.

March 27 To Daniel Smith (enclosure: William P. Owen to Smith, Feb 28, mAJs). ALS, THi (5-0794). *American Historical Magazine,* 6(July 1901):235. Mourns the death of John Samuel Donelson.

March 27 Account with the Nashville Inn for lodging, meals, and wine. ADS, DLC (69). Runs to April 2.

March 29 To John Coffee. ALS, THi (5-0796). Relays information of Coffee's appointment as surveyor of northern Mississippi Territory; mourns the death of John Samuel Donelson.

March 29 *To Francis Smith.* 105

March 31 To George Graham (enclosure: Hugh Young to AJ, March 14). LS, DNA-RG 107 (M221-74). Discusses troop reassignments in Louisiana and Young's survey of the military road.

March 31 From Eleazar Wheelock Ripley (enclosure: William A. Trimble to Ripley, March 10). ALS, DLC (22). Relays reports from his military department.

April 1 From William Orlando Butler. ALS, DLC (22). Explains that he resigned his army commission to marry Eliza Todd of Kentucky.

April 1 From James McDonald. ALS, DLC (22). Requests extension of his leave of absence in order to settle accounts before resigning his army commission.

April 2 *From Edmund Pendleton Gaines.* 106

April 2 From Benjamin Franklin Harney (enclosure: Thomas S. Rogers et al. to George Graham, Feb 8). ALS, DNA-RG 94 (M566-97). Recommends A. Grass for appointment as army lieutenant.

April 2 From Joseph Gardner Swift. ALS, DLC (22). Promises attention to Andrew J. Donelson; discusses appointment of Simon Bernard.

April 3 From George Graham (enclosures: William Rabun to Graham, March 18; Archibald Clark to David B. Mitchell, and William Gibson to Mitchell, Feb 26, all DLC-22). LS, DLC (22); LC, DNA-RG 107 (M6-9). Encloses letters from Georgia reporting Indian attacks.

April 4 Account with John & Newton Sewell for blacksmith work in 1816 and 1817. ADS, DLC (22).

April 5 From Andrew Jackson Donelson. ALS, DLC (5-0801; mAJs); Typed extract, DLC (5-0803). Reports arrival at West Point.

April 5 From George Graham (enclosure: Ninian Edwards to Graham, Feb 21, DLC-22). LS, DLC (22); LC, DNA-RG 107 (M6-9). Warns of hostile disposition of Indians along upper Mississippi River; reports ordering riflemen from Green Bay to Prairie du Chien.

April 6 From Edmund Pendleton Gaines (enclosures: Alexander McCulloch to Gaines, and Gaines to William McIntosh, April 2; Gaines to Richard M. Sands, March 25 and April 2). ALS, DLC (22). Proposes to stop Seminole attacks in Georgia by destroying their villages in Florida; accuses the Spanish and British of aiding the Indians.

April 7	From Adam Gibbs Goodlett. ALS, DLC (22). Describes his journey from Nashville to southern Alabama.
April 7	From George Graham. LC, DNA-RG 107 (M6-9). Gives instructions for repair of the military road between Columbia, Tennessee, and Madisonville, Louisiana.
April 7	From James W. Harris. ALS endorsed by AJ, DLC (71). Lexington *Kentucky Reporter,* May 28. Gives measurement of AJ's line of defense at New Orleans in 1815.
April 7	From Andrew Ross. ALS, DLC (22). Requests the sentence of his court-martial.
April 8	To John Coffee. ALS, THi (5-0804). Forwards Coffee's commission as surveyor.
April 8	From James Gadsden. ALS, DLC (22). Complains of delay by the board of engineers in reaching New Orleans to assess the fortifications there.
April 8	Stephen Harriman Long to Robert Butler (enclosure: Joseph G. Swift to Long, March 23). ALS, DLC (22). Reports for duty with an explanation of the previous orders under which he has acted.
April 9	To Thomas Langford Butler. ALS, John W. Kaufman, Philatelic Auction No. 135 (March 12, 1988), Lot 938 (mAJs). Promises to aid him in obtaining a position with John Coffee's northern Mississippi Territory survey.
April 9	From W. H. Bedford. ADS, DLC (69). Lexington *Kentucky Reporter,* April 30. Certifies that John Thomas and Henry P. Helm were near Baton Rouge about March 20, 1815.
April 11	*To George Graham.* 107
April 11	To William W. Worsley and Thomas Smith (enclosures: John Thomas to AJ, March 29; David B. Morgan to AJ, Jan 8; extract of AJ to troops at New Orleans, March 14, all 1815; W. H. Bedford to AJ, April 9; Thomas Childress to AJ, cApril). LS matched fragments in James C. Bronaugh's hand, DLC (22 and 59; 5-0809); Printed, Lexington *Kentucky Reporter,* April 23 (5-0823). Bassett, 2:284–89 (extract). Condemns again those who claim he withdrew his criticism of the conduct of the Kentucky troops at the Battle of New Orleans.
April 11	From George Graham (enclosures: Alexander Macomb to Graham, March 14; Talbot Chambers to Macomb, Jan 20, DLC-22). LS, DLC (22); LC, DNA-RG 107 (M6-9). Forwards letters relating to the military situation at Green Bay.
April 12	Rufus Lathrop Baker to Robert Butler (enclosures: William A. Trimble to John Sibley, March 21; Trimble to Eleazar W. Ripley, March 28, April 1). ALS, DNA-RG 107 (M222-19). Encloses reports for AJ's orders.
April 14	From George Gibson. ALS, DNA-RG 107 (M221-73). Submits a summary of quartermaster accounts and stores at New Orleans.
April 15	Samuel Houston to Robert Houston. LC, DNA-RG 98 (mAJs). Orders cessation of the removal of intruders from reservations north of the Tennessee River.
April 16	From Isaac Lewis Baker. ALS, DLC (22). Informs AJ of his resigna-

tion from the army; applies for prospective position as assistant inspector general.

April 16 From David Campbell (1779–1859). ALS, DLC (22). Introduces a Mr. Rawlins.

April 16 James McMillan Glassell to Daniel Parker (enclosures: Benjamin F. Harney to AJ, April 2; Thomas S. Rogers et al. to George Graham, Feb 8). ALS, DNA-RG 94 (M566-97). Forwards recommendations of A. Grass.

April 16 Robert Butler to Thomas Adams Smith. LC, DNA-RG 98 (mAJs). Orders 8th Infantry paymaster to Fort Hampton to pay promptly salaries in arrears.

April 18 *From Arkansas Cherokees (to AJ and Return Jonathan Meigs, 1740–1823).* 109

April 18 James McMillan Glassell to George Graham. ALS, DNA-RG 107 (M221-74). Discusses arrangements for Cherokee negotiations.

April 19 From Solomon P. Sharp. ALS, THi (5-0827). Asks AJ's assistance in getting James McGoodin a surveyor's position.

April 20 From Richard Butler. ALS, DLC (22). Bassett, 2:291 (extract, attributed to Robert Butler). Announces arrival of Truxton; gives family news.

April 20 Thomas Adams Smith to Robert Butler (enclosure: Joseph Kean to Smith, Feb 15). ALS with ANS by AJ to accept resignation, DLC (22). Recommends acceptance of Kean's resignation.

April 22 *To George Graham.* 111

April 22 To Abram Maury. ALS, DLC (71). Bassett, 6:462. Discusses progress on the Reid-Eaton biography.

April 22 To Joseph Gardner Swift. LS, NWM (5-0833). Thanks him for promised attention to Andrew J. Donelson; opposes army commissions for foreigners.

April 22 Robert Butler to Eleazar Wheelock Ripley. LC, DNA-RG 98 (mAJs). Orders riflemen to St. Louis and other troops to military road duty.

April 22 Robert Butler to Thomas Adams Smith. LC, DNA-RG 98 (mAJs). Orders preparation to transfer infantry companies to Muscle Shoals.

April 22 James McMillan Glassell to Edmund Pendleton Gaines. Copy, DNA-RG 107 (M221-77). Authorizes punishment of Seminoles for Georgia murders.

April 22 *Division Order.* 113

April 23 Robert Butler to Edmund Pendleton Gaines. LC, DNA-RG 98 (mAJs). Orders court-martial of William Wilson.

April 24 James McMillan Glassell to George Graham. Abstract, DNA-RG 107 (M22-10). Discusses military road.

April 24 Robert Butler to Stephen Harriman Long. LC, DNA-RG 98 (mAJs). Orders Long to report to Thomas A. Smith at St. Louis.

April 25 From Hugh Young. ALS, DLC (22). Reiterates report of his survey work.

April 25 James McMillan Glassell to George Graham (enclosure: AJ to William H. Crawford, Nov 16, 1816). ALS, DNA-RG 107 (M221-74). Encloses copy of letter discussed in April 24 communication.

April 29 To Andrew Jackson Donelson. ALS, DLC (5-0842, mAJs). Announces death of John Samuel Donelson.

April 29	To George Graham. LS, DNA-RG 107 (M221-74); Extract, DNA-RG 46 (5-0843). Reports on military road construction; asserts that protection of the frontier from hostile Seminoles is his primary military objective.	
[April]	From Washington Jackson. ALS, DLC (71). Lexington *Kentucky Reporter,* Sept 3. Recommends James C. Wilkins and Nicholas C. Hall for information on the action of Kentucky militia in 1815.	
[cApril]	From Thomas Childress. ANS, DLC (18). Lexington *Kentucky Reporter,* April 30. Certifies that several Kentucky militia officers stayed in Nashville, April 17–20, 1815.	
[cApril]	Memorandum re assignment of Stephen Harriman Long. AN, DLC (21).	
May 1	Account and receipt of Frederick Pinkley for $37.50 for the construction of a carriage house. DS in AJ's hand, DLC (22).	
May 3	From John Bradstreet. ALS, DLC (22). Inquires if Matthew Codd was promoted to colonel for bravery at the Battle of New Orleans.	
May 4	From John Waller Overton. ALS, DLC (22). Estimates costs due in *Alfred M. Douglass, executor* v. *Jackson & Hutchings.*	
May 7	To Robert Butler. LS, DLC (22). Bassett, 2:293–94. Requests copies of documents relating to the conduct of the Kentucky militia at New Orleans.	
May 7	From Robert Brent. LC, DNA-RG 99 (5-0845). Announces appointments of Cary Nicholas as battalion paymaster at New Orleans and Robert Searcy as temporary battalion paymaster at Nashville.	
May 8	From James Gadsden. ALS, DLC (22). Supports Simon Bernard's plans for strengthening the defenses around New Orleans; praises AJ's April 22 Division Order.	
May 8	From Edmund Pendleton Gaines (enclosures: Gaines to José Masot, April 8; Masot to Gaines, April 12; David Brearley to Masot, April 10, 16, 18, 20, and 22; Masot to Brearley, April 11, 16, and 21). LS, DLC (22). Reports on negotiations with the governor at Pensacola for the passage of provisions to Fort Crawford.	
May 8	From Edmund Pendleton Gaines. ALS, DLC (22). Promises prompt action to halt the Seminole attacks on frontier settlements.	
May 9	*To Isabella Butler Vinson.*	114
May 9	From George Graham. LS, DLC (22); LC, DNA-RG 75 (M15-4); LC, DNA-RG 107 (M6-9). Argues against moving the Indian factory near Natchitoches; asserts that the army is expected to aid Indian agents and factors when possible.	
May 9	Robert Butler to Eleazar Wheelock Ripley. LC, DNA-RG 98 (mAJs); Extract, DNA-RG 94 (mAJs). Orders investigation of reported activities of a Spanish agent among Indians near the Texas border; orders a detail to assist in marking the military road.	
[May 11]	To James Winchester. AL fragment, THi (5-0850). Complains of ill health.	
May 13	*To George Graham.*	115
May 13	From George Gibson. ALS, DLC (22). Reports receipt of funds from Washington and his duties assessing claims for damage incurred during the Battle of New Orleans.	
May 13	From James C. Wilkins. ALS with ANS by Nicholas C. Hall, DLC	

(22). Bassett, 2:294. Recounts flight of the Kentucky militia during the Battle of New Orleans.

May 14 From George Graham. LS, NNMAI (5-0855); LC, DNA-RG 75 (M15-4); Copies, DLC (22), DNA-RG 46 (5-0856). *ASP, Indian Affairs,* 2:141. Relays Monroe's decision to negotiate with Cherokees for tribal lands east of the Mississippi in exchange for those west of the river.

May 14 From James C. Wilkins (enclosure: Wilkins to AJ, May 13). ALS, DLC (22). Promises further testimony regarding the right bank retreat during the Battle of New Orleans; refers AJ to John Metcalf of Kentucky.

May 15 Account with McKiernan & Stout for carriage repairs for $1.75, with receipt for payment March 9, 1820. ADS with AJ endorsement, DLC (28).

May 16 From George Graham (to AJ, Joseph McMinn, and David Meriwether; enclosures: Thomas Jefferson to Cherokee Indians, Jan 9, 1809, DLC-4; Commission of AJ, McMinn, and Meriwether to negotiate with the Cherokee Nation, May 16). LS, DLC (22); LC and Copy, DNA-RG 75 (M15-4, T494-1); Copy, DNA-RG 46 (5-0857). *ASP, Indian Affairs,* 2:141–42. Sends instructions regarding negotiations for the relocation of the Cherokees west of the Mississippi.

May 16 Commission of AJ, Joseph McMinn, and David Meriwether to negotiate with the Cherokee Nation. DS, DLC (22); Copies, DNA-RG 59 (5-0859), InHi (5-0860).

May 20 To John Coffee. ALS, THi (5-0862). Bassett, 2:295 (extract). Discusses the survey of lands in northern Mississippi Territory.

May 20 From George Graham. LS, DLC (22); DNA-RG 107 (M6-9). Suspends removal of intruders from Cherokee lands north of the Tennessee River.

May 20 From Samuel Shaw. ALS with ANS by AJ to grant request, DLC (22). Requests a transfer from St. Louis to Norfolk.

May 21 From George Graham. LS with AJ endorsement ordering transfer, CtY (5-0865); LC, DNA-RG 107 (M6-9). Requests that Lieutenant James Monroe be ordered to report to the war department.

May 21 From James Monroe. Extract, *The Autograph,* Thomas F. Madigan (Dec 1922), Item 666 (5-0867). Requests that his nephew, Lieutenant James Monroe, be allowed to attend West Point; outlines plans for a tour of the North and Northwest.

May 22 To Robert Butler. LS, DLC (22). Protests Jonathan Eppler's account.

May 24 To John Coffee. ALS, James S. Leonardo (5-0868). Recommends Benjamin Smith for deputy surveyor.

May 24 From William Cocke. ALS, DLC (22). Requests removal of intruders from Chickasaw lands.

May 24 From Return Jonathan Meigs (1740–1823). ALS, DLC (22). Bassett, 2:295–96 (extract). Introduces John D. Chisholm, representative of the Arkansas Cherokees for upcoming treaty; gives opinion regarding the Cherokees' best course of action to preserve their existence.

May 24 From James Winchester. Copy, T (5-0870). Defends his conduct as commander at Mobile in January 1815.

May 26 To John Bradstreet. LS, NcD (5-0874). Denies that Matthew Codd was promoted to colonel at New Orleans.

May 26 To George Graham. Abstract, DNA-RG 107 (M22-10). Supports claim that Patrick H. Martin should have received a lieutenant's salary.

May 26 From George Graham (enclosure: John Brown, J. Cox, and Uriah Allison to Graham, May 13, DNA-RG 107, M221-73). LC, DNA-RG 75 (M15-4). Requests that army contractors be notified of supplies needed at impending Cherokee treaty negotiations.

May 27 To George Graham (enclosure: William A. Trimble to Eleazar W. Ripley, April 1, DNA-RG 107, M222-19). LS, OkTG (5-0877). Reports preparations to depart for Cherokee negotiations; discusses the wisdom of moving an Indian factory from Natchitoches.

May 28 From Daniel Parker. LC, DNA-RG 94 (M565-5). Establishes standard procedures governing resignations from the army.

May 29 To James McMillan Glassell. ALS endorsed by David Meriwether, June 20, and Copy, DLC (22 and 23). Appoints him secretary to the commissioners negotiating a treaty with the Cherokees.

May 29 To David Holmes. LS, LNHiC (5-0882). Discusses certification of claims for pay by men of Madison County, Mississippi Territory.

May 29 *To Rachel Jackson.* 117

May 31 To George Graham. LS, Andrew J. Donelson, Jr. (mAJs). Presents complaints against Chickasaw agent, William Cocke.

May 31 From Pierre LeBreton Duplessis. Abstract, DLC (5-0884). Sends newspaper clipping on the conduct of the Kentucky militia at New Orleans.

June 1 From Edmund Pendleton Gaines (enclosures: George Graham to Gaines, March 18; Gaines to Daniel Hughes, May 13). LS, DLC (22). Protests war department orders assigning troops to nonmilitary duties.

June 1 From Edmund Pendleton Gaines (enclosures: Gaines to John M. Davis and to José Masot, May 12; Masot to Gaines, May 17; Masot to Davis, May 17 and 19; Davis to Masot, May 19; Davis to Gaines, May 26). ALS, DLC (22). Sends correspondence re negotiations for the release of provisions at Pensacola.

June 1 Account with United States for pay, clothing, forage, and subsistence for AJ and servants. DS, DNA-RG 217 (5-0887). Runs to December 31.

June 2 From James Monroe. ALS, DLC (22). Bassett, 2:296 (extract). Promises to write later on AJ's Division Order of April 22; discusses relations involving Spain and England.

June 4 From William Allen Trimble (enclosure: Joaquin de Arredondo to Diasabet, Oct 25, 1816, DLC-21). ALS with AJ endorsement to await war department advice, DLC (22). Sends translation of Spanish commission given the Caddo chief.

June 5 James McMillan Glassell to Paul Hyacinte Perrault. LC, DNA-RG 98 (mAJs). Instructs him to continue military road survey from Shoal Creek to the Maury County line.

June 6 From George Graham (enclosure: Graham to John Childress, June 6, DLC-22). LS, DLC (22); LC, DNA-RG 75 (M15-4). Transmits letter

	discussing confiscation of the property of intruders on Cherokee lands.
June 6	James McMillan Glassell to Lewis B. Willis. ALS copy, DLC (22); LC, DNA-RG 98 (mAJs). Orders construction of military road from Cypress Creek to the Tennessee border.
June 7	From Hugh Young. ALS, DLC (22). Reports preparations for constructing the military road north from Madisonville, Louisiana.
June 8	From James Gadsden. ALS, DLC (22). Reports progress of examination of Louisiana coastal defenses and deplores the appointment of Simon Bernard as army engineer.
June 9	Robert Butler to Eleazar Wheelock Ripley. LC, DNA-RG 98 (mAJs). Orders Lieutenant James Monroe to Washington.
June 11	To George Graham. Copy, DNA-RG 46 (5-0889). *ASP, Indian Affairs,* 2:142. Reports progress on the military road and urges early date for land sales in northern Mississippi Territory.
June 11	To James Monroe. Copy certified by James M. Glassell, DLC (22). *TPUS,* 18:111–12. Recommends John W. Walker for territorial governor of Alabama.
June 11	From William Allen Trimble (enclosure: Trimble to Eleazar W. Ripley, June 4, DLC-27). ALS, DLC (22). Transmits letter presenting evidence of Spanish incitement of Indians in Louisiana.
June 11	Arthur Peronneau Hayne to Rachel Jackson. ALS, DLC (22). Appreciates the favors given his family upon their arrival in Tennessee.
[June] 11	*To Rachel Jackson.* 117
June 12	To James Monroe. LS, Sw (5-0895); Copy, DLC (22). Recommends James M. Glassell for assistant adjutant or inspector general.
June 15	Robert Butler to George Graham. ALS, DNA-RG 107 (M221-73). Reports on arrangements to supply Cherokee treaty negotiations.
June 16	From White Youngs. ALS, DNA-RG 94 (M566-96). Recommends Farley Eddy for army commission.
June 17	From Henry H. Minton. ALS, DNA-RG 94 (M566-96). Recommends Farley Eddy for army commission.
June 19	From Daniel Todd Patterson. ALS with AJ endorsement, DLC (22). Bassett, 2:297–98 (extract). Defends his actions at the Battle of New Orleans and praises AJ's letters to the Lexington *Kentucky Reporter.*
June 20–July 8	Minutes of the negotiations with the Cherokee Nation for an exchange of their eastern tribal land for lands in Arkansas. Copy partly in Anthony Palmer's hand and Drafts in James M. Glassell's hand, DLC (23); AD fragment partly in Glassell's hand, DLC (4).
June 21	*To Robert Butler.* 118
June 21	To John Coffee. ALS, THi (5-0898). Bassett, 2:298 (extract). Discusses Cherokee negotiations; suggests a course Coffee should follow during upcoming land sales.
June 23	To James Monroe. AL draft partly in James M. Glassell's hand, DLC (23). Reports transfer of Monroe's nephew; discusses upcoming Cherokee negotiations.
June 26	From Robert Brent. LS, DLC (23). Solicits opinion on payment of troops.
June 26	From Alexander McCoy. ALS with ANS by Return Jonathan Meigs (1740–1823), DNA-RG 75 (M208-7). Requests withholding of

	funds due John Walker from Meigs until the ownership of Robert Grierson's slaves is settled.
June 26	From Lewis B. Willis. ALS, DLC (23). Reports on construction of the military road in northern Mississippi Territory.
June 27	From Robert Breckinridge McAfee. Printed, Lexington *Kentucky Reporter,* July 16 (mAJs). Defends his *History of the Late War in the Western Country* (Lexington, 1816).
June 27	From Return Jonathan Meigs (1740–1823). ALS, DLC (23). Relays James Gilmore's request for volunteers to remove intruders from the Cherokee nation.
June 27	James McMillan Glassell to James Gilmore. LC, DNA-RG 98 (mAJs). Authorizes company of volunteers to remove intruders from Cherokee lands.
June 28	To Cherokee Indians. Copy, DLC (23). Emphasizes necessity to exchange eastern Cherokee land for Arkansas land.
June 29	From Arkansas Cherokees (to AJ, Joseph McMinn, and David Meriwether). LS by proxy and Copy, DLC (23). Demand the land promised to them in exchange for lands east of the Mississippi.
June 30	From Edmund Pendleton Gaines (enclosures: James E. Dinkins to Gaines, June 1, DLC-22; Gaines to Seminole chiefs, May 10). ALS, DLC (23). Reports lack of progress in negotiations with the Seminoles.
July 1	Agreement witnessed by AJ in which John Brown as agent for William Kelly promises to deliver to Return Jonathan Meigs (1740–1823) slaves taken from Broom, a Cherokee chief. Copy, DNA-RG 107 (M222-23).
July 2	To Charles Hicks (from AJ, Joseph McMinn, and David Meriwether). Copy, DLC (23). Bassett, 2:302. Urge inclusion of Arkansas chiefs in Cherokee council; demand that the treaty be explained to all delegates.
July 2	*From Eastern Cherokees (to AJ, Joseph McMinn, and David Meriwether).* 120
July 2	Order releasing Richard Hudson, intruder on Cherokee lands, from confinement. DS, DLC (23).
[July 2]	From William Simmons. ALS matched fragments, DLC (75) and ICHi (mAJs). Asks for particulars about the death of his son.
July 3	From Richard Brown and Thomas Wilson (to AJ, Joseph McMinn, and David Meriwether). Copy, DLC (23). Bassett, 2:302. State the eastern Cherokees' refusal to meet with John D. Chisholm and their fear of the proposed treaty terms.
July 3	From John D. Chisholm (to AJ, Joseph McMinn, and David Meriwether). ALS, DNA-RG 75 (M208-7). Defends his character from aspersions of the Cherokee committee.
July 4	To Cherokee Indians (from AJ, Joseph McMinn, and David Meriwether). ALS copy and Copy, DLC (23); Copy, DNA-RG 75 (T494-1). Bassett, 2:299–300. Explain the meaning of the commissioners' June 28 talk.
[cJuly 4]	From [Joseph McMinn] to AJ and David Meriwether. AL, DLC (23). Suggests delay in answering Eastern Cherokees.

July 6	From Hugh Young. ALS, DLC (23). Describes progress in laying out the military road between Madisonville, Louisiana, and the Pearl River.	
[cJuly 6]	*To Eastern Cherokees (from AJ, Joseph McMinn, and David Meriwether).*	124
July 8	To George Graham (from AJ, Joseph McMinn, and David Meriwether). AL draft, DLC (23). Bassett, 2:300–304. Relate the course and results of Cherokee negotiations.	
July 8	From Lewis B. Willis. ALS with ANS by AJ ordering preparation of a ferry and defining the jurisdiction, DLC (23). Reports difficulty in obtaining a ferry across the Tennessee River; asks in which jurisdiction he is located.	
July 8	Agreement with Doublehead et al. to pay compensation for ceded lands north of the Tennessee River. ADS in AJ's hand, signed also by David Meriwether and Joseph McMinn, DNA-RG 217 (5-0909). With receipts of John Walker, John D. Chisholm, and Return J. Meigs (1749–1823), dated July 9.	
July 8	Treaty with Cherokee Indians. DS, DNA-RG 11 (M668-4); Draft in James M. Glassell's hand and Copy, DLC (23). *ASP, Indian Affairs,* 2:129–31.	
[July 8]	Memorandum on payment to Cherokees for land north of the Tennessee River to be ceded to the United States. AN, DLC (59; 5-0912).	
July 9	To George Graham (from AJ, Joseph McMinn, and David Meriwether; enclosure: Agreement to pay compensation, July 8). Photocopy of LS, THer (mAJs); ALS copy signed by AJ for McMinn and Meriwether, DLC (23). Bassett, 2:305. Explain payments made to secure ratification of the Cherokee treaty.	
July 9	*To George Graham.*	125
July 9	To George Graham. Abstract, *ABPC* (1931–32), p. 535 (5-0916). Discusses prospective visit of a Cherokee delegation with James Monroe in October.	
July 9	To George Graham (from AJ, Joseph McMinn, and David Meriwether). ALS by AJ, also signed by McMinn and Meriwether, DNA-RG 107 (M222-19). Recommend William Rockhold to supply the articles promised in the Cherokee treaty.	
July 9	To George Graham (from AJ, Joseph McMinn, and David Meriwether). ALS by McMinn, also signed by AJ and Meriwether, InHi (5-0917). Recommend that Cherokee agent Return J. Meigs (1740–1823) be given an assistant.	
July 9	To George Graham (from AJ, Joseph McMinn, and David Meriwether). ALS by McMinn, also signed by AJ and Meriwether, InHi (5-0920). Recommend that the United States subsidize the movement of Cherokees to Arkansas.	
July 9	To James Monroe (from AJ, Joseph McMinn, and David Meriwether). LS, NN (5-0923). Recommend Isham Randolph as census taker of the Cherokees in Arkansas.	
July 9	Robert Butler to Samuel Shaw. LC, DNA-RG 98 (mAJs). Orders him to report to Norfolk.	
July 10	To George Graham (from AJ and Joseph McMinn). ALS by Mc-	

	Minn, also signed by AJ, DNA-RG 107 (M221-74). Recommend John Brown (1779–1843) as census taker of eastern Cherokees.	
July 10	To George Graham (from AJ, Joseph McMinn, and David Meriwether). LS, DNA-RG 217 (5-0925). Submit bill for \$449.12½ covering board, whiskey, and forage during the treaty negotiations.	
July 10	From Edmund Pendleton Gaines (enclosures: Cappachimico to James E. Dinkins, May 29, DLC-22; Sanders Donoho to Gaines, June 23; David E. Twiggs to Gaines, June 29). ALS, DLC (23). Bassett, 2:305–307 (extract). Blames the failure of negotiations with the Seminoles on the interference of Alexander Arbuthnot; reports on construction of a military road from Fort Crawford to Georgia.	
July 11	From James Gilmore. ALS, DLC (23). Reports burning squatters' houses along the Sequatchie River.	
July 12	From George Graham. LS, DLC (23); LC, DNA-RG 107 (M6-9). Reports forwarding three letters to James Monroe.	
July 13	*To John Coffee.*	126
July 14	Account with United States for AJ's travel expenses as Cherokee treaty commissioner. DS, DLC (23).	
July 15	Deed from John Coffee to John Gray Blount in execution of September 1815 AJ agreement with Blount. DS with AJ endorsement, DLC (19).	
July 17	From George Graham (enclosure: Graham to [James Bankhead], July 17, DLC-23). LS, DLC (23); LC, DNA-RG 107 (M6-9). Encloses copy of order for occupying the area near the St. Mary's River to close the slave trade.	
[July 17]	From Gideon Morgan, Jr. ALS, DNA-RG 75 (M208-7). Describes John Walker's attempt to secure payment of a claim against the government.	
July 19	From Arthur Peronneau Hayne. ALS, DLC (23). Reports preparations for Milledgeville land sales.	
July 22	*To George Graham.*	128
July 22	Receipt from Robert Butler for \$4,000 for quartermaster's account. ADS duplicate, DNA-RG 217 (5-0932).	
July 23	To John Adair (enclosures: Adair to William P. Anderson, Aug 28, 1815; Anderson to John Reid, Oct 17, 1815, both DLC-71; James C. Wilkins to AJ, May 13; Washington Jackson to AJ, [April 1817]; Detachment report of Kentucky militia, Jan 13, 1815, DLC-67). Copy, DLC (71). Bassett, 2:309–19. Charges Adair with spreading falsehoods concerning the conduct of Kentucky militia at New Orleans.	
July 23	To George Graham (enclosures: Farley Eddy to Robert Butler, June 4; White Youngs to AJ, June 16; Henry H. Minton to AJ, June 17; George P. Peters to Butler, June 18). LS, DNA-RG 94 (M566-96). Sends recommendations supporting Eddy for lieutenant.	
July 23	From Robert Butler. LC, DNA-RG 98 (5-0938). *Nashville Clarion,* Aug 19. Denies John Adair's charge that Butler was responsible for misreporting action of Kentucky militia at New Orleans.	
July 23	From Levi Colbert. LS by proxy with ANS by AJ to forward to secretary of war, DNA-RG 107 (M221-74). Inquires about overdue payment for ceded Chickasaw lands.	

July 24	*To James McMillan Glassell.*	129
July 25	To Thomas Smith. Printed, William Martin, *The Self Vindication of Colonel William Martin* . . . (Nashville, 1829), pp. 24–25 (11-0770). States his belief that William Martin (1765–1846) excited mutiny among troops in December 1813.	
July 25	From Robert Brent. LC, DNA-RG 99 (5-0945). Seeks opinion concerning the stationing of paymasters within the Southern Division.	
July 29	To William Clark (from AJ, Joseph McMinn, and David Meriwether). Printed, Washington *National Intelligencer,* Sept 24 (5-0946). Outline the features of the Cherokee treaty, particularly as they involve Arkansas lands.	
July 29	From Jane Nelson. ALS, DLC (23). Seeks restitution for property allegedly taken by AJ's troops.	
July 30	To George Graham (enclosures: Accounts, July 14, for AJ's travelling expenses, and, July 30, for James M. Glassell's services at Cherokee negotiations). Abstract, DNA-RG 107 (M22-10). Encloses accounts.	
July 30	From George Graham. LS, DLC (23); LC, DNA-RG 75 (M15-4). Proposes a fort to maintain peace between the Osage and Cherokee nations in Arkansas.	
July 30	From Winfield Scott (enclosure: Scott to George Graham, July 28). ALS, T (5-0947). Transmits copy of a letter discussing the congressional medals voted War of 1812 officers.	
July 30	Robert Brownlee Currey to Samuel Houston. DS in AJ's hand with ANS by AJ to preserve it, DLC (23). Acknowledges receipt of a letter to John Adair at the Nashville post office.	
July 30	Account for James McMillan Glassell's service as secretary to the Cherokee treaty commission. DS, DLC (23).	
July 31	From Hezekiah Niles. ALS, DLC (23). Requests a recommendation of *Niles' Register* for publication.	
July 31	Certification by Samuel Houston of pay due Anthony Palmer. ADS duplicate with NS by AJ to pay Palmer's account, DNA-RG 217 (mAJs).	
Aug 1	From Richard Brown. LS by proxy (John Thompson), DLC (23). Complains about intruders on Cherokee lands.	
Aug 1	From George Graham (to AJ, Joseph McMinn, and David Meriwether). LS, DLC (23); LC and Copy, DNA-RG 75 (M15-4, M208-7); Copy, DNA-RG 46 (5-0952). *ASP, Indian Affairs,* 2:143. Discusses arrangements to fulfill the conditions of the Cherokee treaty and the probability of Senate ratification.	
Aug 3	From Nathan Guilford. Printed form signed with ANS, DLC (23). Seeks information on Mississippi Territory lands for the Western Emigrant Society.	
Aug 4	To Andrew Jackson Donelson. ALS, DLC (5-0953). Bassett, 2:320 (extract). Imparts advice on proper conduct.	
Aug 4	From James Monroe. ALS with AJ endorsement, DLC (23); Copy, NN (5-0956). Bassett, 2:319. Asserts that all orders from the secretary of war must be obeyed, but promises to discuss the issue more fully later.	

Aug 5	*From Arthur Peronneau Hayne.* 130
Aug 8	Robert Butler to Eleazar Wheelock Ripley. LC, DNA-RG 98 (mAJs). Approves Ripley's response to war department order directing Charles Wollstonecraft to Washington.
Aug 8	Robert Butler to Eleazar Wheelock Ripley. LC, DNA-RG 98 (mAJs). Authorizes visit to Washington on public business.
Aug 9	From George Graham (enclosure: Graham to Return J. Meigs, 1740–1823, Aug 9, DNA-RG 75, M15-4). LS, DLC (23); LC and Extract, DNA-RG 75 (M15-4, M208-7); Copy, DNA-RG 46 (5-0960). *ASP, Indian Affairs,* 2:144. Describes arrangements to distribute supplies to Cherokees; authorizes AJ to withhold appointment of Nicholas Byers as assistant Cherokee agent.
Aug 11	James McMillan Glassell to George Graham (enclosure: Levi Colbert to AJ, July 23). ALS, DNA-RG 107 (M221-74). Acknowledges AJ's receipt of July 17 letter from the war department.
Aug 12	To Robert Brent. LS, NhD (5-0961). Approves the present method of paying the troops; requests that funds be sent the paymaster at Nashville.
Aug 12	To Thomas Langford Butler. ALS, William C. Cook (mAJs). Discusses controversy with John Adair re Kentucky troops at New Orleans.
Aug 12	*To John Coffee.* 132
Aug 12	To James Monroe (enclosures: Daniel Parker to Eleazar W. Ripley, June 11, DNA-RG 94, M565-5; Ripley to Parker, July 20, DNA-RG 94, M566-96; AJ to Graham, Feb 26; Division Order, April 22). LS, NN (5-0969). Bassett, 2:320–21. Reiterates his conviction that war department orders to subordinate officers must be routed through the commanding officer.
Aug 12	Certification of Alfred Flournoy's good conduct as army lieutenant. DS, DNA-RG 94 (5-0968).
Aug 14	From George Graham (enclosure: William H. Crawford to AJ, Jan 27, 1816). LS with AJ endorsement, NNMAI (5-0977); LC and Copy, DNA-RG 75 (M15-4, M208-7); Copies, DLC (23), DNA-RG 46 (5-0980). *TPUS,* 18:135–36. Asserts that the federal government lacks authority to seize livestock of intruders on Cherokee lands.
Aug 14	*From Unknown.* 134
Aug 15	From John Lowry. ALS, ICHi (5-0984). Reports the course of two disputes concerning property titles.
Aug 16	From George Graham. LS, NNMAI (5-0988); LC, DNA-RG 75 (M15-4). Reports approval of expense accounts of AJ and James M. Glassell.
Aug 18	To Nathan Guilford. LS, OHi (5-0990). Promises to respond to his queries about Mississippi Territory at a later time.
Aug 18	From Adam Gibbs Goodlett. ALS, DNA-RG 94 (M566-97). Resigns as army surgeon.
Aug 19	To George Graham. Extract, Parke-Bernet Catalog (March 26, 1957), Item 107 (5-0992); Extract, Bassett, 2:322 (5-0991). Dismisses objections to the Cherokee treaty; acknowledges order for a military post on the Arkansas River.

Aug 19	From Thomas Tudor Tucker. LS, DLC (23). Encloses $109.06 for AJ's expenses as Cherokee treaty commissioner.
Aug 20	Robert Butler to Thomas Adams Smith (enclosure: George Graham to AJ, July 30). LC, DNA-RG 98 (mAJs). Orders establishment of post on the Arkansas River.
Aug 21	To John Coffee. LS, THi (5-0993). Introduces Captain Farmer and Mr. Nisbit, who intend to purchase Alabama lands.
Aug 21	Robert Butler to Eleazar Wheelock Ripley. LC, DNA-RG 98 (mAJs). Directs order to Charles Wollstonecraft.
Aug 21	Account of Mrs. [R. P.] Cannon for Rachel Jackson with John Baird for cloth, with receipts of payment. DS, DLC (23).
Aug 23	To James D. Miller. ALS, DLC (23). Complains of excessive charge for the repair of a wagon.
Aug 23	From Samuel Brown. ALS, DLC (23). Suggests that AJ call on John Brown (1757–1837) while visiting Kentucky.
Aug 23	Account with James D. Miller for $14 for the repair of a wagon, with AJ's ANS, Aug 26, stating he paid only $10 of the account. AD, DLC (23).
Aug 25	From William Cocke. ALS, DLC (23). Discusses payment of a Cherokee chief for horses held by the Chickasaws; inquires re payments to Chickasaws for ferrying AJ's troops on return from Natchez expedition.
Aug 25	From Edmund Pendleton Gaines (enclosure: Gaines to Murder Creek settlers, July 12). ALS, DLC (23). Bassett, 2:322–23 (extract). Explains his refusals to protect squatters on land obtained by the Treaty of Fort Jackson; reports his effort to capture Indians responsible for killing a white settler.
Aug 25	From Joseph McMinn. ALS with ANS by AJ, T (5-0995). States approval of AJ's August 19 letter to George Graham; requests information on the military road to New Orleans.
Aug 26	To George Graham (enclosure: Graham to Return J. Meigs, 1740–1823, Aug 9, DNA-RG 75, M15-4). Abstract, DNA-RG 107 (M22-10). Returns letter appointing Nicholas Byers as agent for Cherokee removal and recommends Samuel Houston instead.
Aug 26	To Return Jonathan Meigs, 1740–1823 (enclosure: George Graham to AJ, Aug 9). ALS, THi (5-0999). Amelia W. Williams and Eugene C. Barker, eds., *Writings of Sam Houston* (8 vols.; Austin, Texas, 1938–43), 5:243–44. Explains his disapproval of Nicholas Byers's appointment and recommends instead Samuel Houston to be assistant at the Cherokee Agency.
Aug 26	To [Hezekiah Niles]. Printed extract, DLC (5-1000). Praises *Niles' Register.*
Aug 28	From George Graham. LS, NNMAI (5-1001); LC, DNA-RG 75 (M15-4). Explains delay in distribution of Chickasaw annuity.
Aug 29	From Joseph McMinn. ALS, DLC (23). Proposes to replace a government check lost by Cherokee chief John Walker.
Aug 30	From George Henry Nixon. ALS, DLC (23). Complains re nonpayment of residents of the Pearl River settlements, Mississippi Territory, for goods and services rendered during the War of 1812.

Aug 30	From Thomas Adams Smith. LC, MoHi (5-1002). Complains of a shortage of military doctors; requests enlarged recruiting district for Rifle Regiment; reports on Indian movements in Illinois Territory.	
Aug 30	Account with Robert Smiley for tailoring. DS, DLC (24). Runs to January 21, 1818.	
Aug 31	From Edmund Pendleton Gaines (enclosure: David E. Twiggs to Gaines, Aug 11). ALS, DLC (23). Bassett, 2:323–24 (extract). Reports plans for action against the Seminoles.	
[Aug]	From Thomas Langford Butler. ADS, DLC (71). *Cincinnati Commercial,* June 8, 1880. Contradicts John Adair's account of the source of arms for Kentucky militia at New Orleans.	
Sept 1	From Joseph McMinn. ALS, DLC (23). Approves AJ's recommendation of Samuel Houston for assistant Cherokee agent.	
Sept 2	To George Graham. Abstract, DNA-RG 107 (M22-10). Acknowledges receipt of Graham's August 14 letter.	
Sept 2	*To James Monroe.*	135
Sept 8	To William Martin (1765–1846). Photocopy of ALS, T (mAJs). Discusses pay of Patrick H. Martin, deceased.	
Sept 8	To Winfield Scott (enclosure: Unknown to AJ, Aug 14). ALS draft, T (5-1008); Copies, THi (5-1010), NWM (mAJs). Bassett, 2:325. Inquires whether Scott has criticized AJ's April 22 order.	
Sept 8	From Charles McClung. ALS with AJ endorsement, DLC (23). Discusses title to land he and AJ purchased from Robert Cotton.	
Sept 9	*To James Monroe.*	135
Sept 9	From Robert Brent (enclosure: Brent to Cary Nicholas, Sept 8). LC, DNA-RG 99 (5-1011). Encloses letter for Nicholas.	
Sept 9	From Return Jonathan Meigs (1740–1823). Copy, DNA-RG 75 (M208-7). States preference for William Smith as assistant Cherokee agent.	
Sept 9–30	James McMillan Glassell to Daniel Parker. LS, DNA-RG 94 (M566-101). Conveys AJ's protest of the August 22 order to Charles Wollstonecraft.	
Sept 9	Angus W. McDonald to Robert Butler. ALS with ANS by AJ denying request, DLC (23). Seeks extension of furlough.	
Sept 10	To John Henry Eaton. Extract, Anderson Galleries Catalog (Nov 1935), p. 194 (5-1012). Comments on the Kentucky militia controversy.	
Sept 10	To James Monroe. Printed, Octavia Zollicoffer Bond, *The Family Chronicle and Kinship Book* (Nashville, 1928), pp. 452–53 (5-1013). Recommends Richard C. Cross for appointment to West Point.	
Sept 11	*From William Carroll.*	137
Sept 14	From Hugh Young. ALS, DNA-RG 77 (5-1014). Describes the survey of the military road from Madisonville, Louisiana, to the Tennessee River.	
Sept 15	To John Quincy Adams. LS, DNA-RG 59 (M439-5). Recommends William Donnison, Jr., for secretary of Alabama Territory.	
Sept 15	Account and receipt of Kirkman, Jackson & Erwin with AJ and John Henry Eaton for transporting picture frames from Philadelphia to Nashville. ADS with ANS by Eaton, DLC (31).	

Sept [15]	Account with John Henry Eaton for picture frames, newspaper subscriptions, and loan. DS with AJ endorsement, DLC (31). Runs to October 1822.	
Sept 16	Receipt for $75 charged to AJ's account from Edward George Washington Butler to Thomas Kirkman. ADS, DLC (23).	
Sept 16	Receipt from Edward George Washington Butler for $298, for personal expenses paid by AJ as his guardian (endorsed on account of Aug 19, 1816). DS in AJ's hand signed by Butler, DLC (23).	
Sept 18	From Lewis Evans. ALS, ICHi (5-1019). Recommends William Edward West to paint AJ's portrait.	
[cSept 25]	Memorandum directing letter (not found) to the secretary of war. ANS, DNA-RG 77 (5-1022).	
Sept 27	From James Monroe. ALS, DLC (23). Bassett, 2:325. Promises to discuss AJ's April 22 Division Order after he has recovered from recent travels.	
Sept 28	*To John Coffee.*	138
Sept 29	To John Coffee. ALS, THi (5-1026). Describes John Hutchings's illness and discusses management of his farm in Alabama Territory.	
Sept 29	From George Graham (enclosure: Graham to Samuel Houston, Sept 29). LC, DNA-RG 75 (M15-4). Encloses Houston's commission as Cherokee subagent.	
Sept 30	To John Coffee. ALS, THi (5-1030). Relays John Hutchings's instructions regarding pay as surveyor; requests further help in securing an overseer.	
Sept 30	*From Tochelar and The Glass.*	139
Sept 30	From Hugh Young (enclosure: Map of the military road, 1817, DNA-RG 77). ALS, ABAU (5-1032). Reports in detail on his survey of the military road from Madisonville, Louisiana, to the Tennessee River.	
Oct 1	*From Edmund Pendleton Gaines.*	140
Oct 1	Account with Thomas Yeatman for sundries. DS with AJ endorsement, DLC (70). Runs to December 7, 1819.	
[Oct] 2	From John Rhea. ALS, DLC (23). Reports election of judges and senator by the Tennessee legislature.	
Oct 3	From Eleazar Wheelock Ripley. ALS, DNA-RG 94 (M566-100). Reports death of Charles Wollstonecraft.	
Oct 3	Thomas R. Mercein to James McMillan Glassell. ALS, DLC (23). Reports delivery of AJ's letters to Winfield Scott.	
Oct 4	*From Winfield Scott.*	142
Oct 5	*From James Monroe.*	144
Oct 6	To John Coffee. ALS, THi (5-1101). Encloses settlement of an account between Mr. Briant [John Bryan?] and John Hutchings; complains that his Alabama overseer has not yet arrived.	
Oct 6	Letter of introduction and certification re Francis Booby's New Orleans service. Copy, KyClHi (5-1100).	
[Oct 9]	From [Hugh Young]. AL fragment, DLC (5-1103). Reports regarding duties as topographical engineer.	
Oct 11	From George Graham. LS, DLC (23); LC, DNA-RG 107 (M6-9). Encloses instructions for Samuel Houston from Return J. Meigs (1740–1823).	

Oct 16 Daniel Parker to James McMillan Glassell (enclosure: Parker to AJ and Jacob J. Brown, July 9, 1816). LS with AJ endorsement, DLC (23); LC, DNA-RG 94 (M565-5). Justifies orders to Charles Wollstonecraft and Eleazar W. Ripley.

Oct 17 To [George Graham] (enclosures: Hugh Young to AJ, Sept 14; Tochelar and The Glass to AJ, Sept 30; Map of the military road, 1817). Extract, DNA-RG 77 (5-1105). Praises Young's military road survey; urges the prompt sale of public land in the Alabama Territory.

Oct 17 Robert Butler to Daniel Parker. ALS with ANS by AJ, DNA-RG 94 (M566-98); LC, DNA-RG 98 (mAJs). Recommends William R. Jouett for army appointment.

Oct 19 Robert Butler to Hugh Young. LC, DNA-RG 98 (mAJs). Orders survey between Tennessee and Black Warrior rivers.

Oct 20 To Andrew Jackson Donelson. ALS, DLC (5-1108). Discusses plans to visit John Hutchings; urges Donelson to write.

Oct 21 To William Lee. LS, DNA-RG 217 (5-1115). Encloses receipt of Robert Butler for $1,500.

Oct 21 From John Adair. Printed, Lexington *Kentucky Reporter,* Oct 29 (5-1111). Defends action of Kentucky militia at the Battle of New Orleans.

Oct 21 From Robert Bell. ALS with ANS by AJ, DLC (23). Requests $100 to pay taxes on the Edward Butler estate near Pittsburgh, Pennsylvania, and gives receipt for same.

Oct 21 From [Peter Hagner]. LC, DNA-RG 217 (5-1114). Adjusts AJ's quartermaster account.

Oct 22 *To James Monroe.* 148

Oct 23 From Edmund Pendleton Gaines (enclosures: Gaines to Eleazar W. Ripley, Oct 18; William Rabun to Gaines, Sept 17). LS with concluding paragraph and postscript in Gaines's hand, DLC (23). Reports his response to Indian activities along the Florida border.

Oct 24 Samuel Houston to Angus W. McDonald. LC, DNA-RG 98 (mAJs). Denies furlough extension.

Oct 25 From George Graham. LS, DLC (23); LC and Extract, DNA-RG 75 (M15-4, M271-2). Inquires about the prospect of purchasing Chickasaw land in Kentucky, Ohio, and Tennessee; discusses payment of Chickasaw annuity.

Oct 25 Robert Butler to Joseph Woodruff. LC, DNA-RG 98 (mAJs). Grants permission for Woodruff to go to Washington to settle accounts.

Oct 26 Robert Butler to George Graham (enclosure: Hugh Young to AJ, Sept 30). ALS, DNA-RG 77 (mAJs). Encloses report.

Oct 27 From George Graham. LS, DLC (23); LCs, DNA-RG 75 (M15-4), DNA-RG 98 (5-1122). Requests military assistance for construction of an Indian factory at Sulphur Fork on the Red River.

Oct 27 Account of Rachel Jackson with Martha Adams for clothing. DS, DLC (26). Runs to March 3, 1819.

Oct 29 Account with Brahan & Hutchings for shoes, paper, rope, and other merchandise. ADS, A-Ar (5-1123). Runs to January 10, 1820.

Oct 30 From George Graham (enclosure: Graham to Edmund P. Gaines, Oct 30, *ASP, Indian Affairs,* 2:159). LS, DLC (23); LC, DNA-RG 107 (M6-9). Encloses letter regarding movement against the Seminoles.

Oct 30	From George Graham. LC, DNA-RG 107 (M6-9). Orders repair of the military road from Columbia, Tennessee, to Madisonville, Louisiana.
[Oct?]	To George Graham. Abstract, DNA-RG 107 (M22-10). Discusses his division orders.
Nov 2	Robert Butler to Paul Hyacinte Perrault. Copy, DNA-RG 94 (M566-111); LC, DNA-RG 98 (mAJs). Orders topographical survey between Fort Montgomery and Savannah.
Nov 3	From José Masot. LS and Translation, DLC (23). Bassett, 2:333. Reports the return to William Peacock of two slaves who had fled to Pensacola.
Nov 5	Receipt from Samuel Scott & Co. for $20 for boat plank. DS in AJ's hand, Mrs. H. A. Brewer (mAJs).
Nov 5	Receipt from Joseph Wyatt for $15 for boat. DS in AJ's hand, Mrs. H. A. Brewer (mAJs).
Nov 6	From George Graham. LS, DLC (23); LC, DNA-RG 75 (M15-4). Promises to receive Arkansas Cherokee delegation headed to Washington; outlines plans for sales of Alabama lands.
Nov 6	From [Peter Hagner]. LC, DNA-RG 217 (5-1125). Acknowledges receipt of AJ to William Lee, October 21, and the crediting of $1,500 to AJ's account.
Nov 6	From David P. Hillhouse. ALS, DLC (23). Solicits information on planting techniques for eventual publication.
Nov 6	From William Lee. LC, DNA-RG 217 (5-1126). Notifies AJ of the transfer of his quartermaster accounts to the third auditor.
Nov 7	Will of John Hutchings appointing AJ guardian of Andrew Jackson Hutchings and AJ, John Coffee, and Stockley Donelson Hutchings, executors. DS in AJ's hand, signed by Hutchings and witnesses, THi (5-1127); Copy, Mrs. Richard H. Gilliam, Jr. (5-1129).
Nov 8	From Tishomingo. LS by proxy (James Colbert), DLC (23). Recommends James Neelly to replace William Cocke as Chickasaw agent.
Nov 9	From Edmund Pendleton Gaines. ALS, DLC (23); Copy, DNA-RG 107 (M222-19); Extracts, DNA-RG 46 (5-1132), DNA-RG 233 (5-1134). *ASP, Indian Affairs,* 2:160 (extract). Reports on Indian activities and troop movements; discusses agricultural possibilities of land between Forts Montgomery and Gaines.
Nov 9	From Eleazar Wheelock Ripley. ALS, DLC (23). Announces his imminent departure for Washington and explains redeployment of his troops.
Nov 13	From George Graham (enclosures: Graham to Edmund P. Gaines, to James Bankhead, and to William Rabun, Nov 12, DLC-23). LS, DLC (23); LC, DNA-RG 107 (M6-9). Encloses letters directing the occupation of Amelia Island.
Nov 13	From Eleazar Wheelock Ripley. ALS, DLC (23). Reports his expected departure for Washington on November 14.
Nov 19	Robert Butler to George Graham. ALS, DNA-RG 107 (M221-73). Reports forwarding Graham's October 25 letter to AJ near Huntsville.
Nov 19	Account with John Newnan for medical advice for John Hutchings,

	with receipt for payment in full, Dec 12, 1820. DS by proxy (Samuel M. Price) with AJ endorsement, A-Ar (8-0019).	
Nov 21	To Eli Hammond. ALS, THi (5-1145). Orders payment of $90 to Daniel Giggers for construction of a cotton gin at Melton's Bluff.	
Nov 21	*From Edmund Pendleton Gaines.*	150
Nov 22	Account with Saunders & Chandler for cloth. ADS, DLC (69). Runs to May 9, 1818.	
Nov 24	From George Graham. LS, DLC (23); LC, DNA-RG 107 (M6-9). Acknowledges receipt of Hugh Young's topographical report on the military road.	
Nov 24	Account with William McKnight for tuition of Andrew Jackson, Jr., and Andrew Jackson Hutchings. AD, THi (5-1147).	
Nov 25	Aaron Jordan Booge to Robert Butler. ALS, DLC (23). Thanks AJ and Butler for past favors and informs them of his current activities as army chaplain.	
Nov 26	From Edmund Pendleton Gaines (enclosure: Mathew Arbuckle to Gaines, Nov 30). ALS, DLC (23). Reports skirmish with the Seminoles near Fowltown.	
Nov 26	From George Graham (enclosures: Robert Brent to Graham, Nov 12; Graham to Brent, Nov 26). LS, DLC (23). Discusses payment of troops.	
Nov 27	From George Graham. LC, DNA-RG 107 (M6-9). Encloses contract (not found) with Camillus Griffith to supply troops in Louisiana, Mississippi, and Alabama.	
Nov 27	From John Rhea. ALS, DLC (23). Bassett, 2:335–36. Attempts to mediate misunderstanding between AJ and James Monroe over Stephen H. Long's orders.	
Dec 1	*To George Graham.*	151
Dec 1	Robert Butler to William Lindsay. LC, DNA-RG 98 (mAJs). Orders him to organize recruits and proceed to Mobile.	
Dec 1	Robert Butler to Thomas Adams Smith (enclosure: George Graham to AJ, Oct 27). LC, DNA-RG 98 (mAJs). Directs him to supply soldiers for protection and construction at Sulpher Fork on the Red River.	
Dec 1	James McMillan Glassell to Daniel Parker. ALS, DNA-RG 94 (M566-101). Reports AJ's satisfaction with Parker's explanation of the order to Charles Wollstonecraft.	
Dec 2	To [William Allen Trimble]. Copies, DLC (23), Ms-Ar (5-1151). Warns of possible Seminole attacks in Alabama and orders him to provide adequate forces in the area.	
Dec 2	*From Edmund Pendleton Gaines.*	153
Dec 2	*From James Monroe.*	155
Dec 3	*To Winfield Scott.*	156
Dec 4	To Andrew Jackson Donelson. ALS, DLC (5-1161). Comments on court-martial of Alden Partridge; warns of men's wickedness and corruption.	
Dec 4–6	Proceedings in the courts-martial of John Buyrns and Carter Whitington. ADS by Angus W. McDonald also signed by William Davenport with ANS by AJ approving the verdict, DLC (23).	

Dec 5	William Allen Trimble to Robert Butler. ALS with ANS by AJ to consult war department, DLC (23). Suggests the sale of public property at Forts Selden and Claiborne.	
Dec 6	*To Richard Butler.*	158
Dec 6	George Graham to Robert Butler. LS with ANS by AJ directing Butler to forward items to Graham, DLC (23). Announces appointment of Henry Sherburne as Chickasaw agent; requests another copy of AJ to Graham, February 12.	
Dec 8	*To William Berkeley Lewis.*	159
Dec 10	From William Lee (enclosure: Statement of paymaster accounts, Nov 28, DLC-69). LC, DNA-RG 217 (5-1173). Sends correction to paymaster accounts of November 12 and 26.	
Dec 11	From John Caldwell Calhoun (enclosure: Calhoun to Edmund P. Gaines, Dec 9, DLC-23). LS with AJ endorsement, DLC (23); LC, DNA-RG 75 (M15-4). Encloses letter permitting Gaines to cross the Florida border, if necessary, to break up marauding Seminole forces.	
Dec 12	From Robert Brent. LC, DNA-RG 99 (5-1174). Suggests that AJ call upon Cary Nicholas for a copy of letter of December 12.	
Dec 12	From John Caldwell Calhoun. LS with ANS by AJ ordering preparations, DLC (23); LC, DNA-RG 107 (M6-9). Directs AJ to provide a detachment at New Orleans to cooperate with naval Captain John D. Henley in an assault on Galveston.	
[Dec 13]	From [William Allen Trimble]. AL fragment with AN fragment by AJ, DLC (75). Discusses troop assignments for the 8th Military Department.	
Dec 16	To Andrew Jackson Donelson. ALS, DLC (5-1175). Urges that he write his grandfather, Daniel Smith.	
Dec 16	*To George Graham [John Caldwell Calhoun].*	161
Dec 17	To Samuel Carswell. Extract, John Heise Catalog 2461, Item 229 (5-1179). Introduces George W. Martin.	
Dec 17	To George Washington Martin. Photocopy of ALS, MsSM (5-1180). Requests information about the claim of John Donelson's (c1718–86) heirs before Congress.	
Dec 17	From John Caldwell Calhoun (enclosures: Calhoun to Edmund P. Gaines and to James Bankhead, Dec 16, DLC-23). LS, DLC (23); LC and Copies, DNA-RG 75 (M15-4, M271-2). Encloses letters permitting Gaines to attack the Seminoles in Florida if necessary and discusses removal of intruders from Amelia Island.	
Dec 18	From Samuel Houston. ALS, Tx (5-1184). Discusses delegation of Arkansas Cherokees to Washington, preparations for Cherokee emigration to Arkansas, and supply problems at the Cherokee Agency.	
Dec 19	From Mathew Arbuckle (enclosure: Peter Muhlenberg, Jr., to Arbuckle, Dec 16). LS, DLC (23). Reports his response to a concentration of Seminoles on the Apalachicola River threatening the expedition to supply Fort Scott.	
Dec 19	From John Caldwell Calhoun. LS, DLC (23); LC, DNA-RG 107 (M6-9). Sends for consideration design of the congressional medal honoring AJ's War of 1812 service.	
Dec 20	*To James Monroe.*	162

Dec 21	From William Oliver Allen. ALS, DNA-RG 94 (M566-102). Resigns army post.	
Dec 21	From Richard Brown. ALS by proxy with AJ endorsement, DLC (23). Complains of whites stealing livestock from Cherokees.	
Dec 22	From Eleazar Wheelock Ripley. ALS, DLC (23). Explains that illness has delayed his travel to Washington.	
Dec 22	Receipt from Joseph Wyatt for $16.50 paid by Richard Massey for salt and whiskey for AJ and John Hutchings. DS, Mrs. H. A. Brewer (mAJs).	
Dec 23	To James Monroe. LS, MH-H (5-1196). Reveals a plot by squatters north of the Tennessee River to manipulate the upcoming February land sales.	
Dec 24	From John Caldwell Calhoun. LS, DLC (23); LC, DNA-RG 75 (M15-4). Suggests that AJ "seize the moment" of annuity distribution to procure relinquishment of Chickasaw lands in Tennessee and Kentucky.	
Dec 24–25	From John Rhea. ALS, DLC (23). Bassett, 2:341. Argues against AJ's resignation.	
Dec 25	To James Jackson, Jr. LS by proxy, THer (mAJs). Discusses ownership of the slave Dick.	
Dec 25	Archimedes Donoho to Robert Butler. ALS with AJ endorsement directing the letter forwarded for approval, DNA-RG 94 (M566-96). Resigns army commission.	
Dec 26	*From John Caldwell Calhoun.*	163
Dec 26	Receipt from E. Shields for $10 paid by Richard Massey for a ferry boat for AJ and John Hutchings.	
Dec 27	To [John Caldwell Calhoun]. Abstract, DNA-RG 107 (M22-10). Reports forwarding statement of receipts and expenditures.	
Dec 27	From John Caldwell Calhoun. LS, DLC (23); LC, DNA-RG 75 (M15-4). Calculates the amount owed Chickasaws for 1817 as $19,350.	
Dec 28	From James Monroe. ALS copy, NN (5-1209). *Cincinnati Commercial,* Jan 8, 1880 (extract). Defends new regulations regarding issuance of war department orders; urges AJ not to retire.	
Dec 29	To Robert Butler. ALS, DLC (23). Orders arrest of those accused of stealing livestock from Cherokees.	
Dec 29	From John Brown. DS in AJ's hand, witnessed by AJ and John Overton and endorsed by AJ, DLC (23). Authenticates the theft of hogs from Cherokees by Thomas Billingsley and other whites.	
Dec 29	From John Caldwell Calhoun (enclosures: Calhoun to Edmund P. Gaines, Dec 26, DLC-23; Order by Calhoun, Dec 29). ALS with AJ endorsement, DLC (23); LC, DNA-RG 107 (M6-9). Bassett, 2:343. Explains that policy governing the issuance of war department orders is compatible with AJ's views.	
Dec 29	Order by John Caldwell Calhoun stating that the war department will issue directives to a subordinate commander only in emergency situations. DS, DLC (23); LC, DNA-RG 107 (M6-9).	
Dec 29	Receipt of William Hill for $1.68¾ from Harrison Saunders for ferry charges owed by AJ. DS, DLC (69).	

Dec 30	To John Caldwell Calhoun (enclosure: AJ to George Graham, Feb 12). LS, Sc (5-1212). *Calhoun Papers,* 2:46. Reports that land proposed for an armory and foundry along Shoal Creek has no owner and that he has ordered cooperation with the naval operation against Galveston.
Dec 30	From John Caldwell Calhoun. LS, LS duplicate, and Copy, DLC (23); LC, DNA-RG 75 (M15-4). Requests that Cherokee Indians led by Gideon Morgan, Jr., be used in the campaign against the Seminoles.
Dec 30	From Eleazar Wheelock Ripley. ALS, DLC (23). Describes his efforts at Washington regarding the 8th Military Department.
Dec 30	From James Sanders, Edward Ward, and Peter Moseley. ALS with AJ endorsement, DLC (23). Solicit $50 for the building of a schoolhouse; with receipt for $50, in AJ's hand signed by Samuel Scott, January 1, 1818.
Dec 31	From Joseph McMinn. ALS, Stanley F. Horn (5-1214). Describes his efforts to convince the Cherokees to move west of the Mississippi River.
Dec 31	Robert Butler to James Dorman. LC, DNA-RG 98 (mAJs). Directs him to apprehend the men accused of driving off Cherokee stock.
Dec 31	Robert Butler to William Allen Trimble. LC, DNA-RG 98 (mAJs). Orders him to retain troops at Natchitoches, to report the names of absent officers, and to cooperate with the naval expedition against Galveston.
1817	Statement of AJ's accounts with Andrew Jackson Hutchings regarding Alabama plantations. DS by John Coffee, A-Ar (5-0661). Runs to August 31, 1825.
[1817]	To [George Gibson]. ANS, DNA-RG 217 (5-0655). Orders payment of $100 to Thomas Maples for 1815 freight charges.
[1817]	To [George Gibson]. ANS, DNA-RG 217 (5-0659). Orders payment of $150 to Mrs. Allard for cypress logs used in 1815.
[1817]	To William Piatt [George Gibson]. ANS, DNA-RG 217 (5-0657). Orders payment of $93.33⅓ to Mathias Ory for food, lodging, and forage in 1815.
[1817]	To [William Jones et al.] (from AJ, John McNairy, Robert Butler, Robert Weakley, John Waller Overton, John Coffee, James Jackson, Jesse Wharton, and John Patton Erwin). Copy, DNA-RG 46 (5-0664). *Nashville Whig,* June 8, 1838. Recommend Robert Searcy and John Sommerville for president and cashier of the Nashville branch of the Bank of the United States.
[c1817]	From George Washington Campbell. ALS, DLC (5-0651). Introduces [Samuel P. P.] Fay of Massachusetts.
[c1817]	From Tishomingo. LS by proxy, DLC (59). Reports sending notification of upcoming negotiations to an Indian nation.

1818

Jan 1 — To Thomas Beale. AL draft, DLC (23). *Nashville Whig,* Feb 28 (dated Jan 20). Thanks the New Orleans Volunteer Company of Riflemen for a commemorative sword.

Jan 1 — From William Bradford. ALS, DLC (23). Reports his arrival at the Arkansas River and discusses disputes between Cherokees and Osages.

Jan 1 — Account and receipt with United States for $2,905.70 covering pay, forage, clothing, and subsistence. DS, DNA-RG 217 (5-1222). Runs to June 30.

Jan 1 — Account with James Jackson & Co. for financial, mercantile, and real estate transactions. AD, DLC (26). Bassett, 2:412–14. Runs to April 1, 1819.

Jan 2 — From Winfield Scott. ALS, DLC (23); Copies, DLC (23), THi (5-1224), NWM (mAJs). Bassett, 2:344–45. Declines to duel over the misunderstanding provoked by Scott's condemnation of AJ's April 22 Division Order.

Jan 6 — To John Caldwell Calhoun. Photocopy of LS, THer (5-1226). Acknowledges receipt of Calhoun's letter of December 17, 1817.

Jan 6 — To John Caldwell Calhoun. LS, DLC (75). Declines to suggest changes to the congressional medal honoring his War of 1812 service.

Jan 6 — To Peter Hagner. LS, DNA-RG 217 (5-1227). Encloses receipt of $2,000 by his acting quartermaster, Robert Butler.

Jan 6 — *To James Monroe.* 166

Jan 6 — To Cary Nicholas. LS, DNA-RG 217 (5-1236). Requests a pay increase for Robert Butler.

Jan 6 — From Mathew Arbuckle (enclosure: Edwin Sharpe to Arbuckle, Dec 31, 1817, DNA-RG 94, M566-104). LS, DLC (23); Extract, DNA-RG 94 (M566-104). Reports on skirmishes with Indians and supply problems at Fort Scott.

Jan 7 — James McMillan Glassell to Daniel Parker. ALS, DNA-RG 107 (M221-78). Requests an explanation of the inscription on the congressional medal to be awarded to AJ.

Jan 9 — To John Caldwell Calhoun. Abstract, DNA-RG 107 (M22-11). Acknowledges receipt of Calhoun's letter of December 24, 1817.

Jan 9 — Receipt from Peter H. Martin for $8. ADS, DLC (23).

Jan 10 — From B. S. Bulfinch. ALS, DLC (23). Pledges as a newspaper editor in Winchester, Virginia, to defend AJ from slanders.

Jan 10 — From John Caldwell Calhoun (enclosures: Samuel Shaw to Calhoun, 1817; Henry Shaw to Calhoun, Jan 10, DLC-23). LS, DLC (23); LC, DNA-RG 107 (M6-9). Refers Samuel Shaw's request for a furlough.

[cJan 10] — Certification of James Henderson's service as lieutenant during the War of 1812. DS, DNA-RG 94 (5-1237).

Jan 11 — *To Robert Henry Dyer et al.* 168

Jan 11 — To Joseph McMinn. Copy (dated 1819), DNA-RG 46 (5-1244). *ASP, Military Affairs,* 1:767. Informs McMinn of the call for volunteers from Tennessee to fight the Seminoles.

Jan 12 — To John Caldwell Calhoun. LS, MiU-C (5-1254); Copy, DNA-RG

233 (5-1258); Extract, DNA-RG 46 (5-1261). Bassett, 2:347. Justifies his call for 1,000 Tennessee volunteers to fight the Seminoles; asks for maps of the Seminole territory.

Jan 12 To Daniel Todd Patterson. Copy, DNA-RG 45 (M125-58). Asks naval protection for supply ships en route from New Orleans to Fort Scott.

Jan 12 To William Rabun. Extract, Milledgeville *Georgia Journal,* Feb 3 (mAJs; 5-1279). Sends notification of AJ's instructions to fight the Seminoles and his authority to request a call of militia.

Jan 12 From Mathew Arbuckle (enclosures: Robert Irvin to Arbuckle, Dec 23, 1817, DLC-23; Edwin Sharpe to Arbuckle, Dec 31, 1817, and Milo Johnson to Arbuckle, Jan 7, DNA-RG 94, M566-104). LS, DLC (23); Copies, DNA-RG 107 (M221-77), DNA-RG 233 (5-1245); Extracts, DNA-RG 46 (5-1253), DNA-RG 94 (M566-104). *ASP, Military Affairs,* 1:695. Reports on expedition against Fowltown and on the shortage of provisions at Fort Scott.

Jan 12 From Edmund Pendleton Gaines (enclosures: Mathew Arbuckle to Gaines, Dec 20, 21, 1817; Peter Muhlenberg, Jr., to Arbuckle, Dec 16, 19, 1817; Thomas Glascock to Gaines, Jan 10, DLC-23). ALS and LS duplicate (dated 1812), DLC (23); LC, DNA-RG 98 (5-1264); Copy, DNA-RG 94 (5-1269). Reports on troop movements, hostile Indian activities, and the state of supplies along the southern Georgia border.

Jan 12 From Edmund Pendleton Gaines (enclosures: George Graham to Gaines, Nov 12; Gaines to John C. Calhoun, Dec 4, 15, 30, all 1817, DLC-23). ALS and LS duplicate, DLC (23); LC, DNA-RG 98 (5-1273); AL draft, DNA-RG 94 (5-1275). Reports capture of Amelia Island.

Jan 12 From John H. Gibson. ALS, DLC (23). Agrees to raise volunteers to fight the Seminoles.

Jan 12 From John Rhea. ALS, DLC (23). Bassett, 2:348. Praises Monroe's annual message and refers vaguely to similarity of AJ's and the president's views.

Jan 13 To John Caldwell Calhoun. Copy, DNA-RG 233 (5-1280). *ASP, Military Affairs,* 1:744. Requests quartermaster's funds sent to Fort Scott.

Jan 13 From James Dorman. ALS with ANS by AJ approving, DLC (23). Requests approval of continued construction of a military road through Alabama Territory.

Jan 13 From William Berkeley Lewis. ALS, DLC (71). Bassett, 6:463–64. Discusses the controversies over AJ's April 22 Division Order and Kentucky troops at New Orleans; urges AJ not to resign.

Jan 14 *To John Coffee.* 169

Jan 14 To John Donelson (1787–1840). Extract, Octavia Zollicoffer Bond, *The Family Chronicle and Kinship Book* (Nashville, 1928), p. 170 (5-1285). Announces his imminent departure for Georgia to lead troops against the Seminoles.

Jan 14 From William Savin Fulton. ALS, DLC (23). Volunteers to serve in AJ's army.

Jan 15 From William Allen Trimble. ALS, DLC (23); Extract, DNA-RG 94

(M566-105). Reports on effort to raise a Choctaw company, troop dispositions along the Florida border, and conditions at Fort Crawford.

Jan 15 Minutes of Cumberland Lodge 8, listing AJ and other subscribers for the purchase of a lot for a new Masonic hall in Nashville. AD, T (5-1286).

Jan 16 Receipt of Shadrach Howard for $13.50 from Richard Massey, overseer for AJ and John Hutchings. DS, Mrs. H. A. Brewer (mAJs).

Jan 17 From John Caldwell Calhoun (enclosures: Calhoun to James Bankhead, Jan 15; Calhoun to Edmund P. Gaines, Jan 16, DLC-23). LS, DLC (23); LC, DNA-RG 107 (M6-9). Transmits copies of orders regarding Amelia Island and the Seminole campaign.

Jan 19 To Joseph McMinn. ALS endorsed with ANS regarding the return of the document, DLC (24); Copy, DNA-RG 46 (5-1295). *ASP, Military Affairs,* 1:767. Reports raising two regiments of West Tennessee volunteers to fight the Indians.

Jan 19 From Edmund Pendleton Gaines (enclosures: John Nicks to Gaines, Jan 3; Thomas Glascock to Gaines, Jan 18, DLC-23). LS, DLC (24); LC, DNA-RG 98 (5-1293); ALS draft, DNA-RG 94 (5-1289). Reports on supplies.

Jan 19 Rachel Jackson to George Gibson. Printed, *Potter's American Monthly,* 5(1875):820 (5-1294). Thanks Gibson for a present and chides him for his bachelorhood.

Jan 19 James McMillan Glassell to Robert Henry Dyer and Thomas Williamson. Copy, DLC (24). Washington *National Intelligencer,* March 9, 1819. Orders rendezvous of Tennessee volunteers at Fayetteville, January 31.

[cJan 19] To John Caldwell Calhoun. LS, ScU (5-1287). Acknowledges receipt of $19,350 for the Chickasaw Nation; complains of the Nashville Bank's refusal to loan money for the upcoming Seminole campaign.

Jan 20 To Mathew Arbuckle. Copy, DNA-RG 46 (5-1297). *ASP, Military Affairs,* 1:765. Promises efforts to relieve Fort Scott.

Jan 20 To John Caldwell Calhoun (enclosures: Mathew Arbuckle to AJ, Dec 19; Peter Muhlenberg, Jr., to Arbuckle, Dec 16, both 1817, DLC-23). LS, MiU-C (5-1298); Copies, DNA-RG 233 (5-1302, -1307); Extract, DNA-RG 46 (5-1313). *ASP, Military Affairs,* 1:696–97. Describes the route and supply system for the Tennessee volunteers' march south; responds amicably to Calhoun's December 29 letter.

Jan 20 *To Edmund Pendleton Gaines.* 171

Jan 20 To Return Jonathan Meigs (1740–1823). LS, DNA-RG 217 (mAJs). Accepts services of up to 200 Cherokee warriors, to be commanded by Samuel Houston.

Jan 20 From George Gibson. ALS, DLC (24). Sends a plan (not found) of the old Spanish fortifications in New Orleans.

Jan 20 Receipt by Alexander Campbell Wilder Fanning for $2,000 from AJ for quartermaster expenditures. DS, DNA-RG 217 (5-1317).

[Jan 20] To Thomas Glascock. Copies, DNA-RG 94 (M566-105), DNA-RG 98 (5-1322). Orders him to rescue Peter Muhlenberg, Jr.'s detachment on the Apalachicola River but to initiate no offensive maneuvers until AJ arrives.

Jan 21	To John Caldwell Calhoun. ALS, DNA-RG 107 (M221-78). *Calhoun Papers,* 2:84. Submits account for Cherokee treaty negotiations.
Jan 21	To Arthur Peronneau Hayne. Copy, DNA-RG 107 (M221-78). *Annals of Congress,* 15th Cong., 2nd sess., p. 2365. Orders him to march the Tennessee volunteer troops from Fayetteville to Fort Scott.
Jan 21	To Arthur Peronneau Hayne. Copy, DNA-RG 107 (M221-78). Authorizes Hayne to draw upon the secretary of war for funds.
Jan 21	To Edward Livingston. LS, Charles Apfelbaum (mAJs). Acknowledges receipt of a bronze statue of Napoleon.
Jan 21	To James Monroe. ALS, NN (5-1323). Bassett, 2:349–50. Announces commencement of Seminole campaign; suggests that future government deposits be directed to the Nashville branch of the Bank of the State of Tennessee to reward their aid in financing his army.
Jan 21	From Anthony Butler. ALS, DLC (24). Introduces Morgan A. Heard of Kentucky.
Jan 21	James Gadsden to John Caldwell Calhoun. ALS, DNA-RG 107 (M221-77). Announces that AJ has authorized Arthur P. Hayne to draw on war department funds.
Jan 21	James Gadsden to Peter Hagner (enclosures: Receipts of Robert Butler and Arthur P. Hayne, Jan 21). ALS, DNA-RG 217 (mAJs). Transmits receipts to be transferred to AJ's credit.
Jan 21	Receipt by Robert Butler for $1,200 from AJ on account of the quartermaster department. ADS, DNA-RG 217 (mAJs).
Jan 21	Receipt by Arthur Peronneau Hayne for $3,622 from AJ for quartermasters' and contractors' expenditures. ADS, DNA-RG 217 (mAJs).
Jan 22	Robert Butler to William Allen Trimble (enclosures: George Graham to AJ, Oct 27; Butler to Thomas A. Smith, Dec 1, both 1817). LC, DNA-RG 98 (mAJs). Directs Trimble to order detachment to relieve Smith's troops from duty at Sulphur Fork on Red River.
Jan 24	From John B. Bibb. ALS, DLC (24). Recommends Morgan A. Heard of Kentucky.
Jan 24	From Anthony Butler. ALS, DLC (24). Introduces John Hull of Kentucky.
Jan 24	From Amos Edwards. ALS, DLC (24). Recommends Robert F. Crittenden, commanding a band of Kentucky volunteers.
Jan 24	From Edmund Pendleton Gaines (enclosures: Mathew Arbuckle to Thomas Glascock, Jan 18, DLC-23; Robert Irvin to Glascock, Jan 20, DLC-24; Glascock to Gaines, Jan 22, DLC-24). ALS, DLC (24); AL draft (dated Jan 23) and Copy, DNA-RG 94 (5-1335, -1337); LC, DNA-RG 98 (5-1339). Reports that "there is no prospect of peace" with the Indians along the southern frontier.
Jan 25	From John Breathitt. ALS, DLC (24). Recommends Robert F. Crittenden, captain of the Kentucky volunteers.
Jan 26	From Benjamin Howard. ALS, DLC (24). Seeks aid to recover pay for his service as a surgeon in the Louisiana militia in 1814–15.
Jan 27	*To John Caldwell Calhoun.* 172
Jan 27	To John Coffee. ALS, THi (5-1344). Bassett, 2:352. Authorizes Coffee and James Jackson to act as his agents at Huntsville land sales.

Jan 27 To Rachel Jackson. ALS, S. Howard Goldman (5-1346). Heiskell, 3:289. Describes his journey to Huntsville, Alabama Territory.

Jan 27 To United States House of Representatives. DS, DNA-RG 233 (5-1350). *ASP, Public Lands,* 3:371–72. Requests compensation of the heirs of John Donelson (c1718–86) with the 10,000 acres of land promised by Georgia for surveying performed by Donelson.

Jan 27 From Thomas Eastland. ALS, DLC (24). Introduces Robert F. Crittenden.

Jan 27 From Washington L. Hannum. ALS, DLC (24). Introduces John Hull of Russellville, Kentucky.

Jan 27 From John Haywood. ALS, DLC (24). Introduces Brady, one of AJ's troops.

Jan 29 From John Caldwell Calhoun. LS, DLC (24); LC, DNA-RG 75 (M15-4); Extracts, DNA-RG 46 (5-1402), DNA-RG 233 (5-1400). *ASP, Military Affairs,* 1:697 (extract). Approves AJ's call for 1,000 Tennessee volunteers for the Seminole campaign.

Jan 29 From Return Jonathan Meigs (1740–1823). ALS draft, DNA-RG 217 (mAJs). Discusses organization of Cherokee warriors for Seminole campaign.

Jan 31 To Tennessee Volunteers. Printed, *Nashville Whig,* Jan 31 (5-1419). Praises their patriotism and urges subordination and discipline.

Jan 31 From John Devereux DeLacy (enclosure: Memorial asking redress for Spanish imprisonment of DeLacy, DLC-59). ALS, DLC (24). Discusses settlement of David Allison's estate.

Jan 31 From Edmund Pendleton Gaines (enclosure: Clinton Wright to Gaines, Jan 26, DLC-24). ALS, DLC (24); AL draft, DNA-RG 94 (5-1409); LC, DNA-RG 98 (5-1403). Informs AJ of troop movements, provisions, Indian activities, and topography of the southern border.

Jan 31 Receipt of Branch Jones for $3 from Richard Massey on account of Hutchings and AJ. DS, Mrs. H. A. Brewer (mAJs).

[cJan] To John Coffee. ALS fragment, THi (7-0110). Offers financial assistance to Catherine D. Hutchings and discusses land purchase.

Feb 1 From Edmund Pendleton Gaines. ALS, DLC (24); LC, DNA-RG 98 (5-1421); Copy, DNA-RG 94 (5-1423). Details supplies at Georgia forts.

Feb 1 From Arthur Peronneau Hayne (enclosure: Circular calling for volunteer troops, Feb 1). ALS, DLC (24). Reports that bad weather has delayed the rendezvous of the West Tennessee volunteers.

Feb 2 From George Gibson. ALS, DLC (24). Suggests that troops be sent down the Apalachicola River into Florida to secure a supply route from New Orleans.

Feb 4 From William Allen Trimble. ALS, DLC (24). Details plans for sending supplies from New Orleans up the Apalachicola River and discusses the disposition of troops in his department.

Feb 5 To Andrew Jackson Donelson. ALS, DLC (5-1428). Bassett, 2:352–53 (extract). Recounts his orders to fight the Seminoles and expresses a desire to retire.

Feb 5 To John Henry Eaton (enclosures: Winfield Scott to AJ, Jan 2; AJ to Rachel Jackson, Feb 5). ALS, DLC (24). Bassett, 2:352. Proposes to treat Scott's letter "with silent contempt."

Feb 5 To Rachel Jackson. Extract, *The Collector,* No. 845 (1976), Item J-236 (5-1437). Describes his progress to Georgia.
Feb 5 From Edmund Pendleton Gaines. ALS, DLC (24); ALS draft, DNA-RG 94 (5-1431); Extract, DNA-RG 98 (5-1434). Discusses troop dispositions and supply arrangements.
Feb 5 From [Peter Hagner]. LC, DNA-RG 217 (5-1436). Acknowledges receipt of Alexander C. W. Fanning's account forwarded by AJ.
Feb 6 From John Caldwell Calhoun. LC, DNA-RG 107 (M6-10); Extracts, DNA-RG 46 (5-1444), DNA-RG 59 (5-1439), DNA-RG 233 (5-1440, -1442). *ASP, Military Affairs,* 1:697 (extract). Approves AJ's measures for the Seminole campaign; explains delay in dispatching paymasters to AJ's command.
Feb 8 From Edmund Pendleton Gaines. AN, DLC (24). Transmits a sketch (not found) of "the country before us."
Feb 8 From Clinton Wright. ALS, DLC (24). Reports hostility of the Mikasuki Indians.
Feb 9 From William Rabun. LS, DLC (24); LC, G-Ar (5-1445). Reports on muster of Georgia militia.
Feb 10 To John Caldwell Calhoun. LS, DNA-RG 107 (M221-78); Copy, DNA-RG 59 (6-0001); Extracts, DNA-RG 46 (6-0003), DNA-RG 233 (6-0004, -0006). *ASP, Military Affairs,* 1:697 (extract). Condemns the Georgia militia for returning home; reports on the supply situation at Fort Scott.
Feb 10 To Rachel Jackson. ALS, DLC (24). Bassett, 2:353. Describes his movements; complains that "Georgia at present does not display much patriotism."
Feb 10 *To William Rabun.* 173
Feb 10 From Christopher Keiser. Copy, DLC (24). Reports on provisions at Fort Mitchell.
Feb 10–11 Statement of David Brearley et al. charging David Brydie Mitchell, Creek agent, with misconduct. AD abstract in AJ's hand, NN (6-0009).
Feb 11 To Arthur Peronneau Hayne. Extract, DNA-RG 153 (6-0015). Relays information regarding provisions at Fort Gaines.
Feb 11 From Thomas L. Trotter. ALS, DLC (24). Offers medical services to sick soldiers near Fayetteville.
Feb 12 From John Caldwell Calhoun. Extract, DNA-RG 75 (M15-4). Returns the account AJ sent January 21 and asks him to supply the dates of his service as Cherokee treaty commissioner.
Feb 12 From John Coffee (enclosure: Advertisement of Cotton Port, n.d., *Nashville Whig,* Feb 21, 1818, mAJs). ALS, DLC (24). Bassett, 2:353–54 (extract). Regrets his inability to accompany AJ; reports on land sales at Huntsville.
Feb 12 *From John Henry Eaton.* 174
Feb 12 From George Gibson. ALS, DLC (24). Bassett, 2:354 (extract). Discusses progress of expedition to supply Fort Scott; relays reports of George Woodbine's presence among the Seminoles.
Feb 12 *From James Jackson.* 177
Feb 12 From William Allen Trimble. LS with ANS postscript, DLC (24).

Fears George Woodbine and the Seminoles will prevent supplies from ascending the Apalachicola and suggests AJ capture St. Marks.

Feb 13 From Mathew Arbuckle. LS, DLC (24). Discusses supplies at Fort Scott.

Feb 13 From Arthur Peronneau Hayne. ALS, DLC (24). Reports that only two-thirds of the West Tennessee volunteers are well armed.

Feb 13 William Allen Trimble to Robert Butler (enclosure: Disposition of force in 8th Military Department, Feb 5). Extract, DNA-RG 107 (M221-79). Explains his noncompliance with Butler's January 22 order to detach troops up Red River.

Feb 14 *To John Caldwell Calhoun.* 180

Feb 14 To Rachel Jackson. Abstract, *ABPC* (1905), p. 570 (6-0043). Discusses the impending campaign against the Seminoles.

Feb 14 From Thomas Williamson. ALS, DLC (24). Notifies AJ of the strength and position of his volunteer regiment.

Feb 15 From John Michael O'Connor. ALS, DLC (24). Sends his translation of Simon François Gay de Vernon, *Treatise on the Science of War and Fortification* (New York, 1817).

Feb 15 Mathew Arbuckle to Edmund Pendleton Gaines, referred to AJ (enclosure: Arbuckle to Gaines, Feb 13). Copy, DLC (24). Reports that he will be compelled to abandon Fort Scott if not supplied within eight days.

Feb 16 From José Masot. LS and Translation, DLC (24). Requests the return of two free blacks and two slaves kidnapped and taken into the Alabama Territory.

Feb 16 From William Allen Trimble. ALS duplicate, DLC (24). Describes the convoy sent from New Orleans with provisions for Fort Scott.

Feb 17 From Pathkiller. LS by proxy (Charles Hicks) with ANS by Daniel Hughes, DLC (24). Pledges Cherokee assistance against the Seminoles but indicates concern about pay of warriors.

Feb 19 From John Caldwell Calhoun. LS, DLC (24); LC, DNA-RG 107 (M6-10). *Calhoun Papers,* 2:148–49. Reports that Congress has passed the appropriation bill and has received AJ's suggestion for a foundry and arsenal in the Southeast.

Feb 19 Receipt of Joysson Parmertree for $1.50 for picking cotton for Richard Massey, overseer for AJ and Hutchings. DS by proxy, Mrs. H. A. Brewer (mAJs).

Feb 20 From David Brearley. ALS, DLC (24). *TPUS,* 18:262. Recounts the latest Indian attack near Fort Mitchell.

Feb 21 From David Brearley. ALS, DLC (24). *TPUS,* 18:262–63. Elaborates on his account of the Indian attack and reports that many Indians have volunteered for service against Seminoles.

Feb 22 From Edmund Pendleton Gaines (enclosure: Gaines to Mathew Arbuckle, Feb 22, DLC-24). LS, DLC (24); AL draft, DNA-RG 94 (6-0044); LC, DNA-RG 98 (6-0048). Reports efforts to prevent abandonment of Fort Scott.

Feb 22 From Arthur Peronneau Hayne. ALS, DLC (24). Reports arrival of the Tennessee volunteers at Fort Jackson and asks that supplies meet their continued march at Fort Mitchell.

Feb 22	Account with James B. Houston for a trundle bed, with receipt of payment, November 30, 1819. DS, DLC (70).
Feb 23	From John Caldwell Calhoun. LS, DLC (24); LC, DNA-RG 107 (M6-10). Advises of remittances for supplies and pay of troops.
Feb 23	From William McIntosh. LS by proxy, DLC (24). Requests that more than the previously authorized 1,000 Creek warriors be permitted to join AJ.
Feb 24	From David Brearley (enclosures: Enos Cutler to Brearley, Feb 22; Brearley to Cutler, Feb 24). ALS, DLC (24). Discusses muster of Creek warriors at Fort Mitchell.
Feb 25	From Thomas Glascock. ALS, DLC (24). Reports progress of Georgia militia.
Feb 26	From Big Warrior and Little Prince (Tustunnuggee Hopoie). LS by proxy, DLC (24). Request that AJ accept all Creek warriors with William McIntosh.
Feb 26	To John Caldwell Calhoun. LS, DNA-RG 107 (M221-78); Copies, DNA-RG 233 (6-0050, -0054), DNA-RG 59 (6-0058). *ASP, Military Affairs,* 1:698. Complains of supply problems.
Feb 26	From William McIntosh. LS by proxy, DLC (24). Reports plans to attack a body of hostile Indians and to meet AJ at Fort Scott.
Feb 27	From David Brearley (enclosure: Alexander Arbuthnot to David B. Mitchell, Jan 19, DNA-RG 94, mAJs). ALS, DLC (24). Describes the planned movements of Indian troops to meet AJ at Fort Scott.
Feb 27	From William McIntosh. LS by proxy, DLC (24). Urges AJ to wait at Fort Early for 600 Indian troops.
[Feb]	From George Gibson. Extract, Charles Hamilton Catalog 15 (1966), Item 111 (5-1420). Complains of lack of funds to pay expenses of the quartermaster department.
March 2	From John Stadler Allison (enclosure: Mathew Arbuckle to Allison, Feb 28–March 1). ALS, DLC (24). Reports on search for Edmund P. Gaines, whose boat wrecked.
March 2	From John Caldwell Calhoun. LS, DLC (24); LC, DNA-RG 107 (M6-10). *Calhoun Papers,* 2:169–70. Agrees that the contract system of supply is inefficient; requests evidence to support AJ's allegations against David B. Mitchell.
March 2	Agreement of AJ and John Coffee with John Childress, James Jackson, and John Donelson, Jr. (1787–1840), to purchase lands in Alabama Territory for Thomas Kirkman, John McCrea, and John Goddard of Philadelphia. DS (AJ's signature by Coffee as proxy), THi (6-0064).
March 3	From John Walter Phillips. ALS, DLC (24). Reports arrival of supplies at Fort Early and detachment of troops to Creek Agency.
March 5	From Mathew Arbuckle (enclosures: Arbuckle to Richard M. Sands, Feb 25, March 3; Arbuckle to George Vashon, March 3; Enos Cutler to Arbuckle, March 4, all DLC-24). Copy, DNA-RG 94 (6-0067). Reports lack of supplies at Fort Scott.
March 6	From Mathew Arbuckle (enclosures: Arbuckle to Enos Cutler, March 5, 6). ALS, DLC (24). Sends supplies to AJ's troops.
March 6	From [Edward] Am[brose] Baber. ALS, DLC (24). Announces that provisions have reached Fort Early.

March 6 From Robert Brent (enclosure: Brent to John B. Hogan, March 6). LC, DNA-RG 99 (6-0071). Sends information concerning pay of troops.

March 6 Receipt of P. C. Anderson & Co. for $100 paid by AJ. ADS, DLC (24).

March 7 From Mathew Arbuckle (enclosures: Richard M. Sands to Arbuckle, Feb 28; Enos Cutler to Arbuckle, March 5; Arthur P. Hayne to Arbuckle, March 2). LS, DLC (24). Reports on Indian movements near Fort Scott.

March 8 From Daniel Hughes (enclosure: Thomas Anthony to Hughes, March 8). LS, DLC (24). Reports inability to supply Cherokee warriors intending to join AJ and solicits AJ's judgment of his decision.

[March 8?] Morning report of troops commanded by Edmund Pendleton Gaines. ADS by Robert R. Ruffin with ANS by Robert Butler and AN by AJ regarding the date of the report and troop movements and strength, DLC (69).

March 9 From Arthur Peronneau Hayne (enclosure: Enos Cutler to Hayne, March 5, DNA-RG 107, M221-78). LS and LS duplicate, DLC (24); Copy, DNA-RG 107 (M221-78). Reports that a shortage of supplies has induced him to retreat from Fort Mitchell to Fort Hawkins.

March 10 To John Caldwell Calhoun. LS and LS duplicate, DNA-RG 94 (M566-106). Recommends James M. Glassell for assistant adjutant general.

March 10 From Arthur Peronneau Hayne. LS, DLC (24); LS copy, DNA-RG 107 (M221-78). Reports shipment of supplies from the Creek Agency.

March 10 General order by Robert Butler announcing AJ's assumption of command of troops at Fort Scott and arrangements for march into Florida. LC, DNA-RG 98 (6-0073).

March 13 *From Hopony and Echofixeca.* 182

March [13] From James Alexander. ALS, DLC (24). Reports his movements.

March 14 From John Caldwell Calhoun (enclosures: Calhoun to William A. Trimble, March 4, 7, DLC-24). LS, DLC (24); LC, DNA-RG 107 (M6-10). Encloses copies of letters.

March 14 From John N. McIntosh. ALS, DLC (24). Reports on provisions and Indian movements in the vicinity of Fort Scott.

March 15 From Daniel Hughes. ALS, DLC (24). Transmits a copy of letter from William McIntosh, March 10, relating the Creek army's victory over a force of hostile Indians.

March 15 From John N. McIntosh. ALS, DLC (24). Reports the escape of three black prisoners from Fort Scott.

March 16 From John N. McIntosh. ALS, DLC (24). Reports arrival at Fort Scott of a detachment with supplies.

March 16 From Homer Virgil Milton. LS, DLC (24). Reports arrival with provisions at Fort Scott.

March 16 Receipt of John Easley for $7.25 for labor for AJ and John Hutchings. ADS, Mrs. H. A. Brewer (mAJs).

[March] 16 From William McIntosh. LS by proxy, DLC (24). Describes victory over hostile Indians and requests further orders.

March 17 From Thomas Randolph Broom. Copy with copy of AJ directive to

Edmund P. Gaines re Broom, DNA-RG 94 (M566-103). Explains delay in paying troops.

March 17 From John Caldwell Calhoun (enclosure: Calhoun to Thomas A. Smith, March 16). LS, DLC (24). Encloses letter re establishment of a permanent fort at the mouth of the Yellowstone River.

March 17 From Daniel Hughes et al. LS, DLC (24). Report movement of hostile Indians.

March 19 From Cussetau Micco (to AJ and William McIntosh). LS by proxy, DLC (24). Offers 400 warriors for AJ's army and asks for a guarantee that Cherokee property rights will be respected.

March 19 From Arthur Peronneau Hayne. LS, DLC (24); Copy, DNA-RG 107 (M221-78). Reports marching plans of the Tennessee volunteers, commends officers, and regrets that sickness will prevent him from accompanying the troops.

March 19 From John N. McIntosh. LS, DLC (24). Describes plans to forward provisions from Fort Scott to Fort Gadsden.

March 19 From William McIntosh (enclosure: McIntosh to AJ, March 16). LS by proxy, DLC (24). Asks advice concerning the route his troops should follow to join AJ, their provisions, and the treatment of prisoners.

March 19 From Little Prince (to AJ and William McIntosh). LS by proxy and LS duplicate by proxy, DLC (24). Appoints McIntosh to lead Creek warriors; pledges friendship to AJ, but hopes the war against the Seminoles will not result in further loss of Creek lands.

March 21 From William Rabun. LS, DLC (24); LC, G-Ar (6-0079); Copies, DNA-RG 75 (M271-2), DNA-RG 107 (M221-79), DNA-RG 233 (6-0081). *ASP, Military Affairs,* 1:774–75. Requests troops to protect against Indian hostilities near Telfair County, Georgia.

March 22 To William McIntosh. ALS draft endorsed on McIntosh to AJ, March 16 and 19, DLC (6-0085). Instructs him to rendezvous at the bluff on the Ochlockonee River.

March 22 From David Brydie Mitchell. ALS, DLC (24). *Georgia Historical Quarterly,* 28(1944):101–104. Denies David Brearley's charges of misconduct.

March 22 Robert Butler to John N. McIntosh. LC, DNA-RG 98 (mAJs). Arranges for the departure of William McIntosh's troops from Fort Scott; requires an explanation for the delay of supply boats.

March 24 Edmund Pendleton Gaines to Robert Butler. LS, DLC (24). Announces the arrests of David Brearley and George M. Brooke.

March 24 To Edmund Pendleton Gaines. LS, DNA-RG 94 (M566-105); LC, DNA-RG 98 (6-0087). Seeks approval to suspend the arrests of David Brearley and George M. Brooke.

March 24 From Sanders Donoho. ALS with ANS by AJ ordering Robert Butler to announce transfer, DLC (24). Assents to the transfer of Henry M. Simons.

March 24 From Edmund Pendleton Gaines (enclosure: David E. Twiggs et al. to Gaines, March 24, DLC-24). LS, DLC (24); AL draft, DNA-RG 94 (M566-103); LC, DNA-RG 98 (6-0088). States that he will not suspend the arrests of Brearley and Brooke, but will acquiesce should AJ do so.

March 24 From William McIntosh. LS by proxy, DLC (24). Promises to rendezvous with AJ on March 28.

March 24 From William Allen Trimble (enclosure: John Rogers to Trimble, March 24). ALS, DLC (24). Defends his conduct in supplying Fort Scott.

[March 24] From Edmund Pendleton Gaines. LC, DNA-RG 98 (5-1221); AL draft, DNA-RG 94 (M566-108). Requests assignment of William W. Lear as subaltern officer in 7th Infantry.

March 25 To John Caldwell Calhoun. LS, DNA-RG 107 (M221-78); Copies, DNA-RG 46 (6-0089), DNA-RG 84 (6-0109), DNA-RG 233 (6-0115, -0125, -0133); Extract, THi (6-0143). *ASP, Military Affairs,* 1:698–99. Describes campaign; discloses plans to capture St. Marks.

March 25 To Edmund Pendleton Gaines. LC, DNA-RG 98 (6-0145). Asks the terms by which a private sloop was chartered to supply Fort Gadsden.

March 25 To José Masot. Copies, DNA-RG 46 (6-0151), DNA-RG 84 (6-0154), DNA-RG 94 (6-0156, -0158), DNA-RG 233 (6-0161, -0165, -0168). Bassett, 2:355–56. Warns against interference with the transport of supplies through Florida to Fort Crawford.

March 25 To Isaac McKeever. Copy, DNA-RG 45 (M125-58). *SDoc* 100, 15th Cong., 2nd sess. (Serial 15), pp. 18–19. Requests naval support for his movement against St. Marks.

March 25 From Edmund Pendleton Gaines. AL draft, DNA-RG 94 (6-0147). States conditions by which he chartered the sloop *Phoebe Ann.*

March 25 From Edmund Pendleton Gaines. LC, DNA-RG 98 (6-0150); AL draft, DNA-RG 94 (M566-105). Requests the appointment of subaltern officers.

March 25 From John N. McIntosh. ALS and LS duplicate with AL postscript, DLC (24). Describes preparations for William McIntosh's march to join AJ and explains the delay of supply boats bound for Fort Gadsden.

March 25 From John N. McIntosh. ALS, DLC (24). Promises to investigate the delay of supply boats sent to Fort Gadsden.

March 25 Robert Butler to John N. McIntosh. LC, DNA-RG 98 (mAJs). Requests that he supply William McIntosh's troops for their march to join AJ.

March 26 To John Coffee. ALS, THi (6-0170). Discusses the effect of supply problems on the movements of his troops.

March 26 *To Rachel Jackson.* 183

March 26 To José Masot. Translations (Spanish), Archivo Histórico Nacional, Madrid (mAJs); Typed translation, SpSAG (6-0177). Promises to investigate Masot's February 16 complaint when time allows; states that he intends to enter Florida in pursuit of Indians and may occupy Fort St. Marks.

March 26 From John N. McIntosh. LS, DLC (24). Reports on provisions at Fort Scott.

March 26 Robert Butler to Daniel Parker. LS, DNA-RG 94 (M566-105); LC, DNA-RG 98 (mAJs). Announces AJ's appointment of subaltern officers.

March 26 Daniel Parker to Robert Butler. LS, DLC (24); LC, DNA-RG 94

	(M565-5). Discusses transfer of artillery officers between the Northern and Southern Divisions.	
March 26	Receipt for $4 from James H. Owen to Richard Massey on account of AJ and John Hutchings. DS, Mrs. H. A. Brewer, (mAJs).	
March 27	From John N. McIntosh. LS, DLC (24). Discusses provisions at Fort Scott and troops departing to join AJ.	
March 28	From George Gibson. ALS, DLC (24). Announces the arrival of supplies at Fort Gadsden.	
March 28	From George Gibson. ALS, DLC (24). Reports the departure of ships for St. Marks and the arrival of supplies at Fort Gadsden.	
March 29	From George Gibson. ALS, DLC (24). Reports on troop movements to and from Fort Gadsden.	
March 29	From Arthur Peronneau Hayne. ALS, DLC (24). Suggests that AJ organize the volunteers from East Tennessee into a separate company.	
March 31	From Thomas Passon. ALS, DLC (24). Seeks furlough for ill Tennessee volunteers at Hartford, Georgia; expects to lead the remainder to join AJ in two weeks.	
March	Account of AJ and John Hutchings with Branch Jones for blacksmithing, with Jones's receipt acknowledging payment by John Coffee, April 22, 1819. ADS, Mrs. Richard H. Gilliam (6-0062).	
April 1	From Arthur Peronneau Hayne (enclosure: Hayne to commanding officers at Charleston, Savannah, and Augusta, March 19). ALS, DLC (24). Seeks permission to go to Washington to settle his accounts; encloses an order to arrest Louis Magnan for the murder of William Chisum.	
April 3	From Edmund Pendleton Gaines (enclosure: Thomas Glascock to Gaines, April 3, DLC-24). LS, DLC (24); LC, DNA-RG 98 (6-0184); AL draft, DNA-RG 94 (6-0180). Describes his march across Florida and the discovery of scalps in a Seminole village.	
April 4	From Aaron Jordan Booge. ALS, DLC (24). Requests transfer from Fort Montgomery to AJ's army.	
April 4	From B. G. Cray. DS, DLC (24). Certifies that cattle seen near Mikasuki were taken from the Georgia frontier.	
April 4	From George Gibson. ALS, DLC (24). Requests instruction regarding provisions for AJ's army.	
April 6	*To Francisco Caso y Luengo.*	186
April 6	To Kentucky gentleman. Extract, *Augusta Chronicle & Georgia Gazette,* July 1 (mAJs). Describes discovery of scalps at Mikasuki town.	
April 6	From John N. McIntosh. LS, DLC (24). Reports the arrival of food and supplies at Fort Scott.	
April 7	*From Francisco Caso y Luengo.*	188
April 7	To Francisco Caso y Luengo. LS and Translation, SpSAG (6-0217, -0219); Copies, DNA-RG 46 (6-0221), DNA-RG 84 (6-0223), DNA-RG 94 (6-0225), DNA-RG 233 (6-0229, -0231, -0233). *ASP, Military Affairs,* 1:705. Refuses to delay the occupation of St. Marks.	
April 7	From Francisco Caso y Luengo. ALS and Translations, DNA-RG 94 (6-0287, -0291, -0293); ALS copy, SpSAG (6-0286); Translations, DLC (24), DNA-RG 46 (6-0296), DNA-RG 233 (6-0298, -0302,	

	-0306). Bassett, 2:357. Protests seizure of Fort St. Marks; requests transportation to Pensacola.
April 7	To Francisco Caso y Luengo. LS and Translation, SpSAG (6-0235, -0237); Copies, DNA-RG 46 (6-0238), DNA-RG 84 (6-0239), DNA-RG 94 (6-0240), DNA-RG 233 (6-0243, -0245, -0248). *ASP, Military Affairs,* 1:706. Justifies occupation of St. Marks.
April 8	*To John Caldwell Calhoun.* 189
April 8	To Rachel Jackson. ALS, DLC (24). Bassett, 2:357–58. Recounts the occupation of St. Marks and the capture of Josiah Francis and Alexander Arbuthnot.
April 8	To Daniel Todd Patterson. Copy, DNA-RG 45 (M125-58). Praises services of Isaac McKeever and requests continued naval cooperation.
April 8	From John N. McIntosh. ALS, DLC (24). Reports the arrival of Tennessee volunteers at Fort Scott and his order that they proceed to Fort Gadsden.
April 8	Robert Butler to William King. LC, DNA-RG 98 (mAJs). Orders the execution of Josiah Francis and Homathlemico.
April 8	Certification that Alexander Arbuthnot acknowledged authorship of a letter to David Brydie Mitchell, January 19. ANS, DNA-RG 94 (mAJs).
[cApril 8]	From John M. Davis. ADS, ICHi (6-0061). Reports on ammunition supplies of brigades on the Florida frontier.
April 9	To John Caldwell Calhoun. Copies, DNA-RG 84 (6-0331), DNA-RG 233 (6-0332, -0335). *ASP, Military Affairs,* 1:700. Announces the death in battle of the Seminole chief Kenhajee and the hanging of Josiah Francis and Homathlemico.
April 9	To George Gibson. ALS, DLC (6-0338); Extract, DNA-RG 46 (6-0341). *ASP, Military Affairs,* 1:753 (extract). Orders cartridges from Fort Gadsden and reports the surrender of sixty-five Seminoles.
April 9	To Unknown. Extract, *Nashville Clarion,* May 12 (mAJs, 6-0342). Recounts his campaign from Fort Gadsden to St. Marks.
April 9	From Francisco Caso y Luengo. ALS and Translation, DLC (24); ALS copy, SpSAG (6-0337). Protests the arrest of an army deserter.
April 9	From George Vashon. ALS, DLC (24). Encloses receipts (not found) of John Hull; reports on Alexander Arbuthnot's imprisonment.
April 10	*To Rachel Jackson.* 191
April 10	To Rachel Jackson. ALS, MH-H (6-0346). Expresses pleasure at the receipt of her letter of February 20 (not found).
April 10	From Daniel Bissell. ALS, DLC (24). Reports his arrival in New Orleans, where ill health has delayed his assumption of command.
April 11	From John Caldwell Calhoun (enclosure: Calhoun to Arthur P. Hayne, April 11, DLC-24). LS, DLC (24); LC, DNA-RG 107 (M6-10). Approves Hayne's request to come to Washington to settle his accounts.
April 11	From George R. Clayton. LS, DLC (24). Outlines the conditions by which the Georgia treasury will exchange drafts from the Bank of the United States to purchase supplies for the army.
April 12	From George Gibson. ALS, DLC (24). Reports the dispatch of supplies from Fort Gadsden.

April 13	From William Stephen Mitchell. ALS, DLC (24). Describes an attack by Creek troops and Tennessee volunteers on a band of hostile Indians.	
April 13	General order by Robert Butler promoting Indian officers. Copy endorsed by AJ, DLC (24); LC, DNA-RG 98 (mAJs).	
April 14	To William McIntosh. ALS, DLC (6-0349). Orders him to send cattle to the front of the line.	
April 15	*To United States Troops near Suwannee River.*	192
April 15	From José Masot. LS and Translations, DNA-RG 94 (6-0352, -0363, -0366, -0368, -0372); Translations, DLC (24), DNA-RG 46 (6-0356), DNA-RG 59 (M116-4), DNA-RG 84 (6-0361), DNA-RG 233 (6-0378, -0385, -0388, -0396). Bassett, 2:359–60. Discusses permission for transport of provisions through Florida to Fort Crawford.	
April 16	From William Stephen Mitchell. ALS, DLC (24). Reports a skirmish between friendly Creeks and the Seminoles.	
April 17	Commission appointing AJ and Isaac Shelby to negotiate a treaty with the Chickasaw Indians. Copies, DLC (24), DNA-RG 59 (6-0399).	
April 18	From Thomas Glascock. ALS, DLC (24). Suggests a route the Georgia militia should take home at the campaign's conclusion.	
April 18	Report of Middle Tennessee Supreme Court reversal of circuit court decision in *Thomas Crutcher, AJ, and Alfred Balch, executors of William Terrell Lewis* v. *Frederick Stump*. Copy, T (6-0401).	
April 20	*To John Caldwell Calhoun.*	193
April 20	To Rachel Jackson. ALS, DLC (24). Bassett, 2:360. Recounts his victory at Bowlegs' Town.	
April 20	To William Rabun. Extract, *Niles' Register,* May 23 (6-0459). Notifies him that the Georgia militia is ordered to Hartford for discharge.	
April 20	From Robert Brent. LC, DNA-RG 99 (6-0404); Copy, DNA-RG 46 (6-0402); Copy (dated April 30), DNA-RG 153 (mAJs). Gives instructions on payment of troops.	
April 20	From Edmund Pendleton Gaines (enclosure: William Bee, Jr., to Gaines, April 20, DLC-24). LS with ALS copy of reply by James M. Glassell approving the leave, DLC (24); AL draft, DNA-RG 94 (6-0449); LC, DNA-RG 98 (6-0451). Recommends that Bee be granted leave to settle his accounts.	
April 20	From Edmund Pendleton Gaines (enclosure: William King to Gaines, April 19, DLC-24). LS, DLC (24); AL draft, DNA-RG 94 (6-0452); LC, DNA-RG 98 (6-0457). Details his brief pursuit of the Seminoles beyond Bowlegs' Town.	
April 20	From Thomas Glascock et al. ALS, DLC (24). Offer congratulations on behalf of the Georgia militia.	
April 20	From Thomas Williamson. LS, DLC (24). Blames Creek troops for the Seminoles' escape during the assault on Bowlegs' Town.	
April 20	Caroline Butler Bell to Rachel Jackson. ALS, DLC (24). Consoles her on the absence of AJ and discusses Donelson family matters.	

April 20 Isaac Hill to William King. ALS with ANS approvals by Edmund P. Gaines and by AJ, DNA-RG 94 (M566-107). Resigns lieutenancy.

April 20 General order by Robert Butler making troop dispositions for the return march and conveying AJ's congratulations to the Georgia militia. LC, DNA-RG 98 (mAJs).

April 22 From John Caldwell Calhoun (enclosure: Act regulating army staff, April 14, DLC-24). LS with AN by AJ directing James Gadsden's response, DLC (24); LC, DNA-RG 107 (M6-10). Sends notification of promotions and reassignments of George Gibson, James Gadsden, William Cumming, and Milo Mason.

April 24 From William McIntosh. LS by proxy (William S. Mitchell), DLC (24). Requests compensation for two horses lost in action.

April 26 Robert Butler to John Benjamin Hogan (enclosure: Robert Brent to Hogan, March 6, DNA-RG 99). LC, DNA-RG 98 (mAJs). Orders him to join AJ at Fort Scott.

April 26 General order by Robert Butler establishing a military court to try Alexander Arbuthnot and Robert Christie Ambrister. LC, DNA-RG 98 (6-0464); Copies, DNA-RG 59 (M116-4), DNA-RG 46 (6-0460), DNA-RG 94 (6-0463), DNA-RG 153 (mAJs), DNA-RG 233 (6-0462). *ASP, Military Affairs,* 1:721.

[April] 26 To John Caldwell Calhoun. LS (dated March 26), MiU-C (6-0466); Copies, DNA-RG 46 (6-0470), DNA-RG 233 (6-0473, -0476, -0480); Copy (dated March 26), DNA-RG 84 (6-0471). Bassett, 2:363–64. Reports his return to St. Marks; claims evidence implicates the British for inciting the Indians; proposes to return to Nashville.

April 26–28 Record of the courts-martial of Alexander Arbuthnot and Robert C. Ambrister. DS with originals of documents in evidence and additional documents, DNA-RG 94 (mAJs); DS draft by James M. Glassell and Copy, DNA-RG 153 (mAJs); Copies, DNA-RG 46 (mAJs), DNA-RG 233 (mAJs); Extract (Arbuthnot trial only), DNA-RG 159 (M116-4); AD fragment partly in Glassell's hand, DLC (24). *ASP, Military Affairs,* 1:721–34.

April 27 To José Masot. Copies, DNA-RG 46 (6-0482), DNA-RG 84 (6-0486), DNA-RG 94 (6-0488, -0492), DNA-RG 233 (6-0496, -0499, -0506); Translations, SpSAG (6-0508), Archivo Histórico Nacional, Madrid (mAJs), Archivo General de la Nacion Mexico (mAJs). *ASP, Military Affairs,* 1:706–707. Accuses Spain of aiding the Seminoles.

April 27 From Enos Cutler. ALS, DLC (24). Reports on the supply situation at Fort Scott.

April 27 From William Lindsay. ALS, DLC (24). Reports disposition of cargo seized from a Spanish schooner at St. Marks.

[April 27] To James McMillan Glassell. ANS endorsed on Alexander Arbuthnot to David B. Mitchell, Jan 19, DNA-RG 94 (6-0330). Directs him to present Arbuthnot's letter to the military court.

April 28 From Mathew Arbuckle. ALS, DLC (24). Requests a court of inquiry to investigate his conduct as commander of Fort Scott.

April 28 From Robert Carr Lane. ALS, DLC (24). States that he has resigned and asks to be relieved from duty as army surgeon.

April 28 Robert Butler to James McMillan Glassell. ALS, DNA-RG 153 (mAJs). Reports that AJ is moving his encampment and discusses arrangements for communications from the court-martial.

April 28 Robert Butler to William Lindsay. LC, DNA-RG 98 (mAJs). Orders liberation of the crew of the captured Spanish schooner.

April 28 Robert Butler to Abraham L. Sands. LC, DNA-RG 98 (mAJs). Orders him to examine Spanish works at Pensacola.

April 28 General order by Robert Butler appointing John Stadler Allison to the court trying Alexander Arbuthnot and Robert Christie Ambrister. LC, DNA-RG 98 (6-0513); Copies, DLC (24), DNA-RG 94 (6-0510), DNA-RG 153 (mAJs), DNA-RG 233 (6-0512). *ASP, Military Affairs,* 1:731.

April 29 To Alexander Campbell Wilder Fanning. LS and Copy, NHpR (6-0528, -0529). Orders him to dispatch the captured Spanish schooner to Pensacola.

April 29 General order by Robert Butler approving the death sentence by hanging given by the military court to Alexander Arbuthnot, but changing the sentence given Robert Christie Ambrister to death by firing squad. DS, DNA-RG 94 (6-0514); LC, DNA-RG 98 (6-0517); Copies, DNA-RG 153 (6-0520), DNA-RG 233 (6-0524); Copy fragment, DLC (71). *ASP, Military Affairs,* 1:734.

April 30 From Thomas Glascock. ALS, DLC (24); Copies, DNA-RG 75 (M271-2), DNA-RG 107 (M221-78), DNA-RG 233 (6-0531). *ASP, Military Affairs,* 1:776. Reports the massacre of friendly Indians at Chehaw village by Obed Wright's Georgia militia.

May 2 From John Caldwell Calhoun (to AJ and Isaac Shelby; enclosure: Commission, April 17). LS and Copy, DLC (24); LC and Copy, DNA-RG 75 (M15-4, M271-2); Copy, DNA-RG 46 (6-0537). *ASP, Indian Affairs,* 2:173–74. Informs them of appointments to negotiate a cession of Chickasaw lands and gives instructions.

May 2 From William Hambly and Edmund Doyle. LS, DNA-RG 94 (6-0539); Copies, DLC (24), DNA-RG 46 (6-0543), DNA-RG 107 (M222-20), DNA-RG 233 (6-0548, -0552, -0555). *ASP, Foreign Relations,* 4:577–78. Testify that the Spanish commander at Fort St. Marks knowingly aided Indians who attacked American settlements.

May 3 From Daniel Bissell. ALS, DLC (24). Reports sending rations to Fort Crawford via Pensacola.

May 3 From Jacob R. Brooks and Peter Cone. DS, DNA-RG 94 (6-0558); Copies, DLC (24), DNA-RG 107 (M222-20), DNA-RG 233 (6-0560, -0561). *ASP, Foreign Relations,* 4:578. Testify that stolen cattle from Georgia were found with the property of the commander of Fort St. Marks.

May 3 From Andrew F. Fraser and Daniel F. Sullivan. DS, DNA-RG 94 (6-0563); Copies, DLC (24), DNA-RG 107 (M222-20), DNA-RG 233 (6-0565). *ASP, Foreign Relations,* 4:578. Certify that cattle stolen from Georgia were found in St. Marks.

May 3 From James Gadsden. ALS, DNA-RG 94 (6-0570); ALS copy, DLC (24); Copies, DNA-RG 46 (6-0566), DNA-RG 107 (M222-20), DNA-RG 233 (6-0573, -0576, -0578). *ASP, Foreign Relations,*

4:578. Testifies that the Spanish commander of Fort St. Marks regularly gave "aid and comfort" to the Seminoles.

May 3 From David Emanuel Twiggs. LS endorsed by William Hambly, DNA-RG 94 (6-0582); Copies, DLC (24), DNA-RG 46 (6-0580), DNA-RG 233 (6-0584), DNA-RG 107 (M222-20). *ASP, Foreign Relations,* 4:578. Testifies that the Spanish commander of Fort St. Marks acknowledged that Seminole property was stored within the fort.

May 3 Robert Butler to Daniel Parker. LS, DNA-RG 107 (M221-77); LC, DNA-RG 98 (mAJs). *ASP, Military Affairs,* 1:703–704. Reports AJ's movements, March 26–May 2.

May 4 To William Davenport. ALS, PHi (6-0585). Bassett, 2:364–65. Boasts of success of Florida campaign and announces his intention to occupy Pensacola.

May 4 To Rachel Jackson. Extract, *ABPC* (1934–35), p. 613 (6-0591). Expresses concern about her illness but announces intention to march to Pensacola before returning home.

May 4 From Edmund Pendleton Gaines. ALS, DNA-RG 94 (6-0587); LC, DNA-RG 98 (6-0590). Reports on troop strength.

May 4 From George Gibson et al. LS by George P. Peters, DNA-RG 94 (M566-108). Recommend Selah Kirby for post surgeon.

[May 4] To John Caldwell Calhoun (enclosure: George Gibson et al. to AJ, May 4). LS, DNA-RG 94 (M566-108). Recommends Selah Kirby as post surgeon.

May 5 *To John Caldwell Calhoun.* 197

May 5 To Edmund Pendleton Gaines. LS, DNA-RG 94 (6-0636); LC, DNA-RG 98 (6-0640). Places Gaines in command of the troops east of the Apalachicola River and leaves instructions for garrisoning Fort St. Marks and Fort Gadsden.

May 5 To John W. Hill. ALS, THi (6-0642). Orders him to purchase provisions for the return of the Tennessee volunteer troops.

May 5 From William McIntosh. Extract, *Niles' Register,* June 20 (6-0644). Requests an investigation of the massacre at Chehaw village.

May 5 From Daniel Todd Patterson (enclosure: Benjamin W. Crowninshield to Patterson, March 27). ALS, DLC (24). Promises continued naval cooperation.

May 5 From Hugh Young (enclosure: Sketch of Indian and Negro towns on the Suwannee River, DNA-RG 77, mAJs). ALS, Ernest Dibble (mAJs); Copy, DNA-RG 77 (6-0645). *Florida Historical Quarterly,* 55(1977):325. Submits a topographical report of the route between Fort Gadsden and the Suwannee River in Florida.

May 5 Robert Butler to Edmund Pendleton Gaines. ALS, DNA-RG 94 (M566-105); LC, DNA-RG 98 (mAJs). Orders that AJ's Indian guide John Blount and his clan be protected in settling on their former lands.

May 5 Edmund Pendleton Gaines to Robert Butler (enclosure: General order, May 5). ALS, DLC (24). Promises to attend to AJ's wishes re John Blount; encloses order re troop disposition.

May 6 To John Caldwell Calhoun. LS, ScU (6-0658). Promises to have depositions taken regarding the charges against David B. Mitchell.

May 6 Account with Benjamin Fort Smith for provisions and lodging. AD with ANS by AJ showing account paid July 1, DLC (70). Runs to May 29.

May 7 To John Caldwell Calhoun (enclosures: Thomas Glascock to AJ, April 30; AJ to John M. Davis, to William Rabun, and to Chehaw Indians, all May 7). AL in James Gadsden's hand, DNA-RG 107 (M221-78); Copies, DNA-RG 75 (M271-2), DNA-RG 233 (6-0661). Bassett, 2:368–69. Reports the massacre of friendly Indians at Chehaw village by Obed Wright's Georgia militia.

May 7 To Chehaw Indians. Copies, DNA-RG 107 (M221-78), DNA-RG 75 (M271-2), DNA-RG 233 (6-0665). *ASP, Military Affairs,* 1:776–77. Promises amends for the unprovoked attack on their village by Georgia militia; urges them to remain at peace.

May 7 To John M. Davis (enclosures: AJ to John C. Calhoun, May 5 and 7; AJ to Chehaw Indians, to Thomas Glascock, and to William Rabun, May 7). Copies, DLC (24), DNA-RG 75 (M271-2), DNA-RG 107 (M221-77), DNA-RG 233 (6-0669). *ASP, Military Affairs,* 1:775. Orders arrest of Obed Wright for the attack on the Chehaw village.

May 7 To Edmund Pendleton Gaines. LS, DNA-RG 94 (6-0673). Arranges for the disposition of the schooner *Chance* and its crew.

May 7 To Thomas Glascock. Extract, Washington *National Intelligencer,* June 8 (6-0675). Expresses outrage at attack on Chehaw village; reports ordering Obed Wright's arrest.

May 7 To W. W. Mallory and Richard Maher. Abstract, Carnegie Book Shop Catalog 182 (1953), Item 205 (6-0676). Gives instructions regarding a mission to Fort Scott.

May 7 *To William Rabun.* 202

May 7 From Edmund Pendleton Gaines (enclosure: McQueen McIntosh to William J. McIntosh, March 8). AL, DNA-RG 75 (M271-2). Transmits testimony regarding the involvement of Creek agent David B. Mitchell in smuggling slaves.

May 7 James Gadsden to John Caldwell Calhoun (enclosure: McQueen McIntosh to William J. McIntosh, March 8). ALS, DNA-RG 75 (M271-2). Forwards statement accusing David B. Mitchell of smuggling slaves.

May 7 Order to pay John Baptiste $26 for piloting ships into Florida harbors. Abstract, Charles Hamilton Catalog 127 (April 1980), Item 112 (6-0659).

May 8 From John M. Davis. ALS, DLC (25). Promises execution of AJ's order concerning the arrest of Obed Wright.

May 8 From John M. Davis. ANS endorsed on account of W. W. Mallory and Richard Maher for pay as express riders, TM (6-0684). Acknowledges receipt of packet delivered by Mallory and Maher.

May 8 General order by Robert Butler detailing enforcement of discipline among troops. LC, DNA-RG 98 (mAJs).

May 10 To Edmund Pendleton Gaines. LC, DNA-RG 98 (6-0686). Describes crossing to the west side of the Apalachicola River and the burial of Clinton Wright.

May 11 From Alexander Campbell Wilder Fanning. ALS, DLC (25). Reports

	on activities of Seminoles led by Peter McQueen and on desertions from Fort St. Marks.	
May 11	From Thomas Glascock. ALS with endorsement by AJ docketing an enclosure (not found), DLC (25). Discusses pay of Georgia militia and responses to the attack on the Chehaw village.	
May 11	From Daniel Parker. LC, DNA-RG 94 (M565-5). Requests that AJ report on the number, grade, and stations of Southern Division officers, pursuant to the House resolution of April 20.	
May 11	Account with William McKnight for tuition for Andrew Jackson, Jr., Andrew Jackson Hutchings, and Sergeant Day. AD, THi (6-0689).	
May 12	William Bee, Jr., to Robert Butler. ALS, DLC (25). Discusses discharge of Georgia troops and attack on Chehaw village.	
May 15	From [Peter Hagner]. LC, DNA-RG 217 (6-0691). Calculates that AJ's military account has a balance due of $3,582.84.	
May 15	Report of circuit court judgment for AJ against John Smith T as prosecution bail for Thaddeus Holt. Copy and extract, TNDa (6-0696, -0695).	
May 17	From Edmund Pendleton Gaines (enclosure: Francis W. Brady to Gaines, May 13, DLC-25). ALS, DLC (25); LS draft and Copy, DNA-RG 94 (6-0701, -0698); LC, DNA-RG 98 (6-0705). Discusses the burial of Clinton Wright and reports arrival of the schooner *Chance*.	
May 17	From Edmund Pendleton Gaines (enclosures: Daniel Parker to William King, Oct 31, 1817, DLC-23, 26). ALS, DLC (25); ALS draft, DNA-RG 94 (6-0709); LC, DNA-RG 98 (6-0708). Forwards letter which Gaines feels thwarts the waging of the Seminole War.	
May 18	*From José Masot.*	203
May 19	From William Wyatt Bibb (enclosures: Thomas Figures to Bibb, May 16, DLC-25). ALS, DNA-RG 94 (M566-103); Copies, DNA-RG 46 (6-0760, -0766), DNA-RG 59 (M116-4), DNA-RG 75 (M271-2), DNA-RG 233 (6-0772, -0776). *ASP, Military Affairs,* 1:745–46. Details Indian attacks in southern Alabama Territory and requests funds to pay the militia.	
May 19	From White Youngs. LS, DLC (25). Requests permission to participate in the Florida campaign.	
May 23	*From José Masot.*	205
May 23	*To José Masot.*	206
May 23	From Trueman Cross (enclosures: Cross to José Masot, May 17, 19; Masot to Cross, May 18). ALS, DLC (25). Announces his arrival at Pensacola with supplies for Fort Crawford and discusses negotiations to ascend the river.	
May 24	To José Masot (enclosure: AJ to Masot, May 23). Copies, DNA-RG 46 (6-0862), DNA-RG 94 (6-0865), DNA-RG 233 (6-0867, -0869, -0871); Translations, SpSAG (6-0873), Archivo Histórico Nacional, Madrid (mAJs), Archivo General de la Nacion Mexico (mAJs). *ASP, Military Affairs,* 1:712. Sends notification of his entrance into Pensacola and cautions against resistance.	
May 24	*To [Luis Piernas].*	210
May 24	From José Masot. LS and Translations, DNA-RG 94 (6-0874, -0893, -0896); Copies, SpSAG (6-0879), Archivo Histórico Na-	

cional, Madrid (mAJs), Archivo General de la Nacion Mexico (mAJs); Translations, DLC (25), DNA-RG 46 (6-0883), DNA-RG 59 (M116-4), DNA-RG 84 (6-0890), DNA-RG 233 (6-0902, -0911, -0920). Bassett, 2:372–73. Denies charges of Spanish aid to the Seminoles and protests AJ's occupation of Pensacola.

May 24 — Caroline Butler Bell to Rachel Jackson. ALS, DLC (25). Discusses family matters and her possible journey to Nashville.

May 25 — *To José Masot.* 210

May 27 — Account of Rachel Jackson with Saunders & Chandler. AD, DLC (26). Runs to October 12; with receipt for payment, January 15, 1819.

May 27 — Robert Butler to Thomas Wright or [Robert Beall]. LC, DNA-RG 98 (mAJs). *New York Evening Post,* July 1 (extract). Orders arms to Pensacola.

May 28 — From José Masot. LS, DLC (25). Encloses the terms of capitulation of Fort Barrancas.

May 28 — Proposals by José Masot for the surrender of Pensacola, with AJ's response. DS and English translation, DNA-RG 94 (mAJs); Copies and Spanish translations, Archivo Histórico Nacional, Madrid (mAJs), Archivo General de la Nacion Mexico (mAJs); English translations, DLC (25), DNA-RG 45 (M125-58), DNA-RG 59 (mAJs), DNA-RG 233 (mAJs). *ASP, Military Affairs,* 1:719–20.

[May 28] — [Robert Butler to Robert Beall]. Extract, *New York Evening Post,* July 1 (mAJs). Countermands May 27 order.

May 29 — From José Masot. LS, DLC (25). Reports dispute regarding implementation of Article 14 of agreement for surrender of Pensacola.

May 29 — From José Masot (enclosures: Rosters of Havana Regiment, Louisiana Regiment, black troops, corps of artillery, engineering corps, and civil department at Fort Barrancas, DLC-69). LS, DLC (25). Encloses reports of Spanish troops surrendered at Fort Barrancas.

May 29 — Robert Butler to Edmund Pendleton Gaines. LS and Copy, DNA-RG 94 (M566-105); LCs, DNA-RG 98 (mAJs). Announces occupation of Pensacola; orders inquiry into delay of supplies.

May 29 — General orders justifying the occupation of Pensacola, appointing officers, and describing procedures for governing the province. Copies, DNA-RG 59 (M116-4), DNA-RG 107 (M222-20), DNA-RG 45 (M125-58); Translation, SpSAG (6-0939). Bassett, 2:374–75.

May 29 — General order by Robert Butler praising the troops for bravery in their occupation of Pensacola and Fort Barrancas. Copies, DNA-RG 59 (M116-4), DNA-RG 107 (M222-20), DNA-RG 233 (mAJs); Extract, FHi (6-0443). *ASP, Military Affairs,* 1:720.

May 30 — To Edmund Pendleton Gaines. ALS, DNA-RG 94 (M566-105); LC, DNA-RG 98 (6-0944). Orders the purchase of clothing for three friendly Indians.

May 30 — *From John M. Davis.* 211

May 30 — From George West. ALS, DLC (25). Complains about supply problems encountered in returning a detachment of sick and wounded volunteers to Tennessee.

May 31 — Robert Butler to Zachariah McGirtt and Thomas H. Boyles. LC,

DNA-RG 98 (mAJs). Washington *National Intelligencer,* July 15. Authorizes them to raise troops to scout for Indians between the Perdido River and Mobile.

May — Account with James Glasgow Martin for merchandise purchased by Rachel Jackson. AD, DLC (25).

[May] — From John Innerarity. Abstract, Heartman's Book Auctions (1953), Item 77 (6-0536). Describes his authority.

June 1 — From William Rabun. LS, DLC (25); LC, G-Ar (6-0945); Copies, DNA-RG 75 (M271-2), DNA-RG 107 (M221-79), DNA-RG 233 (6-0946). Bassett, 2:375–76. Disputes AJ's power over Georgia militia Captain Obed Wright.

June 1 — Receipt for provisions supplied by Camillus Griffith to Tennessee volunteer troops from June 1 to June 14. DS copy, DLC (69).

June 1 — Memorandum of AJ's account with United States for pay of troops. DS, DNA-RG 217 (mAJs); Copy, DLC (70). Runs to August 5.

June 2 — To John Caldwell Calhoun. LS, DNA-RG 107 (M221-78); Copies, DNA-RG 46 (6-0951), DNA-RG 233 (6-0954, -0957, -0960). *ASP, Military Affairs,* 1:707–708. Introduces John Blount and William Hambly, whom AJ sends to Washington.

June 2 — To John Caldwell Calhoun (enclosures: AJ to José Masot, May 23, 24, 25; Masot to AJ, May 23, 24; Proposals for the surrender of Pensacola, May 28; General order justifying the occupation of Pensacola, May 29; Hugh Young's topographical sketch from the Apalachicola River to Pensacola, 6-0651; Depositions of Richard Brickham and John Bonner, [May 25], William Hambly, June 2, and James L. Bell and William Russell, n.d., DNA-RG 107, M222-20). Copies, DNA-RG 46 (6-0962), DNA-RG 84 (6-0975), DNA-RG 233 (6-0981, -0988, -0997). Bassett, 2:379–81. Describes and justifies his occupation of Pensacola.

June 2 — To Edmund Pendleton Gaines. ALS, DLC (6-1003); LC, DNA-RG 98 (6-1007). Describes the capture of Fort Barrancas and complains of persistent problems with supplies.

June 2 — *To Rachel Jackson.* 212

June 2 — *To James Monroe.* 213

June 2 — From George B. McKnight. ALS, DNA-RG 94 (M566-109). Resigns as surgeon's mate.

June 2 — From Susannah Stiggins. ALS with an ANS from AJ to Rachel Jackson, June 2, directing delivery, and ADS receipt by Samuel Edmunds, Oct 28, DLC (25). Requests delivery of the slave girl Lisa to David Tate.

June 2 — *From Christopher Vandeventer.* 216

June 2 — Robert Butler to Edmund Pendleton Gaines (enclosure: General order praising troops, May 29). LCs, DNA-RG 98 (mAJs). Announces AJ's imminent departure and instructs Gaines on duties.

June 3 — Robert Butler to Paul Hyacinte Perrault. Copy, DNA-RG 94 (M566-111); LC, DNA-RG 98 (mAJs). Requires immediate progress on the survey ordered November 2, 1817.

June 4 — To Robert Brent. LS, NhD (6-1022). Accounts for the expenditure of paymaster funds.

June 4	Robert Butler to [Milo Mason]. LC, DNA-RG 98 (mAJs). Orders him to furnish supplies to John Blount and other Indians travelling to Washington.
June 4	Receipt from James Craine Bronaugh for $25.25 for expenses incurred in travelling to St. Stephens. ADS, DLC (25).
June 4	Receipt from Morgan A. Heard for $690 for expenses incurred by the quartermaster department. ADS, DLC (69).
June 4	Receipt from John Maul for $5,000 for expenses incurred by the quartermaster department. ADS, DLC (69).
June 4	Abstract of money paid by AJ for expenses of the Seminole campaign. Copies, DLC (70), DNA-RG 217 (mAJs). Runs to July 3.
June 6	From Edmund Pendleton Gaines (enclosure: Duncan L. Clinch to Gaines, May 1, DLC-24). LS with endorsement stating that the letter was received Aug 18, 1821, DLC (25); ALS draft, DNA-RG 94 (6-1030); LC, DNA-RG 98 (6-1024). Discusses the court-martial of David Brearley and Seminole activities in Florida.
June 6	From Edmund Pendleton Gaines. LC, DNA-RG 98 (6-1036); AL draft, DNA-RG 94 (M566-103). Introduces Thomas Biddle, Jr.
June 8	Notice of delinquent taxes for 1816 owed by AJ and Samuel Donelson for 178 acres of land on Pond Lick Creek in Wilson County. Printed, Clarksville *Weekly Chronicle,* Aug 5 (mAJs).
June 8–21	Abstract of purchases made by AJ to supply the Tennessee volunteers' return march. Copies, DLC (69), DNA-RG 217 (mAJs).
June 8–25	Receipts from Aaron Short, Jesse Colman, John K. Irby, John Kirkhane, Andrew Moore, Thomas Greer, Benjamin Baldwin, David Campbell, John Elliott, William Seale, Daniel Taylor, William Cooper, Nathan Garrett, Isaac H. Green, John W. Hill, Thomas Carmichael Hindman, William Russell, William Williams, and James Walker for payments of Seminole campaign expenses. DSs, DNA-RG 217 (6-1037 to -1076); DS duplicates and Copies, DLC (69).
June 10	From John Maul. ALS, DLC (25). Sends mail packet from John M. Davis and adds that quartermaster funds have not arrived at Fort Montgomery.
June 11	From Eleazar Wheelock Ripley. ALS with AJ endorsement, DLC (25). Reports arrival at New Orleans and discusses plans for recruiting.
June 12	From Robert Brent. LC, DNA-RG 99 (6-1045); Copy, DNA-RG 94 (M566-111). Reports payment of Georgia militia and friendly Creeks who served in Florida.
June 12	Account with John C. Hicks for china for $100, with receipt by John W. Allen, August 18. AD, THi (6-1046).
June 12	Account with John C. Hicks and John W. Allen for china and silver plate for $200. Abstract, Bassett, 2:408 (6-1043).
June 12	Receipt from Robert Newton for reimbursement of $12 left with an ill soldier under his command. DS, DLC (69).
June 14	Receipts from William Hunter and Samuel B. McKnight for compensation for horses killed in action. DS and DS duplicate, DNA-RG 217 (6-1050); DLC (69).

June 15 From Francis Philip Fatio. ALS with AJ endorsement, DLC (25). Requests aid in the recovery of slaves stolen from his plantation near St. Augustine.

June 15 Account with Alpha Kingsley for cloth, paper, books, and sundry merchandise. DS, THi (6-1055). Runs to April 20, 1819.

June 16 From Gabriel William Perpall. ALS with AJ endorsement summarizing contents, DLC (25); Copy, NN (6-1057). Discusses ownership of the slave Polydore and complains that nearly 300 slaves have been taken by Seminoles from their Florida owners.

June 17 From Robert Brent (enclosures: Brent to John B. Hogan, June 15, 17, DLC-25). LS, DLC (25); LC, DNA-RG 99 (6-1060). Sends copies of correspondence discussing payment of Tennessee troops.

June 17 James McMillan Glassell to Robert Butler (enclosure: Edmund P. Gaines to John C. Calhoun, June 14). ALS with AJ endorsement on the enclosure directing letter to the secretary of war, DLC (25). Complains of regulations regarding officers' forage allowance.

June 17 Eleazar Wheelock Ripley to Robert Butler (enclosure: Proposed recruiting regulations, n.d., DLC-59). LS, DLC (25). Transmits a plan for Southern Division recruitment for AJ's consideration.

June 18 From Edmund Pendleton Gaines. ALS, DLC (25); LC, DNA-RG 98 (6-1061); AL draft, DNA-RG 94 (6-1063). Reports on movements of the Seminoles and the troops in Florida.

June 19 From Thomas F. Hunt (enclosure: Abstract of money received and expended in May, June 3, DLC-69). ALS, DLC (25). Discusses accounts of the quartermaster department in New Orleans.

June 20 From Joseph McMinn. ALS and Copy, DLC (25); Extract, DNA-RG 46 (6-1067). *ASP, Military Affairs,* 1:768 (extract). Congratulates AJ on the capture of St. Marks and Pensacola and relates the progress of Cherokee negotiations.

June 21 From Richard Whartenby. ALS, DLC (25). Recommends Trueman Cross as paymaster of the 1st Infantry.

June 22 From James Dorman. ALS, DNA-RG 94 (M566-104). Recommends promotion of Thomas Cook.

June 23 From Milo Mason (enclosure: John C. Calhoun to Mason, April 18, DLC-24). ALS with ANS by AJ to require delivery of $100,000 in quartermaster funds to pay expenses of Tennessee troops, DLC (25). Reports his appointment as interim quartermaster general of the Southern Division and requests a furlough.

June 23 Receipt from Reuben Humphreys for the transfer of corn, flour, and bacon to the 8th Infantry. DS, DNA-RG 217 (6-1077); DS duplicate, DLC (69).

June 25 From John Benjamin Hogan. LS, DLC (25); Copy, DNA-RG 46 (6-1079). Requests instructions about the pay of militia.

June 25 From Reuben Humphreys. ALS with ANS by AJ directing referral to war department, DNA-RG 94 (M566-104). Recommends promotion of Thomas Cook.

June 25 From Milo Mason. ALS, DLC (25). Notifies AJ of supplies and money furnished William Hambly for John Blount's journey to Washington.

June 25	From Hugh Young. ALS, DNA-RG 94 (M566-104). Recommends promotion of Thomas Cook.
June 25	Receipt from William Harris for provisions. DS, DNA-RG 217 (6-1078); DS duplicate, DLC (69).
June 26	General order by Robert Butler discharging the Tennessee volunteers. LC, DNA-RG 98 (6-1081); Copy, DLC (25).
June 26	Receipt from John Benjamin Hogan for $38,700 for pay of Tennessee volunteer troops. ADS, DLC (69)
June 27	To [John Caldwell Calhoun]. Abstract, DNA-RG 107 (M22-11). Desires more funds to pay the troops.
June 27	From Isaac Shelby (enclosures: John C. Calhoun to Shelby, May 13, DLC-25; Calhoun to AJ and Shelby, May 2; Commission appointing AJ and Shelby, April 17). ALS with ANS by AJ docketing receipt, DLC (25); ALS copy, WHi (6-1083). Asks AJ to make the necessary arrangements for Chickasaw negotiations.
June 27	Receipt from William Harris for $500 for Tennessee volunteer forage accounts. DS, DLC (69).
June 28	To John Caldwell Calhoun. Abstracts, DNA-RG 107 (M22-11), DLC (75). Reports drawing bills to pay Tennessee troops.
June 28	To John Benjamin Hogan. Copy, DNA-RG 46 (6-1087). Reports obtaining $70,000 from a Franklin, Tennessee, bank and orders immediate payment of Tennessee volunteers.
June 28	Bills of exchange in favor of Mathew D. Cooper for $1,000 for pay of troops. DS duplicate, T (6-1085); Copy, DLC (25).
June 29	James Gadsden to John Caldwell Calhoun. ALS, DNA-RG 107 (M221-77). Promises that AJ will reply to Calhoun's April 22 letter when health permits.
June 29	Receipt from Robert Butler for one horse to be sold, the funds going to the United States. DS, DNA-RG 217 (6-1088).
June 30	From Benjamin [Fort] Smith. Copy, DNA-RG 107 (M221-78). Reports that William S. Mitchell has purchased cattle intended for distribution among the friendly Creeks.
June 30	From James Walker. ALS, DLC (25). Reports that the Columbia branch of the Bank of the State of Tennessee will honor AJ's drafts totaling $30,000.
June 30	James Gadsden to John Caldwell Calhoun. ALS, DNA-RG 107 (M221-77). Discusses the responsibility of subordinate officers for Obed Wright's attack on the Chehaw village and complains of the interference of civil authorities in Wright's arrest.
June 30	Receipt from William Savin Fulton for $127.20 for services as AJ's private secretary. DS, DLC (69).
June 30	Account with Andrew Jackson Hutchings for expenses and assets relating to Hutchings's plantations. D, THi (6-1090). Runs to April 20, 1827.
June–July	Account with United States for expenses of Seminole campaign (enclosures: Abstract of purchases made, June 8–21; Abstract of money paid, June 4–July 3). Copy, DLC (70).
July 1	To John Benjamin Hogan. Copy, DNA-RG 46 (6-1095). Discusses pay of troops.

July 1	Receipt from John Benjamin Hogan for $30,000 to pay the Tennessee volunteers. ADS duplicates, DLC (70), DNA-RG 217 (mAJs).	
July 1	Account with United States for pay, clothing, forage, and subsistence. DS, DNA-RG 217 (6-1096). Runs to September 30.	
July 2	From John Quincy Adams. LC and AL draft, DNA-RG 59 (M40-15, 6-1097); Copy, DNA-RG 46 (6-1098). Relays President Monroe's decision that Obed Wright be arrested by civil authorities and tried by a special commission.	
July 2	*From George Mercer Brooke.*	217
July 2	From John Benjamin Hogan. Copy, DNA-RG 46 (6-1103). Defends procedures in paying the Tennessee volunteers.	
July 2	Receipt by John Benjamin Hogan for $105,400 from AJ to pay the Tennessee volunteer troops. ADS duplicates, DLC (70), DNA-RG 217 (mAJs).	
[July 2]	From William Stone. ALS (dated June 2) with ANS by AJ to require Stone to furnish the original returns, WHi (6-1020, mAJs). Requests that abstract for provisions issued at Fort Montgomery be signed.	
July 3	From Mathew Arbuckle. ALS duplicate, DNA-RG 94 (6-1105). Requests exoneration of his conduct as commander at Fort Scott.	
July 6	From John Benjamin Hogan (enclosures: Robert Brent to Hogan, June 15, 17, 18; William H. Crawford to Benjamin Cox, June 18). LS with AL postscript, DLC (25). Reports completion of payment of the Tennessee volunteer troops; requests transfer.	
July 7	*To Isaac Shelby.*	219
July 7	From John Benjamin Hogan. ALS, DLC (25). Discusses final arrangements for payment of Tennessee volunteer troops.	
July 7	Robert Butler to Eleazar Wheelock Ripley. LC, DNA-RG 98 (mAJs). Authorizes minor changes in recruiting service; requests report of officers and justification for Ripley's long absence at Washington.	
July 8	To John Caldwell Calhoun. LS, ScU (6-1113). Complains that funds designated to pay army expenses have not arrived.	
July 8	To John Caldwell Calhoun (enclosures Benjamin F. Smith to AJ, June 30; AJ to William McIntosh and to David B. Mitchell, July 8). DNA-RG 107 (M221-78). Requests orders regarding effort to distribute captured cattle among the friendly Creeks.	
July 8	*To William McIntosh.*	220
July 8	To David Brydie Mitchell. Copies, DNA-RG 107 (M221-78). Protests William S. Mitchell's purchase of captured cattle that AJ had ordered given to friendly Creeks.	
July 10	To William Harris (enclosure: Arthur P. Hayne to Harris, July 11, DLC-25). Copy, DNA-RG 233 (6-1120). Orders the settlement of quartermaster accounts for Tennessee volunteer troops.	
July 12	From Alexander Campbell Wilder Fanning. ALS, DLC (25). Reports the activities of the Seminoles around St. Marks and the supply problems at the fort.	
July 13	To John Caldwell Calhoun. Copy, DNA-RG 46 (6-1121). *ASP, Indian Affairs,* 2:178. Suggests payment of annuities to the Chicka-	

saws for previously ceded lands to facilitate negotiation of a new treaty.

July 13 To Chifubie (spurious). Copy, DNA-RG 279 (mAJs). Grants land east of Suwannee River on condition of peaceful relations with the United States and its citizens.

July 13 From John Caldwell Calhoun. LC, DNA-RG 107 (M6-10). Requests copies of documents relating to AJ's expedition in Florida; discusses quartermaster accounts.

July 13 From Alexander Campbell Wilder Fanning. ANS, DLC (25). Reports capture of two deserters.

July 14 *To Andrew Jackson Donelson.* 222

July 14 Toast at Nashville public dinner: The United States "should shew foreign nations, that under a *pretence of neutrality,* her rights are not to be outraged." Printed, *Nashville Whig,* July 18 (6-1125).

July 16 From Mathew Arbuckle. LS, DNA-RG 94 (6-1126). Defends himself against charges of misconduct while in command of Fort Scott.

July 17 From James Colbert. LS and Copy, DNA-RG 75 (M271-2); Copy, WHi (6-1138); Copy (dated 1816), DNA-RG 46 (5-0305). *ASP, Indian Affairs,* 2:102–103 (dated 1816). Reports Chickasaw opposition to further land cessions.

July 17 From Edmund Pendleton Gaines (enclosures: Gaines to Fort Scott commanding officer, June 28; David E. Twiggs to Gaines, June 25; Gaines to Arbuckle, June 26; General order by James M. Glassell, June 25, all DLC-25). ALS, DLC (25); LC, DNA-RG 98 (6-1140); ALS draft, DNA-RG 94 (6-1144). Reports on recent troop reassignments, Indian negotiations, and rumors of Spanish influence on Seminoles near St. Augustine.

July 19 *From James Monroe.* 224

July 21 From John Caldwell Calhoun (enclosure: List of AJ letters received by the war department, DLC-75). LS, DLC (25); LC, DNA-RG 107 (M6-10). Requests duplicates of any unreceived correspondence sent to the war department since February.

July 21 Cary Nicholas to James Gadsden. ALS with ANS by AJ recommending Thomas L. Lloyd, DNA-RG 94 (M566-109). Requests that Gadsden introduce Lloyd to AJ and support his effort to gain an army appointment.

July 22 From Edward George Washington Butler. ALS, DLC (25). Relates news from West Point.

July 22 From John M. Davis. Abstract, DLC (6-1148). Discusses offers of peace from certain Indian chiefs to William McIntosh.

July 22 From Isaac Shelby. ALS draft, WHi (6-1151). Agrees that more money will be needed to secure Chickasaw lands in Kentucky and Tennessee.

July 22 Promissory notes for $116.66⅔, signed by AJ and John Coffee and payable to the trustees of the Cypress Land Company, February 1, 1821, and February 1, 1822, with ANS by James Jackson regarding renewal of the notes, December 30, 1821. DS, THi (6-1149).

July 24 *To James Colbert.* 228

July 24 From Crabb & Rousseau. ALS, Mrs. H. A. Brewer (mAJs). Present for payment an account for medical treatment of slaves, October 1817 to July 1818.

July 27 From John Caldwell Calhoun. LS, DLC (25); LC, DNA-RG 107 (M6-10); Extract, DNA-RG 92 (6-1159). Corrects misunderstanding regarding quartermaster accounts.

July 27 From Daniel Parker. LS, DLC (25); LC, DNA-RG 94 (M565-5). Reports the resignation of Judge Advocate Rider Henry Winder and asks that AJ recommend a replacement.

July 27 From Daniel Ross. ALS with AJ endorsement, DNA-RG 107 (M221-78). Solicits help to secure more land from the Cherokee cession for his family.

July 27 Receipt from Joel Lamberth to Richard Massey for $5.50 on account of AJ and Hutchings. DS, Mrs. H. A. Brewer (mAJs).

July 28 From John Caldwell Calhoun. LS with AJ endorsement directing that General Gaines execute the order, DLC (25); Copy certified by Robert Butler, DNA-RG 94 (M566-105); LCs, DNA-RG 107, DNA-RG 98 (M6-10, 6-1160). Orders AJ to seize the cattle purchased by William S. Mitchell and either distribute them to the Creeks or sell them.

July 28 From [Peter Hagner]. LC, DNA-RG 217 (6-1162). Reports issuance of $40,000 for the quartermaster department.

July 28 From Thomas Sidney Jesup. LS with AJ endorsement, DLC (25); LC, DNA-RG 92 (6-1163). Reports funds available for the quartermaster department in the Southern Division.

July 28 From Henry Sherburne. ALS with AJ endorsement, DLC (25). Discusses prospects of Chickasaw negotiations and reports on Chickasaw annuity payments.

July 28 Receipt from [?] Woods to Richard Massey for $11.75 for flour and crocks for the farm of AJ and Hutchings. DS, Mrs. H. A. Brewer (mAJs).

July 29 George Strother Gaines to Robert Butler. ALS, DLC (25). Requests that a detachment of troops be sent to the Choctaw factory.

July 30 From John Caldwell Calhoun (enclosures: Calhoun to Henry Sherburne and to Isaac Shelby, both July 30, DLC-25). LS with ANS by AJ directing a reply and discussing his plans for the Chickasaw negotiations, DLC (25); LC, DNA-RG 75 (M15-4); Copy, DNA-RG 46 (6-1165). *ASP, Indian Affairs,* 2:178. Explains delay in paying the Chickasaw annuity.

July 30 From Thomas Sidney Jesup (enclosure: Amount and distribution of Southern Division funds, DLC-25). LS with AJ endorsement, DLC (25); LC, DNA-RG 92 (6-1166). Sends updated accounting of funds allotted to the Southern Division.

July 31 To John Caldwell Calhoun (enclosure: James Colbert to AJ, July 17). LS, DNA-RG 75 (M271-2). *Calhoun Papers,* 2:446–47. Complains that the quartermaster department still lacks funds and that the forage allowance for Southern Division officers is inadequate.

July 31 To Isaac Shelby (enclosure: James Colbert to AJ, July 17). LS, KyLoF (6-1167). Reports his failure to meet with James Colbert; promises to notify Shelby of time and place for Chickasaw negotiations.

July 31	James Gadsden to John Caldwell Calhoun. ALS, DNA-RG 107 (M221-78). Promises that he will carry to Washington documents regarding the trials of Arbuthnot and Ambrister.	
Aug 1	To William Rabun. LS, G-Ar (6-1175). Washington *National Intelligencer,* Nov 23. Refutes Rabun's charges of military despotism.	
Aug 1	From James Gadsden. LC, DNA-RG 77 (6-1168). *Florida Historical Quarterly,* 15(1937):242–48. Reports on the condition of forts in Florida; stresses the importance of Florida to the defense of the country.	
Aug 1	From Robert Carter Nicholas (d. 1836). ALS with ANS by AJ directing a denial, DLC (25). Requests a year's furlough to attend to private matters.	
Aug 3	To Mathew Carey. Extract, Edward Eberstadt & Sons Catalog 130 (1952), Item 316 (6-1179). Thanks Carey for a gift of books.	
Aug 3	To Andrew Jackson Donelson. ALS, DLC (6-1180; mAJs). Urges him to write home more.	
Aug 3	Robert Butler to Milo Mason. LC, DNA-RG 98 (mAJs). Orders Mason to report to Nashville with funds to pay the expenses of Tennessee troops in the Florida campaign.	
Aug 4	To James Colbert. Abstract, DLC (25). Announces that ill health prevents his meeting Colbert on the Tennessee River and requests that Colbert come to Nashville; argues that the Chickasaws should relinquish their lands in Tennessee and Kentucky.	
Aug 5	*To Richard Keith Call.*	230
Aug 5	From Nathaniel Frye (enclosures: Bill of exchange in favor of Mathew D. Cooper, June 28; Statement of Bowie & Kurtz re bill of exchange, Aug 5, both DLC-25). LS, DLC (25); LC, DNA-RG 99 (6-1184). Inquires about discrepancies in paymaster accounts.	
Aug 5	Receipt from Cary Nicholas for $7,000 for the Brigade of Tennessee Volunteer Mounted Gunmen. ADS duplicates, DLC (70), DNA-RG 107 (mAJs).	
Aug 6	From James Gadsden (enclosure: John C. Calhoun to AJ, July 21). ALS, DLC (25). Forwards letter and speculates on government action in regard to Florida.	
Aug 7	To Edmund Pendleton Gaines. ALS, DNA-RG 94 (M566-105); Copy, NN (6-1186); LC, DNA-RG 98 (6-1190); Extracts, DNA-RG 46 (6-1194), DNA-RG 107 (M221-81), DNA-RG 233 (6-1197). Bassett, 2:384–85 (extract). Gives orders for the capture of St. Augustine if evidence substantiates Spanish incitement of the Indians.	
Aug 7	To Joseph Saul. Extract, Charles Hamilton Catalog 27 (May 1968), Item 124 (6-1200). Complains of ill health.	
Aug 7	From James Gadsden. ALS, DLC (25). Reports that he has written Calhoun, is copying documents relating to the Florida campaign, and will depart for Washington on August 12.	
Aug 8	From James Colbert. ALS, DNA-RG 75 (M271-2). Appoints a date and place for Chickasaw treaty talks.	
Aug 8	From Edmund Pendleton Gaines. LC, DNA-RG 98 (6-1201); ALS draft, DNA-RG 94 (6-1205). Reports on fortifications at Pensacola.	

Aug 9 To John Caldwell Calhoun (enclosures: Robert Butler to Daniel Parker, May 3; Proceedings of the Alexander Arbuthnot court-martial; AJ to Francisco Caso y Luengo, April 6, 7; Caso y Luengo to AJ, April 7; AJ to José Masot, March 25, April 27; Masot to AJ, May 23). LS, DNA-RG 107 (M221-78). Transmits copies of documents; recommends George Gibson and James C. Bronaugh for quartermaster general and surgeon general, respectively.

Aug 9 From William Lindsay (enclosures: General orders of April 28 and July 23). ALS, DLC (25). Reports intention to take leave, September 5; protests transfers of officers from his battalion.

Aug 10 *To John Caldwell Calhoun.* 231

Aug 10 To James Monroe. ALS, NN (6-1213). Bassett, 2:385–87. Argues that Spanish incitement of Seminole hostilities justifies the retention of Pensacola and St. Marks and an attack against St. Augustine.

Aug 10 From Matthew Lyon. ALS with AJ endorsement to reply at leisure, DLC (25). Bassett, 1:259 (extract). Asks help in settling Jacob Purkill's claim for a slave impressed to work on New Orleans defenses in 1814.

Aug 10 From David Brydie Mitchell. Copy, DNA-RG 107 (M221-78). Explains the disposition of cattle captured from the Seminoles.

Aug 10 James Gadsden to John Caldwell Calhoun (enclosures: AJ to Edmund P. Gaines, Aug 7; David E. Twiggs to Gaines, June 25, DLC-25; Gabriel W. Perpall to AJ, June 16). ALS, NN (mAJs). Encloses letters.

Aug 11 *To Isaac Shelby.* 234

Aug 11 From John Caldwell Calhoun. LC, DNA-RG 107 (M6-10). *Calhoun Papers,* 3:23–24. Requests report on the construction of the military road from the Tennessee River to Mobile and New Orleans; orders the expenditure of funds for a road from Columbia to Madisonville.

Aug 12 From Return Jonathan Meigs (1740–1823). ALS, DLC (25). Requests permission to use militia to remove intruders from Cherokee lands.

Aug 13 From Enos Cutler. LC, DNA-RG 94 (6-1226). Refers Robert C. Nicholas's request for a furlough.

Aug 13 From John Ford. ALS with AJ endorsement, DNA-RG 107 (M221-78). Offers assistance to troops building the road from New Orleans to Mobile, if the road crosses his property.

Aug 13 Frances Duncan Hayne to Rachel Jackson. ALS, DLC (25). Thanks Rachel for her hospitality.

Aug 14 To James Dorman. ALS, PHi (6-1229). Gives orders concerning military road construction.

Aug 14 From John Caldwell Calhoun (enclosure: Calhoun to Edmund P. Gaines, Aug 14, DLC-25). LS and Copy, DLC (25); LC, DNA-RG 107 (M6-10); Copy, DNA-RG 233 (6-1227). *ASP, Military Affairs,* 1:734–35. Sends copy of order directing the return of St. Marks and Pensacola to the Spanish and the retention of Fort Gadsden.

Aug 15 From Eleazar Wheelock Ripley. ALS, DLC (25). Reports on officers under his command; suggests a detachment to explore the Red River.

Aug [17] To Richard Keith Call. ALS fragment, DLC (6-1233); Extract, FHi (6-1235). *The Collector* (Jan 1906), p. 28 (extract). Asks him to gather evidence justifying the Florida campaign.

Aug 18 To John Caldwell Calhoun. Copy, DNA-RG 46 (6-1237). *ASP, Indian Affairs,* 2:179. Discusses preparations for the Chickasaw negotiations.

Aug 18 To Peter Hagner. LS, DNA-RG 217 (6-1243). Acknowledges receipt of a treasury draft to be applied to the quartermaster accounts.

Aug 18 To Thomas Sidney Jesup. Extract, Robert F. Batchelder Catalog 44 [1983?], Item 243 (6-1245). Acknowledges the receipt of funds from the quartermaster general.

Aug 18 To Henry Sherburne. Abstract, Charles Hamilton Catalog 120 (June 7, 1979), Item 143 (6-1246). Orders him to pay the Chickasaw annuity at the treaty negotiations in October.

Aug 18 From John Caldwell Calhoun. LS, PHC (6-1240); LC, DNA-RG 75 (M15-4). *Calhoun Papers,* 3:39–40. Reports arrangements to fund AJ's quartermaster corps; discusses forage allowance and the Chickasaw annuity.

Aug 18 From Edward Livingston. ALS, DLC (71). Praises AJ's recent campaign in Florida; discusses the significance of ceremonies honoring Richard Montgomery.

Aug 19 *To James Monroe.* 236

Aug 19 From Daniel Bissell (enclosure: Departmental orders by Eleazar W. Ripley, June 10). ALS, DLC (25). Recommends that Trueman Cross be ordered to Washington.

Aug 19 Robert Butler to Edmund Pendleton Gaines (enclosure: John C. Calhoun to AJ, July 28). LS with ANS postscript, DNA-RG 94 (M566-105); LCs, DNA-RG 98 (mAJs). Orders Gaines to seize illegally purchased livestock, distribute the cattle among the Creeks, and sell the horses for quartermaster funds.

[cAug 19] Memoranda re orders to invade Florida. AD in James Gadsden's hand, DLC (26).

Aug 21 To James Monroe. LS, NN (6-1255). Introduces James Walker and supports his plan to establish mail stages between Nashville and Madisonville, Louisiana.

Aug 22 To John Caldwell Calhoun. LS, DLC (mAJs). Supports John Coffee's claim for the forage allowance granted cavalrymen during the War of 1812.

Aug 22 From John Caldwell Calhoun (enclosure: Calhoun to Thomas A. Smith, March 16). LS with AJ endorsement approving the order, DLC (25); LC, DNA-RG 107 (M6-10). *American Historical Association Annual Report, 1899,* 2:138. Discusses Missouri River posts; proposes to transfer Mississippi River posts above Rock River to the Northern Division.

[Aug 22] Order to reimburse Daniel Rawlings for a horse purchased by Charles Kavanaugh, June 11, 1815, with Rawlings's receipt. Abstract, John Heflin Catalog (January 1981), Item 849 (6-1258).

Aug 24	To Thomas Cooper. LS, MiDbEI (6-1259); Photocopy of LS, DLC (71). Bassett, 6:464–66. Defends his campaign in Florida.
Aug 24	Account of AJ, Rachel Jackson, and James Jackson with R. P. Garrett for dry goods. DS, DLC (25). Runs to October 29.
Aug 25	To Daniel Parker. ALS, DNA-RG 94 (M566-107). Recommends Stockley D. Hays as judge advocate.
Aug 25	To Isaac Shelby. ALS, WHi (6-1263). Bassett, 2:391–92 (extract). Discusses arrangements for the Chickasaw negotiations.
Aug 25	From James Thompson (enclosures: [Thompson] to Robert H. Dyer and to Thomas Williamson, Aug 25, DNA-RG 217, mAJs). LS with AJ endorsement, DLC (25); LC, DNA-RG 217 (6-1268). Requests additional evidence for charges levelled against Turk & Henderson, army contractors.
Aug 25	From Decius Wadsworth. LC, DNA-RG 156 (6-1269). Cancels AJ's requisition of ordnance for St. Marks.
[cAug 25]	From Isaac Shelby. AL draft, WHi (6-1266). Discusses arrangements for the Chickasaw negotiations and agrees that a strong stand will be necessary to secure a treaty.
Aug 26	Robert Butler to William Eastin. LC, DNA-RG 98 (mAJs). Discusses contract to supply Chickasaw treaty commissioners.
Aug 26	Receipt from Abraham Day to William Eastin for bacon purchased for AJ and Hutchings. ADS with AJ endorsement regarding settlement of the debt, Mrs. H. A. Brewer (mAJs).
Aug 27	From Thomas Sidney Jesup. LS, DLC (25); LC, DNA-RG 92 (6-1270). Reports transmittal of $10,000 to Eleazar W. Ripley for quartermaster accounts.
Aug 27	From Joseph McMinn (enclosures: John C. Calhoun to McMinn, July 29). ALS, DLC (25). Discusses relations with the Cherokees.
Aug 27	Robert Butler to Return Jonathan Meigs (1740–1823). LS, DNA-RG 75 (M208-7); LC, DNA-RG 98 (mAJs). Authorizes a call for militia to remove intruders from Cherokee lands.
Aug 28	From John Caldwell Calhoun. LS, DLC (25); LC, DNA-RG 107 (M6-10). *Calhoun Papers,* 3:74–75. Solicits opinion on the proposal to change army regulations governing rations.
Aug 28	From Paul Hyacinte Perrault. ALS, DLC (25). Regrets that the topographical survey of the southern frontier has been delayed by his illness.
Aug 28	From Joseph Saul. ALS with AN by AJ directing acknowledgment of the deposit to the secretary of war, DLC (25). Reports the deposit of $30,000 in the New Orleans branch of the Bank of the United States.
Aug 28	From Christopher Vandeventer. LC, DNA-RG 107 (M6-10); Copy, DNA-RG 192 (6-1271). Solicits amendments to the proposed system of depots for army provisions.
Aug 30	From William Eastin. ALS with AJ endorsement, DLC (25). Discusses a problem in the army's accounts with the Bank of Tennessee at Franklin; reports agreement to supply provisions during Chickasaw negotiations.
Aug 30	Contract between William Eastin and Robert Butler for provisioning the Chickasaw negotiations. Copy, DLC (25).

Aug 31 — To Edward Livingston. ALS, NjP (mAJs; 6-1272). Bassett, 6:466–68. Regrets Calhoun's order to Gaines for the return of St. Marks and Pensacola to the Spanish.

[Aug] 31 — Trueman Cross to Robert Butler (enclosures: Cross to Daniel Bissell and Bissell to Cross, Aug 19). ALS (dated July 31), DLC (25). Requests orders to Washington or a furlough.

[Aug] — To John Caldwell Calhoun. Abstract, DNA-RG 107 (M22-11). Sends copies of letters from José Masot.

Sept 1 — To Robert Butler. ALS, DLC (25). Instructs him to write letters concerning troop movements and preparations for the Chickasaw negotiations.

Sept 1 — From William Rabun. LS, DLC (25); LC, G-Ar (6-1275). Bassett, 2:392–93. Accuses AJ of failing to protect Georgia settlers while seeking glory in Florida and of exceeding his orders in the case of Obed Wright.

Sept 1 — From Hugh Young. ALS, DLC (25). *TPUS,* 18:407–408. Reports his failure to meet William W. Bibb and the opposition of Chickasaws to any land cession.

Sept 1 — Robert Butler to Edmund Pendleton Gaines (enclosure: John C. Calhoun to Gaines, Aug 14, DLC-25). LS with ANS, DNA-RG 94 (M566-105); LCs, DNA-RG 98 (mAJs). Relays orders regarding the evacuation of Florida.

Sept 1 — Robert Butler to Henry Sherburne. LC, DNA-RG 98 (mAJs). Acknowledges letters (not found) from Sherburne to AJ; discusses distribution of rations and annuities at the Chickasaw negotiations.

Sept 2 — To Mathew Arbuckle. Copy, DNA-RG 94 (6-1276). States that he finds little to criticize in Arbuckle's conduct while commander of Fort Scott and will submit the case to the secretary of war.

Sept 2 — To John Caldwell Calhoun (enclosure: Mathew Arbuckle to AJ, July 3, 16; AJ to Arbuckle, Sept 2). ALS, DNA-RG 94 (6-1279). Sends for Calhoun's decision documents relating to Arbuckle's conduct.

Sept 2 — From John Caldwell Calhoun. LS, DLC (25); Extract, DNA-RG 107 (M6-10). *Calhoun Papers,* 3:91–92. Urges the submission of all accounts against the contractor Benjamin G. Orr.

Sept 2 — From James Eakin. LC, DNA-RG 217 (6-1281). Discusses AJ's military accounts.

Sept 3 — From William C. Beard. ALS, DLC (25). Claims innocence of the charges of insubordination.

Sept 3 — From [Peter Hagner]. LC, DNA-RG 217. Acknowledges Robert Butler's receipt for $10,000 credited to AJ's account.

Sept 3 — Robert Butler to John Caldwell Calhoun (enclosure: Butler to Richard I. Easter, Sept 3). LS, DNA-RG 107 (M221-80); LC, DNA-RG 98 (mAJs). Reports on repair of road between Columbia, Tennessee, and Madisonville, Louisiana.

Sept 5 — From Thomas Henry. ALS, DLC (25). Sends documents regarding disposition of the personal property of John Henry, deceased.

Sept 5 — From Decius Wadsworth. ALS, DLC (25); LC, DNA-RG 156 (6-1284). Promises to supply forts at Mobile and New Orleans with new artillery.

Sept 6 Robert Butler to William Lindsay. LC, DNA-RG 98 (mAJs). Informs him that the protested personnel transfers were legal; refuses leave of absence.

Sept 7 To Andrew Jackson Donelson. ALS, DLC (6-1285). Congratulates him on his progress at West Point.

Sept 8 From John Caldwell Calhoun (enclosure: Calhoun to Edmund P. Gaines, Aug 14, DLC-25). LS and Extracts, DLC (25, 71); LC, DNA-RG 107 (M6-10); Extract, DNA-RG 233 (6-1286). *Calhoun Papers,* 3:109–11. Acknowledges receipt of documents on the Florida campaign; justifies administration policy with regard to Florida.

Sept 8 From Edmund Pendleton Gaines (enclosure: Gaines to John C. Calhoun, Sept 8, DLC-25). LS, DLC (25); LC, DNA-RG 98 (6-1288); ALS draft, DNA-RG 94 (6-1291). Details actions to stop Indian attacks in southern Alabama Territory.

Sept 9 From John M. Davis. ALS, DLC (25). Suspects that the Milledgeville postmaster, Walter Jones, stole the missing dispatches from AJ to John C. Calhoun.

Sept 10 From John Caldwell Calhoun. LS, DLC (25); LC, DNA-RG 107 (M6-10). *Calhoun Papers,* 3:116. Sends a copy of the new regulations governing forage allowances.

Sept 10 From James Dorman (enclosure: Estimate of provisions required commencing September 1, DLC-70). LS, DLC (25). Reports failure of the army contractor to deliver provisions to Camp Parker, Alabama Territory.

Sept 10 Robert Butler to John Caldwell Calhoun. LS, DNA-RG 107 (M221-77); LC, DNA-RG 98 (mAJs). Conveys AJ's approval of Calhoun's orders to Thomas A. Smith; discusses quartermaster accounts.

Sept 10 Robert Butler to Henry Sherburne. LC, DNA-RG 98 (mAJs). Authorizes him to draw bills to pay the Chickasaw annuity in cash if the Indians object to payment in goods.

Sept 11 To John Caldwell Calhoun (enclosures: Daniel Ross to AJ, July 27; John Ford to AJ, Aug 13). ALS, DNA-RG 107 (M221-78). Discusses quartermaster accounts; reports that the Chickasaws demand their annuity in cash.

Sept 11 From John Caldwell Calhoun (to Commissioners for holding Indian treaties). Copies, DLC (25), DNA-RG 46 (mAJs), DNA-RG 233 (mAJs); LC, DNA-RG 75 (M15-4). *ASP, Indian Affairs,* 2:431. Outlines procedures for issuance of rations during treaty negotiations.

Sept 12 From James Dorman (enclosure: Dorman to AJ, Sept 10). ALS, DLC (25). Reports continued refusal of the contractor to supply Camp Parker, Alabama Territory.

Sept 12 From Thomas Sidney Jesup. ALS, DLC (25); Extract, DNA-RG 92 (6-1297). Reports sending funds to supply Fort Hawkins and transmits revised regulations governing forage and transportation.

Sept 15 *From George Mercer Brooke.* 239

Sept 15 From [James Gadsden]. AL fragment, DLC (75). Discusses investment in Alabama lands.

Sept 15 Robert Butler to Trueman Cross. LC, DNA-RG 98 (mAJs). Relays

AJ's denial of Cross's request for orders to proceed to Washington.

Sept 16 From Edmund Pendleton Gaines (enclosures: Mathew Arbuckle to Gaines, Aug 31; Little Prince et al. to Gaines, Sept 6; Gaines to Little Prince et al., Sept 16, all DLC-25; Description by Granville Leftwich of Negroes delivered to Fort Gadsden, n.d., DLC-59). ALS, DLC (25); LC, DNA-RG 98 (6-1301); Copy, DNA-RG 94 (6-1303). Reports on the location and activities of hostile Indians in Florida.

Sept 16 From Arthur Peronneau Hayne. ALS, DLC (25). Discusses his financial situation; claims that most approve AJ's actions in Florida.

Sept 16 From Thomas Sidney Jesup. ALS, DLC (25); LC, DNA-RG 92 (6-1307). Reports disbursement of $1,000 to Hugh McCall for quartermaster accounts in Savannah.

Sept 16 Robert Butler to Richard Ivy Easter. LC, DNA-RG 98 (mAJs). Orders $25,000 sent to Reuben Humphreys for the supply of James Dorman's detachment.

Sept 17 To Robert Butler. ALS, ICarbS (6-1308). Sends account (not found) of horses lost in the Florida campaign.

Sept 17 Account with Robert Smiley for tailoring, with Smiley's receipt for payment in full, December 15. DS, THi (6-1310).

Sept 18 Robert Butler to William C. Beard. LC, DNA-RG 98 (mAJs). States that Beard's case will be decided by court-martial at an early date.

Sept 18 Robert Butler to Thomas Henry (enclosure: Butler to Daniel Hughes, Sept. 18). DNA-RG 98 (mAJs). Encloses order for the delivery of John Henry's property.

Sept 19 Affidavit certifying that William Pillow was wounded at the battle of Talladega. ANS, DNA-RG 15 (6-1312).

[cSept 19] Memorandum for report on commissary department. AD draft, DLC (59).

Sept 20 To John Caldwell Calhoun (enclosures: Robert Butler to Calhoun, Sept 19, DNA-RG 107, M221-77; Report on commissary department, Sept 19). LS, DNA-RG 107 (M221-81). *Calhoun Papers,* 3:145–46. Supports a change in the system of army contractors.

Sept 20 To Andrew Jackson Donelson. ALS, DLC (6-1314). Predicts that the Chickasaw treaty will conclude his "official career."

Sept 20 Division order by Robert Butler requiring quartermasters to report on supplies purchased because of contractor failure. DS, DLC (25); LC, DNA-RG 98 (mAJs).

Sept 21 To John Caldwell Calhoun. LS, ScU (6-1316). Accounts for purchases of provisions under his command.

Sept 21 To Joseph Saul. LC, DLC (63). Directs him to pay to Thomas F. Hunt the $30,000 deposited to AJ's credit at the Bank of the United States at New Orleans.

Sept 21 Receipt from James H. Owen for $7.25 for weaving cloth for AJ and Hutchings. ADS, Mrs. H. A. Brewer (mAJs).

Sept 21 Account of Richard Massey with AJ and Hutchings for expenses as overseer. AD, Mrs. H. A. Brewer (mAJs).

Sept 24 From John Caldwell Calhoun (enclosures: Calhoun to Edmund P. Gaines, Sept 1, 23, both DLC-25). ALS, DLC (25); LC, DNA-RG

	107 (M6-10). *Calhoun Papers,* 3:158. Transmits copies of orders regarding military activities in Florida.	
Sept 24	From Edmund Pendleton Gaines (enclosures: Gaines to John C. Calhoun and to William King, both Sept 20, DLC-25). ALS, DLC (25); LC, DNA-RG 98 (6-1319); AL draft, DNA-RG 94 (6-1321). Reports murder of six men by Seminoles and proposes to attack the Seminoles in eastern Florida upon the arrival of reinforcements.	
Sept 24	From Arthur Peronneau Hayne. Extract, Thomas Hart Benton, *Thirty Years' View . . .* (2 vols.; New York, 1856), 1:173 (mAJs). Criticizes James Monroe's Florida policy.	
Sept 24	From Daniel Parker. LS, DLC (25); LC, DNA-RG 94 (M565-6). States that the war department agrees with AJ's assessment of the conduct of Mathew Arbuckle and declines further investigation.	
Sept 24	Receipt from Charles Plant for $7.70 for beef for AJ and Hutchings. DS by proxy, Mrs. H. A. Brewer (mAJs).	
Sept 25	Receipt from Crabb & Rousseau for medical services, with account, August 3, of corn, fodder, hogs, and cotton seed offered in payment. DS with AJ endorsement regarding the form of payment, Mrs. H. A. Brewer (mAJs).	
Sept 27	From John Beaty (enclosures: Protests, July 2 and Aug 3, for nonpayment of bills of exchange). ALS, DLC (25). Requests assistance to secure payment for goods furnished to the army.	
Sept 28	*From James Gadsden.*	241
Sept 29	From John Caldwell Calhoun. LS, DLC (25); LC, DNA-RG 107 (M6-10). Desires prompt settlement of quartermaster accounts; reports arrangements to pay Chickasaw annuity in cash; gives tentative approval to John Ford's proposal.	
Sept 29	From Robert Jetton. ALS, DLC (25). Reports regarding settlement of account for the expenses of his detachment.	
Sept 29	Confidential journal of the negotiations with the Chickasaws. DS partly in Robert Butler's hand, signed by Butler, AJ, and Isaac Shelby, and Copy, DLC (62, 25); DS copy, DNA-RG 75 (T494-1). Williams, *Beginnings of West Tennessee,* pp. 283–300. Runs to October 20.	
Oct 1	From William Wyatt Bibb. ALS, DLC (25). Bassett, 2:393–94 (extract). Gives evidence that the Spanish in Pensacola encouraged Indian attacks in Alabama Territory.	
Oct 1	Account with United States for pay, forage, clothing, and subsistence. ADS, DNA-RG 217 (6-1335). Runs to December 31, with AJ's receipt, January 5, 1819.	
Oct 2	From [Peter Hagner]. LC, DNA-RG 217 (6-1336). Adjusts AJ's accounts with the United States.	
Oct 2	Receipt to Henry Sherburne for $37,550 to pay the annuity to the Chickasaw Nation. Copy, DLC (25).	
Oct 5	To George Washington Campbell. ALS, MoSM (6-1343); Copy, DLC (mAJs). Bassett, 2:395–98. Describes and justifies his Florida campaign.	
Oct 9	To William Berkeley Lewis (from Isaac Shelby and AJ). Copies, DLC (62), DNA-RG 75 (T494-1). Williams, *Beginnings of West Tennessee,* p. 286. Request report on the extent of North Carolina	

grants claimed by the Chickasaw nation within Kentucky and Tennessee.

Oct 10 From William Berkeley Lewis (to Isaac Shelby and AJ). Copies, DLC (62), DNA-RG 75 (T494-1). Williams, *Beginnings of West Tennessee,* pp. 287–88. Reports on land grants within the Chickasaw nation.

Oct 10 From Thomas Adams Smith. LS, DNA-RG 94 (M566-112); LC, MoHi (6-1352). Resigns from the army.

Oct 10 From Thomas Adams Smith. LS, DLC (25); LC, MoHi (6-1351). Discusses arrangements to settle his accounts.

Oct 12 To Chickasaw Indians (from Isaac Shelby and AJ). DS, WHi (6-1353); Copies, DLC (62), DNA-RG 75 (T494-1). Williams, *Beginnings of West Tennessee,* pp. 290–94. Urge exchange of Chickasaw claims in Tennessee and Kentucky for lands west of the Mississippi River.

Oct 12 From Marcus Brutus Winchester (to Isaac Shelby and AJ; enclosure: Inventory of goods shipped to commissioners, Oct 9). Copies, DLC (62), DNA-RG 75 (T494-1). Williams, *Beginnings of West Tennessee,* pp. 288–90. Reports the arrival and condition of goods shipped for use by the Chickasaw commissioners.

Oct 12 *From Hugh Young.* 243

Oct 14 From Edmund Pendleton Gaines (enclosure: Charles Bullock to Daniel E. Burch, Oct 7, DLC-25). ALS, DLC (25); LC, DNA-RG 98 (6-1357); ALS draft, DNA-RG 94 (6-1359). Sends additional information of reported murders by Indians.

[cOct 14] Claims of George Harpole and Drury Bettis for horses lost during the 1813 Creek campaign, including AJ's affidavits testifying that Thomas Bradley served as a captain in the Creek war. ADS, DNA-RG 46 (6-1325, -1331).

Oct 15 From William King. Copies, DNA-RG 107 (M221-81), DNA-RG 233 (6-1361). *ASP, Military Affairs,* 1:751–52. Reports a clash between volunteer troops and the Seminoles.

Oct 15 Talbot Chambers to Robert Butler (enclosure: Statement of James B. Thompson, Oct 14, DLC-70). ALS with ANS by AJ approving, DLC (25). Requests that AJ order Joseph Selden to 9th Military Department headquarters in St. Louis for investigation.

Oct 17 Memorandum of AJ and William Berkeley Lewis regarding the distribution of $20,000 to be paid for land reserved to George and Levi Colbert by the September 20, 1816, Chickasaw treaty. Copies, DLC (62), DNA-RG 75 (T494-1). Williams, *Beginnings of West Tennessee,* p. 296.

Oct 18 Receipt from N. Mitchell, agent for Samuel Scott & Co., for $93.15¼, payment for the estate of John Hutchings. DS, A-Ar (6-1363).

Oct 19 To Charles D. McLean and George Tunstall. Printed, *Nashville Whig,* Oct 24 (6-1376). Announces the signing and the terms of the Chickasaw treaty.

Oct 19 *Rachel Jackson to Andrew Jackson Donelson.* 244

Oct 19 Treaty ceding Chickasaw lands in Tennessee and Kentucky for $300,000. DS signed by AJ, Isaac Shelby, and Chickasaw chiefs,

DNA-RG 11 (M668-5); Copy, DNA-RG 59 (6-1365). *ASP, Indian Affairs,* 2:164–65.

Oct 20 To Thomas Kirkman. ALS, DLC (25). *American Historical Magazine,* 4(1899):99–100. Arranges the payment of goods to Levi and George Colbert for their cooperation in the Chickasaw negotiations.

Oct 20 To John McKee. ALS, A-Ar (6-1377). Announces conclusion of Chickasaw treaty; introduces David Smith, who wishes to establish a store within the Choctaw Nation.

Oct 20 From Levi Colbert. LS by proxy, DLC (25). Requests unspecified favor in connection with the Chickasaw treaty.

Oct 20 From James Monroe. Copies, NN (6-1378), DLC (25), NcU (mAJs); Abstract in Monroe's hand, NN (6-1380). Parton, 2:524–25. States his satisfaction with the motives of AJ's conduct relative to Florida; suggests that AJ justify his actions for the record in a letter to the secretary of war.

Oct 22 From Edmund Pendleton Gaines (enclosure: Alexander C. W. Fanning to Gaines, Oct 2, DLC-25). LS, DLC (25); LC, DNA-RG 98 (6-1382); ALS draft, DNA-RG 94 (6-1383). Relays rumors of an imminent surrender of Seminoles at Suwannee.

Oct 22 From Eleazar Wheelock Ripley. ALS, DLC (25). Reports the approach of Spanish troops at the Louisiana border and the precautionary mobilization of U.S. forces.

Oct 23 To John Caldwell Calhoun (enclosures: Depositions of Sebastian Caro, Sept 7; Joseph Esteeven Caro, Sept 10; Carlos Baron, Sept 13; Joaquin Barelas, George Skeate, Carlos Lavalle, and William Cooper, Sept 18; Santiago Dauphin, Joseph Bonifay, and Pedro Senac, Sept 19). LS, DNA-RG 107 (M222-20). Encloses depositions asserting Spanish complicity in Seminole attacks across the border.

Oct 23 To John Caldwell Calhoun (from Isaac Shelby and AJ). LS, DNA-RG 75 (T494-1). Report concluding Chickasaw treaty.

Oct 25 Deed to William White Crawford of 320 acres on the north fork of the Deer River in the Western District of Tennessee for $1. Copy, TBHay (6-1385)

Oct 26 Account with Alexander Porter for cloth and sundries. DS, DLC (28). Runs to February 9, 1820.

Oct 30 To John Caldwell Calhoun (from AJ and Isaac Shelby; enclosures: James Colbert to AJ, July 17, Aug 8; AJ to Colbert, July 24). LS, DNA-RG 75 (M271-2); Copy with AJ endorsement, OCX (mAJs); Copies, DLC (25), THi (6-1388), T (6-1392). Bassett, 2:399–401. Announce conclusion of the Chickasaw treaty and justify the payment promised to the Colberts to facilitate agreement.

Oct 30 To John Caldwell Calhoun (from Isaac Shelby and AJ). LS, DNA-RG 75 (M271-2). Report drawing bills for $2,303.15¼ for expenses while negotiating the Chickasaw treaty.

Oct 30 *To James Monroe.* 245

Oct 30 From [Daniel Parker] (to AJ and Jacob Jennings Brown). LC, DNA-RG 94 (M565-6). Demands regimental reports on clothing and equipage expenses.

Oct 31	From Eleazar Wheelock Ripley. Copy, DNA-RG 107 (M221-81). Reports on response to Spanish movements in Texas; complains of weakness of his force.
Oct 31	From Levi Whiting (enclosures: Daniel Parker to Edmund P. Gaines, Oct 5, and to Loring Austin, Oct 6, DLC-25; Eleazar W. Ripley to John C. Calhoun; Whiting to Willis Foulk, both Oct 31, DLC-26). ALS, DLC (26); LC, DNA-RG 98 (6-1399). Encloses documents relative to an 8th Infantry detachment.
Nov 1	From Eleazar Wheelock Ripley. ALS, DLC (26). Complains of the expense of supplying Pensacola and Fort Gadsden.
Nov 1	Robert Butler to Thomas Adams Smith. ALS, James S. Corbitt (mAJs). Reports forwarding to Washington Smith's resignation.
Nov 2	From James Dorman (enclosure: Return of troops at Camp Pike for October, DLC-70). ALS, DLC (26). Requests a surgeon attached to his command.
Nov 2	Account with Henry Terrass for baked goods. DS, DLC (27). Runs to June 8, 1819.
Nov 5	Ralph Eleazar Whitesides Earl to Rachel Jackson. ALS, THi (6-1400). Sends an account and some medicine from Nashville.
Nov 7	From Edmund Pendleton Gaines. ALS, DLC (26); AL draft, DNA-RG 94 (6-1403); Extract, DNA-RG 98 (6-1402). Reports his arrival in East Florida and recent movements of Indians there.
Nov 9	John A. Heard, William Edward Butler (agent for AJ), and Thomas Carr to Georgia General Assembly. DS, DNA-RG 233 (6-1405). *HRDoc* 31, 15th Cong., 2nd sess. (Serial 18), pp. 3–5. Request passage of resolution to Congress supporting land grant claims by John Donelson's (c1718–86) heirs and others.
Nov 10	Deed to Enoch Deason for 270 acres on the Duck River in Bedford County for $1. Copy, TSBe (6-1414).
Nov 12	Order from Daniel Parker that those sentenced to hard labor be put to work on fortifications in Louisiana. DS, DLC (70); LC, DNA-RG 98 (mAJs).
Nov 13	From John Caldwell Calhoun (enclosure: Nathaniel Frye to Calhoun, Nov 10, DLC-26). LS, DLC (26); LC, DNA-RG 75 (M15-4). *TPUS,* 18:466. Appoints John McKee to pay the Choctaw warriors in the U.S. service; approves of the Chickasaw treaty.
Nov 14	From Edmund Pendleton Gaines. ALS, DLC (26); LC, DNA-RG 98 (6-1416); AL draft, DNA-RG 94 (6-1420). Reports peace overtures of the Seminoles and his favorable response.
Nov 15	*To James Monroe.* 246
Nov 15	To Eleazar Wheelock Ripley. Copy, DNA-RG 107 (M221-81). Discounts threat of Spanish invasion from Texas; urges that "every disposable soldier" be detailed to completion of the military road.
Nov 15	From Robert McGregor Walmsley. ALS, DLC (26). Requests leave of absence.
Nov 16	From Harry Toulmin (enclosure: Deposition of William Pierce, Oct 4, DLC-25). ALS, DLC (26). *TPUS,* 18:468–69. Sends deposition testifying to Spanish aid of the Seminoles; reports that Pensacola is now quiet.
Nov 16	James Gadsden to John Henry Eaton (enclosure: Benjamin W.

Crowninshield to Daniel T. Patterson, March 27, DLC-24). Copy, DLC (26). Sends evidence that the navy was directed to cooperate with AJ's Florida campaign.

Nov 16 — Share of stock in the Marathon Town Company (Alabama Territory) purchased for $10. DS with endorsement by AJ transferring stock to John Coffee, April 26, 1826, A-Ar (6-1432).

Nov 18 — From Joseph Coppinger (enclosure: "A citizen" [Coppinger] to editor of *New-York Columbian,* Aug). ALS, DLC (26). Solicits support for his plan to help new immigrants find work.

Nov 20 — *From John Henry Eaton.* 248

Nov 20 — From Edmund Pendleton Gaines (enclosures: Interrogatories to and answers by David Brearley, DLC-24, 26). ALS, DLC (26); LC, DNA-RG 98 (6-1435); ALS draft, DNA-RG 94 (6-1436). Sends Brearley's testimony regarding David B. Mitchell's conduct at the Creek Agency.

Nov 20 — Account with Thomas Ramsey & Co. for curtain calico, with receipt for payment in full, October 4, 1819. DS, DLC (27).

Nov 21 — Richard Keith Call to George Strother Gaines. LC, DLC (63). States that as Gaines has requested troops at the Choctaw factory for "menial Service" and not for protection of property, AJ refuses the request.

Nov 22 — From William Triplett. ALS with AJ endorsement that a letter has been written to James Monroe, DLC (26). Solicits support for his application as Choctaw factor.

Nov 23 — From Andrew Jackson Donelson. ALS, DLC (26). Discusses his studies at West Point and the abuse of some cadets.

Nov 24 — To Andrew Jackson Donelson. ALS, DLC (6-1438). Assesses the value of a military education; reiterates his opposition to "parsimony."

Nov 24 — From Edmund Pendleton Gaines (enclosure: Gaines to John C. Calhoun, Nov 24). Cover with AJ endorsement questioning the constitutionality and effectiveness of the proposed plan, DLC (26). Encloses letter discussing punishment for desertion.

Nov 24 — *To Isaac Shelby.* 250

Nov 25 — To John Caldwell Calhoun (enclosures: Eli B. Clemson to Thomas A. Smith, Feb 22; Smith to Clemson, Feb 24; Smith to Callender Irvine and to Daniel Parker, March 5; Parker to Smith, June 26; Smith to Robert Butler, July 31; Calhoun to Irvine, July 31; Irvine to John Whistler and to Willoughby Morgan, Aug 12; Talbot Chambers to Butler, n.d. [Sept 12], Sept 19, all DNA-RG 107, M222-20). LS, DNA-RG 107 (M222-20); Copy, DLC (63). Submits documents on Clemson's arrest for Calhoun's opinion; recommends that Bellefontaine, Missouri Territory, remain a depot for supplies.

Nov 25 — From William H. Mann. ALS with AJ endorsement directing a recommendation, DNA-RG 94 (M566-109). Solicits patronage in securing army commission.

[cNov 25] — Memorandum re the case of Eli B. Clemson. AN, DLC (60).

Nov 26 — From Donelson Caffery. ALS, DLC (26). Discusses his recent wedding, crops, and the death of Severn Donelson.

Nov 26 From Daniel Parker (enclosures: Eleazar W. Ripley to John C. Calhoun, Oct 31; Parker to Ripley, to Edmund P. Gaines, and to Mobile commander, Nov 26, all DLC-26). LS, DLC (26); LC, DNA-RG 94 (M565-6). Sends copies of orders regarding transfer of an 8th Infantry detachment to New Orleans.

Nov 27 To Eleazar Wheelock Ripley. Copy, DNA-RG 107 (M221-81); Extract, DNA-RG 94 (M566-123). Reiterates the insignificance of Spanish troop movements in Texas; suggests that the 8th Infantry detachment work on the military road.

Nov 27 Richard Ivy Easter to Edmund Pendleton Gaines and to Eleazar Wheelock Ripley. ALS to Gaines, DNA-RG 94 (M566-108); LC to Gaines, DNA-RG 98 (mAJs); LCs to Ripley, DLC (63), DNA-RG 98 (mAJs); Copy to Ripley, DNA-RG 94 (M566-123). Orders investigation of deficient regimental reporting regarding clothing and camp equipage.

Nov 28 *To John Caldwell Calhoun.* 251

Nov 28 From Edmund Pendleton Gaines (enclosure: Gaines to John C. Calhoun, Nov 24, DLC-26). ALS, DLC (26); LC, DNA-RG 98 (7-0006); AL draft, DNA-RG 94 (7-0007). Encloses a revised draft of his letter discussing the best means to discourage desertion.

Nov 29 To James Monroe. ALS, NN (7-0009). Recommends Anthony Butler for territorial governor of Arkansas.

Nov 29 To Isaac Shelby. ALS, NHi (7-0012). Passes on John C. Calhoun's congratulations for the Chickasaw treaty.

Nov 29 *From Andrew Jackson Donelson.* 253

Nov 30 To John Caldwell Calhoun. Copy, DLC (63). *Calhoun Papers,* 3:318–19. Acknowledges receipt of Calhoun's letter of November 13.

Nov 30 From Edmund Pendleton Gaines (enclosures: Gaines to Mathew Arbuckle, Oct 24, DLC-25; Joel Spencer to Arbuckle, Nov 9; Arbuckle to Gaines, Nov 15; Arbuckle to Creek chiefs, Nov 13, all DLC-26). LS, DLC (26); LS copy, DNA-RG 94 (7-0014); LC, DNA-RG 98 (7-0013); Copy, DNA-RG 107 (M221-81). Reports seizure and distribution of part of the cattle detained at the Creek Agency.

Nov 30 From Eleazar Wheelock Ripley (enclosure: 8th Department orders, Nov 20). ALS, DLC (26). Discusses arrangements for completing the military road between New Orleans and Mobile.

Dec 1 From Kirkman & Jackson. Typed copy, Mrs. Uhland O. Redd (7-0017). Send account of funds advanced to Andrew J. Donelson.

Dec [1] From James Gadsden (enclosure: Memorandum by Wilkins Tannehill with endorsement by Gadsden, DLC-75). ALS, DLC (26). Asks AJ to oversee collection by the Nashville Bank of funds owed Gadsden.

Dec 3 From Daniel Parker. LS with AJ endorsement requiring Robert Butler to issue an order, DLC (26); LC and Copy, DNA-RG 94 (M565-6, M566-102). Demands delinquent quarterly reports from Southern Division surgeons.

Dec 5 From [Daniel Parker]. LC, DNA-RG 94 (M565-6). Arranges for the enlistment of troops to ascend the Missouri River.

Dec 6	From Samuel Houston. ALS with AJ endorsement, Tx (7-0019). Recounts his conflict with Cherokee leader John Walker and Senator John Williams.
Dec 7	To James Monroe. ALS, NN (7-0037); Copy, NcU (mAJs); Extract, DLC (26). Parton, 2:526–27. Approves of Monroe's message to Congress; warns of Indian hostilities if Pensacola is restored to Spain; supports Chickasaw agent Henry Sherburne's wish for a transfer.
Dec 7	To Cary Nicholas (enclosure: Certificate of Uriah Blue, Nov 22, 1816, mAJs). ALS, DNA-RG 94 (7-0041). Orders payment of two Indians for services rendered the United States.
Dec 7	From Daniel Parker. LS, DLC (26); LC, DNA-RG 94 (M565-6); Copy, DNA-RG 107 (M222-20). *Calhoun Papers,* 3:362. Notifies commanding officers of a change in the means of supplying the army.
Dec 8	From Richard Ivy Easter. ALS, DLC (26). Forwards AJ's mail to the Hermitage from Nashville.
Dec 8	*From Isaac Shelby.* 255
Dec 8	Richard Ivy Easter to Edmund Pendleton Gaines. ALS, DNA-RG 94 (M566-108); LCs, DLC (63), DNA-RG 98 (mAJs). Approves the Seminole policy reported in Gaines's November 14 letter.
Dec 8	Receipt to John Coffee for the payment of $1,258.56 for the estate of John Hutchings. DS, THi (7-0044).
Dec 10	To John Caldwell Calhoun (enclosure: William H. Mann to AJ, Nov 25). ALS, DNA-RG 94 (M566-109). Recommends Mann for army appointment.
Dec 11	To David Campbell (1753–1832). ALS, THer (7-0046). Offers to recommend Campbell's son John (1777–1859) for any civil office; expresses satisfaction with the Chickasaw treaty.
Dec 12	From George Poindexter. ALS, DLC (26). Heiskell, 3:143–45. Recounts his support of AJ against the efforts of congressional enemies to criticize the Florida campaign.
Dec 12	From Henry Sherburne. ALS, DLC (26). Discusses investigation of a robbery committed by several Indians.
Dec 12	Deed to James Winchester for one-eighth interest in 5,000 acres at Chickasaw Bluffs on the Mississippi River. Copies, TMSh (7-0048), THi (7-0050, -0054); Abstract, TNDa (7-0058).
Dec 13	From Pathkiller (enclosure: Joseph McMinn to Dick Justice, Dec 4). LS by proxy, DLC (26). Discusses a recent Cherokee council with McMinn; complains of failure to comply with terms of the treaty of July 8, 1817.
Dec 14	From John Henry Eaton. ALS, DLC (26). Heiskell, 3:145–46. Advises AJ not to come to Washington to defend his Florida campaign; predicts the course of the recent Chickasaw treaty in Congress.
Dec 14	From Isaac Shelby. Printed, *Nashville Whig,* Nov 11, 1828 (mAJs; 7-0059). Congratulates AJ on the purchase of land in the Alabama Territory and the recent Nashville ball in his honor.
Dec 15	*From Robert Butler.* 256
Dec 15	From John Caldwell Calhoun. LC, LC draft (dated Nov 16), Draft

in an unknown hand, and Copy, DNA-RG 75 (M15-4, M271-2, 7-0060); Copy, DNA-RG 233 (7-0062). *ASP, Indian Affairs,* 2:704. Orders restriction of settlement on Oklahoma lands acquired by treaty with the Quapaw and Osage tribes.

Dec 16 Receipt from Thomas Hickman for $41.15 for court costs in *Edward Williams* v. *William Edwards*. DS, THi (7-0063).

Dec 18 From John Rhea. ALS, DLC (26). Bassett, 2:403–404. Discusses the congressional investigation of the Florida campaign; reports offering a resolution to confirm land granted to AJ at the Treaty of Fort Jackson.

Dec 19 From Eleazar Wheelock Ripley (enclosure: Ripley to John C. Calhoun, Dec 30, 1817, DLC-23). ALS, DLC (26). Discusses personnel matters pertaining to his department.

Dec 21 From Anthony Wayne Butler. ALS, DLC (26). Claims ill health prevents his entering Yale College.

Dec 21 *From James Monroe.* 257

Dec 21 *From John Overton.* 259

Dec 23 From Thomas Claiborne. ALS, DLC (26). Reports attempts in Congress to censure AJ for the Florida campaign.

Dec 26 From Edmund Pendleton Gaines. ALS, DLC (26); LC, DNA-RG 98 (7-0071); Copy, DNA-RG 107 (M221-86); ALS draft, DNA-RG 94 (7-0072). Doubts the willingness of hostile Seminoles to make peace with the United States.

Dec 28 *To Andrew Jackson Donelson.* 262

Dec 28 To Washington Jackson. ALS, DLC (26). *American Historical Magazine,* 4(1899):101. Promises to pay drafts for the benefit of George and Levi Colbert and Andrew J. Donelson; approves Donelson's conduct in the West Point controversy.

Dec 28 From Isaac Lewis Baker. ALS, DLC (26). Promises to introduce in the Louisiana legislature a resolution supportive of the acquisition of Florida; reports hard economic times in New Orleans.

Dec 28 From John Caldwell Calhoun. LS, DLC (26); LC (dated Dec 22) and AL draft (dated Dec 22) with additions in James Monroe's hand, DNA-RG 107 (M7-1, 7-0074). Justifies his refusal to arrest Col. Eli B. Clemson for desertion and his orders to move the army depot from Bellefontaine to St. Louis.

Dec 28 From John Caldwell Calhoun. LS, DLC (26); LC and LS draft, DNA-RG 107 (M7-1, 7-0081). *Calhoun Papers,* 3:431–32. Agrees that hostile Spanish movements in the southwest are unlikely; concurs on the efficacy of AJ's proposed operations in Florida without authorizing action; discusses the Yellowstone expedition.

Dec 28 Account with Marshall & Watkins for carpeting and a coat. ADS with AJ endorsement, DLC (26).

Dec 28 Order by Daniel Parker directing the release of Eli B. Clemson from arrest and the removal of supplies from Bellefontaine to St. Louis. DS, DLC (26).

Dec 29 From Edmund Pendleton Gaines (enclosures: Gaines to José Coppinger, Dec 28, DLC-26; Alexander C. W. Fanning to Gaines, Nov 27, DLC-28). LS with ANS by AJ regarding assignment of a quartermaster to Gaines's department, DLC (26); LS copy and AL draft,

	DNA-RG 94 (7-0093, -0096); LC, DNA-RG 98 (7-0089). Reports the capture of three American citizens near St. Augustine and rumors of the Spanish supplying the Indians with arms.
Dec 30	*To John Caldwell Calhoun.* 263
Dec 30	From John McNairy. ANS, DLC (26). Transmits an affidavit of Reuben Bullard stating that Bullard's son John was underage when he enlisted in the army and should be discharged.
Dec 30	From Henry Sherburne. ALS, DLC (26). Reports the conclusion of an investigation of a robbery committed by several Chickasaws.
Dec 31	To Isaac Shelby. ALS, NIC (7-0100). Reports on complications that have delayed ratification of the Chickasaw treaty.
Dec 31	From Joseph Delaplaine. ALS, DLC (26). Sends a prospectus of his "National Panzographia."
[Dec]	From Richard Ivy Easter. ANS, DLC (26). Sends a book and mail to the Hermitage from Nashville.
[Dec]	From James Pitchlynn. LS, DNA-RG 107 (M221-81). Bassett, 2:406–407 (extract). Suggests terms by which the Choctaws might exchange their lands east of the Mississippi River for lands west.
[Dec]	To James Pitchlynn. ALS, DNA-RG 107 (M221-98). Gives opinion regarding terms the government would offer to exchange Choctaw lands for lands west of the Mississippi.
1818	Account of Jackson & Hutchings with James Jackson & Co., with an explanatory note by John Coffee. DS, Mrs. H. A. Brewer (mAJs).
[1818]	From Robert Irvin. ALS, Benjamin H. Caldwell, Jr. (37-0493). Complains of fraud by Thomas Anthony, commissary at Fort Mitchell.
[1818]	Estimate by Reuben Humphreys of money required by James Dorman's command for work on the military road. DS endorsed by AJ regarding an order for partial payment, DLC (25).
[1818–22]	To Unknown. Abstract, *ABPC* (1904), p. 656 (5-1220). Introduces James Craine Bronaugh.

1819

Jan 2	From Edmund Pendleton Gaines. LS, DLC (26); LC, DNA-RG 98 (7-0113). Discusses incident at St. Augustine and reports the capture of four deserters.
Jan 2	From Felix Grundy. ALS, DLC (72). Bassett, 6:469–70. Urges AJ to go to Washington to answer charges lodged against him in Congress for the execution of Arbuthnot and Ambrister.
Jan 4	*To John Coffee.* 266
Jan 4	From James Gadsden. ALS, DLC (26). Reports on ordnance stores at New Orleans and Mobile.
Jan 5	From John Caldwell Calhoun. LS, DLC (26); AL draft and LC, DNA-RG 107 (7-0117, M7-1). *American Historical Association Annual Report, 1899,* 2:151–52. Discusses possible retaliation for Indian depredations in Missouri River area and encloses a letter (not found) complaining of cruel treatment of soldiers in 9th Military Department.

Jan 5	Memorandum of AJ's account with James Jackson & Co. ADS with AJ endorsement, DLC (26).
Jan 6	Agreement between John Overton, James Winchester, and AJ establishing surviving partnership rights to lands jointly owned at the junction of the Wolf and Mississippi rivers. Copies, DNA-RG 60 (7-0121), THi (7-0125); LC, TMSh (mAJs); Typed copy, TM (mAJs).
Jan 7	Receipt for Davidson County taxes for 1819. Printed form with ms insertions and AJ endorsement, DLC (26).
Jan 8	From James Dorman. ALS, DLC (26). Requests funds for quartermaster's department.
Jan 8	From William Kenner & Co. ALS, DLC (26). Sends madeira, port, champagne, claret, and cognac, a gift from Richard Butler.
Jan 11	Account with Kirkman & Jackson for expenses of Andrew J. Donelson and Edward G. W. Butler at West Point. ADS, LNHiC (7-0127).
Jan 12	To William Berkeley Lewis. ALS, NNPM (7-0132). Reports his arrival in Knoxville and expectation of reaching Washington in ten days.
Jan 12	From Edmund Pendleton Gaines (enclosures: José Coppinger to Gaines [Jan 3]; James M. Glassell to Coppinger, Jan 4; Coppinger to Glassell, and Glassell to Coppinger, Jan 5, DLC-26). ALS, DLC (26); ALS copy, DNA-RG 94 (7-0129), LC, DNA-RG 98 (7-0131). Sends copies of correspondence with the governor of St. Augustine.
Jan 12	Report of the House Military Affairs Committee condemning the executions of Alexander Arbuthnot and Robert Christie Ambrister. AD, DNA-RG 233 (7-0172). *HRDoc* 82, 15th Cong., 2nd sess. (Serial 20).
Jan 12	Minority Report of the House Military Affairs Committee exonerating AJ of misconduct in the executions of Alexander Arbuthnot and Robert Christie Ambrister. AD, DNA-RG 233 (7-0138). *HRDoc* 86, 15th Cong., 2nd sess. (Serial 22).
Jan 12	Agreement between John Overton, James Winchester, James Trimble, AJ, John Christmas McLemore, and John Brown re John Ramsay's claim to lands on Mississippi River adjoining land owned by Overton, Winchester, and AJ. ADS in Overton's hand, THi (7-0134).
Jan 14	From George Blaney (enclosure: Walker K. Armistead to Hugh Young, Jan 14, DLC-26). ALS, DLC (26); LC, DNA-RG 77 (7-0183). Encloses directive ordering Young to New Orleans.
Jan 15	Accounts of Rachel Jackson with Saunders & Chandler for fabric. ADS, DLC (26, 28).
Jan 16	From Edmund Pendleton Gaines (enclosures: James M. Glassell to Gaines, Jan 12; Statement of Augustus Santee, n.d., DLC-59). LS, DLC (26). Reports on and solicits advice on citizens held at St. Augustine; discusses sickness among troops in Florida.
Jan 17	From James Gadsden. ALS, DLC (26). Reports difficulties in construction of fortress at Mobile due to lack of plans and material.
Jan 19	From John M. Davis. LS, DLC (26). Expresses his friendship for AJ.
Jan 19	From Edmund Pendleton Gaines (enclosure: Map of Harbor of St. Augustine, n.d., DLC, mAJs). ALS, DLC (26); ALS draft, DNA-RG 94 (7-0187); LC, DNA-RG 98 (7-0189). Sends map.

[Jan 19]	Mary Donelson Caffery to Rachel Jackson. ALS (dated 1818), THi (7-0184). Mourns the death of their brother Severn Donelson and reports news of her family.
Jan 21	From Arthur Peronneau Hayne. ALS, DLC (26). Thomas Hart Benton, *Thirty Years' View* . . . (2 vols.; New York, 1856), 1:173 (extract). Discusses an alleged assault on his character by Governor Rabun of Georgia.
Jan 21	From Arthur Peronneau Hayne. ALS, DLC (26). Projects reasons for the investigation of AJ and the Seminole War; asserts that most citizens and the administration heartily support AJ's actions.
Jan 23	Account with Hall, Gwinn & Co. for clothing. ADS with postscript to Rachel Jackson, DLC (26).
Jan 25	To John Quincy and Louisa Catherine Adams. DS by proxy, MHi (7-0190). Declines dinner invitation.
Jan 25	To Rachel Jackson. ALS, Anonymous (mAJs). *The Autograph* (Dec 1911):29 (7-0192). Reports on congressional debate of his conduct in Florida.
Jan 25	To William Berkeley Lewis. ALS, NN (7-0193). *New York Public Library Bulletin* 4(1900):159–60. Details congressional investigation of Florida invasion.
Jan 26	From Edmund Pendleton Gaines (enclosures: José Coppinger to Gaines, Jan 18; Gaines to Coppinger, Jan 24, DLC-26). ALS, DLC (26); ALS copy, DNA-RG 94 (M566-117); LC, DNA-RG 98 (7-0201). Transmits correspondence.
Jan 26	Richard Keith Call to Eleazar Wheelock Ripley. LC, DLC (63). Orders Robert Beall to remain on departmental duty until April 1.
Jan 26	Auditor's report re AJ's account of Oct 2, 1818. LC, DNA-RG 217 (7-0197).
Jan 27	Receipt from John Gardiner for warrants for land purchased in Colbert County, Alabama. ADS with AJ endorsement, DLC (26).
Jan 28	From William Lee. LC, DNA-RG 217 (7-0208). Informs AJ that his accounts are closed.
Jan 28	From Allen McLane. ALS with AJ endorsement, DLC (26). Praises AJ's military career.
Jan 28	From Gurdon Saltonstall Mumford. Printed, *Richmond Enquirer,* Feb 23 (mAJs; 7-0209). Transmits resolutions of Republican Committee of New York City praising AJ's career and approving actions in Florida.
Jan 28	Robert Butler to Daniel Parker. ALS, DNA-RG 94 (M566-128). Reports that officers of Tennessee Volunteers in Florida campaign were appointed for that service.
Jan 28	Richard Keith Call to Edmund Pendleton Gaines. ALS, DNA-RG 94 (M566-115); LCs, DLC (63), DNA-RG 98 (mAJs). Informs him that Robert Beall will serve until April 1.
Jan 29	From Daniel Parker. ALS, DLC (26). Discusses discharge of John Reuben Bullard.
Jan 30	To Rachel Jackson. ALS, T (7-0210). Reports on the congressional debate re his actions in Florida.
Jan 30	*To William Berkeley Lewis.* 268
Jan 30	From Robert Butler. ALS endorsed by James Monroe ordering a re-

	port, DNA-RG 107 (M221-80). Argues that his brevet rank is too low.	
Jan 30	John Canfield Spencer to John Caldwell Calhoun (referred to AJ). ALS, DNA-RG 94 (M566-127). Commends Daniel Riddle.	
Jan 30	Account with Saunders & Chandler for sundries. ADS, OClWHi (7-0218). Runs to July 21.	
Jan 31	*To Andrew Jackson Donelson.*	270
[Jan]	Account for keeping horses in Frederick, Maryland. AD fragment, DLC (72).	
Feb 1	To John Caldwell Calhoun (enclosure: William King to Robert Butler, Dec 7, 1818). LS, DNA-RG 107 (M221-81). Transmits letter and requests funds.	
Feb 2	To Gurdon Saltonstall Mumford. Printed, *Richmond Enquirer,* Feb 23 (mAJs; 7-0223). Acknowledges letter and resolution of the Republican Committee of New York City.	
Feb 2	To Francis Preston. ALS, MHi (7-0224). Bassett, 2:409–10. Discusses the Florida campaign investigation and the Clay-Crawford alliance.	
Feb 4	From William Bradford. Copy, DNA-RG 94 (7-0227). Reports that hostilities between the Osages and the Cherokees have increased and war threatens to erupt.	
Feb 4	From William King. Copies, DNA-RG 107 (M221-80), DNA-RG 153 (7-0231), DNA-RG 233 (7-0232). *ASP, Military Affairs,* 2:186. Reports the arrival of a Spanish expedition at the Barrancas.	
Feb 4	From Daniel Parker. LS, DLC (26); LC, DNA-RG 94 (7-0233). Asks AJ's opinion re the abandonment of Forts Edward and Osage.	
[Feb 4]	From Thomas H. Boyles. ALS, DLC (26). Reports on the arrival of Spanish troops in Pensacola and resumption of Spanish rule.	
Feb 5	From John Caldwell Calhoun (enclosure: Abner Lacock to Calhoun, Feb 3, DLC-26). LS and Copies, DLC (26); Copies, DLC (24), DNA-RG 46 (7-0234); LC, DNA-RG 107 (M6-10). *ASP, Military Affairs,* 1:768. Transmits inquiry from the Senate committee investigating the Seminole War and requests AJ to reply.	
Feb 5	To John Caldwell Calhoun. Copies, DNA-RG 233 (7-0235), DNA-RG 46 (7-0238); Copy fragment, DLC (24). Bassett 2:410–11. Recounts for congressional committee events which led to march into Pensacola.	
Feb 5	From Abraham H. Quincy. ALS, DLC (26). Praises AJ's career and denounces his maligners.	
[Feb] 6	*To Rachel Jackson.*	271
Feb 10	To John Henry Eaton. LS, NHi (7-0245); AL draft with revisions in AJ's hand, DLC (28). Answers questions re Treaty of Fort Jackson and Indian relations in Florida; reports that he is about to leave for New York.	
Feb 10	From William King (enclosures: King to John M. Echeverri, Echeverri to King, Feb 5, DNA-RG 94). Copies, DNA-RG 94 (7-0254), DNA-RG 107 (M221-80), DNA-RG 153 (7-0252), DNA-RG 233 (7-0249). *ASP, Military Affairs,* 2:187. Reports the transfer of Pensacola to Spanish authority and asks for the arrest of Thomas F. Hunt for failure to report for duty.	

Feb 10	Account with Samuel Van Dyke Stout & Co. for carriage repairs. ADS, DLC (28). Runs to March 9, 1820.
Feb 12	Account of United States with John Strother. Printed form with ms insertions and certified by AJ, DNA-RG 46 (7-0264).
Feb 13	From Edmund Pendleton Gaines (enclosure: Gaines to John C. Calhoun, Feb 12, DLC-26). ALS, DLC (26); ALS draft, DNA-RG 94 (7-0267); LC, DNA-RG 98 (7-0269). Informs AJ of his reestablishing a post west of Okefenokee Swamp.
Feb 14	Frances Duncan Hayne to Rachel Jackson. ALS, DLC (26). Announces the birth of a daughter and congratulates her on the termination of AJ's difficulties.
Feb 15	To Andrew Jackson Donelson. ALS, DLC (7-0273). Reports on his itinerary to New York and asks that Donelson and Edward G. W. Butler meet him there.
Feb 15	From William Mooney. Printed, *Niles' Register,* March 6 (7-0276). Sends resolutions of the Tammany Society in praise of AJ's conduct in Florida.
Feb 16	From Daniel Bissell (enclosures: Alexander Gray to Bissell, Feb 8; Account of Gray, n.d.). LS, DNA-RG 94 (M566-121). Forwards Gray's resignation and account.
Feb 16	Account with United States for treaty negotiations. ADS, DNA-RG 217 (7-0278).
[Feb 17]	Resolution of the Mississippi legislature commending AJ's actions in Florida. DS, Ms-Ar (mAJs). Natchez *Mississippi Republican,* Feb 23.
[Feb 18]	From Thomas Cadwalader and Isaac Worrell. Printed, Baltimore *American and Commercial Advertiser,* Feb 22 (mAJs; 7-0288). Greet AJ on behalf of the 1st Division, Pennsylvania militia.
Feb 18	To Thomas Cadwalader and Isaac Worrell. LS, DLC (28; 7-0285). Baltimore *American and Commercial Advertiser,* Feb 22 (mAJs; 7-0287). Expresses appreciation for the tribute of the citizens and militia of Philadelphia.
Feb 18	To William Mooney. Printed, *Niles' Register,* March 6 (7-0284). Acknowledges receipt of resolutions of the Tammany Society.
Feb 18	From James Gadsden. ALS, DLC (26). Expresses regret that he is not with AJ and predicts that the congressional investigation will end in AJ's favor.
[Feb 18]	Toast at public dinner in Philadelphia: "The memory of Benjamin Franklin." Printed, *Niles' Register,* March 6 (7-0283).
Feb 19	Account with United States for Seminole campaign. DS, DNA-RG 217 (7-0289).
Feb 20	From John Brown (1757–1837). ALS, DLC (26). Praises AJ's career.
[Feb 21]	Toast at public dinner in New York: "The governor of the state—De Witt Clinton." Printed, *Niles' Register,* March 6 (7-0308).
Feb 23	From Cadwallader David Colden (enclosure: Citation making AJ a "FREEMAN AND CITIZEN" of New York City, DLC-26). Printed, *Niles' Register,* March 6 (7-0309). Praises AJ's military career.
Feb 23	To Cadwallader David Colden. LS draft, DLC (28; 7-0310). *Niles' Register,* March 6. Expresses appreciation for tribute.
Feb 23	*Rachel Jackson to Ralph Eleazar Whitesides Earl.* 272

Feb 24	Draft Report of the Senate Select Committee on the Seminole War and Florida invasion. AD with revisions, DNA-RG 46 (7-0316).	
Feb 25	To James Monroe. LS, DNA-RG 59 (M439-10). Recommends William Laval as collector of customs, Pensacola.	
Feb 25	From James Gadsden. ALS, DLC (26). Inquires about the outcome of the Seminole investigation; reports that Henry Clay's reputation has suffered; urges AJ to come to New Orleans from New York.	
Feb 27	From Edward Johnson. Printed, Baltimore *American and Commercial Advertiser,* March 1 (mAJs; 7-0386). Praises AJ's services.	
Feb 27	To Edward Johnson. Draft, DLC (7-0384). Baltimore *American and Commercial Advertiser,* March 1. Expresses appreciation for reception in Baltimore.	
Feb 27	From William Darby. ALS, THi (7-0372). Seeks office in Florida.	
Feb 27	From Edmund Pendleton Gaines (enclosure: Daniel E. Burch to Gaines, Feb 26, DLC-26). ALS, DLC (26); Copy, DNA-RG 94 (7-0375); LC, DNA-RG 98 (7-0378). Transmits report on activities along the coast of eastern Florida; discusses Indians and military activities in the area.	
Feb 27	From Edmund Pendleton Gaines. LS, DLC (26); AL draft, DNA-RG 94 (7-0380); LC, DNA-RG 98 (7-0382). Discusses supplies for Forts Gadsden and Scott.	
Feb 28	From David Brearley. ALS, DLC (26). Requests furlough and retirement for John R. Corbaly.	
Feb	Account with Hall, Gwinn & Co. for sundries. ADS with AJ endorsement, DLC (28). Runs to February 29, 1820.	
[Feb]	From John Henry Eaton. AL fragment, DLC (75). Queries AJ about 1818 Florida invasion.	
March 1	From John Berry, Richard K. Heath, and John E. Howard. LS, DLC (26). *Niles' Register,* March 6. Praise AJ's services to the country.	
March 1	To Richard K. Heath. LS draft, DLC (26) *Niles' Register,* March 6. Expresses his gratification for tribute.	
March 1	From DeWitt Clinton. LC, NNC (mAJs). Expresses regret at failing to meet while AJ was in New York.	
[March 1]	Remarks and toast at public dinner in Baltimore: "What I have done sir, was for my country . . . I have no fear but my country will do me justice. . . ." Printed, *Niles' Register,* March 6 (7-0391).	
[cMarch 1]	Deposition of Robert Butler re the Florida invasion. Copy with AJ endorsement, DNA-RG 46 (7-0826).	
March 3	Statement of Robert Butler re purchase of Florida land by John Donelson (1787–1840). DS, DNA-RG 46 (7-0393); Copy, DNA-RG 233 (7-0397). *ASP, Military Affairs,* 1:754.	
March 3	Deposition of George Gibson re Florida invasion. Copy with AJ endorsement, DNA-RG 46 (7-0833). *ASP, Military Affairs,* 1:753.	
March 3	Mary Donelson Caffery to Rachel Jackson. ALS, DLC (26). Laments death of her daughter, Jane Caffery Earl.	
March 3	Account with Gordon & Walker for sundries. ADS with AJ endorsement, DLC (26).	
March 6	*From John Caldwell Calhoun.*	273
March 6	From Arthur Peronneau Hayne (enclosures: Hayne to Talbot Chambers; to John M. Davis; and to Eleazar W. Ripley; all Feb 18). ALS,	

DLC (26). Bassett, 2:412 (extract). Reviews his forthcoming inspection tour and new procedure for returns; states his pleasure over AJ's decision to go to Washington.

March 6 — Account with Richmond & Flint for tableware and jewelry. ADS, DLC (28). Runs to December 11.

March 7 — To James Monroe. LS, NN (7-0413). Recommends appointment of William Laval to a civil post.

March 7 — From Edmund Pendleton Gaines. ALS draft, DNA-RG 94 (7-0410); LC, DNA-RG 98 (7-0412). Reports news of arrival of a Spanish force at Barrancas.

March 7 — Robert Butler to Henry Atkinson. LC, DNA-RG 98 (mAJs). On AJ's behalf, orders Atkinson to command of the 9th Military Department.

March 7 — Robert Butler to Daniel Bissell. LC, DNA-RG 98 (mAJs). Relieves Bissell of command of the 9th Military Department.

[March 7] — To Robert Butler (enclosure: John C. Calhoun to AJ, March 6). ALS, DLC (26). Orders occupation of posts along the Missouri River.

March 8 — *To Thomas McCorry.* 276

March 8 — To James Monroe. LS, DNA-RG 59 (M439-14). Recommends Edward B. Randolph as marshal in Florida.

March 8 — To James Monroe. Abstract, Anderson Galleries, Sale 2324 (Feb 1929), Item 230 (7-0417). Recommends Samuel Hawkins as boundary commissioner between United States and Spanish possessions.

March 9 — To John Caldwell Calhoun. LS, DNA-RG 107 (M222-21). Requests order to pay Hugh Young for topographical services.

March 9 — From Richard Riker. ALS, DLC (26). Recommends William Theobald Wolfe Tone for war department and commends AJ's actions in Florida.

March 9 — Rachel Jackson to Ralph Eleazar Whitesides Earl. ALS, DLC (26). Asks Earl to send "pretty that you saide was of no use to you," to buy shoes, and to check for letters from AJ.

March 10 — From Anthony Wayne Butler. AL fragment, DLC (75). Reports that he is still in New York.

March 12 — To John Caldwell Calhoun. LS, DNA-RG 94 (M688-10). Recommends Edward C. McDonald for West Point.

March 12 — From Robert White, Hugh Holmes, and D[abney] Carr. Printed, *Richmond Enquirer,* March 26 (mAJs). Invite AJ to public dinner in Winchester.

March 12 — To [Robert White, Hugh Holmes, and Dabney Carr]. Printed, *Richmond Enquirer,* March 26 (mAJs). Accepts invitation.

March 12 — From Edmund Pendleton Gaines. ALS, DLC (26); LC, DNA-RG 98 (7-0422); Copy, DNA-RG 94 (7-0420). Transmits map of eastern Florida.

March 13 — From John Caldwell Calhoun (enclosure: Calhoun to Jacob J. Brown, March 11, DLC-26). LS, DLC (26); LC, DNA-RG 107 (M6-10). Encloses letter to Brown re military operations along the Mississippi and Missouri rivers.

March 18 — From James Pitchlynn. Copy, DNA-RG 46 (mAJs). *ASP, Indian Affairs,* 2:229. Discusses possibility of Choctaw removal to west of the Mississippi.

March 18 — *Rachel Jackson to William Davenport.* 277

March 18 — Rachel Jackson to Catherine Walker. ALS by proxy, THer (7-0428). Acknowledges letter to Jane Caffery Earl and reports details of her death.

March 18 — Resolution of the Pennsylvania House of Representatives commending AJ. Printed, *Richmond Enquirer,* March 26 (mAJs).

March 20 — From Daniel Parker (enclosure: Talbot Chambers to Parker, Feb 20, DLC-26). LS, DLC (26); LC, DNA-RG 94 (7-0430). Sends extract of Chambers's report.

March 23 — From Edmund Pendleton Gaines. LS, DLC (26); AL draft, DNA-RG 94 (7-0431); LC, DNA-RG 98 (7-0433). Reports on illness of troops on Amelia Island and speculates about the impact of the acquisition of Florida on Indians and fugitive blacks in the area.

March 24 — From George Gibson. ALS, DLC (26). Discusses a bill of exchange on John Innerarity, cosigned by AJ (not found); reports passage of resolutions by the Pennsylvania House of Representatives approving AJ's Seminole campaign.

March 25 — From Enoch Parsons. Copy, DLC (26). *Knoxville Register,* March 30. Praises AJ's service to his state and country and congratulates him on triumph over his enemies.

March 25 — To Enoch Parsons. Copy, DLC (28). *Knoxville Register,* April 6 (7-0436). Acknowledges congratulations.

March 25 — From Hugh Lawson White. Printed, *Knoxville Register,* March 30 (7-0440). Praises AJ's military services at the Battle of New Orleans and in Florida.

March 25 — To Hugh Lawson White. Printed, *Knoxville Register,* April 6 (7-0438). Expresses appreciation.

March 26 — To Rachel Jackson. Printed extract, American Art Association Sale (April 8, 1926), Item 255 (7-0441). Reports his arrival in Knoxville.

March 26 — *To William Berkeley Lewis.* 278

March 28 — From Daniel Parker. Printed form signed with AJ endorsement and Copy, DLC (26). Orders that commanding officers of garrisons and posts will detail soldier to help assistant commissary.

March 29 — From John Caldwell Calhoun (enclosures: Commission to negotiate Choctaw treaty, March 29; Calhoun to John McKee, March 29). LS, DLC (26). Bassett, 2:414. Appoints AJ, John McKee, and Daniel Burnet as Choctaw commissioners.

March 29 — *From Thomas Hill Williams.* 278

March 29 — Commission to negotiate with Choctaw Indians. DS by James Monroe and John C. Calhoun, DLC (26).

March 30 — From Richard Gilliam Dunlap (enclosure: Joseph McMinn to Dunlap with AJ endorsement, Feb 22, 1818, DLC-24). ALS, DLC (26); Copy, DNA-RG 46 (7-0444). *ASP, Military Affairs,* 1:767. Discusses his intentions in 1818 to raise a volunteer company and march to Fort Scott and the support his proposal received from McMinn.

April 1 — Account with United States for pay and expenses. DS, DNA-RG 217 (7-0446). Runs through June 30.

April 3 — *To John Coffee.* 279

April 3 — To John Gordon. ALS, THi (7-0458). Informs him that the Chickasaw treaty has been remitted to Chickasaw agent Henry Sherburne.

April 5	From Ephraim Hubbard Foster et al. Copy, DLC (26). Invite AJ to a public dinner in Nashville.	
April 5	From Thomas F. Hunt. Copy, DNA-RG 94 (7-0460). Relates reasons for his failure to comply with AJ's order of November 27, 1818, transferring him to Pensacola.	
April 5	From John Jackson. ALS, DLC (26). Declines purchase of Florence, Alabama, stock.	
April 6	From John Overton and Nashville Citizens. Printed, *Nashville Whig,* April 10 (7-0449). Welcome AJ's return to Nashville and praise his services.	
April 6	To John Overton and Nashville Citizens. Printed, *Nashville Whig,* April 10 (7-0451). Thanks them.	
April 6	From Elizabeth Jackson. ALS, DLC (26). Reports on possible family relations in County Fermanagh, Ireland.	
April 6	From Reuben Kemper. ALS with AJ endorsement, DLC (26). Reports favorable decisions on most of his Florida claims and thanks AJ for his influence; urges him to recommend Alexander Anderson for secretary of Florida territory; states that Winfield Scott's pamphlet is "unworthy of your notice."	
April 6	From Joseph McMinn. ALS draft and Copies, DLC (26); Extract, DNA-RG 46 (7-0463). *ASP, Military Affairs,* 1:768 (extract). Discusses events leading to the call-up of the Tennessee volunteers in January 1818.	
April 6	Toast at public dinner in Nashville: "Isaac Shelby, late Gov. Kentucky—The revolutionary patriot and distinguished hero." Printed, *Nashville Whig,* April 10 (mAJs).	
April 7	*From Isaac Lewis Baker.*	281
April 8	*To Willie Blount.*	282
April 8	From Eleazar Wheelock Ripley (enclosure: Confidential report of the officers and department, April 8). LS with postscript in Ripley's hand, DLC (26). Transmits report.	
April 8	Robert Butler to Eleazar Wheelock Ripley. Copy, DNA-RG 94 (M566-123); LC, DNA-RG 98 (mAJs). Requests report on military road.	
April 9	From [James Scallan]. ALS fragment, DLC (75). Requests aid in securing a civil or naval appointment.	
April 10	Robert Butler to Milo Mason. LC, DNA-RG 98 (mAJs). Transmits orders.	
April 13	To William King. LS, DNA-RG 153 (7-0470); LC, DLC (63); Copy, DNA-RG 233 (7-0473). *ASP, Military Affairs,* 2:176. Approves conduct and evacuation of Penascola.	
April 13	To James Winchester. ALS, THi (7-0475). *Taylor-Trotwood Magazine,* 10(March 1910):396. Advises Winchester on running the line between the Chickasaw nation and the state of Tennessee.	
April 13	Richard Keith Call to Thomas H. Boyles. LC, DLC (63). Authorizes payment of Boyles's claim and promises to investigate claim for a wagon.	
April 13	Richard Keith Call to Talbot Chambers. LC, DLC (63). Encloses letter (not found) complaining of cruel punishment and directs investigation.	

April 14	Richard Keith Call to John Caldwell Calhoun. ALS, DNA-RG 107 (M221-80); LC, DLC (63). *Calhoun Papers,* 4:21–22. Acknowledges Calhoun's letter of January 5 informing AJ of complaint of cruel punishment in the 9th Military Department and states that complaint will be investigated.	
April 14	Receipt from Henry Terrass for groceries. ADS, THi (7-0478).	
April 15	To Edmund Pendleton Gaines. LS, THi (7-0479); LC, DLC (63). Approves his course re the commandant at St. Augustine; expresses regret for the difficulties Gaines has faced because of lack of funds; discusses charges against Gaines in the Senate report on the Florida invasion.	
April 15	From James Gadsden. ALS with AJ endorsement, DLC (26). Bassett, 2:414–16. Commends AJ's restraint in dealing with critics and recommends a new biography of AJ.	
April 15	*From John McCrea.*	283
[April 15]	From James Gadsden. AL fragment, DLC (75). Sends bill of exchange and requests funds.	
April 16	Robert Butler to Eleazar Wheelock Ripley. Copy, DNA-RG 94 (M566-123); LC, DNA-RG 98 (mAJs). On AJ's behalf forbids abandonment of Fort Bowyer.	
April 16	Richard Keith Call to John Caldwell Calhoun (enclosures: William King to AJ, Feb 4, 10; King to John M. Echeverri and Echeverri to King, Feb 5, DNA-RG 107, M221-80). ALS, DNA-RG 107 (M221-80); LC, DLC (63). *Calhoun Papers,* 4:25. Transmits letters on the transfer of Pensacola.	
April 17	From Henry Atkinson. ALS, DLC (26). Nichols, *Missouri Expedition,* pp. 93–94. Reports arrival at Pittsburgh en route to Missouri as per orders.	
April 18	*From Willie Blount.*	285
April 18	From Willie Blount. ALS with AJ endorsement, DLC (26). Recalls that, in a meeting with AJ and John Cocke previous to the Creek campaign, Cocke pledged to supply provisions for the East and West Tennessee troops.	
April 18	From James Gadsden. ALS, DLC (26). Criticizes Robert Butler's deposition on Florida and states that he himself plans to file one.	
April 18	Account with James Jackson & Co. for Andrew Jackson Hutchings. ADS, A-Ar (7-0483). Runs to October 25.	
April 19	From Eleazar Wheelock Ripley. ALS, DLC (26). Reports loss of a schooner and stores for Fort Gadsden.	
April 20	*To John Clark.*	287
April 21	From William Bradford. LS, DLC (26). Relates that he has had no response to nineteen previous communications; criticizes the congressional investigation of AJ.	
April 21	From Richard Ivy Easter. ALS, DLC (26); Extract, DNA-RG 46 (7-0490). *ASP, Military Affairs,* 1:766–67 (extract). Reports conversation with John Forsyth while in Washington re call up of Tennessee troops for Seminole War.	
April 21	From Richard Ivy Easter. ALS, DLC (26). Denies that AJ appointed officers during Seminole War.	
April 21	From Richard Ivy Easter. LS, DLC (26). Reports conversation with	

	Return J. Meigs (1740–1823) while in Washington that documents relating to Cherokee spoliations claims are at Meigs's home.	
April 21	From Alexander Campbell Wilder Fanning. ALS, DNA-RG 107 (M221-86). Asks AJ's intervention with officials in Washington to reinstate disallowed pay and about status of captured blacks.	
April 21	From Henry Sherburne. ALS with AJ endorsement, DLC (26). Asks if William Colbert, whose name is missing from those to be paid pursuant to the Chickasaw treaty, is actually entitled to receive $100, and whether there was any talk in Washington re his transfer to a station "more Comfortable & productive."	
April 22	*To John McKee.*	288
April 22	From James Gadsden. ALS, DLC (26). Expresses regret that AJ did not return to Tennessee via Louisiana; comments on the Senate report and explains his failure to go to Washington.	
April 24	*To Edmund Pendleton Gaines.*	289
April 24	From Zachariah McGirtt. ALS, DLC (26). Asks AJ to issue orders for the payment of his volunteers for forage and horses.	
April 24	Order transmitting the proceedings of Stoughton Gantt's court-martial to the secretary of war. DS by Robert Butler, DLC (26); LC, DNA-RG 98 (mAJs); Copy, DNA-RG 391 (7-0497).	
April 25	*From Robert Butler.*	290
April 26	*From Richard Mentor Johnson.*	292
April 26	From Samuel Swartwout. ALS, DLC (72). Bassett, 6:470–72. Asks Jackson to recommend [William?] Colden to accompany Monroe on his western trip; warmly praises AJ's career.	
April 27	From William Trigg, Jr. ALS, DLC (26). Asks for letter of introduction for Pensacola and discusses a debt to AJ.	
April 28	From Abner Lawson Duncan. ALS, DLC (26). States that he will revise and send James Gadsden's deposition on the Seminole campaign; condemns the Senate report.	
April 29	From John Blake White. ALS, DLC (26). Transmits a copy of his *The Triumph of Liberty, or, Louisiana Preserved, a National Drama, in Five Acts* (Charleston, 1819) and praises AJ's services.	
April 29	[Peter Hagner] to Robert Butler. LS, DLC (26); LC, DNA-RG 217 (7-0502). Returns receipt for correction to close AJ's account with United States.	
April 30	From John Jackson. ALS, DLC (26). Announces engagement of Englishman William Frost as AJ's gardener.	
April 30	From Joseph McMinn. ALS, DLC (26). Reports that recent negotiations with the Cherokees conflict with earlier agreements and requests his intervention with the secretary of war.	
[April]	From James Gadsden. ALS fragment, DLC (75). Discusses southern defenses and the Lacock committee report.	
May 1	To Smith Thompson. LS, DLC (7-0503). Recommends Cary Nicholas as purser, Pensacola.	
May 1	From Michael McKinsey (enclosure: Petition of Pensacola residents, n.d.). ALS, DNA-RG 59 (M439-11). Asks recommendation for appointment as keeper of Pensacola archives.	
May 1	Eleazar Wheelock Ripley to Robert Butler. Copy, DNA-RG 94	

	(M566-123). Reports that Fort Bowyer was dismantled in November 1818.	
May 1	Eleazar Wheelock Ripley to Robert Butler. Copy, DNA-RG 94 (M566-123). Reports on construction of military road.	
May 3	*From James Gadsden.*	294
May 4	To John Coffee. ALS, THi (7-0505). Expresses desire to visit Coffee before Monroe's arrival and urges him to see that there is enough corn at his farm for the fall and winter.	
May 4	From Henry Atkinson. ALS, DLC (27). Reports arrival of his troops at Pittsburgh.	
May 5	*From Andrew Jackson Donelson.*	296
May 6	From Anthony Wayne Butler. ALS, DLC (27). Reports on his debts and intention to transfer from Yale to Princeton.	
May 8	Account with William Arthur for tombstone for John Hutchings. ADS with AJ endorsement, THi (7-0507).	
May 10	From George Gibson. ALS, DLC (27); LC, DNA-RG 192 (7-0510). Asks AJ to appoint an assistant commissary for the detachment working on the military road from the Tennessee River to New Orleans.	
May 10	Richard Keith Call to John Caldwell Calhoun. ALS, DNA-RG 107 (M221-81); LC, DLC (63). Encloses documents (not found) re shortage of clothing for troops in the 9th Military Department and discusses commissary problems.	
May 10	Receipt from Robert Smiley for clothing and sundries. ADS with AJ endorsement, THi (7-0512). Runs to September 16.	
May 12	From William O. Winston. ALS, DLC (27). *Cincinnati Commercial,* Jan 8, 1880 (extract). In response to AJ's letter (not found) reports that Winfield Scott showed him correspondence with AJ in March 1818.	
May 12	Robert Butler to Eleazar Wheelock Ripley. Copy, DNA-RG 94 (M566-123); LC, DNA-RG 98 (mAJs). Demands explanation for failure to report on the construction of the military road.	
May 13	To George Gibson. LS and Extract, DNA-RG 192 (7-0515, -0519). Reports his recovery from an illness and on Richard M. Johnson's drafts at Philadelphia and Washington.	
May 15	*To Henry Atkinson.*	298
May 15	From Henry Atkinson. ADS, DLC (27). Nichols, *Missouri Expedition,* p. 95 (extract). Reports that his regiment will reach St. Louis in early June.	
May 16	From "A Citizen." ALS, DLC (27). *TPUS,* 18:631–33. Congratulates AJ on the report of the House of Representatives; discusses the activities of the collector of customs at Mobile, Addin Lewis, who is unfriendly to AJ.	
May 16	From Edmund Pendleton Gaines. AL draft, DNA-RG 94 (7-0521). Informs AJ, on behalf of Monroe, of the president's travel to Huntsville.	
May 17	*To Andrew Jackson Donelson.*	299
May 17	From James Rogers. ALS, DLC (27). Announces AJ's election to the Philadelphia Hibernian Society for the Relief of Emigrants from Ireland.	

May 18 Richard Keith Call to Reuben Humphreys. LC, DLC (63). Requests a statement from contractor on failure to furnish supplies for detachment constructing military road.

May 20 From David Scott. ALS, DLC (27). Asks AJ for recollections of the character of his brother Luther Scott, now deceased, an army officer under AJ at New Orleans.

May 21 From Robert Henry Dyer. ALS with ANS by Thomas Williamson, DNA-RG 46 (7-0528). *ASP, Military Affairs,* 1:768–69. States that AJ neither appointed officers nor organized Tennessee volunteers for the Seminole expedition.

May 23 From Henry Atkinson. ALS, DLC (27). Nichols, *Missouri Expedition,* p. 96. Reports the arrival with the detachment at the mouth of the Cumberland River.

May 24 To Zachariah McGirtt. LC, DLC (63). States that there is no allowance for back forage but there will be compensation for back rations and horses lost or killed.

May 24 From John Clark. ALS, DLC (27). Bassett, 2:416–18. Discusses his planned pamphlet on William H. Crawford and Crawford's hostility to AJ.

May 26 From Samuel Carswell. ALS, DLC (27). Announces that he is forwarding AJ's certificate of membership in the Hibernian Society by Capt. [Milo] Mason.

May 27 Eleazar Wheelock Ripley to Robert Butler. Copy, DNA-RG 94 (M566-123). Defends progress of work on military road.

May 29 From Return Jonathan Meigs (1740–1823). ALS, DLC (27). Forwards papers re Cherokee spoliation claims.

May 30 From Reuben Humphreys (enclosure: Certificate of James Fleming, April 1, DLC-70). ALS, DLC (27). Transmits certificate of agent for Camillus Griffith, justifying his failure to furnish supplies to detachment along the military road.

May 31 From Alexander Macomb. ALS, NjP (7-0532). Introduces Dr. [Joseph Pynchon] Russell.

May 31 From James Monroe. ALS, DLC (27); Copy, NN (7-0534). Bassett, 2:418–19 (extract). Suggests plan whereby AJ and Winfield Scott can settle their differences.

May 31 Robert Butler to Henry Atkinson. LC, DNA-RG 98 (mAJs). Acknowledges letter of May 15; asks for notice of arrival of provisions at St. Louis for Missouri expedition.

May 31 Robert Butler to Peter Hagner. LC, DNA-RG 98 (mAJs). Returns corrected receipt to close AJ's account with the United States.

June 1 Robert Butler to George Gibson. LC, DNA-RG 98 (mAJs). Informs Gibson that Robert Lyman has been appointed acting assistant commissary for the upper end of the military road.

June 1 Robert Butler to Eleazar Wheelock Ripley. Copy, DNA-RG 94 (M566-123); LC, DNA-RG 98 (mAJs). Orders report on military road.

June 1 Order assigning Henry Atkinson to command of the 9th Military Department. LC, DNA-RG 391 (7-0540).

June 4 From Arthur Peronneau Hayne. ALS, DLC (27). Sends draft of his deposition on the Seminole invasion, which Abner L. Duncan is revising.

June 5 — From James Gadsden (enclosure: Deposition of Isaac McKeever, June 5). ALS, DLC (27). Encloses McKeever's deposition on Seminole invasion; states that he will forward his own deposition, now being revised by Abner L. Duncan, shortly.

June 5 — From Edward Livingston. ALS, DLC (72). Asks AJ to assist [Bernard de Marigny] in procuring a pair of carriage horses.

June 5 — Deposition of Isaac McKeever re Florida invasion. ADS with AJ endorsement, DNA-RG 46 (7-0809). *ASP, Military Affairs,* 1:763.

June 6 — From James Gadsden. ALS, ICHi (7-0542). States that his and Arthur P. Hayne's depositions on the Seminole invasion will be forwarded shortly.

June 6 — Eleazar Wheelock Ripley to Robert Butler. Copy, DNA-RG 94 (M566-123). Requests six-month furlough to prepare accounts for settlement.

June 7 — From Henry Atkinson. ALS, DLC (27). Reports arrival in St. Louis and preparations for the Missouri expedition.

June 7 — From Isaac Lewis Baker. ALS, DNA-RG 94 (M566-123). Recommends Ogden Langstaffe for the army medical staff.

June 7 — From Joseph McMinn (enclosure: John C. Calhoun to McMinn, May 6). ALS, DLC (27). Encloses Calhoun's opinion re purchases under leases with the Cherokee Indians and awaits president's views.

June 8 — From Matthew Lyon. ALS, DLC (27). Asks AJ to urge John H. Eaton to support his renewed effort in the Senate for remuneration under the Sedition Act.

June 9 — Toast at a public dinner in Nashville in honor of James Monroe: "Congress of the U. States—The representatives of a free nation; may they never act from any [other] motives than to protect the constitution, and for the best interest of their country." Printed, *Nashville Whig,* June 12 (7-0546).

June 10 — From James Cage. ALS, DNA-RG 59 (7-0547). Asks AJ to urge Monroe to gain release of his brother, Richard H. Cage, held prisoner by the Spanish since 1813.

June 10 — From Speaker et al. LS by proxy, DLC (27). Ask AJ for his interpretation of the 1816 Cherokee treaty.

June 10 — Order approving the sentences in the courts-martial of William McHenry, John Waters, and Lewis H. Dumbleton, privates of the 4th Infantry Regiment. ADS by Edmund P. Gaines, DNA-RG 94 (7-0552).

June 12 — To James Monroe. ANS, DNA-RG 94 (M688-10). Reminds Monroe of his pledge to alert the United States Military Academy that Frederick L. Guion, a cadet, will arrive late.

June 12 — From Arthur Peronneau Hayne (enclosures: Deposition on the Florida invasion, June 12; Hayne to John C. Calhoun, Feb 9, 13, March 13, 28, Calhoun to Hayne, March 7, April 11, all 1818, DLC-24). ALS, DLC (27). Transmits documents and pledges to join AJ in Nashville before a trip to Washington if he desires.

June 12 — From John Benjamin Hogan. Copy, DNA-RG 94 (M566-122). Details his arrest by William King and requests court-martial.

June 12	Deposition of Arthur Peronneau Hayne re invasion of Florida. DS, DLC (27); Copy with AJ endorsement, DNA-RG 46 (7-0837). *ASP, Military Affairs,* 1:768.
June 16	From William Theobald Wolfe Tone. ALS, DLC (27). Sends his *Essay on the Necessity of Improving our National Forces* (New York, 1819) and denounces attacks on AJ.
June 17	From "C." Printed, *Nashville Whig,* July 3 (mAJs). Urges increased speed in completion of military road.
June 17	From [Peter Hagner]. LC, DNA-RG 217 (7-0555). Certifies that AJ's account with the treasury department is closed.
June 17	From Edward Livingston. ALS with AJ endorsement, DLC (27). Removes the restriction of the color gray from the carriage horses for Bernard de Marigny.
June 19	From Henry Atkinson. ALS, DLC (27). Reports on preparations for the Missouri expedition.
June 21	Robert Butler to Peter Hagner. LC, DNA-RG 98 (mAJs). Forwards paper re settlement with Camillus Griffith.
June 22	From James Pitchlynn. ALS, DNA-RG 75 (M271-2); Copy, DNA-RG 46 (7-0558). *ASP, Indian Affairs,* 2:231. Reports that many Choctaws are inclined to meet with commissioners to negotiate a treaty.
June 23	From Richard Taylor, Sr., et al. Printed, Washington *National Intelligencer,* July 19 (7-0560). Invite AJ to a dinner for President Monroe in Louisville and praise his military achievements.
June 24	To Richard Taylor, Sr., et al. Copy, DLC (37; 7-0562). Lexington *Kentucky Reporter,* July 7 (mAJs); Washington *National Intelligencer,* July 19 (7-0564). Accepts dinner invitation.
June 25	Toast at a public dinner in Louisville, Kentucky: "Domestic manufactures essential to the prosperity and real independence of our country." Printed, Washington *National Intelligencer,* July 19 (mAJs).
June 26	From James Gadsden (enclosure: Deposition on the Florida invasion, June 30). ALS, DLC (27). Encloses deposition.
June 27	From Richard Mentor Johnson. ALS, DLC (27). *RegKyHi,* 39(1941):45–46. Urges intervention with the president for cash advances for the Missouri expedition.
June 29	From James Gadsden. ALS with AJ endorsement, DLC (27). Asks AJ to see that a bill of exchange for $2,375 on the Nashville Bank is honored and funds are remitted to him in New Orleans.
June 30	Toast at a public dinner at Frankfort, Kentucky, honoring James Monroe: "The state of Kentucky—justly distinguished for patriotism and correct republican principles." Printed, *Richmond Enquirer,* July 23 (mAJs).
June 30	Receipt for subscriptions to *National Register* and the *City of Washington Gazette,* ADS in hand of Jonathan Elliot, DLC (29). Runs to November 12, 1820.
June 30	Deposition of James Gadsden re Florida invasion. Copy, DNA-RG 46 (7-0790). *ASP, Military Affairs,* 1:761–62.
June 30	Account with United States for pay as major general. ADS by Cary

	Nicholas with AJ endorsement, DLC (29). Runs to December 31, 1820.	
June	Receipt to Milo Mason for $98. Abstract, Charles Hamilton Catalog 41, Item 121 (7-0538).	
July 1	Account with United States for pay and expenses. DS, DNA-RG 217 (mAJs). Runs to September 30.	
July 1	Abstract of payments made to field and staff officers. AD, DNA-RG 217 (mAJs). Runs to October 1.	
July 2	From James Morrison. Printed, Lexington *Kentucky Gazette,* July 9 (mAJs). Invites AJ to Lexington dinner honoring the president.	
July 2	Robert Butler to Daniel Parker (enclosures: Report of Perrin Willis, June 14; Levi Whiting to Butler, June 16; Willis to Eleazar W. Ripley, June 14; Field notes of Willis, n.d., M566-123). LS, DNA-RG 94 (M566-123); LC, DNA-RG 98 (mAJs). Transmits documents re military road.	
July 3	To James Morrison. Printed, Lexington *Kentucky Gazette,* July 9 (mAJs); Extract, DLC (23). Accepts invitation to dinner.	
July 3	Account with Thomas Deaderick for grindstone. ADS with AJ endorsement marked paid March 13, [1823], DLC (27).	
July 3	Rachel Jackson to Ralph Eleazar Whitesides Earl. ALS, DLC (27). Asks him to check post office for letters.	
July 5	*To [James Monroe].*	300
July 5	To James Monroe. ALS, NN (7-0567). Recommends Richard K. Call, William S. Fulton, James Gadsden, and William Laval for appointments in Florida; asks him to remind John C. Calhoun of the promise of two cannon for the Nashville Town Company and requests cannon captured at Pensacola in 1814.	
July 6	From James Gadsden. ALS, DLC (27). States willingness to accompany AJ to Washington; doubts that Joseph G. Swift conspired with William H. Crawford against AJ.	
July 7	*From Arthur Peronneau Hayne.*	302
July 9	From John Quincy Adams. LC, DNA-RG 59 (M40-15). Informs AJ that the Spanish chargé d'affaires has recommended the release of Richard H. Cage from prison in Mexico and encloses United States passport for James Cage to Mexico.	
July 10	From Eleazar Wheelock Ripley (enclosures: William C. Beard to John C. Carr, June 18; Carr to Beard, June 18, DNA-RG 107, M221-86; Beard to Robert L. Coomb, June 9; Beard to H. A. Bullard, and Bullard to Beard, June 14; Beard to Ripley, June 22; Ripley to Beard, and to John Dick, July 9, DLC-27). ALS with AJ endorsement forwarding enclosures to the president and observing that the military's duty lies in suppressing armed combinations formed contrary to law, DLC (27); Copy, DNA-RG 107 (M221-86). Reports a purported armed expedition to Texas and asks for instructions.	
July 11	Henry Atkinson to John Caldwell Calhoun. ALS, DLC (mAJs). Reports on progress of the Missouri expedition and notes that "a copy of this communication is transmitted to Maj. Gen. Jackson."	
July 12	From Eleazar Wheelock Ripley. Copies, DNA-RG 94 (M566-123; 7-0570), DNA-RG 107 (M221-86, -87). Discusses his decision to order the crossroad from Bay of St. Louis to the Pearl River.	

July 13 To John Clark. LS, TxU (7-0576); ALS draft, DLC (27). Bassett, 2:419–21. Acknowledges earlier letters and reminds Clark of his wish to have a copy of Clark's publication on William H. Crawford before concluding his answer to the Senate report on the Seminole investigation.

July 14 To [James Rogers]. Copy, DLC (27). Acknowledges election to membership in the Hibernian Society.

July 14 Richard Ivy Easter to John Quincy Adams (enclosure: Michael McKinsey to AJ with petition, May 1). ALS, DNA-RG 59 (M439-11). Sends recommendation for appointment of McKinsey as keeper of the provincial archives in West Florida.

July 14 Richard Ivy Easter to John Caldwell Calhoun (enclosure: Isaac L. Baker to AJ, June 7). ALS, DNA-RG 94 (M566-123). Sends recommendation of Ogden Langstaffe.

July 16 From Daniel Parker. LS, DLC (27); LC, DNA-RG 94 (7-0580). Requests that Richard I. Easter be ordered to Washington to settle accounts before accepting his resignation.

July 16 Robert Butler to Eleazar Wheelock Ripley. Copy, DNA-RG 94 (M566-123); LC, DNA-RG 98 (mAJs). Denies furlough requests, but will accept resignation.

July 19 From John Caldwell Calhoun. LS, DLC (27); LC, DNA-RG 107 (M6-10); Copy, DNA-RG 94 (M566-129). *Calhoun Papers,* 4:158–59. Orders economy in quartermaster disbursements.

July 19 Daniel Parker to [Robert Butler?] (enclosure: Proceedings of court-martial of Stoughton Gantt, Dec 8, 1818, DNA-RG 153). LS, DLC (27); LC, DNA-RG 98 (mAJs). Returns court-martial proceedings to AJ for review.

July 20 To Edward Livingston. ALS, NjP (mAJs). Bassett, 6:473. States that he has found horses for Bernard de Marigny; comments on the Florida investigation and his health.

July 20 Tennessee Land Grant for six acres in Sumner County. DS by Joseph McMinn and Daniel Graham, T (7-0582).

July 22 From George Poindexter. ALS, DLC (27). Discusses the location of the military road.

July 23 *To Andrew Jackson Donelson.* 303

July 24 To John Caldwell Calhoun (enclosures: William C. Beard to John C. Carr, and Carr to Beard, June 18; Beard to Robert L. Coomb, June 9; Beard to H. A. Bullard, and Bullard to Beard, June 14; Beard to Eleazar W. Ripley, June 22; Ripley to Beard, July 9, and to John Dick, July 7, M221-86). LS in Richard K. Call's hand, DNA-RG 107 (M221-86); LC, DLC (63). *Calhoun Papers,* 4:172–73. Reports filibustering attempt on Texas.

July 24 To Eleazar Wheelock Ripley. LC, DLC (63); Copy, DNA-RG 107 (M221-86). Approves orders re the threatened invasion of Texas; cautions that the military must await request of civilian authority before acting.

July 26 From John Henry Eaton. ALS and Copy, DLC (27). In response to AJ's inquiry, states that he informed the Senate committee investigating the Florida invasion that AJ, who was in Washington, would answer committee queries; discusses the Senate report.

July 29 From Thomas Kirkman. ALS, DLC (27). Encloses invoice of Kirkman & Erwin for sundries purchased by AJ.

July 29 Deposition of James Craine Bronaugh re testimony on invasion of Florida. ADS, DLC (27); Copy with AJ endorsement, DNA-RG 46 (7-0822). *ASP, Military Affairs,* 1:766.

July 30 To William Berkeley Lewis. ALS, NNPM (7-0588). Discusses personal business involving Thomas Claiborne, James Jackson, AJ, and Lewis.

July 30 From Henry Atkinson. ALS, DLC (27). Reports on the Missouri expedition.

July 30 Deposition of Richard Keith Call re testimony on Florida invasion. ADS, DLC (27); Copy with AJ endorsement, DNA-RG 46 (7-0818). *ASP, Military Affairs,* 1:766.

July 31 *To Eleazar Wheelock Ripley.* 305

July 31 From John Caldwell Calhoun (enclosure: Callender Irvine to Calhoun, June 9, extract in DLC-27). LS with AJ endorsement forwarding a copy to Daniel Bissell requiring a report on charges against Eli B. Clemson, DLC (27); LC, DNA-RG 107 (M6-10). *Calhoun Papers,* 4:194–95. Reports investigation into charges of negligence against Clemson.

July 31 From John McKee. ALS, ICHi (7-0591). Reports that Choctaw negotiations may not be as successful as originally thought.

[cJuly 31] Notes re military road and draft of letter to Eleazar W. Ripley. AD, DLC (27).

Aug 1 *To James Gadsden.* 307

Aug 2 From George Gibson (enclosure: New York *National Advocate,* July 31, extract). ALS, DLC (27). Sends news clipping reporting that Spain is unlikely to ratify treaty with the United States for fear of alienating Great Britain.

Aug 2 Richard Keith Call to John Caldwell Calhoun (enclosures: Eleazar W. Ripley to AJ, July 12; AJ to Ripley, July 31; Alexander C. W. Fanning to AJ, April 26). ALS, DNA-RG 107 (M221-86); LC, DLC (63). On AJ's behalf forwards letters re military road and Fanning's letter re claim for double rations, which AJ supports.

Aug 4 To John McKee. LC, DLC (63). Expresses confidence that McKee will persuade the Choctaws to negotiate.

Aug 4 To Eleazar Wheelock Ripley. LC, DLC (63). Suggests following George Poindexter's recommendation of running military road through Columbia, Mississippi, if consistent with the public interest.

Aug 4 From Richard Mentor Johnson. ALS, DLC (27). *RegKyHi,* 39(1941):178–79. States that he has not lost support of the voters for defending AJ; regrets Henry Clay's course and attitude and urges AJ not to be rash; agrees to investigation of charges of malfeasance in supplying the Missouri expedition.

Aug 4 Deed to John Tait for 100 acres on Stone's River, Davidson County. Copy, TNDa (7-0593).

Aug 6 To Andrew Jackson Donelson (enclosure: AJ to Sylvanus Thayer, Aug 6). ALS, DLC (7-0595). Sends money, comments on the hard times, and urges him to room again with Joshua Baker (1799–1885).

Aug 6 To Sylvanus Thayer. ALS, NWM (7-0599). Requests that Andrew J.

Donelson and Joshua Baker (1799–1885) be allowed to room together again at West Point.

Aug 6 From Daniel Parker. LS, DLC (27); LC, DNA-RG 94 (M565-6). Informs AJ that the secretary of war intends to require economy in the quartermaster's department.

Aug 7 To [John Caldwell Calhoun]. Abstract, DNA-RG 107 (M22-12). Sends instructions to Edmund P. Gaines re possible capture of St. Augustine.

Aug 7 From David Holmes. ALS, DLC (27). Discusses debt of General John Thomas of Kentucky.

Aug 8 From Edward Livingston. Typed copy, DLC (72). Thanks AJ for his assistance in the purchase of horses for Bernard de Marigny; offers services in writing AJ's response to Senate report if the relevant documents are sent to him.

Aug 8 From John Williams Walker. ALS, DLC (27). Introduces Henry Hitchcock, Alabama secretary of state.

Aug 10 From John Caldwell Calhoun. LC, DNA-RG 107 (M7-1). *Calhoun Papers,* 4:224–26. Calls attention to irregularities in the medical department in Southern Division.

Aug 10 General order for the court-martial of William King. DS by Daniel Parker, DLC (27); LC, DNA-RG 98 (mAJs); Copy, DNA-RG 153 (mAJs).

Aug 11 From Daniel Parker. AL fragment (in clerk's hand), DLC (75); LC, DNA-RG 94 (7-0600). Transmits all war department vouchers and correspondence re William King's court-martial.

Aug 12 *Agreement with Malachi Nicholson.* 312

Aug 13 From Louis Alexis. ALS with AJ endorsement, DLC (27). Asks for certificate approving pay for powder which was remanufactured for the American troops in New Orleans.

Aug 13 *From John McKee.* 313

Aug 14 From Edmund Pendleton Gaines. ALS, DLC (27); AL draft fragment, DNA-RG 94 (7-0611). States that he will send proceedings of general court-martial of John M. Davis; reports that many leaders in Georgia do not sustain the Senate report on the Florida invasion.

Aug 17 *To William Berkeley Lewis.* 314

Aug 17 Robert Butler to Daniel Parker. LS, DNA-RG 94 (M566-119). Acknowledges Parker's letter to AJ of July 16 and others addressed to Butler; reports on travel plans of Richard I. Easter and on court-martial of Daniel Riddle.

Aug 17 Richard Keith Call to Edmund Pendleton Gaines (enclosure: Daniel Parker to AJ, Aug 6). ALS, DNA-RG 94 (M566-122); LC, DLC (63). On AJ's behalf, orders court-martial of John B. Hogan.

Aug 17 Richard Keith Call to John Benjamin Hogan. LC, DLC (63). On AJ's behalf, informs him of court-martial pursuant to his request of June 12.

Aug 17 Richard Keith Call to Eleazar Wheelock Ripley. LC, DLC (63). Forwards circular of the secretary of war re economy in the quartermaster department and recommends adoption of policy to effect it.

Aug 18 From John Clark. ALS, DLC (27). Bassett, 2:424–26 (extract). Reports that he hopes to publish his pamphlet on Crawford before Congress convenes; expresses regret that he has no further information on the cabinet disagreement re AJ's arrest; discusses the slave trade at Amelia Island.

Aug 18 From George Gibson. ALS with AJ endorsement, DLC (27). Reports that Abner Lacock and Nathan Towson are candidates for appointment as paymaster general, but that Towson will probably receive the nomination; reports consensus in Washington that Spain will ratify treaty with the United States.

Aug 18 From Arthur Peronneau Hayne. ALS, DLC (27). Urges AJ to request a year's leave of absence for his health; suggests that the Senate report has "exhalted" AJ's reputation; recommends John Duncan, his brother-in-law, as an aide.

Aug 18 From Daniel Parker. LS with AJ endorsement, DLC (27); LC, DNA-RG 94 (7-0620). On behalf of the secretary of war, asks that Daniel Bissell be ordered back to his command.

Aug 19 From Daniel Parker. LC, DNA-RG 94 (7-0621). Forwards additional documents for William King's court-martial.

Aug 19 From Eleazar Wheelock Ripley. ALS, DLC (27). Reports on the military road.

Aug 19 Richard Keith Call to Daniel Bissell (enclosure: Callender Irvine to John C. Calhoun, June 9, extract, DLC-27). LC, DLC (63). Asks that a report be made on charges against Eli B. Clemson.

Aug 20 To John Coffee. ALS, TMM (7-0629). Heiskell, 3:198. Congratulates him on the birth of Andrew Jackson Coffee and tells of company at the Hermitage.

Aug 20 To Joseph McMinn. ALS draft, LS copy in William B. Lewis's hand with corrections in AJ's hand (dated Aug 22), LS copy, DLC (27). Sends draft of report, depositions, and secret journal of the proceedings of the Chickasaw treaty.

Aug 20 From Edmund Pendleton Gaines (enclosures: Gaines to Robert Butler, Aug 20; Daniel Parker to Gaines, Aug 10, 11; Gaines to William King, Aug 20; Gaines to James E. Dinkins, Aug 20, DLC-27). ALS, DLC (27); Copy, DNA-RG 94 (7-0632). Reports King's arrest and progress of John B. Hogan's court-marital.

Aug 20 Eleazar Wheelock Ripley to Robert Butler (enclosure: Ripley to John C. Calhoun, Aug 20). ALS, DLC (27); Copy, DNA-RG 94 (mAJs). Encloses resignation and explains conduct re military road.

Aug 20 Eleazar Wheelock Ripley to John Caldwell Calhoun. ALS with AJ endorsement ordering him to Washington to settle accounts, and ALS duplicate, DNA-RG 94 (7-0622, -0625). Resigns army commission.

Aug 20 Edmund Pendleton Gaines to Robert Butler. ALS with AJ endorsement, DLC (27). Transmits correspondence re arrest of William King.

Aug 20 Deposition of William Berkeley Lewis re Chickasaw treaty and salt lick reserve. ADS and ADS Copy (dated Aug 24), DLC (27).

Aug 22 Robert Butler to Richard Ivy Easter. LC, DNA-RG 98 (mAJs). Orders him to Washington to settle accounts.

Aug 22 Division Order disapproving panel for court-martial of Stoughton Gantt. DS by Robert Butler, DNA-RG 153 (mAJs); LC, DNA-RG 98 (mAJs).

Aug 23 To Edward Livingston. ALS, NjP (mAJs). Bassett, 6:474. Expresses regret that he cannot recommend Livingston's son for secretary of Florida because he has already recommended Richard K. Call.

Aug 23 From Robert Butler. LS, DLC (27). *Nashville Whig,* Dec 22. Discusses the circumstances of the salt lick reserve under the Chickasaw treaty.

Aug 23 Deposition of George Bell, Boyd McNairy, and Thomas Eastland re salt lick reserve and Chickasaw treaty. ADS also signed by Bell and Eastland, and Copy, DLC (27, 28). *Nashville Whig,* Dec 22.

Aug 24 To John Caldwell Calhoun (enclosures: James Pitchlynn to AJ, June 22; John McKee to AJ, Aug 13; Council of the Choctaw Nation to James Monroe, Aug 12, DLC-27; AJ to Eleazar W. Ripley, Aug 24). LS, DNA-RG 75 (M271-2); LC (dated Aug 25, 1820), DLC (63). *Calhoun Papers,* 4:271–72, 5:336–37. Discusses the failed talks with the Choctaws and suggests that Indian affairs should be legislated rather than negotiated.

Aug 24 To Eleazar Wheelock Ripley. LC, DLC (63); Copy, DNA-RG 75 (M271-2). Informs him that treaty with Spain is not likely to be ratified and, because of Spanish "treachery and perfidy," directs him to defend Mobile and New Orleans.

Aug 25 *To James Jackson.* 316

Aug 25 To [Joseph McMinn] (enclosures: Depositions of William B. Lewis, Aug 20; of Richard K. Call, Aug 25; of Richard I. Easter, Aug 27; of George Bell, Boyd McNairy, and Thomas Eastland, Aug 23; James C. Bronaugh to AJ, Aug 26; Robert Butler to AJ, Aug 23; and Confidential Journal of Negotiations with the Chickasaw Indians, Sept 29, 1818). ALS draft, DLC (27). Bassett, 2:426. Transmits report re salt lick reserve of 1818 Chickasaw treaty.

Aug 25 Deposition of Richard Keith Call re salt lick reserve and the Chickasaw treaty. ADS with AJ endorsement, ADS copy (undated), ADS copy with AJ endorsement (dated Aug 27), DLC (27, 28). *Nashville Whig,* Dec 22.

Aug 26 From James Craine Bronaugh. ALS with AJ endorsement and Copy (dated Aug 24), DLC (27, 28). *Nashville Whig,* Dec 22. Discusses the salt lick reserve and the Chickasaw treaty.

Aug 27 To Edward Livingston (enclosure: Receipt of Samuel Cromwell, Aug 27). ALS, NjP (mAJs). Announces that horses purchased for Bernard de Marigny of New Orleans are in transit via Samuel Cromwell and requests payment of $440.25 for bill drawn on James Jackson.

Aug 27 From John Caldwell Calhoun (enclosures: Callender Irvine to Eli B. Clemson, June 4; Clemson to Irvine, July 4; Irvine to Calhoun, Aug 23, DLC-27). LS, DLC (27); LC, DNA-RG 107 (M6-10). Transmits letters, which strengthen Calhoun's impressions of Clemson's innocence.

Aug 27 Receipt of Samuel Cromwell for two horses to be delivered to New Orleans for Bernard de Marigny. AD in AJ's hand, signed by Cromwell and John H. Eaton as witnesses, NjP (mAJs).

Aug 27	Deposition of Richard Ivy Easter re salt lick reserve and Chickasaw treaty. ADS with AJ endorsement and Copy, DLC (27). *Nashville Whig,* Dec 22.	
Aug 28	From Samuel Swartwout. ALS with AJ endorsement, DLC (72). Introduces Adolphus Loss.	
Aug 28	Deed to Daniel Cherry for lot in Gallatin, Tennessee. ADS, TGSum (7-0636).	
Aug 29	From William White Crawford. ALS, Mrs. H. A. Brewer (mAJs). Reports on expenses for transporting corn and cotton seed from Melton's Bluff to Florence, Alabama.	
Aug 30	Account of Rachel Jackson with Richmond & Flint for a gold watch. ADS, DLC (27).	
[cAug 30]	To Louis Alexis. AL draft, DLC (27). States that accounts for the remanufacture of powder at New Orleans ought to be paid; suggests that his letter be sent to Washington in support of payment.	
Aug 31	Milo Mason to Robert Butler. ALS, DLC (27). Reports his arrival in Rhode Island in accordance with AJ's order.	
Aug 31	Division order confirming the sentence in the court-martial of John M. Davis. DSs by Robert Butler, DNA-RG 153 (mAJs), DNA-RG 94 (M566-119); LC, DNA-RG 98 (mAJs).	
[cAug 31]	To Robert Butler. LS with revisions and postscript in AJ's hand, DLC (28). Confirms the sentence of John M. Davis and transmits documents and orders convening court-martial of William King.	
Sept 1	From Eleazar Wheelock Ripley. LS, DLC (27); Copy, DNA-RG 107 (M221-86). Discusses supply problems encountered with the military road.	
Sept 2	Division order for the court-martial of William King. DS by Robert Butler, DNA-RG 94 (M566-123).	
Sept 4	From Edmund Pendleton Gaines. LS, DLC (27); AL draft, DNA-RG 94 (7-0608). Reports that he will enforce the war department circular demanding economy; contradicts John B. Hogan's statement that he has endured a long detention without being court-martialed.	
Sept 6	From Henry Atkinson (enclosure: Thomas Biddle to Atkinson, Aug 24, DLC-26). ALS, DLC (27). Reports on the Missouri expedition; blames steamboats for delay.	
Sept 7	To John Caldwell Calhoun. LS, THi (7-0639); LC, DLC (63). *Calhoun Papers,* 4:304–306. Encloses report of James C. Bronaugh (not found) and states that he did not intend division orders to interfere with reporting to the surgeon general; discusses William King's court-martial and anticipated charges against Eleazar W. Ripley.	
Sept 7	To John Caldwell Calhoun. LC, DLC (63). *Calhoun Papers,* 4:306. Encloses letter from James Morris of Kentucky (not found) and states that sample of gunpowder supplied by Dr. Boswell is of superior quality.	
Sept 7	*To George Gibson.*	318
Sept 7	From Richard Ivy Easter. ALS, DLC (27). Discusses a publication reputedly written by John P. Erwin.	
Sept 7	From Lewis Livingston. ALS, DLC (27). Asks for a military appointment should war erupt with Spain.	

Sept 8 — To George Gibson. ALS, DNA-RG 192 (7-0646). Encloses letter from William Carroll (not found).

Sept 8 — From George Washington Campbell. AL fragment, DLC (75). Reports the death of his three eldest children from a fever; discusses Russian attitudes toward Spanish-American affairs; describes St. Petersburg and Moscow.

Sept 8 — From John Rhea. ALS, DLC (27). Expresses regret that he will not be able to see AJ in Nashville.

Sept 8 — Division order requiring surgeons to report to the surgeon general in Washington and to division headquarters. Printed, DLC (70); LC, DNA-RG 98 (mAJs).

Sept 9 — *To Richard Keith Call.* 319

Sept 9 — From Joseph McMinn. ALS, DLC (27). States that he has examined the secret journal of the Chickasaw negotiation and concluded that AJ did not know of William B. Lewis's salt lease until it was completed; suggests that AJ prepare a statement that will not reveal the existence of the journal.

Sept 9 — Receipt from Stockley Donelson Hutchings for $33 for enclosing grave of John Hutchings. ADS, THi (7-0653).

Sept 10 — To James Monroe. LS, Paul Banks (7-0655). Reports death of John Childress, marshal for West Tennessee, and recommends delay in appointing a replacement.

Sept 11 — From Eleazar Wheelock Ripley. ALS, DLC (27); Copy, DNA-RG 107 (M221-86). Reports a six-month delay in receiving orders from Daniel Parker; announces again his resignation and intention to proceed to Washington to settle accounts.

Sept 11 — Robert Butler to Daniel Parker. ALS, DNA-RG 94 (mAJs); LC, DNA-RG 98 (mAJs). Forwards Eleazar W. Ripley's resignation and states that he will forward copies of correspondence with Ripley re military road.

Sept 11 — Robert Butler to Eleazar Wheelock Ripley (enclosures: Division order, Sept 8; Order to James B. Many, Sept 11, DNA-RG 94). Copies, DNA-RG 94 (mAJs), DNA-RG 98 (mAJs). Acknowledges resignation; orders him to turn over command to officer next in rank, to send report on military road, and to proceed to Washington to close accounts.

Sept 12 — To Abram Maury. Abstract, Carnegie Book Shop Catalog 333, Item 229 (7-0657). Recommends [Francis W.] Brady for a clerkship in the Tennessee Senate.

[cSept 12] — From James Craine Bronaugh. ALS, DLC (59). Discusses possible duel between John H. Eaton and Andrew Erwin.

Sept 13 — *To Joseph McMinn.* 321

Sept 13 — To James Monroe. LS, NN (7-0658). Discusses vacancy in West Tennessee marshalcy.

Sept 13 — From James Pitchlynn. ALS, DNA-RG 107 (M221-86). Bassett, 2:429. Discusses divisions among the Choctaws re removal and negotiations with the United States.

Sept 15 — From James Monroe. ALS, DLC (mAJs). Reports that his health is improved and that the depositions included in AJ's of July 23 (not found) have been forwarded to John Q. Adams to "promote the object intended by you"; expresses hope that Spain will soon ratify the treaty with the United States.

Sept 16 From James Craine Bronaugh. ALS, DLC (27). Sends report (not found) on the health of troops.

Sept 16 From Edmund Pendleton Gaines (enclosure: Mathew Arbuckle to Gaines, Sept 5, extract, DLC-27). ALS, DLC (27); ALS copy, DNA-RG 94 (7-0664). Inquires about the disposition of cattle refused by the Creek Indians.

Sept 16 Receipt from Edmond Cooper for $65 payment on subscription to Masonic Hall, Nashville. AD in AJ's hand, signed by Cooper, DSC (7-0662).

Sept 17 *To Andrew Jackson Donelson.* 322

[Sept] 18 *To John Clark.* 323

Sept 21 To [Unknown]. Abstract, Joseph Rubinfine, Catalog 77 (Feb 1984), Item 34 (7-0671). States that receipts must be submitted to the secretary of war.

Sept 22 To James Monroe. AD (address page only), DNA-RG 59 (M439-13). Recommends Robert Purdy for marshal.

Sept 22 Robert Butler to Daniel Parker. ALS, DNA-RG 94 (M566-123); LC, DNA-RG 98 (mAJs). Transmits correspondence among AJ, Eleazar W. Ripley, and Perrin Willis re military road and other matters.

Sept 23 From Samuel Bunch. ALS with AJ endorsement and Copy, DLC (27); Copy, DNA-RG 46 (7-0673). *ASP, Military Affairs,* 1:769. Reports on his service during 1812–13 in East Florida under John Williams.

Sept 23 From Pleasant Moorman Miller. ALS with AJ endorsement and Copy, DLC (27); Copy, DNA-RG 46 (7-0676). *ASP, Military Affairs,* 1:769. Reports on his service in East Florida under John Williams.

Sept 23 From Hugh Young. Copy, DNA-RG 107 (M222-21). Outlines objectives of the topographical engineers in the South.

Sept 23 Robert Butler to Daniel Parker. ALS, DNA-RG 94 (M566-123); LC, DNA-RG 98 (mAJs). Transmits correspondence re military road and other matters.

Sept 24 *From James Houston.* 325

Sept 24 From Eleazar Wheelock Ripley (enclosure: Department order promulgating the proceedings in courts-martial of William C. Beard and German Senter, April 14, DLC-26). ALS, DLC (27). Reports on courts-martial of Beard, Senter, and Daniel Riddle.

Sept 25 To Samuel Swartwout. LS, DLC (75). States that Adolphus Loss may not find employment in Tennessee as a surveyor but that John Coffee may need a deputy.

Sept 25 *To William Williams.* 325

Sept 25 From John Brown (1779–1843). ALS with AJ endorsement, DLC (27). States that John Williams, like AJ, wants to renew their friendship.

Sept 25 From [Daniel Parker]. LC, DNA-RG 94 (7-0679). On behalf of John C. Calhoun, acknowledges AJ's letters, directs that no volunteers be called out at present re Spanish affairs, and discusses courts-martial of William King and John B. Hogan.

Sept 26 Memorandum of a conversation between James L. Armstrong and

	Theodorick Fowlk Bradford. ADS in AJ's hand, DLC (27). Recounts conversation wherein Bradford admitted that he, not Andrew Erwin, authored an attack against John H. Eaton.
Sept 27	From James Gadsden. ALS with AJ endorsement regarding slaves of John Hutchings's estate, DLC (27). States that the information re the Clay-Crawford intrigue to injure James Monroe came to him confidentially and the informant refuses to allow the use of his name.
Sept 29	To Joseph McMinn (enclosures: AJ to Isaac Shelby, Aug 11, 1818; AJ and Shelby to John C. Calhoun, Oct 30, 1818). ALS copy, DLC (27). Sends letters that should have been annexed to his report on the Chickasaw treaty and salt lick reserve.
Sept 29	*To James Monroe.* 330
Sept 30	To John Caldwell Calhoun (enclosure: Samuel Houston to AJ, Sept 30). LS, DNA-RG 94 (M566-122); ALS copy, DLC (27). *Calhoun Papers,* 4:354–55. Recommends Samuel Houston as Cherokee agent in Arkansas.
Sept 30	To [Unknown]. Printed extract, Thomas S. Woodward, *Woodward's Reminiscences of the Creek, or Muscogee Indians* (Montgomery, Ala., 1859), p. 5 (mAJs). Commends Woodward as "a brave, intrepid and gallant soldier."
Sept 30	From Richard Ivy Easter. ALS, DLC (27). Reports that he has called on David Meriwether, who will furnish his letter to the secretary of war, and that Easter will see John Clark on the latter's return to Milledgeville; discusses the circumstances of the court-martial of John M. Davis.
Sept 30	From Samuel Houston. ALS, DNA-RG 94 (M566-122). Requests recommendation as Cherokee agent.
Sept 30	From Thomas and Ann Puckett. ALS with AJ endorsement, DLC (27). Inquire about slaves captured after the massacre at Fort Mimms.
Oct 1	Account with United States for services as major general, Southern Division. DS with insertions in AJ's hand, DNA-RG 217 (7-0696). Runs to December 31.
Oct 2	*To Robert Young Hayne.* 333
Oct 2	To James Monroe. Extract, NN (7-0701). Expresses hope that the treaty with Spain has been ratified but also urges preparation "for any emergency."
Oct 2	From John M. Davis. ALS with AJ endorsement stating that upon official notification of Micajah Crupper's reinstatement, he will remit Davis's punishment and restore him to command, DLC (27). Discusses his court-martial and requests a review of the case.
Oct 2	Richard Keith Call to John Caldwell Calhoun (enclosures: Eleazar W. Ripley to AJ, Sept 1, 11; James Pitchlynn to AJ, Sept 13). ALS, DNA-RG 107 (M221-86). Sends copies of letters.
Oct 3	From Henry Atkinson. ALS, DLC (27). Nichols, *Missouri Expedition,* p. 114. Reports arrival of the Missouri expedition near the Council Bluffs.
Oct 4	To John Caldwell Calhoun. Abstract, DNA-RG 107 (M22-13). Discusses Robert Butler's account.
Oct 4	From Edmund Pendleton Gaines (enclosures: Duncan L. Clinch to

José Coppinger, Aug 29, Sept 25; Deposition of Rosalia Damberville, Aug 23; Coppinger to Clinch, Sept 13; Gaines to Clinch, Oct 4, all DLC-27). ALS, DLC (27); ALS draft, DNA-RG 94 (M566-118). Forwards documents re attack on Damberville by Theophilus Williams, James Ennis, and others, and discusses arrangements for their trial.

Oct 4 — From Edmund Pendleton Gaines. ALS, DLC (27); AL draft, DNA-RG 94 (7-0703). Sends proceedings of court-martial of John B. Hogan and asks decision thereon; reports that he is still seeking information on David B. Mitchell, an "abandoned calumniator."

Oct 7 — To James Monroe. ALS, NN (7-0707). Encloses letter from John Brahan (not found) and recommends William Atwood as U.S. marshal in Alabama.

Oct 8 — *To John Brown (1779–1843).* 335

Oct 8 — To John Caldwell Calhoun (enclosures: Henry Atkinson to AJ, Oct 6; Thomas Biddle to Atkinson, Aug 24, DLC-26). ALS, Robert V. Remini (mAJs); ALS copy, DLC (63). *Calhoun Papers,* 4:367–68. Transmits letters re Missouri expedition and relations with the Pawnee Indians.

Oct 8 — To James Monroe. Abstract, Thomas F. Madigan, *The Autograph* (1929), p. 43 (7-0710). Encloses letter from Robert F. Crittenden (not found) and recommends him as register of the land office in Arkansas Territory.

Oct 10 — From James Gadsden. ALS, DLC (27). Discusses their friendship, Gadsden's arduous duties, and his financial problems.

Oct 12 — To Andrew Jackson Donelson. ALS, DLC (7-0712). Relates that he has heard from Edward G. W. Butler but not him; sends $100 and advises him on his future course.

Oct 12 — To Edmund Pendleton Gaines. LS, NHpR (7-0716); AL copy signed by proxy, DLC (27). Suggests that the Talladega Indians will probably want the cattle Gaines wrote about on September 16, although he is authorized to sell them if necessary.

Oct 16 — From John Brown (1779–1843). ALS, DLC (28). Bassett, 2:438. Apologizes for his misunderstanding in trying to renew friendship between AJ and John Williams.

Oct 17 — Edmund Pendleton Gaines to John Caldwell Calhoun (enclosures: David B. Mitchell to Gaines, Oct 7, 1817; Gaines to David E. Twiggs, Nov 20, 1817; Twiggs to Gaines, Nov 21, 1817; Daniel E. Burch to Twiggs, Oct 6; Twiggs to Gaines, Oct 7, all in DLC-27). LS copy endorsed "copy for Major Genl. Jackson," DLC (28). *ASP, Military Affairs,* 2:125–30. Vindicates his conduct in the Seminole War and attacks David B. Mitchell.

[Oct 19] — From Josiah Meigs. LC, DNA-RG 49 (7-0718). Sends patents for land in Franklin County, Alabama.

Oct 20 — From David Brearley. ALS, DLC (28). States that he will forward his recollections on the conduct of David B. Mitchell and William Bowen as soon as possible.

Oct 20 — From David Brearley (enclosure: Charges and specifications against Edmund P. Gaines, Oct 20). ALS, DLC (28); Copy, DNA-RG 107 (M221-84). Encloses charges against Gaines and requests his arrest.

Oct 20 Charges and specifications by David Brearley against Edmund Pendleton Gaines. DS, DLC (28); DS copy with revisions in Brearley's hand, DNA-RG 107 (M221-84).

Oct 21 *From John Overton.* 336

Oct 22 Ezra Stiles Ely to Rachel Jackson. ALS, DLC (28). Thanks her for hospitality at the Hermitage and expresses his hope that AJ will become a Christian; sends her the first volume of his *Quarterly Theological Review.*

Oct 23 From David Brearley (enclosure: Revised charges against Edmund P. Gaines, Oct 20). ALS, DLC (28). Sends duplicate with revisions of charges and specifications against Gaines.

Oct 23 From Stockley Donelson Hays. Extracts, DNA-RG 94 (M566-118), DNA-RG 107 (M222-21). Reports that he believes the treaty with Spain will not be ratified and that there is evidence of a Spanish buildup in Pensacola.

Oct 27 From Stockley Donelson Hays. ALS, DLC (28). Reports on yellow fever in Mobile area and on his intention to proceed to Cantonment Montpelier, where he will await Daniel Bissell and the commencement of the court-martial of William King.

Oct 27 Reuben Humphreys to Robert Butler. LS, DLC (28). Requests instructions on expenditure of public funds.

Oct 28 From James Gadsden. ALS, DLC (28). Suggests that the United States must occupy Spanish territory if the treaty with Spain is rejected and that he and Lewis Livingston be selected for AJ's staff.

Oct 28 Account with William White Crawford for services as overseer from September 15, 1818, to October 15, 1819, for AJ and as Andrew Jackson Hutchings's guardian. AD signed by Crawford, THi (6-1298).

Oct Confidential Report by Arthur Peronneau Hayne on the Southern Division of the Army for 1819. ADS, DNA-RG 159 (mAJs); ADS copy, DNA-RG 94 (mAJs).

Nov 2 From William Bradford. ALS, DNA-RG 107 (M221-86). Reports that he has almost settled the hostility between the Cherokee and Osage Indians.

Nov 2 From John Clark (enclosure: Deposition of Thomas Moore, n.d.). ALS with AJ endorsement to be "filed and carefully preserved," DLC (28). Thanks him for pamphlet by "A Citizen of Tennessee," discusses progress on his own publication, and encloses Moore's statement re cabinet division over AJ's arrest.

Nov 3 From Elbert Woodward. Copy, DNA-RG 107 (M222-21). Reports the repair of the Barrancas.

Nov 6 From James Gadsden. ALS, DLC (28); Copy, DNA-RG 107 (M221-86). Reports on the defenses of Mobile Point and proposes plan to correct situation.

Nov 7 From Edmund Pendleton Gaines (enclosure: James E. Dinkins to Gaines, Oct 22, DLC-28). ALS, DLC (28); AL draft, DNA-RG 94 (M566-119; 7-0845); Copy, DNA-RG 107 (M222-21). Reports strengthening of Pensacola's defenses and requests four companies of artillery for southern border.

Nov 7 From [Thomas Sidney Jesup?]. AL, DLC (7-0841). Advocates the seizure of Florida, Cuba, and a port on the coast of Africa if Spain fails to ratify treaty with the United States.

Nov 8 From James Gadsden. ALS, DLC (28). Thanks AJ for his advice on the collectorship at Pensacola and again expresses a desire for joint service in the event of war with Spain; discusses joint purchase of lots in Florence, Alabama.

[Nov 9] From Howell Rose et al. (enclosure: Resolutions of the Alabama legislature). LS, DLC (20). *Nashville Whig,* Nov 24. Send resolutions praising AJ's career and service to the country.

Nov 9 To Howell Rose et al. LS, NjP (7-0848). *Nashville Whig,* Nov 24. Thanks the Alabama legislature for resolutions.

Nov 9 Resolutions of the Alabama legislature commending AJ's military career. AD, DLC (20). *Nashville Whig,* Nov 24.

Nov 9 Bill of sale for the slave Eli from John Brahan to John Overton. DS by AJ as witness, THi (7-0724).

Nov 9 Receipt to John Coffee and Stockley Donelson Hutchings for payments from the estate of John Hutchings. DS also signed by Catherine Hutchings, Mrs. Richard H. Gilliam, Jr. (7-0847).

Nov 10 From Robert Young Hayne. Printed, (DLC-72) Bassett, 6:474–75. Thanks AJ for pamphlet by "A Citizen of Tennessee"; urges him to visit South Carolina and expresses the hope that John H. Eaton and Andrew Erwin have avoided a duel.

Nov 10 From Alexander A. White. ALS, DLC (28). Asks for recommendation as agent to the Caddo Indians.

Nov 12 Zachary Taylor to Robert Butler. ALS with AJ endorsement first granting then denying request, DLC (28). Asks permission to remain at Louisville until the Ohio River is navigable, so that he can move family to New Orleans.

Nov 15 To John Caldwell Calhoun. Copy, DNA-RG 92 (7-0855). Recommends Joseph Kingsbury as assistant deputy quartermaster.

Nov 15 To John Caldwell Calhoun (enclosures: Confidential report of Arthur P. Hayne, Oct; Hugh Young to AJ, Sept 23; Charges and specifications by David Brearley against Edmund P. Gaines, Oct 20; Richard K. Call to AJ, Nov 15). LS with postscript in AJ's hand, DNA-RG 107 (M221-86); LC, DLC (63); Extract, DNA-RG 92 (7-0852). *Calhoun Papers,* 4:410–11. Transmits and supports reports of Hayne, Young, and Call; calls Brearley's charges against Gaines "vexatious"; laments lack of supplies for completion of military road.

Nov 15 From Richard Keith Call. ALS, DNA-RG 107 (M221-86). Reports on the military road.

Nov 15 Deed to William Edward Butler transferring AJ's interest in the John Ramsay claim. ADS, THi (7-0850).

Nov 16 To David Brearley. LC, DLC (63). States that he has forwarded the charges against Edmund P. Gaines to the war department.

Nov 16 To Andrew Jackson Donelson. ALS, DLC (7-0863). Chastises him for not writing.

Nov 16 To James Monroe. ALS, NN (7-0867). Bassett, 2:439–40. Reports on his investigation of the military road; discusses the failure of Spain to ratify the treaty and his desire to retire.

Nov 16 To James Monroe. ALS, DLC (7-0871). Asks for clemency for an "unfortunate youth."

Nov 17 From James Houston. ALS with AJ endorsement "that if funds could be [secured] I would take them—an answer final as soon as I could hear from Florence," DLC (28). Bassett, 2:440. Describes the family of the slave Peter whom AJ hoped to reunite.

Nov 17 From Hugh Young. ALS, DLC (28). Reports that the survey along the Gulf Coast has been hampered by a lack of boats.

Nov 19 To Robert Butler. ALS, DLC (28). Sends proceedings of the court-martial of John B. Hogan with instructions for drafting the order approving same; discusses Reuben Humphreys's requests for pay procedures.

Nov 19 Robert Butler to Reuben Humphreys. LC in Butler's hand, DNA-RG 98 (mAJs). Explains pay procedures.

Nov [19] Division order (dated Nov 18) approving proceedings in the court-martial of John B. Hogan. DS by Robert Butler, DNA-RG 153 (mAJs); LC, DNA-RG 98 (mAJs).

Nov 20 From James Gadsden. ALS, DNA-RG 107 (M221-86). Discusses the need for a road from New Orleans to Chef Menteur.

Nov 20 Robert Butler to Henry Atkinson. LC, DNA-RG 98 (mAJs). Conveys AJ's approbation of the Missouri expedition.

Nov 20 Robert Butler to Zachary Taylor. LC, DNA-RG 98 (mAJs). States that he will submit Taylor's request for delay to AJ, but notes that 8th Military Department is short of officers.

Nov 21 To Andrew Jackson Donelson. ALS, THi (7-0873). Bassett, 2:440–42. Again urges him to write and points out the advantages of regular communication.

Nov 21 From James Gadsden. ALS, DLC (28). Discusses contractors' failure to provide supplies; pronounces pamphlet by "A Citizen of Tennessee" an "able vindication."

Nov 21 Memorandum by Robert Butler re submission of the record of the court-martial of John Benjamin Hogan to Daniel Parker. LC, DNA-RG 98 (mAJs).

Nov 22 To John Caldwell Calhoun (enclosures: Stockley D. Hays to AJ, Oct 20, extract; James E. Dinkins to Edmund P. Gaines, Oct 22, M222-21; Elbert Woodward to AJ, Nov 3; Gaines to AJ, Nov 7). LS, DNA-RG 107 (M222-21); LC, DLC (63). *Calhoun Papers,* 4:425–26. Sends information on situation at Pensacola and Mobile Point and on defense preparations.

Nov 22 To James Edward Dinkins. Copy, DNA-RG 94 (M566-118); LC, DLC (63). Directs him, if ordered by the commanding officer at Fort Bowyer, to march a portion of his forces to defend Mobile Point.

Nov 22 To the Commanding Officer of Fort Bowyer. LS, AMobM (7-0877); LC, DLC (63). Exhorts him to keep a close watch on the Spanish and to request military assistance from James E. Dinkins if needed.

Nov 22 To Edmund Pendleton Gaines (enclosures: Stockley D. Hays to AJ, Oct 20, extract; AJ to James E. Dinkins, Nov 22). LS, DNA-RG 94 (M566-118); LC, DLC (63). Informs him of orders to Dinkins and the commander at Fort Bowyer.

Nov 22 To James Monroe. ALS, NN (7-0881). Bassett, 2:442. Transmits

	Thomas Moore's deposition and mentions documents published in the Milledgeville *Georgia Journal* substantiating the Amelia slave trade rumor.	
Nov 22	*From Thomas Jefferson.*	337
Nov 22	*From Christopher Vandeventer.*	338
Nov 22	Resolutions of the Tennessee legislature commending AJ's and Edmund P. Gaines's conduct in Florida. Printed, *Journal of the Senate of Tennessee* (Murfreesboro, [1819]), pp. 109–110 (mAJs).	
Nov 23	To John Clark. ALS, DLC (28). Bassett, 2:442–43 (extract). Congratulates him on election as governor of Georgia and on his information regarding the Amelia Island slave trade.	
Nov 23	To William Berkeley Lewis. ALS, NN (7-0895). *New York Public Library Bulletin,* 4(1900):161–62. Asks him to retrieve documents from the Tennessee legislature re the salt lick reserve for appending to answer to the Senate committee report on the Florida invasion.	
Nov 23	From Henry Atkinson. ALS, DLC (28); Copy, DNA-RG 107 (M221-86). Nichols, *Missouri Expedition,* pp. 117–18 (extract). Reports establishment of military post at the Council Bluffs.	
Nov 25	From Richard Ivy Easter. ALS, DLC (28). States that he awaits the arrival of his accounts in Washington; relates rumor that Spain has ratified the treaty and discusses gubernatorial election in Georgia.	
Nov 25	From George Gibson. ALS, DLC (28). Reports news that treaty has not been ratified; discusses his health and that of John C. Calhoun.	
Nov 27	Robert Butler to Edmund Pendleton Gaines. LC, DNA-RG 98 (mAJs). Remits sentence imposed on John M. Davis.	
Nov 29	*To John Henry Eaton.*	339
Nov 29	*To James Monroe.*	342
Nov 29	From John Clark (enclosure: Deposition of Thomas Moore, n.d.). ALS with AJ endorsement, DLC (28). Acknowledges pamphlet sent by AJ and arrangements for republication in Georgia; discusses progress on his pamphlet and sends another copy of Moore's statement.	
Nov 30	To John Caldwell Calhoun. LS, DNA-RG 94 (M566-115). Recommends Thomas J. Ayer for army appointment.	
[Nov]	Receipt from Z. Tate, collector of taxes for Lauderdale County, for $18.75, paid by AJ as guardian for Andrew Jackson Hutchings. ADS with AJ endorsement, A-Ar (7-0726).	
[Nov]	Memorandum on the Florida campaign. AD fragment, DLC (59).	
Dec 1	From David Brearley. LS, DLC (28). Discusses the conduct of Creek agent David B. Mitchell and William Bowen during the winter of 1817–18.	
Dec 1	From Daniel Parker. LS, DLC (28); LC, DNA-RG 94 (7-0903). Advises that the president desires continuation of John M. Davis's pay during suspension.	
Dec 2	From Edmund Pendleton Gaines (enclosures: Micajah Crupper to Gaines, Nov 12 and 28). ALS draft, DNA-RG 94 (M566-117). Transmits letters re sale of cattle taken from Seminole Indians.	
Dec 3	To Andrew Jackson Donelson. ALS, DLC (7-0904). Acknowledges letter of November 7 (not found) and urges continued correspondence.	

Dec 3	From David Brearley (enclosure: Brearley to AJ, Dec 1). ALS with AJ endorsement, DLC (28). Transmits letter.
Dec 3	From William White Crawford. ALS, DLC (28). Reports on the damage to AJ's Alabama cotton gin and on the corn and cotton harvest.
Dec 3	From James Gadsden. ALS with AJ endorsement, DLC (28). Complains about contractors; inquires about Florence and Cypress Land Company stock.
Dec 4	To Arthur Peronneau Hayne. LS with postscript in AJ's hand, UkENL (7-0907). Washington *National Intelligencer,* Jan 17, 1820 (lacking postscript). Responds to news that William Laval is a candidate for sheriff of the Charleston District; informs Hayne of his intention to retire once his memorial to Congress is acted upon.
Dec 5	To John Caldwell Calhoun (enclosures: William Bradford to AJ, Nov 2; James Gadsden to AJ, Nov 20). LS, DNA-RG 107 (M221-86); LC draft (dated Nov 1819), DLC (63). Transmits letters re the salt springs and the military road.
Dec 5	From Henry Atkinson. ALS, DLC (28). Reports on the status of the Missouri expedition.
Dec 5	From Edmund Pendleton Gaines (enclosures: Gaines to John C. Calhoun, Dec 4; John Clark to Gaines, Nov 30; Thomas E. Hardee to Clark, Nov 11; A. B. Sheehee to Clark, Nov 24; John Nicks to Gaines, Nov 23, extract; Duncan L. Clinch to Gaines, Nov 27, extract, all DLC-28). ALS draft, DNA-RG 94 (7-0911). States that he has received the orders through Christopher Vandeventer concerning the possible invasion of Florida and awaits AJ's orders.
Dec 6	From William Bradford. ALS, DLC (28). Introduces Talbot Chambers and requests to be ordered to Washington to settle his accounts.
Dec 7	From William Bradford. LS, DNA-RG 107 (M221-86). Reports on western Cherokees.
Dec 7	From Daniel Parker. LS with AJ endorsement ordering Robert Butler to issue necessary orders, DLC (28); LC (dated Dec 8), DNA-RG 94 (7-0913). Encloses copy of the paymaster general's report (not found) and on behalf of Calhoun asks that several orders concerning payments be issued.
Dec 8	From Henry Atkinson (enclosures: Talbot Chambers to Atkinson, Dec 8; John Whistler to [Chambers], Dec 1; James McGunnegle to Chambers, Dec 7, DNA-RG 107, M221-86). ALS, DLC (28). Discusses Chambers's accounts; sends statements on Eli B. Clemson's conduct.
Dec 8	From Edmund Pendleton Gaines (enclosure: Gaines to John C. Calhoun, Dec 8). ALS draft, DNA-RG 94 (M566-119). Transmits copy of request for tools for entrenching in reoccupation of Florida.
Dec 10	To James Monroe. ALS, NN (7-0914); ALS draft, DLC (28). Bassett, 2:446–47. Acknowledges confidential orders of November 22 from Christopher Vandeventer, relates that necessary orders have been issued, and recommends staff appointments of James Gadsden and Lewis Livingston.
Dec 11	*To John Caldwell Calhoun.* 344
Dec 11	Richard Keith Call to Edmund Pendleton Gaines (enclosure: Christo-

pher Vandeventer to AJ, Nov 22). LC, DLC (63). Transmits copy of Vandeventer's letter and directs preparations to carry the order into effect.

Dec 11 Robert Butler to Zachary Taylor. LC, DNA-RG 98 (mAJs). Orders him to proceed to post without delay.

Dec 12 From James Monroe. ALS, DLC (28). Bassett, 2:447–48. Details relations with Spain and requests AJ not to resign from army.

Dec 12 Richard Keith Call to James B. Many (enclosure: Christopher Vandeventer to AJ, Nov 22). LC, DLC (63); Copy, DNA-RG 107 (M221-86). Transmits copy of Vandeventer's letter and directs preparations to carry the order into effect.

Dec 13 Richard Keith Call to John Symington. LC, DLC (63). Orders preparations for invasion of Florida.

Dec 14 From James Johnson (enclosures: James Johnson to Richard M. Johnson, Sept 20; Talbot Chambers to James Johnson, May 20, 22, 23; Chambers to Daniel Bissell, May 21; James Johnson to Chambers, May 22, 23, 24; John Whistler to James Johnson, May 23; Deposition of Levi Craig, Nov 22; William Stackpole and Regiles Whiting to John C. Calhoun, Nov 20, DLC-27). ALS, DLC (28). *RegKyHi*, 35(1937):320. Transmits correspondence.

Dec 14 Report on the memorials of Thomas Carr, John A. Heard, and AJ. AD draft, DNA-RG 233 (7-0918). *ASP, Public Lands*, 3:416–18. Reports favorably on claims for land in the bend of the Tennessee River and suggests Alabama as site for compensation.

Dec 15 From James Gadsden. ALS, DLC (28). Discusses the Spanish treaty, the military status in Florida, and land purchased in Florence.

Dec 15 From Edmund Pendleton Gaines (enclosure: Gaines to John C. Calhoun, with estimate of supplies for the 9th Military Department, Dec 15, DLC-28). ALS draft, DNA-RG 94 (7-0929). Transmits copy of his letter to the secretary of war re invasion of Florida.

Dec 15 From Arthur Peronneau Hayne. ALS, DLC (28). Reports on the inspection of troops and fortifications in Charleston and his plans for inspections elsewhere.

Dec 18 Robert Butler to Daniel Parker. LC, DNA-RG 98 (mAJs). States that John M. Davis was restored to command and pay by order of November 27.

Dec 21 Account with Rapier & Simpson for sundries. ADS, THer (7-0931). Runs to January 30, 1821.

Dec 22 Receipt from Malachi Nicholson for pork consumed on Andrew Jackson Hutchings's farm. AD in AJ's hand signed by Nicholson with AJ endorsement, THi (7-0933).

Dec 22 Daniel Parker to [Robert Butler]. LS, DNA (28); LC, DNA-RG 98 (mAJs). Accepts Eleazar W. Ripley's resignation.

Dec 23 From Daniel Bissell. ALS, DLC (28). Reports receipt of AJ's orders of December 12 (not found), those of the secretary of war of November 22, and the steps he has taken to implement them.

Dec 24 From John Caldwell Calhoun. LS, DLC (28); LC and Copy, DNA-RG 107 (M7-1, 7-0939); Copy, DNA-RG 94 (7-0935). Bassett, 2:449. Asks for report on the number and distribution of the troops of the Southern Division and a plan of campaign for probable invasion of Florida.

Dec 24 From John Caldwell Calhoun (enclosure: Calhoun to James Gadsden, Dec 24, DLC-28). LS, DLC (28); LC (dated Dec 1819), DNA-RG 107 (M6-10). *Calhoun Papers,* 4:506. Authorizes construction of road between Chef Menteur and New Orleans, as suggested by Gadsden.

Dec 25 *From John Henry Eaton.* 345

Dec 26 From Abraham L. Sands. ALS, DLC (28). Regrets that in the event of war he will be unable to serve under AJ because he is in St. Croix, Michigan Territory, to settle an estate.

Dec 27 To John Caldwell Calhoun (enclosure: James Gadsden to AJ, Nov 6). LS, DNA-RG 107 (M221-86); LC, DLC (63). Reports the defenselessness of Fort Bowyer.

Dec 27 From Charles Cassedy. ALS, DLC (28). Details claim of Mad Wolf to women and children taken during Creek campaign.

Dec 28 To John Caldwell Calhoun (enclosure: William King to AJ, Feb 4; Proceedings of court-martial of King, DNA-RG 153, mAJs). LS, DNA-RG 153 (7-0942); LC, DLC (63); Extracts, DNA-RG 233 (7-0946, -0948). *ASP, Military Affairs,* 2:186, 198 (extract). Transmits proceedings.

Dec 28 To John Henry Eaton. Printed, Parton, 2:671–72 (7-0950). Discusses AJ's memorial to the Senate.

Dec 29 Robert Butler to Daniel Parker. LC, DNA-RG 98 (mAJs). Transmits proceedings of court-martial of William King for the president's confirmation.

Dec 30 To Henry Atkinson. LC, DLC (63). Expresses satisfaction with his conduct of the Missouri expedition.

Dec 30 To Andrew Jackson Donelson. ALS, DLC (7-0953). Pauline Wilcox Burke, *Emily Donelson of Tennessee* (2 vols.; Richmond, Va., 1941), 1:79 (extract). Informs him that he has requested the secretary of war to grant an early examination of Donelson, and, should he pass, an order to join AJ's staff.

Dec 30 To James Monroe. ALS, DLC (7-0956). Introduces Joshua Baker (1799–1885), brother of Isaac L., of the engineer corps.

Dec 30 From Auguste Macarty. ALS, DLC (28). Sends memorial of the people of New Orleans (not found) re land in the city and asks AJ to forward it to the president.

Dec [30] From [Henry Atkinson] (enclosures: Atkinson to William Bradford, Dec 15; Report of Gabriel Field, Dec 9, DNA-RG 107, M221-86). AL fragment, DLC (75). Reports on status of Cantonment Missouri.

Dec 31 To John Caldwell Calhoun. LS, DNA-RG 94 (M566-124). Recommends Mosby McDaniel for army appointment.

Dec 31 To John Caldwell Calhoun (enclosures: Henry Atkinson to AJ, Nov 23; William Bradford to AJ, Dec 7; Talbot Chambers to Atkinson, Dec 8; John Whistler to [Chambers], Dec 1; James McGunnegle to Chambers, Dec 7, DNA-RG 107, M221-86). LS, DNA-RG 107 (M221-86); LC, DLC (63). Transmits documents.

Dec 31 From John Caldwell Calhoun. LS, DLC (28); LC and AL draft, DNA-RG 107 (M7-1, 7-0958). *Calhoun Papers,* 4:530. Outlines course of action should Congress authorize the occupation of Florida.

[1819] From Martha Bradstreet. ALS fragment, ICHi (7-0105). Praises AJ's military accomplishments.

[1819] Memorandum of accounts re AJ and John Coffee. AD in Coffee's hand, THi (7-0112).

[1819] Memorandum of private letters to be written. AD, DLC (28).

[1819] Receipt from William White Crawford for $60 for superintending AJ's farm near Florence, Alabama. AD in AJ's hand, also signed by Crawford, DLC (58).

[c1819] From Decker & Black. Typed copy, Ruth Crownover (mAJs); Extract, Current Company Catalog 2 (5-0652). Contract with AJ for carpentry work on a house west of Cypress Creek in Alabama Territory.

[1819–20] To Richard Keith Call. ALS, PHi (7-0108); Photocopy of ALS, DLC (7-0966). Requests that he make out duplicate for the payment of postmaster accounts and requisitions letter paper, wafers, and quills.

[1819–20] Memorial to the U.S. Senate re conduct during the Florida invasion. Draft, DLC (28); DS in James C. Bronaugh's hand, signed by proxy in an unknown hand, with revisions in John H. Eaton's hand and others', DNA-RG 46 (7-0728). *Annals of Congress,* 15th Cong., 2nd sess., Appendix, pp. 2308–2328.

[1819–20] Memorandum on the Salt Lick Reserve. ADS fragment, DLC (59). Discusses the salt lick reserve of the 1818 Chickasaw treaty.

[1819–20] Rachel Jackson to "Dear Sister." Printed, *American Art Association Catalog* (April 8, 1926), Item 289 (7-0111). Arranges for the care of a slave girl.

1820

Jan 1 From Edmund Pendleton Gaines (enclosure: Edmund Doyle to Gaines, Nov 29, 1819). LS, DNA-RG 107 (M221-89). Reports steps taken pursuant to orders of November 22, 1819, and on the disposition of the Seminoles.

Jan 1 Accounts with United States for fuel and quarters. DS and DS duplicate, DNA-RG 217 (7-0968, -0972). Runs to April 1821.

Jan 3 *From George Gibson.* 348

Jan 4 To Edmund Pendleton Gaines. ALS, THi (7-0975). Acknowledges letters and states that Gaines will be informed about Florida reoccupation upon receipt of orders from the war department.

Jan 4 To Robert Lyman. LC, DLC (63). Orders payment for quartermaster's department.

Jan 5 From Robert Mottrom Ball. ALS with AJ endorsement, DLC (28). Accepts appointment as army post surgeon.

Jan 6 *To John Clark.* 349

Jan 7 To Edward Livingston. ALS, NjP (mAJs). Bassett, 3:1–2. Discusses Congress, relations with Spain, and his memorial; inquires about horses sent for Bernard de Marigny.

Jan 7	To Smith Thompson. ALS, DNA-RG 45 (7-0983). Recommends reinstatement of Gaston Davezac in navy.	
Jan 7	From Daniel Bissell (enclosures: Ygnacio Perez to William C. Beard, Oct 31; Beard to Perez, Oct, [Nov 8]; and Beard to [Bissell], [Nov] 10, all 1819). LS with AJ endorsement, DNA-RG 107 (M221-86). Sends documents re forces on the Sabine River.	
Jan 7	Richard Keith Call to Daniel Bissell. LC, DLC (63). Communicates orders re storage of supplies for possible Florida reoccupation.	
Jan 8	To Daniel Bissell. LC, DLC (63). Sends charges and specifications against John N. McIntosh (not found) to which he directs Bissell's "immediate attention."	
Jan 8	To Reuben Humphreys. LC, DLC (63); Copy, DNA-RG 107 (M221-86). Denies furlough and points out Humphreys's misunderstanding of previous order re winter quarters.	
Jan 8	From James Gadsden. ALS, ScU (7-0985). Reports on repair of fortifications in vicinity of New Orleans and Mobile; advises on the best time for traveling.	
Jan 10	To John Caldwell Calhoun (enclosures: Estimate of ordnance required for reduction of Pensacola, Barrancas, and St. Marks, [cJan 10]; Estimate of supplies required for quartermaster department, [cJan 10]). LS, DNA-RG 107 (M221-86); LC, DLC (63). Bassett, 3:2–6. Outlines the arrangements necessary for the reoccupation of Florida.	
Jan 10	To George Gibson. Photocopy of AL (incomplete). Christie, Manson, and Woods Catalog (Oct 1977), p. 13 (7-0989). Discusses the Spanish treaty and William H. Crawford's machinations.	
Jan 10	Memorandum of payments by John Coffee to AJ et al., creditors of the estate of John Hutchings. AD, Mrs. H. A. Brewer (mAJs).	
[cJan 10]	Estimate of ordnance required for reduction of Pensacola, Barrancas, and St. Marks. DS, DNA-RG 107 (M221-86).	
[cJan 10]	Estimate of supplies required for quartermaster department. DS, DNA-RG 107 (M221-86).	
Jan 11	From William C. Beard. ALS, DLC (28). Requests order to proceed to Washington to settle accounts.	
Jan 12	*Affidavit of Thomas Childress.*	351
Jan 12	From John Coffee (enclosure: Memorandum of accounts between Brahan & Hutchings and Jackson & Hutchings, [Jan 12]). ALS, DLC (28). Reports payment of accounts, for which AJ owes him $317.35¼; reports that Bennett Smith may sue the executors of the Hutchings estate.	
Jan 12	Deposition of James Jackson, Jr., re Pensacola land speculation. ADS, DLC (28).	
[Jan 12]	Memorandum of accounts between Brahan & Hutchings and Jackson & Hutchings. AD with AN (dated Jan 15) drawing $317 on AJ, THi (7-0991).	
Jan 13	From John Henry Eaton. AL fragment, DLC (75). Discusses relations with Spain, treasury deficit, the Missouri question, and the delay in the presentation of AJ's memorial.	
Jan 13	Deposition of John Donelson (1787–1840) re Pensacola land speculation. ADS, DLC (28). Bassett, 3:6–7.	

Jan 13	Deposition of John Jackson re Pensacola land speculation. ADS, DLC (28).
Jan 15	To James Monroe. ALS, NN (7-0993). Bassett, 3:7–8. Reports on efforts to restore order in the 8th Military Department; discusses Spanish affairs and the political combination of William H. Crawford and John Forsyth.
Jan 17	To John Caldwell Calhoun. LS, DNA-RG 107 (M221-86); LC, DLC (63). Bassett, 3:8–9. States that troops will be kept on the military road until needed elsewhere; reports on Eleazar W. Ripley and John N. McIntosh.
Jan 17	To John Caldwell Calhoun. LS, DNA-RG 75 (M271-3). *Calhoun Papers,* 4:581. Recommends William S. May as agent for the Arkansas Cherokees.
Jan 17	From James Gadsden. ALS, DLC (28). Reports New Orleans rumors that Congress will not authorize the reoccupation of Florida and that Spanish ships are in the area of Pensacola; recommends plan of operation in Florida; discusses land purchases in Florence, Alabama.
Jan 18	To John Caldwell Calhoun. LS, David K. Wilson (7-0997). Recommends Montgomery Bell for manufacturing ordnance and a site on the Harpeth River for an armory.
Jan 18	From Edmund Pendleton Gaines (enclosures: John C. Calhoun to AJ, Dec 24, 1819; Gaines to Calhoun, Jan 14). ALS, DLC (28). Transmits documents concerning reoccupation of Florida.
Jan 18	Account with William Cumming for purchase of a slave, Tom, for $455. ADS by James J. Hanna, DLC (28).
Jan 20	James Edward Dinkins to Robert Butler. ALS, ICHi (7-1001). Reports on defense at the Barrancas.
Jan 21	To John Caldwell Calhoun. ALS, DLC (7-1003); LC, DLC (63). Bassett, 3:9–11 (extract). Proposes a campaign in Florida if authorized by Congress.
Jan 21	Joseph N. Chambers to Richard Keith Call. ALS, DLC (28); LC, DNA-RG 98 (mAJs). Announces temporary absence of Daniel Bissell but promises transmittal of communications of January 7 and 8 to him upon his return.
Jan 22	From John Caldwell Calhoun. LS, DLC (28); LC, DNA-RG 107 (M6-10). *Calhoun Papers,* 4:591. States that he informed the president about Eleazar W. Ripley's conduct, but Monroe declined to address the matter.
Jan 22	Receipt from John Waller Overton for fees of $352.12½ in the case *Jackson & Hutchings* v. *Benjamin Rawlings*. ADS, THi (7-1010).
Jan 23	*From John Caldwell Calhoun.* 352
Jan 23	Richard Keith Call to John Caldwell Calhoun (enclosures: Daniel Bissell to AJ, Jan 7; Ygnacio Perez to William C. Beard, Oct 31, 1819; Beard to Perez, Oct, [Nov 8], 1819; and Beard to [Bissell], [Nov] 10, 1819). ALS, DNA-RG 107 (M221-86). Transmits documents re troops on the Sabine River.
[Jan 23]	To John Coffee. ALS, THi (11-1070). Discusses lawsuit by Bennett Smith against John Hutchings's executors and the settlement of the case against Benjamin Rawlings.

Jan 25	From Edmund Pendleton Gaines. ALS, DLC (28). Discusses report of James E. Dinkins re Spanish force at Pensacola.	
Jan 25	From John Rawles. ALS, DLC (28). Inquires about military land warrant and money he had sent from Savannah.	
Jan 25	Account with Joseph Wright for table linens. ADS with AJ endorsement, also signed by John Wright, DLC (28).	
Jan 27	To John Caldwell Calhoun. ALS, THi (7-1012). Transmits memorial from New Orleans citizens re sale of federal land.	
Jan 27	To Auguste Macarty. ALS, LN (7-1015). Acknowledges letter and memorial and informs him that he has sent it to Washington.	
Jan 28	From James Pitchlynn. LS by proxy, DNA-RG 107 (M221-98). Urges negotiations with the Choctaws and requests appointment as interpreter.	
Jan 29	Richard Keith Call to John Caldwell Calhoun (enclosures: Edmund P. Gaines to AJ, Jan 1; Edmund Doyle to Gaines, Nov 19, 1819). ALS, DNA-RG 107 (M221-86). Transmits letters.	
Jan 30	*From James Jackson Hanna.*	353
Jan 30	Richard Keith Call to Robert Lyman. LC, DLC (63). On AJ's behalf orders settlement of commissary department accounts.	
Jan 31	To Daniel Bissell. LC, DLC (63); Copy, DNA-RG 107 (M221-86). Orders Bissell to investigate the removal of troops from the north end of the military road under command of Reuben Humphreys.	
Jan 31	*To Andrew Jackson Donelson.*	354
[cJan]	To [Daniel D. Tompkins]. Copy, DLC (59). Defends actions during Florida invasion.	
Feb 1	*To George Gibson.*	355
Feb 1	From Milo Mason. ALS, DLC (28). Resigns army staff position.	
Feb 3	Receipt from John Barnett for $724 and release of AJ as security for Robert Barnett. ADS also signed by Richard K. Call, Adam Young by proxy (William Barnett), DLC (1).	
Feb 4	Richard Keith Call to William C. Beard. LC, DLC (63). Denies furlough.	
Feb 5	From John Caldwell Calhoun. LS, DLC (28); LC, DNA-RG 107 (M6-10); Extract, DNA-RG 94 (M566-132). *Calhoun Papers,* 4:636–37. Advises that AJ's plan for reoccupation of Florida is approved, but that Congress probably will not authorize action until fall; discusses Eleazar W. Ripley's conduct and the appointment of David Brearley as Cherokee agent in Arkansas.	
Feb 6	From James Gadsden (enclosure: Gadsden to AJ, Feb 6). ALS, DLC (28). Concurs in AJ's decision re political opponents; discusses Florence, Alabama, stock.	
Feb 6	From James Gadsden. LS, DLC (28). Reports on the strength of the garrisons and fortifications at St. Augustine, Pensacola, and St. Marks.	
Feb 7	General order suspending William King from the army. LC, DNA-RG 98 (mAJs).	
Feb 9	To Andrew Jackson Donelson. ALS, DLC (7-1024). Informs him that John C. Calhoun has advised that he continue at West Point until June unless Congress authorizes Florida invasion.	
Feb 9	From Daniel Bissell (enclosure: Thomas F. Hunt to Joseph N. Cham-	

bers, Jan 26). LS, DLC (28). Reports on supplies and the arrest of John N. McIntosh.

Feb 11	To John Caldwell Calhoun. LS, DNA-RG 107 (M688-15). Recommends Abram Poindexter Maury, Jr., for appointment to West Point.
Feb 12	To James Craine Bronaugh. ALS, DLC (28). Bassett, 3:13–15. Thanks him for information concerning John Williams's charges re salt lick reserve and criticizes congressional inaction on the reoccupation of Florida.
Feb 14	From Daniel Bissell. LS, DLC (28); Copy, DNA-RG 107 (M221-86). Reports that the removal of troops and artillery from the north end of the military road has been corrected.
Feb 14	From Jacob Jennings Brown. ALS draft, MiU-C (7-1026). Requests furlough for Fabius Whiting.
Feb 14	From George Gibson. ALS, DLC (28). Discusses the Missouri compromise, the reoccupation of Florida, and the appointment of a brigadier general.
Feb 16	To Andrew Erwin. LS with ANS by James Younger for William Norwill, sheriff: "I certify that I Delivered a Copy of the within to the wife of A. Erwin the said A. Erwin not being at home nor in the County This 18 Day of Febuary 1820," T (7-1028). Advises him of the time for taking depositions in the *Jackson* v. *Erwin* case.
Feb 17	From John Caldwell Calhoun. LCs, DNA-RG 107 (M6-10). Transmits statement by quartermaster general (not found) re Richard I. Easter's accounts and urges AJ to assist Easter in making a satisfactory adjustment of the $21,901.08 he owes.
Feb 17	From Return Jonathan Meigs, 1740–1823 (enclosures: John C. Calhoun to Meigs, Jan 8 and 29). ALS, DLC (28). Reports re intruders upon Cherokee lands.
Feb 18	Bill of sale for $475 for the slave Ned from David H. Bell. DS by James J. Hanna, DLC (28).
Feb 18	General order regulating recruitment of blacks, mulattoes, and underage boys. Printed form signed by Daniel Parker with AJ endorsement, ICHi (7-1030); LC, DNA-RG 98 (mAJs).
Feb 20	Edmund Pendleton Gaines to Robert Butler (enclosure: James E. Dinkins to James M. Glassell, Feb 5, DLC-28). ALS, DLC (28); AL draft (endorsed for AJ), DNA-RG 94 (7-1032). Transmits letter re Pensacola.
Feb 21	To Henry Atkinson. LC, DLC (63); Copy, DNA-RG 107 (M221-86). Acknowledges his report of December 30, 1819, and praises his conduct; advises him concerning Indians and encroachment upon their lands.
Feb 21	From Daniel Parker. LC, DNA-RG 94 (M565-6). Encloses copy of James Gadsden's letter (not found) re stationing artillery.
Feb 21	From Perrin Willis. ALS, DLC (28); LC, DNA-RG 98 (7-1034). Sends documents (not found) re supply problems along the military road.
Feb 23	*To John Coffee.* 357
Feb 23	From John Henry Eaton. AL fragment, DLC (75). Announces that Rufus King has presented AJ's memorial before the Senate with the suggested revisions.

Feb 25	From Cary Nicholas (enclosures: Nathan Towson to Nicholas, Jan 29; Joseph Lovell to John C. Calhoun, Jan 22; Nicholas to Towson, Feb 15; Stockley D. Hays to Nicholas, Feb 15). ALS, DNA-RG 107 (M221-86). Sends documents re charges that he paid troops working on the military road in depreciated paper currency.	
Feb 26	To Abner Underwood. ALS copy, DLC (28). Advises him to remove from Cherokee lands and to stop trading without permission.	
Feb 26	Order for the removal of intruders from the Cherokee lands. ADS copy, DLC (28).	
Feb 27	From Robert Butler. ALS, DLC (28). Encloses letters from Edmund P. Gaines to Butler and from Daniel Parker to William McDonald (neither found).	
Feb 27	From James Scallan (enclosures: Department orders of Jan 1 and 8, DLC-28; Description of open causeways, and Sketches of bridges on the southern end of the military road, n.d., DLC-59; Statement of extra labor, Descriptions of completed causeways and bridges, n.d., DLC-70). ALS, DLC (70). Reports on the military road.	
Feb 27	Richard Keith Call to John Caldwell Calhoun (enclosure: AJ to Henry Atkinson, Feb 21). ALS, DNA-RG 107 (M221-86). Transmits letter.	
Feb 28	To Daniel Bissell. LC, DLC (63); Copy, DNA-RG 107 (M221-86). Acknowledges letter of February 14 re the removal of the troops and discusses the military road.	
Feb 28	To John Caldwell Calhoun. LC, DLC (63). *Calhoun Papers,* 4:689–90. Requests instructions re the removal of intruders from Cherokee lands.	
Feb 28	To Edmund Pendleton Gaines. LC, DLC (63). Reports Spanish reinforcement of Pensacola.	
Feb 28	*To Return Jonathan Meigs (1740–1823).*	358
Feb 29	To Andrew Jackson Donelson. ALS, DLC (7-1036). Informs him that he will send $440 for his and Edward G. W. Butler's expenses as soon as possible.	
Feb 29	From Robert Lyman (enclosures: Lyman to John A. Rogers, Jan 31, DLC-28; George Gibson to Lyman, Aug 23, Sept 30, 1819, DLC-27). LS, DLC (28). Discusses the delay in discharging claims against the quartermaster's department.	
Feb 29	From Cary Nicholas. ALS, DNA-RG 94 (M566-130). Asks AJ to recommend William Alexander for army post.	
[cFeb]	From James Craine Bronaugh. ALS fragment, ICHi (7-0964). Commends AJ's memorial to the U.S. Senate.	
March 2	To John Caldwell Calhoun (enclosures: Reuben Humphreys to Robert Butler, Oct 27, 1819; Nathan Towson to Cary Nicholas, Jan 29; Joseph Lovell to Calhoun, Jan 22; Nicholas to Towson, Feb 15; Stockley D. Hays to Nicholas, Feb 15; Statement of Richard K. Call, March 2, DNA-RG 107, M221-86; AJ to Humphreys, Jan 8; Butler to Humphreys, Nov 19, 1819). LS, DNA-RG 107 (M221-86); LC, DLC (63). Transmits correspondence re troops on the military road, winter quarters, and pay in depreciated currency.	
March 2	To John Caldwell Calhoun (enclosure: Cary Nicholas to AJ, Feb 29).	

LS, DNA-RG 94 (M566-130). Recommends William Alexander for army post.

March 4 — To Thomas Watson. Printed, *New York Times,* Nov 4, 1927 (7-1039). Declares that he was born in South Carolina.

March 4 — From William Bradford (enclosure: Cherokee Council to [Bradford and Reuben Lewis], Feb 10). LS, DNA-RG 107 (M221-86). *TPUS,* 19:169–70. Reports on Osage-Cherokee tensions for which he blames the Cherokees.

March 4 — From Arthur Peronneau Hayne. ALS, DLC (28). Requests copy of AJ's memorial, commends the conduct of James E. Dinkins, and discusses the court-martial of William King.

March 4 — From Reuben Humphreys (enclosure: John N. McIntosh to Humphreys, cDec 1819, DLC-29). ALS, DLC (28); Copy, DNA-RG 107 (M221-86). Discusses supplies and equipment on the military road; renews request for a leave of absence.

March 9 — To John Caldwell Calhoun (enclosure: James E. Dinkins to Robert Butler, Jan 20). LS, DNA-RG 107 (M221-86); LC, DLC (63). *Calhoun Papers,* 4:706–707. Transmits letter and discusses the status of Richard I. Easter's account.

March 11 — *From John Henry Eaton.* 359

March 13 — From Return Jonathan Meigs, 1740–1823 (enclosure: List of intruders on Cherokee lands, March 13, DLC-70). LS, DLC (28). States that he has distributed to intruders AJ's orders but fears not all will leave.

March 13 — Statement of funds paid to general officers. DS by William Lee, DNA-RG 233 (7-1040).

March 14 — To James Monroe. ALS, NN (7-1043). Recommends Samuel R. Overton for appointment.

March 14 — From Daniel Bissell (enclosure: William C. Beard to Bissell, March 8). LS, DLC (28). Reports on the garrisons on the Sabine River and at Fort St. Philip and Fort Claiborne.

March 15 — *To George Gibson.* 363

March 15 — *From John Caldwell Calhoun.* 365

March 15 — From John Henry Eaton (enclosure: Memorandum of Rufus King, Eaton, and William Pinkney, Feb). ALS, DLC (28). Heiskell, 3:150–51. Sends page proof of AJ's memorial (not found) and memorandum detailing further revisions.

March 15 — From Return Jonathan Meigs (1740–1823). ALS, DLC (70). States that Isaiah Walker is not an intruder on Cherokee lands.

March 17 — From Peter Hagner. LS, DLC (28); LC, DNA-RG 217 (7-1049). Inquires about a draft of $25,000 in favor of Thomas Camp.

March 19 — From Edmund Pendleton Gaines (enclosures: James Bankhead to Gaines, March 9; Don Juan Lowe to Bankhead, Feb 23; Bankhead to Lowe, Feb 26, DLC-28; José Coppinger to Lowe, Sept 9, 1819, DLC-29). LS with AN, DLC (28). Discusses slave smuggling from the West Indies across the Florida line.

March 19 — From James Scallan. ALS, DNA-RG 107 (M221-86). Reports on topography between Baton Rouge and Madisonville and the advantages of a crossroad from the military road to the Mississippi River.

March 20 — From George Gibson. ALS, DLC (28). Reports the popularity of AJ's memorial and believes that Congress will not adopt the president's recommendation re Florida.

March 21 To Andrew Jackson Donelson. ALS, DLC (7-1050). Announces he is sending a note for $500 on the Bank of Pennsylvania by another letter.

March 21 To Andrew Jackson Donelson. ALS, DLC (7-1053). Congratulates him on his studies and informs him of $500 note sent for his return to Tennessee.

March 21 Promissory note from James Jackson and AJ to Jenkin Whiteside for $1,000. DS with ANS by John Nichol, executor of Charles McAlister, assignee, CtY (7-1056).

March 21 Deed of release from Jenkin Whiteside for one-third of the Allison lands. ADS, T (7-1058).

March 21 Account with James Glasgow Martin & Co. for sundries. DS, DLC (31). Runs to December 1, 1821.

March 22 From James Scallan. ALS, DLC (28). Relates information on Bogue Chitto, lying between the Mississippi River and the military road.

March 22 Receipt from Berryhill & McKee for sugar and coffee. ADS, DLC (28).

March 25 To John Caldwell Calhoun (enclosures: John N. McIntosh to Reuben Humphreys, cDec, 1819, DLC-29; Daniel Bissell to AJ, Feb 14; AJ to Bissell, Jan 31, Feb 18; Humphreys to AJ, March 4). LS, DNA-RG 107 (M221-86); LC, DLC (63). *Calhoun Papers,* 4:732. Sends documents re construction of the military road.

March 26 Robert Butler to Daniel Parker. ALS, DNA-RG 94 (M566-132). Transmits documents re Dr. John Trevitt's report and clarifies reporting division returns.

March 27 From John Caldwell Calhoun. ALS, ScU (7-1061). Sends presidential message recommending the postponement of the Florida occupation and discusses reasons for delay.

March 29 From George Gibson. ALS, DLC (28). Bassett, 3:19. Acknowledges congressional delay in authorizing reoccupation of Florida.

March 31 To John Caldwell Calhoun. LS, DNA-RG 107 (M221-86); LC, DLC (63). *Calhoun Papers,* 4:743–44. Acknowledges receipt of the foreign relations committee report, and states that he will incur no great expenses until Congress authorizes the reoccupation of Florida.

[March] Memoranda on Henry Randolph Storrs's report. AD fragments, DLC (59, 60).

April 1 From George Gibson. ALS, DLC (28). Comments again on AJ's memorial and intended resignation and Richard I. Easter's departure for Nashville.

April 2 From John Henry Eaton. ALS, DLC (28). Heiskell, 3:151–52. Reports on the reception of AJ's memorial in the Senate; discusses AJ's accounts and the dispute between John Williams and John Overton over charges in Overton's pamphlet, *A Vindication,* that Williams had entered Florida without authorization in the 1813 military campaign.

April 3 To Unknown. LS copy with revisions by AJ, DLC (28). Denounces Henry R. Storrs's report.

April 3 From Arthur Peronneau Hayne. ALS, DLC (28); Extract, DNA-RG

107 (M222-21). Reports death of his daughter, Martha Ann; discusses AJ's memorial and his intention to resign from army.

April 4 From William Young. ALS, DLC (28). States he kept no journal of the campaign to East Florida in 1813 but gives his recollections.

April 6 To Peter Hagner (enclosure: Thomas L. Butler to Thomas Camp, Oct 11, 1814). LS with postscript in AJ's hand, DNA-RG 217 (7-1065). Sends copy of order directing the transfer of funds to John T. Wirt.

April 7 From John Macrae Washington (enclosure: Return of ordnance and ordnance stores at Fernandina, March 31, DLC-70). ALS, DLC (28). Sends return.

April 7 Richard Keith Call to John Caldwell Calhoun (enclosure: James Scallan to AJ, March 19). ALS, DNA-RG 107 (M221-86); LC, DLC (63). Reports the arrival in Nashville of Richard I. Easter, who will be sent to Washington as soon as his vouchers are placed in order.

April 12 To Daniel Bissell. LC, DLC (63). Acknowledges the abandonment of Fort Claiborne; advises against large expeditions except where the frontier is endangered.

April 12 To Reuben Humphreys. LC, DLC (63). Endorses his return to the north end of the military road; observes that Humphreys must gain permission of his commanding officers before a furlough can be granted.

April 12 Richard Keith Call to Daniel Parker. ALS, DNA-RG 94 (M566-131); LC, DLC (63). On AJ's behalf requests copy of the court-martial proceedings against David Brearley and a statement of the number of friendly Creeks employed in the Seminole campaign.

April 13 To Andrew Erwin and Henry Crabb. LS by proxy (Oliver B. Hays), T (mAJs). Notifies them that he will take the deposition of Jenkin Whiteside on May 17.

April 13 From John Caldwell Calhoun (enclosures: Calhoun to Henry Atkinson and to Henry Leavenworth, April 10, DLC-28). LC, DNA-RG 107 (M6-11). Transmits letters re suspension of the Missouri expedition.

April 14 From John Hamlin Camp. ALS, DNA-RG 217 (7-1068). States that the receipts kept by his late brother, Thomas Camp, have been destroyed.

April 15 To James Monroe. ALS, NN (7-1070); Copy, DLC (28). Bassett, 3:20. Acknowledges message to Congress on relations with Spain and informs the president that he wishes to resign from the army.

April 15 From James Gadsden. ALS with AJ endorsement, DLC (28). Writes that he will not leave Mobile Point before July 1, when he will visit AJ at the Hermitage; hopes that AJ will accompany him to Washington and the Northeast.

April 16 From John Henry Eaton. ALS, DLC (29). Heiskell, 3:152–55. Expresses pleasure that AJ agrees to changes in the memorial, and urges him to ignore the Storrs report.

[April 16] *To Andrew Jackson Donelson.* 366

April 18 From Daniel Parker. LC, DNA-RG 94 (7-1077). Sends copy of a letter (not found) from Nathan Towson to Simeon Knight, who has never reported according to orders.

April 20 To Peter Hagner (enclosure: John H. Camp to AJ, April 14). LS,

	DNA-RG 217 (7-1078). States that he has been unable to obtain Thomas Camp's vouchers.
April 20	From George Gibson. ALS, DLC (29). Reports on Congress, John Cocke's inquiry into the mode of letting contracts, and the arrival of the Spanish minister.
April 20	Account with Kerr & Co. for coffee. ADS with AJ endorsement, DLC (29).
April 22	From Daniel Bissell (enclosures: Dominick A. Hall to Bissell, Dec 31, 1819, DLC-28; Statement of federal grand jurors, Louisiana, April 20; Jacques P. Villeré to Bissell, April 20; Hall to Bissell, April 20). LS, DLC (29). Informs AJ of his response to the request for a force to guard pirate prisoners in the New Orleans jail.
April 24	From [Peter Hagner]. LC, DNA-RG 217 (7-1080). Reports on the Thomas Camp account and encloses letter (not found) to Camp's father.
April 25	From John Caldwell Calhoun. LC, DNA-RG 107 (M6-11). *Calhoun Papers,* 5:75. Expresses the hope that Richard I. Easter will settle his accounts and advises that an intersecting route with the military road is worthy of consideration after a survey and estimate of expenses.
April 26	Division of the estate of William Terrell Lewis, signed by AJ, Thomas Crutcher, and A. Foster, executors. Copy, TNDa (mAJs).
April 27	To John Caldwell Calhoun. LC, DLC (63). Notifies him of the receipt of Edmund P. Gaines's letter of March 19 re the illicit introduction of slaves and free blacks on the frontier of Georgia and solicits orders on the matter.
April 27	From Edward George Washington Butler. ALS, DLC (29). Informs AJ that Andrew J. Donelson has received the $500 bank note; asks to borrow a similar amount and seeks advice on a military post.
April 27	From James Pitchlynn. ALS, DNA-RG 107 (M222-22). Anna Lewis, *Chief Pushmataha, American Patriot* (New York, 1959), pp. 131–32. Announces that the Choctaws are willing to exchange their land and asks AJ to inform the president.
April 28	From Henry Atkinson. LS, THi (7-1081). Reports on sickness of troops on the Missouri expedition and on James Johnson's failure to fulfill his supply contract.
April 30	To John Caldwell Calhoun (enclosures: William Bradford to AJ, March 4; Cherokee Council to [Bradford and Reuben Lewis], Feb 10). LS, DNA-RG 107 (M221-86). *TPUS,* 19:169. Transmits documents re Cherokee-Osage quarrels.
April 30	From James Gadsden. ALS, DLC (29). Praises AJ's memorial and discusses the election in Louisiana.
May 1	From William Cocke. ALS, DNA-RG 107 (M221-89). Informs AJ that Alabamians are anxious for a Choctaw land cession.
May 1	From Silas McBee. ALS, DNA-RG 107 (M222-21). Reports that Choctaws seem inclined to cede their land.
May 3	From George Gibson. ALS, DLC (29). Discusses Spanish minister and failure to ratify treaty; mentions that Henry R. Storrs and John Cocke have not yet reported on Gibson's procedures as commissary general.

May 3	Daniel Parker to Richard Keith Call. LS, DLC (29); LC, DNA-RG 94 (M565-6). States that the proceedings of David Brearley's court-martial will be forwarded shortly.	
May 3	Account of Rachel Jackson with R. P. Garrett for fabric and a dress. ADS, DLC (29). Runs to May 16.	
May 5	From William McLean Berryhill. ALS, DNA-RG 94 (7-1084). Recommends Stewart Cowan for army appointment.	
May 6	*To Andrew Jackson Donelson.*	367
May 6	From George Gibson. ALS, DLC (29). Reports on Spanish negotiations and suggests that the president will probably urge the reoccupation of Florida and refuse AJ's resignation.	
May 6	From Josiah Meigs (enclosure: Oliver Wolcott to Meigs, April 2, DLC-28). ALS, DLC (29). Sends a quotation from a friend and classmate praising AJ's service.	
May 7	Robert Butler to Daniel Bissell. LC, DNA-RG 98 (mAJs). Inquires into Simeon Knight's failure to report.	
May 7	Robert Butler to Daniel Parker. LC, DNA-RG 98 (mAJs). Acknowledges letter of April 18 and encloses 8th Military Department order of February 5 (not found) re Simeon Knight's failure to report for duty.	
May 8	From Daniel Bissell (enclosures: Duncan L. Clinch to Bissell, May; Bissell to Clinch, May 7). LS, DLC (29). Reports that the military road will be completed by early June; forwards Clinch's request for a furlough.	
May 8	Daniel Parker to Richard Keith Call (enclosures: Proceedings of the court-martial of David Brearley, May 10–June 25, 1818, DLC-29; Statement of the number of friendly Indians employed in the Seminole War, May 1, DLC-70). LS, DLC (29); LC, DNA-RG 94 (M565-6). Transmits requested documents.	
May 9	From Paul Hyacinte Perrault. ALS, DLC (29). Transmits map and report of his survey (not found).	
May 10	From Daniel Bissell (enclosures: John C. Calhoun to Bissell, March 10; Bissell to Calhoun, April 11; Decius Wadsworth to John Symington, March 8, DLC-28). LS, DLC (29); Copy, DNA-RG 107 (M222-21). Discusses orders re ordnance, disapproved by the secretary of war.	
May 12	To John Caldwell Calhoun (enclosures: William Cocke to AJ, May 1; Silas McBee to AJ, May 1; James Pitchlynn to AJ, April 27). LS, DNA-RG 107 (M221-89). Suggests that exchange of land with the Choctaws may now be possible.	
May 12	From Walker Keith Armistead. LC, DNA-RG 77 (7-1092). Submits for inspection the orders to Paul H. Perrault (not found).	
May 13	Account with Samuel Green for posts and fencing. AD in AJ's hand, signed by Green, DLC (29).	
May 15	To Daniel Bissell. LC, DLC (63). Approves response to the request for troops by the governor of Louisiana.	
May 15	To John Caldwell Calhoun. Extract, Charles Frederick Heartman, *Rare Americana* (Nov 23, 1929), Item 212 (mAJs). Introduces Francis Jones, a new cadet at West Point.	

May 15 To John Caldwell Calhoun. LS, NjP (mAJs). Recommends Lewis Livingston as legation secretary in France.

May 15 To Peter Hagner. ALS, THi (7-1096). Discusses the Thomas Camp account.

May 15 To Lewis Livingston (enclosures: AJ to John C. Calhoun, and to James Monroe, May 15). LS, NjP (mAJs). Transmits letters of recommendation.

May 15 To James Monroe. LS, NjP (mAJs). Recommends Lewis Livingston as secretary to legation in France.

[May 15] To Andrew Jackson Donelson. ALS, DLC (7-1094). Introduces Francis Jones.

May 16 From John Caldwell Calhoun. LS, DLC (29); LC, DNA-RG 107 (M6-11). Reports reduced army appropriation and suggests suspension of construction of the military road unless completed shortly.

May 16 From John Caldwell Calhoun (enclosure: Calhoun to William Bradford, May 12, DLC-29). LS, DLC (29); LC, DNA-RG 107 (M15-4). Acknowledges letters from Bradford and the Cherokees.

May 16 From John Hamlin Camp. ALS, DLC (29). Reports that the receipts of his brother, Thomas Camp, were destroyed.

May 16 From Christopher Rankin. ALS with AJ endorsement, DLC (29). Informs him that Mississippi congressmen have arranged AJ and Thomas Hinds's appointment as commissioners to the Choctaw Indians.

May 17 *To John Caldwell Calhoun.* 369

May 20 Richard Keith Call to Daniel Bissell (enclosure: Call to Reuben Humphreys, May 20). LC, DLC (63). Transmits letter.

May 20 Richard Keith Call to Reuben Humphreys. LC, DLC (63). Orders repair of military road.

May 22 Richard Keith Call to Daniel Bissell. LC, DLC (63). Informs him of repair of the military road; denies Duncan L. Clinch's furlough.

May 23 From John Clark. ALS, DLC (29). Sends portion of his pamphlet, *Considerations on the Purity of the Principles of William H. Crawford, Esq. . . .* (Augusta, Ga., [1820]).

May 23 From James Monroe. Copies, DLC (7-1098). Stanislaus Murray Hamilton, ed., *The Writings of James Monroe* (7 vols.; New York, 1898–1903), 6:126–30. Discusses AJ's request to resign, leaving decision to AJ.

May 24 From John Caldwell Calhoun. LS, DLC (29); LC (dated May 23), DNA-RG 107 (M15-4); Copy (dated May 23), DNA-RG 46 (mAJs). Bassett, 3:23–24. Asks AJ to serve as Choctaw treaty negotiator.

May 29 To Intruders on Cherokee Lands. ADS copy, DLC (29). Announces that all on tribal lands without permits will be removed.

May 29 From Daniel Parker. LC, DNA-RG 94 (M565-6). Encloses letter from Thomas Granbery (not found) re conduct of officers in Mississippi.

May 30 Samuel Hodge to Rachel Jackson. ALS, DLC (29). Discusses religious duties.

May 31 From Mycajah Hendrick et al. ALS, DNA-RG 107 (M221-89). Protest their removal from Cherokee reservation.

June 1 From John Caldwell Calhoun. ALS with AJ endorsement, DLC (29). *Calhoun Papers,* 5:164–65. Acknowledges AJ's letters of April 15 and May 5 (neither found); regrets his decision to retire; discusses politics and foreign relations and states that class rank will determine placement of Andrew J. Donelson and Edward G. W. Butler.

June 3 From Thomas I. Moore et al. Typed copy, G-Ar (7-1108). Thaddeus Brockett Rice, *History of Greene County, Georgia, 1786–1886* (Spartanburg, S.C., c1961), p. 330. Invite AJ to dinner in Greensborough, Georgia.

June 3 To Thomas I. Moore et al. Typed copy, G-Ar (7-1109). Accepts invitation.

June 3 From Edmund Pendleton Gaines (enclosure: Gaines to John C. Calhoun, June 3). ALS, DLC (29). Sends estimate (not found) for repairs of fortifications in Charleston harbor.

June 3 From Edmund Pendleton Gaines. LS, DLC (29). Thanks AJ for his letter of April 27 (not found) and his remarks on Storrs's report; proposes to go to Washington to settle accounts, visiting forts en route.

June 3 Toast at dinner in Greensborough, Georgia: "The Governor of Georgia." Printed, Thaddeus Brockett Rice, *History of Greene County, Georgia, 1786–1886* (Spartanburg, S.C., c1961), p. 331 (mAJs).

June 3 Deed of release to the estate of David Allison. Copy, Wilkes County, Georgia, Deed Book (7-1106). Duplicates lost deed of August 3, 1812, for all Allison lands in Tennessee.

June 4 To Alexander and John Allison. Typed copy, G-Ar (7-1110). Encloses copies of depositions (not identified) taken in Greensborough.

June 4 From Daniel Bissell (enclosure: Department order to James Scallan, June 1). LS, DLC (29). Reports ordering repair of military road.

June 4 From Daniel Bissell. LS, DLC (29). States that he has ordered troops formerly at work on the military road to Ripley Barracks.

June 5 *From Edward George Washington Butler.* 369

June 7 *From John Rodgers, Sr.* 371

June 8 From Michael Nourse. Printed form with ms insertions, endorsed by AJ asserting that the note is a forgery, DLC (29). Informs AJ that a note drawn by T. E. Butler, Robert Butler, and AJ for $5,000 has been protested for nonpayment.

June 9 From John McKee. ALS, DLC (29). States he has drawn on AJ or James Jackson for $230, according to his memorandum (not found).

June 10 From Arthur Peronneau Hayne. ALS, DLC (29); Extract, DNA-RG 107 (M222-21). Bassett, 3:24–25 (extract). Discusses Alabama farm and confirms army resignation.

June 10 From William Lee (enclosure: Lee to David Meriwether, Jesse Franklin, and AJ, June 10). ALS, DLC (29); LC, DNA-RG 217 (7-1111). Transmits letter.

June 10 From William Lee (to David Meriwether, Jesse Franklin, and AJ). ALS, DLC (29); LC, DNA-RG 217 (7-1112). Asks for evidence of credit for the $1,000 debt as Indian commissioners.

June 14 Richard Keith Call to Reuben Humphreys. LC, DLC (63). Orders a detachment for the removal of intruders from Cherokee lands; reiterates order for repairs on the military road.

June 14	Account with Francis Alexander for medical treatment on AJ's and Andrew Jackson Hutchings's farms in Alabama. AD with AN and endorsement by AJ, A-Ar (7-1113).
June 15	To John Caldwell Calhoun (enclosure: Mycajah Hendrick et al. to AJ, May 31). LS, DNA-RG 107 (M221-89); LC, DLC (63). Bassett, 3:25–26. Informs him of action in regard to the removal of intruders from the Indian lands and progress on the military road; endorses the petition of John Pace.
June 15	From Return Jonathan Meigs (1740–1823). ALS, DLC (29). Discusses removal of Cherokee intruders.
June 16	Robert Butler to Daniel Parker (enclosure: Butler to Daniel Bissell, May 7). LC, DNA-RG 98 (mAJs). Transmits documents re Simeon Knight's failure to report.
June 19	To John Caldwell Calhoun. Copies, DLC (29), DNA-RG 46 (7-1115); LC, DLC (63). *ASP, Indian Affairs,* 2:230–31. Agrees to serve as commissioner for the Choctaw negotiations and outlines suggestions.
June 19	To Christopher Rankin. Copy, DLC (29). Bassett, 3:27. Announces AJ's appointment as Choctaw treaty commissioner.
June 19	From John Caldwell Calhoun. LS, DLC (29); LC, DNA-RG 107 (M6-11). Demands cooperation from Daniel Bissell in erection of barracks at Baton Rouge.
June 19	From George Gibson. ALS with AJ endorsement, DLC (29). States there is no news regarding relations with Spain.
June 19	From John Ross. ALS, DLC (29). Gary Moulton, ed., *Papers of Chief John Ross* (2 vols.; Norman, Okla., 1985), 1:40–41. Discusses the removal of intruders from Cherokee lands.
June 20	To James Monroe. ALS and Extract, NN (7-1117, -1125); Copy, T (7-1121). Bassett, 3:28–29. Informs Monroe that he will not retire from the army at present.
June 21	To John Clark. Abstract, Emily Driscoll, *Autographs, Manuscripts, Drawings, Association Books,* No. 27 (Nov 1968):31 (7-1126). Thanks him for pamphlet and discusses Georgia politics.
June 21	Richard Keith Call to Daniel Bissell. LC, DLC (63). Orders investigation of charges of military misconduct in Mississippi.
June 21	Richard Keith Call to John Caldwell Calhoun (enclosure: Petition of John Pace, n.d., DNA-RG 75, M208-8). ALS, DNA-RG 107 (M221-89); LC, DLC (63). Forwards petition.
June 23	To Daniel Bissell. LC, DLC (63). Authorizes discretion in the assignment of troops for the summer; endorses his action in the dispute over arms.
June 23	From William Montrose Graham. ALS, DLC (29). Reports the arrival of a detachment from Reuben Humphreys's company at the military ferry on the Tennessee River and the need for rations.
June 23	Richard Keith Call to Paul Hyacinte Perrault. LC, DLC (63). Acknowledges his communication of May 9.
June 26	To Henry Atkinson. LC in Richard K. Call's hand, DLC (63). Discusses 9th Military Department.

June 26	To John Caldwell Calhoun. ALS, S. Howard Goldman (7-1127); ALS copy, DLC (63). Discusses the dispute between the ordnance department and Daniel Bissell.
June 26	From Elijah Montgomery. ALS, DLC (29). Requests a furlough.
June 28	From Reuben Humphreys (enclosure: Thomas S. Jesup to Humphreys, Jan 20, DLC-28). ALS, DLC (29). Discusses shortage of funds, the military road, and his command.
June 28	Richard Keith Call to Return Jonathan Meigs (1740–1823). ALS, DNA-RG 75 (M208-8); ALS copy, DLC (29); LC with AN by AJ, DLC (63). Discusses removal of intruders from Cherokee lands.
June 29	Richard Keith Call to William Montrose Graham. ALS copy and LC fragment, DLC (29, 63). Issues orders for the removal of intruders from the Cherokee lands.
June 29	Richard Keith Call to Reuben Humphreys (enclosure: Call to Humphreys, May 20). LC with AN by AJ, DLC (63). Discusses order of May 20 regarding the military road and the failure to carry it out.
June 30	Richard Keith Call to Matthew Strong Massey. LC, DLC (63). Orders funds for subsistence and transportation of forces on the military road.
[cJune-Aug]	To William Berkeley Lewis. ALS, NN (8-1322). Bassett, 2:408 (dated 1819). Discusses arrangements for painting the Hermitage.
July 1	To Richard Keith Call. Printed, *The Collector* (Sept 1901):130–31 (7-1131). Appoints Call to remove intruders from Cherokee and Creek lands and issues instructions.
July 1	From John Price. ADS with AJ endorsement, THi (7-1133). Transmits account with John Peck for coffin and tombstone of John Hutchings.
July 5	To Michael Nourse. ALS, PHi (7-1135). Declares he was never a surety for T. E. Butler and Robert Butler.
July 6	To John Clark. Abstract, Dodd, Mead & Company Catalog 66 (Jan 1903), Item 116 (7-1137). Defends his conduct against slanders by William H. Crawford.
July 6	From James Gadsden. ALS, DLC (29). Expects to depart from the Rigolets shortly; discusses Louisiana elections.
July 7	From James Scallan. ALS, DNA-RG 107 (M221-89). Reports on the military road.
July 7	Receipt from Isaac Peairs for medical treatment of a slave, Jack. AD in AJ's hand, signed by Peairs and Richard I. Easter, DLC (24).
[cJuly 7]	To Robert Butler. AN, DLC (29). Directs him to implement orders of the secretary of war of June 19.
July 8	To John Caldwell Calhoun (enclosures: AJ to James Scallan, July 7, 8; Robert Butler to Daniel Bissell, July 8, M221-89). LS with postscript in AJ's hand (dated July 9), DNA-RG 107 (M221-89); LC in AJ's hand, DLC (63). Informs him that orders in accordance with Calhoun's of June 19 have been issued; discusses Thomas F. Hunt and Henry Chotard; reports on military road.
July 8	To John Caldwell Calhoun. LC in AJ's hand, DLC (63). Reports the illness of Richard I. Easter and requests extension of time to settle his accounts.

July 8	To William Lee. LS, NhD (7-1138); LC, DLC (63). Discusses accounts of treaty commissioners.	
July 8	*From Richard Keith Call.*	372
July 8	From James Scallan. ALS, DNA-RG 107 (M221-89). Reports on inns on the military road within the Choctaw nation.	
July 9	To John Caldwell Calhoun (enclosure: John Rodgers, Sr., to AJ, June 7). ALS, NcD (7-1141). Bassett, 3:29 (extract). Reports on removal of intruders from Cherokee lands and complaints about unfulfilled treaty provisions.	
July 10	*To George Gibson.*	374
July 10	From William Lee. LS with AJ endorsement, DLC (29); LC, DNA-RG 217 (7-1148). Asks for information regarding an 1815 account of $60,461.11 intended as presents for Indians.	
July 12	From John Caldwell Calhoun (enclosure: Calhoun to AJ and Thomas Hinds, July 12). LS with AJ endorsement, DLC (29); LC, DNA-RG 75 (M15-4); Copy, DNA-RG 46 (7-1149). *ASP, Indian Affairs,* 2:231. Announces AJ's appointment as Choctaw negotiator.	
July 12	From John Caldwell Calhoun (to AJ and Thomas Hinds; enclosures: Commission of AJ and Hinds as Choctaw treaty negotiators, July 13; Extracts of Calhoun to William Clark, and Calhoun to Clark and Auguste Chouteau, both May 8, 1818; Extract from Quapaw treaty, [Aug 18, 1818], DLC-25). LS with AJ endorsement, DLC (29); LC, DNA-RG 75 (M15-4); Copy, DNA-RG 46 (7-1150). *ASP, Indian Affairs,* 2:231–32. Transmits commission and instructions re Choctaw treaty.	
July 12	From Richard Keith Call. ALS, DLC (29). Discusses removal of intruders from Cherokee lands.	
July 13	Commission of AJ and Thomas Hinds to negotiate treaty with Choctaw Indians. DS by James Monroe and John Q. Adams, DLC (29); Copy, DNA-RG 59 (7-1152).	
July 14	From William Mitchell. ALS, DNA-RG 94 (M688-15). Asks for recommendation for his son, Jacob D. Mitchell, to West Point.	
July 15	To William Berkeley Lewis. ALS, NN (7-1158). *New York Public Library Bulletin,* 4(1900):162. Declares the state loan office bill to be unconstitutional.	
July 15	*From William Berkeley Lewis.*	376
July 15	Memorial By Davidson County citizens against the state loan office bill. DS, T (mAJs). *Nashville Whig,* July 26.	
July 16	*To William Berkeley Lewis.*	378
July 16	From Richard Keith Call. ALS, DLC (29). Again reports on removal of intruders from Cherokee lands.	
July 18	To John Caldwell Calhoun (enclosure: William Mitchell to AJ, July 14). LS, DNA-RG 94 (M688-15). Recommends Jacob D. Mitchell for West Point.	
July 19	To John Coffee. Typed copy, CoHi (7-1169). Discusses his efforts to defeat the state loan office bill.	
July 19	From Hugh Young. ALS with AJ endorsement, DLC (29). Asks AJ to settle Young's debt to James C. Bronaugh; discusses his topographical report and future surveys.	
July 20	From John Caldwell Calhoun. LS with AJ endorsement, DLC (29);	

LC, DNA-RG 107 (M6-11). Approves measures taken for removal of intruders from Cherokee lands and discusses removal of intruders from Creek areas.

July 21 To John McKee. AL fragment in James C. Bronaugh's hand, DLC (7-1175). Discusses upcoming negotiations with the Choctaw nation.

July 21 From John Caldwell Calhoun. LS, DLC (29); LC, DNA-RG 107 (M6-11). Encloses congressional resolution of May 11 on the reduction of the army and asks for AJ's response.

July 21 From Read Fort. ALS by proxy with AJ endorsement, DNA-RG 46 (7-1172). Expresses willingness to exchange eastern land for land in Arkansas.

July 23 From Richard Keith Call. ALS, DLC (29). Reports on removal of intruders from Indian lands.

July 24 *To John Caldwell Calhoun.* 381

July 26 To John Caldwell Calhoun. LC with AN by AJ, DLC (63). Bassett, 3:30–31. Reports that Richard K. Call will require three months to remove intruders from Cherokee lands and that Edmund P. Gaines has been ordered to remove intruders from Creek lands in Georgia.

July 26 From Daniel Bissell (enclosures: John Jones to Bissell, July 13; Jones to Richard Whartenby, July 10; Whartenby to Jones, July 12). LS with AJ endorsement, DLC (29). Discusses construction of barracks at Baton Rouge.

July 28 To William Lee. LC, DLC (63). Details the distribution of $60,461.11 to Indians in 1815.

July 28 From Levi Whiting (enclosure: Petition of Thomas Wright et al., n.d., DNA-RG 94, M566-132). LC, DNA-RG 98 (7-1179). Sends paper requesting discharge of Ira Drew, a soldier, and requests approval.

July 31 *To Richard Keith Call.* 382

July 31 From John Caldwell Calhoun (enclosures: James Monroe to Western Cherokee Chiefs, March [13], 1818, DLC-24; Calhoun to William Bradford, Sept 9, 1818, DLC-25; Calhoun to Reuben Lewis, Nov 18, 1818, and March 9, 1819, DLC-26; Calhoun to Lewis, Aug 2, 1819, DLC-27; Lewis to Calhoun, Jan 21, DLC-28). LS with AJ endorsement, DLC (29); LC, DNA-RG 107 (M6-11). *Calhoun Papers,* 5:303–304. Approves settlement of command dispute at Baton Rouge; discusses military road and removal of intruders from Indian lands; grants Richard I. Easter additional time to settle his accounts.

Aug 2 *To John Caldwell Calhoun.* 384

Aug 3 From Robert Butler. LC in Butler's hand, DNA-RG 98 (7-1184). Reports that he found no letter from William King re order to shoot deserters.

Aug 4 From Reuben Humphreys. ALS with AJ endorsement, DLC (29). Discusses his requisition for $1,000, progress on the military road, and condition of his troops.

Aug 5 To John Caldwell Calhoun. ALS, DNA-RG 107 (M221-89); LC, DLC (63). Encloses inspection report of James C. Bronaugh (not found) and recommends removal of sick to Baton Rouge; suggests that funds for negotiations with Choctaws be deposited at Natchez, where money will be accepted at par.

Aug 6 To Richard Keith Call (enclosure: John C. Calhoun to AJ, July 20).

ALS, THi (7-1185). Transmits copy of letter on the removal of intruders from the Creek lands and asks that a copy be forwarded to Edmund P. Gaines.

Aug 6 To Return Jonathan Meigs, 1740–1823 (enclosure: AJ to Richard K. Call, Aug 6). Extract, King V. Hostick Catalog (1976), Item 17 (7-1190). Asks that he forward enclosed letter.

Aug 6 From Arthur Peronneau Hayne (enclosure: Hayne to AJ, Aug 6). ALS, DLC (29). Sends his resignation from the army and discusses AJ's decision to remain in service.

Aug 6 From Arthur Peronneau Hayne. ALS, DNA-RG 94 (7-1187). Resigns as inspector general of the Southern Division.

Aug 7 To John Caldwell Calhoun (from Thomas Hinds and AJ). ALS in Hinds's hand also signed by AJ with internal address and address cover in his hand, DNA-RG 107 (M221-89); ALS copy in AJ's hand, also signed by Hinds, DLC (29). Announce that they will begin Choctaw negotiations October 1 and request that funds be drawn on the Bank of Mississippi.

[Aug 7] Memorandum of accounts between Edward G. W. Butler and AJ. AD, DLC (29).

Aug 8 Memorandum on negotiating with the Choctaws. ADS by Thomas Hinds with AJ endorsement, DLC (29).

Aug 8 Account of Rachel Jackson with Oldfield & Co. for fabric. AD, DLC (29).

Aug 9 *To John Caldwell Calhoun.* 385

Aug 9 From Pleasant Moorman Miller. ALS, DLC (29). In response to AJ's queries of August 3 (not found), discusses the bank scheme in Tennessee and election prospects.

Aug 9 Memorandum on the peace establishment of the army. DS, DNA-RG 107 (M221-89); LC, DLC (63); Copy, DLC (7-1191).

Aug 9 Advertisement for Indian rations for Choctaw negotiations, signed by AJ. Printed, *Nashville Whig*, Aug 9 (mAJs).

Aug 10 To John Caldwell Calhoun (enclosures: Arthur P. Hayne to AJ, April 3 and June 10). ALS, DNA-RG 107 (M221-89); LC, DLC (63). *Calhoun Papers*, 5:323–24. Sends Hayne's resignation and requests the appointment of James Gadsden as division inspector general.

Aug 10 To Arthur Peronneau Hayne. LC, DLC (63). Reports that his resignation has been forwarded to the secretary of war.

Aug 10 From John Caldwell Calhoun. LS, DLC (29); AL draft, DNA-RG 107 (7-1202). *Calhoun Papers*, 5:324–25. Reaffirms orders of June 14 re expenses for seeds, utensils, etc.

Aug 11 To James Monroe. Copy, DLC (29). Recommends Isaac McKeever for naval promotion.

Aug 11 To Smith Thompson. Copy, DLC (29). Recommends Isaac McKeever for naval promotion.

Aug 12 To Reuben Humphreys. LC, DLC (63). States that funds requested were ordered to be forwarded; orders him to report thereon and to join his detachment once repairs on the military road are completed.

Aug 17 From Richard Keith Call. ALS, DLC (29). Discusses removal of intruders from Cherokee lands.

Aug [17]	From John Rogers, [Jr.]. LS, DNA-RG 75 (M271-3). Discusses Cherokee removal to Arkansas territory.
Aug 18	To Daniel Bissell. LC, DLC (63). In compliance with the order from the secretary of war, again orders reinforcement of Baton Rouge.
Aug 18	From Thomas Sidney Jesup (enclosure: Plan for army reorganization, n.d.). ALS, DLC (29). Sends copy of his report to the secretary of war and discusses need for an original military system for the United States.
Aug 19	To John Caldwell Calhoun. LC, DLC (63). Acknowledges Calhoun's letter of July 31, discusses removal of Creek and Cherokee intruders, and reports that Richard I. Easter's accounts will be settled satisfactorily.
Aug 19	To Isaac McKeever. ALS, DLC (29). States that he has recommended him for promotion.
Aug 19	Richard Keith Call to Edmund Pendleton Gaines. LC, DLC (63). Orders detachment for removal of intruders from Creek lands.
Aug 20	From Reuben Humphreys. ALS with AJ endorsement, DLC (29). Acknowledges instructions of August 12 and informs AJ that he has not received the funds requested.
Aug 21	From Christopher Vandeventer. LS, DLC (29); LC, DNA-RG 75 (M15-5); Copy, DNA-RG 46 (7-1214). *ASP, Indian Affairs,* 2:232. Reports that funds for the Choctaw treaty will be forwarded to Natchez; discusses terms for negotiations and reserves for mixed-bloods.
Aug 24	To Reuben Humphreys. LC, DLC (63). Regrets that Humphreys has not received the funds from Matthew S. Massey; states that his expenses will be paid; reiterates his order to proceed to Baton Rouge once the military road is completed.
Aug 24	To Matthew Strong Massey. LC, DLC (63). Orders him to advance funds needed by Reuben Humphreys's detachment.
Aug 24	To John McKee. ALS fragment, DLC (7-1216). *Southern Historical Association Publications,* 2(1898):15–16 (7-1219). Discusses the forthcoming Choctaw talks.
Aug 24	Appointment of Samuel Ragland Overton as secretary to the Choctaw commissioners. Copies, DNA-RG 75 (T494-1), DNA-RG 46 (7-1221). *ASP, Indian Affairs,* 2:233.
Aug 24–Nov 10	Journal of Choctaw treaty negotiations. DS fragment (begins Oct 19) signed by AJ and Thomas Hinds, Anonymous (7-1227); Copy, DNA-RG 46 (7-1246).
Aug 25	From William Lee. Printed form with ms insertions, DLC (29). Announces transmission of $20,000 for Choctaw treaty negotiations.
Aug 27	From Reuben Humphreys. ALS, DLC (29). Introduces a Mr. McDonald who can answer complaints of a Choctaw chief against him.
Aug 29	From Richard Keith Call. ALS, DLC (29). Reports the removal of intruders from the Cherokee lands in Georgia and plans for intruder removal north of the Tennessee River.
Aug 29	From William Lee (to David Meriwether, AJ, and Jesse Franklin). ALS, DLC (29). Reports credit of $1,000 to their account, thereby closing it.

Aug 31	To John McKee. ALS, DLC (7-1224). *Southern Historical Association Publications,* 2(1898):16 (7-1226). Inquires about a permit for Capt. [Samuel B.] Marshall to transport goods into the Choctaw nation.
Aug 31	Robert Butler to Daniel Parker (enclosure: Arthur P. Hayne to AJ, Aug 6). LS, DNA-RG 94 (M566-132); LC, DNA-RG 98 (mAJs). Transmits Hayne's resignation.
Aug 31	Memorandum of contract of AJ and Thomas Hinds with William Eastin and William Berkeley Lewis for rations for the Choctaw negotiations. Copies, DNA-RG 75 (T494-1), DNA-RG 46 (7-1222). *ASP, Indian Affairs,* 2:233.
Sept 1	From Joshua Baker (1799–1885). ALS, DNA-RG 94 (M688-14). Requests that AJ recommend an immediate examination of Alexander McFaddin for admission to West Point.
Sept 1	From Daniel Bissell. LS, DLC (29). Requests furlough to attend to private business in the St. Louis area when public lands are sold.
Sept 1	From Daniel Bissell. LS, DLC (29). Discusses in greater detail his furlough request.
Sept 1	From Edmund Pendleton Gaines (enclosure: Gaines to Mathew Arbuckle, Sept 1). ALS, DLC (29). Reports order to Arbuckle to remove intruders from Creek lands.
Sept 2	*To John Caldwell Calhoun.* 388
Sept 2	To John Rogers, [Jr.]. LC, DLC (63). Discusses allegedly undelivered supplies awarded the Cherokees in the 1817 treaty and tells Rogers he must prove allegation.
Sept 2	From Edmund Pendleton Gaines. ALS with AJ endorsement directing introduction of Dr. [Charles N.] McCoskry, DLC (29). Reports the settlement of his accounts in Washington and his efforts to gather more information on the investigation into the Florida invasion.
Sept 3	From Alexander Campbell Wilder Fanning. ALS, DLC (29). Discusses the health of his troops at St. Marks and Fort Gadsden and requests that they be transferred.
Sept 4	From Francis Saunders. ALS, DNA-RG 94 (M688-22). Requests recommendation for his son, Thomas F. Saunders, to West Point.
Sept 6	To Henry Atkinson. LC, DLC (63). Discusses situation in 9th Military Department.
Sept 6	To John Duncan. ALS and Typed copy, CLU-C (7-1306, -1309). Suggests Florence, Alabama, as place to settle.
Sept 8	To [John Caldwell Calhoun]. Abstract, Parke-Bernet Catalog (Feb 19, 1945), Item 306 (7-1314). Inquires about a warrant for a young man entering West Point.
Sept 8	Receipt for Tennessee and Davidson County taxes for 1820. Printed form with ms insertions, THi (7-1311).
Sept 10	Deed from Charlotte and Isaac Lewis Baker for town lot in Nashville and land in Giles County. Copies, TNDa (7-1315), TPGil (7-1317).
Sept 11	From Richard Ivy Easter. ALS with AJ endorsement accepting resignation and directing Robert Butler to issue orders for appointment of Andrew J. Donelson as aide-de-camp, ICHi (7-1325). Resigns as aide-de-camp.
Sept 11	To Richard Ivy Easter. LC, DLC (63). Accepts resignation.

Sept 12	Decision in case of *William Hadley* v. *AJ, Andrew Jackson Hutchings, and Daniel Cherry.* AD with AJ endorsement, T (7-1328).	
Sept 12	Receipt from John Hoggatt for shoeing horses. DS, DLC (70).	
Sept 13	To William Lee. LS, DNA-RG 217 (7-1356). Acknowledges receipt of $20,000 for the Choctaw negotiations.	
Sept 13	From James Craine Bronaugh (enclosures: Bronaugh to German Senter, July 16; Senter to Bronaugh, July 30, DNA-RG 94, M566-136). ALS, DNA-RG 94 (7-1353); Copy, DNA-RG 107 (M221-90). Sends Senter's resignation and requests court-martial.	
Sept 13	From Edmond Folsom (to AJ and Thomas Hinds). ALS, DNA-RG 75 (M271-3); Copy, DNA-RG 46 (7-1355). *ASP, Indian Affairs,* 2:232. Reports opposition of the Choctaws at Six Towns to exchange or sale of land.	
Sept 14	To John Caldwell Calhoun (enclosures: James C. Bronaugh to German Senter, July 16; Senter to Bronaugh, July 30; Bronaugh to AJ, Sept 13). LS, DNA-RG 94 (7-1358); Copy, DNA-RG 107 (M221-90). Recommends dropping Senter from the army rolls.	
Sept 14	From Benjamin Delavan. ALS, DLC (29). *Cincinnati Commercial,* Jan 8, 1881. Pronounces Francis S. Belton "a Slanderer and a Coward" for his statements re Delavan's character.	
Sept 14	*From Cary Nicholas.*	389
Sept 15	To John Caldwell Calhoun (enclosure: Cary Nicholas to AJ, Sept 14). LS, DNA-RG 107 (M221-89); LC, DLC (63). Bassett, 3:32–33 (extract). Reports his departure for the Choctaw country; discusses removal of intruders from the Cherokee lands and depreciated currency in Nashville.	
Sept 17	From Richard Keith Call. ALS copy, DNA-RG 107 (M221-89). Reports on removal of intruders from the Cherokee lands.	
Sept 17	Richard Keith Call to John Caldwell Calhoun (enclosure: Call to [AJ], Sept 17). ALS, DNA-RG 107 (M221-89). Sends report re intruders on Cherokee lands.	
Sept 20	From Daniel Bissell. LS, DLC (29). Reports that he has dispatched two companies to Baton Rouge.	
Sept 20	Agreement with Samuel Bell for digging a well on Andrew Jackson Hutchings's farm. DS also signed by Bell, THi (7-1362).	
Sept 20	Division order appointing Andrew Jackson Donelson as aide-de-camp. DS by Robert Butler, DNA-RG 94 (M566-132); LC, DNA-RG 98 (mAJs).	
Sept 24	From Edmund Pendleton Gaines. ALS, DLC (29). Reports the receipt of instructions re intruders on the Creek lands holding permits from the sub-agent.	
Sept 25	From James Gadsden. ALS, DLC (29). Reports on his trip to Washington and New York.	
Sept 27	Account with John Buchanan for planks. DS with AJ endorsement, DLC (29).	
Sept 29	Account with Marshall & Watkins for fringe. AD with AJ endorsement, DLC (29).	
Sept 30	*To Rachel Jackson.*	390
Sept	Account with James B. Houston for sundries. ADS with AJ endorsement, DLC (30). Runs to March 10, 1821.	

Oct 1	Endorsement of George W. Gardner & Co., Washington, D.C., as agents for claims against the government. Printed, Washington *National Intelligencer,* Oct 19 (7-1374).	
Oct 2	To John Caldwell Calhoun. Abstract, DNA-RG 107 (M22-14). Encloses report of Richard K. Call on removal of intruders from Cherokee lands.	
Oct 2	To George Poindexter. LS in Samuel R. Overton's hand, THi (7-1375). Discusses forthcoming Choctaw talks.	
Oct 2	From James Scallan (enclosures: Description of causeways, n.d.; Description of bridges, n.d., DLC-70; Statement of extra labor performed, [May 31], DLC-28). ALS, DLC (29). Forwards continuation of his report on the military road.	
Oct 2	Account of Benjamin Ducker with David Whitesides for planks for the Hermitage. AD with AJ endorsement, DLC (29).	
Oct 3	*To Choctaw Indians.*	391
Oct 3	Rachel Jackson to Richard Keith Call. ALS, ViHi (7-1379). Regrets that she did not see him before his departure.	
Oct 3	Account of Malachi Nicholson with William Griffin for work on Andrew Jackson Hutchings's farm. AD signed by Griffin and endorsed by AJ, A-Ar (7-1383).	
Oct 4	From John Caldwell Calhoun. LS, DLC (29); LC, DNA-RG 107 (M6-11). States intention to pay salaries and expenses in specie or in notes of specie-paying banks.	
Oct 5	Account of James Jackson Hanna with Thomas N. Cameron for medical treatment of slave, Tom. ADS, DLC (29). Runs to October 12.	
Oct 6	From Edmond Folsom and [Middleton] Mackay. ALS in Folsom's hand also signed by Mackay, DNA-RG 75 (M271-3). Report on efforts to persuade Choctaws to attend treaty negotiations.	
Oct 6	Decision in *Thomas Crutcher, Andrew Jackson, and Alfred Balch, Executors of William Terrell Lewis* v. *Peter Bennett.* DS, TKL (mAJs).	
Oct 10	To Choctaw Indians. Copies, DNA-RG 75 (T494-1), DNA-RG 46 (7-1254). *ASP, Indian Affairs,* 2:235–37. Urges Choctaws to exchange lands for compensation in Arkansas.	
Oct 11	*To John Caldwell Calhoun.*	392
Oct 13	To Choctaw Indians. Copies, DNA-RG 75 (T494-1), DNA-RG 46 (7-1265). *ASP, Indian Affairs,* 2:238. Discusses area and terms of the proposed land exchange.	
Oct 14	From John Caldwell Calhoun. LS, DLC (29); LC and Copy, DNA-RG 75 (M15-5, M208-8). Approves methods of removal of intruders from Cherokee lands and Cherokee proposal for protecting themselves against intruders.	
Oct 15	From John Hull (enclosures: Philip Wager et al. to Edmund P. Gaines, Sept 30; Order by Gaines disapproving court-martial sentence, Sept 30). ALS, DNA-RG 107 (M222-21). Discusses his court-martial and dismissal and requests reversal of the sentence.	
Oct 16	To John Caldwell Calhoun (enclosure: John Hull to AJ, Oct 15). LS, DNA-RG 107 (M221-89). Transmits letter, praises Hull, and suggests that if Hull's statements are true his sentence was too harsh.	
Oct 17	*To Choctaw Indians.*	393

Oct 17	Advertisement by Mourning E. Parish of the apprehension of the slave Tom. *Richmond Enquirer,* Oct 17 (mAJs).
Oct 18	From Cyrus Kingsbury (to AJ and Thomas Hinds). ALS, DNA-RG 75 (M271-3); Copy, DNA-RG 46 (7-1385). *ASP, Indian Affairs,* 2:232–33. Submits plan for education of the Choctaws.
Oct 18	Treaty of Doak's Stand with the Choctaw Indians. DS, DNA-RG 11 (M668-5); Copy, DNA-RG 46 (7-1279). *ASP, Indian Affairs,* 2:224–25.
Oct 19–21	To John Caldwell Calhoun (from AJ and Thomas Hinds; enclosures: Read Fort to AJ, July 21; Edmond Folsom to AJ, Sept 13; Folsom and [Middleton] Mackay to AJ, Oct 6; Joel H. Vail et al. to AJ, Oct 19; Pushmataha et al. to AJ and Hinds, Oct 20; Account of AJ and Hinds re Choctaw Treaty, Oct [21]). LS also signed by Hinds, DNA-RG 75 (T494-1); Copy (dated Oct 21), DNA-RG 46 (7-1291); Copy, Anonymous (7-1230); Extracts, DNA-RG 46, DNA-RG 94 (mAJs). *ASP, Indian Affairs,* 2:241–43. Report conclusion of the Choctaw treaty.
Oct 19	From Pushmataha et al. Copies, Anonymous (7-1228), DNA-RG 46 (7-1289). *ASP, Indian Affairs,* 2:241. Request that mixed-blood Alexander Hamilton be given land in fee simple.
Oct 19	From Joel H. Vail et al. LS, DNA-RG 46 (7-1389). Request U.S. citizenship.
Oct 20	From Apuckshunnubbe et al. (to AJ and Thomas Hinds). Copies, Anonymous (7-1229), DNA-RG 46 (7-1290). Petition to sell two tracts reserved by Treaty of Mount Dexter of 1805.
Oct 20	From Pushmataha et al. (to AJ and Thomas Hinds). DS, DNA-RG 75 (M271-3). Petition for the appointment of Robert Cole as chief of the upper Choctaw towns, replacing Apuckshunnubbe.
Oct 20	Richard Keith Call to Daniel Bissell. LC, DLC (63). Denies request for furlough until Florida situation is resolved; allows Bissell to attempt an exchange of commands with Henry Atkinson.
Oct 21	List of donations made to the Choctaw chiefs. Copies, Anonymous (7-1240), DNA-RG 46 (7-1301). *ASP, Indian Affairs,* 2:244.
Oct [21]	Account of AJ and Thomas Hinds with United States re Choctaw negotiations. Copies, Anonymous (7-1242), DNA-RG 46 (7-1303). *ASP, Indian Affairs,* 2:244.
Oct 23	Account with Smith & Chisholm for leather belts for slaves on AJ's and Andrew Jackson Hutchings's farm in Alabama. ADS, A-Ar (7-1392).
Oct 24	From Isaac Lewis Baker. AL matched fragments, ICHi (mAJs), DLC (72); Typed copy, DLC (75). *Cincinnati Commercial,* Jan 8, 1881 (extract). Reports his arrival in Natchez and on friends, including Abner L. Duncan and George Poindexter.
Oct 24	From John McKee. ALS, DLC (29). Reports the death of Margaret F. Butler and encloses documents (not found) re the theft of horses from relatives of the Indian Little Leader.
Oct 25	From John Caldwell Calhoun (enclosure: George Graham to AJ, Aug 14, 1817). LS, DLC (29); LC, DNA-RG 107 (M15-5). Acknowledges Richard K. Call's report on the removal of intruders from Cherokee lands, but questions legality of seizing slaves and stock.

Oct 25	From George Poindexter. LS and Typed copy, DLC (29, 72); Copy, Ms-Ar (7-1395). *Cincinnati Commercial,* Jan 8, 1881 (extract). Extols success of the Choctaw negotiations and discusses his disagreements with Thomas Hinds and William S. Hamilton.	
Oct 26	From Trueman Cross. ALS, DLC (29). Reports his appointment as assistant inspector general for the Southern Division.	
Oct 28	Account of Rachel Jackson with R. Buchanan for fabric. ADS, DLC (29).	
Nov 1	From Thomas Jefferson Ayer. ALS, DLC (29). Complains of the slowness of his court-martial.	
Nov 2	From Edmond Folsom. Copy, DNA-RG 107 (M221-89). Agrees to gather the Choctaws in Arkansas onto treaty lands provided he is paid $1,000 per acre for his land as requested.	
Nov 3	From Stockley Donelson Hutchings. ALS, THi (7-1399). Requests recommendation of William Atwood for marshal of Alabama.	
Nov 4	Agreement between AJ and Nelson P. Jones terminating management of AJ's Alabama farm. DS in hand of John Coffee, also signed by Jones and witnessed by Coffee, James Jackson and Samuel Savage, and AD draft, THi (7-1402, -1405).	
Nov 6	From John Caldwell Calhoun. LS, DLC (29); LC, DNA-RG 107 (M6-11). *Calhoun Papers,* 5:427. Approves the discharge of the deserter Welch and expresses the hope that it will influence favorably the Choctaw negotiations.	
Nov 10	From Eden Brashears. Extract, DNA-RG 107 (M222-21). Reports that Choctaws wish the boundary of their reservation clearly marked as soon as possible.	
Nov 10	From Peter Hagner (enclosure: Hagner to John P. Erwin, Nov 10, DNA-RG 217, mAJs). LS, DLC (29); LC, DNA-RG 217 (7-1406). Sends letter to Erwin for transmittal and discusses the account of Robert Searcy.	
Nov 10	Account of AJ with United States re Choctaw treaty negotiation expenses, Oct 21 through Nov 10. DS, Anonymous (7-1244); Copy, DNA-RG 46 (7-1304). *ASP, Indian Affairs,* 2:244.	
Nov 11	Richard Keith Call to Henry Atkinson. LC, DLC (63). Approves measures taken to identify the tribe to which certain murderers belong.	
Nov 12	*From Stockley Donelson Hays.*	397
Nov 13	To Daniel Bissell (enclosure: Thomas J. Ayer to AJ, Nov 1). LC, DLC (63). Sends letter for his consideration.	
Nov 13	To John Caldwell Calhoun (enclosure: Edmond Folsom to AJ, Nov 2). LS, DNA-RG 107 (M221-89); LC, DLC (63). Reports Samuel R. Overton's departure for Washington with the Choctaw treaty; discusses the negotiations and John Hersey.	
Nov 13	To Alexander Campbell Wilder Fanning. LC, DLC (63). Discusses the health of Fanning's garrison and regrets delay in his reply.	
Nov 13	To James Monroe. ALS, NN (7-1410). Introduces Samuel R. Overton.	
Nov 13	Receipt from Jenkin Whiteside for legal services in *Bennett Smith* v. *John Hutchings's Executors.* ADS with AJ endorsement, A-Ar (7-1412).	

Nov 14 From Henry Atkinson. ALS, ICHi (7-1414). Encloses letter of Alphonso Wetmore (not found) explaining unappropriated sums.

Nov 17 From Henry Atkinson. Copy, DNA-RG 107 (M221-89). Reports on severe punishments ordered by Talbot Chambers.

Nov 18 Account with Richmond & Flint for watch trinkets for Rachel Jackson. ADS with ANS by AJ, DLC (29).

Nov 20 To James Jackson. Typed copy, Mrs. Uhland O. Redd (7-1417). Discusses the bank scheme in Tennessee, his crops, and the case of *Bennett Smith* v. *John Hutchings's Executors*.

Nov 23 To John Clark. ALS, ICHi (7-1420). Thanks him for his pamphlet that discusses the political fate of William H. Crawford and Thomas W. Cobb.

Nov 23 Account with John E. Linn for clothing. Printed, *Historical Outlook,* 14(Jan 1923):14 (7-1418).

Nov 24 Account with Edward Jones for medical expenses. AD, DLC (29). Runs to December 8.

Nov 25 To John Caldwell Calhoun. LS, DNA-RG 99 (mAJs); LC, DLC (63). Requests that the paymaster in Nashville be allowed to serve also as quartermaster; informs him of Cary Nicholas's departure for Washington to settle accounts and requests appointment of Milo Mason or Edward J. Lambert as successor.

Nov 25 *To Nelson P. Jones.* 399

Nov 25 From John Caldwell Calhoun (enclosures: Jacques P. Villeré to James Monroe, Oct 27, extract; Calhoun to Villeré, Nov 25, DLC-29). LS, DLC (29); LC, DNA-RG 107 (M6-11). Transmits correspondence with the governor of Louisiana requesting a new military post on the Sabine River and asks AJ to use his discretion in troop assignments.

Nov 27 From Samuel Sacket. Abstract, DLC (mAJs). Recommends Gilbert Story as ensign.

Nov 29 *To William King.* 400

Nov 30 To John Caldwell Calhoun (enclosures: Eden Brashears to AJ, Nov 10, extract; Stockley D. Hays to AJ, Nov 12). LS, OkTGil (8-0003); LC, DLC (63). *Calhoun Papers,* 5:459–62. Approves seizure of intruders' stock on Cherokee lands and gives ideas on Choctaw boundaries; recommends George Gibson or Cary Nicholas for Choctaw agent.

Nov 30 From Daniel Bissell. LS, DLC (29). States that his furlough request was conditional on Florida situation; corrects misunderstanding re exchange of commands with Henry Atkinson.

Nov 30 From John Caldwell Calhoun. AL in unknown clerk's hand, DLC (29); LC, DNA-RG 107 (M6-11). Bassett, 3:34. Requests return of the device of the medal sent AJ in December 1817 so that the medal can be completed.

Dec 8 *To Henry Atkinson.* 402

Dec 8 To John Caldwell Calhoun (enclosure: Henry Atkinson to AJ, Nov 17). LS, DNA-RG 107 (M221-89); LC, DLC (63). Sends letter re corporal punishment of deserters under Talbot Chambers's command.

Dec 8 From Henry Atkinson. ALS, PHi (8-0011). Reports the surrender of an Indian murderer and encloses a map, field notes of the country between the Mississippi and Missouri rivers, and a sketch of barracks (none found).

Dec 8 *From James Gadsden.* 403

Dec 10 Account with Anthony Wayne Johnson, tinsmith. ADS with AJ endorsement, DLC (29). Runs to October 7, 1823.

Dec 11 To Mad Wolf and James Fife. Copy, GHi (8-0015). Informs them that cattle taken from the Seminoles were distributed to the friendly Creeks and discusses payments to indemnify their losses at the hands of the Red Sticks.

Dec 11 From Pathkiller. LS, DNA-RG 107 (M221-89). *ASP, Indian Affairs,* 2:504. Solicits support of a petition.

Dec 12 From James Monroe. Abstract, Edward Eberstadt & Sons Catalog 129 (1951), Item 93 (8-0017). Introduces a Mr. Somerville who has been appointed a professor at Cumberland College.

Dec 13 *To John Coffee.* 404

Dec 14 From John Caldwell Calhoun. LS, DLC (29); LC, DNA-RG 107 (M6-11). Encloses letter of Richard W. Habersham to Calhoun, December 4 (M221-89), re the attendance of army officers as witnesses at the trial of intruders on Cherokee lands.

Dec 15 To John Caldwell Calhoun. LC, DLC (63). Encloses memorandum (not found) by Alexander Hamilton, mixed-blood, who seeks compensation for his army service.

Dec 15 Andrew Jackson Donelson to Daniel Bissell. LC, DLC (63). Reiterates AJ's decisions on Bissell's furlough and exchange of commands with Henry Atkinson; discusses troop assignments along the Sabine River.

Dec 16 *To Ellen Jackson Kirkman.* 406

Dec 16 From David Caldwell (enclosure: Certificate, April 20, 1814, DLC-66). ALS with AJ endorsement, DLC (29). Encloses certificate re his horse, lost in service on the Creek campaign, and requests compensation.

Dec 16 From John Caldwell Calhoun (enclosure: Calhoun to John W. Taylor, Dec 12, *Calhoun Papers,* 5:480–90). AL in unknown clerk's hand, DLC (29). Sends report on the reduction of the army.

[cDec 16] *To Richard Keith Call.* 408

Dec 18 From James Scallan. ALS, DLC (29). Thanks AJ for the praise of his report on the military road; informs AJ of his marriage and employment as auctioneer; urges the appointment of Abner L. Duncan as judge of the U.S. District Court in Louisiana.

Dec 20 Andrew Jackson Donelson to Daniel Bissell (enclosure: John C. Calhoun to AJ, Nov 25). LC, DLC (63). Revises orders re troop assignment along the Sabine River.

Dec 21 *To John Caldwell Calhoun.* 409

Dec 24 From Daniel Bissell (enclosure: Abraham L. Sands to Richard Whartenby, Nov 16, extract). LS, DLC (29). Reports organization of court-martial for Thomas J. Ayer's trial.

Dec 24 From James Gadsden. ALS, DLC (29). Reports on activities at Mobile Point and Dauphin Island.

Dec 28 To John Caldwell Calhoun. ALS, DNA-RG 107 (M221-89). States his belief that the device of the medal was returned to Washington, but had ordered a search for it nonetheless; confirms that a profile likeness will be sent shortly.

Dec 28 From William Lee. LS, DLC (29); LC, DNA-RG 217 (8-0030). Requests information on arms used by the Tennessee Brigade of Mounted Volunteers in 1818–19.

Dec 31 From Edmund Pendleton Gaines. ALS with AJ endorsement, DLC (29). Thanks AJ for introductions of surgeons Charles N. McCoskry and Robert French; discusses removal of intruders from Creek lands and William H. Crawford's political prospects in Virginia.

[1820] From James McMillan Glassell. ALS with AJ endorsement, DLC (60). Introduces Winston Wright Lear, son of William W. Lear, 4th Infantry.

[1820] From Alfred Thruston. ALS, DLC (60). Thanks him for hospitality at the Hermitage and sets price for horses left behind.

[1820] Receipt from Thomas Barnett for payment of taxes on Andrew Jackson Hutchings's farm. ADS with AJ endorsement, A-Ar (7-0962).

[1820] Memorandum of money belonging to the estate of William Donelson. AD with AJ endorsement, DLC (70).

[1820] Cover note for report re military road to New Orleans. AD, DLC (59).

Index

Page-entry numbers between 419 and 582 refer to the Calendar. Numbers set in boldface indicate identification of persons. The symbol * indicates biographical information in the *Dictionary of American Biography*; the symbol †, in the *Biographical Directory of the United States Congress.*